PAGE 52

ON THE ROAD

and insider tips

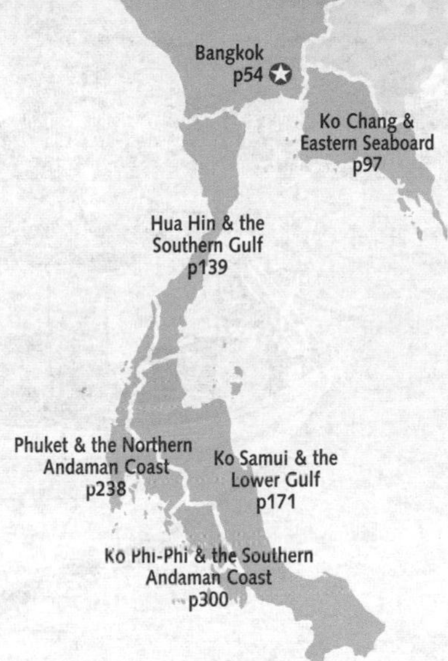

PAGE 397

SURVIVAL GUIDE

VITAL PRACTICAL INFORMATION TO HELP YOU HAVE A SMOOTH TRIP

THIS EDITION WRITTEN AND RESEARCHED BY

Brandon Presser

Celeste Brash, Austin Bush

welcome to Thailand's Islands & Beaches

Best Beach Ever

Thailand's beaches are legendary; tall palms angle over pearlescent sand, coral gardens flourish in the shallow seas and beach parties are liberally lubricated with alcohol and fun. With a long coastline (actually, two coastlines) and jungle-topped islands anchored in azure waters, Thailand is a tropical getaway for the hedonist and the hermit, the prince and the pauper. And in between the kissing cousins of sea and sky are dramatic limestone mountains standing sentinel. Perhaps as impressive as the beaches themselves is the variation of seaside holidays to be had. Scale the sheer sea cliffs of Krabi, cavort with gentle whale sharks at pinnacles off of Ko Tao and Ko Pha-Ngan, toe the curling tide alongside gypsy fishermen in Trang, gorge on seafood snacks among the steamy stalls of Hua Hin or relish perfectly practised butler service at your luxury digs in Phuket. The adventure awaits.

Gorge-ous Thailand

It may be the beaches that bring you to Thailand, but it's the food that'll lure you back for seconds. Adored around the world, Thai cuisine expresses fundamental aspects of Thai culture: it is generous and warm, outgoing and nuanced, refreshing and relaxed. And it is much more delicious in its native setting. Each Thai dish relies on fresh and local ingredients – from pun-

Bays of peach-tinged sand, cotton hammocks swinging lazily between palm trunks, castle-like karsts emerging from the deep. These dreams of a tropical paradise become a reality along the coasts of southern Thailand.

(left) Long-tail boat on Hat Hin Khom, Ko Phi-Phi Don
(below) Elephant on a beach in Krabi

gent lemongrass and searing chillies to plump seafood and crispy fried chicken. With a tropical abundance, a varied national menu is built around the four fundamental flavours: spicy, sweet, salty and sour. And then there are the regional differences, which propel travellers on eating tours around the country. Lucky for you, dear beachgoer, these days it's quite easy to sample the kaleidoscope of national flavours without leaving the comforts of your island getaway.

Sun-Kissed Smiles

Whether it's the glimmering eye of the meditative *wâi* (palms-together Thai greeting) or the mirthful smirk of passers-by, it's hard not to be charmed by the Land of Smiles. The moniker is not only apt but also well earned in a kingdom where hospitality has aged like a fine wine. Thailand has long been Southeast Asia's mama-san, inviting foreigners from near and far to indulge in the kingdom's natural splendours. This utopian recipe is perfected along the beaches and islands where the heady mix of seascapes, soaring limestone towers and equatorial sunshine provides the perfect backdrop to expertly run resorts catering to whimsy with flair and a desire to please.

Thailand's Islands & Beaches

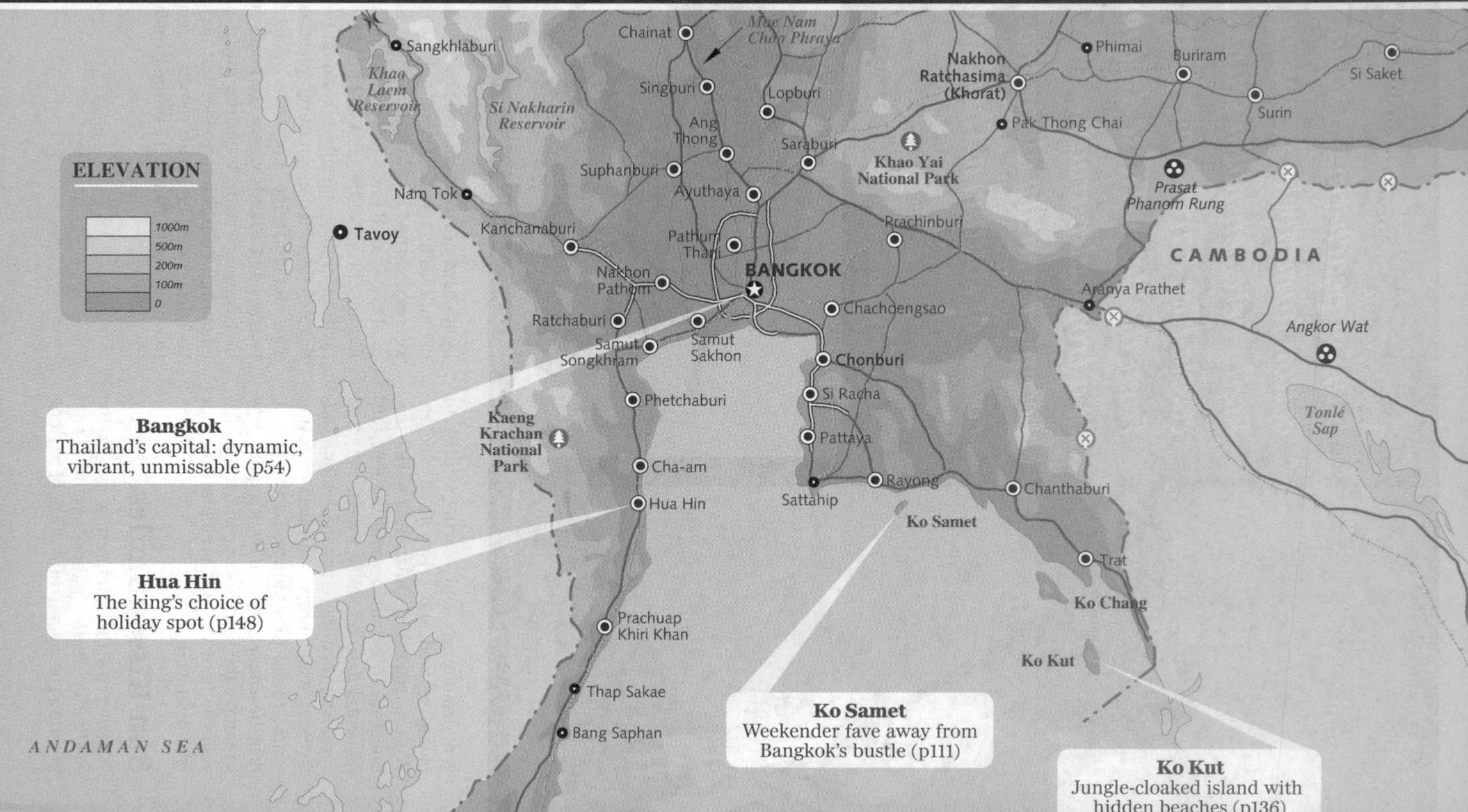

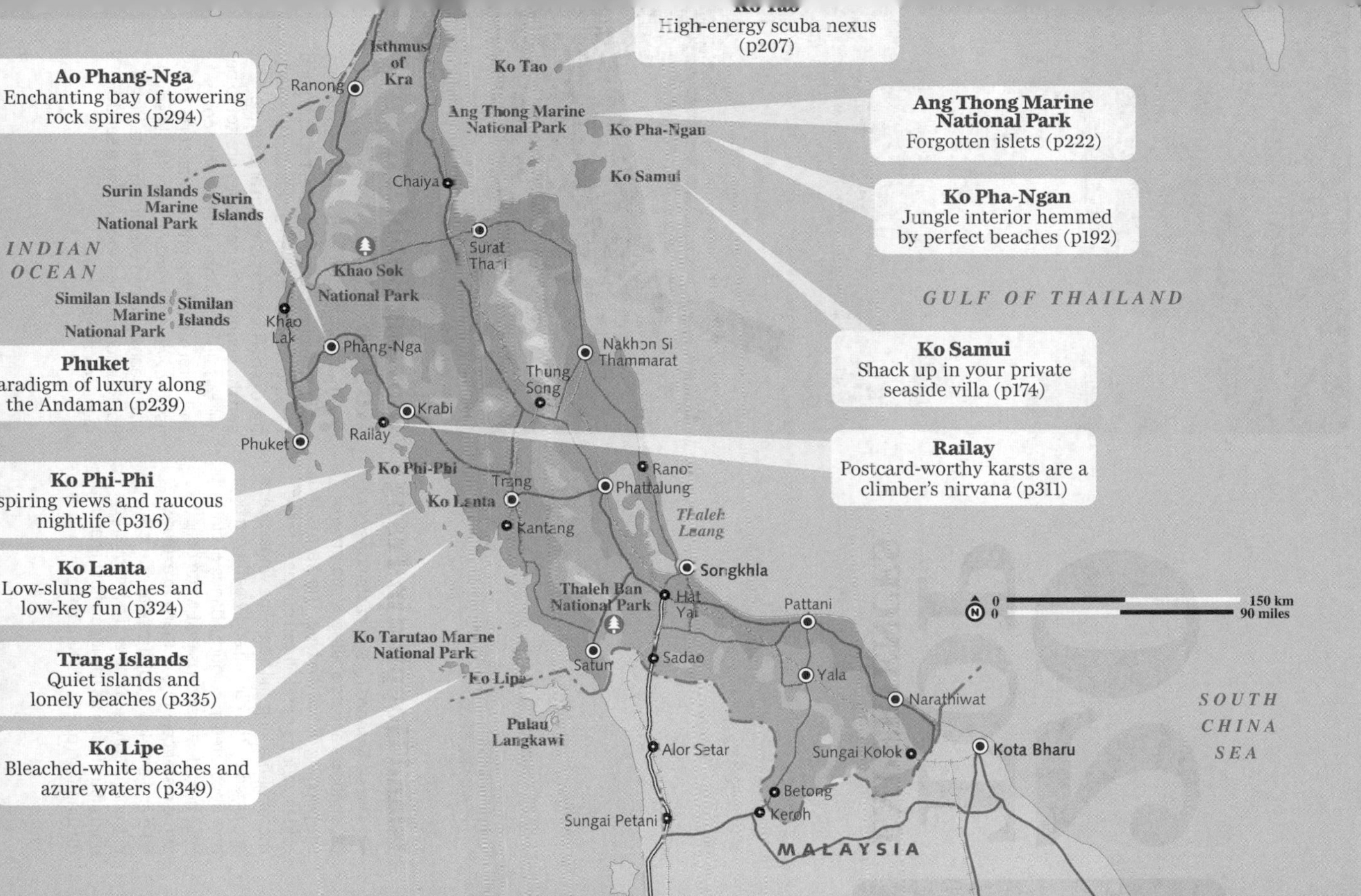
High-energy scuba nexus (p207)
Ao Phang-Nga
Enchanting bay of towering rock spires (p294)
Ang Thong Marine National Park
Forgotten islets (p222)
Ko Pha-Ngan
Jungle interior hemmed by perfect beaches (p192)
Ko Samui
Shack up in your private seaside villa (p174)
Railay
Postcard-worthy karsts are a climber's nirvana (p311)
Phuket
Paradigm of luxury along the Andaman (p239)
Ko Phi-Phi
Inspiring views and raucous nightlife (p316)
Ko Lanta
Low-slung beaches and low-key fun (p324)
Trang Islands
Quiet islands and lonely beaches (p335)
Ko Lipe
Bleached-white beaches and azure waters (p349)
INDIAN OCEAN
GULF OF THAILAND
SOUTH CHINA SEA
MALAYSIA
Isthmus of Kra
Ranong
Ko Tao
Ang Thong Marine National Park
Ko Pha-Ngan
Ko Samui
Chaiya
Surin Islands Marine National Park
Surin Islands
Surat Thani
Khao Sok National Park
Similan Islands Marine National Park
Similan Islands
Khao Lak
Phang-Nga
Nakhon Si Thammarat
Thung Song
Krabi
Railay
Phuket
Ko Phi-Phi
Trang
Phattalung
Ko Lanta
Kantang
Thaleh Ban National Park
Songkhla
Hat Yai
Pattani
Ko Tarutao Marine National Park
Satun
Sadao
Yala
Ko Lipe
Narathiwat
Pulau Langkawi
Alor Setar
Sungai Kolok
Kota Bharu
Betong
Keroh
Sungai Petani
0 150 km
0 90 miles

20 TOP EXPERIENCES

Island Hopping in Trang

1 The early-morning sun casts honey-like shadows across another deep-green isle popping out of the blue. The warm wind ruffles your hair and all you can hear is the motor of the long-tail boat. The whole scene is framed by the carved and weathered boat bow decorated in colourful bands of cloth. Your next destination is that white beach in the distance – one of many to explore, hike and snorkel – but the boat ride is so extraordinarily relaxing and gorgeous, you enjoy it as much as the idea of being at your destination (p335). Ko Kradan (p340)

Blowing Bubbles in Ko Tao

2 The dive-master's island, Ko Tao (p207) is the cheapest and easiest spot around to learn how to strap on a tank and dive into the deep. The water is warm and gentle, and the submarine spectacles are not to be missed. Just offshore, scenic rocky coves and coral reefs frequented by all sorts of fish provide a snorkelling 'aperitif'. Its small size means you can explore all of its jungle nooks and crannies, looking for a sandy niche to call your own.

1

MUM62/ SHUTTERSTOCK ©

2

KRAIG LIEB/LONELY PLANET IMAGES ©

K.MBERLEY COOLE/LONELY PLANET IMAGES ©

Ko Pha-Ngan

3 Famous for its sloppy Full Moon Parties and all-night techno fun, Ko Pha-Ngan (p192) has graduated from a sleepy bohemian island to full-on attraction for migrating party people. The beach shanties have been transformed into boutiques, so comfort seekers have an alternative to Ko Samui. And on the northern and eastern coasts, the ascetic hammock hangers can still escape enough of the modern life to feel like a modern castaway (a well-fed one, of course). Just offshore is Sail Rock, one of the gulf's best dive sites.

Rock Climbing in Railay

4 Whether you're a pro or have never grabbed a notch hole in your life, Railay's rock-climbing scene (p311) will get you scrambling skywards with joy. With around 500 bolted routes of limestone walls overlooking some of the world's most spectacular scenery – vertical grey spires decorated in greenery surrounded by crystalline sea and white beaches – even the shortest jaunt guarantees thrills. Seasoned climbers could stay for months. For even more adventure, try deep-water soloing where the climb ends with a splash in the water below.

Ko Ratanakosin's Temple Treasures

5 Not only is the artificial island of Ko Ratanakosin (p55) the birthplace of modern Bangkok, it's also among the city's most atmospheric 'hoods. Home to the bulk of Bangkok's must-see sights, such as the Emerald Buddha Wat Phra Kaew and Wat Pho, Ko Ratanakosin also holds several low-key treasures, including the hectic amulet market and the delightful Museum of Siam. Better yet, the area can be approached via a scenic trip on the Chao Phraya Express boat, and the sights can be linked via our custom walking tour (p65). Wat Phra Kaew (p55), Bangkok

5

JOHN ELK III/LONELY PLANET IMAGES ©

Touring Ko Lanta

6 By motorbike or túk-túk (pronounced *đúk đúk*), getting off the tourist beaches of Ko Lanta (p324) is a ticket to a wonderland of friendly Muslim fishing villages and gentle jungle scenery. Don't miss Ban Lanta with its Wild West–era streets and arty shops, then continue down the east coast that's had little influence from tourism. For natural beauty, Ko Lanta Marine National Park is hard to beat – and there are plenty of caves and slinky blonde beaches to stop at along the way.

6

GLENN VAN DER KNIJFF/LONELY PLANET IMAGES ©

Kayaking in Ao Phang-Nga

7 While other visitors squeeze onto crowded speedboats to get blurry glimpses of Ao Phang-Nga National Park's (p295) spectacular limestone-tower-studded bay, kayakers get to enjoy it in slow silence. Cavort with flying lizards, banded sea snakes or helmeted hornbills. Glide past rock art inside sea caves, picnic on secluded beaches and swim in silky water. At nightfall, illuminate your senses amid the bay's famed bioluminescence.

Live-Aboard Cruising to Richelieu Rock

8 The world-renowned dive sites dotting the crystal seas of the Surin and Similan Islands Marine National Parks are some of the best spots in the country to strap on a scuba mask and dive deep. The ultimate prize, however, is distant Richelieu Rock (p278), accessible only to those who venture north towards the so-called Burma Banks on a live-aboard diving trip (p291). The horseshoe-shaped outcrop acts as a feeding station luring manta rays and whale sharks.

7

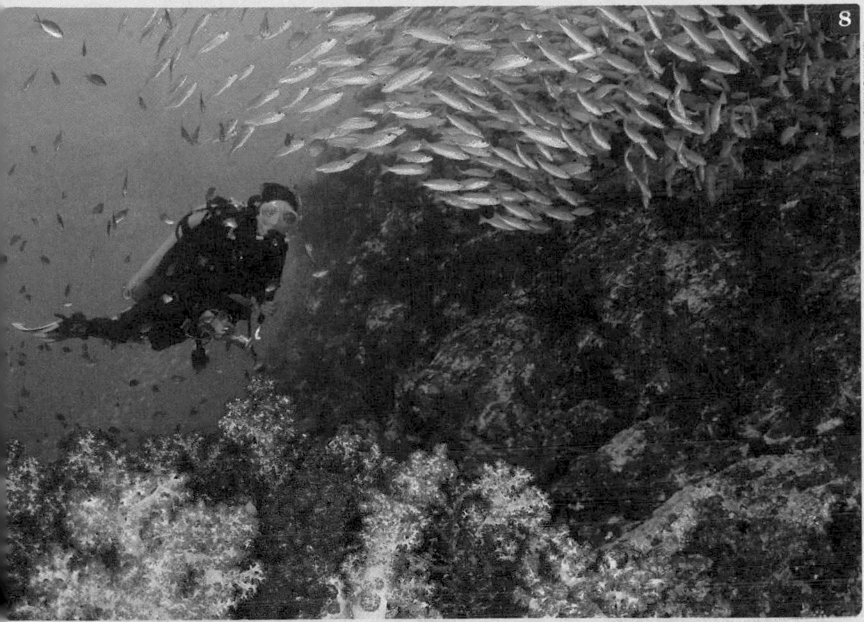

8

9

Thai-Style Beaches of Hua Hin

9 The king's choice, Hua Hin (p148) is a fine fit for city and sea creatures. The beaches are long and wide, the market meals are fantastic and there's also Thai culture. Explore the quiet beaches south of the city for a more secluded feel, hike to the top of a headland shrine or master the sea and the wind with a kiteboard lesson. And of course feast like a Thai morning, noon and night.

Design Your Dream Holiday in Ko Samui

10 Eager to please, Samui (p174) is a civilised beach-resort island for the vacationing masses, many of whom fly in and out having made hardly any contact with the local culture. Chaweng is a luxurious stretch of sand where sun-worshippers come to see and be seen. However, there are still sleepy spits reminiscent of Samui's old moniker, 'Coconut Island', and a few gentle coves for families who need to get in and out quickly. Samui also boasts a thriving health scene with yoga, meditation, detox retreats and other yins to the island's partying yang.

Luxury in Phuket

11 As if a private pool, your own staff and views over turquoise seas weren't enough, add some classic Thai style to the deal. Staying at a luxury resort in Phuket (p239) is about extreme pampering. Sure, you can find high-end digs in hundreds of other places around the globe, but no other destination can replicate the sweetness of the smiles, the glimmer of gold off a Buddha statue or the hint of plumeria wafting through the air. When you're not at the spa, try diving, lounging, hiking, kayaking...it's up to you.

MICK ELMORE/LONELY PLANET IMAGES ©

JOE CUMMINGS/LONELY PLANET IMAGES ©

Jim Thompson's House

12 The former home of an American silk entrepreneur may seem a strange estination, but Jim Thompson's House (p60) Bangkok is definitely worth the visit. In he late 1950s, Thompson assembled four ntique wooden houses and filled them with n exquisitely selected collection of Asian art nd antiques. Competent guided tours escort isitors through the structures, pointing out etails that the casual observer wouldn't otice. Also check out the attached art centre, ccompanying cafe/restaurant and shop selling Thompson's famed silk.

Ko Chang

13 Ko Chang's (p97) rugged landscape conceals some of Southeast Asia's best-preserved wilderness. The island's craggy mountainous interior is home to a veritable Jurassic Park of flora and fauna. The abounding biodiversity includes exotic reptiles, Technicolor birds and even some friendly elephants. Although developers have snared all of the attractive beachfront real estate there are still plenty of sand-fringed nooks in the east and south that feel decidedly off the beaten path.

14

Comparing Ko Lipe's Beaches

14 Which is better: Hat Pattaya or Sunrise Beach (p349)? Most visitors will leave with an opinion but everyone will have had an awesome time researching the question. Pattaya is a perfect arc of the whitest white with long-tails bobbing in its azure bay. But there are a lot of seafood barbecues and volleyball nets, hmmm. Sunrise is more golden and stretches on till it curves at the sight of majestic Ko Adang. A few people lounge in the sun and it beckons you to do the same. For us, it's a draw.

Discovering the Ko Yao Islands

15 Shhh, it's only about an hour from Phuket Town to the serene banks of the low-key Ko Yao Islands (p297) that float, cloaked in obscurity, right in the heart of stunning Ao Phang-Nga. Swap girly bars for wholesome Muslim fishing communities and late-night parties for quiet sunrises over outlying limestone isles. One of the region's most luxurious resorts is found here but mostly the islands are a place for fan-cooled huts to lay your head after days of diving, rock climbing and mountain biking.

Ang Thong Marine National Park

16 When Alex Garland wrote his cult novel *The Beach* (which later became a movie starring Leonardo DiCaprio), he must have been dreaming about Ang Thong Marine National Park (p222). Known as Mu Ko Ang Thong in Thai, this stunning archipelago contains 42 small islands featuring sheer limestone cliffs, hidden lagoons, perfect peach-coloured beaches and an interesting menagerie of tropical creatures. Ang Thong is best explored as a day trip from Ko Samui.

15

ANGELA MARIA LOBEFARO/GETTY IMAGES ©

16

BLAINE HARRINGTON III/CORBIS ©

17

18

Weekending in Ko Samet

17 So close to Bangkok and oh so pretty, Ko Samet (p111) is the perfect beach when your time is pinched. The jungle eclipses development, the sand and sea are tropically proportioned and a wooded coastal trail skirts between rocky headlands and a string of beautiful coves. People watch by day, party by night on the popular northern beaches or hide away on the southern beaches for a well-earned nap. When your vacation is over, board the boat and be back in Bangkok by lunchtime.

Beautiful Ko Phi-Phi

18 One of Thailand's most famous spots, Ko Phi-Phi (p316) deserves all the praise it gets. Stunning azure waters, gorgeous beaches and breath-taking limestone cliffs make it a great spot for diving, snorkelling and even rock climbing. After dark, it turns into a hedonistic mess, with dazed-eyed twenty-somethings carrying around minibuckets of sweet cocktails and nursing them like drunken Easter Bunnies. Morning headaches are guaranteed.

PANITHANKS/ SHUTTERSTOCK ©

CHRISTER FREDRIKSSON/LONELY PLANET IMAGES ©

Solitude on Ko Kut

19 Thailand's last large island frontier and a verdant canvas of dense jungle hemmed by pristine beaches – perfect for uninterrupted afternoons of sun worship and calm evenings accented by the meditative hum of the cicada. Although Ko Kut's (p136) topography is similar to many of the other islands in the kingdom, with rainforest and waterfalls hidden deep within, its location at the tip of the Ko Chang archipelago means that the coastal waters glimmer with a unique emerald tint.

The Gong Show in Patong

20 Patong (p258) is the best and the worst that southern Thailand has to offer: sugary sand beaches and jet-ski pollution, wall-to-wall shopping and inflated prices, first-rate cabaret shows and prostitution. This is the heart of the Andaman's action, including many dive centres, great hotel deals and this coast's wildest nightlife. Expect busy cityscapes, tourist T-shirts that could make Hugh Hefner blush and lots of 'Mistah want massage?' But also don't be surprised if, after some days on the beach and at the mall, you kind of enjoy it.

need to know

Currency
» Thai baht (B)

Language
» Thai

When to Go

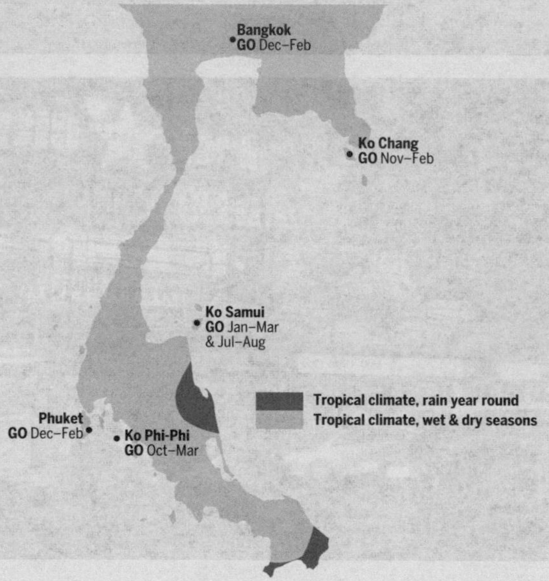

Bangkok
GO Dec–Feb

Ko Chang
GO Nov–Feb

Ko Samui
GO Jan–Mar & Jul–Aug

Phuket
GO Dec–Feb

Ko Phi-Phi
GO Oct–Mar

Tropical climate, rain year round
Tropical climate, wet & dry seasons

High Season (Nov–Mar)

» A cool and dry season follows the monsoons, meaning the landscape is lush and temperatures are comfortable.

» Western Christmas and New Year's holidays bring crowds and inflated rates to the beaches.

Shoulder Season (Apr–Jun)

» Although April, May and June are generally very hot and dry, the sea breeze provides plenty of natural air-con.

Low Season (Jul–Oct)

» The Andaman and gulf coasts take turns being pummelled by monsoon rains.

» Weather is generally favourable along the southern gulf in July and August.

» Some islands shut down and boats are limited during stormy weather.

Setting Your Budget

Budget Less Than
1500B

» Basic guest-house room: 300-1000B

» Excellent market and street-stall meals

» One or two evening drinks

» Get around with a mix of walking and public transport

Midrange
1500-3000B

» Flashpacker guest-house or midrange hotel room: 1000-2500B

» Western lunches and seafood dinners

» Several evening beers

» Motorbike hire

Top End Over
3000B

» Boutique hotel room: 2500B and beyond

» Fine dining

» Private tours

» Car hire

Money
» ATMs are widespread and charge a 150B foreign-account fee. Visa and MasterCard accepted at upmarket establishments.

Visas
» 30-day visas for international air arrivals; 15-day visas at land borders; 60-day visas from a Thai consulate before leaving home.

Mobile Phones
» Thailand is on a GSM network; inexpensive prepaid SIM cards are available. 3G on HSPA+ technology is currently available around Bangkok.

Transport
» Extensive and affordable buses, cheap domestic air connections, slow and scenic trains. It's easy to rent cars and motorcycles.

Websites
» **Tourism Authority of Thailand** (TAT; www.tourismthailand.org) National tourism department covering info and special events.

» **Thaivisa** (www.thaivisa.com) Expat site.

» **Lonely Planet** (www.lonelyplanet.com/thailand) Country profile and what to do and see.

» **Bangkok Post** (www.bangkokpost.com) English-language daily newspaper.

» **Thai Language** (www.thai-language.com) Online dictionary and Thai tutorials.

» **Thai Travel Blogs** (www.thaitravelblogs.com) Thailand-based travel blogger.

Exchange Rates

Australia	A$1	32B
Canada	C$1	31B
China	Y10	40B
Euro zone	€1	44B
Japan	¥100	38B
New Zealand	NZ$1	25B
Russia	R10	10B
UK	£1	50B
USA	US$1	30B

For current exchange rates see www.xe.com.

Important Numbers

Thailand country code	☎66
Emergency	☎191
International access codes	☎001, 007, 008, 009 (different service providers)
Operator-assisted international calls	☎100
Tourist police	☎1155

Arriving in Thailand
» **Suvarnabhumi International Airport**

Airport Bus Every hour from 6.10am to 9pm (150B).

Airport Rail Link Local service (45B, 30 minutes) to Phaya Thai station; express service (150B, 15 minutes) to Makkasan station.

Taxi Meter taxis 220B to 380B plus 50B airport surcharge and tolls; about an hour to the city depending on traffic.

FLYING TO THE ISLANDS
If you plan on spending the bulk of your Thailand time in the islands consider flying directly to Phuket or Ko Samui from a variety of international destinations rather than connecting through Bangkok. Phuket International Airport (HKT) is serviced by heaps of airlines that connect the gateway to the Andaman with faraway cities like Seoul, Kuala Lumpur, Hong Kong, Singapore, Jakarta, Moscow, St Petersburg, Stockholm, Brussels, Perth and Brisbane. Ko Samui's airport (USM) is significantly smaller, but there are direct flights to Hong Kong, Kuala Lumpur and Singapore.

Everyone needs a helping hand when they visit a country for the first time. There are phrases to learn, customs to get used to and etiquette to understand. The following section will help demystify Thailand so your first trip goes as smoothly as your fifth.

Language

Don't know a lick of Thai? In most places you don't need to. Tourist towns are well stocked with English speakers. Bus drivers, market vendors and even taxi drivers are less competent speakers. In small, less touristy towns, it helps to know how to order food and count in Thai. With just a few phrases, you'll be rewarded with big grins.

Thais have their own script, which turns educated Westerners into illiterates. Street signs are always transliterated into English, but there is no standard system so spellings vary widely and confusingly. Not all letters are pronounced as they appear. Confounding, huh?

Booking Ahead

While it's very easy to score walk-in bookings at many midrange and budget spots, we recommend booking your first few nights in advance. The following phrases will help you when booking accommodation.

Hello.	สวัสดี	sà-wàt-dee
I would like to book a room.	ขอจองห้องหน่อย	kŏr jorng hôrng nòy
a single room	ห้องเดี่ยว	hôrng dèe·o
a double room	ห้องเตียงคู่	hôrng đee·ang kôo
My name is...	ผม/ดิฉันชื่อ...	pŏm/dì-chăn chêu ... (m/f)
from... to... (date)	จากวันที่ ... ถึงวันที่ ...	jàhk wan têe ... tĕung wan têe ...
How much is it...?	... ละเท่าไร	... lá tôw-rai
per night	คืน	keun
for two people	สำหรับสองคน	săm·ràp sŏrng kon
Thank you.	ขอบคุณ	kòrp kun

What to Wear

In general, light, loose-fitting clothes will prove the most comfortable in the tropical heat throughout the year. It's worth bringing one reasonably warm sweater for the odd cool evening (or the blasting air-con on the plane). If you plan to visit a temple, you will need shirts with long sleeves and full-length pants. While sandals are definitely the way to go, you should bring one pair of nice shoes for the occasional night out in Bangkok or Phuket.

What to Pack

» Passport

» Credit card

» Driving licence

» Phrasebook

» Power converter

» GSM mobile phone

» Mobile phone charger

» Sunscreen

» Mosquito repellent with DEET

» Anti-itch cream (for sandfly bites)

» Light, long-sleeve shirts

» Breathable pants

» Hat

» Sunglasses

» Beach towel

» Comfortable sandals

» Torch/headlamp

» Camera

» Antibiotics

Checklist

» Make sure your passport is valid for at least six months.

» Purchase your international and domestic flight tickets.

» Visit the Thai consulate for a tourist visa if you're planning to stay for more than 30 days.

» Organise travel insurance and diver's insurance.

» Visit the doctor for check up and medical clearance if you intend on scuba diving.

Etiquette

The Thais are generally very understanding and hospitable, but there are some important taboos that permeate the various aspects of local life. The best way to win over the Thais is to smile – any visible anger or arguing is embarrassing; the locals call this 'loss of face'. Never disrespect the royal family with disparaging remarks, and also treat objects depicting the king (like money) with respect.

» Temples

When visiting a temple, it's important to dress neatly and conservatively. As with most interiors, it is expected that you remove all footwear. When sitting, keep your feet pointed away from any Buddha images. Women should never touch a monk or a monk's belongings – it is best to stay at a palpable distance to avoid accidental bumps.

» At the beach

Avoid public nudity – in fact most Thai will swim fully clothed. Away from the sand, men should wear shirts and women should be appropriately dressed (no bikinis).

Bargaining

» When to bargain

Bargaining forms the crux of almost any commercial interaction in Thailand. There are no set rules. If you're purchasing something like souvenirs or clothes, it's best to buy in bulk – the more T-shirts you buy, the lower the price will go.

» When not to bargain

Bargaining is very seldom taboo. You shouldn't bargain in restaurants and at petrol stations, and you should never haggle for a better price at a high-end hotel. Accommodation bargaining is, however, fair game at most Thai-run beach establishments.

Money

In general, paying for your food, drinks, entertainment and souvenirs is a lot easier with cash than card. For the most part, midrange and top-end hotels will take a credit card, as will most diving outfits, but expect to pay an additional 'processing fee' (of two to three per cent) when you swipe your Visa or Mastercard (the two preferred cards).

It should be noted that withdrawing money comes with a hefty withdrawal fee – usually around 150B to 200B. Consider making an educated guess as to how much you plan on spending each day and withdraw your money accordingly. You will find ATMs at (or near) almost all 7-Elevens. Many islands, however, have limited withdrawal facilities, so it's best to read the Information sections of each of our destinations for pre-planning.

what's new

For this new edition of Thailand's Islands & Beaches, our authors have hunted down the fresh, the transformed, the hot and the happening. These are some of our favourites. For up-to-the-minute recommendations, see lonelyplanet.com/thailand.

Full Speed Ahead to Sand & Sun

1 It's easier than ever to reach your slice of paradise as heaps of international flights service Phuket and Ko Samui directly. A slew of additional domestic links means that you don't have to pause in Bangkok on your search for azure waters and powder-white beaches.

Diving Diversity

2 Ko Tao is no longer just for beginners. Technical divers are now exploring underwater caves and others are even casting off their scuba gear for lung-stretching free dives. (p207)

Flashpacker Digs in BKK

3 The last couple of years have seen a flashpacker revolution in Bangkok and new hostels, such as NapPark, are combining high-tech dorm beds, pub-like communal areas and loads of fun activities. (p54)

Restored Sino-Portuguese Architecture

4 Phuket has long been a port of call for international traders and recently much of Phuket Town's Sino-Portuguese architecture has been restored to its former lustre – you can even call one of the buildings, Phuket 346, home! (p246)

Climbing Ko Yao Noi

5 Railay is undoubtedly the big cheese when it comes to rock climbing, but its reputation has meant a glut of visitors. Link up with Mountain Shop Adventures for a more secluded climbing experience off the coast of Phuket. (p297)

Serviced Villas

6 The next iteration in luxury vacations has arrived in Thailand – private villas. Seclusion seekers will relish the privacy of a serviced stay that comes with all of the trappings of a resort but without the gaggles of holidaymakers. Go green at Ko Jum Beach Villas. (p332)

Point-&-Click Travel Agencies

7 Sure, you'll find swarms of travel agents lining the backpacker-y nooks of the country, but internet savvy has finally washed up along the shores of Thailand – it's now easier than ever to book your activities and transportation with the click of a button. Try Ko Pha-Ngan's Backpackers Thailand. (p206)

nahm

8 After helming a Michelin-starred London restaurant and penning two best-selling books, Australian chef David Thompson has finally opened a branch of nahm in Bangkok. (p78)

if you like...

Beaches

From intimate coves to sandy coastlines, Thailand's beaches are beauty queens and draw a steady crowd of international sun-seekers. Long gone are the days of having paradise to yourself, but the scenery is still supreme.

Trang Islands A serene archipelago where each islet is more idyllic than the next. Toe the sand from your hammock then take a dip in the house reef (p335)

Ko Kut Miles of unpopulated sand arc around lonely Ko Kut – don't miss Khlong Chao, the crème de la crème of creamy, dreamy beaches (p136)

Ko Pha Ngan The original beach bum island hosts boisterous Full Moon Parties and a whole lot of hammock-hanging in between (p192)

Ko Lipe A handsome reward for those who put in a bit more legwork to get here – crystal-white sand beckons the click of a camera on Hat Pattaya (p349)

Similan Islands Just as stunning above the sea as below it. Strewn boulders punctuate the otherwise pearly white and deep blue uninterrupted vistas (p293)

Diving & Snorkelling

The warm clear waters of the Gulf of Thailand and the Andaman Sea harbour a variety of underwater landscapes and marine species that rank Thailand among the world's top diving destinations. The Andaman is the regional blockbuster, while the gulf is good for beginners.

Surin & Similan Islands Marine National Parks With some of the world's top diving spots, these Andaman islands have dramatic rocky gorges, hard and soft coral reefs and a laundry list of marine life; live-aboard trips depart from Khao Lak (p278 & p293)

Ko Lanta Nearby feeding stations for manta rays, whale sharks and other large pelagic fish earn this Andaman island high diving marks (p325)

Ko Tao With affordable dive schools, shallow waters and year-round conditions, Ko Tao is the kingdom's scuba-training island. Its near-shore reefs mean you can go snorkelling right after breakfast (p207)

Ko Phi-Phi Surprisingly decent dives orbit the ultimate party haven nestled between the craggy towers (p317)

Great Food

Thai food is fabulously flavoured, remarkably convenient and ridiculously cheap. Street stalls spring up wherever there are appetites, night markets serve everyone dinner, and family restaurants deliver colourful plates of traditional recipes.

Curries The soup that eats like a meal, Thai curry is pungent, fiery and colourful. Bangkok delivers a variety of flavours from across the country, while the south cooks up curry stock with heaping portions of stewed fish.

Seafood Grilled prawns, spicy squid stir-fries, crab curries, fried mussels – get thee to the coast and dine on the fruits of the sea.

Fruits Whole meals are made up of the luscious variety of Thai fruits, which are sold in abundance at day markets or displayed like precious jewels in glass cases by roaming vendors.

Isan cuisine The food that fuels labour, the northeast's triumvirate of dishes – *gài yâhng* (grilled chicken), *sôm·đam* (spicy green papaya salad) and *kôw nĕe·o* (sticky rice) – is, perhaps ironically, a perennial stall-food fave in the south.

Cooking courses Learn how to replicate the tricks of the trade at local cooking schools in Bangkok (p63), Phuket (p245) and Ko Samui (p179)

If you like...nightlife, then a night (or 12!) in Bangkok is a must. You're also apt to find plenty of boozing and cruising down in Phuket and Ko Samui, and don't forget the veritable beeline of backpackers that move between Ko Pha-Ngan and Ko Phi-Phi.

Five-Star Pampering

No one does luxury better than Thailand. After all, the Land of Smiles boasts the original flavour of Asian hospitality. The country's larger islands boast some of the finest five-star properties that the world has to offer (and some are surprisingly inexpensive).

Phuket Enjoy a parade of upmarket accommodation along the silky western sands of Phuket. Even if you're not crashing, it's worth coming by for cocktails (p239)

Ko Samui Quieter than Phuket, Samui knows how to blend posh digs with quiet seclusion – the island's myriad peninsulas offer private paradises to those who open their wallets (p179)

Bangkok Intense competition among hotels has kept prices low in the capital, so splurge on a fancy crash pad at one of the city's luxury headliners (p67)

Khao Lak Known mostly for the diving, Khao Lak has a small cluster of five-star properties that are easier on the wallet than the Phuket picks nearby (p292)

Ko Pha-Ngan Emerging from backpackerdom, Ko Pha-Ngan has a small handful of upmarket options nestled along the quiet waters (p196)

Adventure Sports

After one too many days of beach lazing, get the blood pumping with one of Thailand's many adventure activities. Sure, there's plenty of scuba, but you'll find just as many thrilling things to do without strapping on a tank.

Rock climbing in Railay The Andaman's signature limestone outcrops come to a dramatic climax in Railay – look up high and spots hundreds of dangling climbers (p311)

Jungle trekking in Ko Chang Have your *Heart of Darkness* moment deep in the thick jungles of Ko Chang – a large tract of mostly untouched foliage (p126)

Kayaking in Phang-Nga Gaze towards the heavens from the comfort of your kayak as the jagged stone pierces the lazy clouds above (p296)

Ziplining in Phuket Go gibbon-style through the vast acreage of sweaty palms and swing through the canopy, catching glimpses of the secreted forest below (p239)

Rock climbing in the Ko Yaos Far less touristy than the towers at Railay, quiet Ko Yao Noi is the upcoming climbing destination for adventure seekers in the know (p297)

Back to Basics

Don't trust the backtalk – there are still heaps of places in Thailand where you can go to rid yourself of the world's woes. Sling up the cotton hammock, lie down and enjoy.

Ko Lao Liang Lost between the Trang Islands and the Ko Tarutao archipelago, Ko Lao Liang has but one low-key place to stay hidden betwixt twin turrets of stone (p342)

Ko Phra Thong Near the muddy flats of Ranong, Ko Phra Thong is a glittering gem along the Andaman Sea where older tourists like to gather to return to their backpacker roots (p287)

Ko Pha-Ngan Things may be moving upscale, but Ko Pha-Ngan still has myriad nooks that have yet to see any sign of true development (p192)

Ko Wai Ko Wai? Ko Why Not! One of the smaller flecks of sand in the Ko Chang archipelago silently floats in the sea after the day-trippers depart before sunset (p134)

Bang Saphan Yai Tucked along the mainland's overlooked upper gulf region, Bang Saphan Yai basks in its back-to-Thai lifestyle – bamboo huts are aplenty (p166)

month by month

Top Events

1 **Songkran**, April

2 **Loi Krathong**, November

3 **Full Moon Party**, Monthly

4 **Vegetarian Festival**, October

5 **HM the King's Birthday**, December

January

The weather is cool and dry in Thailand, ushering in the peak tourist season when Europeans escape dreary winter weather.

Chinese New Year

Thais with Chinese ancestry celebrate the Chinese lunar new year (dates vary) with a week of house-cleaning and fireworks. Phuket, Bangkok and Pattaya all host citywide festivities, but in general Chinese New Year *(drùd jeen)* is a family event.

February

Still in the high season swing, snowbirds flock to Thailand for sun and fun.

Makha Bucha

One of three holy days marking important moments of Buddha's life, Makha Bucha *(mah·ká boo·chah)* falls on the full moon of the third lunar month and commemorates Buddha preaching to 1250 enlightened monks who came to hear him 'without prior summons'. A public holiday, it's mainly a day for temple visits. Organisations and schools will often make merit as a group at a local temple.

March

Hot and dry season approaches, and the beaches start to empty out. The winds kick up ushering in kite-flying and kiteboarding season. This is also Thailand's semester break, and students head out on sightseeing trips.

Pattaya International Music Festival

Pattaya showcases pop and rock bands from across Asia at this free music event, attracting bus loads of Bangkok university students.

April

Hot, dry weather sweeps across the land as the tourist season winds down, except for one last hurrah during Songkran. Make reservations well in advance since the whole country is on the move for this holiday.

Songkran

Thailand's traditional new year (12–14 April) starts out as a respectful affair then degenerates into a water war. Morning visits to the temple involve colourful processions of the sacred Buddha images, which are ceremoniously sprinkled with water. Elders are shown respect by younger family members by having water sprinkled on their hands. Afterwards Thais load up their water guns and head out to the streets for battle: water is thrown, catapulted and sprayed from roving commandos and outfitted pick-up trucks at willing and unwilling targets. Bangkok is the epicentre of the battle. Innocent bystanders shelter indoors until the ammunition runs out.

May

Leading up to the rainy season, festivals encourage plentiful rains and bountiful harvests. This is an underappreciated shoulder season when prices are lower and tourists are few.

Royal Ploughing Ceremony

This royal ceremony employs astrology and ancient Brahman rituals to kick off the rice-planting season. Sacred oxen are hitched to a wooden plough and part the ground of Sanam Luang in Bangkok. The ritual was revived in the 1960s by the king, and Crown Prince Maha Vajiralongkorn has assumed the ceremony's helm.

June

In some parts of the region, the rainy season is merely an afternoon shower, leaving the rest of the day for music and merriment.

Hua Hin Jazz Festival

Jazz groups descend on this royal retreat for a musical homage to the king, an accomplished jazz saxophonist and composer.

July

With the start of the rainy season, the religious community and attendant festivals prepare for Buddhist Lent, a period of reflection and meditation.

Khao Phansaa

The day after Asahna Bucha, the day the lord Buddha delivered his first sermon, marks the beginning of Buddhist Lent (the first day of the waning moon in the eighth lunar month), the traditional time for men to enter the monkhood and when monks typically retreat

(above) Devotees at the Jui Tui temple during the Vegetarian Festival (p250) in Phuket Town
(below) Thai teenagers at Th Khao San in Bangkok during Songkran (p25)

inside the monastery for a period of study and meditation. During Khao Phansaa, worshippers make offerings of candles and other necessities to the temples and attend ordinations.

August

Overcast skies and daily showers mark the middle of the rainy season. The predictable rain just adds to the ever-present humidity.

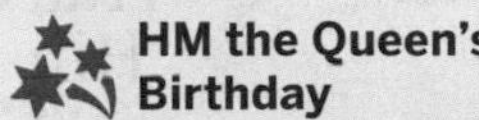

HM the Queen's Birthday

The Thai Queen's Birthday (12 August) is a public holiday and national mother's day. In Bangkok, the day is marked with cultural displays along Th Ratchadamnoen and Sanam Luang.

October

Religious preparations for the end of the rainy season and the end of Buddhist Lent begin. The monsoons are reaching the finish line (in most of the country)

Vegetarian Festival

Usually held in late September or early October, the Vegetarian Festival is a holiday from meat taken for nine days (during the ninth lunar month) in adherence with Chinese Buddhist beliefs of mind and body purification. Cities with large Thai-Chinese populations, such as Bangkok, Hua Hin, Pattaya, Trang and Krabi, are festooned with yellow banners heralding vegetarian vendors, and merit-makers dressed in white shuffle off for meditation retreats. In Phuket the festival gets extreme, with entranced marchers turning themselves into human shish kebabs.

November

The cool, dry season has arrived and if you get here early enough, you'll beat the tourist crowds. The landscape is lush: perfect for trekking and waterfall-spotting.

Loi Krathong

One of Thailand's most beloved festivals, Loi Krathong is celebrated on the first full moon of the 12th lunar month. The festival thanks the river goddess for providing life to the fields and forests, and asks for forgiveness for the polluting ways of humans. Small handmade origami-like boats made from banana leaves (called *kràthong* or *grà·tong*) are sent adrift in the country's waterways. They're decorated with flowers, and incense, candles and coins are placed in them.

December

The peak of the tourist season has returned with fair skies and a holiday mood.

HM the King's Birthday

Honouring the king's birthday on 5 December, this public holiday hosts parades and merit-making events; it is also recognised as national father's day. Th Ratchadamnoen Klang in Bangkok is decorated with lights and regalia. Everyone wears pink shirts, pink being the colour associated with the monarchy.

Choose your own Beach Adventure

How far will you travel to find your perfect beach? Pick a starting point based on your travel priorities, then fill in the blanks.

Start

Seeking popular Hotspots

I'll take a one-hour flight or the night train from Bangkok, but I don't want to spend an entire day travelling.

When it comes to accommodation, I tend to pick...

...backpacker digs.

...something family-friendly or luxurious.

Scuba diving...

...sounds great.

...is not for me.

My top activity is...

...relaxing on a beach.

...rock climbing.

When it comes to food...

...I'm all about seafood.

...Thai staples are fine.

...I want an eclectic mix.

The perfect resort...

...is on a quieter beach with a youthful vibe.

...has an international standard of excellence.

Ko Lanta p324

Hua Hin p148

Ko Tao p207

Railay p311

Ko Samui p174

Phuket p238

Ko Chang (Andaman Coast) p275

Trang Islands p335

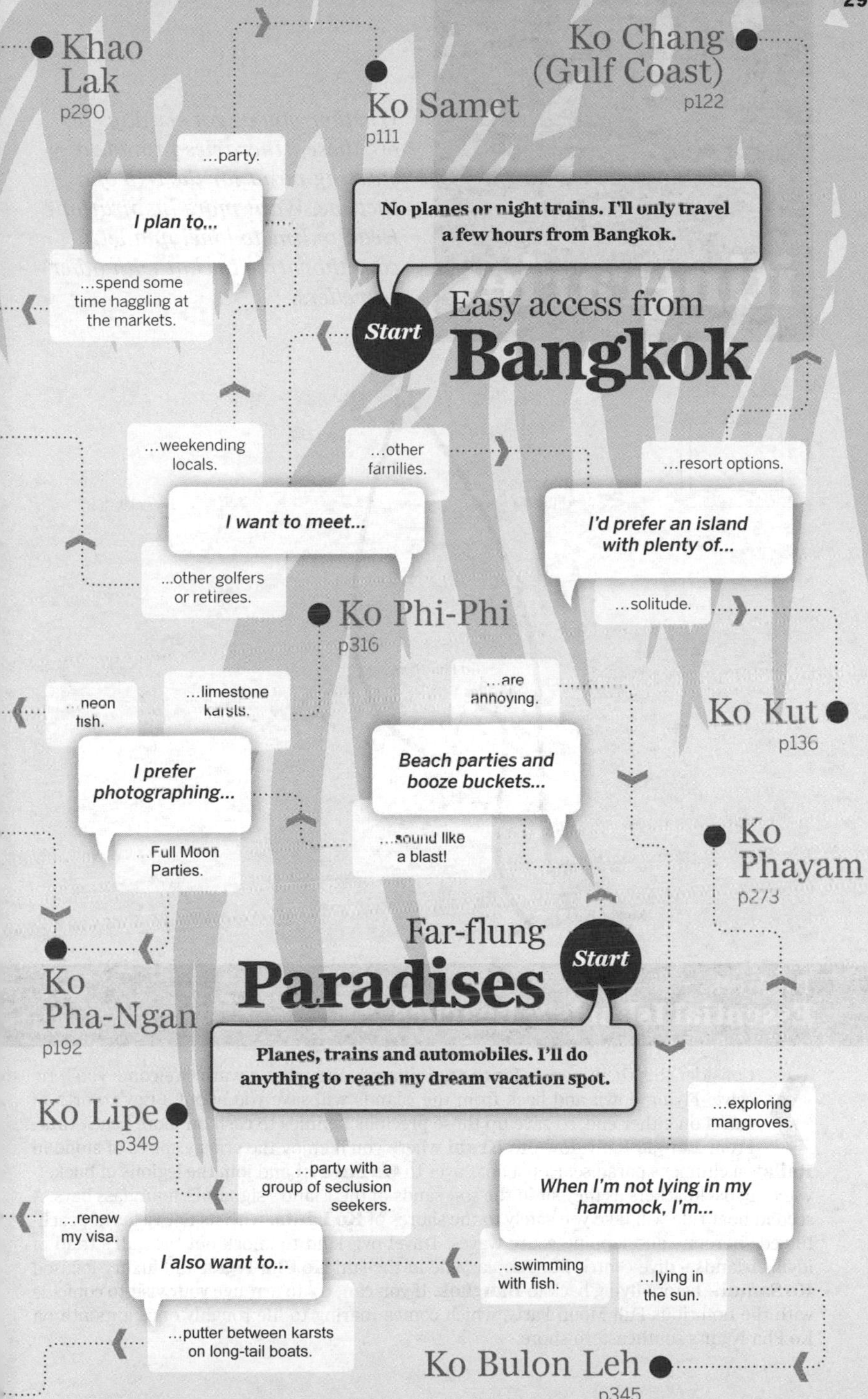

Easy access from
Bangkok
Start
No planes or night trains. I'll only travel a few hours from Bangkok.
I want to meet...
...weekending locals.
...other families.
...other golfers or retirees.
I plan to...
...party.
...spend some time haggling at the markets.
I'd prefer an island with plenty of...
...resort options.
...solitude.
Khao Lak
p290
Ko Samet
p111
Ko Chang (Gulf Coast)
p122
Ko Kut
p136
Far-flung
Paradises
Start
Planes, trains and automobiles. I'll do anything to reach my dream vacation spot.
Beach parties and booze buckets...
...are annoying.
...sound like a blast!
I prefer photographing...
...neon fish.
...limestone karsts.
...Full Moon Parties.
When I'm not lying in my hammock, I'm...
...exploring mangroves.
...swimming with fish.
...lying in the sun.
I also want to...
...party with a group of seclusion seekers.
...renew my visa.
...putter between karsts on long-tail boats.
Ko Phi-Phi
p316
Ko Phayam
p273
Ko Pha-Ngan
p192
Ko Lipe
p349
Ko Bulon Leh
p345

itineraries

Whether you've got six days or 60, these itineraries provide a starting point for the trip of a lifetime. Want more inspiration? Head online to lonelyplanet.com/thorntree to chat with other travellers.

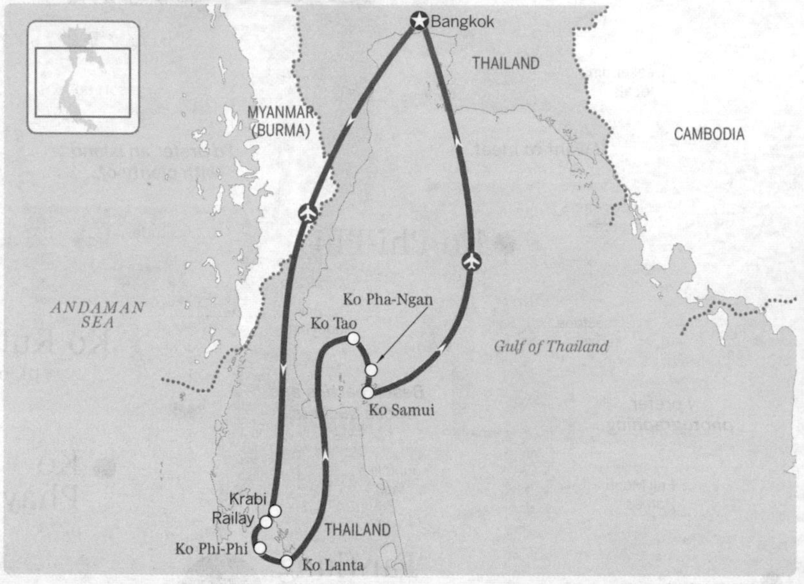

Two Weeks

Essential Islands & Beaches

Consider this the itinerary for the uninitiated, and what a warm welcome you'll receive. Flying down and back from the islands will save you about a day's worth of travel on either end, so save up those precious pennies to cash on more beach time.

From **Bangkok**, fly down to **Krabi** where you'll enjoy the craggy spires of stone in **Railay**, a climber's paradise. Hop a boat over to **Ko Phi-Phi** and join the legions of bucket-wielding backpackers as they sit in the soft sands of the island's signature hourglass bays. A second boat ride will take you safely to the shores of **Ko Lanta**, with its flat vistas of peach-tinged shoreline and lapping azure waves. Travel overland to knock out the gulf's triad of idyllic islands – dive-centric **Ko Tao**, lazy, lie-in-the-sun **Ko Pha-Ngan** and luxury-focused **Ko Samui** – before flying back to **Bangkok**. If you can, try to arrange your visit to coincide with the notorious Full Moon Party, which comes roaring to life roughly once a month on Ko Pha-Ngan's southeastern shore.

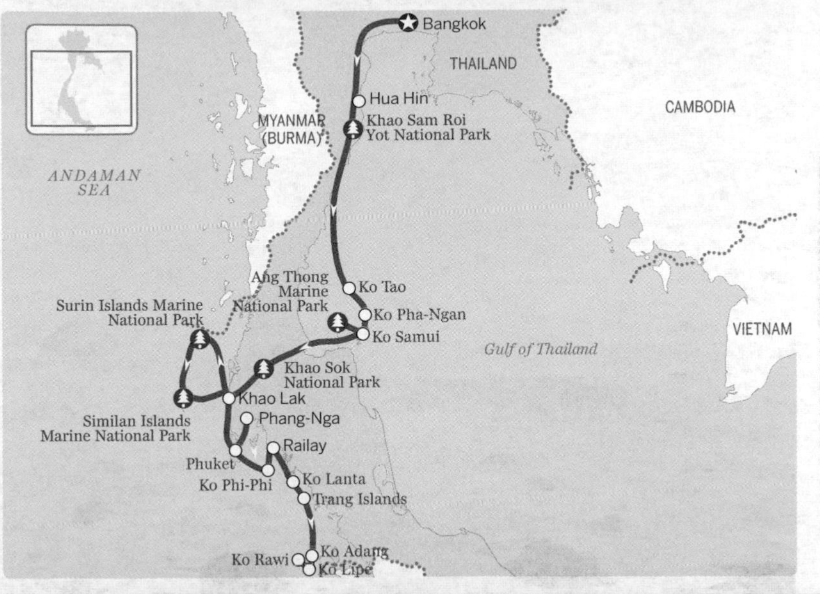

One Month

The Full Monty

A month, you say? There are thousands of perfectly good itineraries to think up but, well, why not consider a hammock tour extraordinaire. Not just any old beach trip, this is enough time to really get to know southern Thailand's islands, beaches and jungle-clad parks. Start your journey in Thailand's capital, **Bangkok**, before following the coastline south. Your first stop is **Hua Hin**, the king's preferred holiday destination and home to a thriving local and expat scene that cavorts among seafood markets and charming shanty piers. Hike the craggy hills of quiet **Khao Sam Roi Yot National Park** before making your way out to **Ko Tao**. Strap on your tank and dive with the fish below before moving over to **Ko Pha-Ngan** for some subdued beachside relaxing. **Ko Samui**, next door, offers a bit more variety and has a magical stash of holiday fodder to suit every budget and desire – don't miss the chance to do a day trip out of the wild islets of **Ang Thong Marine National Park** (which are said to have inspired Alex Garland's *The Beach*). Swap coasts with a stop in **Khao Sok National Park**, known to be one of the oldest stretches of jungle in the world. If time permits, hop on a live-aboard diving excursion in **Khao Lak** to explore the kingdom's finest diving treasures lurking in the **Surin** and **Similan Islands Marine National Parks** near the Burmese border. Travel down the coast to **Phuket** and sample Thailand's finest iteration of luxury hospitality; spend a night in Patong if you dare. Paddle around the limestone karsts of quiet **Phang-Nga** then sleep beneath the ethereal crags of **Ko Phi-Phi** after a spirit evening (no pun intended) of beach dancing and fire twirling. Scale the stone towers of **Railay**, next door, zoom around the flat tracts of land on mellowed-out **Ko Lanta**, then hop on a boat bound for the **Trang Islands** – paradise found. One last archipelago awaits those who travel further south towards the Malaysian border. **Ko Lipe** is the island of choice for those looking for something social, but let the local *chow lair* (sea gypsies; also spelt *chao leh*) lead you to silent **Ko Adang** or **Ko Rawi** next door if you're looking to get away from it all.

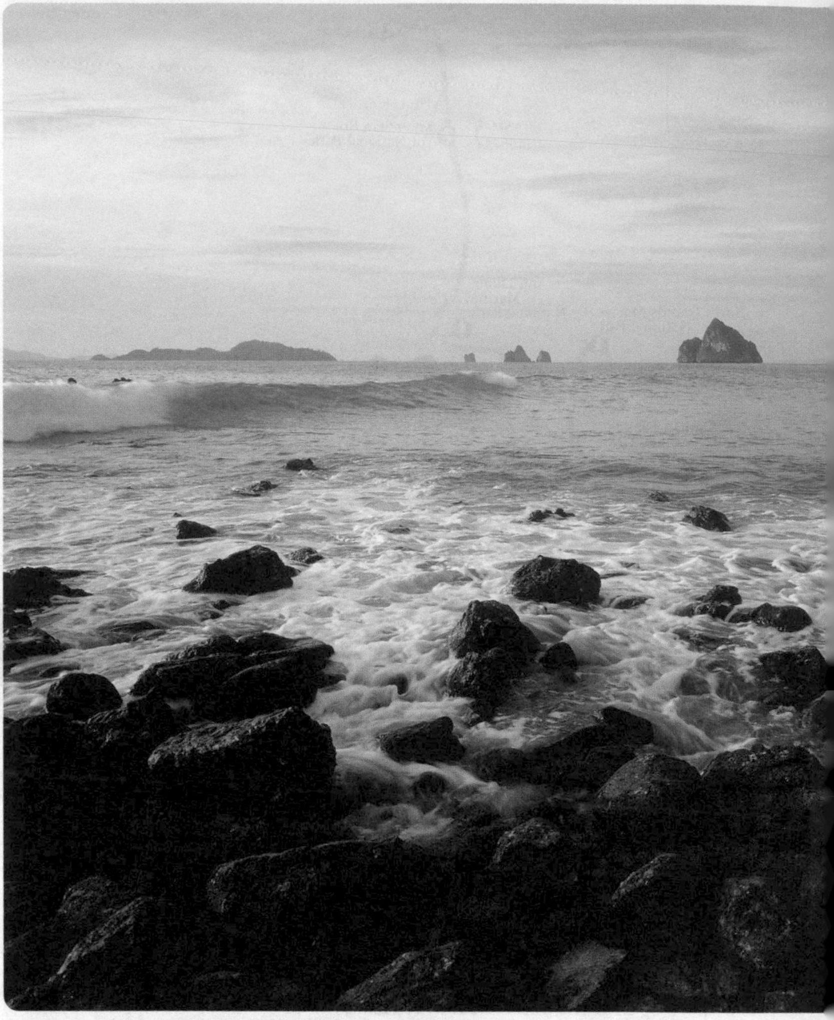

» (above) Ko Kradan (p340)
» (left) Bungalows on Ko Lipe (p34

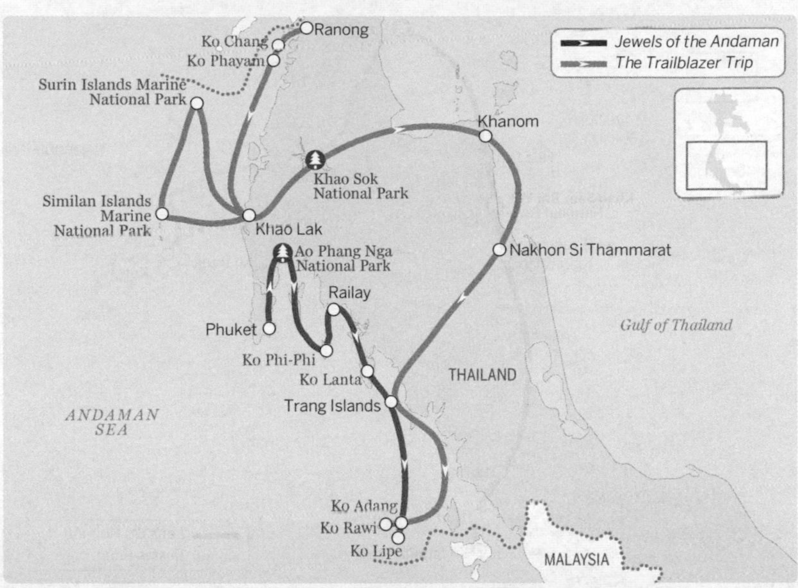

Two Weeks
Jewels of the Andaman

Dreams of perfect beaches, silky sands and emerald waters come true along the Andaman coast, where limestone crags soar skyward creating infinite moments for that perfect photo-opp. Do not pass 'Go', do not collect $200, just head directly to **Phuket** to start your journey down one of the finest stretches of coastline in the world. Cruise through the limestone karsts of **Ao Phang-Nga National Park**, which give Halong Bay a run for its money. **Ko Phi-Phi's** hourglass bays further south can't be beat, especially when the sun sets behind the earthen crown of Ko Phi-Phi Leh just offshore. Let the towers of stone in **Railay** cast anthropomorphic shadows on the sands, then sail down to **Ko Lanta**, a flat island best explored by motorbike. Savour the secrets of the **Trang Islands**, like the hidden emerald lagoon or the untouched house reef of **Ko Kradan**, then make your way to the Malaysian border where you'll find tiny **Ko Lipe** protected by its looming neighbour, **Ko Adang**.

Three Weeks
The Trailblazer Trip

Buck the travel trends and blaze your own trail through some of the lesser-known beaches and islands of southern Thailand. Start in **Ranong**, a rather inauspicious welcome mat to the region, then connect to the nearby island of **Ko Phayam** and 'little' **Ko Chang** (not to be confused with the 'big' Ko Chang near Cambodia). Trade diver tips in **Khao Lak** further south and join a live-aboard up to the Burmese border. Then switch coasts, stopping in **Khao Sok National Park** to enjoy a spot of submarine cave diving. Reward yourself with lazy beach days once you reach the gulf's **Khanom**. Explore the rich, temple-filled, cultural centre of **Nakhon Si Thammarat** further south before returning to the Andaman coast for a few more days of island-hopping. Choose among the lonely stone specks of the **Trang Islands** – perhaps **Ko Kradan** or **Ko Sukorn** – then wander south for a camping excursion with the *chow lair* on whisper-quiet **Ko Adang** or **Ko Rawi**.

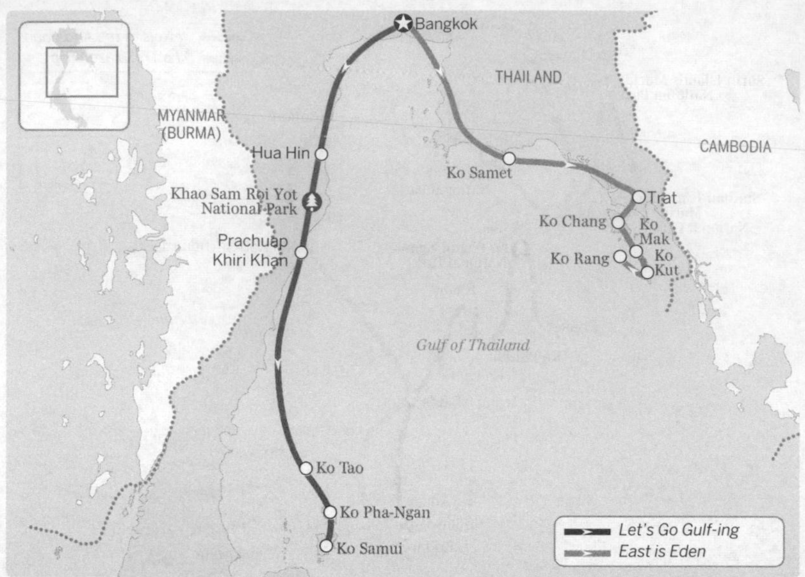

Two Weeks

Let's Go Gulf-ing

With less dramatic weather than its Andaman counterpart, Thailand's gulf is solid choice for a beach holiday almost any time of year. Start in **Bangkok** and travel overland down to **Hua Hin**, home to the king's holiday palace. Gorge on fresh fish at the markets before heading for the hills of **Khao Sam Roi Yot National Park**. Towering limestone, hidden temples and quiet beaches await those with the luxury of time. Roll through the sleepy seaside villages of **Prachuap Khiri Khan** then grab a boat from Chumphon and hit the cool gulf waters, stopping first in **Ko Tao** – where you can learn all the tricks of the diving trade – before moving on to **Ko Pha-Ngan** to live out your castaway fantasies on one of the island's quiet beaches. Fete the Full Moon before leaving, then set your sights on **Ko Samui**, the area's largest island and undoubted master of luxury dream holidays. Quainter lodging options and diverse restaurants also stretch as far as the eye can see.

Ten Days

East is Eden

Thailand's southern treasures are undoubtedly the kingdom's major drawcards, but if you're pushed for time or heading into Cambodia, it's worth exploring the eastern gulf. From **Bangkok** head to rustic **Ko Samet,** where Bangkokians let loose on weekends. Follow the coast to sleepy **Trat** then hop on a boat for one of the Ko Chang archipelago's many islands. Ride elephants and hike the interior of jungle-topped **Ko Chang**, the largest and most developed island in the region. Get further off the beaten track on secluded **Ko Mak** or rugged **Ko Kut**. Hardcore Robinson Crusoes can go one step further on neighbouring, ultra-simple **Ko Kham** or **Ko Rayang** for some stunning coral. Alternatively, hit up to **Ko Rang** for a genuine *Survivor* experience, sans pesky host, cameramen and tribal councils.

Diving & Snorkelling

Best Place to Learn

Ko Tao Fantastic frenetic dive energy and scores of shallow dive sites that are often visited by plankton-chewing whale sharks. This is the best (and cheapest) place in Thailand to lose your scuba virginity. Sail Rock (closer to Ko Pha-Ngan) and Chumphon Pinnacle are the star sites.

Best Live-Aboards

Khao Lak The gateway to the hushed tropical archipelagos of the Surin and Similan Islands. Explore the myriad dive sites on a live-aboard trip and check out Richelieu Rock – a stunning diving spot near the Burmese border discovered by Jacques Cousteau.

Best Marine Life

Ko Lanta A top spot for crystal clear waters and loads of marine life, including recurrent visits by manta rays and the odd whale shark. Try the submerged pinnacles at Hin Daeng and Hin Muang.

Best Snorkelling

Ko Phi-Phi A triumphant comeback after the tsunami and loads of shimmering reefs swaying under perfectly clear waters. Ko Mai Phai and Ko Nok are great snorkelling spots, while Hin Bida and Ko Bida Nok are the local diving faves.

Diving

Those who have explored the deep can undoubtedly agree with Jacques Cousteau: 'the sea, once it casts its spell, holds one in its net of wonder forever'. In fact, when Mr Cousteau sang that sea's praises, he was probably talking about the Land of Smiles, since he himself discovered several of the sites explored by many today. Those who are willing to strap on some scuba gear can easily access this stunning realm, which rivals the beauty of the kingdom's idyllic onland scenery, so often captured in photographs and postcards, then flaunted to jealous friends back home.

Planning Your Trip

The monsoon rains and peak tourist season are two factors determining when to go and which islands and beaches to pick. The severity of the rainy weater varies between seasons and coasts, and there are dry and wet microclimates as well.

When to Go

Generally speaking, the Gulf of Thailand has a year-round dive season, while the Andaman coast has optimal diving conditions between December and April. The southwestern monsoon seems to affect the Ko Chang archipelago more than other eastern gulf coast dive sites; hence, November to early May is the ideal season for those islands.

HITTING THE UNDERWATER JACKPOT

Most divers come to Thailand with the hope of hitting the underwater jackpot; spotting an elusive whale shark – the largest fish in the sea – with a giant mouth that can measure about 2m wide (so just imagine how big their bodies are!) Don't worry: they are filter feeders, which means that they mostly feed on plankton, krill and other tiny organisms. In fact, divers often report that adult whale sharks are quite friendly and enjoy swimming through the stream of bubbles emitted by divers. Usually these gentle creatures gravitate towards submerged pinnacles. They often hang out at a site for several days before continuing on, so if rumours are flying around about a recent sighting, then strap on your scuba gear and hit the high seas. Most diving instructors we encountered said that they personally average around three to seven sighting per year. In the past there were 'spotting seasons', but recent shifts in weather patterns mean that they can be spotted at any time of the year.

Manta ray sightings are more frequent during the prime diving months on the Andaman side, while whale sharks usually make an appearance throughout the year on the gulf side.

December–February Days are mostly rain-free and under the waves you'll find a conglomeration of large pelagics at the feeding stations along the Andaman coast.

April–June Along the gulf things are pretty quiet at this time, and the weather holds out nicely allowing for good visibility underwater.

Try to avoid the following times.

June–September The monsoon rains arrive on the Andaman coast, some hotels shut down and boat travel can be interrupted by storms.

October–December The gulf coast gets the brunt of its rainy season during this period.

Pre-Booking

It is not necessary to pre-book any diving excursions in Thailand unless you plan on doing a live-aboard up to the Surin and Similan Islands Marine National Parks. Diving packages can be arranged in advance through the operator of your choosing, especially if you are looking for a diving deal that includes accommodation. However, in most destinations, such as Ko Tao (p207) and Ko Phi-Phi (p317), you'll find that a solid infrastructure has been set up to support those who decide to give diving a go at the last minute. Consult the destination coverage for detailed information about linking up with a recommended operator.

Costs

Scuba can be a costly venture when compared to many of the world's other leisure sports. Diving in Thailand is significantly cheaper than in most other nations around the world, which makes it a wonderful place for newbies to cut their teeth, or for seasoned scubaphiles to take a sea-themed vacation. Generally, it is more prudent to sign up for a diving package, which usually consists of a set number of dives. A 10-dive package goes for around 7000B to 10,000B on the more affordable beaches. Another popular option is a two- or three-dive day trip, which shuttles divers to the area's best sites. Day-trip prices largely depend on how far the boat will travel as petrol prices are at a premium. Figure around 2500B for a day trip from Ko Pha-Ngan and up to around 5000B for a trip out to Hin Daeng and Hin Muang from Ko Lanta.

Often diving costs can include 'free' accommodation provided by your outfitter. Note that lodging is only free on the days that you dive.

See p37 for information about course pricing and check out p38 for details on live-aboard pricing.

Where to Dive

Thailand's unique coastal topography sits at the junction of two distinct oceanic zones – the Andaman waters wash in from the west, while the gulf coast draws its waters from the islands of Indonesia and the South China Sea. Although marine life is somewhat similar on both sides of the peninsula, each region has telltale differences that easily distinguish one from the other. An ideal diving vacation in Thailand would involve stops along both bodies of water.

Diving the Andaman

When the weather is right, the Andaman Sea has some of the finest diving in Southeast Asia. Many would argue that the Andaman has better diving than the gulf, but this is mostly attributed to excellent visibility during the few months of favourable sea conditions. After several post-tsunami evaluations of the coral reefs in the Andaman, most divers agree that the damage was surprisingly small. In fact, some say that the sea shines a more brilliant blue in recent years. At least 210 hard corals and 108 species of reef fish have been recorded here, and encounters with large pelagic creatures are quite frequent along the southern provinces.

Live-aboard dive trips regularly depart Khao Lak (p291) and Phuket (p239) for the quiet archipelagos further west known as the Surin and Similan Islands. To the south, Ko Phi-Phi (p317), Ko Lanta (p325) and even little Ko Lipe (p351) are great places to hang your rucksack and put on some fins.

Exploring the Gulf

The best part about diving the Gulf of Thailand is that sea conditions are generally favourable throughout the year. This C-shaped coastline is about twice as long as the Andaman side and changes drastically as it links the Malaysian border to Thailand's eastern neighbour, Cambodia. The southwestern gulf coast has the finest diving spots, located near the islands of Ko Tao (p207) and Ko Pha-Ngan (p195). Ko Tao currently certifies more divers than any other place in the world. Pattaya (p103), just a quick two-hour hop from the Bangkok bustle, offers a few memorable dives as well, including a couple of wrecks. On the far eastern side of the coast, the Ko Chang archipelago (p128) provides for some pleasant scuba possibilities, although choppy seas limit the season to between November and May.

Safe Diving

Before You Dive

Before embarking on a scuba-diving trip, carefully consider the following points to ensure a safe and enjoyable experience:

» Make sure you have a current diving certification card from a recognised scuba-diving instructional agency. If you have not dived in the last six months, insist on a brush-up tutorial to refresh your memory on how to operate your gear.

» Make sure you visit a doctor before diving for the first time. A doctor's clean bill of health is expected at all dive schools if you are a newbie. Asthmatics will not be allowed to dive.

» Ensure you're healthy and feel comfortable diving. Make sure to be very hydrated on the days you dive.

» Never dive alone, and if you are diving a site for the first time, make sure you are accompanied by an instructor or divemaster who knows the site well.

» Remember that your last dive should be completed 24 hours before you fly. It is, however, fine to dive soon after arriving by air.

» Make sure your insurance policy covers diving injuries. If it doesn't, purchase additional coverage at www.diversalertnetwork.org.

Decompression Chambers

For the amount of diving throughout Thailand, the kingdom has a surprisingly limited number of medical facilities dedicated to diving accidents.

Decompression (hyperbaric) chambers can be found at most major hubs, including Bangkok, Ko Samui (p191), Pattaya and Phuket (p245). Ko Tao has an emergency chamber – most injuries are dealt with on Ko Samui. Injured divers out of Khao Lak are generally rushed south to Phuket (about an hour away). We advise you to ask your operator of choice about the nearest chamber. Also, make sure that there is an emergency supply of oxygen on your dive boat.

Coursework

Thailand is one of the best places in the world to learn how to dive. The dive school market is saturated, which means that you'll get top-notch instruction for practically nothing, as everyone is eagerly competing for your dime. If you are looking for the best bang for your baht, we recommend getting certified on Ko Tao (p207), where coursework starts at 9000B to 9800B depending on the type of licence you receive. Ko Tao is also a great place to continue your diving education – see p208 for additional information about going from 'zero to hero'.

Beyond Ko Tao, there are plenty of places to get certified, though you're looking at an extra 3000B to 6000B for your Open Water certificate. Ko Pha-Ngan (p195), Ko Phi-Phi (p317), Khao Lak (p291) and Ko Lanta (p325)

PRESERVING THAILAND'S REEFS

Thailand's underwater kingdom is incredibly fragile and it's worth taking some time to educate yourself on responsible practices while you're visiting. Here are a few of the more important sustainable practices, but this is by no means an exhaustive list.

» Whether on an island or in a boat, take all litter with you – even biodegradable material like apple cores – and dispose of it back on the mainland.

» Remember that it is an offence to damage or remove coral in marine parks.

» Don't touch or harass marine animals.

» Never rest or stand on coral since touching or walking on it will damage it. It can also create some nasty cuts.

» If you have a boat, be aware of the rules in relation to anchoring around the reef, including 'no anchoring areas'. Be very careful not to damage coral when you let down the anchor.

» If you're diving, check that you are weighted correctly before entering the water and keep your buoyancy control well away from the reef. Ensure that equipment such as secondary regulators and gauges aren't dragging over the reef.

» If you're snorkelling (and especially if you are a beginner), practise your technique away from coral until you've mastered control in the water.

» Hire a wetsuit rather than slathering on sunscreen, which can damage the reef.

» Watch where your fins are – try not to stir up sediment or disturb coral.

» Do not enter the water near a dugong, including when swimming or diving.

» Do not take any shells home with you – it's illegal.

round out Thailand's top five places to lose your scuba virginity.

Live-Aboards

The live-aboard industry has been steadily growing in Thailand over the past 20 years. Most live-aboards are based out of Khao Lak, just north of Phuket on the Andaman coast. These live-aboard excursions are all-inclusive (lodging on the boat, food, scuba gear, guides) and vary in length from two to five nights. Check out p291 for more information, and note that there are no diving live-aboards in the gulf.

Freediving

Freediving is a type of underwater exploration where an individual diver goes below the waves without scuba equipment or snorkel gear. A single dive is performed solely on your ability to hold your breath. Advanced freedivers have tapped into the mammalian diving reflex in which the human body changes its blood flow and oxygen circulation to allow for a seemingly inordinate amount of time submerged. While it is often popular as a competitive sport (depth and time challenges), travellers can find opportunities in a relaxed environment. Currently, one of the top spots to try the sport is on Ko Tao (p211) in the southern gulf. Beginner courses (usually two days of diving) cost around 5000B.

For more information on freediving check out **AIDA International** (International Association for Development of Apnea; www.aidainternational.org) and **CMAS** (World Underwater Federation; www.cmas.org).

Technical Diving

Often called tec diving by those in the industry, technical diving is an advanced scuba diving involving additional equipment and, most notably, a tank of mixed breathing gases to allow for deeper dives. Technical diving is often taken on as a recreational sport for those interested in exploring deep wrecks and caves.

Underwater caving has really taken off in recent years, and there are several operators on Ko Tao (p212) that offer one-day/one-night trips out to the submerged grottos in Khao Sok National Park.

Snorkelling

Snorkelling is popular choice for those who cringe at the thought of breathing air out of a tank; it's also a great option for those who are simply on a tighter budget. Many islands, including the Trang island chain (p335), Ko Tao (p209), Ko Pha-Ngan (p195), Ko Phi-Phi (p318) and the islands in the Ko Chang archipelago (p128) have phenomenal snorkelling spots right off shore.

Tours

Lately, snorkel tours are becoming just as popular as diving day trips; in fact, many dive operators are now starting to offer snorkel outings as well. Expect to pay between 500B and 1000B for a day trip depending on how far you travel to find favourable conditions. Often a snorkelling component gets tied into larger day trips that take in virgin islands and hidden topographical wonders.

High-end excursions usually use fancy speedboats and expensive equipment, while cheaper deals tend to focus more on the social aspect of the trip, taking customers to so-so reefs. Consider chartering your own speedboat or long-tail boat if you are serious about snorkelling. With a little research, it's not too difficult to scout out undisturbed reefs nearby.

On Your Own

Orchestrating your own snorkelling adventure is a cinch – there are loads of resorts and dive shops spread through Thailand's islands and beaches that rent out gear for 100B to 200B per day. If you plan on snorkelling under your own steam, it is best to follow the same simple rules that you would for scuba:

» Bring a buddy with you.

» Wear a lifejacket if you are an unsure swimmer, or are unsure of riptides.

» Test your gear before entering deep water.

» If you explore unguided, make sure to have a fundamental knowledge of the reef life.

» Let someone on land know that you are going snorkelling, just in case something happens to you and your buddy.

» Wear sunscreen on the back of your arms, knees and neck.

» Wear a thin wetsuit (3mm) if you are sensitive to prolonged time in the water.

Eat & Drink Like a Local

When to Go

Summer Thailand's hot season (March to June) is the best time of year for fruit. Durian, mangoes, mangosteen and lychees are all at their juicy peak during these months.

Rainy Season One holiday to look out for during the rainy season (June to October) is Thailand's annual vegetarian festival (typically held in late September or early October). The festival is particularly celebrated in towns with large Chinese populations, such as Bangkok, Phuket Town and Trang. It's also worth mentioning that if you find yourself in predominantly Muslim areas during Ramadan (typically August or September), food may be relatively scarce during the daylight hours.

Where to Go

Bangkok Cheap but tasty street eats, just about every regional Thai cuisine and a diverse international food scene make Bangkok the number one place in Thailand to eat.

Trang Seemingly concealed in this quiet southern town are lauded Thai-Chinese restaurants, timeless cafes and some of the country's best southern Thai food.

Incendiary curries, oodles of noodles, fresh seafood and the tropical fruit you've been dreaming about – Thailand has it all. But what many visitors aren't aware of is that by eating in guest-house restaurants and tourist-frequented stalls, they're often experiencing a gentrified version of Thai food. In an effort to help you experience the true flavours of Thailand, we've put together an entire section to inspire and familiarise you with the dishes of Bangkok and southern Thailand. For a more general scoop on Thai food, see p382.

Food Experiences

Top Local Restaurants

Krua Apsorn, Bangkok (p77) This award-winning restaurant has a thick menu of decadent Bangkok- and central Thailand–style fare.

Poj Spa Kar, Bangkok (p77) Allegedly the city's oldest restaurant, Poj Spa Kar also has links with the former palace kitchen.

Jay Fai, Bangkok (p77) This lauded open-air shophouse specialises in seafood-heavy stir-fries that blur the line between Thai and Chinese cuisines.

Bharani, Bangkok (p81) Come here for rich, meaty boat noodles, a central Thai fave.

Pan & David Restauarant, Ko Si Chang (p103) Excellent Thai food in addition to Western treats such as homemade ice cream and French-pressed coffee.

Mum Aroi, Pattaya (p107) This rare gem serves fantastic Thai food in the midst of mediocre tourist fare.

Rang Yen Garden, Cha-am (p147) Deep in the heart of Thai vacation territory, this garden-side spot serves up local favourites.

Night Market, Hua Hin (p155) The undeniable favourite in the king's preferred town – go for the succulent crab curry.

Kanya, Ko Tao (p217) Scrumptious home-style dishes spun by a native Ko Taoian up the jungle road from central Sairee.

Cookies Salad, Ko Pha-Ngan (p204) The name may not sound particularly Thai, but the curries are treasured family recipes.

Ka Jok See, Phuket (p249) Down tasty Thai treats, then toss the dishes aside and dance on the tables.

Mama's Restaurant, Khao Lak (p292) Unbeatably delicious riffs on seafood classics – don't miss Mama's fishcakes.

BACKPACKER FOOD *AUSTIN BUSH*

It all began with an order of Hat Yao fried rice, a bizarre concoction of rice fried with ketchup and chicken breast, enveloped in a thin omelette. Now, I've eaten lots of Thai dishes in nearly every region of Thailand and have never come across anything quite like Hat Yao fried rice. I'd also never seen a green curry the way it was served the next night: soupy and impotent, and laden with carrots, cauliflower and potatoes. In fact, once I sought it out, I discovered an entire repertoire of food on Ko Pha-Ngan's Hat Yao that I'd never encountered previously. This genre of cuisine, characterised by unrecognisable interpretations of local and foreign dishes, dull flavours, a strong vegetarian bias, facsimile menus, mystery ingredients and even more mysterious origins, I called Backpacker Food.

The simple fact that Backpacker Food exists begs the question: why does one need comfort food when on the road? Isn't the point of travelling to try new things? Admittedly, there are times when a tender tummy might require familiar flavours, and perhaps this is when a queasy Italian would order the spaghetti carbonara, or when a nauseous native of the islands would choose the pork chop Hawaiian. (I'm still not exactly sure who would order Contigi prawn, fried chicken mayonnaise, no name falafel-style chicken or cauliflower cheese.) But the ubiquity of such menu items on Hat Yao suggested that they were the norm rather than the exception.

Backpacker breakfasts in particular seemed to have the least in common with the local cuisine. The English, with their 'Full English Breakfast' seemed to dominate this area, while the Swiss, with their muesli (often little more than oatmeal with a few cornflakes thrown in), have also had a palpable, though unpalatable, impact. And the ubiquitous 'American Breakfast' of instant coffee, lighter-than-air white bread, warm hotdogs and oily fried eggs isn't doing much to promote the image of American food abroad, and certainly isn't a good way to start the day.

Even if you do make an effort to go 'local', Thai-style Backpacker Food is often just as bizarre as, if not more so, the quasi-Western food. Authentic southern Thai cooking is a vibrant seafood-based cuisine that is among the most full-flavoured in the country, if not the world. But the guest-house kitchens of Hat Yao put out consistently weak Thai-style salads, limp tasteless stir-fries, barely there curries and oddly enough, despite being on an island, very few seafood dishes.

Luckily, if the lack of authentic Thai food on Ko Yao is getting to you, you could always order *kôw pàt à·me·rí·gan*, 'American fried rice' – rice fried with ketchup, sliced hotdogs and sweet raisins, topped with a fried egg. Despite the name, the dish is found throughout Thailand and is particularly popular among Thai children and university students. It was, as far as I could tell, the only authentically Thai dish on the restaurant menus of Hat Yao.

CAN I DRINK THE ICE?

Among the most common concerns we hear from first-time visitors to Thailand is about the safety of the country's ice. At the risk of sounding fatalistic, if it's your first time in Thailand, the ice is probably the least of your concerns – you're most likely going to get sick at some point. Considering that you're exposing yourself to a different cuisine and a new and unfamiliar family of bacteria and other bugs, it's virtually inevitable that your body will have a hard time adjusting.

In most cases this will mean little more than an upset tummy that might set you back a couple hours. You can avoid more serious setbacks, at least initially, by trying to frequent popular restaurants and vendors where dishes are prepared to order and only drinking bottled water.

And the ice? We've been lacing our drinks with it for years and have yet to trace it back to any specific discomfort.

Lanta Seafood (p330) The best seafood on Ko Lanta. Try the snapper with turmeric and garlic.

Cheap Eats

Chinatown, Bangkok (p78) Enjoy noodle soups, fried dishes and savoury snacks along the streets of Bangkok's most hectic 'hood.

Food Plus, Bangkok (p78) A narrow alleyway in the centre of town filled with countless cheap curries.

MBK Food Court, Bangkok (p78) A cheap, clean and tasty introduction to Thai and Thai-Chinese staples.

Soi 38 Night Market, Bangkok (p81) Who says dinner needs a wine list, or even a roof?

Laem Din Market, Ko Samui (p185) Where the local go for inexpensive nibbles and fresh produce.

Trang Night Market, Trang (p334) The best night market on the Andaman coast will have you salivating over bubbling curries, fried chicken and fish, *pàt tai* and an array of Thai desserts

Krabi Night Market, Krabi (p303) Near the Khong Kha pier, this market has excellent, authentic Thai food – despite the English menus.

Local Food Market, Ko Phi-Phi (p322) Easily the cheapest place for grub on this rather overpriced island. Try the smoked catfish.

Cooking Courses

A standard one-day course usually features a shopping trip to a local market to choose ingredients, followed by preparation of curry pastes, soups, curries, salads and desserts.

Khao, Bangkok (p63)

Helping Hands, Bangkok (p64)

Koh Chang Thai Cookery School, Ko Chang (p127)

KaTi, Ko Chang (p127)

Buchabun Art & Crafts Collection, Hua Hin (p153)

Samui Institute of Thai Culinary Arts, Ko Samui (p179)

Mom Tri's Boathouse, Phuket (p255)

Blue Elephant Restaurant & Cookery School, Phuket (p245)

Phuket Thai Cookery School, Phuket (p245)

Pum Thai Cooking School, Phuket (p245)

Krabi Thai Cookery School, Ao Nang (p308)

Railay Thai Cookery School, Railay (p313)

Pum Restaurant & Cooking School, Ko Phi-Phi Don (p318)

Time for Lime, Ko Lanta (p327)

Local Specialties

In both Bangkok and southern Thailand, geography and the country's predominant minorities – Muslims and the Chinese – have resulted in different but profound influences on the local cuisine.

Bangkok Cuisine

Bangkok is Thailand's melting pot and, not surprisingly, just about every regional or ethnic cuisine is available in the city. Strictly speaking though, the food of Bangkok has been shaped by the climate and crops of central Thailand, the city's immigrants and the refined dishes of the royal court.

People in Bangkok are fond of sweet/savoury flavours, and many dishes include freshwater fish, pork, coconut milk and palm sugar – common ingredients in the central Thai plains. Because of the city's proximity to the Gulf of Thailand, Bangkok eateries also serve a wide variety of seafood. Chinese labourers and vendors introduced a huge variety of noodle and wok-fried dishes to the city as many as 200 years ago. They also influenced the city's cuisine in other ways: beef is not widely eaten in Bangkok due to a Chinese-Buddhist teaching that forbids eating 'large' animals. A final significant influence on food in Bangkok has been the royal court, which has been producing sophisticated and refined takes on central Thai dishes for nearly 300 years. Although originally available only within palace walls, the dishes have spread over time and are now available across the city.

Must-eat Bangkok dishes include:

Pàt tai Thin rice noodles stir-fried with dried and/or fresh shrimp, bean sprouts, tofu, egg and seasonings, and traditionally served with lime halves, a few stalks of Chinese chives and a sliced banana flower.

Yam Ƅlah dùk foo Fried shredded catfish, chilli and peanuts served with a sweet/tart mango dressing.

Đôm yam Lemon grass, kaffir lime leaf and lime juice give this soup its characteristic tang; fresh chillies or an oily chilli paste provide it with its legendary sting.

Yen đah foh Combining a slightly sweet crimson-coloured broth with a variety of meat balls, cubes of blood and crispy greens, *yen đah foh* is probably both the most intimidating and the most popular noodle dish in Bangkok.

Kà·nŏm bêuang The old-school version of these taco-like snacks comes in two varieties, sweet and savoury.

Gaang sôm Central Thailand's famous 'sour soup' often includes freshwater fish, vegetables and/or herbs, and a thick, tart broth.

Mèe gròrp Crispy noodles made the old-school way with a sweet/sour flavour – most likely a former palace recipe – are a dying breed.

Gŏoay đĕeo reua Known as boat noodles because they were previously served from canals in central Thailand, these intense pork- or beef-based bowls are among the most full-flavoured of Thai noodle dishes.

Southern Thai Cuisine

Don't say we didn't warn you: southern Thai cooking is undoubtedly the spiciest regional cooking style in a land of spicy regional cuisines. The food of Thailand's southern provinces also tends to be very salty, and seafood, not surprisingly, plays an important role, ranging from fresh fish that is grilled or added to soups, to pickled or fermented fish or served as sauces or condiments. Two of the principal crops in the south are coconuts and cashews, both of which find their way into a variety of dishes. In addition to these, southern Thais love their greens, and nearly every meal is accompanied by a platter of fresh herbs and veggies, and a spicy 'dip' of shrimp paste, chillies, garlic and lime. Specific southern greens to look out for include *sà·đor* (a pungent green beanlike vegetable also known as stink bean), *lôok nee·ang* (a round dark-green bean) and *mót ree·ang* (similar to large, dark-green bean sprouts).

Dishes you are likely to come across in southern Thailand include the following:

Gaang đai Ƅlah An intensely spicy and salty fish curry that includes *đai Ƅlah* (salted fish stomach); much tastier than it sounds.

Kà·nŏm jeen nám yah This dish of thin rice noodles served with a fiery currylike sauce is

BEYOND THE STREET STALL

Read any magazine or newspaper article about eating in Thailand and you will inevitably find gushing references to the glories of the country's street food. While much of the food sold from mobile carts and streetside stalls is indeed very tasty, it certainly isn't the case that *only* street food is good. In fact, in our research, we've found that the best places to eat are anything but mobile. Rather, we recommend the long-standing, family-owned restaurants typically found in aged Sino-Portuguese shophouses. The cooks at such places have likely been serving the same dish – or limited repertoire of dishes – for several decades, and really know what they're doing. The food may cost slightly more than on the street, but the setting is usually more comfortable and hygienic, plus you're eating a piece of history. While such restaurants rarely have English-language menus, you can usually point to a picture or dish. If that fails, turn to p423 and practise your Thai.

So do indulge in a street cart or two as they're an essential part of the Thailand experience, but be sure to try a few old-school restaurants as well.

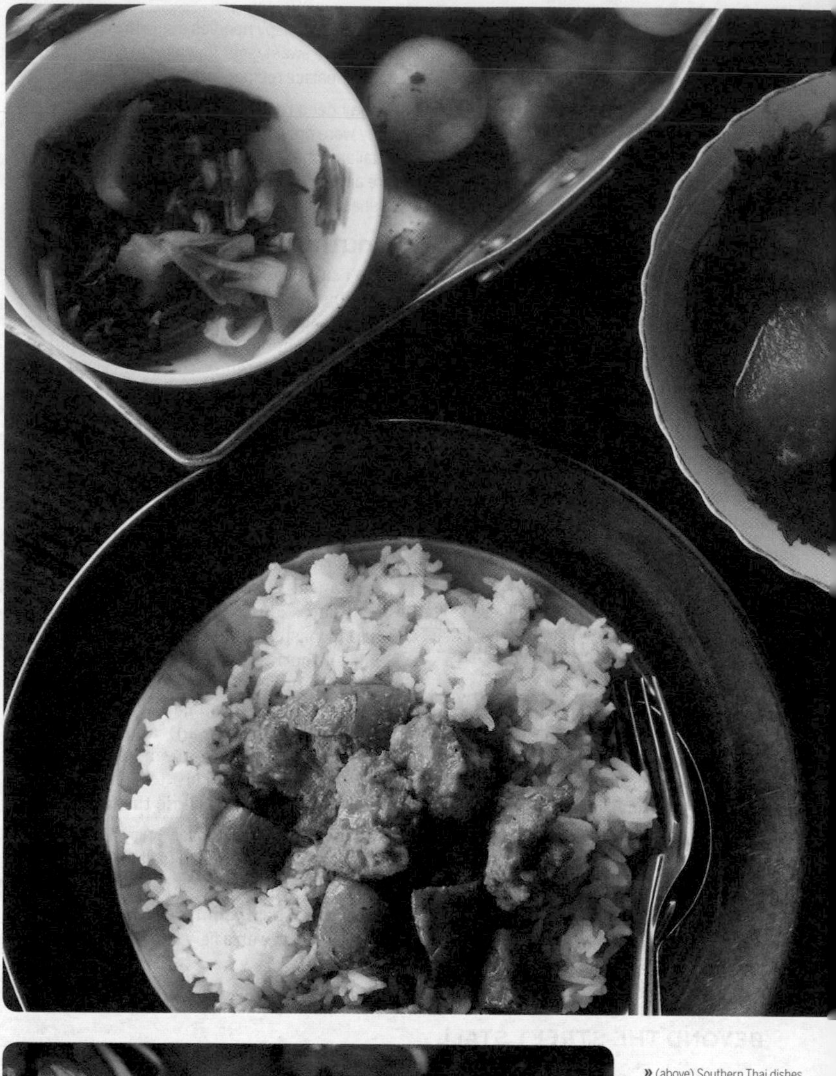

AUSTIN BUSH/LONELY PLANET IMAGES ©

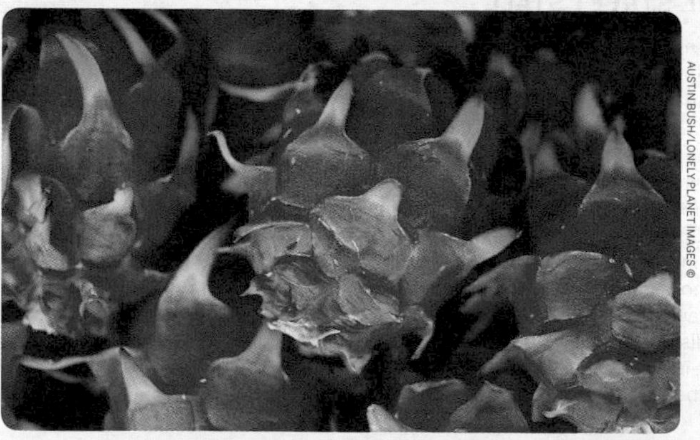

» (above) Southern Thai dishes
» (left) Dragon fruit at Or Tor Kor Ma
(p90), Bangkok

COFFEE, SOUTHERN STYLE

In virtually every town or city in southern Thailand you'll find numerous old-world cafes known locally as *ráhn goh·Ъée*. The shops are almost exclusively owned by Thais of Chinese origin, and often seem suspended in time, typically sporting the same decor and menu for decades. Characteristics of *ráhn goh·Ъée* include marble-topped tables, antique mugs and dishes, and an almost exclusively male clientele that also seems not to have budged since opening day. Some of the most atmospheric *ráhn goh·Ъée* in Thailand can be found in the town of Trang (p335).

The beans used at *ráhn goh·Ъée* are sometimes grown abroad, but are roasted domestically. Although the beans are as black as the night, the drink typically tends to lack body. This may be due to the brewing method, which involves pouring hot water through a wind-sock-like piece of cloth that holds the loose grounds. Typically, *goh·Ъée* is served over a dollop of sweetened condensed milk and a tablespoon (or more) of sugar in small, handleless glasses. For those lacking a sweet tooth, try *goh·Ъée or* (black coffee), or just ask them to hold the sugar. All hot coffee drinks are served with a 'chaser' of weak green tea.

Ráhn goh·Ъée are also a great place for a quick bite. Upon arriving at the more traditional ones, you'll be greeted by a tray of steamed Chinese buns, sweet snacks, such as sticky rice wrapped in banana leaf, or baked goods.

always accompanied by a tray of fresh vegetables and herbs.

Kôw yam A popular breakfast, this dish includes rice topped with sliced herbs, bean sprouts, dried prawns, toasted coconut and powdered red chilli served with a sour/sweet fish-based sauce.

Gaang sôm Known as *gaang lĕu·ang* (yellow curry) in central Thailand, this sour/spicy soup gets its hue from the liberal use of turmeric, a root commonly used in southern Thai cooking.

Ngóp Something of a grilled curry, this dish combines coconut cream, a herb paste and seafood, all wrapped in a banana leaf and grilled until firm.

Gài tôrt hàht yài The famous deep-fried chicken from the town of Hat Yai gets its rich flavour from a marinade containing dried spices.

Kôo·a glîng Minced meat fried with a fiery curry paste and served with a platter of fresh vegetables and herbs is a southern staple.

Pàt sà·đor This popular stir-fry of 'stink beans' with shrimp, garlic, chillies and shrimp paste is both pungent and spicy.

Thai-Muslim Cuisine

Muslims are thought to have first visited southern Thailand during the late 14th century. Along with the Quran, they brought with them a cusine based on meat and dried spice from their homelands in India and the Middle East. Nearly 700 years later, the impact of this culinary commerce can still be felt.

While some Muslim dishes such as *ro·ti,* a fried bread similar to the Indian *paratha,* have changed little, if at all, others such as *gaang mát·sà·màn* are a unique blend of Thai and Indian/Middle Eastern cooking styles and ingredients. In more recent years, additional Muslim dishes have arrived via contact with Thailand's neighbour to the south, Malaysia.

Common Thai-Muslim dishes include the following:

Kôw mòk Biryani, a dish found across the Muslim world, also has a foothold in Thailand. Here the dish is typically made with chicken and is served with a sweet/sour dipping sauce and a bowl of chicken broth.

Sà·dé (satay) These grilled skewers of meat probably came to Thailand via Malaysia. The savoury peanut-based dipping sauce is often mistakenly associated with Thai cooking.

Má·đà·bà Known as *murtabak* in Malaysia and Indonesia, these are *ro·ti* that have been stuffed with a savoury or sometimes sweet filling and fried until crispy.

Súp hăhng woo·a Oxtail soup, possibly another Malay contribution, is even richer and often more sour than the 'Buddhist' Thai *đôm yam*.

Sà·làt kàak Literally 'Muslim salad' (*kàak* is a slightly derogatory word used to describe people or things of Indian and/or Muslim origin), this dish combines iceberg lettuce, chunks of firm tofu, cucumber, hard-boiled egg and tomato, all topped with a sweet peanut sauce.

Gaang mát·sà·màn 'Muslim curry' is a rich coconut milk–based dish, which, unlike most Thai curries, gets much of its flavour from dried spices. As with many Thai-Muslim dishes, there is an emphasis on the sweet.

Thai-Chinese Cuisine

Immigrants from southern China have been influencing Thai cuisine for centuries, and it was Chinese labourers and vendors who most likely introduced the wok and several varieties of noodle dishes to Thailand. Their dishes live on in Bangkok and across southern Thailand, particularly in towns with large Chinese populations such as Trang and Phuket Town.

Thai-Chinese dishes you're likely to run across in Bangkok and southern Thailand include:

Mŏo yâhng Roast pig – skin, fat and all – typically eaten as part of a yam cha brunch, is a speciality of the southern city of Trang.

Đìm sam Yam cha is a favourite breakfast or brunch meal among Trang's Chinese community.

Kôw kăh mŏo Braised pork leg served over rice, often with sides of greens and a hard-boiled egg, is the epitome of the Chinese-style one-dish meal.

Kôw man gài Chicken rice, originally from the Chinese island of Hainan, is now found in just about every corner of Thailand.

Bà·mèe Chinese-style wheat and egg noodles are typically served with slices of barbecued pork, a handful of greens and/or wontons.

Sahlah Ɓow Chinese-style steamed buns are a favourite at old-school Chinese-style coffee shops across southern Thailand.

Gŏoay đěeo kôoa gài Wide rice noodles fried with little more than egg, chicken, squid and garlic oil, is a popular dish in Bangkok's Chinatown.

Oh đôw Small chunks of taro fried with egg and tiny oysters, and topped with deep-fried pork rind – a specialty of Phuket Town.

Loh bà Deep-fried savoury snacks served with a slightly sweet dipping sauce is another Phuket Town delicacy.

Goh·Ɓée – Chinese-style coffee – see p45.

Travel with Children

Best Regions for Kids

Ko Samui & the Lower Gulf

Older children can strap on a mask and snorkel Ko Tao without worry. Ko Samui's northern beaches are popular with pram-pushers and toddlers, while Chaweng appeals to older kids.

Phuket & the Northern Andaman Coast

As well as the beach, Phuket has amusements galore, but steer clear of the Patong party scene. There are at least a dozen islands along this coast where families can frolic in the sea.

Ko Chang & Eastern Seaboard

Families with children of all ages flock to Ko Chang. Shallow seas are kind to young swimmers and low evening tides make for good beachcombing. Older kids will like the interior jungle, elephant camp and mangrove kayaking.

Hua Hin & the Southern Gulf

Hua Hin attracts an international crowd and has a long sandy coastline for pint-sized marathons and hillside temples for monkey spotting. Phetchaburi's cave temples often deliver a bat sighting. Ban Krut and Bang Saphan Yai are so casual you can wake up and play in the waves before you brush your teeth.

Thailand for Children

Thais are serious 'cute' connoisseurs and exotic-looking foreign children rank higher on their adorable meter than stuffed animals and fluffy dogs. Children are instant celebrities and attract almost paparazzi-like attention that eclipses the natural shyness of Thai people.

Babies do surprisingly well with their new-found stardom, soaking up adoration from gruff taxi drivers who transform into loving uncles wanting to play a game of peekaboo (called *já ăir*). If you've got a babe in arms, the food vendors will often offer to hold the child while you eat, taking the child for a brief stroll to visit the other vendors.

At a certain age, kids develop stranger anxiety, which doesn't mix well with the Thai passion for children. For the preschool set, who are becoming self-conscious but still have major cute quotient, we recommend sticking to tourist centres instead of trotting off to far-flung places where foreigners, especially children, will attract too much attention.

To smooth out the usual road bumps of dragging children from place to place, check out Lonely Planet's *Travel with Children*, which contains useful advice on how to cope with kids on the road, with a focus on travel in developing countries.

EATING WITH KIDS

Dining with children, particularly with infants, in Thailand is a liberating experience as the Thais are so fond of kids. Take it for granted that your babies will be fawned over, played with, and more often than not, carried around, by restaurant wait staff. Regard this as a much-deserved break, not to mention a bit of free cultural exposure.

Because much of Thai food is so spicy, there is also an entire art devoted to ordering 'safe' dishes for children, and the vast majority of Thai kitchens are more than willing to oblige.

In general Thai children don't start to eat spicy food until primary school. Before then they seemingly survive on *kôw nĕe•o* (sticky rice) and jelly snacks. Other kid-friendly meals include chicken in all of its nonspicy permutations – *gài yâhng* (grilled chicken), *gài tôrt* (fried chicken) and *gài pàt mét má•môo•ang* (chicken stir-fried with cashew nuts) – as well as *kài jee•o* (Thai-style omelette). A mild option includes *kôw man gài,* Hainanese chicken rice.

Children's Highlights

Of the many destinations in Thailand, children will especially enjoy the beaches, as most are shallow, gentle bays good for beginner swimmers. The further south you go, the clearer the water and where there are near-shore reefs curious fish will swim by for a visit. Please, however, be aware of rip tides and take all sea-related warnings with the utmost seriousness. Many of the beach resorts, such as Phuket and Ko Chang, also have wildlife encounters, waterfall spotting and organised water sports ideal for children aged six years and older.

Bangkok is great fun for those in awe of construction sites: the city is filled with cranes, jackhammers and concrete-pouring trucks. Then there's the above-ground Skytrain and shopping malls complete with escalators (a preschool favourite). The city's immense shopping options will appeal to the tweens and teens.

Kids on a train kick might like an overnight journey. They can walk around on the train and they're assigned the lower sleeping berths with views of the stations.

Even the temples can be engaging places for children. The climbs to the hilltop temples are a great way to expend energy and some of the forested hills have resident monkeys and cave shrines. Merit-making at a Buddhist temple is surprisingly kid-friendly – there's the burning joss sticks, the bowing in front of the Buddha and the rubbing of gold leaf on the central image. It is a very active process that kids can be a part of. Most temples also have a fortune-telling area, where you shake a bamboo container until a numbered stick falls out. The number corresponds to a printed fortune. A variation on this is to make a donation into a pot (or in some cases an automated machine) corresponding to the day of the week you were born and retrieve the attached fortune.

Planning & Practicalities

Amenities specially geared towards young children – such as child-safety seats for cars, high chairs in restaurants or nappy-changing facilities in public restrooms – are virtually nonexistent in Thailand. Therefore parents will have to be extra resourceful in seeking out substitutes or just follow the example of Thai families (which means holding smaller children on their laps much of the time).

Baby formula and nappies (diapers) are available at minimarkets and 7-Elevens in the larger towns and cities, but the sizes are usually small, smaller and smallish. If your kid wears size 3 or larger, head to Tesco Lotus, Big C or Tops Market stores. Nappy rash cream is sold at the pharmacies.

Hauling around little ones can be a challenge. Thailand's footpaths are often too crowded to push a pram, especially today's full-size SUV versions. Instead opt for a compact umbrella stroller that can squeeze past the fire hydrant and the mango cart and that can be folded up and thrown in a túk-túk. A baby pack is also useful but make sure that the child's head doesn't sit higher than yours: there are lots of hanging obstacles poised at forehead level.

Health & Safety

For the most part parents needn't worry too much about health concerns, although it pays to lay down a few ground rules (such as regular hand washing) to head off potential medical problems. Children should be warned not to play with animals as rabies is relatively common in Thailand and many dogs are better at barking and eating garbage than being pets.

Mosquito bites often leave big welts on children. If your child is bitten, there are a variety of locally produced balms that can reduce swelling and itching. All the usual health precautions apply (see p416).

Children familiar with urban environments will do well in Thailand's cities, where traffic is chaotic and pedestrian paths are congested. Thai cities are very loud and can be a sensory overload for young children. Be sure that your child cooperates with your safety guidelines before heading out as it will be difficult for them to focus on your instructions amid all the street noise.

regions at a glance

Bangkok

Culture/History ✓✓✓
Food ✓✓✓
Shopping ✓✓✓

Classic Siam

Once a show of strength after the devastating war with Burma, Bangkok's royal Buddhist temples are now both national pilgrimage sites and the country's greatest displays of classical art and architecture.

More is Better

This multiwatt megacity peddles excess in every permutation, from the skyscrapers and luxe malls to the never-ending traffic jams and late-night after-hours clubs. Food is everywhere, and shopping flourishes in crisp modern malls and humble streetside markets.

Toast the Stars

The quintessential night out in Bangkok is still a plastic table filled with sweating Beer Chang but this aspirational city capitalises on its skyscraper towers with half a dozen rooftop bars. Music clubs and entertainment zones lure the young and hip.

p54

Ko Chang & Eastern Seaboard

Beaches ✓✓
Diving ✓
Small Towns ✓✓

A Herd of Islands

Overland travellers en route to coastal Cambodia and Russian package tourists claim Ko Chang for its tropical ambience, dive sites and thriving party scene. Quiet Ko Kut excels in seaside seclusion, Ko Mak boasts a laid-back island vibe and little Ko Wai has the prettiest views you've ever seen.

Provincial Prominence

Tourists often overlook the eastern seaboard's small towns of Chanthaburi, famous for a weekend gem market, and Trat, a transit link to Ko Chang. But these provincial towns are charming for their ordinariness and middle-class prosperity, which is not found on the islands.

p97

Hua Hin & the Southern Gulf

Culture/History ✓
Beaches ✓✓
Small Towns ✓✓

Royal Coast

Thai kings escaped Bangkok's stifling climate in Hua Hin. Modern Bangkokians have followed in their footsteps, stopping in Phetchaburi to tour a historic hilltop palace and cave shrines. The region's coastline is long, inviting and not nearly as crowded as every other beach resort in Thailand. Honeymooners and families will appreciate this short cut to the beach.

Surf & Turf

This region is both sea and city for beach-lovers looking for a sense of place. Little Prachuap Khiri Khan has stunning karst scenery, and Hua Hin and Phetchaburi boast atmospheric shophouse districts indicative of Thailand's coast settled by Chinese merchants.

p139

Ko Samui & the Lower Gulf

Beaches ✓✓✓
Diving✓✓
Nightlife ✓✓

Diver Down
The three Samui sister islands have been pursued by smitten island-hoppers for decades. With warm gentle seas and wallet-friendly prices, Ko Tao remains one of the world's best places to learn how to dive. Just offshore are snorkelling spots that make fish-spotting fun and easy.

Bronzing Bodies
Ko Pha-Ngan is known for lunar parties and coastal loafing. Gone are the thatch shacks but the layabout vibe remains. Professional Ko Samui caters to international tastes and active vacationers. A day-trip dreamboat, Ang Thong Marine National Park is a stunning collection of hulking limestone mountains jutting out of azure seas.

p171

Phuket & the Northern Andaman Coast

Resorts ✓✓✓
Diving ✓✓
Nightlife ✓✓

Cousteau Territory
Big fish, pristine coral, clear waters – diving and snorkelling sites orbit the world-renowned Similan and Surin Islands all the way up to the Burmese border. Most visitors pack a snorkel set in their day bags for impromptu sessions. Hop on a live-aboard to maximise your diving pleasure as you cavort with manta rays and the occasional whale shark at Richelieu Rock.

Just Phuket
Thailand's leading international beach destination excels in comfort for the holidaying masses. Resorts specialise in design and pampering, and the modern convenience of an airport delivers time-crunched visitors from sky to shore faster.

p238

Ko Phi-Phi & the Southern Andaman Coast

Diving ✓✓
Food ✓✓
Culture ✓

Under the Sea
The southern Andaman lives in the shadow of the northern Andaman and the southern gulf, but dive deep around Ko Lanta and Ko Phi-Phi, and you'll begin to wonder why. The undersea pinnacles at Hin Muang and Hin Daeng are quietly world class. Ko Phi-Phi also has some of the finest snorkelling in the kingdom – don't miss an early morning session with docile reef sharks.

To Market
Trang and Krabi have excellent night markets where you can browse for your perfect noodles, grilled fish or spicy salads. On islands, beach barbeques take pride of place and you'll be beckoned nightly to iceboats filled with the day's catch.

p300

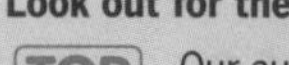

Look out for these icons:

TOP CHOICE Our author's recommendation

A green or sustainable option

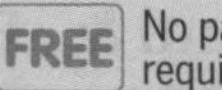

FREE No payment required

See the Index for a full list of destinations covered in this book.

On the Road

Bangkok

Includes »

Best Places to Eat

- » nahm (p78)
- » Krua Apsorn (p77)
- » Bo.lan (p80)
- » Kai Thort Jay Kee (p78)
- » MBK Food Court (p78)

Best Places to Stay

- » AriyasomVilla (p73)
- » Metropolitan (p71)
- » Siam Heritage (p71)
- » Siam@Siam (p70)
- » Lamphu Tree House (p68)

Why Go?

If all you want to do is kick back on a peaceful beach, at first glance Bangkok will seem like a transit burden full of concrete towers instead of palm trees. But once you tire of sea breezes you'll better appreciate Bangkok's conveniences, sophistication and fast pace.

This big, crowded, polluted and seemingly chaotic Asian megacity is many things to many people, but no one calls it boring. For the visitor, the impact is immediate. Everywhere you look the streets and waterways are alive with commuters. School kids run without sweating, smiling vendors create mouth-watering food in push-away kitchens, monks rub bare shoulders with businessmen in air-conditioned malls... With its mix of the historic and contemporary, dangerously appealing shopping and some of the most delicious and best-value eating on earth, the City of Angels is surely one of the most invigorating destinations in Asia.

When to Go

According to the World Meteorological Organisation, Bangkok is one of the hottest cities in the world. To make things worse, there's very little fluctuation in the temperature, and the average high sways between a stifling 32°C and an incrementally more stifling 34°C. The rainy season runs from approximately May to October, during which the city receives as much as 300mm of rain a month. Virtually the only break from the relentless heat and humidity comes during Bangkok's winter, a few weeks of relative coolness in December/January.

History

As capital cities go, Bangkok is a fairly recent invention. Following the sacking of Ayuthaya by the Burmese (p361), King Taksin established the Thai capital at Thonburi, on the west bank of Mae Nam Chao Phraya (Chao Phraya River). But in 1782 Rama I (King Phraphutthayotfa Chulalok; r 1782–1809) founded the Chakri dynasty (p362) and promptly moved his capital across the river to the modest village of Bang Makok (current-day Bangkok).

Buddhist relics from Ayuthaya, Thonburi and Sukhothai were re-enshrined in towering new temples and the city expanded rapidly around the royal compound at Ko Ratanakosin. Under Rama IV (King Mongkut; r 1851–68) and his son Rama V (King Chulalongkorn; r 1868–1910), Bangkok and the country began to modernise, adopting and integrating Western customs, styles and architecture. Europeans flocked to the city to negotiate trade contracts and increase their influence in the region.

In 1932 Thailand saw the end of absolute monarchy and the beginnings of a turbulent political era. From that momentous shift of power until the present day, Bangkok has witnessed 19 attempted coups d'état, half of which have resulted in a change of government. The most recent, in September 2006, saw controversial Prime Minister Thaksin Shinawatra ousted without a shot being fired following months of protests in the capital. However, previous political ructions were not so peaceful and on a handful of occasions mass demonstrations have ended in the military massacring protesters.

During the 1970s Bangkok became an R&R base for American troops fighting in Vietnam and its reputation as 'sin city' was born. During the 1980s and '90s Thailand's economy and Bangkok's skyline grew rapidly. But when the Bangkok stock market collapsed in 1997 the city, the country and indeed most of the region ground to an economic halt.

Much of Bangkok's most recent history has been defined by intermittent and sometimes violent political unrest between the Yellow Shirts, made up of the educated elite aligned with the monarchy and the military, and the Red Shirts, comprised of supporters of the exiled prime minister Thaksin Shinawatra. In 2008, Yellow Shirt protestors shut down Bangkok's airports for two weeks, and in 2010, the opposition Red Shirt protestors staged a two-month siege of the city's central shopping district that ended in violent clashes with the military.

The Red/Yellow conflict came to the forefront in national elections in July 2011. Thanks to Thaksin's enduring popularity, the Red Shirt–linked Pheu Thai party dominated. Their candidate for prime minister, Yingluck Shinawatra, Thaksin's younger sister and a political novice, will most likely facilitate the return of her brother to Thailand, possibly inciting yet another era of political instability.

Sights

Thailand's islands and beaches are not particularly well stocked with traditional Thai 'sights', so it's well worth taking in a few while you're in Bangkok. Fortunately, the capital is home to some of the most impressive wát (temples) and palaces in the country. Many are conveniently concentrated on Ko Ratanakosin, Thonburi and nearby Dusit, all of which border the Banglamphu hotel district.

Keep in mind that Thai temples are sacred places, especially those with a royal connection, and visitors should dress and behave appropriately. Wear shirts with sleeves, long pants or skirts past the knees, and closed-toed shoes. Sarongs and baggy pants are available on loan at the entry area for Wat Phra Kaew. Shoes should be removed before entering buildings. When sitting in front of a Buddha image, tuck your feet behind you to avoid the offence of pointing your feet towards a revered figure.

KO RATANAKOSIN & BANGLAMPHU เกาะรัตนโกสินทร์/บางลำพู

Most of Bangkok's must-sees reside in compact, walkable Ko Ratanakosin, the former royal district. Wat Arun is just a short ferry ride across the river in Thonburi.

Banglamphu has a slow, old-world local feel in parts and a 24-hour festival vibe around the Th Khao San area of guest houses, hotels, restaurants and bars. If your trip to Thailand is more about partying than sightseeing, then this is the place for you.

TOP CHOICE Wat Phra Kaew TEMPLE

(วัดพระแก้ว/พระบรมมหาราชวัง; Map p60; admission 350B; 8.30am-3.30pm; 503 & 508, Tha Chang) Also known as the Temple of the Emerald Buddha, Wat Phra Kaew is an architectural wonder of gleaming gilded stupas,

Bangkok Highlights

1. Skipping between sightseeing spots aboard the **Chao Phraya Express** (p94)
2. Exploring the streets of old Bangkok, including **Ko Ratanakosin** (p65), on foot
3. Learning to make authentic Thai dishes at one of Bangkok's numerous cooking schools, such as **Khao** (p63)
4. Toasting the stars and the twinkling skyscraper lights atop a rooftop bar, such as **Moon Bar at Vertigo** or **Sirocco Sky Bar** (p83)
5. Getting blissfully pounded into submission at one of the city's terrific value massage venues and spas, including **Ruen-Nuad Massage Studio** (p63)

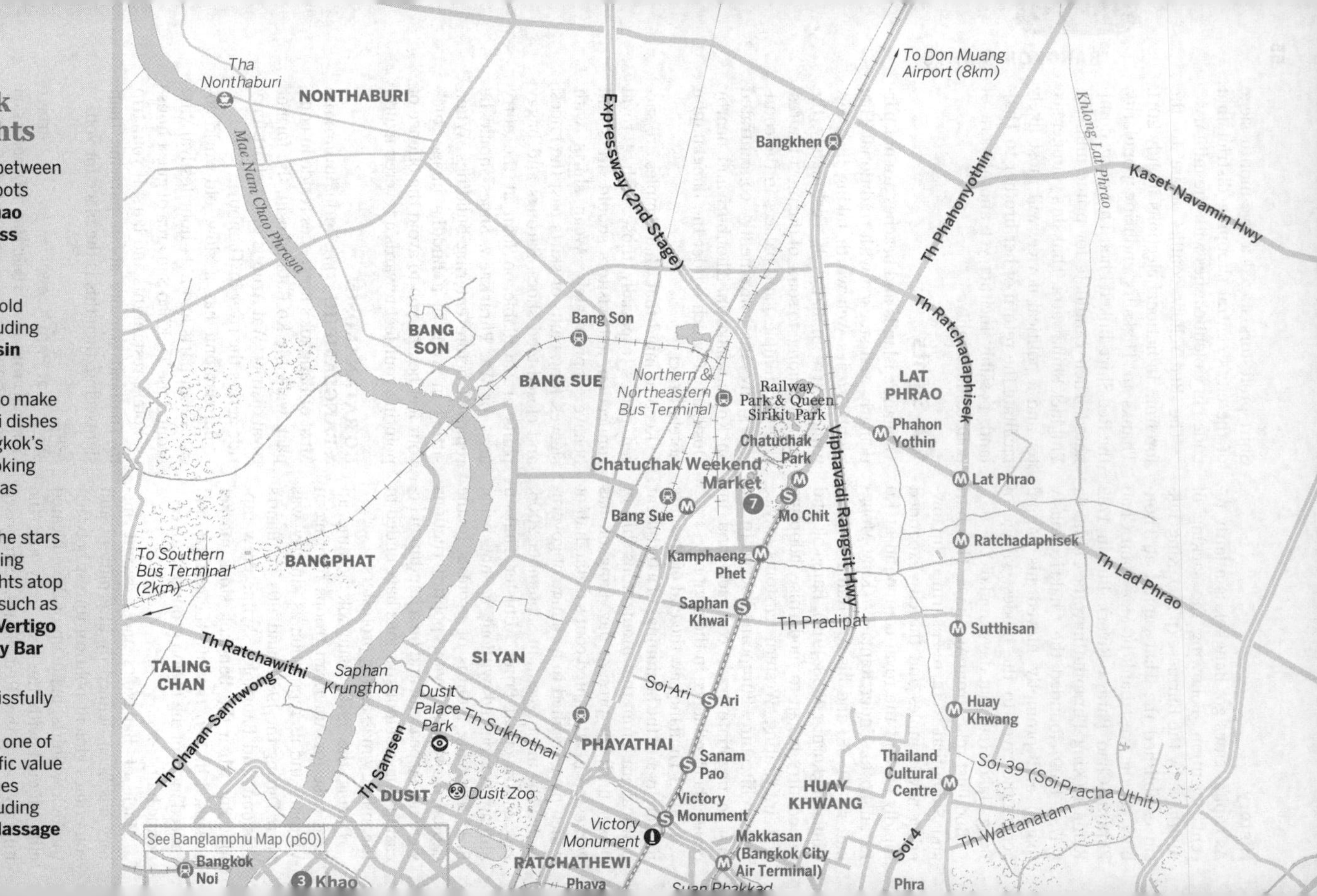

6 Being a houseguest at the city's most beautiful former residence, **Jim Thompson's House** (p60)

7 Burning baht at one of the world's largest markets, the **Chatuchak Weekend Market** (p90)

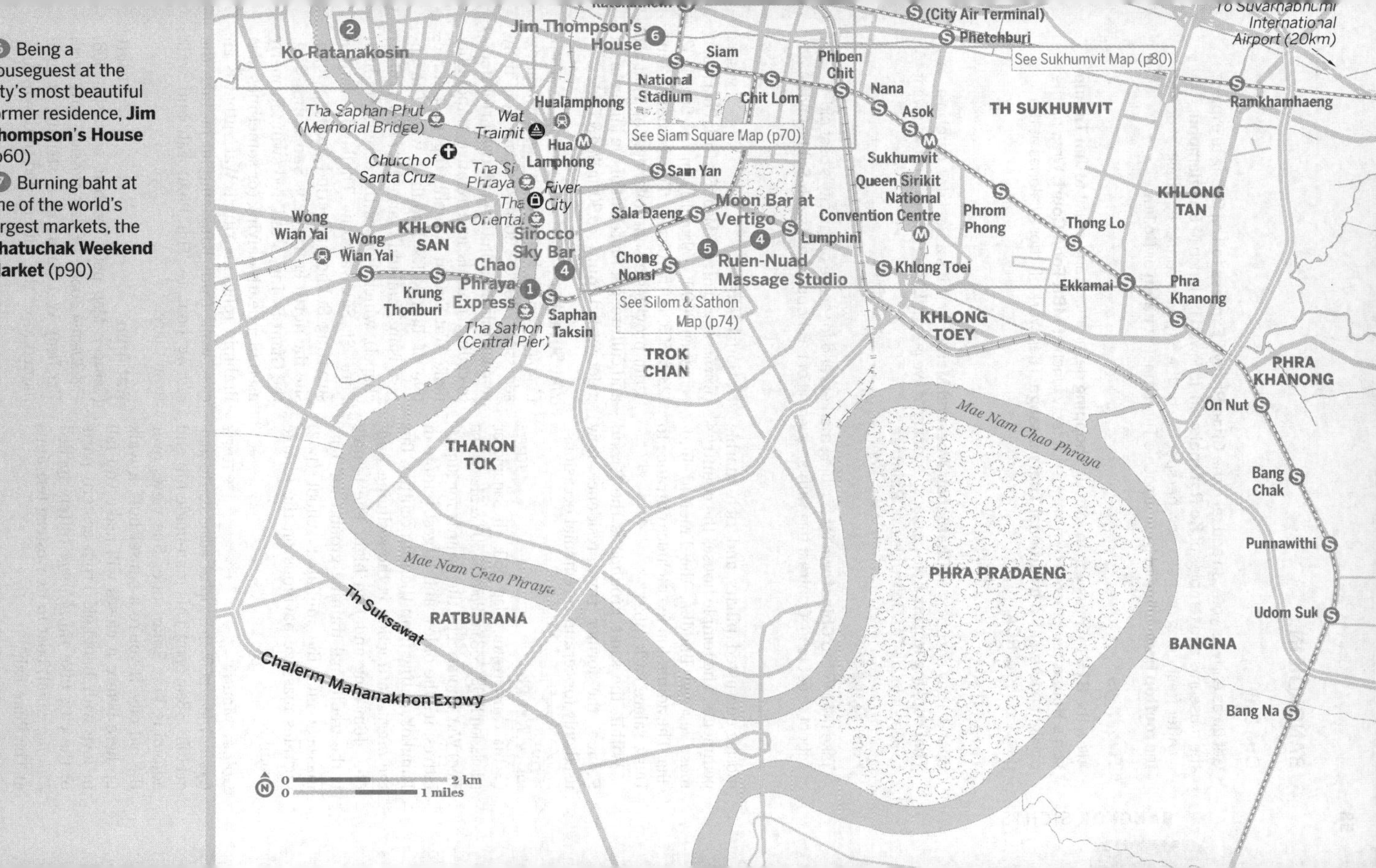

BANGKOK IN...

One Day

Get up as early as you can and take the **Chao Phraya Express** to Tha Chang to explore the museums and temples of **Ko Ratanakosin**, followed by lunch in **Banglamphu**.

After freshening up, get a new perspective on the city with sunset cocktails at one of the **rooftop bars**, followed by an upscale Thai dinner at **nahm** or **Bo.lan**.

Two Days

Allow the **BTS** to whisk you to various **shopping** destinations and a visit to **Jim Thompson's House**, punctuated by a cheap but tasty lunch at **MBK Food Court**. Wrap up the daylight hours with a **traditional Thai massage**. Then work off those calories at the dance clubs of **RCA**.

Three Days

Spend a day shopping at **Chatuchak Weekend Market** or, if it's a weekday, enrol in a **Thai cooking lesson**. Enjoy a classy evening of live jazz at **Living Room**, or, if you want to keep it local, Thai folk music at **Raintree**.

Four Days

Take the MRT to **Chinatown** for bustling markets and for some of the city's best old-school street food. Contrast this with an evening of bar-hopping along **Th Sukhumvit**.

mosaic-encrusted pillars and rich marble pediments. The temple houses the country's most revered Buddha, the Emerald Buddha. The admission fee includes entrance to Dusit Palace Park (p62).

Within the same grounds is the **Grand Palace**, the former royal residence now used only for certain ceremonial occasions.

TOP CHOICE **Wat Pho** TEMPLE

(วัดโพธิ์ (วัดพระเชตุพน; Map p60; Th Sanamchai; admission 100B; ⌚8am-9pm; 🚌508 & 512, ⛴Tha Tien) Wat Pho sweeps the awards for superlatives: it's the oldest and largest temple in Bangkok, dating from the 16th century. But the *biggest* attraction is the reclining Buddha, 46m long and 15m high. The temple is the traditional training ground for Thai massage and the affiliated school (p63) operates massage pavilions on the temple grounds.

Golden Mount TEMPLE

(ภูเขาทอง; Map p60; Th Boriphat; admission to summit 10B; ⌚8am-5pm) This man-made hill and adjoining **Wat Saket** offer fine views over the old city. If you're a sunset buff, a walk up here before it closes will make you fall in love with Bangkok. From eastern parts of the city, take the *klorng* (often spelled *khlong;* canal) boat to its western terminus at Tha Phan Fah.

National Museum MUSEUM

(พิพิธภัณฑสถานแห่งชาติ; Map p60; Th Na Phra That 1; admission 200B; ⌚9am-3.30pm Wed-Sun; 🚌32, 123 & 503, ⛴Tha Chang) The National Museum provides a solid overview of Thai art and culture; get more out of the museum on a docent-led **tour** (⌚9.30am Wed & Thu).

Wat Suthat TEMPLE

(วัดสุทัศน์/เสาชิงช้า; Map p60; Th Bamrung Meuang; admission 20B; ⌚8.30am-4.30pm) The truly remarkable Buddha image, colourful floor-to-ceiling murals and relative tranquillity make Wat Suthat arguably the most attractive of Bangkok's Buddhist wát. The appeal is in Thailand's largest *wí·hăhn* (main chapel), which houses the serene 8m-high Phra Si Sakayamuni, Thailand's largest surviving Sukhothai-period bronze. Opposite the north entrance is **Sao Ching-Cha**, the Giant Swing, a tall, red swing formerly used in a death-defying (or sometimes not) Brahmin religious ritual. Wat Suthat is an easy walk from Banglamphu, or take the *klorng* boat to Tha Phan Fah and walk from there.

Wat Arun TEMPLE

(วัดอรุณฯ; Map p60; Thonburi; admission 50B; ⌚8.30am-4.30pm; ⛴river-crossing ferry from Tha Tien) Wat Arun is a striking temple named after the Indian god of dawn, Aruna. It looms large on Chao Phraya River's west bank, looking as if it were carved from granite; a closer inspection reveals a mosaic made of broken porcelain covering the imposing 82m Khmer-style *prang* (tower).

Museum of Siam MUSEUM
(สถาบันพิพิธภัณฑ์การเรียนรู้แห่งชาติ; Map p60; Th Maha Rat; admission 300B; ⏲10am-6pm Tue-Sun; 🚌32 & 524, ⛴Tha Tien) A new addition to the royal district, this museum explores the origins of the Thai people and their culture with surprisingly modern and engaging exhibits.

Amulet Market MARKET
(ตลาดพระเครื่องวัดมหาธาตุ; Map p60; Th Maha Rat; ⏲7am-5pm; ⛴Tha Chang) This arcane and fascinating market claims both the sidewalks along Th Maha Rat and Th Phra Chan, as well as a dense network of covered market stalls near Tha Phra Chan. The trade is based around small talismans carefully prized by collectors, monks, taxi drivers and people in dangerous professions.

Songkran Niyomsane Forensic Medicine Museum & Parasite Museum MUSEUM
(พิพิธภัณฑ์นิติเวชศาสตร์สงกรานต์นิยมเสน; Map p60; 2nd fl, Forensic Pathology Bldg, Siriraj Hospital, Th Phrannok, Thonburi; admission 40B; ⏲9am-4pm Mon-Sat; ⛴Tha Wang Lang) This gory institution contains the various appendages and remnants of famous murders, including the bloodied T-shirt from a victim who was stabbed to death with a dildo. Next door, the Parasite Museum continues the queasy theme. The easiest way to reach the museum is by taking the river-crossing ferry from Tha Wang Lang (on the Thonburi side) or Tha Chang. At the exit of the pier, turn right to enter Siriraj Hospital, and follow the green signs that say 'Museum'.

CHINATOWN & PHAHURAT เยาวราช (สำเพ็ง)/พาหุรัด

Gold shops, towering neon signs and shopfronts spilling out onto the sidewalk – welcome to Chinatown (also known as Yaowarat). The neighbourhood's energy is at once exhilarating and exhausting, and it's fun to explore at night when it's lit up like a Christmas tree and there's lots of street food for sale. The area is a short taxi ride or a longish walk from the MRT stop at Hua Lamphong.

Wat Traimit TEMPLE
(วัดไตรมิตร; Temple of the Golden Buddha; Map p56; cnr Th Yaowarat & Th Charoen Krung; admission 40B; ⏲8am-5pm Tue-Sun; ⛴Tha Ratchawong, Ⓜ Hua Lamphong) The main attraction at Wat Traimit is undoubtedly the impressive 3m-tall, 5.5-tonne, solid-gold Buddha image, which gleams like, well, gold. Sculpted in the graceful Sukhothai style, the image was 'discovered' some 40 years ago beneath a stucco or plaster exterior when it fell from a crane while being moved to a new building within the temple compound. It has been theorised that the covering was added to protect it from marauding hordes, either during the late Sukhothai period or later in the Ayuthaya period when the city was under siege by the Burmese.

The structure is also home to the **Yaowarat Chinatown Heritage Center** (admission 100B; ⏲8am-5pm Tue-Sun), a small but engaging museum with multimedia exhibits on the history of Bangkok's Chinatown and its residents.

THÀNŎN KHAO SAN

Almost 30 years after locals on the Khao San Rd, as it's known, first started converting their homes into guest houses for smelly backpackers – known jokingly in Thai as *fa·ràng kêe ngók* ('stinky foreigners') – Banglamphu has evolved into a clearing house for travellers unlike anywhere else on earth. At any time of day or night, Th Khao San is mobbed by travellers from across the globe, mingling with beggars, hawkers, transvestites and street performers, and surrounded by stallholders offering hair-braiding, body-piercing, pirated CDs, hippy jewellery, handicrafts, fake brand-name clothes, Thai fast food, cold beers and croaking wooden frogs, among other things. Think of it as a backpacker cabaret in which you are both a spectator and a participant.

Critics claim Th Khao San cocoons travellers from the real Thailand. It's true that many people leave Bangkok having seen just this short stretch of road, but its reputation is not really fair. Today, Banglamphu has become a major entertainment district for young Bangkokians, who add the Thai spice long missing from this dish.

Banglamphu

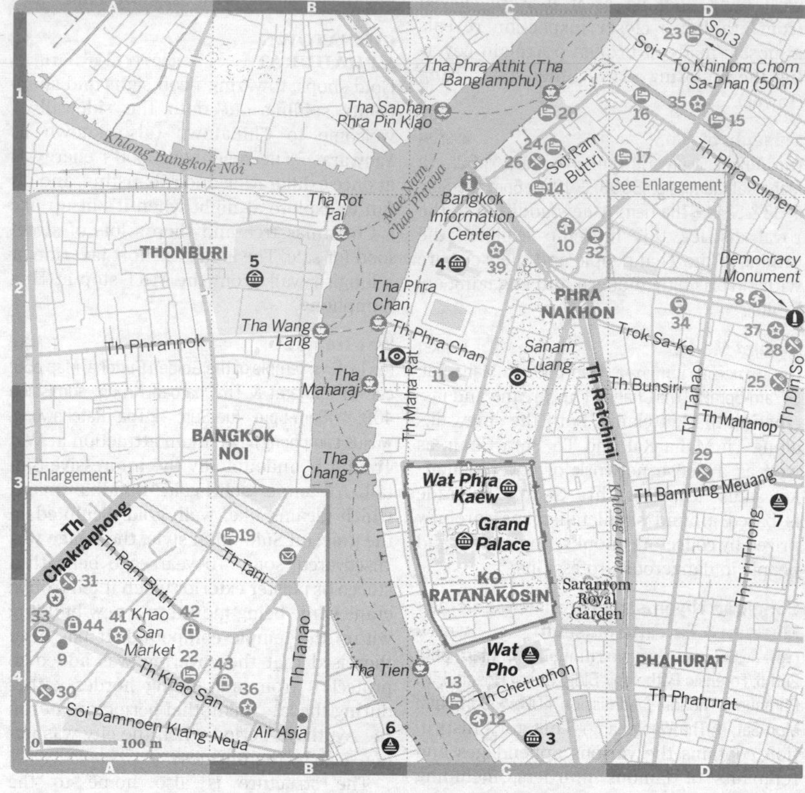

Talat Mai MARKET

(ตลาดใหม่; Soi 6/Trok Itsaranuphap, Th Yaowarat; 73, 159 & 507, Tha Ratchawong, M Hua Lamphong) 'New Market' is a narrow covered alleyway between tall buildings. Even if you're not interested in food, the hectic atmosphere and exotic sights and smells culminate in something of a surreal sensory experience. The market is best visited during the busy morning hours, from about 6am to 10am.

FREE **Wat Mangkon Kamalawat** TEMPLE

(วัดมังกรกมลาวาส; Neng Noi Yee; cnr Th Mangkorn & Th Charoen Krung; 9am-6pm; 73, 159 & 507, Tha Ratchawong, M Hua Lamphong) Clouds of incense, stick-rattling fortune telling and the sounds of chanting form the backdrop at this Chinese-style Mahayana Buddhist temple. Dating back to 1871, it's the largest and most important religious structure in the area. During the annual Vegetarian Festival (p67), religious and culinary activities are particularly active here.

Phahurat Market MARKET

(ตลาดพาหุรัด; cnr Th Phahurat & Th Chakraphet; 82, 169 & 507, Tha Saphan Phut (Memorial Bridge)) Hidden behind the slick India Emporium mall is Phahurat Market, an endless bazaar uniting flamboyant Bollywood fabric, photogenic vendors selling *paan* (betel nut for chewing) and several shops stocked with delicious northern Indian–style sweets. Nearby, in an alley off Th Chakraphet is **Gurdwara Siri Guru Singh Sabha** (Th Phahurat; 9am-5pm), reportedly the second-largest Sikh temple outside India.

OTHER AREAS

TOP CHOICE **Jim Thompson's House** MUSEUM

(Map p70; www.jimthompsonhouse.com; 6 Soi Kasem San 2; admission adult/child 100/50B;

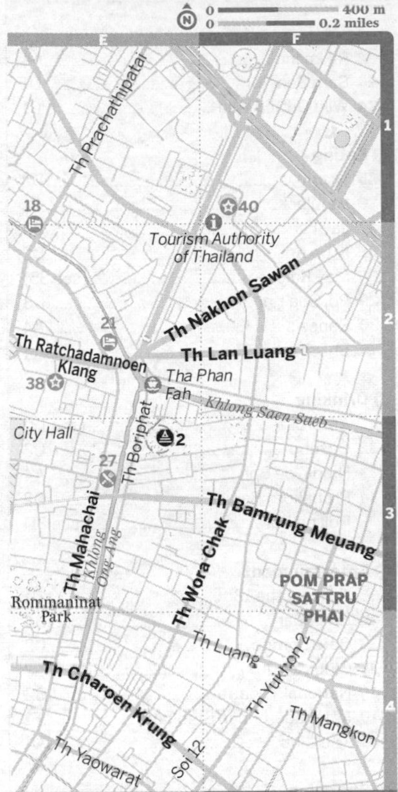

⌚9am-5pm, compulsory tours in English & French every 20min; ⛴klorng taxi Tha Hua Chang, 🚉National Stadium) This leafy compound is the former home of the eponymous US silk entrepreneur and art collector. Born in Delaware in 1906, Thompson briefly served in the Office of Strategic Services (forerunner of the CIA) in Thailand during WWII. When he settled in Bangkok after the war, his neighbours' handmade silk caught his eye and piqued his business sense; he sent samples to fashion houses in Milan, London and Paris, gradually building a steady worldwide clientele.

In addition to exquisite Asian art, Thompson collected parts of various derelict Thai homes in central Thailand and had them reassembled in their current location in 1959. One departure from tradition is the way each wall has its exterior side facing the house's interior, thus exposing the wall's bracing system. His small but splendid Asian art collection and his personal belongings are also on display in the main house.

Thompson's story doesn't end with his informal reign as Bangkok's best-adapted foreigner. While out for an afternoon walk in the Cameron Highlands of western Malaysia in 1967, Thompson mysteriously disappeared. That same year his sister was murdered in the USA, fuelling various conspiracy theories. Was it a CIA conspiracy? Business rivals? Or a man-eating tiger? No-one knows. *Jim Thompson: The Unsolved Mystery* by William Warren and *The Ideal Man* by Joshua Kurlantzick are good sources of information on Thompson's career, residence and subsequent intriguing disappearance.

TOP CHOICE Ancient City MUSEUM

(เมืองโบราณ; www.ancientcity.com; adult/child 400/300B; ⌚8am-5pm; 🚉Bearing & access by taxi or bus) East of Bangkok in the suburb of Samut Prakan is an unusual attraction. The Ancient City is an 80-hectare outdoor museum with 109 scaled-down replicas of Thailand's most famous historic monuments, including some that no longer survive. Visions of Legoland may spring to mind, but the Ancient City is architecturally sophisticated and definitely worth the trip.

Air-con bus 511 travels from the east end of Th Sukhumvit to Samut Prakan's bus terminal, then you board minibus 36, which passes the entrance to Ancient City.

Suan Phakkad Palace Museum MUSEUM

(วังสวนผักกาด; Map p56; Th Sri Ayuthaya; admission 100B; ⌚9am-4pm; 🚉Phaya Thai) An overlooked treasure, Suan Phakkad is a collection of eight traditional wooden Thai houses that was once the residence of Princess Chumbon of Nakhon Sawan and before that a lettuce farm – hence the name. Within the stilt buildings are displays of art, antiques and furnishings, and the landscaped grounds are a peaceful oasis complete with ducks, swans and a semienclosed garden.

FREE Erawan Shrine SHRINE

(ศาลพระพรหม; San Phra Phrom; Map p70; cnr Th Ploenchit & Th Ratchadamri; ⌚6am-8pm; 🚉Chit Lom) When the Erawan Hotel was being built in the 1950s a series of construction disasters occurred. They stopped soon after this shrine to the Hindu god Brahma was erected. The hotel was a huge success and

Banglamphu

Top Sights
- Grand Palace ... C3
- Wat Pho ... C4
- Wat Phra Kaew ... C3

Sights
- 1 Amulet Market ... B2
- 2 Golden Mount ... E3
- 3 Museum of Siam ... C4
- 4 National Museum ... C2
- 5 Songkran Niyomsane Forensic Medicine Museum & Parasite Museum ... B2
- 6 Wat Arun ... B4
- 7 Wat Suthat ... D3

Activities, Courses & Tours
- 8 Grasshopper Adventures ... D2
- 9 Khao ... A4
- 10 Sor Vorapin Gym ... C2
- 11 Wat Mahathat ... C2
- 12 Wat Pho Thai Traditional Medical and Massage School ... C4

Sleeping
- 13 Arun Residence ... C4
- 14 Baan Sabai ... C1
- 15 Diamond House ... D1
- 16 Fortville Guesthouse ... D1
- 17 Lamphu House ... D1
- 18 Lamphu Tree House ... E1
- 19 NapPark Hostel ... B3
- 20 Navalai River Resort ... C1
- 21 Old Bangkok Inn ... E2
- 22 Rikka Inn ... A4
- 23 Sam Sen Sam ... D1
- 24 Wild Orchid Villa ... C1

Eating
- 25 Arawy ... D2
- 26 Hemlock ... C1
- 27 Jay Fai ... E3
- 28 Krua Apsorn ... D2
- May Kaidee ... (see 35)
- 29 Poj Spa Kar ... D3
- 30 Ranee's ... A4
- 31 Shoshana ... A4

Drinking
- Amorosa ... (see 13)
- 32 Gazebo ... C2
- 33 Hippie de Bar ... A4
- 34 Pranakorn Bar ... D2
- Rolling Bar ... (see 21)

Entertainment
- 35 Ad Here the 13th ... D1
- 36 Brick Bar ... B4
- 37 Café Democ ... D2
- 38 Club Culture ... E2
- 39 National Theatre ... C2
- 40 Ratchadamnoen Stadium ... F1
- 41 The Club ... A4

Shopping
- 42 Saraban ... A4
- 43 Shaman Bookstore ... B4
- 44 Shaman Bookstore ... A4

ever since people have come here to pray for luck and fortune.

Ban Kamthieng MUSEUM

(บ้านคำเที่ยง; Map p80; Siam Society, 131 Soi 21/Asoke, Th Sukhumvit; adult/child 100/50B; 9am-5pm Tue-Sat; MSukhumvit, Asok) An engaging house museum, Ban Kamthieng transports visitors to a northern Thai village complete with informative displays of daily rituals, folk beliefs and everyday household chores, all within the setting of a traditional wooden house.

Dusit Palace Park PALACE

(วังสวนดุสิต; Map p56; bounded by Th Ratchawithi, Th U-Thong Nai & Th Ratchasima; adult/child 100/50B, free with Grand Palace ticket; 9.30am-4pm; 18, 28 & 515) Elegant Dusit Palace Park is a former royal palace with serene green space and multiple handicraft museums. The must-see is the 1868 **Vimanmek Teak Mansion**, reputedly the world's largest golden teakwood building.

FREE **Lumphini Park** PARK

(สวนลุมพินี; Map p74; bounded by Th Phra Ram IV, Th Witthayu (Wireless Rd), Th Sarasin & Th Ratchadamri; 5am-8pm; MSi Lom & Lumphini, Sala Daeng) Named after Buddha's birthplace in Nepal, central Bangkok's largest and most popular public park is crisscrossed by walking trails and has tranquil lawns, wooded glades and a large artificial lake with pedalos for hire. It's a great place to watch Bangkokians unwind: practising t'ai chi in the early morning, running, working out, taking part in outdoor aerobics classes or just unleashing the kids on the grass. From mid-February to April, Lumphini is a favourite spot for kite fighting. Year round, it's the best place in Bangkok to spot ginormous monitor lizards.

FREE Church of Santa Cruz CHURCH
(โบสถ์ซางตาครูส; Map p56; Th Kuti Jiin; Sat & Sun; Tha Pak Talat (Atsadang)) Dating back to 1913, this Catholic church holds relatively little interest unless you visit on a Sunday. But the surrounding neighbourhood, a former Portuguese concession dating back to the Ayuthaya period, is worth a wander for its old-school riverside atmosphere and Portuguese-inspired cakes, *kà·nŏm fa·ràng*.

Activities

Bangkokians regard traditional massage as a vital part of preventative health care and they frequent massage parlours more regularly than gyms. There are literally thousands of massage places in Bangkok, ranging from luxury spas to cheap-and-cheerful foot-massage joints. Note that a man asking for an 'oil massage' can sometimes lead to techniques that aren't on the curriculum at Wat Pho. If you're not looking for a 'happy ending', avoid parlours where the masseuses are young and wear short skirts.

Depending on the neighbourhood, prices for massages tend to stay fixed: around 250B for a foot massage and around 500B for a body massage.

Ruen-Nuad Massage Studio MASSAGE
(Map p74; 0 2632 2662; 42 Th Convent; Thai massage per hr 350B; 10am-9pm; M Si Lom, Sala Daeng) Set in a refurbished wooden house, this charming place successfully avoids both the tackiness and New Agedness that characterise most Bangkok massage joints. Prices are reasonable, too.

Health Land SPA, MASSAGE
(www.healthlandspa.com; Thai massage 2hr 450B) Ekamai (Map p80; 0 2392 2233; 96/1 Soi 10, Soi 63/Ekamai, Th Sukhumvit; 9am-11pm; Ekkamai); Sathon (Map p74; 0 2637 8883; 120 Th Sathon Neua; 9am-11pm; Chong Nonsi); Sukhumvit (Map p80; 0 2261 1110; 55/5 Soi 21/Asoke, Th Sukhumvit; 9am-midnight; M Sukhumvit, Asok) A winning formula of affordable prices, expert treatments and pleasant facilities has created a small empire of Health Land centres.

Wat Pho Traditional Thai Medical and Massage School MASSAGE
(Map p60; 0 2622 3550; 392/25-28 Soi Pen Phat; Thai massage per hr 220B; 8am-6pm; 508 & 512, Tha Tien) This is the nation's premier massage school. Students of traditional Thai medicine offer air-con service in this location, but the pavilions inside the temple are more atmospheric. Lessons in Thai massage are also available (see p64).

Divana Massage & Spa SPA, MASSAGE
(Map p80; 0 2261 6784; www.divanaspa.com; 7 Soi 25, Th Sukhumvit; spa treatments from 2500B; 11am-11pm Mon-Fri & 10am-11pm Sat & Sun; M Sukhumvit, Asok) Edging towards the spa end of the spectrum, Divana retains a unique Thai touch with a private and soothing setting in a garden house.

Courses

Khao COOKING
(Map p60; 08 9111 0947; www.khaocookingschool.com; D&D Plaza, 68-70 Th Khao San; lessons 1500B; 9.30am-12.30pm & 1.30-4.30pm) Khao was started up by an authority on Thai food and features instruction on a wide variety of authentic dishes. Located in the courtyard behind D&D Inn.

Phussapa Thai Massage School MASSAGE
(Map p80; 0 2204 2922; www.thaimassage-bangkok.com/nuat1_egl.htm; 25/8 Soi 26,

> ### WHAT'S YOUR NAME AGAIN?
>
> The name Bangkok is derived from Bang Makok, meaning 'Place of Olive Plums', the name of a village that predates the arrival of the capital in 1782. The full official title of the capital is 'Krungthep mahanakhon amon rattanakosin mahintara ayuthaya mahadilok popnopparat ratchathani burirom udomratchaniwet mahasathan amonpiman avatansathit sakkathattiya visnukamprasit'. Thais abbreviate it to Krung Thep (City of Angels). Pretty much the only place you'll find the full name spelled out is on the very wide sign in front of City Hall (Map p60); bring your wide-angle lens.

MAKING SENSE OF BANGKOK

Mae Nam Chao Phraya (Chao Phraya River) divides Bangkok from the older city of Thonburi. Bangkok can be further divided into east and west by the main railway line feeding Hualamphong station. The older part of the city, crowded with historical temples, bustling Chinatown and the popular travellers' centre of Banglamphu (home of the famous Khao San Rd) is sandwiched between the western side of the tracks and the river. East of the railway is the new city, devoted to commerce with its attendant skyscrapers and shopping centres, particularly the Siam Sq, Sukhumvit and Silom districts.

A note about streets: throughout this book, *thànŏn* (street) is abbreviated as 'Th'. A soi is a small street that runs off a larger street. The address of a site located on a soi will be written as 33 Soi 3, Th Sukhumvit, meaning on Soi 3 off Th Sukhumvit. Smaller than a soi is a *tràwk* (alley).

Th Sukhumvit; tuition from 6000B; ⌚9am-4pm; 🚊Phrom Phong) This places is run by a longstanding Japanese resident of Thailand and offers a basic course in Thai massage, which spans 30 hours over five days. There are shorter courses in foot massage and self massage. Thai massage is also available for 250B per hour.

Helping Hands COOKING
(☎08 4901 8717; www.cookingwithpoo.com; lessons 1200B; ⌚8.30am-1pm Mon-Sat) This popular cookery course was started by a native of Khlong Toey's slums and is held in her neighbourhood. Courses, which must be booked in advance, span four dishes and include a visit to Khlong Toey Market and transportation to and from Emporium shopping centre (see Map p80).

Wat Mahathat MEDITATION
(Map p60; 3 Th Maha Rat; 🚌32, 201 & 503, ⛴Tha Maharaj & Tha Chang) This temple is home to two independently operating meditation centres. The **International Buddhist Meditation Center** (☎0 2222 6011; www.centermeditation.org; Section 5, Wat Mahathat; donations accepted) offers daily meditation classes at 7am, 1pm and 6pm. Taught by English-speaking Phrasuputh, classes last three hours. The **Meditation Study and Retreat Center** (☎0 223 6878; www.meditation-watmahadhat.com; Wat Mahathat; donations accepted) offers a regimented daily program of meditation.

Wat Pho Thai Traditional Medical and Massage School MASSAGE
(Map p60; ☎0 2622 3550; www.watpomassage.com; 392/25-28 Soi Phen Phat; tuition from 5000B; ⌚8am-6pm; 🚌508 & 512, ⛴Tha Tien) Offers basic and advanced courses in traditional massage. The school is outside the temple compound in a restored Bangkok shophouse on unmarked Soi Phen Phat – look for Coconut Palm restaurant.

Sor Vorapin Gym THAI BOXING
(Map p60; ☎0 2282 3551; www.thaiboxings.com; 13 Th Kasab, Th Chakraphong; tuition per day/month 500/9000B; 🚌2, 15, 44 & 511, ⛴Tha Phra Athit (Banglamphu)) Specialising in training foreign students of both genders, this gym is a sweaty run from Th Khao San.

Baipai Thai Cooking School COOKING
(☎0 2561 1404; www.baipai.com; 8/91 Soi 54, Th Ngam Wong Wan; lessons 1800B; ⌚9.30am-1.30pm & 1.30-5.30pm Tue-Sat) Housed in an attractive suburban villa, and taught by a small army of staff, Baipai offers two daily lessons of four dishes each. Transportation is available.

Tours

If you're not travelling with a group but would like a guide, recommended outfits include the following:

Tour with Tong GUIDED TOURS
(☎0 81835 0240; www.tourwithtong.com; day tour from 1000B) Guided tours in and around Bangkok.

Thai Private Tour Guide GUIDED TOURS
(☎0 81860 9159; www.thaitourguide.com; day tour from 2000B) Chob and Mee get good reviews.

Bangkok Private Tours GUIDED TOURS
(www.bangkokprivatetours.com; full-day walking tour 3400B) Customised walking tours of the city.

Bangkok Food Tours GUIDED TOURS
(☎08 9126 3657; www.bangkokfoodtours.com; half-day tour 950-1300B) Half-day culinary

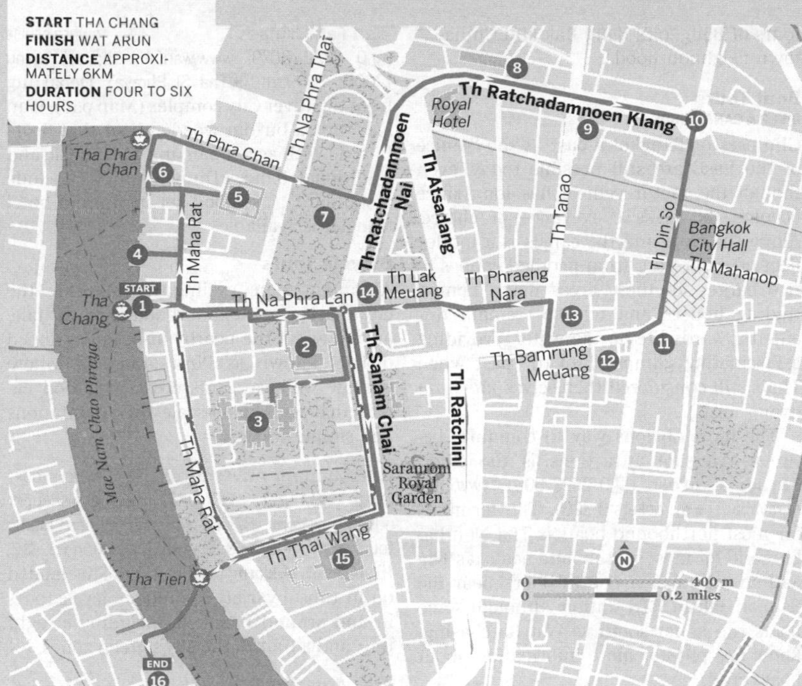

Walking Tour
Old Bangkok

The bulk of Bangkok's 'must-see' destinations are found in the former royal district, Ko Ratanakosin, and neighbouring Banglamphu. Start early to beat both the heat and the hordes and remember to dress modestly for the temples.

Start at 1 **Tha Chang** and proceed to the main gate of 2 **Wat Phra Kaew** and the 3 **Grand Palace**.

Return to Th Maha Rat and proceed north. Turn left into 4 **Trok Tha Wang**, a narrow alleyway holding a seemingly hidden classic Bangkok neighbourhood. Returning to Th Maha Rat, continue moving north. On your right is 5 **Wat Mahathat**, one of Thailand's most respected Buddhist universities. Across the street, turn left into crowded Trok Mahathat to discover the cramped 6 **amulet market**.

Exiting at Tha Phra Chan, cross Th Maha Rat and continue east, passing even more traditional Thai medicine shops and amulet vendors until you reach 7 **Sanam Luang**, the 'Royal Field'.

Cross Th Ratchadamnoen Nai and go north, turning right at the Royal Hotel. On your left is 8 **Th Ratchadamnoen Klang**, Bangkok's own Champs Élysées. Continuing east, you'll see the 9 **October 14 Memorial**, commemorating the civilian demonstrators who were killed on 14 October 1973 by the military during a prodemocracy rally. Ahead you'll see the four-pronged 10 **Democracy Monument**.

Turn right down Th Din So and continue south until you reach the unmistakable 11 **Wat Suthat** and **Sao Ching-Cha**, both lesser-known landmarks.

Cut through the 12 **religious shops** along Th Bamrung Meuang for a lunch stop at 13 **Poj Spa Kar**.

After lunch, turn left on Th Phraeng Nara, crossing Khlong Lawt, and continue west along Th Lak Meuang until you reach the street's namesake and home of Bangkok's city spirit, 14 **Lak Meuang**.

Head south along Th Sanam Chai and turn right onto Th Thai Wang, which will escort you to the entrance of 15 **Wat Pho**, home of the giant reclining Buddha.

Finally, head to Tha Tien to catch the cross-river ferry to Khmer-influenced 16 **Wat Arun**.

tours of Bangkok's Bang Rak and Chinatown neighbourhoods.

Boat Tours

RIVER & CANAL TRIPS

Glimpses of Bangkok's past as the 'Venice of the East' are still possible today, even though the motor vehicle has long since become the city's conveyance of choice. Along the river and the canals is a motley fleet of watercraft, from paddled canoes to rice barges. In these areas many homes, trading houses and temples remain oriented towards life on the water, providing a fascinating glimpse into the past when Thais still considered themselves *jôw nám* (water lords).

The most obvious way to commute between riverside attractions is the **Chao Phraya Express** (0 2623 6001; www.chaophrayaboat.co.th; tickets 9-32B). The terminus for most northbound boats is Tha Nonthaburi and for most southbound boats it's Tha Sathon (also called Central Pier), near the Saphan Taksin BTS station, although some boats run as far south as Wat Ratchasingkhon. See p94 for more information about boat travel.

Long-tail boats are Bangkok icons and can be chartered for tours of the Thonburi *klorng,* particularly Khlong Bangkok Yai and Khlong Bangkok Noi. You'll find boat drivers at Tha Chang (Map p60), Tha Saphan Phut (Map p56), Tha Oriental (Map p56) and Tha Si Phraya (Map p56). Rental costs from about 1000B an hour (it costs more the closer you are to an expensive hotel). Feel free to negotiate.

DINNER CRUISES

Perfect for romancing couples or subdued families, dinner cruises swim along Chao Phraya River, basking in the twinkling city lights at night, far away from the heat and noise of town. Cruises range from downhome to sophisticated, but the food generally ranges from mediocre to forgettable.

Loy Nava DINNER CRUISE
(0 2437 4932; www.loynava.com; set menu 1766B; 6-8pm & 8.10-10.10pm; Tha Si Phraya) Operating since 1970, and quite possibly the original Bangkok dinner cruise, Loy Nava offers two daily excursions, both departing from Tha Si Phraya, near River City (Map p56). Vegetarian menu available.

Wan Fah Cruises DINNER CRUISE
(0 2222 8679; www.wanfah.in.th; set menu 1200B; 7-9pm; Tha Si Phraya) Departing from the River City complex (Map p56), Wan Fah runs a buxom wooden boat that floats in style with accompanying Thai music and traditional dance. Dinner options include a standard or seafood set menu and hotel transfer is available.

Bicycle Tours

Although some cycling tours tackle the city's urban neighbourhoods, many take advantage of the nearby lush, undeveloped district known as Phra Pradaeng, where narrow walkways crisscross irrigation canals that feed small-scale fruit plantations and simple villages.

Grasshopper Adventures BICYCLE TOURS
(Map p60; 0 2280 0832; www.grasshopperadventures.com; 57 Th Ratchadamnoen Klang; tours from 750B; 8.30am-6.30pm Mon-Fri; 2, 15, 44 & 511, klorng taxi Phan Fah) This lauded outfit runs a variety of unique bicycle tours in and around Bangkok, including a night tour and a tour of the city's green zones.

ABC Amazing Bangkok Cyclists BICYCLE TOURS
(Map p80; 0 2665 6364; www.realasia.net; 10/5-7 Soi 26, Th Sukhumvit; tours from 1000B; daily tours depart at 8am, 10am or 1pm; Phrom Phong) ABC has operated for more than a decade, offering bike-based tours that purport to reveal the 'real' Asia by following the elevated walkways of the city's rural canals.

Festivals & Events

In addition to these main festivals, there's always something going on in Bangkok. Check the website of **TAT** (www.tourismthailand.org) or the **Bangkok Information Center** (www.bangkoktourist.com) for exact dates.

Chinese New Year NEW YEAR
Thai-Chinese celebrate the lunar New Year with a week of traditional performances, lion dances and fireworks; February/March.

Songkran NEW YEAR
Thai New Year has morphed into a full-scale water war; mid-April.

Royal Ploughing Ceremony TRADITIONAL
The crown prince commences rice-planting season at Sanam Luang; early May.

BANGKOK FOR CHILDREN

There aren't a whole lot of attractions in Bangkok meant to appeal directly to the little ones, but there's no lack of locals willing to provide attention. The website www.bambi-web.org is a useful resource for parents in Bangkok.

Although not specifically child-targeted, the Museum of Siam (p59) has lots of interactive exhibits that will appeal to children.

Dusit Zoo (Map p56; Th Ratchawithi; adult/child 100/50B; 8am-6pm; 18, 28 & 515, Phaya Thai & access by taxi) covers 19 hectares with caged exhibits of more than 300 mammals, 200 reptiles and 800 birds, including relatively rare indigenous species such as banteng, gaur, serow and some rhinoceros. There are shady grounds, plus a lake in the centre with pedalos for hire and a small children's playground.

The oceans have been brought indoors at the **Siam Ocean World** (Map p70; www.siamoceanworld.co.th; basement, Siam Paragon, Th Phra Ram I; adult/child 900/700B; 10am-9pm; Siam) shopping-centre aquarium. Gaze into the glass-enclosed deep-reef zone or view the daily feeding of penguins and sharks.

Lumphini Park (p62) is a trusty ally in the cool hours of the morning and evening for kite-flying (in season) as well as stretching the legs and lungs. Nearby, kids can view lethal snakes become reluctant altruists at the adjacent anti-venom-producing snake farm at the **Queen Saovabha Memorial Institute** (off Map p74; www.saovabha.com; cnr Th Phra Ram IV & Th Henri Dunant; adult/child 200/50B; 9.30am-3.30pm Mon-Fri, to 1pm Sat & Sun; M Si Lom, Sala Daeng).

MBK Center (p88) and Siam Paragon (p89) both have bowling alleys to keep the older ones occupied. **Krung Sri IMAX** (Map p70; 0 2129 4631; www.imaxthai.com; Siam Paragon, Th Phra Ram I; tickets 350-450B; Siam) screens special-effects versions of Hollywood action flicks and nature features.

Vegetarian Festival VEGETARIAN
Chinese-Thais visit temples and eschew meat for 10 days in September/October.

Loi Krathong TRADITIONAL
Small lotus-shaped boats made of banana leaf and containing a lit candle are set adrift on Chao Phraya River; early November.

Bangkok World Film Festival FILM
(www.worldfilmbkk.com) Mid-November.

Sleeping

Bangkok boasts more than 400 hotels and guest houses, ranging from cheap backpacker joints to some of the most luxurious lodgings on earth. They are scattered widely, though hotels of a type tend to congregate in certain neighbourhoods.

Banglamphu and the famous (or should that be infamous?) Th Khao San are a tractor beam for backpackers and few are able to escape its pull. This area is conveniently near the river and the monuments and museums of old Bangkok. A long walk north is Thewet, which is refreshingly laid-back and handy for the palaces in Dusit. It's home to a small cluster of good guest houses. Further south, Chinatown is a lively but often-overlooked neighbourhood with a couple of decent options, not to mention some convenient budget choices across from Hualamphong train station.

The riverside area south of Chinatown boasts several big-name, superluxurious hotels with spectacular views, while Th Silom and more recently Th Sathon are home to several new, stylish and well-priced midrange hotels and some chic top-end places. The area around Siam Sq also has several more stately upmarket hotels, plus a handful of budget options. Th Sukhumvit, where you'll find sleaze and class in plentiful supply depending on which soi you're on, is home to a bunch of new boutique and wannabe-boutique places, numerous tour-group oriented midrangers and a smattering of quirky budget and top-end affairs. See p396 for more on accommodation in Thailand.

KO RATANAKOSIN & BANGLAMPHU

Banglamphu, the neighbourhood that includes the backpacker street of Th Khao San, is a well-padded landing zone for jet-lagged travellers. This doesn't necessarily mean it's the only or even the best place to

WHAT TO EXPECT IN BANGKOK

Hotel rooms are generally more expensive in Bangkok than elsewhere in Thailand, but don't fret as there's a huge variety and significant discounts can be had, making accommodation very good value overall. We have divided rooms into the following three categories:

Budget Under 1000B

Midrange 1000B to 3000B

Top End Over 3000B

The prices listed are high-season walk-in rates, but it's worth noting that significant discounts can be found by booking online.

So what do you get for your money? At the budget end, the days of 50B beds in Banglamphu are over, but those counting every baht can still get a fan-cooled dorm bed (or a closet-like room) for between 150B and 200B with a shared bathroom. The more you're willing to pay, the more likely you are to get a towel, hot water and air-con. If you require privacy and your own bathroom, paying in the realm of 700B or so can get you a serviceable, but generally characterless, room.

The biggest mixed bag of all, the midrange level starts out with the high-quality guest houses, then moves into a grey area of mediocrity. Above 1000B, the hotels have all the appearance of a hotel back home – a bellboy, uniformed desk clerks and a well-polished lobby – but without the predictability. If you're on a lower midrange budget, and aren't so keen on aesthetics, some very acceptable rooms can be had for between roughly 1500B and 2000B. If your budget is near the higher end of the scale, it really pays to book ahead, as online discounts can be substantial.

Bangkok's growing array of top-end hotels typically include amenities such as pool, spa, fitness and business centres, and overpriced internet connections. The famous brands generally provide more space, while 'boutique' hotels emphasise ambience. In the top tier, rooms start at more than 10,000B, but in most of the luxurious design and boutique hotels, and the vast majority of the international brands, you're looking at about 6000B to 9000B, before hefty online discounting. Keep in mind that the hotels in this category will generally add a 10% service charge plus 7% tax to hotel bills.

stay in town, but prices are generally low and standards relatively high. Neighbouring Ko Ratanakosin is seeing an increasing number of boutique-type riverside places.

TOP CHOICE Lamphu Tree House HOTEL $$
(Map p60; ☎0 2282 0991; www.lamphutreehotel.com; 155 Wanchat Bridge, Th Prachatipatai; r incl breakfast 1500-2100B; 🚌56, 58 & 516, ⛴Tha Phra Athit (Banglamphu), ⛴klorng taxi Tha Phah Fah; ❄@📶🏊) Despite the name, this attractive midranger has its feet firmly on land and as such, represents brilliant value. Rooms are attractive and inviting, and the rooftop bar, pool, internet, restaurant and quiet canal-side location ensure that you may never feel the need to leave.

Diamond House HOTEL $$
(Map p60; ☎0 2629 4008; www.thaidiamondhouse.com; 4 Th Samsen; r 2000-2800B, ste 3600B; 🚌32 & 516, ⛴Tha Phra Athit (Banglamphu); ❄@📶) Despite sharing real estate with a rather brash Chinese temple, there's no conflict of design at this eccentric, funky hotel. Most rooms are loft style, with beds on raised platforms, and are outfitted with stained glass, lush dark colours and chic furnishings.

Arun Residence HOTEL $$$
(Map p60; ☎0 2221 9158; www.arunresidence.com; 36-38 Soi Pratu Nok Yung; r incl breakfast 3500-3800B; 🚌123 & 508, ⛴Tha Tien; ❄@📶) The six rooms here manage to feel both homey and stylish, some being tall and loft-like, while others combine two rooms (the best is the top-floor suite with its own balcony). There are inviting communal areas, including a library, a rooftop bar and a restaurant.

NapPark Hostel HOSTEL $
(Map p60; ☎0 2282 2324; www.nappark.com; 8 Th Tani; dm 550-750B; ⛴Tha Tien; ❄@📶) This exceedingly well-done hostel features dorm rooms of various sizes, the smallest and

most expensive of which boasts six pod-like beds outfitted with power points, mini-TV, reading lamp and wi-fi.

Old Bangkok Inn HOTEL **$$$**
(Map p60; ☎0 2629 1787; www.oldbangkokinn.com; 609 Th Phra Sumen; r incl breakfast 3190-6590B; klorng taxi Tha Phan Fah;) The 10 rooms in this refurbished antique shophouse are decadent and sumptuous, making it the perfect honeymoon hotel.

Fortville Guesthouse HOTEL **$**
(Map p60; ☎0 2282 3932; www.fortvilleguesthouse.com; 9 Th Phra Sumen; r 650-970B; 32, 33, 64 & 82, Tha Phra Athit (Banglamphu);) The design concept of this unique new hotel is a bit hard to pin down, but rooms are stylishly minimal, and the more expensive include perks such as fridge, balcony and free wi-fi.

Navalai River Resort HOTEL **$$$**
(Map p60; ☎0 2280 9955; www.navalai.com; 45/1 Th Phra Athit; r incl breakfast 2900-4800B; 32, 33, 64 & 82, Tha Phra Athit (Banglamphu);) The latest thing to go up on breezy Th Phra Athit, this chic hotel has 74 modern rooms, many looking out over Chao Phraya River.

Baan Sabai HOTEL **$**
(Map p60; ☎0 2629 1599; baansabai@hotmail.com; 12 Soi Rongmai; r 190-600B; 53 & 516, Tha Phra Athit (Banglamphu);) Truly living up to its name (Comfortable House), this rambling old building holds dozens of plain but comfy rooms, at a variety of prices.

Wild Orchid Villa HOTEL **$**
(Map p60; ☎0 2629 4378; www.wildorchidvilla.com; 8 Soi Chana Songkhram; r 280-1800B; 32, 33, 64 & 82, Tha Phra Athit (Banglamphu);) The cheapies here are some of the tiniest we've seen anywhere, but all rooms are clean and neat, and come in a bright, friendly package.

Lamphu House HOTEL **$**
(Map p60; ☎0 2629 5861; www.lamphuhouse.com; 75-77 Soi Ram Buttri; r 200-950B; Tha Phra Athit (Banglamphu);) Tucked off Soi Ram Buttri, you'll forget how close to Th Khao San you are in this quiet, homey budget hotel.

Rikka Inn HOTEL **$$**
(Map p60; ☎0 2282 7511; www.rikkainn.com; 259 Th Khao San; r 1150-1450B; 53 & 516, Tha Phra Athit (Banglamphu);) Boasting tight but attractive rooms, a rooftop pool and a central location, the Rikka is one of several great-value midrange hotels changing the face of Th Khao San.

Sam Sen Sam GUEST HOUSE **$**
(Map p60; ☎0 2628 7067; www.samsensam.com; 48 Soi 3, Th Samsen; r 590-2400B; Tha Phra Athit (Banglamphu);) This bright, refurbished villa gets good reports about its friendly service and quiet location.

CHINATOWN & PHAHURAT

Bangkok's Chinatown isn't the most hospitable part of town, but for those who wish to stay off the beaten track it's an area where travellers can remain largely anonymous.

Shanghai Mansion HOTEL **$$$**
(☎0 2221 2121; www.shanghai-inn.com; 479-481 Th Yaowarat; r 1500-3500B, ste 4000B; Tha Ratchawong;) This award-winning boutique hotel screams Shanghai c 1935 with stained glass, an abundance of lamps, bold colours and tongue-in-cheek Chinatown kitsch.

Baan Hualampong GUEST HOUSE **$**
(☎0 2639 8054; www.baanhualampong.com; 336/20-21 Trok Chalong Krung; dm incl breakfast 150B, r incl breakfast 290-800B; Hua Lamphong;) Simple but homey, this guest house is a short walk from Hualamphong, Bangkok's main train station.

@ Hua Lamphong BUDGET HOTEL **$**
(☎0 2639 1925; www.at-hualamphong.com; 326/1 Th Phra Ram IV; dm 200B, r 690-1000B; Tha Ratchawong, Hua Lamphong;) Tidy hostel located across the street from the train station.

HAVE YOUR SAY

Found a fantastic restaurant that you're longing to share with the world? Disagree with our recommendations? Or just want to talk about your most recent trip?

Whatever your reason, head to lonelyplanet.com, where you can post a review, ask or answer a question on the Thorntree forum, comment on a blog, or share your photos and tips on Groups. Or you can simply spend time chatting with like-minded travellers. So go on, have your say.

Siam Square

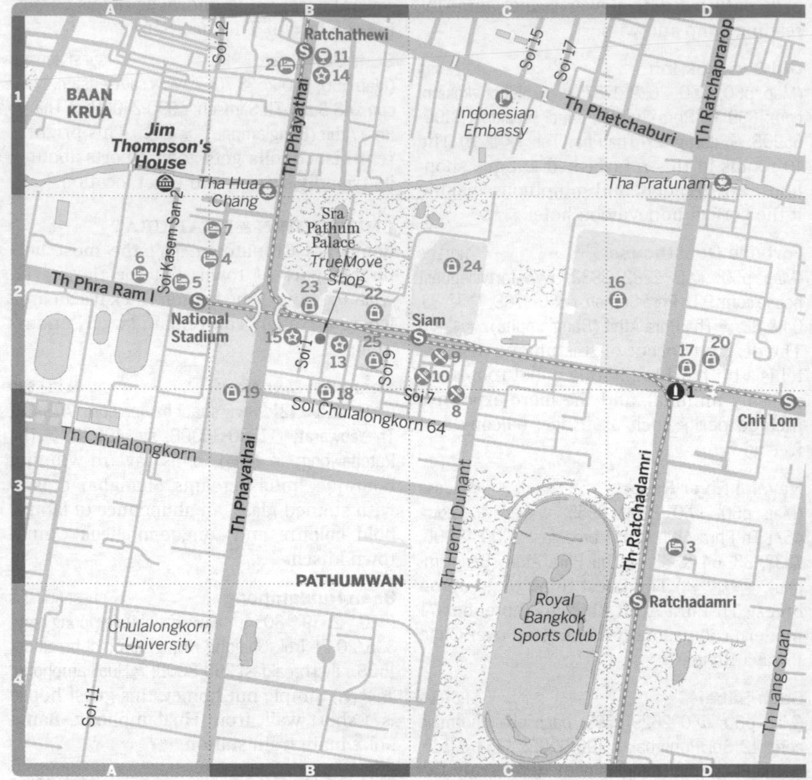

SIAM SQUARE

Siam Sq lies conveniently along both BTS lines. A low-key, DIY traveller community bunks down on Soi Kasem San 1.

TOP CHOICE Siam@Siam HOTEL $$$

(Map p70; ☎0 2217 3000; www.siamatsiam.com; 865 Th Phra Ram I; r incl breakfast 5000-7000B; National Stadium;) A seemingly random mishmash of colours and materials result in a style one could only describe as 'junkyard' – but in a good way, of course. The rooms, which continue the theme, are located between the 14th and 24th floors, and offer terrific city views, free wi-fi and breakfast.

Lub*d HOSTEL $

(Map p70; ☎0 2634 7999; www.lubd.com; Th Pha Ram I; dm 550B, r 1350-1800B; National Stadium;) There are 24 dorms here (including ladies-only dorms), each with only four beds, and a few private rooms, both with and without bathrooms. There's an inviting communal area stocked with free internet, games and a bar, and thoughtful facilities ranging from washing machines to a theatre room.

Hansar HOTEL $$$

(Map p70; ☎0 2209 1234; www.hansarbangkok.com; 3 Soi Mahadlekluang 2, Th Ratchadamri; r incl breakfast 5500-24,000B; Ratchadamri;) The brand-new Hansar can lay claim to that elusive intersection of style and value. All 94 rooms here have huge bathrooms and giant desks, but the smallest (and cheapest) studios are probably the best deal, as they have a kitchenette, washing machine, stand-alone tub, free wi-fi and balcony. Located a short walk from BTS Ratchadamri.

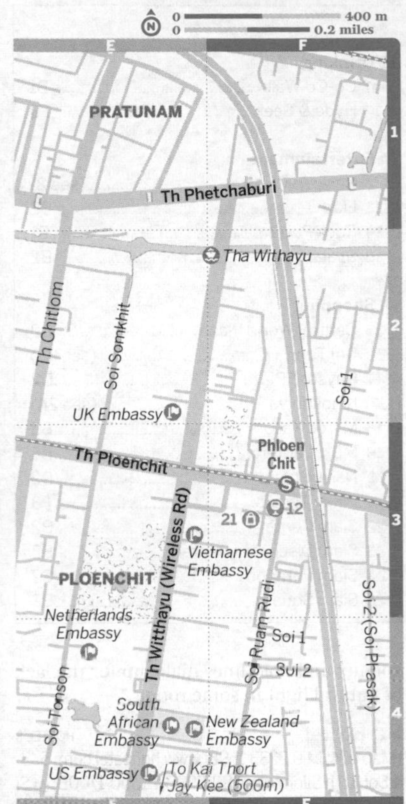

LIT HOTEL **$$$**

(Map p70; ☎0 2612 3456; www.litbangkok.com; 36/1 Soi Kasemsan 1; r incl breakfast 7000-10,000B; Siam;) This funky new hotel has a variety of rooms united by a light theme. Check out a few, as they vary significantly, and some features, including a shower that can be seen from the living room, aren't necessarily for everybody. Also check the website for online discounts.

Asia Hotel HOTEL **$$$**

(Map p70; ☎0 2217 0808; www.asiahotel.co.th; 296 Th Phayathai; r incl breakfast 3700-4800B, ste incl breakfast 8000-10,000B; klorng taxi Tha Ratchathewi, Ratchathewi;) A recent renovation has the rooms of this tourist-group staple looking more modern than the 1970s-era lobby would suggest.

Wendy House HOTEL **$**

(Map p70; ☎0 214 1149; www.wendyguesthouse.com; 36/2 Soi Kasem San 1; s/d 900/1050B; klorng taxi Tha Ratchathewi, National Stadium;) The rooms here are small, but spotless and well maintained, and they come packed with amenities ranging from TV to fridge.

SILOM, SATHON & RIVERSIDE

The city's financial district along Th Silom is not the most charming area of town, but it is conveniently located for nightspots and the BTS and MRT. The adjacent riverside area is home to some of Bangkok's most famous luxury hotels.

TOP CHOICE **Siam Heritage** HOTEL **$$$**

(Map p74; ☎0 2353 6101; www.thesiamheritage.com; 115/1 Th Surawong; r incl breakfast 3000-3500B, ste incl breakfast 4500-9000B; MSi Lom, Sala Daeng;) Tucked off busy Th Surawong, this classy boutique hotel oozes homey Thai charm – probably because the owners also live in the same building. Rooms are decked out in silk and dark woods with genuinely thoughtful design touches and good amenities.

Metropolitan HOTEL **$$$**

(off Map p74; ☎0 2625 3333; www.metropolitan.como.bz; 27 Th Sathon Tai; r incl breakfast 4951-5768B, ste incl breakfast 6945-21,186B; MLumphini;) The exterior of the former YMCA has changed relatively little, but a peek inside reveals one of Bangkok's sleekest hotels. Urban minimalism rules here, except where it concerns the size of the two-storey penthouse suites. Breakfast is either American or 'organic' and the attached nahm (p78) is Bangkok's best upscale Thai restaurant.

Mandarin Oriental HOTEL **$$$**

(☎0 2659 9000; www.mandarinoriental.com; 48 Soi 40/Oriental, Th Charoen Krung; r incl breakfast 12,799-14,799B, ste incl breakfast 23,999-140,999B; hotel shuttle boat from Tha Sathon/Central Pier;) The classic Oriental stays rooted in its past as the first luxury hotel in Bangkok and a haven for legendary literary names.

Baan Saladaeng HOTEL **$$**

(Map p74; ☎0 2636 3038; www.baansaladaeng.com; 69/2 Th Sala Daeng; r incl breakfast 1300-2300B; MSi Lom, Sala Daeng;) Of the handful of pint-sized boutique hotels along Th Sala Daeng, Baan Saladaeng is the most welcoming. The lobby's cheery primary-colour theme carries into the 11 rooms, of

Siam Square

Top Sights
Jim Thompson's House ... A1

Sights
1 Erawan Shrine ... D3
Krung Sri IMAX ... (see 24)
Siam Ocean World ... (see 24)

Sleeping
2 Asia Hotel ... B1
3 Hansar ... D3
4 LIT ... B2
5 Lub*d ... A2
6 Siam@Siam ... A2
7 Wendy House ... B2

Eating
8 Coca Suki ... C3
Crystal Jade La Mian Xiao Long Bao ... (see 1)
9 Food Plus ... C2
MBK Food Court ... (see 19)
10 Som Tam Nua ... C2

Drinking
11 Co-Co Walk ... B1
12 Hyde & Seek ... F3

Entertainment
Calypso Cabaret ... (see 2)
13 Lido ... B2
14 Rock Pub ... B1
15 Scala ... B2

Shopping
16 Central World Plaza ... D2
Doi Tung ... (see 23)
17 Gaysorn Plaza ... D2
Kinokuniya ... (see 24)
18 Marco Tailors ... B3
19 MBK Center ... B3
20 Narai Phand ... D2
21 Pinky Tailors ... F3
22 Siam Center ... B2
23 Siam Discovery Center ... B2
24 Siam Paragon ... C2
25 Siam Square ... B2

which those on the upper floors are the largest and airiest.

Shangri-La Hotel HOTEL $$$
(☎0 2236 7777; www.shangri-la.com; 89 Soi 42/1/ Wat Suan Phlu, Th Charoen Krung; r incl breakfast 6800-7700B, ste incl breakfast 8500-15,600B; Saphan Taksin;) A recent facelift has the longstanding Shangri-La looking better than ever. Reasonable rates, an attractive riverside location, a resort-like atmopshere, and ample activities and amenities make this a good choice for families.

Swan Hotel HOTEL $$
(☎0 2235 9271; www.swanhotelbkk.com; 31 Soi 36, Th Charoen Krung; s/d incl breakfast 1200/1500B; Tha Oriental;) Although still ensconced in the 1960s, the Swan is a good choice for its large rooms, quiet location and classic hotel pool.

All Seasons Sathorn HOTEL $$
(off Map p74; ☎0 2343 6333; www.allseasons-sathorn.com; 31 Th Sathon Tai; r incl breakfast 1800-2500B; MLumphini;) The former King's Hotel has been reborn as this modern attractive budget choice, right in the middle of the embassy district. The primary colours and bold lines make up for the lack of natural light in some rooms.

HQ Hostel HOSTEL $
(Map p74; ☎0 2233 1598; www.hqhostel.com; 5/3-4 Soi 3, Th Silom; dm 380-599B, r 1300-1700B; MSi Lom, Sala Daeng;) This new hostel combines basic but stylish rooms and dorms with inviting communal areas, smack dab in the middle of Bangkok's financial district.

New Road Guesthouse HOSTEL $
(☎0 2630 9371; www.newroadguesthouse.com; 1216/1 Th Charoen Krung; dm fan/air-con 160/250B, r 900-2500B; Tha Si Phraya;) For those on tight budgets, the clean fan dorms are among the cheapest accommodation in all of Bangkok.

If you were hitting the Asian hippy trail back in the 1970s, you would have laid your love beads at a guest house in Soi Ngam Duphli. It remains a budget alternative to Th Khao San, and getting there has been made even easier by the MRT stop at Lumphini.

Penguin House HOTEL $
(☎0 2679 9991; www.penguinhouses.com; 27/23 Soi Si Bamphen; r 800-950B; MLumphini;) The oddly named Penguin is a breath of

LATE-NIGHT TOUCHDOWN

A lot of nail-biting anxiety is expended on international flights arriving in Bangkok around midnight. Will there be taxis into town? Will there be available rooms? Will my family ever hear from me again? Soothe those nagging voices with the knowledge that most international flights arrive late, there are taxis 24/7 and Bangkok is an accommodating place.

If you haven't already made hotel reservations, a good area to look for a bed is lower Sukhumvit – it's right off the expressway and hotels around Soi Nana such as the **Swiss Park** (Map p80; ☎0 2254 0228; 155/23 Soi 11/1, Th Sukhumvit; r 1500-1900B, ste 2900B; Nana;) and the **Federal** (Map p80; ☎0 2253 0175; www.federalbangkok.com; 27 Soi 11, Th Sukhumvit; r incl breakfast 1050-1500B; Nana; @) are used to lots of late-night traffic and won't break the bank. Alternatively, you could always go to Th Khao San, which stays up late, is full of hotels and guest houses, and sees a near-continuous supply of 'fresh-off-the-birds' just like you.

If, for some reason, you can't stray too far from the airport, these places provide a more than adequate roof.

Suvarnabhumi International Airport

The nearest good budget option is Refill Now! (p76).

Grand Inn Come Hotel (☎0 2738 8189-99; www.grandinncome-hotel.com; 99 Moo 6, Th Kingkaew, Bangpli; r incl breakfast from 1800B; @) Solid midranger 10km from the airport, with airport shuttle and 'lively' karaoke bar.

Novotel Suvarnabhumi Airport Hotel (☎0 2131 1111; www.novotel.com; r incl breakfast from 7146B; @) With 600-plus luxurious rooms in the airport compound.

Don Muang Airport

Amari Airport Hotel (☎0 2566 1020; www.amari.com; 333 Th Choet Wutthakat; d incl breakfast from 2001-3350B; @) Directly opposite Don Muang.

fresh air in this area of tired old-timers. Rear rooms will be quieter, and there are a couple of interior rooms that sleep two couples.

ETZzz Hostel HOSTEL $
(☎0 2286 9424; www.etzhostel.com; Soi Ngam Duphli; dm/r 200/900B; M Lumphini;) The rooms at this brand-new shophouse-based hostel are tiny and overpriced, but the tidy dorm, shiny facilities and convenient location are worth considering.

SUKHUMVIT

This seemingly endless urban thoroughfare is Bangkok's unofficial International Zone and also boasts much of the city's accommodation. There's a bit of everything here, from the odd backpacker hostel to sex-tourist hovels and five-star luxury digs. The former two are largely located between Soi 1 and Soi 4, while the latter doesn't begin to appear until you reach Soi 12 or so.

In general, because visitors with larger budgets stay in Sukhumvit, tourist services are more expensive here than in Banglamphu. The trade-off is access to food from virtually every corner of the globe, heaps of nightlife options and easy access to both the BTS and MRT.

TOP CHOICE **Ariyasom Villa** HOTEL $$$
(Map p80; ☎0 2254 880; www.ariyasom.com; 65 Soi 1, Th Sukhumvit; r incl breakfast 4248-9138B; Phloen Chit; @) If you can score a reservation, you'll have access to one of the 24 spacious rooms here, all of which are meticulously outfitted with thoughtful Thai design touches and beautiful antique furniture. There's a spa and an inviting tropical pool, and breakfast is vegetarian and served in the original villa's stunning glass-encased dining room.

72 Ekamai HOTEL $$
(Map p80; ☎02 714 7327; www.72ekamai.com; 72 Soi 63/Ekamai, Th Sukhumvit; r incl breakfast 2100B, ste incl breakfast 2500-2850B; Ekkamai; @) This fun, young-feeling, design-conscious hotel is a great choice. The junior suites are huge and, like all rooms, are well equipped and located a short walk from BTS Ekkamai and lots of nightlife options.

Silom & Sathon

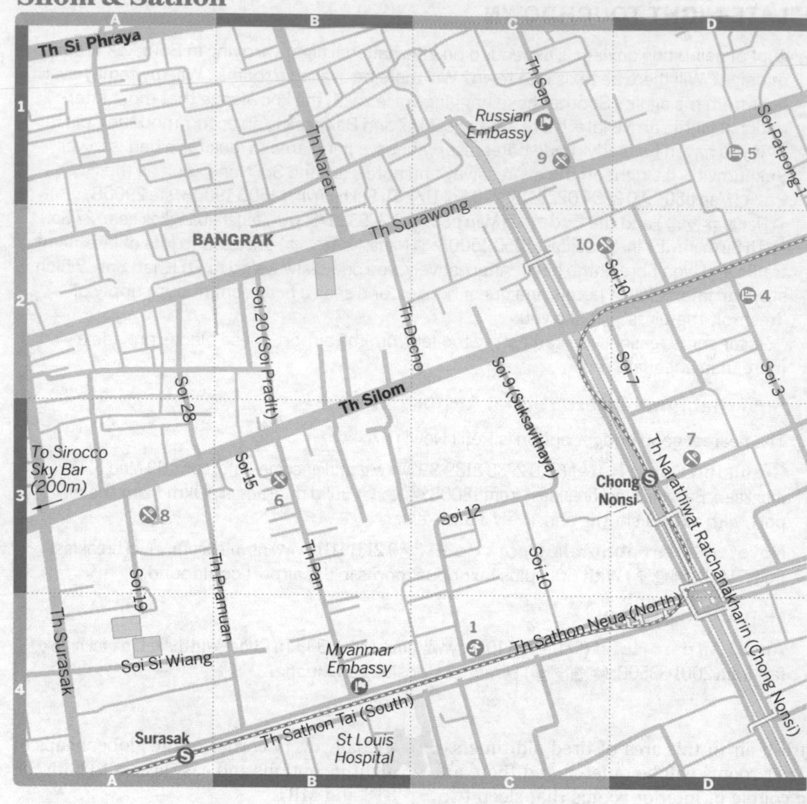

Silom & Sathon

Top Sights
- Lumphini Park F1

Activities, Courses & Tours
1. Health Land C4
2. Ruen-Nuad Massage Studio E3

Sleeping
3. Baan Saladaeng F2
4. HQ Hostel D2
5. Siam Heritage D1

Eating
6. Chennai Kitchen B3
7. FooDie D3
8. Nadimos A3
9. Scoozi C1
10. Soi 10 Food Centres C2
11. Somtam Convent E2

Drinking
12. Balcony E1
13. DJ Station E1
14. G.O.D. E1
15. Telephone E1

Entertainment
16. Tapas Room E1

Shopping
17. Jim Thompson E1

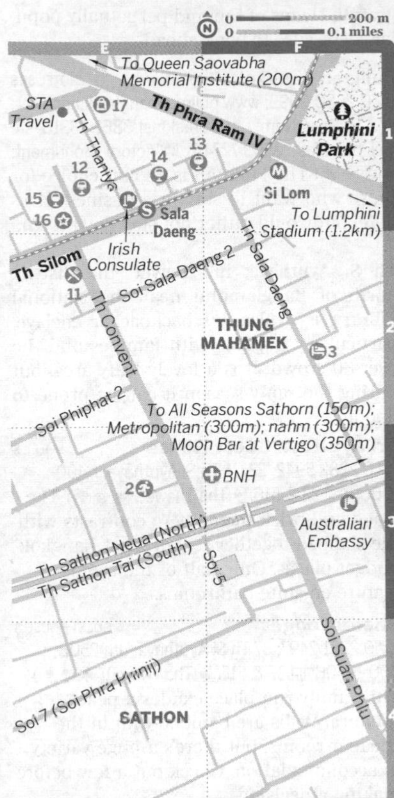

Eugenia HOTEL $$$

(Map p80; 0 2259 0017-19; www.theeugenia.com; 267 Soi 31/Sawatdi, Th Sukhumvit; ste incl breakfast 8107-9911B; Phrom Phong & access by taxi;) Colonial manor houses aren't an indigenous legacy in Thailand but this anachronistic 12-guestroom hotel indulges in the anomaly. Think stuffed animals, four-poster beds and antique furniture, all done with class and style.

Ma Du Zi HOTEL $$$

(Map p80; 0 2615 6400; www.maduzihotel.com; cnr Th Ratchadapisek & Soi 16, Th Sukhumvit; r incl breakfast 5000-12,000B, ste incl breakfast 12,000B; Sukhumvit, Asok;) The name is a play on the Thai phrase for 'come take a look', somewhat of a misnomer for this reservations-only, no walk-ins hotel. Behind its towering gate you'll find an attractive midsized hotel steeped in dark, chic tones and designs.

Sheraton Grande Sukhumvit HOTEL $$$

(Map p80; 0 2649 8888; www.luxurycollection.com/bangkok; 250 Th Sukhumvit; r incl breakfast 3500-10,000B, ste incl breakfast 16,500-55,000B; Sukhumvit, Asok;) This conveniently located business-oriented hotel offers some of the most spacious rooms in town and fills them with a generous array of amenities.

Sacha's Hotel Uno HOTEL $$

(Map p80; 0 2651 2180; www.sachas.hotel-uno.com; 28/19 Soi 19, Th Sukhumvit; r incl breakfast 1800-2500B; Sukhumvit, Asok;) Surprisingly sophisticated rooms at a budget price. Convenient location, too.

Seven HOTEL $$$

(Map p80; 0 2662 0951; www.sleepatseven.com; 3/15 Soi 31/Sawatdi, Th Sukhumvit; r incl breakfast 3290-5290B; Phrom Phong;) Tiny hotel with hip rooms and easy-to-befriend staff.

Stable Lodge HOTEL $$

(Map p80; 0 2653 0017; www.stablelodge.com; 39 Soi 8, Th Sukhumvit; r 1495-1695B; Nana;) A recent renovation has given a bit of life to the simple rooms here, and the spacious balconies still offer great city views.

Despite the general upscale nature of this part of town, there's a decent selection of backpacker hostels:

Suk 11 HOTEL $

(Map p80; 0 2253 5927; www.suk11.com; 1/33 Soi 11, Th Sukhumvit; s incl breakfast 535-695B, d incl breakfast 749-963B; Nana;) This popular guest house is an oasis in the urban jungle that is Th Sukhumvit. The cheaper rooms have shared bathrooms, and although there are nearly 100 rooms, you'll still need to book at least two weeks ahead.

Bed Bangkok HOSTEL $

(Map p80; 0 2655 7604; www.bedbangkok.com; 11/20 Soi 1, Th Sukhumvit; dm incl breakfast 390B, r incl breakfast 800-1200B; Sukhumvit, Asok;) This brand-new hostel manages to maintain a homey feel despite the industrial-design theme. The friendly service makes up for the rather hard dorm beds.

Nana Chart HOSTEL $

(Map p80; 0 2259 6908; www.thailandhostel.com; cnr Soi 25 & Th Sukhumvit; dm incl breakfast 390-550B, r incl breakfast 1200-1800B;

Sukhumvit, Asok;) This tidy, new-ish backpacker hostel packs in 68 plain but more-than-adequate budget rooms, as well as some of the better dorms around with en suite bathrooms.

HI-Sukhumvit HOSTEL $

(Map p80; 0 2391 9338; www.hisukhumvit.com; 23 Soi 38, Th Sukhumvit; dm/s incl breakfast 320/650B, d incl breakfast 900-1300B; Thong Lo;) Located in a quiet residential street a brief walk from the BTS, this friendly hostel excels with its neat dorms and accompanying immense bathrooms.

OTHER AREAS

Many of the following hotels lie outside our neat neighbourhood designations, so they often require a little more effort to reach. This also means that they tend to be located in less hectic parts of the city, perfect for those who'd rather not stay in the thick of it.

If you need to stay near one of Bangkok's two airports, check the accommodation options in the boxed text on p73.

Phra-Nakorn Norn-Len HOTEL $$

(0 2628 8188; www.phranakorn-nornlen.com; 46 Soi Thewet 1, Th Krung Kasem; s incl breakfast 1800B, d incl breakfast 2200-2400B; 32 & 516, Tha Thewet;) Set in an expansive garden compound decorated like the Bangkok of yesteryear, this bright and cheery hotel is an atmospheric if not necessarily great-value place to stay. Rooms are simply furnished, but generously decorated with antiques and wall paintings, and there's wi-fi, massage and endless opportunities for peaceful relaxing.

Refill Now! HOSTEL $

(0 2713 2044; www.refillnow.co.th; 191 Soi Pridi Bhanom Yong 42, Soi 71, Th Sukhumvit; dm/s/d 480/928/1215B; Phra Khanong & access by taxi;) Sporting a look that blends the Habitat catalogue and a Kubrick movie, this hostel is equipped with an achingly hip chill-out area and a massage centre. If you decide you need to leave, there's a túk-túk (pronounced *đúk đúk*; 30B per passenger) to Thong Lo and Phra Khanong BTS stations.

Mystic Place HOTEL $$

(0 2270 3344; www.mysticplacebkk.com; 224/5-9 Th Pradiphat; r incl breakfast 2250-3250B; Saphan Khwai & access by taxi;) This hotel unites 36 individually and playfully designed rooms. One of the rooms we checked out combined a chair upholstered with stuffed animals and walls covered with graffiti. Heaps of fun and perpetually popular, so be sure to book ahead.

Pullman Bangkok King Power HOTEL $$$

(0 2680 9999; www.pullmanbangkokkingpower; 8/2 Th Rang Nam; r incl breakfast 3861-4331B, ste incl breakfast 6803-7274B; Victory Monument;) The Pullman is a great choice for those who want to stay in a business-class hotel but would rather not stay downtown.

Th Si Ayuthaya, in Thewet, the district north of Banglamphu near the National Library, is a pleasant backpacker enclave, particularly popular with families and the over-30 crowd. It is a lovely leafy area, but during the rainy season it can be prone to flooding.

Sri Ayuttaya Guest House HOTEL $

(0 2282 5942; 23/11 Th Si Ayuthaya; r 400-1000B; 32 & 516, Tha Thewet;) The wood-and-brick theme here contrasts with the slapped-together feel of most Bangkok budget places. Only half of the rooms feature en-suite bathrooms.

Shanti Lodge GUEST HOUSE $

(0 2281 2497; 37 Th Si Ayuthaya; dm 250B, r 400-1950B; 32 & 516, Tha Thewet;) This family-run place exudes a peaceful aura. Walls are bamboo-thin in the cheaper rooms, but there's a huge variety of accommodation. Check out a few before making a decision.

Taewez Guesthouse HOTEL $

(0 2280 8856; www.taewez.com; 23/12 Th Si Ayuthaya; r 250-530B; 32 & 516, Tha Thewet;) Popular with French travellers, the cheapest rooms here are plain and share bathrooms, but are good value.

Eating

Nowhere else is the Thai reverence for food more evident than in Bangkok. The city's characteristic scent is a unique blend of noodle stall and car exhaust, and in certain parts of town, restaurants appear to form the majority of businesses, typically flanked by street-side hawker stalls and mobile snack vendors.

To outsiders, the life of an average Bangkokian can appear to be little more than a string of meals and snacks punctuated by the odd job, not the other way around. If you can adjust your stomach clock to fit this schedule, we're confident your stay in Bangkok will be a delicious one indeed.

Despite the global infatuation with Thai food, many visitors go from one mediocre meal to another, mainly at guest-house kitchens and tourist-oriented restaurants catering more to a Western definition of ambience than food. We strongly urge you to break out of the ghetto mentality and explore the small eateries and street stalls of this great city. For tips on eating like a local, see p40.

The standard opening hours for restaurants here are approximately 10am to 11pm daily, but many midrange places close between approximately 2pm and 5pm.

KO RATANAKOSIN & BANGLAMPHU

The old areas of town near the river are full of simple Thai restaurants and, because of the traveller presence, Western and vegetarian food as well.

TOP CHOICE Krua Apsorn THAI $$

(Map p60; Th Din So; mains 70-320B; lunch & dinner Mon-Sat; 2, 25, 44 & 511, klorng taxi Tha Phan Fah;) This homey dining room has served members of the Thai royal family and, back in 2006, was recognised as Bangkok's Best Restaurant by the *Bangkok Post*. Must-eat dishes include mussels fried with fresh herbs, the decadent crab fried in yellow chilli oil and the tortilla Española-like crab omelette.

Jay Fai THAI $$$

(Map p60; 327 Th Mahachai; mains from 250B; 3pm-2am; klorng taxi Tha Phan Fah) You wouldn't think so by looking at the bare-bones dining room, but Jay Fai is known far and wide for serving Bangkok's most expensive – and arguably most delicious – *pàt kêe mow* (drunkard's noodles).

Poj Spa Kar THAI $$

(Map p60; 443 Th Tanao; mains 100-200B; lunch & dinner; 2, 25, 44 & 511, klorng taxi Tha Phan Fah;) Pronounced *pôht sà·pah kahn,* this is allegedly the oldest restaurant in Bangkok, and continues to serve recipes handed down from a former palace cook.

Hemlock THAI $$

(Map p60; 56 Th Phra Athit; mains 60-220B; 4pm-midnight; 32, 33, 64 & 82, Tha Phra Athit (Banglamphu);) This cosy gem has an eclectic range with many items – including lots of veggie options – that don't usually pop up on menus.

Shoshana ISRAELI $$

(Map p60; 88 Th Chakraphong; mains 90-220B; lunch & dinner; 32 & 516, Tha Phra Athit (Banglamphu);) This is one of Th Khao San's best and oldest Israeli restaurants, tucked away in an unnamed, almost secret alley beside the former petrol station.

Khinlom Chom Sa-Phan THAI $$

(off Map p60; 11/6 Soi 3, Th Samsen; mains 75-280B; 11am-2am; 32 & 516, Tha Phra Athit (Banglamphu);) Locals come here for the combination of riverfront views and tasty seafood-based eats. Call ahead to book a riverfront table.

VEGGING OUT IN BANGKOK

Vegetarianism is a growing trend among urban Thais, but veggie restaurants are still generally few and far between.

Banglamphu has the greatest concentration of vegetarian-friendly restaurants, thanks to the non-meat-eating *fa·ràng;* these are typically low-scale stir-fry shops that do something akin to what your hippy roommates have cooking in their kitchens. Examples include **Arawy** (Map p60; 152 Th Din So, Phra Nakhon; dishes 20-30B; 8am-8pm; 10 & 12, klorng taxi Tha Phan Fah), **May Kaidee** (Map p60; www.maykaidee.com; 33 Th Samsen; mains 50-100B; lunch & dinner; 32 & 516, Tha Phra Athit (Banglamphu);), which in addition to three branches around Th Khao San also offers a veggie Thai cooking school, and **Ranee's** (Map p60; 77 Trok Mayom; dishes 70-320B; breakfast, lunch & dinner; 32 & 516, Tha Phra Athit (Banglamphu)), whose menu features a lengthy meat-free section.

Elsewhere in town, **Baan Suan Pai** (Banana Family Park, Th Phahonyothin; mains 15-30B; 7am-3pm; Ari), the MBK Food Court (p78) and Chennai Kitchen (p80) all offer cheap but tasty meat-free meals.

During the Vegetarian Festival in September/October, the whole city goes mad for tofu. Stalls and restaurants indicate their nonmeat menu with yellow banners; Chinatown has the highest concentration of stalls.

CHINATOWN & PHAHURAT

When you mention Chinatown, Bangkokians begin dreaming of noodles, usually prepared by street vendors lining Th Yaowarat, near Trok Itsaranuphap (Soi 6, Th Yaowarat), after dark. The dining is good in the Indian district of Phahurat too.

Old Siam Plaza THAI $

(ground fl, Old Siam Plaza, cnr Th Phahurat & Th Triphet; mains 15-50B; 9am-6.30pm; Tha Saphan Phut (Memorial Bridge)) This mall-bound food court turns seemingly savoury ingredients such as beans and rice into syrupy sweet desserts, right before your eyes.

Th Phadungdao Seafood Stalls THAI $$

(cnr Th Phadungdao & Th Yaowarat; mains 180-300B; dinner Tue-Sun; Tha Saphan Phut (Memorial Bridge), Hua Lamphong) After sunset, this frenetic intersection sprouts outdoor barbecues, iced seafood trays and sidewalk seating.

Royal India INDIAN $$

(392/1 Th Chakraphet; mains 65-250B; lunch & dinner; Tha Saphan Phut (Memorial Bridge) Don't be intimidated by its dark alleyway location. After more than 30 years in business, Royal India remains a reliable destination for North Indian cuisine.

SIAM SQUARE

If you find yourself hungry in this part of Bangkok, you're largely at the mercy of shopping-mall food courts and chain restaurants.

TOP CHOICE **MBK Food Court** THAI $

(Map p70; 6th fl, MBK Center, cnr Th Phra Ram I & Th Phayathai; 10am-9pm; National Stadium;) A great introduction to Thai food for recent arrivals, this mall food court has fresh and flavourful street-stall eats that are translated into English and in air-con comfort. Buy coupons from the ticket desk and then cash in whatever you don't spend.

Kai Thort Jay Kee THAI $

(Soi Polo Fried Chicken; off Map p70; 137/1-3 Soi Sanam Khlii (Polo), Th Witthayu/Wireless Rd; mains 40-300B; 7am-10pm; Lumphini;) Although the *sôm·đam* (spicy green papaya salad), sticky rice and *lâhp* (a Thai-style 'salad' of minced meat) give the impression of a northeastern Thailand–style eatery, the restaurant's namesake deep-fried bird is more southern in origin. Regardless, smothered in a thick layer of crispy deep-fried garlic, it's a true Bangkok experience.

Crystal Jade La Mian Xiao Long Bao CHINESE $$

(Map p70; Urban Kitchen, basement, Erawan Bangkok, 494 Th Ploenchit; dishes 120-400B; lunch & dinner; Chit Lom;) The tongue-twistingly long name of this excellent Singaporean chain refers to the restaurant's signature wheat noodles *(la mian)* and the famous Shanghainese 'soup' dumplings *(xiao long bao)*.

Food Plus THAI $

(Map p70; alleyway btwn Soi 3 & Soi 4, Siam Sq; mains 30-70B; 6am-6pm) This claustrophobic alleyway is bursting with the wares of several *ráhn kôw gaang* (rice and curry stalls). You'll be hard-pressed to spend more than 100B and the flavours are unanimously authentic and delicious.

Som Tam Nua NORTHEASTERN THAI $$

(Map p70; 392/14 Soi 5, Siam Sq; mains 59-130B; 10.45am-9.30pm; Siam;) It can't compete with the street stalls for flavour, but if you need to be seen, particularly while in air-con and trendy surroundings, this is a good place to sample northeastern Thai specialities. Expect a lengthy line at dinner.

Coca Suki CHINESE-THAI $$

(Map p70; 416/3-8 Th Henri Dunant; mains 60-200B; 11am-11pm; Siam;) Immensely popular with Thai families, *sù·gêe* takes the form of a bubbling hotpot of broth and the raw ingredients to dip therein.

SILOM, SATHON & RIVERSIDE

Office workers swarm into the shanty villages of street vendors for lunch, and simple Muslim and Indian restaurants proliferate towards the western end of Th Silom and Th Surawong. But this area is known for its elegant restaurants preparing international fusion and royal Thai cuisine.

TOP CHOICE **nahm** THAI $$$

(off Map p74; 0 2625 3333; Metropolitan Hotel, 27 Th Sathon Tai; set meal 1700B; dinner; Lumphini;) Australian chef and author David Thompson is behind what is quite possibly the best Thai restaurant in Bangkok. Using ancient cookbooks as his inspiration, Thompson has given new life to previously extinct dishes such as smoked fish curry with prawns, chicken livers, cockles and

LOCAL KNOWLEDGE

DAVID THOMPSON: CHEF & AUTHOR

David Thompson is the head chef of both the London and Bangkok branches of Michelin-starred nahm restaurant. He is also the bestselling author of *Thai Food* and *Thai Street Food*.

HOW DO YOU DESCRIBE THE FOOD IN BANGKOK?

The food of Bangkok is more urbane, with the rough and rambunctious tastes of the wild and remote regions polished off. There's a huge Chinese influence here because Bangkok was a Chinese city. The central-plains food, which Bangkok is the epitome of, is refined and has the classic four flavours (sweet, sour, salty and spicy).

WHAT ARE SOME CLASSIC BANGKOK-STYLE DISHES?

I like some of the dishes in Chinatown, whether it be the oyster place I adore, or noodles with fish dumplings or with roast duck. Also *ƀoo pàt pŏng gàrèe* (crab fried with curry powder), when done well, is easy, but is bloody delicious and accessible. And *pàt tai* – well, you can't really escape from the cliché, however delicious it might be.

THE BEST FOOD 'HOOD?

It depends on what I'm looking for. Chinatown, for smoked duck or noodles. But if you want to eat Thai food, you need to go to the markets. Bangkok still has some remnants of the city or villages that it once was. For Muslim food you can go down to the area near Haroon Mosque, near Oriental Hotel (Mandarin Oriental; p71), or for Portuguese cakes, you can go to Santa Cruz (p63). There are still those types of things.

YOUR FAVOURITE RESTAURANT?

It changes all the time. I like Krua Apsorn (p77). It's local. It's good. It's unreformed. It's not too precious. They cook for Thais, they feed Thais and it is Thai.

THE BEST MARKET?

Of course, Or Tor Kor (p90). Even though it's sanitised, its soul has not been expunged from it as it's modernised. There's some great stuff there.

BEST EATING ADVICE FOR A FIRST-TIME VISITOR?

Just bloody well eat it – don't think about it – just eat it. It's so unlikely you'll get sick, but you will kick yourself for not actually just diving in. Go to places that look busiest, because they're busy for a reason. And a bit of food poisoning – well, that adds local colour, doesn't it?

As told to Austin Bush

black pepper. Expect full flavours and artful presentation. Reservations recommended.

Scoozi ITALIAN **$$**

(Map p74; www.scoozipizza.com; 174 Th Surawong; pizzas 100-425B; ⌚lunch & dinner; Ⓜ Si Lom, Sala Daeng; ❄) Scoozi now boasts several locations across Bangkok, but we still think the wood-fired pizzas taste best at this, the original branch.

Nadimos MIDDLE EASTERN **$$**

(Map p74; www.nadimos.com; Baan Silom, cnr Th Silom & Soi 19; mains 70-400B; ⌚lunch & dinner; 15 & 504, Surasak; ❄✎) This semi-formal dining room does tasty versions of all the Lebanese standards, plus quite a few dishes you'd never expect to see this far from Beirut. There are also lots of vegetarian options.

FooDie THAI **$$**

(Map p74; Soi Phiphat 2; mains 80-150B; ⌚lunch & dinner; Chong Nonsi; ❄) This airy, cafeteria-like restaurant boasts a menu of hard-to-find central- and southern-style Thai dishes. Highlights include the *yam som o*, a spicy/sour/sweet salad of pomelo, and the spicy *prik khing pla dook foo*, catfish fried in a curry paste until crispy.

Sukhumvit

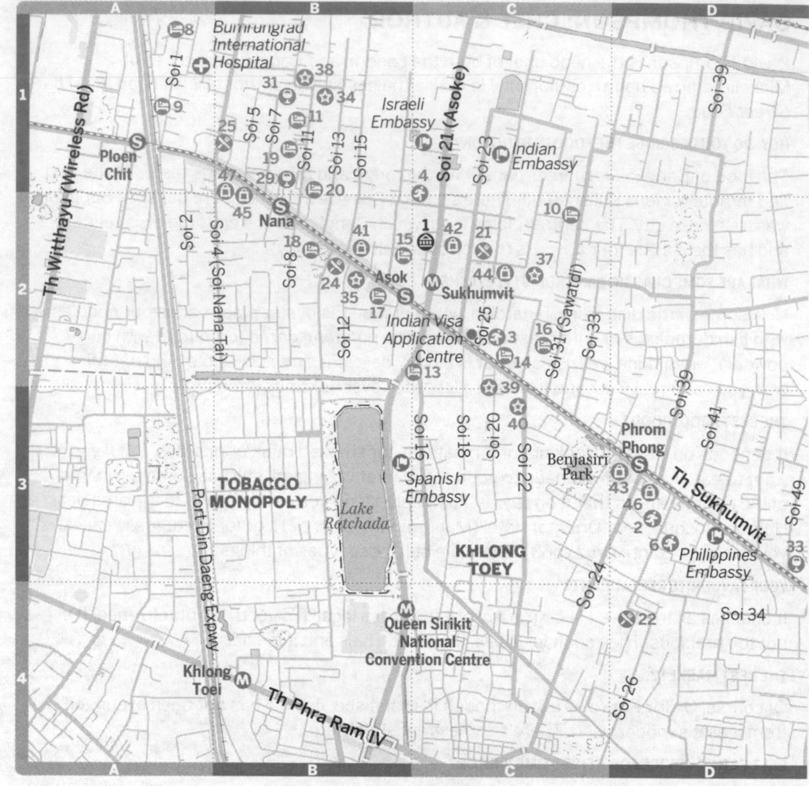

Chennai Kitchen INDIAN **$**
(Map p74; 10 Th Pan; mains 50-150B; ⌚10am-3pm & 6-9.30pm; 🚉Surasak; ❄✎) This thimble-sized restaurant puts out some of the most solid southern Indian vegetarian food in town.

Somtam Convent THAI **$**
(Hai; Map p74; 2/4-5 Th Convent; mains 20-120B; ⌚10.30am-9pm; Ⓜ Si Lom, 🚉Sala Daeng) A less intimidating introduction to the wonders of *lâhp* (a minced meat 'salad'), *sôm-đam* (papaya salad) and other northeastern delights can be had at this popular restaurant.

Soi 10 Food Centres THAI **$**
(Map p74; Soi 10, Th Silom; mains 20-60B; ⌚lunch Mon-Fri; 🚉Sala Daeng, Ⓜ Si Lom) These two adjacent hangar-like buildings tucked behind Soi 10 are the main lunchtime refuelling stations for this area's office staff.

SUKHUMVIT

This avenue is the communal dining room of Bangkok's expat communities.

TOP CHOICE **Bo.lan** THAI **$$$**
(Map p80; ☎0 2260 2962; www.bolan.co.th; 42 Soi Rongnarong Phichai Songkhram, Soi 26, Th Sukhumvit; set meal 1500B; ⌚dinner Tue-Sun; 🚉Phrom Phong) This Australian–Thai couple's scholarly approach to Thai cooking takes the form of seasonal set meals featuring dishes you're not likely to find elsewhere. Reservations recommended.

Nasir Al-Masri MIDDLE EASTERN **$$$**
(Map p80; 4/6 Soi 3/1, Th Sukhumvit; mains 80-350B; ⌚24hr; 🚉Nana; ❄✎) The glimmering stainless-steel exterior beckons to passers-by at this Soi Arabia fave. Middle Eastern meals can be consumed in air-con or street-side for the ambience of a genuine *sheeshah* (waterpipe) cafe.

Myeong Ga KOREAN $$$
(Map p80; ☎0 2229 4658; cnr Soi 12 & Th Sukhumvit; mains 200-550B; ⊙dinner; MSukhumvit, Asok; ❄) Located on the ground floor of Sukhumvit Plaza, the multistorey complex known as Korean Town, this restaurant is the city's best destination for authentic Seoul food.

Soul Food Mahanakorn THAI $$
(Map p80; ☎0 2714 7708; www.soulfoodmahanakorn.com; 56/10 Soi 55/Thong Lor, Th Sukhumvit; mains 120-250B; ⊙dinner; Thong Lo; ❄) This cozy bar/restaurant does tasty but pricey takes on rustic Thai dishes such as *gai tawt hat yai*, southern-style fried chicken, and *gaeng hang lay*, a northern-style pork curry, not to mention deliciously boozy cocktails. Reservations recommended.

Bharani THAI $
(Sansab Boat Noodle; Map p80; 96/14 Soi 23, Th Sukhumvit; mains 50-200B; ⊙10am-10pm; MSukhumvit, Asok; ❄) Bharani dabbles in a bit of everything, from ox-tongue stew to rice fried with shrimp paste. But the real reason to come is for the rich, meaty 'boat noodles' – so called because they used to be sold from boats plying the *klorngs* of Ayuthaya.

Bed Supperclub INTERNATIONAL $$$
(Map p80; ☎0 2651 3537; www.bedsupperclub.com; 26 Soi 11, Th Sukhumvit; mains 450-990B, set meals 790-1850B; ⊙7.30-10pm Tue-Thu, dinner 9pm Fri & Sat; Nana; ❄) Crawl into Bed, a long-standing cutting-edge leader that dabbles in 'modern eclectic cuisine'. Arrive at 9pm sharp for a surprise menu on Fridays and Saturdays.

Boon Tong Kiat Singapore Hainanese Chicken Rice SINGAPOREAN $
(Map p80; 440/5 Soi 55/Thong Lor, Th Sukhumvit; dishes 60-150B; ⊙lunch & dinner; Thong Lo & access by taxi; ❄) Order a plate of the restaurant's namesake and bear witness to how a dish can be simultaneously simple and profound.

Soi 38 Night Market CHINESE-THAI $
(Map p80; Soi 38, Th Sukhumvit; mains 30-60B; ⊙7pm-3am; Thong Lo) After a hard night of clubbing, this gathering of basic Thai-Chinese hawker stalls will look like a shimmering oasis.

OTHER AREAS

Mallika THAI $$
(21/36 Th Rang Nam; mains 70-480B; ⊙10am-10pm Mon-Sat; Victory Monument; ❄) A dream come true: authentic regional Thai (southern, in this case), with a legible English menu, good service and tidy setting. The prices are slightly high for a mum-and-pop Thai joint, but you're paying for quality.

Kaloang Home Kitchen THAI $$
(503-505 Th Samsen; mains 60-170B; ⊙11am-11pm; 32 & 516, Tha Thewet) The laid-back atmosphere and seafood-heavy menu here will quickly dispel any concerns about sinking into Chao Phraya River, and a beer and the breeze will temporarily erase any scarring memories of Bangkok traffic. To find the restaurant, follow Th Si Ayuthaya until you reach the river.

Pathé THAI $$
(cnr Th Lad Phrao & Th Viphawadee; mains 75-160B; ⊙2pm-1am; MPhahon Yothin; ❄) The Thai equivalent of a 1950s-era US diner, this

Sukhumvit

Sights

1	Ban Kamthieng	C2

Activities, Courses & Tours

2	ABC Amazing Bangkok Cyclists	D3
3	Divana Massage & Spa	C2
4	Health Land	C1
5	Health Land	F3
6	Phussapa Thai Massage School	D3

Sleeping

7	72 Ekamai	F4
8	AriyasomVilla	A1
9	Bed Bangkok	A1
10	Eugenia	C2
11	Federal	B1
12	HI-Sukhumvit	E4
13	Ma Du Zi	C2
14	Nana Chart	C2
15	Sacha's Hotel Uno	B2
16	Seven	C2
17	Sheraton Grande Sukhumvit	B2
18	Stable Lodge	B2
19	Suk 11	B1
20	Swiss Park	B1

Eating

	Bed Supperclub	(see 34)
21	Bharani	C2
22	Bo.lan	D4
23	Boon Tong Kiat Singapore Hainanese Chicken Rice	E2
24	Myeong Ga	B2
25	Nasir Al-Masri	B1
26	Soi 38 Night Market	E4
27	Soul Food Mahanakorn	E4

Drinking

28	Bangkok Bar	F4
29	Cheap Charlie's	B1
30	Iron Fairies	E3
31	Nest	B1
32	Tuba	F2
33	WTF	D3

Entertainment

34	Bed Supperclub	B1
35	Club Insomnia	B2
36	Ekamai Soi 5	F3
	Living Room	(see 17)
37	Narz	C2
38	Q Bar	B1
39	Scratch Dog	C2
40	Titanium	C3

Shopping

41	Asia Books	B2
42	Dive Indeed	C2
	Dive Master	(see 42)
43	Emporium	D3
	Kinokuniya	(see 43)
44	Nandakwang	C2
45	Nickermann's	B2
46	Planet Scuba	D3
47	Raja's Fashions	B1

popular place combines solid Thai food, a fun atmosphere and a jukebox playing scratched records.

Drinking

Once infamous as an anything-goes nightlife destination, in recent years Bangkok has been edging towards teetotalism with strict regulations limiting the sale of alcohol and increasingly conservative closing times, with most bars closing around 1am (for places that stay open later, see p84). Likewise, note that smoking has been outlawed at all indoor (and some quasi-outdoor) entertainment places since 2008.

KO RATANAKOSIN & BANGLAMPHU

The area around Th Khao San is one of the city's best destinations for a fun night out.

Hippie de Bar BAR

(Map p60; 46 Th Khao San; 6pm-2am; Tha Phra Athit (Banglamphu)) Popular with locals, Hippie boasts a funky retro vibe, indoor and outdoor seating, and a soundtrack you're unlikely to hear elsewhere in town.

Amorosa BAR

(Map p60; www.arunresidence.com; rooftop, Arun Residence, 36-38 Soi Pratu Nok Yung; 6-11pm; 123 & 508, Tha Tien) It may be the only bar in the area, but that doesn't mean it's any sort of compromise; Amorosa's rooftop location packs killer views of Wat Arun, making it one of the best spots in Bangkok for a riverside sundowner.

Pranakorn Bar BAR

(Map p60; 58/2 Soi Damnoen Klang Tai; 6pm-midnight; klorng taxi Tha Phan Fah) It must have taken a true visionary to transform this characterless multilevel building into a warm, fun destination for a night out. Head to the rooftop for breezy views over Banglamphu.

Rolling Bar BAR

(Map p60; Th Prachathipatai; 6pm-midnight; klorng taxi Tha Phan Fah) An escape from hectic Th Khao San is a good enough excuse to head to this quiet canal-side boozer. Live music and passable bar snacks are reasons to stay.

SIAM SQUARE

Co-Co Walk BAR

(Map p70; 87/70 Th Phayathai; 6pm-1am; Ratchathewi) This covered compound is a lively smorgasbord of pubs, bars and live music popular with Thai university students.

Hyde & Seek BAR

(Map p70; ground fl, Athenee Residence, 65/1 Soi Ruam Rudi; 11am-1am; Phloen Chit;) In addition to having Bangkok's most well-stocked bar and some of the city's best cocktails, Hyde & Seek also does tasty and comforting English-inspired bar snacks and meals.

SUKHUMVIT

WTF BAR

(Map p80; www.wtfbangkok.com; 7 Soi 51, Th Sukhumvit; 6pm-1am Tue-Sun; Thong Lo;) No, not that WTF. Wonderful Thai Friendship is a funky and friendly neighbourhood bar that also has two floors of gallery space. Stop by for great drinks and a bar-snack menu with influences ranging from Macau to Spain, or to check out the latest contemporary-art exhibition.

Cheap Charlie's BAR

(Map p80; Soi 11, Th Sukhumvit; Mon-Sat; Nana) The design concept of this open-air beer corner is best classified as 'junkyard'. The lack of seating compels mingling, making it a great place to meet tourists and long-time residents alike.

Iron Fairies BAR

(Map p80; www.theironfairies.com; Soi 55/Thong Lor, Th Sukhumvit; 5pm-midnight Mon-Sat; Thong Lo;) Imagine, if you can, an abandoned fairy factory in Paris c 1912, and you'll get an idea of the design theme at this popular pub/wine bar. Try to wrangle one of a handful of seats. They claim to serve Bangkok's best burgers here and there's live music after 9.30pm.

Bangkok Bar BAR

(Map p80; Soi Ekamai 2, Soi 63 (Ekamai), Th Sukhumvit; 8pm-1am; Ekkamai;) Bounce with Thai indie kids at this fun bar. There's live music, and the eats are strong enough to make Bangkok Bar a dinner destination.

Tuba BAR

(off Map p80; 34 Room 11-12 A, Soi Ekamai 21, Soi 63 (Ekamai), Th Sukhumvit; Ekkamai & access by taxi;) Part storage room for over-the-top vintage furniture, part friendly local boozer, this bizarre bar certainly doesn't lack character. Indulge in a whole bottle for once and don't miss the delicious chicken wings.

OTHER AREAS

River Bar Café BAR

(405/1 Soi Chao Phraya, Th Rachawithi, Thonburi; 5pm-midnight; Tha Saphan Krung Thon;)

DRINKING WITH THE STARS

Bangkok is one of the few big cities in the world where nobody seems to mind if you slap the odd bar or restaurant on the top of a skyscraper. Note that most of the below do not allow shorts or sandals.

Moon Bar at Vertigo (off Map p74; Banyan Tree Hotel, 21/100 Th Sathon Tai; 5.30pm-1am; M Lumphini) Perched on the top of 61 floors of skyscraper, Moon Bar offers a bird's-eye view of Bangkok. Things can get a bit crowded here come sunset, so be sure to show up early to get the best seats.

Sirocco Sky Bar (off Map p74; The Dome, 1055 Th Silom; 6pm-1am; Saphan Taksin) Descend the sweeping stairs like a Hollywood diva to the precipice bar of this rooftop restaurant that looks over Mae Nam Chao Phraya.

Nest (Map p80; 0 2255 0638; www.nestbangkok.com; 8th fl, Le Fenix Hotel, 33/33 Soi 11, Th Sukhumvit; 5pm-2am; Nana) Perched on the roof of the Le Fenix Hotel, Nest is a chic maze of cleverly concealed sofas and inviting daybeds.

OUT ALL NIGHT

With most pubs and dance clubs closing around 1am, 'One Night in Bangkok' is not quite what it used to be. Thankfully, there are a few places around town that have gained sufficient 'permission' to stay open until the morning hours.

Off Soi Ngam Duphli, **Wong's Place** (27/3 Soi Si Bamphen, Th Phra Ram IV; 8pm-late; Lumphini;), a longstanding backpacker bar, is so late-night that it's best not to show up before midnight. Near Th Khao San, the elevated setting of **Gazebo** (Map p60; 3rd fl, 44 Th Chakraphong; Tha Phra Athit (Banglamphu)) appears to lend it some leniency with the city's strict closing times. On Th Sukhumvit, **Club Insomnia** (Map p80; Soi 12, Th Sukhumvit; admission 200B; 8pm-late; Sukhumvit, Asok) and **Scratch Dog** (Map p80; 0 2262 1234; Windsor Suites Hotel, 8-10 Soi 20, Th Sukhumvit; 8pm-late; Sukhumvit, Asok) employ a Top 40 hip-hop and R&B soundtrack to propel party people (and, it must be said, off-hours working girls) into the morning hours.

For something a bit edgier, ask your friendly taxi driver to escort you to any of the following: **Shock 39**, **Spicy**, **Spice Club**, **Boss** or **Bossy**. These creatively named late-night clubs are all located in central Bangkok and stay open until well past the sunrise. We'd tell you a bit more about them and put them on our maps, but our experience and research suggest that these clubs exist in an alternate late-night reality that only Bangkok taxi drivers can navigate...

Sporting a picture-perfect riverside location, good food and live music, River Bar Café combines all the essentials of a perfect Bangkok night out. Grab a table close to the river to take full advantage of the breeze, as well as to avoid noise fallout from the sometimes overly enthusiastic bands.

Sky Train Jazz Club BAR
(cnr Soi Rang Nam & Th Pahohyothin; 6pm-1am; Victory Monument) A visit to this comically misnamed bar is more like chilling on the rooftop of a stoner friend's apartment than any jazz club we've ever been to. But there are indeed views of the BTS, jazz on occasion and a likeable speakeasy atmosphere. To find it, look for the sign and proceed up the scary graffiti-strewn stairway until you reach the roof.

☆ Entertainment

Nightclubs

The trick in Bangkok is to catch the right club on the right night. To find out what is going on, check **Dudesweet** (www.dudesweet.org) or **Club Soma** (wwww.clubsoma.tumblr.com), organisers of hugely popular monthly parties, or **Paradise Bangkok** (www.zudrangmarecords.com) for retro-themed world music events. Other sources of information include the listings mag **BK** (http://bk.asia-city.com/nightlife) or, if you're partial to the Th Sukhumvit scene, www.thonglor-ekamai.com.

Cover charges for clubs and discos range from 100B to 800B and usually include a drink. Most locals don't show up before 11pm, and everyone needs to show ID. The majority of clubs close at 2am.

RCA NIGHTCLUB
(Royal City Ave; off Th Phra Ram IX; Phra Ram 9 & access by taxi) Formerly a bastion of the teen scene, this Vegas-like strip has finally graduated from high school and hosts party people of every age. Worthwhile destinations include **808 Club** (www.808bangkok.com; admission from 300B), **Flix/Slim** (admission free), **Route 66** (www.route66club.com; admission free) and **Cosmic Café** (admission free).

Tapas Room NIGHTCLUB
(Map p74; www.tapasroom.net; 114/17-18 Soi 4, Th Silom; admission 100B; Si Lom, Sala Daeng) You won't find food here, instead the name is an accurate indicator of the Spanish/Moroccan-inspired vibe of this multilevel den.

Ekamai Soi 5 NIGHTCLUB
(Map p80; cnr Soi Ekamai 5 & Soi 63/Ekamai, Th Sukhumvit; Ekkamai & access by taxi) This open-air entertainment zone is the destination of choice for Bangkok's young and beautiful – for the moment at least. **Demo** (admission free) combines blasting beats and a NYC-warehouse vibe, while **Funky Villa** (admission free), with its outdoor seating and Top 40 soundtrack, is more chilled.

Bed Supperclub NIGHTCLUB
(Map p80; www.bedsupperclub.com; 26 Soi 11, Th Sukhumvit; admission from 600B; Nana) This illuminated tube has been a highlight of the Bangkok club scene for a nearly a decade now. Arrive early to squeeze in dinner (see p81) or, if you've only got dancing on your mind, come on Tuesday for the popular hip-hop nights.

Club Culture NIGHTCLUB
(Map p60; www.club-culture-bkk.com; admission from 200B; Th Ratchadamnoen Klang; klorng taxi Tha Phan Fah) Housed in a seemingly abandoned four-storey building, Club Culture is the quirkiest member of Bangkok's club scene. Opening dates and times can depend on events, so check the website to see what's on.

The Club NIGHTCLUB
(Map p60; www.theclubkhaosan.com; admission free; 123 Th Khao San; klorng taxi Tha Phan Fah) Located smack-dab in the middle of Th Khao San, this cavern-like dance hall hosts a fun mix of locals and backpackers.

Q Bar NIGHTCLUB
(Map p80; www.qbarbangkok.com; 34 Soi 11, Th Sukhumvit; admission from 700B; Nana) This darkened industrial space sees a revolving cast of somebodies, nobodies and working girls. Various theme nights fill the weekly calendar.

Café Democ NIGHTCLUB
(Map p60; www.cafe-democ.com; 78 Th Ratchadamnoen Klang; admission free; klorng taxi Tha Phan Fah) Up-and-coming DJs present their turntable dexterity at this narrow unpretentious club in old Bangkok.

Narz NIGHTCLUB
(Map p80; 112 Soi 23, Th Sukhumvit; admission 500B; Sukhumvit, Asok) The former Narcissus has undergone a recent nip and tuck and now consists of three separate zones boasting an equal variety of music.

Live Music

For the most part, live music in Bangkok means perky Thai pop covers or tired international standards (if you've left town without having heard a live version of 'Hotel California', you haven't really been to Bangkok), but an increasing number of places are starting to deviate from the norm with quirky and/or inspired bands and performances.

Brick Bar BAR
(Map p60; basement, Buddy Lodge, 265 Th Khao San; 8pm-1am; Tha Phra Athit (Banglamphu);) This basement pub hosts a nightly revolving cast of live music for an almost exclusively Thai crowd – most of whom will end the night dancing on the tables.

Living Room LOUNGE
(Map p80; 0 2649 8888; Level I, Sheraton Grande Sukhumvit, 250 Th Sukhumvit; 6.30pm-midnight; Sukhumvit, Asok;) Don't let looks deceive you; every night this bland hotel lounge transforms into the city's best venue for live jazz. Contact ahead of time to

THE PINK MANGO

Bangkok's homosexual community is out and very much open, enjoying lots of local nightspots and even an annual pride parade. **Lesbian Guide to Bangkok** (www.bangkoklesbian.com), **Dreaded Ned** (www.dreadedned.com) and **Fridae** (www.fridae.com) have up-to-date listings and events.

The area around lower Th Silom is Bangkok's gaybourhood. **DJ Station** (Map p74; 8/6-8 Soi 2, Th Silom; admission 200B; 8pm-late; Sala Daeng, Si Lom) and **G.O.D.** (Guys on Display; Map p74; Soi 2/1, Th Silom; admission 280B; 8pm-late; Si Lom, Sala Daeng) get a mixed Thai-*fa·ràng* crowd. For something at conversation level, nearby Soi 4 is home to longstanding **Balcony** (Map p74; www.balconypub.com; 86-88 Soi 4, Th Silom; 5.30pm-1am; Si Lom, Sala Daeng) and **Telephone** (Map p74; 114/11-13 Soi 4, Th Silom; 5pm-1am; Si Lom, Sala Daeng).

If you tire of the Silom scene, Bed Supperclub hosts the popular 'Confidential Sundays', or you can head to Bangkok's 'burbs, where several bars along Th Kamphaeng Phet, including **Fake Club** (Th Kamphaeng Phet, Chatuchak; 9pm-2am; Kamphaeng Phet, Mo Chit) and **el Ninyo** (Th Kamphaeng Phet, Chatuchak; 9pm-2am; Kamphaeng Phet, Mo Chit), are popular on weekends for loud and lushy behaviour.

Bangkok's lesbian scene is pretty much limited to **Zeta** (29/67 Royal City Ave/RCA, off Phra Ram IX; admission 100B; 8pm-2am; Phra Ram 9 & access by taxi).

see which sax master or hide hitter is currently in town.

Saxophone Pub & Restaurant LIVE MUSIC
(www.saxophonepub.com; 3/8 Th Phayathai; 6pm-2am; Victory Monument;) Saxophone is a staple of Bangkok's live-music scene. It's a bit too loud for a first date, but the quality and variety of the music makes it a great destination for music-loving buddies on a night out.

Ad Here the 13th BAR
(Map p60; 13 Th Samsen; 6pm-midnight; Tha Phra Athit (Banglamphu);) Ad Here has everything a neighbourhood joint should have: lots of regulars, cold beer and heart-warming tunes delivered by a masterful house band. The music starts at around 10pm, but you're well advised to arrive earlier if you plan to snag one of the elusive seats.

Tawandang German Brewery BAR
(cnr Th Phra Ram III & Th Narathiwat Ratchanakharin; Chong Nonsi & access by taxi;) It's Oktoberfest all year round at this hangar-sized music hall. The Thai-German food is tasty, the house-made brews are entirely potable and the nightly stage shows are heaps of fun. Music starts at 8.30pm.

Titanium LIVE MUSIC
(Map p80; 2/30 Soi 22, Th Sukhumvit; 8pm-1am; Phrom Phong;) Some come to this cheesy 'ice bar' for the chill and the flavoured vodka, but we come for Unicorn, an all-female rock band.

Raintree LIVE MUSIC
(116/63-64 Soi Th Rang Nam; 6pm-1am; Victory Monument;) This atmospheric pub is one of the few remaining places in town to hear 'songs for life', Thai folk music with roots in the communist insurgency of the 1960s and '70s.

Rock Pub LIVE MUSIC
(Map p70; www.therockpub-bangkok.com; 93/26-28 Th Phayathai; 9.30pm-2am; Ratchathewi;) If you thought the days of heavy metal were long gone, step back in time at this cave-like pub where Iron Maiden posters pass for interior design and black jeans are the unofficial dress code.

Thai Boxing

Lumphini Stadium (Sanam Muay Lumphini; off Map p74; 0 2251 4303; Th Phra Ram IV; Lumphini) and **Ratchadamnoen Stadium** (Sanam Muay Ratchadamnoen; Map p60; 0 2281 4205; Th Ratchadamnoen Nok; 70, 503 & 509, klorng taxi Tha Phan Fah) host Thailand's biggest *moo·ay tai* (also spelled *muay thai*) matches. Ratchadamnoen hosts matches on Monday, Wednesday, Thursday and Sunday at 6.30pm. Lumphini hosts matches on Tuesday and Friday at 6.30pm and Saturday at 5pm and 8.30pm. Foreigners pay 1000/1500/2000B for 3rd-class/2nd-class/ringside seats (advance reservations needed for ringside). Don't buy tickets from the hawkers hanging around outside the stadium.

Traditional Arts Performances

As Thailand's cultural repository, Bangkok offers visitors an array of dance and theatre performances. For background information about these ancient traditions, see p380.

Chalermkrung Royal Theatre THEATRE
(Sala Chalerm Krung; 0 2222 0434; www.salachalermkrung.com; cnr Th Charoen Krung & Th Triphet; tickets 800-1200B; 7.30pm; Tha Saphan Phut (Memorial Bridge)) In a Thai Art Deco building at the edge of the Chinatown-Phahurat district, this theatre provides a striking venue for *kŏhn* (masked dance-drama based on stories from the *Ramakian,* the Thai version of the *Ramayana*), held every Thursday and Friday. The theatre requests that patrons dress respectfully, which means no shorts, tank tops or sandals.

GÀ·TEU·I CABARET

Watching men dressed as women perform tacky show tunes has, not surprisingly, become the latest 'must-do' fixture on the Bangkok tourist circuit. Both **Calypso Cabaret** (Map p70; 0 2653 3960; www.calypsocabaret.com; Asia Hotel, 296 Th Phayathai; tickets 1200B; show times 8.15pm & 9.45pm; Ratchathewi) and **Mambo Cabaret** (0 2294 7381; www.mambocabaret.com; 59/28 Yannawa Tat Mai; tickets 800-1000B; show times 7.15pm, 8.30pm & 10pm; Chong Nonsi & access by taxi) host choreographed stage shows featuring Broadway high kicks and lip-synced pop tunes.

CINEMA STRATEGY

Bangkokians take their movies very seriously. Every mall has its own theatre and it's unlikely that any other city in the world has anything like EGV's Gold Class, a ticket that grants you entry into a cinema with fewer than 50 seats, where you're plied with blankets, pillows, foot-warming stockings and a valet food-and-drink service. There's also Major Cineplex's Emperor Class seat, which for the price of a sticky stool back home entitles you to a sofa-like love seat designed for couples. And if you find Paragon Cineplex's 16 screens and 5000 seats a bit plebeian, you can always apply for Enigma, a members-only theatre.

For something with a bit more character, try the old-school stand-alone theatres at Siam Sq, including **Scala** (Map p70; ☎0 2251 2861; Siam Sq, Soi 1, Th Phra Ram I; Siam) and **Lido** (Map p70; ☎0 2252 6498; Siam Sq, Th Phra Ram I; Siam). For an artsier lineup, RCA's **House** (☎0 2641 5177; www.houserama.com; UMG Bldg, Royal City Ave, near Th Petchaburi; M Phra Ram 9 & access by taxi).

Nearly all movies in Thailand offer screenings with English subtitles – visit **Movie Seer** (www.movieseer.com) for show times. All films are preceded by the Thai royal anthem and everyone is expected to stand respectfully for its duration. And despite the heat and humidity on the streets, keep in mind that all of Bangkok's movie theatres pump the air-con with such vigour that a jumper is an absolute necessity – unless you're going Gold Class, that is.

Aksra Theatre THEATRE
(☎0 2677 8888, ext 5730; www.aksratheatre.com; 3rd fl, King Power Complex, 8/1 Th Rang Nam; tickets 400-600B; shows 7.30-8.30pm Mon-Wed, dinner shows 6.30-9pm Thu-Sun; Victory Monument) Performances of the *Ramakian* are the highlight, using knee-high puppets that require three puppeteers to strike human-like poses. Come early in the week for a performance in the Aksra Theatre, or later for a Thai buffet dinner coupled with a show.

National Theatre THEATRE
(Map p60; ☎0 2224 1352; 2 Th Rachini; tickets 60-100B; Tha Chang) After a lengthy renovation, the National Theatre is again open for business. Performances of *kŏhn*, masked dance-drama often depicting scenes from the *Ramakian*, are held on the first and second Sundays of the month; *lákhon*, Thai dance-dramas, are held on the first Friday of the month; and Thai musical performances are held on the third Friday of the month.

 Shopping

Welcome to a true buyer's market. Home to one of the world's largest outdoor markets, numerous giant upscale malls and sidewalk-clogging bazaars on nearly every street, it's impossible not to be impressed by the amount of commerce in Bangkok. However, despite the apparent scope and variety, Bangkok really only excels in one area when it comes to shopping: cheap stuff. The city is not the place to buy a new Nikon SLR or a (real) Fendi handbag – save those for online warehouses in the US or bargain-basement sales in Hong Kong. Ceramics, dirt-cheap T-shirts, fabric, Asian knick-knackery and yes, if you can deal with the guilt, pirated movies and music – these are the things to stock up on in Bangkok.

The difficulty is finding your way around, since the city's intense urban tangle sometimes makes orientation difficult. A good shopping companion is *Nancy Chandler's Map of Bangkok*, with annotations on all sorts of small and out-of-the-way shopping venues and *đà·làht* (markets).

Bookstores

For a decent selection of English-language books and magazines, branches of **Bookazine** (www.bookazine.co.th) and **B2S** (www.b2s.co.th) can be found at nearly every mall in central Bangkok. The Banglamphu area is home to many of Bangkok's independent bookstores, and Th Khao San is virtually the only place in town to go for used English-language books. You're not going to find any deals there, but the selection is decent.

Asia Books BOOKSTORE
(Map p80; www.asiabook.com; Soi 15, 221 Th Sukhumvit; 8am-9pm; M Sukhumvit, Asok) There are also branches in the Emporium shopping centre (see Map p80) and Siam Discovery Center (p89).

ONE NIGHT IN BANGKOK…IS NOT ENOUGH TO HAVE A SUIT MADE

Clothes can be custom-tailored in Bangkok for prices you'd only dream of back home. But it's important to understand the process if you want to avoid disappointment. If you sign up for a suit, two pairs of pants, two shirts and a tie, with a silk sarong thrown in for US$169 (a very popular offer in Bangkok), the chances are it will look and fit like a sub-US$200 wardrobe. Likewise, it's important to be aware of the going rate to ensure that you're not paying too much.

To avoid these problems, have a firm idea of what you want before walking into a shop. If it's a suit you're after, should the jacket be single- or double-breasted? How many buttons? What style trousers or skirt? Alternatively, bring a favourite garment from home and have it copied. Set aside a week to get clothes tailored (or, if your schedule permits, do the first fitting before you go to the beach and the subsequent ones when you get back). Shirts and trousers can often be turned around in 48 hours or less, but most reliable tailors will ask for two to five fittings for a suit. Treat any tailor that can sew your order in less than 24 hours with extreme caution.

Reputable tailors include the following:

Raja's Fashions (Map p80; 1/6 Soi 4, Th Sukhumvit; ⏲10.30am-8.30pm Mon-Sat; 🚉Nana) With his photographic memory for names, Bobby will make you feel as important as the long list of ambassadors, foreign politicians and officers he's fitted over his family's decades in the business.

Pinky Tailors (Map p70; 888/40 Mahatun Plaza Arcade, Th Ploenchit; ⏲10am-7.30pm Mon-Sat; 🚉Phloen Chit) Custom-made suit jackets have been Mr Pinky's speciality for 35 years. Located behind the Mahatun Building.

Marco Tailors (Map p70; 430/33 Soi 7, Siam Sq; ⏲9am-7pm Mon-Sat; 🚉Siam) Dealing solely in men's suits, this long-standing and reliable tailor has a wide selection of banker-sensibility wools and cottons.

Nickermann's (Map p80; www.nickermanns.net; basement, Landmark Hotel, 138 Th Sukhumvit; ⏲10am-9pm; 🚉Nana) Corporate ladies rave about Nickermann's tailor-made power suits: pants and jackets that suit curves. Formal ball gowns are another area of expertise.

Kinokuniya BOOKSTORE
(www.kinokuniya.com; ⏲10am-10pm) Siam Paragon (Map p70; 3rd fl, Th Phra Ram I; 🚉Siam); Emporium (Map p80; 3rd fl, Th Sukhumvit; 🚉Phrom Phong) The country's largest bookstore has two branches, both featuring multilanguage selections, magazines and children's books.

Saraban BOOKSTORE
(Map p60; 106/1 Th Ram Butri; ⏲9.30am-10.30pm; 🚌2, 15, 44 & 511, ⛴Tha Phra Athit (Banglamphu)) Stocking the largest selection of international newspapers and new Lonely Planet guides on Th Khao San.

Shaman Bookstore BOOKSTORE
Susie Walking Street (Map p60; Susie Walking Street, off Th Khao San; ⏲9am-11pm); Th Khao San (Map p60; Th Khao San; ⏲9am-11pm) With two locations on Th Khao San, Shaman has the area's largest selection of used books. Titles here can conveniently be searched using a computer program.

Department Stores & Shopping Centres

Bangkok may be crowded and polluted, but its department stores are modern oases of order. They're also downright frigid, and Sunday afternoons see a significant part of Bangkok's population crowding into the city's indoor malls to escape the heat. By no accident, the BTS stations also have shaded walkways delivering passengers directly into nearby stores without ever having to set foot on ground level. Most shopping centres are open from 10am or 11am to 9pm or 10pm.

MBK Center MALL
(Mahboonkhrong; Map p70; www.mbk-center.co.th/en; cnr Th Phra Ram I & Th Phayathai; 🚉National Stadium & Siam) This colossal mall has

become a tourist destination in its own right. This is the cheapest place to buy mobile phones and accessories (4th floor) and name-brand knock-offs (nearly every other floor). It's also one of the better places to stock up on camera gear (ground floor and 5th floor), and the expansive food court (6th floor) is one of the best in town (see p78).

Siam Center & Siam Discovery Center MALL
(Map p70; cnr Th Phra Ram I & Th Phayathai; National Stadium & Siam) These linked sister centres feel almost monastic in their hushed hallways compared to frenetic MBK, just across the street. Siam Discovery Center excels in home decor, with the whole 3rd floor devoted to Asian-minimalist styles and jewel-toned fabrics. The attached Siam Center, Thailand's first shopping centre, built in 1976, has recently gone under the redesign knife for a younger, hipper look. Youth fashion is its new focus, and several local labels can be found on the 2nd floor.

Gaysorn Plaza MALL
(Map p70; cnr Th Ploenchit & Th Ratchadamri; Chit Lom) A haute couture catwalk, Gaysorn's spiralling staircases and all-white halls preserve all of fashion's beloved designers in museum-curatorship style. Local fashion leaders occupy the 2nd floor 'Thai Fashion Chic', while the top floor is a stroll through home decor, including a good selection of upscale local art and handicrafts.

Siam Square MALL
(Map p70; btwn Th Phra Ram I & Th Phayathai, Siam) This low-slung commercial universe is a network of some 12 soi lined with tiny, trendy boutiques, many of which are the first ventures of young designers.

Siam Paragon MALL
(Map p70; Th Phra Ram I; Siam) Astronomically luxe brands occupy most floors of Bangkok's biggest and glitziest mall, while the majority of shoppers hang out in the reflecting pool atrium or basement-level food court.

Central World Plaza MALL
(Map p70; cnr Th Ratchadamri & Th Phra Ram I; Chit Lom). This huge mall suffered greatly during the political unrest of April 2010, but the vast majority of shops are again open.

Handicrafts & Decor

The street markets have tonnes of factory-made pieces that pop up all along the tourist route. The shopping centres sell products with a little better quality at proportionally higher prices, but the independent shops sell the best items all round.

Nandakwang TEXTILES
(Map p80; 108/2-3 Soi 23, Th Sukhumvit; 9am-5pm Mon-Sat & 10am-5pm Sun; Sukhumvit, Asok) A Bangkok satellite of a Chiang Mai–based store, Nandakwang sells cheery hand-woven cloth items.

Jim Thompson TEXTILES
(Map p74; www.jimthompson.com; 9 Th Surawong; 9am-9pm; Si Lom, Sala Daeng) The surviving business of the international promoter of Thai silk, this, the largest Jim

BARGAINING 101

Many of your purchases in Bangkok will involve an ancient skill that has long been abandoned in the West: bargaining. Contrary to what you'll see on a daily basis on Th Khao San, bargaining (in Thai, *dòr rahkah*) is not a terse exchange of numbers and animosity. Rather, bargaining Thai style is a generally friendly transaction where two people try to agree on a price that is fair to both of them.

The first rule to bargaining is to have a general idea of the price. Ask around at a few vendors to get a rough notion. When you're ready to buy, it's generally a good strategy to start at roughly 50% of the asking price and work up from there. If you're buying several of an item, you have much more leverage to request and receive a lower price. If the seller immediately agrees to your first price you're probably paying too much, but it's bad form to bargain further at this point. In general, keeping a friendly, flexible demeanour throughout the transaction will almost always work in your favour. And remember, only begin bargaining if you're really planning on buying the item. Most importantly, there's simply no point in getting angry or upset over a few baht. The locals, who inevitably have less money than you, never do this.

COMMON BANGKOK SCAMS

Commit these classic rip-offs to memory and join us in our ongoing crusade to outsmart Bangkok's crafty scam artists.

Gem scam If anyone offers you unsolicited advice about a gem sale, you can be sure that there is a scam involved.

Closed today Ignore any 'friendly' local who tells you that an attraction is closed for a Buddhist holiday or for cleaning. These are set-ups for trips to a bogus gem sale.

Túk-túk rides for 10B Say goodbye to your day's itinerary if you climb aboard this ubiquitous scam. These alleged 'tours' bypass all the sights and instead cruise to all the fly-by-night gem and tailor shops that pay commissions.

Flat-fare taxi ride Flatly refuse any driver who quotes a flat fare. If the driver has 'forgotten' to put the meter on, just say, 'Meter, kha/khap'.

Tourist buses On long-distance buses originating on Th Khao San, well-organised and connected thieves have hours to comb through your bags. This scam has been running for years but is easy to avoid by simply keeping your valuables with you rather than storing them in the baggage area below the bus.

Friendly strangers Be wary of smartly dressed men who approach you asking where you're from and where you're going – usually a set-up for a gem or gambling scam. As the tourist authorities here point out, this sort of behaviour is out of character for Thais and should be treated with suspicion.

Thompson shop, sells colourful silk handkerchiefs, placemats, wraps and cushions.

Doi Tung HANDICRAFTS
(Map p70; www.doitung.com; 4th fl, Siam Discovery Center, Th Rama I; ⌚11am-8pm; 🚇Siam) Earth-coloured ceramics and bright cloths – all handmade by northern Thai artisans – rule at this classy shop.

Thai Home Industries HANDICRAFTS
(35 Soi 40/Oriental, Th Charoen Krung; ⌚9am-6.30pm Mon-Sat; ⛴Tha Oriental) A visit to this temple-like building, a former monks' quarters, is like discovering an abandoned attic full of Asian booty.

Narai Phand HANDICRAFTS
(Map p70; www.naraiphand.com; ground fl, President Tower, 973 Th Ploenchit; ⌚10am-8pm; 🚇Phloen Chit) Souvenir-quality handicrafts are given fixed prices and comfortable air-conditioning at this government-run facility.

Markets

Don't let the bargaining put you off; it's good fun for seller and buyer.

Chatuchak Weekend Market MARKET
(Talat Nat Jatujak; Map p56; ⌚9am-6pm Sat & Sun; Ⓜ Chatuchak Park & Kamphaeng Phet, 🚇Mo Chit) The mother of all markets sprawls over a huge area with 15,000 stalls and an estimated 200,000 visitors a day. Everything is sold here, from snakes to handicrafts to aisles and aisles of clothes. Plan to spend a full day, as there's plenty to see, do and buy (if you see something you like, buy it, as you probably won't find your way back). But come early, ideally around 9am to 10am, to beat the crowds and the heat.

There is an information centre and a bank with ATMs and foreign-exchange booths at the Chatuchak Park offices, near the northern end of the market's Soi 1, Soi 2 and Soi 3. Schematic maps and toilets are located throughout the market.

There are a few vendors out on weekday mornings, and a daily vegetable, plant and flower market opposite the market's southern side. One section of the latter, known as the **Or Tor Kor Market** (Th Kamphaeng Phet; ⌚8am-6pm; Ⓜ Kamphaeng Phet), is Bangkok's most upscale fresh market, which sells fantastically gargantuan fruit and seafood, and has a decent food court as well.

Pak Khlong Market MARKET
(Flower Market; Th Chakkaphet & Th Atsadang; ⌚24hr; ⛴Tha Saphan Phut (Memorial Bridge)) Every night this market near Chao Phraya River becomes the city's largest depot for wholesale flowers.

Talat Rot Fai MARKET
(Th Kamphaeng Phet; 6pm-midnight Sat & Sun; M Kamphaeng Phet) Set in a sprawling abandoned rail yard, this market is all about the retro, from antique enamel platters to secondhand Vespas.

Scuba-Diving Supplies

Most of Bangkok's dive shops are located around Th Sukhumvit.

Dive Indeed OUTDOOR GEAR
(Map p80; 0 2665 7471; www.diveindeed.com; 14/2 Soi 21, Th Sukhumvit; M Sukhumvit, Asok)

Dive Master OUTDOOR GEAR
(Map p80; 0 2259 3191; www.divemaster.net; 16 Asoke Court, Soi 21, Th Sukhumvit; M Sukhumvit, Asok)

Dive Supply OUTDOOR GEAR
(0 2354 4815; www.divesupply.com; 457/4 Th Sri Ayuthaya; Phaya Thai)

Planet Scuba OUTDOOR GEAR
(Map p80; 0 2261 4412/3; www.planetscuba.net; 666 Th Sukhumvit; Phrom Phong)

Information

ATMs, banks, and currency-exchange kiosks are widespread.

Emergency

Fire (199)

Police/Emergency (191)

Tourist police (nationwide call centre 1155; 24hr) English-speaking officers.

Internet & Telephone Access

There's no shortage of internet cafes in Bangkok competing to offer the cheapest and fastest connection. Rates vary depending on the concentration and affluence of net-heads – Banglamphu is cheaper than Sukhumvit or Silom, with rates as low as 20B per hour. Many internet shops are adding Skype and headsets to their machines so that international calls can be made for the price of surfing the web.

A convenient place to take care of your communication needs in the centre of Bangkok is the **TrueMove Shop** (Map p70; www.truemove.com; Soi 2, Siam Sq; 7am-10pm; Siam). It has high-speed internet computers equipped with Skype, sells phones and mobile subscriptions, and can also provide information on city-wide wi-fi access for computers and phones.

Wi-fi, mostly free of charge, is becoming more and more ubiquitous around Bangkok and is available at more businesses and public hotspots than we have space to list here. For relatively authoritative lists of wi-fi hotspots in Bangkok, go to www.bkkpages.com (under 'Bangkok Directory') or www.stickmanweekly.com/WiFi/BangkokFreeWirelessInternetWiFi.htm.

Media

Bangkok 101 (www.bangkok101.com) A monthly city primer with photo essays and reviews of sights, restaurants and entertainment.

Bangkok Post (www.bangkokpost.net) The leading English-language daily with Friday and weekend supplements covering city events.

BK (http://bk.asia-city.com) Free weekly listings mag for the young and hip.

CNNGo (www.cnngo.com/bangkok) Check the Bangkok pages of this online listings mag for quirky news and reviews.

THE INSIDE SCOOP

Several Bangkok residents have taken their experiences to the 'small screen' and maintain blogs and websites about living in Bangkok. Some of the more informative or entertaining include the following sites:

2Bangkok (www.2bangkok.com) News sleuth and history buff follows the city headlines from today and yesterday.

Austin Bush Food Blog (www.austinbushphotography.com/blog) Written by the author of this chapter, the blog focuses on food culture and eating in Bangkok and elsewhere.

Global Post (www.globalpost.com/bio/patrick-winn/articles) Patrick Winn, this online news agency's Southeast Asia Correspondent, is based in Bangkok and has a knack for uncovering all the wacky things that go on in the city.

Greg To Differ (www.gregtodiffer.com) 'Stories, rants and observations on expat life in Asia's craziest city.'

Not The Nation (www.notthenation.com) Thailand's answer to *The Onion*.

Thai Blogs (www.thai-blogs.com) A portal for Thai culture–related blogs.

Medical Services

The following hospitals offer 24-hour emergency service and English-speaking staff. Prices are high, but so is the quality. Use these numbers to call an ambulance.

BNH (Map p74; ☎0 2686 2700; www.bnh hospital.com; 9 Th Convent; Ⓜ Si Lom, Sala Daeng)

Bumrungrad International Hospital (Map p80; ☎0 2667 1000; www.bamrungrad.com; 33 Soi 3/Nana Nua, Th Sukhumvit; Phloen Chit)

Money

Regular bank hours in Bangkok are generally 8.30am to 3.30pm, although branches in busy areas and shopping malls are open later. ATMs are common in all areas of the city. Many Thai banks also have currency-exchange bureaus and there are exchange desks within eyeshot of most tourist areas. Go to 7-Eleven shops or other reputable places to break 1000B bills; don't expect a vendor or taxi to be able to make change on a bill 500B or larger.

Post

Main post office (Th Charoen Krung; ⏲8am-8pm Mon-Fri, 8am-1pm Sat & Sun; Tha Si Phraya)

Toilets

Public toilets in Bangkok are few and far between and your best bet is to head for a shopping centre, fast-food restaurant or our favourite, a luxury hotel. Shopping centres might charge 2B to 5B for a visit; some newer shopping centres have toilets for the disabled. Despite what you'll hear, squat toilets are a dying breed in Bangkok.

Tourist Information

Bangkok Information Center (Map p60; ☎0 2225 7612-4; www.bangkoktourist.com; 17/1 Th Phra Athit; ⏲8am-7pm Mon-Fri & 9am-5pm Sat & Sun; 32, 33, 64 & 82, Tha Phra Athit (Banglamphu) City-specific tourism office provides maps, brochures and directions.

Tourism Authority of Thailand (TAT; ☎1672; www.tourismthailand.org) Head Office (☎0 2250 5500; 1600 Th Petchaburi Tat Mai; ⏲8.30am-4.30pm; Ⓜ Phetchaburi); Banglamphu (Map p60; ☎0 2283 1500; cnr Th Ratchadamnoen Nok & Th Chakrapatdipong; klorng taxi Tha Phan Fah; ⏲8.30am-4.30pm); Suvarnabhumi International Airport (☎0 2134 0040; 2nd fl, btwn Gates 2 & 5; ⏲24hr)

Travel Agencies

Bangkok travel agencies vary greatly in the amount of commission they charge; shop around to compare fares. These are long-running agencies:

Diethelm Travel (☎0 2660 7000; www.diethelmtravel.com; 14th fl, Kian Gwan Bldg II, 140/1 Th Witthayu/Wireless Rd; Phloen Chit)

STA Travel (Map p74; ☎0 2236 0262; www.statravel.co.th; 14th fl, Wall Street Tower, 33/70 Th Surawong; ⏲9am-5pm Mon-Fri, to noon Sat; Si Lom, Sala Daeng)

visit beyond (☎0 2630 9371; www.visit beyond.com; New Road Guest House, 1216/1 Th Charoen Krung; Tha Oriental; ⏲8am-noon & 3-7pm)

ℹ Getting There & Away

Air

Bangkok has two airports. **Suvarnabhumi International Airport** (off Map p56; ☎0 2132 1888; www.bangkokairportonline.com), 30km east of Bangkok, began commercial international and domestic service in September 2006. The airport's name is pronounced *sù·wan·ná·poom*, and it inherited the airport code (BKK) previously used by the old airport at Don Muang. The unofficial airport website has practical information in English, as well as real-time details of arrivals and departures.

At press time, Bangkok's former international and domestic **Don Muang Airport** (off Map p56; ☎0 2535 1111; www.donmuangairportonline.com), 25km north of central Bangkok, served domestic flights by Thai Airways, One-Two-Go and Nok Air.

Bus

Buses using government bus stations are far more reliable and less prone to incidents of theft than those departing from Th Khao San or other tourist centres.

Southern bus terminal (Sai Tai Mai; off Map p56; ☎0 2435 1199; Th Bromaratchachonanee, Thonburi) Located across Saphan Phra Pinklao in the far western suburbs, this terminal serves all points south – hello Phuket, Surat Thani, Krabi, Hat Yai – as well as Kanchanaburi and western Thailand. The easiest way to reach the station is by taxi, or you can take bus 79, 159, 201 or 516 from Th Ratchadamnoen Klang or bus 40 from the Victory Monument.

Eastern bus terminal (Ekamai; Map p80; ☎0 2391 2504; Soi Ekamai/40, Th Sukhumvit; Ekkamai) For buses to cities on or near the eastern gulf coast including Pattaya, Rayong, Chanthaburi and Trat. Ekkamai BTS station is right by the terminal.

Northern & Northeastern bus terminal (Mo Chit; Map p56; ☎for northern routes 0 2936 2841, ext 311/442, for northeastern routes 0 2936 2852, ext 611/448; Th Kamphaeng Phet; Ⓜ Kamphaeng Phet & access by taxi, Mo Chit & access by taxi), commonly called Mor Chit station (*sà·tǎuh·nii mǎw chít*), serves northern and northeastern Thailand.

Minivan

Privately run minivans, called *rót đôo*, are a fast and relatively comfortable way to get between Bangkok and its neighbouring provinces. The biggest minivan stop is just north of the Victory Monument (Map p56), where you can board frequent minivans to the Southern bus terminal (35B, one hour, 6.30am to 9pm). Directly east of the monument are lines to Ko Samet via Ban Phe (200B, 2½ hours, from 6am to 9pm), Pattaya (97B, two hours, from 6am to 8pm) and Suvarnabhumi International Airport (40B, one hour, from 5am to 10.30pm).

Train

Bangkok's main train station is **Hualamphong** (Map p56; ☎nationwide call centre 1690, 0 2220 4334; www.railway.co.th; Th Phra Ram IV; Ⓜ Hua Lamphong). It's advisable to ignore all touts here and avoid the travel agencies. To check timetables and prices for other destinations call the **State Railway of Thailand** (☎nationwide call centre 1690; www.railway.co.th) or look at their website.

Getting Around

Because of parking hassles and traffic jams, and because taxis are cheap and ubiquitous, hiring a car to get around Bangkok is not recommended.

To/From the Airport

At the time of writing there were still two functioning airports in Bangkok; the vast majority of flights are relegated to shiny new Suvarnabhumi, but some domestic flights still fly in and out of the old Don Muang Airport. If you need to transfer between the two, pencil in *at least* an hour, as the two airports are at opposite ends of town. Minivans run between the two airports from 6am to 5pm (30B to 50B).

SUVARNABHUMI INTERNATIONAL AIRPORT

AIRPORT RAIL LINK In 2010 the much-delayed elevated train service linking central Bangkok and Suvarnabhumi International Airport was

TRANSPORT TO/FROM BANGKOK

The following shows travel times and costs to Thailand's most popular beach and island destinations. For more detailed information, be sure to refer to the Getting There & Away chapter of the specific place destination.

DESTINATION	BUS	TRAIN	AIR
Khao Lak	N/A	N/A	1¼hr/from 1480B (to Phuket)
Ko Chang	5hr/248B (to Trat)	N/A	1hr/2890B (to Trat)
Ko Lanta	12hr/720-1080B (to Krabi)	N/A	1¼ hr/from 1590B (to Krabi)
Ko Lipe	14hr/800-1200B (to Satun)	N/A	N/A
Ko Pha-Ngan	8hr/375-550B (to Chumphon), 10hr/379-759B (to Surat Thani)	7 hr/82-480B (to Chumphon), 8-12hr/217-1379B (to Phun Phin, Surat Thani)	1¼hr/from 2800B (to Chumphon), 65min/from 3300B (to Ko Samui), 70min/from 1272B (to Surat Thani)
Ko Phi-Phi	12hr/720-1080B (to Krabi)	N/A	1¼hr/from 1590B (to Krabi)
Ko Samet	4hr/157B (to Ban Phe)	N/A	N/A
Ko Samui	8hr/375-550B (to Chumphon), 10hr/379-759B (to Surat Thani)	7 hr/82-480B (to Chumphon), 8-12hr/217-1379B (to Phun Phin, Surat Thani)	65min/from 3300B (to Chumphon)
Ko Tao	8hr/375-550B (to Chumphon)	7hr/82-480B(to Chumphon)	65min/from 3300B (to Chumphon)
Phuket	N/A	N/A	1¼hr/from 1480B

finally completed. An express service runs, without stops, between Makkasan and Phaya Thai stations and the airport (15 to 17 minutes, 150B), from 6am to midnight. It's worth keeping in mind that this may not be cheaper or faster than a taxi, depending on the size of your group and what time you arrive. Makkasan, also known as City Air Terminal (Map p56), is a short walk from MRT Phetchaburi.

The Airport Rail Link is located on floor B1 of Suvarnabhumi International Airport.

LOCAL TRANSPORT Several air-con local buses serve the airport's public transport centre, a 3km ride on a free shuttle bus from Suvarnabhumi. Bus lines city-bound tourists are likely to use include 551 (Victory Monument), 554 (Don Muang) and 556 (Th Khao San), and minivan line 552 (On Nut BTS station) – fares start at 25B.

From town, you can take the BTS to On Nut, then from near the market entrance opposite Tesco take minivan 522 (25B, about 40 minutes, 6am to 9pm) to the airport. The minivans that park at the east side of the Victory Monument are another alternative (40B, one hour, 5am to 10.30pm)

TAXI As you exit the terminal, ignore the touts and all the signs pointing you to 'official airport taxis' (which cost 700B flat) and descend to the 1st floor to join the generally fast-moving queue for a public taxi. Cabs booked through these desks are legally obliged to use their meter, but they often try their luck so insist by saying, 'Meter, please'. Toll charges (paid by the passengers) vary between 25B and 45B. Note also that there's an additional 50B surcharge added to all fares departing from the airport, payable directly to the driver. The total cost of getting to most destinations in central Bangkok should be about 300B.

DON MUANG AIRPORT

Slow, crowded public bus 59 stops on the highway in front of the airport and carries on to Banglamphu, passing Th Khao San and the Democracy Monument.

As at Suvarnabhumi, public taxis leave from outside the arrivals hall and there is a 50B airport charge added to the meter fare.

The walkway that crosses from Terminal 1 to the Amari Airport Hotel also provides access to Don Muang train station, which has trains to Hualamphong train station every one to 1½ hours between 4am and 11.30am and then roughly every hour between 2pm and 9.30pm (5B to 10B, one hour).

Boat

Once the city's dominant form of transport, public boats still survive along mighty Chao Phraya River and on a few interior *klorng*.

CANAL ROUTES

Over the years, boat services along Bangkok and Thonburi's *klorng* have diminished, but with mounting traffic woes there may be plans to revive these water networks. For now, canal taxi boats run along Khlong Saen Saeb (Banglamphu to Ramkhamhaeng) and are an easy way to get from Banglamphu to Jim Thompson's House, the Siam Sq shopping centres (get off at Tha Hua Chang for both), and other points further east along Sukhumvit – after a mandatory change of boat at Tha Pratunam. These boats are mostly used by daily commuters and pull in to the piers for just a few seconds – jump straight on or you'll be left behind, and try to avoid getting splashed by the foul water. Fares range from 9B to 21B and boats run from approximately 6am to 7pm.

RIVER ROUTES

Chao Phraya Express (☎0 2623 6001; www.chaophrayaboat.co.th) provides one of the city's most scenic (and efficient) transport options, running passenger boats along Chao Phraya River to destinations both south and north of Bangkok. The central pier is known varyingly as Tha Sathon and Saphan Taksin, and connects to the Saphan Taksin BTS station, at the southern end of the city. Visitors are most likely to go northwards, to the stops designated with an N prefix.

Tickets range from 13B to 32B and are generally purchased on board the boat, although some larger stations have ticket booths. Either way, hold on to your ticket as proof of purchase.

The company operates express (indicated by an orange, yellow or yellow and green flag), local (without a flag) and tourist boat (larger boat) services. During rush hour, pay close attention to the flag colours to avoid an unwanted journey to a distant province.

Local (⌚6-8.30am & 3-6pm Mon-Fri; 9-13B) The local line (no flag) serves all company piers between Wat Ratchasingkhon, in south-central Bangkok, and northern Nonthaburi, stopping frequently.

Tourist (⌚9.30am-3.30pm; 19B, one-day pass child/adult 80/150B) The more expensive tourist boat offers heaps of seating and English-language commentary (some of it actually comprehensible). It operates from Tha Sathon to 10 major sightseeing piers, only going as far north as Tha Phra Athit (Banglamphu).

Orange Express (⌚5.50am-6.40pm Mon-Fri, 6am-6.40pm Sat & Sun; 14B) This, the most frequent line, operates between Wat Ratchasingkhon and Nonthaburi with frequent stops.

Yellow Express (⌚6.10-8.40am & 3.45-7.30pm Mon-Fri; 19-28B) The yellow express line operates between Ratburana to Nonthaburi with stops at major piers.

Green-Yellow Express (⌚6.15-8.05am & 4.05-6.05pm Mon-Fri; 11-31B) This rush-hour-only boat takes commuters directly to Pakkret Pier, far north of Bangkok.

Blue Express (⌚7-7.45am & 5.05-6.25pm Mon-Fri; 11-32B) Another rush-hour-only boat takes commuters directly to Nonthaburi.

There are also flat-bottomed cross-river ferries that connect Thonburi and Bangkok. These piers are usually next door to the Chao Phraya Express piers and cost 3B per crossing.

BTS & MRT

The elevated BTS, also known as the Skytrain *(rót fai fáh)*, whisks you through 'new' Bangkok (Silom, Sukhumvit and Siam Sq). The interchange between the two lines is at Siam station, and trains run frequently from 6am to midnight. Fares vary from 15B to 40B. Most ticket machines only accept coins, but change is available at the information booths.

Bangkok's metro (MRT) is most helpful for people staying in the Sukhumvit or Silom areas to reach the train station at Hualamphong. Otherwise the system is mainly a suburban commuter line. Fares cost 15B to 40B. The trains run frequently from 6am to midnight.

Bus

Bangkok's bus service is frequent and frantic, so a bus map (such as *Bangkok Bus Guide* by ThinkNet) is a necessity. Don't expect it to be 100% correct, though; routes change regularly.

Fares for ordinary (non-air-con) buses start at 5B, while air con bus fares begin at 11B.

The following bus lines are useful for tourists who are travelling between Banglamphu and Siam Sq:

Bus 15 From Tha Phra, on the Thonburi side of the river, to Sanam Luang (accessible to Wat Phra Kaew) with stops at MBK Center (connect to BTS) and Th Ratchadamnoen Klang (accessible to Th Khao San).

Bus 47 Khlong Toei Port to Department of Lands, along Th Phahonyothin, in northern Bangkok, with stops along Th Phra Ram IV, MBK Center, Th Ratchadamnoen and Sanam Luang.

Car

If you need private transport, consider hiring a car and driver through your hotel or hire a taxi driver that you find trustworthy. One reputable operator is **Julie Taxi** (☎08 1846 2014; www.julietaxitour.com), which offers a variety of vehicles and excellent service.

Motorcycle Taxi

Motorcycle taxis serve two purposes in Bangkok. Most commonly and popularly they form part of the public transport network, running from the corner of a main thoroughfare, such as Th Sukhumvit, to the far ends of sois that run off that thoroughfare. Riders wear coloured, numbered vests and gather at either end of their soi, usually charging 10B to 20B for the trip (without a helmet unless you ask).

Their other purpose is as a means of beating the traffic. You tell your rider where you want to go, negotiate a price (from 20B for a short trip up to about 150B going across town), strap on the helmet (they will insist for longer trips) and say a prayer to whichever god you're into. Drivers range from responsible to kamikaze, but the average trip involves some time on the wrong side of the road and several near-death

TAXI TIPS

» Never agree to take a taxi that won't use the meter. These drivers usually park outside hotels and in tourist areas. Simply get one that's passing by instead.

» Bangkok taxi drivers will generally not try to 'take you for a ride' as happens in some other countries; they make more money from passenger turnover.

» It's worth mentioning that many Bangkok taxi drivers are in fact seasonal labourers fresh from the countryside and may not know their way around.

» If a driver refuses to take you somewhere, it's probably because they need to return their rental cab before a certain time, not because they don't like how you look.

» Very few Bangkok taxi drivers speak much English; an address written in Thai can help immensely.

» Older cabs may be less comfortable but typically have more experienced drivers because they are driver-owned, as opposed to the new cabs, which are usually rented.

experiences. It's the sort of white-knuckle ride you'd pay good money for at Disneyland, but is all in a day's work for these riders. Comfort yourself with the knowledge that there are good hospitals nearby.

Taxi

Although many first-time visitors are hesitant to use them, in general, Bangkok's taxis are new and spacious, and the drivers are courteous and helpful, making them an excellent way to get around. All taxis are required to use their meters, which start at 35B, and fares to most places within central Bangkok cost 60B to 90B.

Túk-Túk

Some travellers swear by túk-túk, but most have a hard time bargaining a fair price; know how much it should cost to your destination before soliciting a fare. A short trip on a túk-túk should cost at least 50B.

If a túk-túk driver offers to take you on a sightseeing tour, walk away – it's a touting scheme designed to pressure you into purchasing overpriced goods.

Ko Chang & Eastern Seaboard

Includes »

Best Places to Eat

» Mum Aroi (p107)

» Barrio Bonito (p132)

» Cool Corner (p121)

» Pan & David Restaurant (p103)

Best Places to Stay

» Birds & Bees Resort (p107)

» Tubtim Resort (p114)

» Ban Jaidee Guest House (p120)

» Bang Bao Sea Hut (p130)

» Paradise Cottages (p130)

Why Go?

Bangkok Thais have long escaped the urban grind with weekend escapes to the eastern seaboard. Some of the country's first beach resorts sprang up here, starting a trend that has been duplicated wherever sand meets sea. As the country became industrialised, only a few, like Ko Samet beaches, remain spectacular specimens within reach of the capital. Further afield, Ko Chang and its sister islands offer the best 'tropical' ambience in the region but expect crowds.

Just beyond the foothills and the curving coastline is Cambodia, and the east coast provides a convenient, cultural link between the two countries. Many of the mainland Thai towns were at some point occupied by the French during the shifting border days of the colonial era. Migrating travellers who take the time to explore these lesser-known spots will find remnants of Old Siam, tasty market meals and an easygoing prosperity that defines ordinary Thai life.

When to Go

The best time to visit is at the end of the rainy season (usually around November) but before the start of high season (December to March). The weather is cool, the landscape is green and rates are reasonable. Peak season on Ko Chang is during the Christmas and New Year holiday period. Crowds thin in March but this is the start of the hot season.

The rainy season runs from May to October. Some businesses on Ko Chang close for the season and the nearby islands of Ko Wai, Ko Mak and Ko Kut shut completely. Your best monsoon bet is Ko Samet, which is relatively drier.

Ko Chang & Eastern Seaboard Highlights

1. Beachcombing and jungle trekking on **Ko Chang** (p124)
2. Floating the day away on the crystalline waters of **Ko Kut** (p136)
3. Swimming with the fishes in the gin-clear coves of **Ko Wai** (p134)
4. Cove-hopping on pretty **Ko Samet** (p111), so close to Bangkok but so far away
5. Strolling the old city and watching the gem traders in **Chanthaburi** (p116)
6. Running errands with the Thai housewives in the day markets of **Trat** (p119)
7. Avoiding Bangkok's hustle and bustle with an alternative layover in **Si Racha** (p100) and a day trip to **Ko Si Chang** (p102)
8. Admiring the modern masterpiece of Pattaya's **Sanctuary of Truth** (p104), an elaborately carved testament to the artistry of Buddhism and Hinduism
9. Dining on seafood beside the sea everywhere, the primary reason Thais travel to the beach

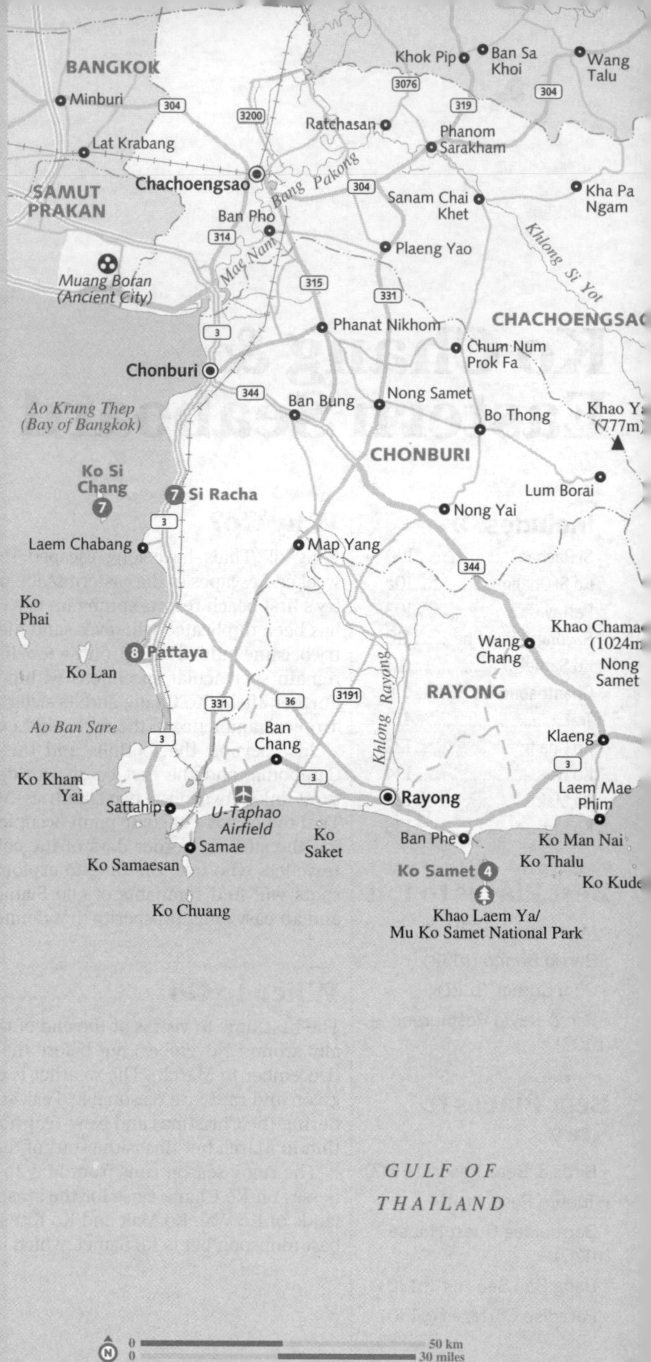

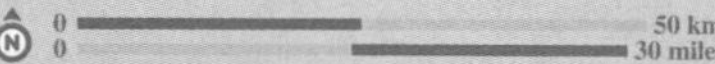

Lam Prachinburi
Sa Kaew
Watthana Nakhon
Huay Jot
Sai Yoi
Khao Chakan
Aranya Prathet
Ang Sila
Non Mak Mun
Poipet
CAMBODIA
Sai Diaw
Non Sao-Eh
Sisophon
Khlong Hat
Khao Takrup (660m)
Wang Mai
Khao Daeng
Thun Khanan
CHANTHABURI
Tamun
Battambang
Khao Soi Dao Nua (1566m)
Pung Ngon
Nong Chek Soi
Takra
Ban Pakard
Khao Chamao/ Khao Wong National Park
Khao Khitchakut National Park
Pong Nam Ron
Psar Pruhm
Pailin
Si Yaek Kong Din
Nong Khla
Makham
Ban Pa-Ah
Tha Mai
Chanthaburi
Chang Thun
Nam Tok Phlio National Park
Nong Sii
Laem Sadet
Ta Chalap
Chak Yai
Laem Singh
Khlung
Pong
Dan Chumpon
Laem Ko Proet
Tha Chot
TRAT
CAMBODIA
Trat
Ban Noen Sung
Bang Kradan
Laem Muang
Laem Ngop
Ao Trat
Tha Sen
Ko Chang
Laem Sok
Mu Ko Chang National Marine Park
Mai Rut
Ko Wai
Ko Kradat
Ko Mak
Ko Rayang
Khlong Yai
Ko Mai Si
Ko Kut
Hat Lek
Krong Koh Kong
348
33
317
3395
3395
317
317
3
3157
3159
3271
3156
3
318

Si Racha ศรีราชา

POP 68,292

A subdued seaside town, Si Racha is a mix of fishing-village roots and modern industry. Waterfront condo towers eclipse a labyrinth of rickety piers and the cargo ships docking at the Laem Chabang port share the shipping channels with simple, multicoloured fishing boats.

Thai towns, especially those with a modern veneer, are adept at disguising themselves to look like every other Thai town. In Si Racha's case, you need a bit of backstory to know that the many Japanese restaurants in town are catering to the international workforce of the nearby Japanese car manufacturers, and the BMWs that are cruising the streets indicate that those too are being produced nearby. In fact, surrounding the Laem Chabang port, Thailand's busiest deep-water port, is a host of industrial factories, petrochemical facilities and chemical plants – the muscle of the Thai manufacturing economy. As a result there's money in this town: the new municipal building is landscaped like a resort and the health park is impeccably maintained.

From a tourism perspective, Si Racha is attractive for what it doesn't have; there are no guest houses, girlie bars or traffic jams. It is also an easy commute to Bangkok's Suvarnabhumi airport if you're looking for a quiet and untouristed place to layover.

Sights

Si Racha's attractions are limited, but the town makes for a pleasant stroll.

Ko Loi ISLAND

This small rocky island is connected to the mainland by a long jetty at the northern end of Si Racha's waterfront and lauded as a local highlight. It has a festival atmosphere centred around a **Thai-Chinese temple** (daylight hrs), decorated by a couple of giant ponds with turtles of every size, from tiny hatchlings to seen-it-all-before seniors. This is also where you can catch the boat to offshore Ko Si Chang.

Health Park GARDEN

The town's waterfront Health Park is possibly one of the best-maintained municipal parks in the country. There are sea breezes, a playground, shady coffee shop with wi-fi, a jogging track and a lot of evening activity.

Sleeping

The most authentic (read: basic) places to stay are the wooden hotels on the piers.

COCK SAUCE BY ANY OTHER NAME

Judging by the phenomenal popularity of Sriracha Hot Chili sauce in the USA, you'd expect the eponymous town to be a veritable sauce temple. But no one in the town of Si Racha seems to know much about the sauce, much less that US haute chefs are using it on everything from cocktails to marinades and that food magazines, like *Bon Appetit*, are profiling it alongside truffle oil as a must-have condiment. (Curiously the culinary world also mispronounces the name of the sauce: Sriracha, an alternative spelling of 'Si Racha', is pronounced 'see-rach-ah' not 'sir-rach-ah'.)

There's a good explanation for all this: the stuff sold in the US was actually invented on home soil. A Vietnamese immigrant living in a suburb of Los Angeles concocted a chilli sauce to accompany noodles based on his memory of Vietnamese hot sauces. His first batches were sold out of his car but eventually his business grew into the Huy Fong Foods company.

Today the company's distinctive rooster logo bottles are distributed in the US and Australia, but not in any Asian countries, according to a company spokesperson. But every now and then you might spot it at a Thai noodle shop. How it is this US-born, Thai-named, Vietnamese-inspired sauce got here, the Huy Fong Foods company does not know.

But that doesn't mean Thailand doesn't have its own version of a vinegar-based chilli sauce *(nám prík sěe rah·chah)*. In fact, many believe that the condiment must have originated in Si Racha and then migrated across Asia to undergo various permutations. In Thailand, Si Racha–style sauces, including such popular brands as Golden Mountain or Sriraja Panich, are used with *kài jee·o* (omelette) and *hŏy tôrt* (fried mussel omelette) and tend to be more homogenous and of a thinner consistency than the rooster brand.

Siriwatana Hotel HOTEL $
(☎0 3831 1037; Soi Siriwatana, Th Jermjompol; r 200B) This wooden stilt hotel sits above the sea – in fact, you can look straight through the squat toilet's hole to the ocean. It's simple, but the basic rooms are cheap.

Samchai HOTEL $
(☎0 3831 1800; Soi 10, Th Jermjompol; r 300B) Look for the sign that says 'Hotel' and you'll find another wooden pier hotel that creeps up the comfort scale. It feels a bit like a port: cement floors with yellow lines wind through the large complex.

Seaview Sriracha Hotel HOTEL $$
(☎0 3831 9000; 50-54 Th Jermjompol; r 900-1200B; ❄@) Rooms are large and comfortable, and some have views of the sea and piers. Rooms facing the street can be a tad noisy, but Si Racha is not Times Square, and a gentle hush settles relatively early.

Eating & Drinking

Si Racha is famous for seafood.

Moom Aroy SEAFOOD $$
(no roman-script sign; dishes 100-350B; ⏲lunch & dinner) Moom Aroy delivers on its name, meaning 'delicious corner'. This is *the* place to enjoy a Si Racha seafood meal with views of the pier and squid rigs. It is north of town; turn left at Samitivet Sriracha Hospital and look for the tank with the 2m fish out front.

Bang Saen SEAFOOD $$
(dishes 100-250B; ⏲lunch & dinner) Do as the Thais do and judge your beach by its seafood restaurants. This beach resort, 18km north of town, isn't good for swimming but weekending Bangkokians and local university students love it for its food and views. You'll need private transport to reach it.

Ko Loi Seafood Stalls SEAFOOD $
(dishes 40-160B; ⏲lunch & dinner) Perched on the Ko Loi jetty, these humble spots specialise in fresh seafood. There is no English menu but it's all good.

Night Square MARKET $
(Th Jermjompol & Th Si Racha Nakorn; dishes from 50B; ⏲5pm) This evening market is a bit small but big enough to feed a street-stall appetite.

Picha Cake Garden BAKERY $
(cnr Th Jermjompol & Th Surasak 1; coffee 40B; ⏲breakfast, lunch & dinner) Baked goodies, coffee and spotless air-con surroundings make this a convenient haven from Si Racha's busy streets. Plus there's wi-fi.

Si Racha

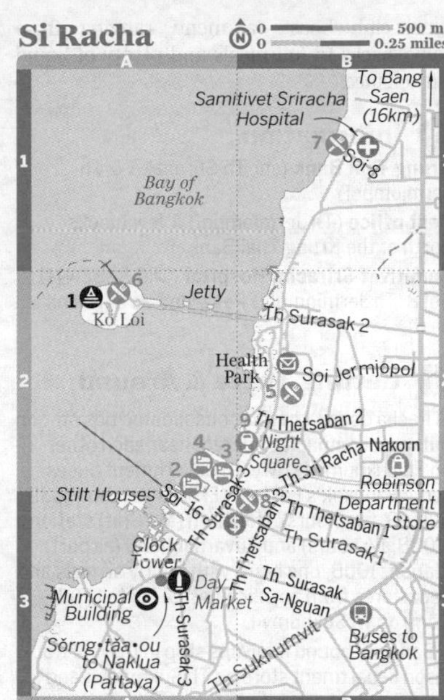

Si Racha

Sights
1 Thai-Chinese Temple A2

Sleeping
2 Samchai A2
3 Seaview Sriracha Hotel A2
4 Siriwatana Hotel A2

Eating
5 Asami Sriracha B2
6 Ko Loi Seafood Stalls A2
7 Moom Aroy B1
8 Picha Cake Garden B3

Drinking
9 Pop Pub B2

Asami Sriracha JAPANESE $$
(Th Jermjompol; dishes 150-250B; ⏲lunch & dinner) Catering to the local Japanese community, this sit-down restaurant does sushi, udon noodle dishes and katsu sets.

Pop Pub BAR
(Th Jermjompol; dishes 60-220B; ⏲5-11pm) More like 'Rock', this waterfront beer-hall-meets-

music-club boasts a menu ranging from salty snacks to full meals and plenty of liquid sustenance.

Information

Krung Thai Bank (cnr Th Surasak 1 & Th Jermjompol)

Post office (Th Jermjompol) A few blocks north of the Krung Thai Bank.

Samitivet Sriracha Hospital (0 3832 4111; Soi 8, Th Jermjompol) Regarded as Si Racha's best.

Getting There & Around

Si Racha doesn't have a consolidated bus station but most companies operate near each other on Th Sukhumvit (Hwy 3). Government buses serve Bangkok's Eastern (Ekamai) station (88B to 155B, two hours), Northern (Mo Chit) station (100B, 1½ hours) and Suvarnabhumi (airport) station (100B, one hour) with hourly arrivals and departures from an office beside IT Mall (Tuk Com) on Th Sukhumvit.

Bangkok-bound minivans stop in front of Robinson department store on Th Sukhumvit and have frequent services to Bangkok's various bus stations (100B to 120B) and Victory Monument (100B).

All the arriving Bangkok buses continue on to Pattaya (50B) and points east. White *sŏrng·tăa·ou* (small pick-up trucks) leave from Si Racha's clock tower to near Pattaya's Naklua market (25B, 30 minutes).

Private bus companies have offices on Th Sukhumvit south of the intersection with Th Surasak and serve the following long-distance destinations: Nong Khai (506B, 12 hours, one evening departure), Khorat (380B, five hours, two evening departures) and Phuket (848B to 1138B, one evening departure).

There is one daily train from Bangkok to Pattaya that stops at Si Racha. It leaves Hua Lamphong station at 6.55am and returns from Si Racha at 2.50pm (3rd class 100B, three hours). Si Racha's train station is 3km east of the waterfront.

Túk-túks (motorised three-wheeled pedicab) go to points around town for 30B to 40B.

Ko Si Chang

เกาะสีชัง

POP 5012

Once a royal beach retreat, Ko Si Chang has a fishing-village atmosphere and enough attractions to fill a day's excursion from Si Racha. Bangkok Thais come on weekends to eat seafood, pose in front of the sea and make merit at the local temples.

Sights

FREE Phra Chudadhut Palace HISTORICAL SITE

(9am-5pm Tue-Sun) This former royal palace was used by Rama V (King Chulalongkorn) over the summer months, but was abandoned when the French briefly occupied the island in 1893. The main throne hall – a magnificent golden teak structure known as Vimanmek Teak Mansion – was moved to Bangkok in 1910 (see p62).

What remains today are fairly subdued Victorian-style buildings indicative of the king's architectural preferences. **Ruen Vadhana** and **Ruen Mai Rim Talay** contain historical displays about the king's visits to the island and his public works programs, including a lecture to the local people on Western tea parties. Up the hill is **Wat Asadang Khanimit**, a temple containing a small, consecrated chamber where Rama V used to meditate. The unique Buddha image inside was fashioned more than 50 years ago by a local monk. Nearby is a stone outcrop wrapped in holy cloth, called Bell Rock because it rings like a bell when struck.

Because this is royal property, proper attire (legs and arms should be covered) is technically required but this place doesn't have an administrative presence so the rules aren't enforced. Sadly, the grounds have fallen into disrepair, which is surprising considering the site's proximity to Bangkok and the reverence usually afforded this revered king.

Cholatassathan Museum AQUARIUM

(admission by donation; 9am-5pm Tue-Sun) Just before you reach the palace, this aquatic museum has a few marine exhibits and a dash of English-language signage. The touch tank is interesting because Thais stand around remarking about which animals are delicious to eat. The Aquatic Resources Research Institute conducts coral research here.

San Jao Phaw Khao Yai TEMPLE

(daylight hrs) The most imposing sight on the island is the ornate Chinese temple, dating back to the days when Chinese traders anchored in the sheltered waters. During Chinese New Year in February, the island is overrun with visitors from the Chinese mainland. There are also shrine caves, multiple platforms and a good view of the ocean. It's east of the town, overlooking the modern-day barges waiting silently in the sea.

Wat Tham Yai Phrik TEMPLE
(วัดถ้ำยายปริก; donation appreciated; ⌚dawn-dusk) This Buddhist monastery is built around several meditation caves running into the island's central limestone ridge and offers fine views from its hilltop *chedi* (stupa). Monks and *mâa chee* (nuns) from across Thailand come to take advantage of the caves' peaceful environment. Someone is usually around to give informal tours and talk about Buddhism; you can also arrange multi-day meditation retreats.

Hat Tham Phang BEACH
On the southwest side of the island, Hat Tham Phang (Fallen Cave Beach) has simple facilities with deckchair and umbrella rental. Swimming isn't recommended but you can soak up all the sun you desire.

Activities

Several locals run **snorkelling** trips to nearby Koh Khang Khao (Bat Island). Ask at Pan & David Restaurant for details.

Sea kayaks are available for rent (150B per hour) on Hat Tham Phang. A nice paddle is down the coast to Koh Khang Khao, which is also a good spot for snorkelling.

Si Chang Healing House MASSAGE
(☎0 3821 6467; 167 Mu 3 Th Makham Thaew; ⌚8am-6pm Thu-Tue) Offers massage and beauty treatments (400B to 800B) in a garden labyrinth opposite Pan & David Restaurant.

Eating

The town has several small restaurants, with simply prepared seafood being your best bet.

TOP CHOICE **Pan & David Restaurant** INTERNATIONAL $$
(☎0 3821 6629; 167 Mu 3 Th Makham Thaew; dishes 50-260B; ⌚breakfast, lunch & dinner Wed-Mon) With free-range chicken, homemade ice cream, French-pressed coffee and excellent Thai dishes, the menu can't go wrong. Phoning ahead for a booking is recommended. The restaurant is 200m from the palace.

Lek Tha Wang SEAFOOD $
(dishes 60-150B; ⌚lunch & dinner) Near the entrance to the palace, this famous restaurant is where Thais go to eat conch and other shellfish. For the rest of us, there's always *đôm yam gûng* (spicy and sour prawn soup) and fried fish.

Information

The island's one small settlement faces the mainland and is the terminus for the ferry. A bumpy road network links the village with all the other sights.

Kasikornbank (99/12 Th Atsadang) Has an ATM and exchange facilities.

Post office (Th Atsadang) Near the pier.

www.koh-sichang.com An excellent source of local information.

Getting There & Around

Boats to Ko Si Chang leave hourly from 7am to 8pm from the Ko Loi jetty in Si Racha (one way 40B). From Ko Si Chang boats shuttle back hourly from 6am to 6pm. Boats leave promptly.

Ko Si Chang's túk-túks will take you anywhere for 40B to 60B. Island tours are available for 250B to 300B: you might need to haggle.

Motorbikes are available to rent on the pier.

Pattaya พัทยา

POP 215,888

Synonymous with prostitution, Pattaya is unapologetic about its bread-and-butter industry. Go-go clubs, massage parlours and girlie bars occupy block after block of the central city, making Bangkok's red-light districts look small and provincial. The city is slightly less seedy in the daylight hours, when families from Russia and Eastern Europe, fresh off a charter flight, might outnumber stiletto-wearing drag queens. More recently, Bangkok Thais have adopted Pattaya as an affordable weekend getaway. They dine beside the sea from a dry location, remarking how much cheaper it is and how much clearer the water is here than in Hua Hin. Does this mean that Sin City is becoming Something-For-Everybody City? Hardly, but there are a few pockets of wholesomeness amid the vice (though it is doubtful that anyone but a missionary would be lured by such a claim).

The city is built around **Ao Pattaya**, a wide crescent-shaped bay that was one of Thailand's first beach resorts in the 1960s. The surrounding area is now Thailand's manufacturing base, transforming the bay from fishing and swimming pool into an industrial port. Some provincial Thais still swim here but we don't think you should as the water is dirty. The oceanfront promenade does, however, provide a scenic stroll under shady trees and a lovely coastal view.

Pattaya & Naklua

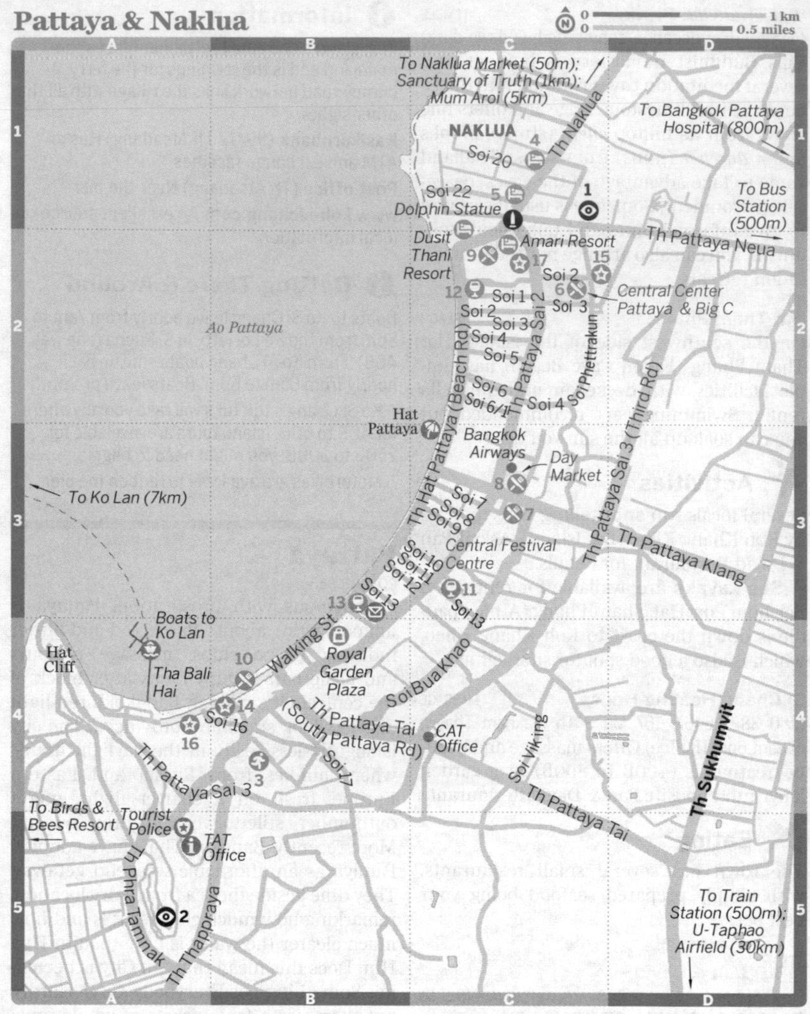

Optimists claim that Hat Jomtien, south of the centre, is a family-friendly scene. True, there are fewer girlie bars, but minus that Jomtien is about two decades away from being retro and in the meantime is decidedly dated with a lot of mediocre tour-group hotels and restaurants. North Pattaya (Pattaya Neua) is fashioning itself as a mini-Bangkok with modern condo towers and respectable corporate hotels. North of the city is **Naklua**, which is a little glossier than Jomtien and a little more promising for Pattaya's alternative tourists.

Sights & Activities

Sanctuary of Truth MONUMENT

(ปราสาทสัจธรรม; ☎0 3836 7229; www.sanctuaryoftruth.com; 206/2 Th Naklua; admission 500B; ⊙8am-6pm) Made entirely of wood (no metal nails) and commanding a celestial view of the ocean, the Sanctuary of Truth is best described as a visionary environment: part art installation, religious shrine and cultural monument. The ornate temple-like complex was conceived by Lek Viriyaphant, a Thai millionaire who spent his fortune on this and other heritage projects (such as Ancient City near Bangkok) that revived and

Pattaya & Naklua

Sights
1 Fairtex Sports Club C1
2 Khao Phra Tamnak A5

Activities, Courses & Tours
3 Thais 4 Life B4

Sleeping
4 Garden Lodge Hotel C1
5 Woodlands Resort C1

Eating
6 Central Festival Food Hall & Park C2
La Baguette .... (see 5)
7 Leng Kee C3
8 Mae Sai Tong C3
9 Mantra C2
10 Nang Nual B4

Drinking
11 Green Bottle C3
12 Gulliver's C2
13 Hopf Brew House B3

Entertainment
14 Blues Factory B4
15 Differ C2
16 Lima Lima A4
17 Tiffany's C2

preserved ancient building techniques and architecture in danger of extinction. In this case, the building will continue to support hand-hewn woodworking skills because it has been under construction for 30 years and still isn't finished.

The sanctuary is constructed in four wings dedicated to Thai, Khmer, Chinese and Indian religious iconography. Every inch of the 20-storey tall building is covered with wood carvings of Hindu and Buddhist gods and goddesses – an artistic consolidation of centuries of religious myths under one unifying roof for greater spiritual enlightenment. For non-Buddhists the experience will be more educational than transcendent as much of the symbolism will be unfamiliar. Regardless, the building and setting are beautiful and the architecture is impressive.

Compulsory tours are led through the building every half hour from 8.30am to 5pm. Thai dancing is on display at 11.30am and 3.30pm. Motorcycle taxis can be hired from Pattaya for 50B to 70B.

Anek Kusala Sala (Viharn Sien) MUSEUM
(อเนกกุศลศาลา (วิหารเซียน); ☎0 3823 5250; off Th Sukhumvit; admission 50B; ⏱9am-5pm) A popular stop for tour groups, this museum contains more than 300 pieces of Chinese artwork, mainly bronze and brass statues depicting historical figures as well as Buddhist, Confucian and Taoist deities. Founded by Sa-nga Kulkobkiat, a Thai national who grew up in China, the museum was founded as a friendship-building project between the two countries, but its greatest success is an impressive collection of art with an unusually high degree of English-language signage (supplemented by a helpful bilingual guidebook available at the ticket office).

The 1st floor is a crowded pavilion of Chinese immortals, from Pangu, the cosmic giant, to Guan Yin, the goddess of mercy. The 2nd-floor terrace is the museum's most dramatic, with larger-than-life-sized statues of Shaolin monks depicting different martial arts poses. Nearby is a touching collection of daily life statues (a fortune teller, dress maker, liquor seller) that visitors place one baht coins on.

The museum is 16km south of central Pattaya; take Th Sukhumvit to the turn-off for Wat Yan Sangwararam. There is a Pattaya-Sattahip *sŏrng·tăa·ou* (25B) that will take you to the turn-off; from there you can hire a motorcycle the remaining 3km to the museum (50B) but finding a ride back to the main road is difficult. You can either negotiate with the driver to wait or come with your own transport.

Ko Lan BEACH
(เกาะล้าน) Day trippers flock to this small island, 7km offshore of central Pattaya, for sun and sand. On weekends, Bangkok's visiting party people bake off hangovers in beach chairs, and the aquamarine sea is sliced and diced by jet-skis, banana boats and other marine merriment. There are about five beaches on the island, easily accessible by motorcycle, but don't expect to find complete seclusion. Boats leave Pattaya's Bali Hai pier (30B, five daily departures) at the southern end of Walking St. The last boat back from Ko Lan is at 6pm.

Hat Jomtien

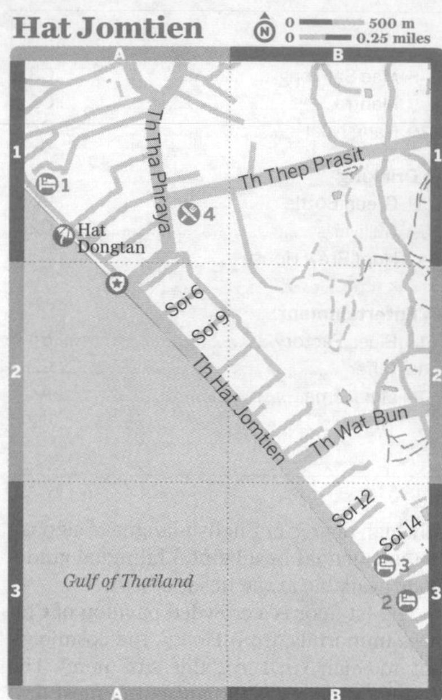

Hat Jomtien

Sleeping

1 Rabbit Resort A1
2 RS Seaside B3
3 Summer Beach Inn B3

Eating

4 Sam's Mexican & American Grill A1

Khao Phra Tamnak VIEWPOINT
(เขาพระตำหนัก; Map p104; daylight hrs) A giant golden Buddha sits on top of this forested hill between Jomtien and South Pattaya (Pattaya Tai) as a reminder that religion has not forsaken this modern-day Gomorrah. The serene Buddha figure of Wat Phra Yai dates back to the days when Pattaya was a small fishing village and from this lofty position you can almost imagine a time before mini-skirts and Beer Chang happy hours. You can walk to the top of the hill from the southern end of Walking St, passing a small Chinese shrine en route.

Fairtex Sports Club FITNESS, MOO·AY TAI
(Map p104; 0 3825 3888; www.fairtex-muaythai.com; 179/185-212 Th Pattaya Neua; per session 800B) Burned-out professionals, martial arts fans and adventurous athletes flock to this resort-style sports camp for *moo·ay tai* (Thai boxing; also spelled *muay thai*) training and a sweat-inducing vacation. Daily sessions include pad work, sparring and clinching, exercise drills and body sculpting work. There are also occasional brushes with fame: domestically famous *moo·ay tai* champions and international mixed martial arts fighters also train here.

Fairtex has been training *moo·ay tai* fighters for 40 years. In 2005, the company opened this sports club to provide Western-style comfort for international visitors interested in fighting and fitness courses. Accommodation packages are available and use of the club's pool and other sports facilities are included.

Flight of the Gibbon OUTDOOR ADVENTURE
(08 9970 5511; www.treetopasia.com; tours from 3000B) This zip-line course extends 3km with 26 platforms through the forest canopy of Khao Kheeo Open Safari in Chonburi, 50 minutes from Pattaya. It is an all-day tour with additional add-on activities, like a jungle obstacle course and a visit to the neighbouring animal zoo. Children 1m tall can do the zip-line independently while younger, shorter kids can ride tandem with an adult.

Festivals

Pattaya International Music Festival MUSIC
In mid-March, Pattaya's oceanfront esplanade is transformed into an outdoor concert venue running for three days of live music. In 2011, bands from Korea, Japan, Malaysia and Laos topped the billing along with Thai favourites such as Modern Dog and Tattoo Colour.

Sleeping

If you're an 'alternative' Pattaya tourist (meaning you aren't a sex tourist or a package tourist), then you should avoid staying in central Pattaya and opt instead for Naklua, Jomtien or parts of Pattaya Neua. Even if you have no desire to visit Pattaya, you might consider an overnight here if you're transiting to Suvarnabhumi International Airport, 110km away, and don't want to layover in Bangkok.

RS Seaside HOTEL $$
(Map p106; 0 3823 1867; www.rs-seaside.com; Th Hat Jomtien; r from 650B;) With small rooms and nice desk staff, RS is a good-value

spot in the package-tour part of town. Two breakfasts are included in the room rate.

Summer Beach Inn HOTEL $$

(Map p106; ☎0 3823 1777; Th Hat Jomtien; r 650-1500B; ❄@) Clean, comfortable rooms come with most of the modern conveniences in a high-rise hotel far from Pattaya's vice.

Rabbit Resort HOTEL $$$

(Map p106; ☎0 3825 1730; www.rabbitresort.com; Hat Dongtan; r from 4000B; ❄@≋) Rabbit Resort has stunning bungalows and villas set in beachfront forest hidden between Jomtien and Pattaya Tai. Furnishings showcase Thai design and art and bathrooms are especially stylish with accents of river stone and granite. It is a lovely escape from Pattaya.

TOP CHOICE **Birds & Bees Resort** HOTEL $$$

(☎0 3825 0556; www.cabbagesandcondoms.co.th; Soi 4, Th Phra Tamnak; r from 4500B; ❄@≋) Retreat into a tropical garden resort bisected by meandering paths and decorated with tongue-in-cheek artwork. Resident rabbits crouch behind the shrubs and kids splash in the pool until they wrinkle like prunes. There's a semi-private beach and an incongruous wholesomeness for a resort affiliated with PDA, the Thai NGO responsible for the country's successful adoption of condom-use and family-planning services.

Garden Lodge Hotel HOTEL $$

(Map p104; ☎0 3842 9109; cnr Soi 20 & Th Naklua; r 950-1450B; ❄≋) Quality rooms with balconies occupy a landscaped garden and shady swimming pool.

Woodlands Resort HOTEL $$$

(Map p104; ☎0 3842 1707; www.woodland-resort.com; cnr Soi 22, 164/1 Th Naklua; r from 3700B; ❄@≋) A surprisingly affordable resort, Woodlands Resort is low-key and professional with a tropical garden and two swimming pools, one with a 'beach' entry for young swimmers. The rooms are light and airy with teak furniture.

Eating

It is a tourist town and there are a lot of overpriced, mediocre restaurants so lower your standards. Most menus are bilingual (usually English and Russian).

TOP CHOICE **Mum Aroi** THAI $$

(☎0 3822 3252; 83/4 Soi 4, Th Naklua; dishes 180-240B; ⏲dinner) 'Delicious corner' is a contemporary glass-and-concrete restaurant perched beside the sea in the fishing village end of Naklua. Old fishing boats sit marooned offshore and crisp ocean breezes envelope diners as they greedily devour fantastic Thai food. Try *sôm·đam Ƀoo* (spicy papaya salad with crab) and *Ƀlah mèuk nêung ma-now* (squid steamed in lime juice). You'll need to charter a baht bus to get here (one way 100B).

Central Festival Food Hall & Park INTERNATIONAL $

(Map p104; Th Pattaya Sai 2; dishes from 60B; ⏲lunch & dinner) The glitziest place to eat a plate of *pàt tai* is in this new Bangkok-style shopping mall.

MOO·AY TAI CHAMPION: YODSAENKLAI FAIRTEX

Khun Yod is a famous *moo·ay tai (muay thai)* fighter but you'd never know it. He is humble and as he is passing into the sunset of his career he is a little stockier than the sinewy kids that can high-kick their opponents in the head. Yod started fighting at eight years old, partly to help his struggling farming family. His first fight was at a temple fair in his home province of Nong Banglamphu and he lost. But since then he earned the nickname 'Computer Wizard' for his technical and methodical fighting style, was a three-time Lumphini champion and has now expanded into the international circuit, winning the super welterweight WBC Muay Thai championship. In the last two years, he has fought in 12 countries and always travels with a supply of Mama noodles and a rice cooker, preferring something akin to Thai food than the local delicacies.

While in Pattaya, Yod recommends an early morning run along the beach road and up Khao Phra Tamnak or a dish of *sôm·đam lao* (Lao-style spicy green papaya salad) from the stand opposite the municipal building. As is customary, Yod adopted the last name of the gym he trains with (Fairtex) where he can be found preparing for a match.

CHARITY SQUAD

A natural counterpoint to the city's prominent debauchery is the city's solid network of charitable organisations. Among the many benevolent servants in Pattaya, Father Ray Brennan, an American priest with the Redemptorist Order who died in 2003, established a lasting and inspiring legacy that today includes six charitable programs under the umbrella of the Redemptorist Foundation. He also founded the Pattaya Orphanage and School for the Deaf, both of which are now operated by the Catholic diocese. All of them succeed thanks to the generosity of benefactors and volunteers.

Pattaya Orphanage (☎0 3842 3468; www.thepattayaorphanage.org; Th Sukhumvit, North Pattaya) was founded in the 1970s when Father Ray was given a baby by a parishioner who could not care for the child. This first child led to many more as word spread that the priest could care for the unintended consequences of the US military presence in the area during the Vietnam War. Today the orphanage cares for children orphaned by modern misfortunes (poverty, drug abuse, HIV/AIDS) and helps find adoptive parents. Those interested in helping the orphanage can sponsor a meal, donate useful items and volunteer for an extended period of time.

Redemptorist Foundation (volunteer@fr-ray.org) operates schools for the blind and disabled and a home and drop-in centre for street children, many of whom may be involved in Pattaya's child-sex industry. The foundation also runs a day-care centre for children of labourers who would otherwise accompany their parents to dangerous work sites. Volunteers rotate through the different centres, teaching English, playing with the children and leading art projects. A six-month commitment is required; contact the foundation for a volunteer handbook that outlines the application process.

If you don't have the time to commit to volunteering, at least stop by **Thais 4 Life** (www.thais4life.com; Soi Yen Sabai Condotel, Th Phra Tamnak; ⏲noon-6pm Mon-Sat), a charity bookstore whose proceeds go to medical treatments for destitute patients, orphanages and school uniform scholarships.

Sam's Mexican & American Grill MEXICAN-AMERICAN **$$**
(Map p106; ☎08 6142 8408; 472/9 Th Tha Phraya, Jomtien Plaza; dishes 80-200B; ⏲closed Sun) When it comes to expat cuisine, Thailand does not excel in Mexican food even though there is a common love of chillies and limes. But Sam's gets the formula right and comes recommended by a displaced Los Angeleno.

Nang Nual THAI **$$**
(Map p104; ☎0 3842 8478; Walking St; dishes 100-200B; ⏲lunch & dinner) Pattaya's most famous seafood restaurant could be a major tourist trap but it keeps its prices affordable and the dishes are pleasant if not spectacular. The outdoor deck gulps in a big view of the bay and you don't have to use sign language to talk to your waiter.

Mae Sai Tong THAI **$**
(Map p104; Th Pattaya Klang; dishes 50B) Next to the day market, this stand is famous for selling *kôw něe·o má·môo·ang* (ripe mango with sticky rice) all year round. Everyone else has to wait for the hot-dry season to compete.

Leng Kee THAI-CHINESE **$**
(Map p104; Th Pattaya Klang; dishes 50-80B; ⏲lunch & dinner) Like Bangkok and other coastal Thai towns, Pattaya has a thriving Chinatown operated by second- and third-generation families who expertly balance their Thai and Chinese heritage. This basic restaurant is a popular lunch stop for duck over rice, but is city-renowned during Chinese New Year when the menu goes vegetarian and includes the festival's golden good-luck noodles.

La Baguette BAKERY **$**
(Map p104; ☎0 3842 1707; 164/1 Th Naklua; dishes from 120B; ⏲breakfast, lunch & dinner) Part of the Woodlands Resort, this sleek cafe has yummy pastries, espresso, and even better crepes. You can also link into its wi-fi network.

Mantra INTERNATIONAL **$$$**
(Map p104; ☎0 3842 9591; Th Hat Pattaya; dishes 240-800B; ⏲dinner Mon-Sat, brunch & dinner Sun) Industrial cool, Mantra is fun even if you can only afford a classy cocktail. The bar is swathed in raw silk and the expansive dining room is cloaked in dark wood. The

menu combines Japanese, Thai and Indian flavours, and everyone comes here for Sunday brunch.

Ban Amphur THAI $
(dishes from 100B; ⌚lunch & dinner) This fishing village 15km south of Pattaya is a dinner destination for Thais. A half-dozen seafood restaurants line the beach road and some are so large the waiters use walkie-talkies. Pick one that doesn't seem lonely or overwhelmed and order all the seafood specialities. You'll have to hire transport to get here.

Drinking

Despite the profusion of noisy, identikit beer bars, there are still some good places for a no-strings-attached drink.

Hopf Brew House BAR
(Map p104; ☎0 3871 0650; Th Hat Pattaya) Moodily authentic in dark wood, the Hopf Brew House is a haven for middle-aged beer aficionados. Beers and pizza are brewed and wood-fired on-site.

Gulliver's BAR
(Map p104; ☎0 3871 0641; Th Hat Pattaya) The neo-colonial facade belies the laid-back sports-bar inside.

Green Bottle BAR
(Map p104; ☎0 3842 9675; 216/6-20 Th Pattaya 2) Cheap beer and lots of cheer can be found at dressed-down Green Bottle, which has been filling glasses since 1988.

Entertainment

Aside from the sex scene, Pattaya does have a youthful club scene centred on Walking St, a semi-pedestrian area with bars and clubs for every predilection.

Lima Lima NIGHTCLUB
(Map p104; Walking St) International DJ scene and a mix of Russian and Western tourists, locals and expats.

Differ NIGHTCLUB
(Map p104; Soi Phettrakun) Popular with weekending Bangkokians, this dance club's slogan is 'feel fun, feel differ'. It's across from Big C.

Blues Factory LIVE MUSIC
(Map p104; ☎0 3830 0180; www.thebluesfactorypattaya.com; Soi Lucky Star, Walking St) This is Pattaya's best venue for no-nonsense live music.

Tiffany's THEATRE
(Map p104; ☎08 4362 8257; www.tiffany-show.co.th; 464 Th Pattaya 2; admission 500-800B; ⌚6pm, 7.30pm & 9pm) Established in 1974, Pattaya probably invented the transvestite cabaret, a show tune-style spectacle of sequins, satin and sentimental songs.

Information

Dangers & Annoyances

So many people are so drunk in this town that all sorts of mayhem ensues (fighting, pickpocketing and reckless driving) after dark. Try to have your wits about you and exit any volatile situation as quickly as possible.

Emergency

Tourist police (☎emergency 1155) The head office is beside the Tourism Authority of Thailand office on Th Phra Tamnak with police boxes along Pattaya and Jomtien beaches.

Internet Access

There are internet places throughout the city and most hotels offer wi-fi or internet terminals.

Media

Explore Pattaya, a free fortnightly magazine, contains information on events, attractions and hotel and restaurant listings. *What's On Pattaya* is a similar monthly publication. *Pattaya Mail* (www.pattayamail.com) is the city's English-language weekly. Pattaya 24 Seven (www.pattaya24seven.com) is an online guide to the city.

Medical Services

Bangkok Pattaya Hospital (☎0 3842 9999; www.bph.co.th; 301 Th Sukhumvit, Naklua; ⌚24hr) For first-class health care.

Money

There are banks and ATMs conveniently located throughout the city.

Post

Post office (Map p104; Soi 13/2, Th Pattaya Sai 2)

Tourist Information

Tourism Authority of Thailand (TAT; Map p104; ☎0 3842 8750; 609 Th Phra Tamnak; ⌚8.30am-4.30pm) Located at the northwestern edge of Rama IX Park. The helpful staff have brochures and maps.

Getting There & Away

Air

Pattaya's airport is U-Taphao International Airport, located 33km south of town; it is an old military base that now receives some commercial flights, especially charters. **Bangkok**

BYPASSING BANGKOK

An expanding network of bus and minivan services now connect the eastern seaboard with Suvarnabhumi airport, meaning that you don't have to transit through Bangkok upon a flight arrival or departure. This is especially alluring to winter-weary visitors or newlyweds eager for a beach retreat. With a little advance planning, Ko Samet is the closest prettiest beach to the airport and its southeastern beaches are serene enough for honeymooners. From the airport bus terminal, check the schedule for Rayong-bound buses and then catch a *sŏrng·tăa·ou* to reach the ferry pier to Ko Samet.

Airways (☎0 3841 2382; www.bangkokair.com; 179/85-212 Th Pattaya Sai 2) flies from here to Phuket (from 3000B) and Ko Samui (3600B).

Boat

A new high-speed ferry service links Pattaya to Hua Hin (adult/child 1500/900B, 3½ hours). Ferries leave Pattaya at 8.30am three times a week in high season (two times in low season) and leave Hua Hin at 12.30pm on the same days. Contact **Thai Living Ferry** (☎0 3836 4515; www.thailivingferry.com) for bookings and info.

Bus

Pattaya's main bus station is on Th Pattaya Neua. Buses serve the following destinations:

Bangkok's Eastern (Ekamai) station (91B, 1½ hours, frequently from 6am to 9pm)

Bangkok's Northern (Mo Chit) station (105B, two hours, frequently from 6am to 9pm)

Bangkok's Suvarnabhumi (airport) station (124B, 1½ hour, hourly 7am to 3pm)

Many 2nd-class provincial buses make stops along Th Sukhumvit (not the bus station); from here you can flag down buses heading to Rayong (83B, 1½ hours) and Si Racha (65B, 30 minutes). You can also catch a white *sŏrng·tăa·ou* from the Naklua market to Si Racha (25B, 30 minutes).

Minibuses go to Ko Chang and Ko Samet for about 250B; travel agencies sell tickets and arrange pick-ups.

Train

One train per day travels between Pattaya and Bangkok's Hualamphong station (3rd class 31B, 3¾ hours). It leaves Bangkok at 6.55am and returns at 2.20pm. Schedules for this service can change, so it's wise to check with the **Pattaya train station** (☎0 3842 9285), off Th Sukhumvit just north of Th Hat Pattaya Neua, before travelling.

Getting Around

Locally known as 'baht buses', *sŏrng·tăa·ou* do a loop along the major roads; just hop on and pay 10B when you get off. If you're going all the way from Jomtien to Naklua you might have to change vehicles at the dolphin roundabout in Pattaya Neua. You can also take a baht bus to the bus station from the dolphin roundabout as well. If you're going further afield, you can charter a baht bus; establish the price beforehand.

Rayong & Ban Phe ระยอง/บ้านเพ

POP 106,737/16,717

You're most likely to be in either of these towns as a transit link en route to Ko Samet. Rayong has frequent bus connections to elsewhere and the little port of Ban Phe has ferry services to Ko Samet. Blue *sŏrng·tăa·ou* link the two towns (25B, 45 minutes, frequent departures).

Sleeping

Rayong President Hotel GUEST HOUSE $
(☎0 3861 1307; Th Sukhumvit, Rayong; r from 550B; ❄) From the bus station, cross to the other side of Th Sukhumvit. The hotel is down a side street that starts next to the Siam Commercial Bank; look for the sign.

Christie's Guesthouse GUEST HOUSE $
(☎0 3865 1976; fax 0 3865 2103; 280/92 Soi 1, Ban Phe; r from 500B; ❄) Christie's is a comfortable place near the pier if you need a room, meal or a book.

Getting There & Away

Buses from Rayong go to/from the following:

Bangkok's Eastern (Ekamai) station (127B to 146B, three hours, hourly 6am to 9.30pm)

Bangkok's Northern (Mo Chit) station (146B, four hours, hourly 6am to 7pm)

Bangkok's Southern (Sai Tai Mai) station (150B, five hours, five daily departures)

Bangkok's Suvarnabhumi (airport) station (165B, 2½ hours, eight daily departures)

Chanthaburi (80B, 2½ hours, frequent)

Buses from Ban Phe's bus station (near Tha Thetsaban) go to/from Bangkok's Eastern (Ekamai) station (157B, four hours, hourly 6am to 6pm). Ban Phe also has frequent minivan services to the following destinations:

Pattaya (250B, two hours, three daily departures)

Bangkok's Victory Monument (250B, four hours, hourly 7am to 6pm)

Laem Ngop (350B, four to five hours, two daily departures) For boats to Ko Chang.

For information about boats to/from Ko Samet see p115.

Ko Samet เกาะเสม็ด

An island idyll, Ko Samet bobs in the sea with a whole lot of scenery: small sandy coves bathed by clear aquamarine water. You'll have to share all this prettiness with other beach lovers as it's an easy weekend escape from Bangkok as well as a major package-tour destination.

But considering its proximity and popularity, Ko Samet is surprisingly underdeveloped with a thick jungle interior crouching beside the low-rise hotels. Most beachfront buildings adhere to the government setback regulations and are discreetly tucked behind the tree line. There are no high-rises or traffic jams (the interior road still isn't paved) and most beach-hopping is done the old-fashioned way, by foot along wooded trails skirting the coastline.

Sights & Activities

On some islands, you beach-hop while on Ko Samet you cove-hop. The coastal footpath traverses rocky headlands, cicada-serenaded forests and one stunning cove after another where the mood becomes successively more mellow the further south you go.

Hat Sai Kaew BEACH

Starting in the island's northeastern corner, Hat Sai Kaew, or 'Diamond Sand', is the island's widest and whitest stretch of sand and has all the hubbub you'd expect of a top-notch beach resort. With sunbathers, sarong-sellers, anchored speedboats loading day-trippers, and restaurants galore – the people-watching here is part of the appeal. At night the scene is equally rambunctious with late-night parties and karaoke sessions.

At the southern end of Hat Sai Kaew are the **prince and mermaid statues** that memorialise Samet's literary role in *Phra Aphaimani*, the great Thai epic by Sunthorn Phu. The story follows the travails of a prince exiled to an undersea kingdom ruled by a lovesick female giant (who has her own lonely statue in Hat Puak Tian in Phetchaburi). A mermaid aids the prince in his escape to Ko Samet, where he defeats the giant by playing a magic flute.

Ao Hin Khok & Ao Phai BEACHES

More subdued than their northern neighbour, Ao Hin Khok and Ao Phai are two gorgeous bays separated by rocky headlands. The crowd here tends to be younger and more stylish than the down-to-earth crew in Hat Sai Kaew and the parties are late-nighters. These two beaches are the traditional backpacker party centres of the island.

Ao Phutsa (Ao Tub Tim) BEACH

Further still is wide and sandy Ao Phutsa (Ao Tub Tim), a favourite for solitude seekers, families and couples who need access to 'civilisation' but not a lot of other stimulation.

Ao Wong Deuan BEACH

A smaller sister to Hat Sai Kaew, **Ao Wong Deuan** is a long, crescent-shaped bay packed with people, mainly package tourists.

Ao Thian BEACH

Ao Thian (Candlelight Beach) is punctuated by big boulders that shelter small sandy spots creating a castaway ambience. It is one of Samet's most casual, easygoing beaches and is deliciously lonely on weekdays. On weekends, Bangkok university students serenade the stars with all-night guitar sessions.

Ao Wai BEACH

The cove 'caboose' is Ao Wai, a lovely beach far removed from everything else (in reality it is 1km from Ao Thian).

Ao Prao BEACH

On the west coast, Ao Prao is worth a visit for a sundowner cocktail but the small beach is outsized by the high-end resorts that promise (but don't deliver) solitude.

BEACH ADMISSION FEE

Ko Samet is part of a national park and charges all visitors an entrance fee (adult/child 200/100B) upon arrival. The fee is collected at the National Parks office in Hat Sai Kaew; *sŏrng·tăa·ou* from the pier will stop at the gates for payment. Hold on to your ticket for later inspections.

Ko Samet

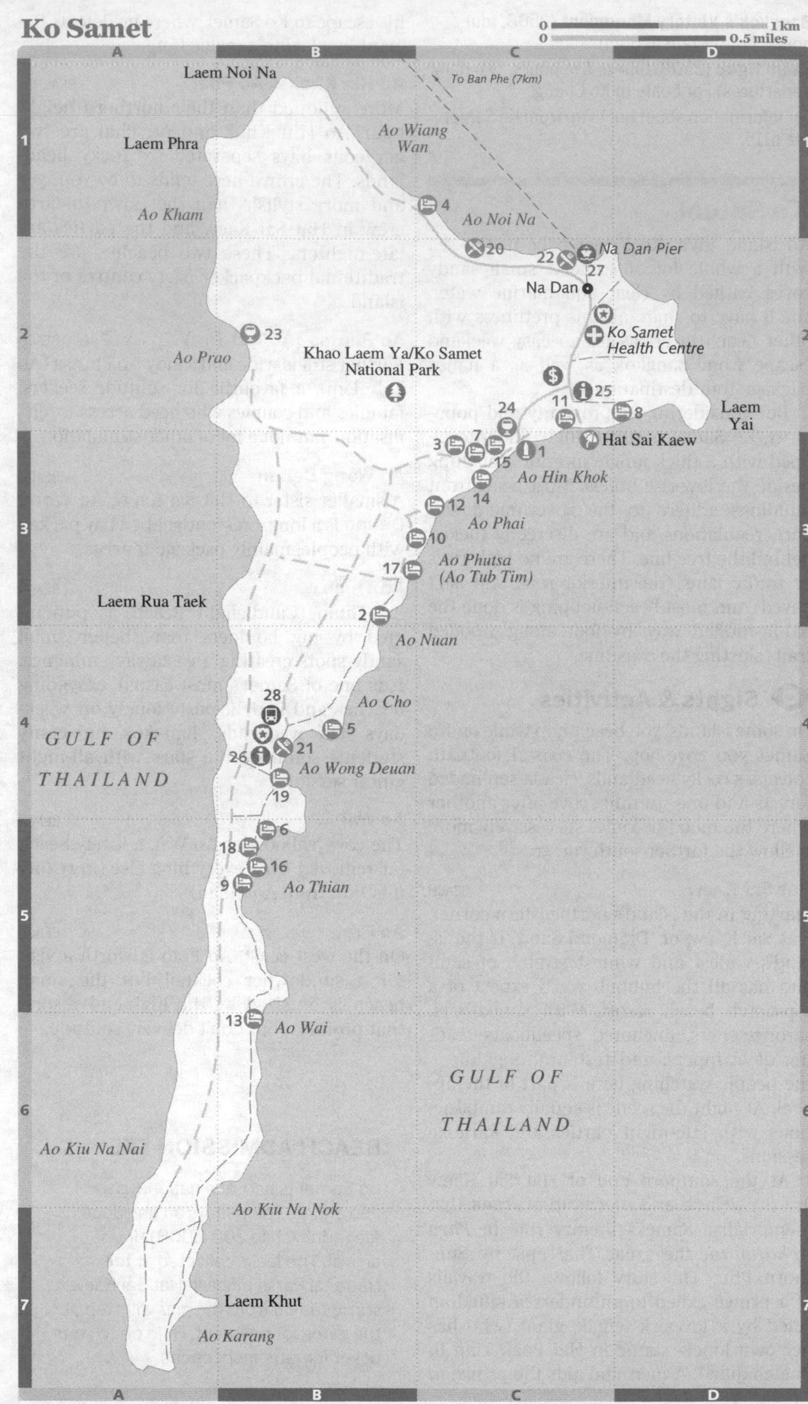
0 1 km
0 0.5 miles
A
B
C
D
1
2
3
4
5
6
7
Laem Noi Na
To Ban Phe (7km)
Ao Wiang Wan
Laem Phra
Ao Kham
4
Ao Noi Na
20
22
Na Dan Pier
27
Na Dan
Ko Samet Health Centre
23
Ao Prao
Khao Laem Ya/Ko Samet National Park
25
11
8
Laem Yai
24
3
7
1
15
Hat Sai Kaew
Ao Hin Khok
14
12
Ao Phai
10
Ao Phutsa (Ao Tub Tim)
17
Laem Rua Taek
2
Ao Nuan
28
Ao Cho
5
GULF OF THAILAND
21
26
Ao Wong Deuan
19
6
18
16
9
Ao Thian
13
Ao Wai
GULF OF THAILAND
Ao Kiu Na Nai
Ao Kiu Na Nok
Laem Khut
Ao Karang

Ko Samet

Sights

1 Prince & Mermaid Statues ... C3

Sleeping

2 Ao Nuan ... B3
3 Ao Pai Hut ... B3
4 Baan Puu Paan ... C1
5 Blue Sky ... B4
6 Candlelight Beach ... B5
7 Jep's Bungalows ... C3
8 Laem Yai Hut Resort ... D2
9 Lung Dam Apache ... B5
10 Pudsa Bungalow ... C3
11 Saikaew Villa ... C2
12 Samed Villa ... C3
13 Samet Ville Resort ... B6
14 Silver Sand ... C3
15 Tok's ... C3
16 Tonhard Bungalow ... B5
17 Tubtim Resort ... B3
18 Viking Holiday Resort ... B5
19 Vongduern Villa ... B4

Eating

20 Ban Ploy Samed ... C2
21 Baywatch Bar ... B4
Jep's Restaurant ... (see 7)
22 Rabeang Bar ... C2
Summer Restaurant ... (see 4)

Drinking

23 Ao Prao Resort ... B2
24 Naga Bar ... C2
Silver Sand Bar ... (see 14)

Information

25 National Parks Main Office ... C2
26 National Parks Office ... B4

Transport

27 Ferry Terminal ... C2
28 Sŏrng·tăa·ou Stop ... B4
Sŏrng·tăa·ou Stop ... (see 27)

Tours

Ko Samet, along with nine neighbouring islands, is part of the Khao Laem Ya/Mu Ko Samet National Park. While there is some development on the other islands, most visitors come for day trips. **Ko Kudee** has a small, pretty sandy stretch, clear water for decent snorkelling and a nice little hiking trail. Ko Man Nai is home to the **Rayong Turtle Conservation Centre**, which is a breeding place for endangered sea turtles and has a small visitor centre.

Agents for boat tours camp out on the popular beaches and have a couple of different boat trips on offer (from 1500B).

Sleeping

Though resorts are replacing bungalows, Ko Samet's accommodation is still surprisingly simple and old-fashioned compared to Thailand's other beach resorts. Weekday rates don't rank well on the value scale (fan rooms start at 800B), but look incredibly attractive considering that weekend and holiday rates increase by as much as 100%.

A word of caution to early risers: Hat Sai Kaew, Ao Hin Khok, Ao Phai and Ao Wong Deuan are the most popular beaches and host well-amplified night-time parties.

HAT SAI KAEW

Laem Yai Hut Resort GUEST HOUSE $
(☎0 3864 4282; Hat Sai Kaew; r 800-1000B; ❄) A colourful collection of weather-worn huts are camped out in a shady garden on the north end of the beach. The laid-back vibe creates an alternative backpacker universe in a firmly rooted package-tour beach.

Saikaew Villa HOTEL $$
(☎0 3864 4144; Hat Sai Kaew; r 800-2000B; ❄) The closest option to the pier, Saikaew Villa has big rooms or small rooms, fan or air-con and conjures up a holiday-camp atmosphere. Quality and privacy varies with each room.

AO HIN KHOK & AO PHAI

Tok's HOTEL $$
(☎0 3864 4072; Ao Hin Khok; r 1500B; ❄) Snazzy villas climb up a landscaped hillside with plenty of shade and flowering plants, making Tok's a respectable midranger.

Jep's Bungalows GUEST HOUSE $$
(☎0 3864 4112; www.jepbungalow.com; Ao Hin Khok; r 500-1600B; ❄@) Good old Jep's still has cheapie fan huts spread across a forested hillside, just like the old days (a mere five years ago). Air-conditioned rooms are the same, just with cooler interior temps.

A WORKING HOLIDAY

You can volunteer to work at Rayong's Turtle Conservation Centre through **Starfish Ventures** (www.starfishventures.co.uk; 4 weeks incl accommodation £800). Activities include monitoring the progress of the turtles, releasing young turtles into the ocean and explaining the project to tourists on day trips from Ko Samet. Accommodation is in a fishing village, and every day you'll go to work in a speedboat across to Ko Man Mai. It's pretty leisurely – you'll be expected to work from 8am to 3pm or 4pm, four days a week – and in your downtime there are good beaches nearby to explore.

Ao Pai Hut GUEST HOUSE $
(☎0 3864 4075; Ao Hin Khok; r 600-1000B; ❄) Same, same as Jep's, this guest house has basic wooden bungalows perched amid the trees.

Silver Sand HOTEL $$
(☎0 3864 4300; www.silversandsamed.com; Ao Phai; r 1500-2200B; ❄@) Contemporary villas with luscious beds and sleek bathrooms provide a needed slice of sophistication to simple Ko Samet. The after-hours action in the Silver Sands bar can be disorderly and is popular with gay travellers.

Samed Villa HOTEL $$
(☎0 3864 4094; www.samedvilla.com; Ao Phai; r 1800-2500B; ❄) Handsome bungalows gaze at the ocean or at a manicured garden and boast a lot of comfort without a lot of hassles.

AO PHUTSA & AO NUAN

TOP CHOICE **Tubtim Resort** HOTEL $$
(☎0 3864 4025; www.tubtimresort.com; Ao Phutsa; r 800-2500B; ❄@) Ranging from fan to fab, Tubtim has a little of everything. More expensive bungalows are pretty and polished, while the cheapies are spare but still within walking distance to the same dreamy beach.

Pudsa Bungalow GUEST HOUSE $$
(☎0 3864 4030; Ao Phutsa; r 700-1500B; ❄) The nicer bungalows near the beach are trimmed with driftwood, but sit beside the main footpath within earshot of late-night blathering. A good option if you are doing the blathering.

Ao Nuan GUEST HOUSE $$
(r 700-2000B) The inventor of chillaxin' on Ko Samet, quirky Ao Nuan has simple wooden bungalows hidden among vegetation. Everyone cool enough to score a room here hangs out in the relaxed restaurant. No phone means no reservations, so just walk on over; it is the only place to stay on a supremely secluded beach.

AO WONG DEUAN & AO THIAN (CANDLELIGHT BEACH)

Ferries run between Ao Wong Deuan and Ban Phe (50B each way), with increased services at the weekend.

To get to Ao Thian, catch a ferry to Ao Wong Deuan and walk south over the headland. It's also a quick walk from here to the west side of the island – look for the marked trail near Tonhard Bungalow.

Blue Sky GUEST HOUSE $
(☎08 1509 0547; r 600-1200B; ❄) A rare budget spot on Ao Wong Deuan, Blue Sky has simple bungalows set on a rocky headland. Though we love cheapies in all their simplicity, budgeters will get better value on other beaches.

Candlelight Beach GUEST HOUSE $
(☎08 1762 9387; r 700-1200B; ❄) On the beach, these fan and air-con bungalows with sea-facing porches have a natural, woody ambience.

Lung Dam Apache GUEST HOUSE $
(☎08 1452 9472; r 800-1200B; ❄) Air-con bungalows sit right smack on the sand and the whole basic collection favours the Thai-country aesthetic of recycled materials.

Tonhard Bungalow GUEST HOUSE $$
(☎08 1435 8900; r 700-1500B; ❄) On a wooded part of the beach, this place has bungalows that vary from basic to less basic. But in return you get a friendly and relaxing setting.

Viking Holiday Resort HOTEL $$
(☎0 3864 4353; www.sametvikingresort.com; r 1200-2000B; ❄@) Ao Thian's most 'upscale' spot with large and comfortable rooms; there's only nine of them so book ahead.

AO WAI

Ao Wai is about 1km from Ao Thian but can be reached from Ban Phe by chartered speedboat.

Samet Ville Resort HOTEL $$$
(☎0 3865 1682; www.sametvilleresort.com; r incl breakfast 2000-5300B; ❄) Under a forest canopy, it's a case of 'spot the sky' at the only resort on this secluded beach. It is an unpretentious sort of place and a tad shabby for resort aficionados. But there is a huge range for all budgets and a great beach.

AO NOI NA

Baan Puu Paan GUEST HOUSE $$
(☎0 3864 4095; r 700-1200B; ❄@) This English-run spot has a breezy setting between the main road and the sea, northwest of the Na Dan pier. If the rates were higher, this would be boutique with its cute cottage colours and a few stand-alone huts squatting above the ocean. Bring a fat book – it's a good place to get away. You'll need private transport to come and go.

Eating & Drinking

Most hotels and guest houses have restaurants that moonlight as bars after sunset. The food and the service won't blow you away, but there aren't many alternatives. Nightly beach barbecues are an island favourite but try to pick one that looks professionally run – meaning that there is a steady stream of dishes being served and people eating rather than looking bored.

On weekends Ko Samet is a boisterous night-owl with provincial tour groups crooning away on karaoke machines or the young ones slurping down beer and buckets to a techno beat. The bar scene changes depending on who is around but there is usually a crowd on Hat Sai Khao, Ao Hin Khok, Ao Phai and Ao Wong Deuan.

Jep's Restaurant INTERNATIONAL $$
(Ao Hin Khok; dishes 60-150B; ⏲breakfast, lunch & dinner) Canopied by the branches of an arching tree decorated with pendant lights, this pretty place does a little of everything right on the beach.

Summer Restaurant INTERNATIONAL $$$
(Baan Puu Paan, Ao Noi Na; dishes 250-400B; ⏲dinner) In a crisp setting overlooking the harbour, Summer savours a globetrotters' culinary scrapbook, from Indian-style chicken tikka to Cajun chicken breasts.

Ban Ploy Samed THAI $$$
(☎0 3864 4188; Ao Noi Na; dishes 300-600B; ⏲dinner) Better than having to haul in your meal, you are hauled to this floating restaurant by a boat-and-pulley system. Fresh seafood dishes, especially the whole steamed fish variety, await.

Rabeang Bar THAI $
(Na Dan; dishes 50-100B; ⏲breakfast, lunch & dinner) Right by the ferry terminal, this over-the-water spot has good enough food to make you forget you have to leave the island.

Naga Bar BAR
(Ao Hin Khok; drinks from 60B) The beachfront bar specialises in drinking games: coin tosses, *moo·ay tai* bouts and whisky buckets to give you courage.

Silver Sand Bar BAR
(Ao Phai; drinks from 60B) Silver Sands progresses (regresses?) from dinner to cocktail buckets and dance floor gyrations and is a popular gay spot.

Baywatch Bar BAR
(Ao Wong Deuan; drinks from 80B) There are a number of chill-out spaces for after-dark beach-gazing. The cocktails are strong and it's a fun evening crowd.

Ao Prao Resort BAR
(Ao Prao; drinks from 80B) On the sunset-side of the island, this resort has a lovely sea-view restaurant perfect for an evening sundowner. You'll need to take private transport here.

Information

There are several ATMs on Ko Samet, including near the Na Dan pier and Ao Wong Deuan.

Internet terminals or wi-fi are available at hotels on most beaches.

Ko Samet Health Centre (☎0 3861 1123; ⏲8.30am-9pm Mon-Fri, 8.30am-4.30pm Sat & Sun) On the main road between Na Dan and Hat Sai Kaew. On-call mobile numbers are posted for after-hours emergencies.

National Parks main office (btwn Na Dan & Hat Sai Kaew) Has another office on Ao Wong Deuan.

Police station (☎1155) On the main road between Na Dan and Hat Sai Kaew. There's a substation on Ao Wong Deuan.

Getting There & Away

Ko Samet is accessible from the mainland piers in Ban Phe. There are dozens of piers in Ban Phe, each used by different ferry companies, but they all charge the same fares (one way/return 50/100B, 40 minutes, hourly 8am to 4pm) and dock at Na Dan, the main pier on Ko Samet. Boats return to the mainland with the same frequency.

If you're staying at Ao Wong Deuan or further south, catch a ferry from the mainland directly to the beach (one way 50B, one hour, two daily departures).

When you buy your ticket on the mainland, you'll get the hard sell for a speedboat trip (2500B for the boat). The boat can hold 10 passengers (250B each) but it is never clear how long you have to wait for that price. But it is always an option if you're in a hurry; the boats go directly to your beach of choice.

Ticket agents on the mainland will also pressure you into pre-booking accommodation with a hefty commission tacked on. You'll be fine if you just show up on the island and start hunting for a room.

Getting Around

Ko Samet's small size makes it a great place to explore on foot. A network of dirt roads connects most of the western side of the island.

Green *sŏrng·tăa·ou* meet arriving boats at the pier and provide drop-offs at the various beaches (20B to 80B, depending on the beach). If drivers don't have enough people to fill the vehicle, they either won't go or they will charge passengers 200B to 500B to charter the whole vehicle.

You can rent motorcycles nearly everywhere along the northern half of the island. Expect to pay about 300B per day. The dirt roads are rough and hazardous, and larger vehicles can leave behind blinding dust clouds. At any rate, make sure to test the brakes before you decide, and drive slowly around curves.

Chanthaburi จันทบุรี

POP 99,819

Chanthaburi is proof that all that glitters is not gold. Here, gemstones do the sparkling, attracting international traders, including Southeast Asians and Africans, dealing in sapphires, rubies, jade and other coloured stones. Thanks to the gem trade and its multicultural history (French, Vietnamese and Chinese), the so-called 'City of the Moon' is surprisingly diverse for a typical Thai town and worth visiting for an appreciation of the economic and religious sanctuary Thailand has long provided in the region.

The old city (also known as the Chantaboon Waterfront community) is the best place to chart the course of immigration and international involvement in the city. The Vietnamese began arriving in the 19th century when Christian refugees escaped religious and political persecution in Cochin China (southern Vietnam). A second wave of Vietnamese refugees followed in the 1920s and 1940s, fleeing French rule, and a third arrived after the 1975 communist takeover of southern Vietnam. The French occupied Chanthaburi from 1893 to 1905, while disputing with Siam over the borders of Indochina.

LOCAL KNOWLEDGE

LIVING WITH HISTORY

Pratapan Chatmalai is the community leader of the Chantaboon Waterfront Community Association. She grew up here and fondly remembers the tight-knit community of culturally diverse people. Today she works to save the stories and the character of the community.

WHAT DOES YOUR ORGANISATION DO?

Now this community is a 'grandma' city. The old city is losing life and the young people have moved away. I want to keep the culture for the next generation to learn about and I'm trying to help the people in the area have a good life. We run the Learning House so that people can come look at the daily life of the past.

WHAT DO YOU RECOMMEND TOURISTS SEE OR DO IN THE OLD CITY?

There is unique history and lifestyle of the past here. Come look at the cathedral, Chinese shrines and old houses. Each house is different and mixes Thai, Chinese and Western styles. Eat at the local restaurants. There are seafood noodles, old-style ice cream and dim sum. If you get tired, you can have a massage in an old Thai-style house.

WHAT IS YOUR FAVOURITE PART OF THE OLD CITY?

I love the whole place because it is a living museum and I can walk along and talk to the people about the past and make them happy.

As told to China Williams

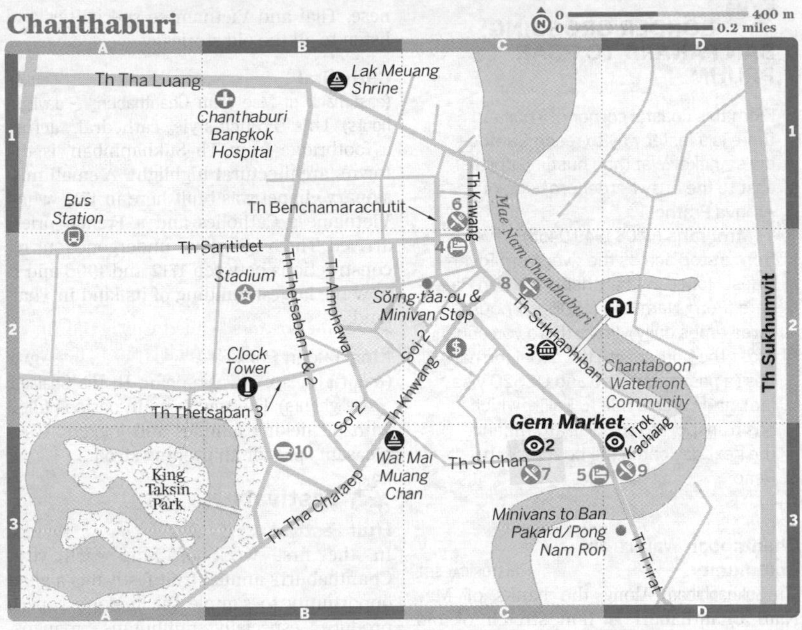

Chanthaburi

Top Sights
Gem Market D3

Sights
1 Cathedral D2
2 Gem Shops C3
3 Learning House C2

Sleeping
4 Kasemsarn Hotel C2
5 River Guest House C3

Eating
6 Chanthorn Phochana C1
7 Muslim Restaurant C3
8 Seafood Noodle Shop C2
9 Sony Yadaw D3

Drinking
10 Coffee Room B3

Sights & Activities

TOP CHOICE **Gem Market** MARKET
(ตลาดพลอย; Th Si Chan & Trok Kachang; ⏰Fri, Sat & Sun) On weekends, the streets and side streets near Th Si Chan (or 'Gem Rd') are overflowing with the banter and intrigue of the hard sell. It has the feel of an average Thai market, incongruously humble considering the preciousness of the commodity. People cluster around makeshift tables or even a trader's outstretched palm, examining small piles of unset stones. In the formal shops, hardnosed inspectors examine the gemstones under magnifying glasses looking for quality and authenticity. This is strictly a spectator sport and not recommended for the uninitiated, but it is a fascinating glimpse at a relatively private trade.

In the hills surrounding Chanthaburi, several sapphire and ruby mines once supplied the palace with fine ornaments prior to the mid-19th century when the mines were developed into commercial operations by Shan (Burmese) traders. These days, locally mined gems are of inferior international quality but the resourceful Chanthaburi traders roam the globe acquiring precious and semi-precious stones, which are in turn traded here to other globetrotters.

The last remaining mine in the area is **Khao Phloi Waen**, 6km from town, which is famous locally for its 'Mekong Whiskey' yellow-coloured sapphire.

BORDER CROSSING: BAN PAKARD TO PSAR PRUHM

From this coastal corner of Thailand, there is a faster way to reach Cambodia's Angkor Wat than hustling northeast to the busy border crossing of Aranya Prathet.

Minivans (☎08 1949 0455) leave from a stop across the river from River Guest House in Chanthaburi to Ban Pakard/Pong Nam Ron (150B, 1½ hours, three times daily). From there you can cross the border with the usual formalities (a passport photo and US$20 visa fee), and catch a ride to Pailin, which has transport to scenic Battambang; the next day catch the boat to Siem Reap.

Chantaboon Waterfront Community HISTORICAL SITE
(Th Sukhaphiban) Along the banks of Mae Nam Chanthaburi is 1km stretch of old wooden shophouses that are valiantly being promoted and preserved as a living history museum. It is an atmospheric stroll through time and place with a uniquely Thai twist: food features more prominently than facts and figures.

Stop by the **Learning House** (☎08 1945 5761; ⏲9am-5pm) for an educational introduction to the community. The 2nd floor displays historic photographs of daily life as well as architectural drawings of the homes' beautifully carved ventilation panels. Much of the community's immigrant past is revealed in these unique panels: there are carvings of Chinese characters and even French fleurs-de-lis.

Farmers and merchants first settled on the fertile river banks some 300 years ago, establishing the area as an agricultural trading post. Chinese traders and economic migrants sought refuge here, thus diversifying the local population. Vietnamese Catholics fled from religious persecution in their home country. And before long the different groups had intermarried until everyone claimed a little bit of each.

Today, the older generation remains in the rickety old houses but through Khun Pratapan's efforts, many domestic tourists are coming for weekend outings to eat Chinese, Thai and Vietnamese specialities and listen to all the old stories.

Cathedral CHURCH
(east bank of Mae Nam Chanthaburi; ⏲daylight hours) This French-style cathedral, across a footbridge from Th Sukhaphiban, is the town's architectural highlight. A small missionary chapel was built here in 1711, when Vietnamese Catholics and a French priest arrived. The original has undergone four reconstructions between 1712 and 1906 and is now the largest building of its kind in Thailand.

King Taksin Park PARK
(สวนสาธารณะสมเด็จพระเจ้าตากสิน; Th Tha Chalaep; ⏲daylight hrs) The town's main oasis is filled with picnicking families and joggers. It's a pleasant spot for an evening stroll.

Festivals

Fruit Festival FOOD
In the first week of June each year, Chanthaburi's annual fruit festival is a good opportunity to sample the region's superb produce, especially rambutans, mangosteens and the ever-pungent durian.

Sleeping

Accommodation can get very busy. Try to book ahead, especially from Friday to Sunday when the gem traders are in town.

River Guest House HOTEL $
(☎0 3932 8211; 3/5-8 Th Si Chan; r 150-400B; ❄@) Standard hotel boxes aren't much to get excited about, but this is as good as it gets in the budget range. The relaxed sitting area and friendly staff are a plus. Try to score a room away from the highway.

Kasemsarn Hotel HOTEL $$
(☎0 3931 1100; www.kasemsarnhotel.net; Th Benchamarachutit 98/1; r 1200-1500B; ❄@) Good enough for visiting Bangkokians, Kasemsarn has large modern rooms with generous weekday discounts.

Eating & Drinking

Seafood Noodle Shop THAI $
(Th Sukhaphiban; dishes 25-50B; ⏲lunch & dinner) The old city, along Mae Nam Chanthaburi, is where you'll find most sightseeing Thais eating this Chanthaburi variation of the basic rice-noodle theme; nearby are other homemade snacks.

Sony Yadaw INDIAN $

(Th Si Chan; dishes 30-100B; ⏲breakfast, lunch & dinner; 🅥) Many South Asian gem dealers stop into this hole-in-the-wall vegetarian restaurant for a home-away-from-home meal.

Chanthorn Phochana THAI-CHINESE $

(☎0 3931 2339; 102/5-8 Th Benchamarachutit; dishes 30-120B; ⏲breakfast, lunch & dinner) A dazzling array of Thai-Chinese meals includes such specialities as stir-fried papaya and local mangosteen wine. Try the Vietnamese spring rolls, and buy a bag of local durian chips (tastier than you think) for your next bus ride. It is totally packed on weekends.

Muslim Restaurant MUSLIM THAI $

(☎08 1353 5174; cnr Soi 4, Th Si Chan; dishes 25-50B; ⏲9.30am-9pm) This tiny place has excellent paratha, *biryani*, curries and chai tea.

Coffee Room CAFE $

(Th Tha Chalaep; drinks from 50B; ⏲breakfast & lunch) Across from King Taksin Park, this urban-style coffee shop is where upscale traders and visitors from Bangkok come to feel a little less provincial.

ℹ Information

Banks with change facilities and ATMs can be found across town.

Bank of Ayudhya (Th Khwang)

Chanthaburi Bangkok Hospital (☎0 3935 1467; Th Tha Luang; ⏲6am-9pm) Part of the Bangkok group; handles emergencies.

ℹ Getting There & Around

Buses operate from Chanthaburi's bus station to the following destinations:

Bangkok's Eastern (Ekamai) station (187B, 3½ hours, hourly 6am to 11.30pm)

Bangkok's Northern (Mo Chit) station (187B, four hours, two daily departures)

Trat (70B, 1½ hours, every 1½ hours 6.30am to 11.30pm)

Khorat (266B, hourly 6am to 6pm) Gateway to the northeast.

Sa Kaew (106B to 137B, hourly 6am to 10pm) Transfer point for buses to Aranya Prathet border crossing.

Minivans leave from a stop near the market and go to Trat (80B) and Rayong (100B). For Ko Samet–bound travellers, take the minivan directly to Ban Phe (120B).

Motorbike taxis around town cost 20B to 30B.

Trat ตราด

POP 21,590

A major mainland transit point for Ko Chang and coastal Cambodia, Trat is under-appreciated for its provincial charms. The guest-house neighbourhood occupies an atmospheric wooden shophouse district bisected by winding sois and filled with typical Thai street life: kids riding bikes, housewives running errands, small businesses selling trinkets and necessities. Since your destination is still so far away, why not stay a little longer and enjoy all the things you can't get on the islands: fresh, affordable fruit; tasty noodles; and tonnes of people-watching.

NATIONAL PARKS NEAR CHANTHABURI

Two small national parks are easily reached from Chanthaburi, and make good day trips. Both are malarial, so take the usual precautions.

Khao Khitchakut National Park (อุทยานแห่งชาติเขาคิชฌกูฏ; ☎0 3945 2074; admission 200B; ⏲8.30am-4.30pm) is 28km northeast of town. The cascade of **Nam Tok Krathing** is the main attraction; though it is only worth a visit just after the rainy season.

To get to Khao Khitchakut, take a *sŏrng·tăa·ou* from next to the post office, near the northern side of the market in Chanthaburi (35B, 45 minutes). The *sŏrng·tăa·ou* stops 1km from the park headquarters on Rte 3249, from which point you'll have to walk. Returning transport is a bit thin so expect to wait or hitch.

Nam Tok Phlio National Park (อุทยานแห่งชาติน้ำตกพลิ้ว; ☎0 3943 4528; admission 200B; ⏲8.30am-4.30pm), off Hwy 3, is 14km to the southeast of Chanthaburi and is much more popular. A pleasant, 1km nature trail loops around the waterfalls, which writhe with soro brook carp. To get to the park, catch a *sŏrng·tăa·ou* from the northern side of the market in Chanthaburi to the park entrance (40B, 30 minutes). You'll get dropped off about 1km from the entrance.

Accommodation is available at both parks; book with the **park reservation system** (☎0 2562 0760; www.dnp.go.th).

Sights

Trat's signature product is a **medicinal herbal oil** (known in Thai as *nám·man lĕu·ang*), touted as a remedy for everything from arthritis to bug bites and available at local pharmacies. It's produced by resident Mae Ang-Ki (Somthawin Pasananon), using a secret pharmaceutical recipe that has been handed down through her Chinese-Thai family for generations. It's said if you leave Trat without a couple of bottles of *nám·man lĕu·ang,* then you really haven't been to Trat.

Another booming business in the city is **swiftlet farming**. Walk down Th Lak Meuang and you'll soon figure out that the top floors of a shophouse have been purposefully converted into a nesting site for a flock of birds who produce the edible nests considered a delicacy among Chinese populations. Swiflets' nests were quite rare (and expensive) because they were only harvested from precipitous sea caves by trained, daring climbers. But in the 1990s, entrepreneurs figured out how to replicate the cave atmosphere in multi-storey shophouses and the business has been a turn-key operation throughout Southeast Asia and here in Trat. Now many municipalities are dealing with the noise pollution of these moneymakers; have a listen for yourself.

Trat Province

Indoor Market MARKET

The indoor market sprawls east from Th Sukhumvit to Th Tat Mai and has a little bit of everything, especially all the things that you forgot to pack. Without really noticing the difference you will stumble upon the **day market**, selling fresh fruit, vegetables and takeaway food.

Sleeping

Trat has many budget hotels housed in traditional wooden houses on and around Th Thana Charoen. You'll find it hard to spend more even if you want to.

TOP CHOICE Ban Jaidee Guest House GUEST HOUSE $

(0 3952 0678; 6 Th Chaimongkol; r 200B; wi-fi) In a charming neighbourhood, this relaxed traditional wooden house has simple rooms with shared bathrooms (hot-water showers). Paintings and objets d'art made by the artistically inclined owners decorate the common spaces. It's very popular and booking ahead is essential.

Residang Guest House GUEST HOUSE $

(0 3953 0103; www.trat-guesthouse.com; 87/1-2 Th Thana Charoen; r 260-600B; air-con, wi-fi) Thick mattresses, hot-water showers, wi-fi – what more do you need? Fan rooms come with breezes and balconies. The owners keep an extensive list of transport information.

Garden Guest House GUEST HOUSE $

(0 3952 1018; 87/1 Th Sukhumvit; r 120-200B) A lovely grandmotherly type runs this guest house festooned with flowers and the flotsam of Thai life. Of the eight rooms, only one has a private bathroom.

Rimklong HOTEL $$

(08 1861 7181; 194 Th Lak Meuang; r 800B; air-con) Trat's first boutique hotel was under construction when we visited; but everything looked promising for the espresso-sipping crowd.

Sawadee GUEST HOUSE $

(0 3951 2392; sawadee_trat@yahoo.com; 90 Th Lak Meuang; r 100-300B) In a converted shophouse, this simple family-run place has fan rooms with shared bathroom.

Pop Guest House GUEST HOUSE $

(0 3951 2392; 1/1 Th Thana Charoen; r 150-500B; air-con, internet) You'll probably end up at Pop without intending to since the owners are generous with their taxi commissions and aggressive

in procuring guests. The rooms are clean and cheap, but if you're an idealistic consumer, promote competition.

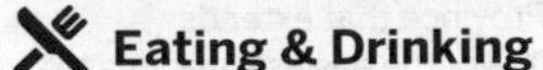

Eating & Drinking

Trat is all about market eating: head to the day market on Th Tat Mai for *gah·faa boh-rahn* (ancient coffee), the indoor market for lunchtime noodles and the night market for a stir-fried dinner.

TOP CHOICE **Cool Corner** CAFE $

(☎08 4159 2030; 49-51 Th Thana Charoen; dishes 50-150B; ⏲breakfast, lunch & dinner) Run by Khun Morn, a modern Renaissance woman (writer, artist and traveller) from Bangkok, Cool Corner is an anchor of Trat's creative expats (both domestic and international) who moved to the city because of its small size, proximity to Bangkok and easygoing way of life. The cafe has a degree of sophistication that you don't usually find in provincial towns and serves up a great vibe, *phat* (cool) beats and darn good mango lassies.

Kluarimklong Cafe THAI $

(☎0 3952 4919; cnr Soi Rimklong & Th Thana Charoen; dishes 70-90B; ⏲lunch & dinner) The winning combination here is delicious Thai food served in modern air-conditioned surroundings. The dishes are surprisingly affordable given the slick decor.

Oscar Bar BAR

(Th Thana Charoen) Trat's artist and expat business owners can be found at this corner bar welcoming the end of the work day.

Shopping

Tratosphere Books BOOKSHOP

(23 Soi Rimklong; ⏲8am-10pm) A good place to browse for secondhand titles and Thai handicrafts. Owner Serge is a fan and promoter of Trat and can point you to some unexplored corners.

Information

Th Sukhumvit runs through town, though it's often referred to as Th Ratanuson.

Bangkok Trat Hospital (☎0 3953 2735; Th Sukhumvit; ⏲24hr) Best health care in the region. It's 400m north of the town centre.

Krung Thai Bank (Th Sukhumvit) Has an ATM and currency-exchange facilities.

Police station (☎1155; cnr Th Santisuk & Th Wiwatthana) A short walk from Trat's centre.

Post office (Th Tha Reua Jang) East of Trat's commercial centre.

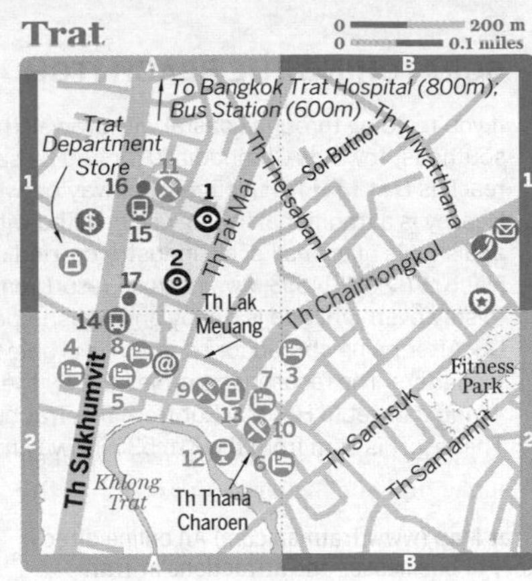

Trat

Sights

1	Day Market	A1
2	Indoor Market	A1

Sleeping

3	Ban Jaidee Guest House	B2
4	Garden Guest House	A2
5	Pop Guest House	A2
6	Residang Guest House	A2
7	Rimklong	A2
8	Sawadee	A2

Eating

9	Cool Corner	A2
	Day Market	(see 1)
10	Kluarimklong Cafe	A2
11	Night Market	A1

Drinking

12	Oscar Bar	A2

Shopping

13	Tratosphere Books	A2

Transport

14	Family Tour (Minivans to Bangkok)	A2
15	Minivans to Chanthaburi	A1
16	Sŏrng·tăa·ou to bus station, Laem Ngop	A1
17	Sŏrng·tăa·ou to Tha Centrepoint (Laem Ngop)	A1

Sawadee@Cafe Net (☎0 3952 0075; Th Lak Meuang; per min 1B; ⏲10am-10pm) Internet and Skype are both available.

Telephone office (Th Tha Reua Jang) Near the post office.

WORTH A TRIP

SCRATCHING THE BEACH ITCH

If you're going through coastal withdrawal, the sliver of Trat Province that extends southeast towards Cambodia is fringed by sandy beaches. One of the easiest beaches to reach is **Hat Mai Rut**, roughly halfway between Trat and the border crossing of Hat Lek. Nearby is a traditional fishing village filled with colourful wooden boats and the sights and smells of a small-scale industry carried on by generations of families. **Mairood Resort** (08 414858; www.mairood-resort.com; Km 53; r 500-1000B;) is a lovely spot to stay overnight and is run by an English-speaking Thai who lived for many years in the US. After being abroad for so long, he is able to explain the unique aspects of this area to foreigners. The resort has simple huts by the sea and in the mangroves.

You can get to Hat Mai Rut from the Trat bus station via Hat Lek–bound *sŏrng·tăa·ou*. The resort is 3km from the Km 53 highway marker.

Trat Map (www.Tratmap.com) An online directory of businesses and attractions in Trat.

Getting There & Around

Air

The airport is 40km from town; a taxi to the airport from Trat town costs a ridiculous 500B.

Bangkok Airways (Trat airport 0 3955 1654-5, in Bangkok 0 2265 5555; www.bangkokair.com) flies to the following destinations:

Bangkok (one way from 2090B, three times daily)

Ko Samui (one way from 3390B, three times weekly) Via Bangkok.

Phuket (one way from 4090B, three times weekly) Via Bangkok.

Bus & Minivans

Trat's bus station is outside of town and serves the following destinations:

Bangkok's Eastern (Ekamai) station (248B, 4½ hours, hourly 6am to 11.30pm)

Bangkok's Northern (Mo Chit) station (248B, 5½ hours, two morning departures)

Bangkok's Suvarnabhumi (airport) station (248B, four to 4½ hours, five daily departures)

Chanthaburi (70B, 1½ hours, every 1½ hours 6.30am to 11.30pm)

Hat Lek (120B to 150B, one hour) Minivans depart when full; morning departures are more frequent.

There are also many in-town options. Minivans to Chanthaburi (80B) leave when full from a stop on Th Sukhumvit north of the indoor market.

Family Tour (08 1996 2216; Th Sukhumvit cnr Th Lak Meuang) runs minivans to Bangkok's Victory Monument (300B, five hours, hourly 8am to 5pm) and continues on to Th Khao San (350B).

Local *sŏrng·tăa·ou* leave from Th Sukhumvit near the market for the bus station (20B to 60B, depending on number of passengers).

Boat

The piers that handle boat traffic to/from Ko Chang are located in Laem Ngop, about 30km southwest of Trat.

There are three piers in Laem Ngop each used by different boat companies, but the most convenient services are through Koh Chang Ferry (from Tha Thammachat) and Centrepoint Ferry (from Tha Centrepoint). See p133 for price and departure details on these ferry services.

From Trat town, shared *sŏrng·tăa·ou* leave from a stop on Th Sukhumvit to Laem Ngop's Tha Centrepoint (50B per person for six passengers, 45 minutes). To reach Tha Thammachat, inquire about pier transfers when you buy your ticket or charter a *sŏrng·tăa·ou* (60B per person for six people or 300B for the vehicle). It should be the same charter price if you want to go directly from Trat's bus station to the pier.

From Bangkok, you can catch a bus from Bangkok's Eastern (Ekamai) station all the way to Tha Centrepoint (250B, five hours, three morning departures). This route includes a stop at Suvarnabhumi (airport) bus station as well as Trat's bus station. In the reverse direction, buses have two afternoon departures from Laem Ngop.

If you want to skip Ko Chang and head straight to the neighbouring islands (Ko Wai, Ko Mak and Ko Kut), see those sections for mainland transport options.

Ko Chang

เกาะช้าง

POP 7033

With steep, jungle-covered peaks erupting from the sea, picturesque Ko Chang (Elephant Island) retains its remote and rugged spirit despite its current status as a package-tour resort akin to Phuket. The island's swathes of sand are girl-next-door pretty but not beauty-queen gorgeous. What it lacks in sand, it makes up for in an unlikely combination: accessible wilderness with a thriving party scene. Convenient forays into a verdant jungle or underwater coral gardens can be enthusiastically toasted at one of Lonely Beach's many beer and bucket parties.

A little more than a decade ago, Ko Chang didn't have 24-hour electricity, was still considered malarial, had few paved roads and fewer motorised vehicles. Today it is still a slog to get here, but there is a constant migration of visitors: Russian package tourists, Cambodia-bound backpackers and beach-hopping couples funnelling through to more remote islands in the Mu Ko Chang National Marine Park. Along the populous west coast are virtual mini-cities with a standard of living that has noticeably outpaced the island's infrastructure, a common problem on many Thai islands: Ko Chang struggles to provide decent sanitation and alternative means of transport to an ever-expanding nonresident population.

Sights

Though Thailand's second-largest island has accelerated into modernity with some understandable growing pains, Ko Chang still has tropically hued seas, critter-filled jungles and a variety of water sports for athletic beach bums.

WEST COAST

The west coast has the island's widest and sandiest beaches and the greatest amount of development. Frequent public *sŏrng·tăa·ou* make beach hopping easy and affordable. It is a good idea to bring swim shoes, especially for children, as many of the beaches are rocky in spots. These shallow, gentle seas are great for inexperienced swimmers, but do be careful of riptides during the storms and the rainy season (May to September).

Hat Sai Khao (White Sand Beach) BEACH

(หาดทรายขาว) The longest, most luxurious stole of sand on the island is packed with package-tour hotels and serious sunbathers. Finding a blanket's-worth of sand can be tough during the high season, unless you wait until the hot hours of the afternoon or hike past KC Grande Resort towards the remarkably low-key backpacker area in the far northern section of the beach. Along the main road, the village is busy, loud and brash – but the extremities provide a convenient break.

Hat Kai Mook (Pearl Beach) BEACH

(หาดไข่มุก) The pearls here are large pebbles that pack the shore and culminate in fish-friendly headlands. Swimming and sunbathing are out but there's good snorkelling. The stylish restaurant Saffron by the Sea is a scenic perch should you prefer to wet your palette instead.

Ao Khlong Prao BEACH

(อ่าวคลองพร้าว) A relaxed counterpoint to Hat Sai Khao's energy, Khlong Prao's beach is a pretty sweep of sand pinned between hulking mountainous headlands and bisected by two estuaries. At low tide, beachcombers stroll the rippled sand eyeing the critters left naked by the receding water. Sprawling luxury resorts dominate Khlong Prao and the primary pastime is sunbathing at seaside pools since high tide tends to gobble up most of the beach.

BORDER CROSSING: HAT LEK TO KRONG KOH KONG

For coastal border crossers, the closest Thai–Cambodian crossing is at the Thai town of Hat Lek into the Cambodian town of Krong Koh Kong. This crossing poises you for transit to Sihanoukville (via Krong Koh Kong) or Ko Chang (via Trat).

If you're leaving Thailand, catch a minivan from Trat's bus station to Hat Lek (120B to 150B) and continue on to Cambodian immigration.

Cambodian tourist visas are available at the border for 1200B (though other borders charge only US$20); payment is only accepted in baht at this border. If you try to debate the issue, be prepared for an argument. Be sure to bring a passport photo and try to avoid some of the runner boys who want to issue a health certificate or other 'medical' paperwork.

From the Cambodian border, take a private taxi (US$10) or moto (US$3) to Koh Kong where you can catch onward transport to Sihanoukville (four hours, one or two departures per day) and Phonm Penh (five hours, two or three departures till 11.30am). You can also use this border to renew your Thai visa, but do note that visas at land borders have been shortened to 15 days. This border crossing closes at 8pm.

Ko Chang

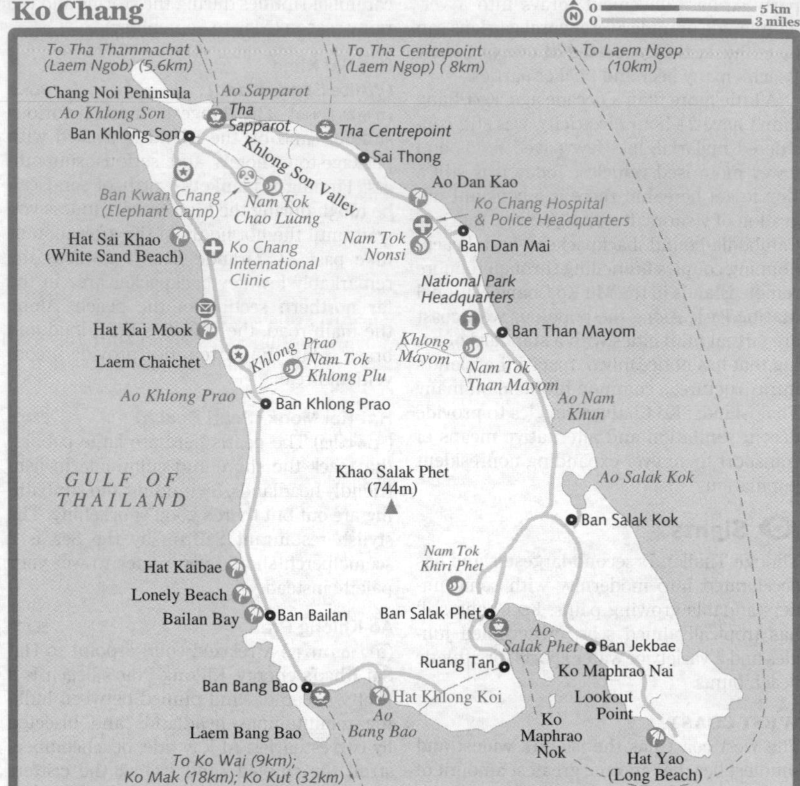

With hired transport, you can depart the beach for some waterfall-spotting. The island's biggest is **Nam Tok Khlong Plu** (park fee 200B; ⏲8am-5pm), a three-tiered cascade with a swimmable pool. It is reached via a 600m jungle path and is most stunning just after the rainy season months and in the morning before the crowds arrive.

Hat Kaibae BEACH

(หาดไก่แบ้) A companion beach to Khlong Prao, Hat Kaibae is a great spot for families and thirty-something couples. A slim strip of sand unfurls around an island-dotted bay far enough removed from the package tour scene that you'll feel self-righteously independent. There's kayaking to the outlying island and low tide provides hours of beachcombing.

Lonely Beach BEACH

The island's backpacker hang-out is the five-o'clock shadow of beaches, a bit scruffy but ready for fun. During the day, most sunbathers are baking off a hangover earned the night before when Lonely Beach becomes the most social place on the island. The music is loud, the drinks are strong and the crowd is youthful and carefree.

Ban Bang Bao VILLAGE

(บ้านบางเบ้า) Nearly at the end of the west coast road, Bang Bao is a former fishing community built in the traditional fashion of interconnected piers. The villagers have swapped their nets for the tourist trade by renting out portions of their homes to souvenir shops and restaurants. Though it isn't a traditional experience, the resulting commercialism is extremely Thai, much like a mainland market with every possible space dedicated to selling something. Follow the pier all the way to the end and you'll find a big blue ocean and boats waiting to take you past the horizon. Most visitors come for a seafood meal and some decide to stay overnight. Wrap up your visit before sunset as taxis become scarcer and more expensive after dark.

Khlong Kloi BEACH

At the eastern end of Ao Bang Bao, Khlong Kloi is a sandy beach that feels a lot like a secret though there are other people here and all the requisite amenities (beer, fruit, food, massage) and a few guest houses if you want the place to yourself. You'll need private transport to get out here.

NORTHERN INTERIOR

Ko Chang's mountainous interior is predominately protected as a national park. The forest is lush and alive with wildlife and threaded by silver-hued waterfalls. For information about hiking tours, see p126).

Ban Kwan Chang ELEPHANT CAMP

(บ้านควาญช้าง; ☎08 1919 3995; changtonc@yahoo.com; ⊙8.30am-5pm) In a beautiful forested setting, this camp offers a quiet and intimate experience with its nine resident elephants. A one-hour visit (900B) involves feeding, bathing and riding an elephant and hotel transfer is included. Be sure to wear mozzie spray.

Pittaya Homkrailas is the camp owner and a well-regarded conservation enthusiast who works to preserve a humane relationship between the elephant and mahout. His interest in environmental and community issues also includes efforts to preserve the southeastern mangroves in Ao Salak Kok on the island's east coast.

EAST COAST

The east coast is still peaceful and undeveloped, mainly undulating hills of coconut and palm trees and low-key fishing villages that have resisted the resort rush of the west coast. You'll need private transport to explore this lost coast of scenic bays and mangrove forests.

Nam Tok Than Mayom WATERFALL

(น้ำตกธารมะยม; park fee 200B; ⊙8am-5pm) A series of three falls along the stream of Khlong Mayom can be reached via the park office near Tha Than Mayom. The view from the top is superb and nearby there are inscribed stones bearing the initials of Rama V, Rama VI and Rama VII.

Ao Salak Kok MANGROVE BAY

(อ่าวสลักคอก) From a hotel developers' perspective, this thick tangle of mangroves is an unprofitable wasteland. But the local population of fisherfolk recognises that its beauty and profit is in its environmental fertility. Mangroves are the ocean's nurseries, fostering the next generation of marine species as well as resident birds and crustaceans.

Thanks to its natural state, the bay is now Ko Chang's leading example of ecotourism. Villagers, working in conjunction with Khun Pittaya, of Ban Kwan Chang elephant park, operate an award-winning program to preserve the environment and the traditional way of life. They rent kayaks through the Salak Kok Kayak Station and run an affiliated restaurant.

Ban Salak Phet VILLAGE

(บ้านสลักเพชร) In the southeast pocket of the island is Ban Salak Phet, a surprisingly bustling Thai community of fisherfolk and merchants plus lots of bike-riding kids and yawning dogs. This is what most of Ko Chang looked like less than a generation ago. Just beyond the commercial heart of the village is **Ao Salak Phet**, a beautiful blue bay serenely guarded by humpbacked islands. Most visitors come for the seafood

ECO VS FUN: DON'T FEED THE ANIMALS

On many of the around-the-island boat tours, operators amaze their guests with a stop at a rocky cliff to feed the wild monkeys. It seems innocent enough and even entertaining but there's an unfortunate consequence. The animals become dependent on this food source and when the boats don't come as often during the low season the young and vulnerable ones are ill-equipped to forage in the forest.

The same goes for the dive or boat trips that feed the fish leftover lunches or bread bought on the pier specifically for this purpose. It is a fantastic way to show young children a school of brilliantly coloured fish but the downside is that the fish forsake the coral reefs for an easier meal. Without the fishes' daily grooming efforts the coral is soon overgrown with algae and will eventually suffocate. Sorry to ruin the fun.

KO CHANG IN...

Four Days

Lay on the beach, roll over to the other side and repeat. Do this until you get sunburned or bored and then rouse yourself out of the sun-induced stupor to explore the island. Do a **day hike** through the jungle or view the island from aboard a **kayak**. Catch a *sŏrng·tăa·ou* to **Bang Bao** for lunch or an early dinner and work off your meal with some souvenir shopping. The next day rent a motorbike and explore the **east coast**.

One Week

Devote a few days to giving back to the island by volunteering at **Koh Chang Animal Project** or **Koh Chang Pony Rehabilitation Project**. Migrate to the nearby islands of **Ko Wai** or **Ko Kut** for a little island sightseeing.

restaurants or to cruise the lonely byways for a secluded beach.

Nam Tok Khiri Phet WATERFALL
(น้ำตกคีรีเพชร) This small waterfall, 2km from Ban Salak Phet, is a 15-minute walk from the road and rewards you with a small, deep plunge pool. It's usually quieter than many of the larger falls and is easily reached if you're in the neighbourhood of Ao Salak Phet.

Activities

Kayaking

Ko Chang cuts an impressive and heroic profile when viewed from the sea aboard a kayak. The water is generally calm and offshore islands provide a paddling destination that is closer than the horizon. Most hotels rent open-top kayaks (from 300B per day) that are convenient for near-shore outings and noncommittal kayakers.

KayakChang KAYAKING
(☎08 7673 1923; www.kayakchang.com; Amari Emerald Cove Resort, Khlong Prao) For more serious paddlers, KayakChang rents high-end, closed-top kayaks (from 1000B per day) that handle better and travel faster. They also lead one- and multi-day trips to other islands in the archipelago.

Salak Kok Kayak Station KAYAKING
(☎08 1919 3995; kayak rentals per hr 100B) On the east side of the island, explore the island's mangrove swamps of Ao Salak Kok while supporting an award-winning ecotour program. Salak Kok Kayak Station rents self-guided kayaks and is a village-work project designed to promote tourism without deteriorating the traditional way of life. The kayak station can also help arrange village homestays and hiking tours.

Hiking

Ko Chang is unusual in Thailand for having a well-developed trekking scene. The island is blessed with lush forests filled with birds, monkeys, lizards and beautiful flowers. Best of all there are a handful of guides who speak English that know and love the forest so that it can be shared with tourists.

Mr Tan from **Evolution Tour** (☎0 3955 7078; www.evolutiontour.com) or Lek from **Jungle Way** (☎08 9247 3161; www.jungleway.com) lead one-day treks (800B to 1400B) through Khlong Son Valley. The trip works up a sweat and then rewards the work with a waterfall swim and a stop at the Ban Kwan Chang elephant camp. Multi-day trips can be arranged through both. Mr Tan also has family-friendly treks and a hike that heads west from Khlong Son to Hat Sai Khao.

Koh Chang Trekking HIKING, BIRD-WATCHING
(☎08 1588 3324; www.kohchangtrekking.info) Bird-watchers should contact Koh Chang Trekking which runs one- and two-day trips (1000B to 2000B) into the national park and hikes to the top of Khao Chom Prasat, two nearby rocky tipped peaks.

Salak Phet Kayak Station HIKING
(☎08 7834 9489; from 1500B) Guides overnight treks on Khao Salak Phet, Ko Chang's highest peak, which rises 744km into the heavens and provides a sunrise and sunset view. Though the altitude might be modest, this is one of the few places in Thailand where you can combine such serious exertion with a coastal landscape; you can choose to sleep in a tent or under the stars.

Volunteering

Koh Chang Animal Project VOLUNTEERING
(☎08 9042 2347; www.kohchanganimalproject.org; Ban Khlong Son) Abused, injured or abandoned animals receive medical care and refuge at this nonprofit centre, established in 2002 by American Lisa McAlonie. The centre also works with local people on spaying, neutering and general veterinarian services, and Lisa is well-known on the island by concerned pet owners and flea-ridden dogs. Volunteers, especially travelling vets and vet nurses, are welcome to donate a bit of TLC and elbow grease for the cause. Call to make an appointment. Most *sŏrng·tăa·ou* drivers know how to get here; tell them you're going to 'Ban Lisa' (Lisa's House) in Khlong Son.

Koh Chang Pony Rehabilitation Project VOLUNTEERING
(☎08 9723 4278; ponyproject.org; Ban Khlong Son) On the same street as Ban Lisa, this centre works to rescue and rehabilitate abused and neglected equines. Volunteers can help feed, clean and exercise the ponies and horses that are recovering from injuries or awaiting adoption in caring environments.

Courses

Break up your lazy days with classes designed to enhance mind and body. Khlong Prao hosts two well-regarded culinary schools. Cooking classes at both are typically four to five hours, include a market tour and cost 1200B per person; book ahead.

Koh Chang Thai Cookery School COOKING
(☎0 3955 7243; Blue Lagoon Bungalows, Khlong Prao) Slices, dices and sautés in a shady open-air kitchen beside the estuary.

KaTi COOKING
(☎0 3955 7252; main road, Khlong Prao) Across from Tropicana Resort, is run by a mother and daughter team teaching family recipes.

Baan Zen YOGA, MEDITATION
(☎08 6530 9354; www.baanzen.com; Khlong Prao; classes from 5500B) Hidden down an unpaved road between Noren Resort and Coco Massage in Khlong Prao. It is a peaceful and relaxing setting for classes in yoga, reiki and meditation.

Sima Massage MASSAGE
(☎08 1489 5171; main road, Khlong Prao; massage per hr 250B; ⏲8am-10pm) Across from Tropicana Resort, and regarded by locals as the best massage on the island – quite an accolade in a place where a massage is easier to find than a 7-Eleven.

Bailan Herbal Sauna SAUNA
(☎08 6252 4744; Ban Bailan, across from Bailan Inn; ⏲4-9pm) Sweating on purpose might seem like a free and unintended consequence of tropical living but, just south of Lonely Beach, Bailan continues an old-fashioned Southeast Asian tradition of the village sauna. Set amid lush greenery, the earthen huts are heated with a health-promoting stew of herbs. There's also massage, facial treatments and a post-steam juice bar.

Sleeping

Ko Chang's package-tour industry has distorted accommodation pricing. In general rates have risen while quality has not, partly because hotels catering to group tours are guaranteed occupancy and don't have to maintain standards to woo repeat visitors or walk-ins. There is also a lot of copy-cat pricing giving value-oriented visitors little to choose from.

A few places close down during the wet season (April to October) and rates drop precipitously. Consider booking ahead and shopping for online discounts during peak season (November to March), weekends and holidays.

WEST COAST

On the west coast, Lonely Beach is still the best budget option, Hat Kai Bae is the

NATIONAL PARK STATUS

Parts of Ko Chang are protected and maintained as a national park. Though their conservation efforts are a bit amorphic, you will be required to pay a 200B park entrance fee when visiting some of the waterfalls (entrance fees are stated in the reviews and payable at the site). **National Park headquarters** (☎0 3955 5080; Ban Than Mayom; ⏲8am-5pm) is on the eastern side of the island near Nam Tok Than Mayom.

Do also be aware that nudity and topless sunbathing are forbidden by law in Mu Ko Chang National Marine Park; this includes all beaches on Ko Chang, Ko Kut, Ko Mak etc.

DON'T MISS

DIVING & SNORKELLING

The dive sites near Ko Chang offer a variety of coral, fish and beginner-friendly shallow waters on par with other Gulf of Thailand dive sites.

The seamounts off the southern tip of the island within the Ko Chang marine park are reached within a 30-minute cruise. Popular spots include **Hin Luk Bat** and **Hin Rap**, rocky, coral-encrusted seamounts with depths of around 18m to 20m. These are havens for schooling fish and some turtles.

By far the most pristine diving in the area is around **Ko Rang**, an uninhabited island protected from fishing by its marine park status. Visibility here is much better than near Ko Chang and averages between 10m and 20m. Everyone's favourite dive is **Hin Gadeng**, spectacular rock pinnacles with coral visible to around 28m. On the eastern side of Ko Rang, **Hin Kuak Maa** (also known as Three Finger Reef) is another top dive and is home to a coral-encrusted wall sloping from 2m to 14m and attracting swarms of marine life.

Ko Yak, **Ko Tong Lang** and **Ko Laun** are shallow dives perfect for both beginners and advanced divers. These small rocky islands can be circumnavigated and have lots of coral, schooling fish, puffer fish, morays, barracuda, rays and the occasional turtle.

Reef-fringed **Ko Wai** features a good variety of colourful hard and soft corals and is great for snorkelling. It is a popular day-tripping island but has simple overnight accommodation for more alone time with the reef.

Dive operators estimate that about 30% of the area's coral reefs were destroyed during the global bleaching phenomenon of 2010. In response park officials closed some areas of the Ko Rang marine park; ask the dive operators which sites are open.

Diving trips typically cost around 2800B to 3500B. PADI Open Water certification costs 14,500B per person. Recently dive shops remain open during the rainy season (June to September) but visibility and sea conditions can be poor. The following are recommend dive operators:

» **BB Divers**
(☎0 3955 8040; www.bbdivers.com) Based at Bang Bao with branches in Lonely Beach, Khlong Prao and Hat Sai Khao.

» **Scuba Zone**
(☎0 3961 9035; www.scuba-kohchang.com) Based at Hat Sai Khao; the instructors come highly recommended.

best-value option and Hat Sai Khao is the most overpriced.

HAT SAI KHAO

The island's prettiest beach is also its most expensive. The northern and southern extremities have some budget and midrange options worth considering if you need proximity to the finest sand. There's a groovy backpacker enclave north of KC Grande Resort accessible only via the beach. We've listed two here but there are more further north.

At the southern end, you can find some good value budget and midrangers but this end of the beach is rocky and lacking sand during high tide.

If you want to splash out, don't do it on Hat Sai Khao where good money will be wasted.

Independent Bo's GUEST HOUSE **$**
(☎08 5283 5581; r 350-550B) A colourful place on the jungle hillside exuding a creative, hippy vibe that Ko Chang used to be famous for. All bungalows are funky and different. The cheapest rooms are 'way, way' up in the jungle. First come, first served.

Rock Sand Beach Resort GUEST HOUSE **$$**
(☎08 4781 0550; www.rocksand-resort.com; r 550-2000B; ❄) Just past Bo's, Rock Sand takes budget accommodation up a notch. Simple fan bungalows share bathrooms, while the highest-priced air-con rooms look out over the sea. The restaurant is popular and hovers over the clear blue water.

Koh Chang Hut Hotel HOTEL **$$**
(☎08 1865 8123; r 600-1500B; ❄📶) Next to Plaloma Cliff Resort at the southern end of the beach, this cliff-side hotel puts you

within walking distance of the beach without spending a lot of baht. More expensive oceanfront rooms drink in the view, while cheaper streetside rooms are noisier.

Keereeelé HOTEL $$
(0 3955 1285; www.keereeele.com; r 2000B;) An excess of 'e's in the name doesn't detract from the merits of this new multistorey hotel on the interior side of the road. The rooms are modern and comfortable and some have views of the verdant mountains behind. Beach access is 300m via sidewalks so you don't have to play chicken with traffic.

Sai Khao Inn GUEST HOUSE $$
(0 3955 1584; www.saikhaoinn.com; r 800-1800B;) A garden setting on the interior side of the road, Sai Khao Inn has a little bit of everything – bungalows, concrete bunkers, big rooms, even rooms for taxi drivers (according to the brochure).

AO KHLONG PRAO

Ao Khlong Prao is dominated by high-end resorts and just a few budget spots peppered in between. There is a handful of cheapies on the main road that are within walking distance to the beach, though traffic can be treacherous and noisy.

Blue Lagoon Bungalows GUEST HOUSE $
(08 6330 0094; r 600-1000B;) An exceedingly friendly garden spot, Blue Lagoon has simple wooden bungalows with private decks beside a peaceful estuary. A wooden walkway leads to the beach.

Tiger Huts GUEST HOUSE $
(08 1762 3710; r 600B) The only thing that separates these wooden huts from labourer shanties is indoor plumbing. They are low on comfort and hospitality, but high on location claiming the widest and prettiest part of the beach. The neighbouring resorts must be very jealous.

Aana HOTEL $$$
(0 3955 1539; www.aanaresort.com; r from 7000B;) Private villas perch prettily above the forest and Khlong Prao, kayaking distance from the beach. The rooms are effortlessly romantic and have verandahs and views.

Lin Bungalows GUEST HOUSE $$
(08 4120 1483; r 800-1200B;) Opposite Blue Lagoon, a variety of sealed concrete bungalows facing the beach.

Baan Rim Nam GUEST HOUSE $$
(08 7005 8575; www.iamkohchang.com; r from 1100B;) Converted fisherman's-house-turned-guest house teeters over a mangrove-lined river; kayaks and dialled-in advice free of charge.

Sofia Resort GUEST HOUSE $$
(0 3955 7314; www.jussinhotel.net; r 900-1200B;) Great price for the comfort factor but the trade-off is the location on the main road without direct beach access.

Boonya Resort GUEST HOUSE $
(0 3955 7361; r from 800B;) Another main road option that would be a fab find if the beds weren't bare springs.

HAT KAIBAE

Hat Kaibae has some of the island's best variety of accommodation, from boutique hotels to budget huts and midrange bungalows. It is a great beach for families and flashpackers.

TOP CHOICE **KB Resort** HOTEL $$
(0 1862 8103; www.kbresort.com; r 2000-3500B;) Lemon yellow bungalows have cheery bathrooms and pose peacefully beside the sea. Listen to the gentle lapping surf while the kids construct mega-cities in the sand. Skip the overpriced fan bungalows, though.

Buzza's Bungalows GUEST HOUSE $
(08 7823 6674; r from 400B;) Solid concrete bungalows with porches face each other creating a laid-back travellers ambience. It is a short and hassle-free stroll to the beach.

Kaibae Hut Resort HOTEL $$
(0 3955 7142; r 700-2500B;) Sprawling across a scenic stretch of beach, Kaibae Hut has sane prices and a variety of lodging options – slightly worn fan huts, fancier concrete bungalows and modern hotel-style rooms. A large open-air restaurant fires up nightly barbecues and there's plenty of room for free-range kids.

Garden Resort HOTEL $$
(0 3955 7260; www.gardenresortkohchang.com; r from 2500B;) On the interior side of the main road, Garden Resort has picture-window bungalows blossoming in a shady garden with a salt-water swimming pool. The owners are friendly and kid-oriented, thanks to their own child.

GajaPuri Resort & Spa HOTEL $$$
(☎0 2713 7689; www.gajapuri.com; r from 6900B; ❄@≋) Polished wooden cottages gleam with quintessential Thai touches so that you have a sense of place and pampering. Oversized beds with crisp linens, sun-drenched reading decks and a pretty beach are even more luxurious if you score an online discount.

Porn's Bungalows GUEST HOUSE $
(☎08 9251 9233; www.pornsbungalows-kohchang.com; r 800-900B) Kaibae's resident rasta scene hangs out in a shady coconut grove beside the beach; wooden fan bungalows with hot-water showers. First come, first served.

Siam Cottage GUEST HOUSE $
(☎08 9153 6664; www.siamcottagekohchang.com; r 500-800B; ❄) Rickety wooden bungalows packed perpendicular to the beach don't afford much privacy but a nice slice of sand is right at your feet.

LONELY BEACH

A backpacker party fave, Lonely Beach is one of the cheapest places to sleep on the island, though oceanfront living has mostly moved upmarket, pushing the penny-pinchers into the interior village. If you've been flashpackerised, there are several creative midrangers that will save you from carbon-copy resorts. This end of the island is less developed and the jungle broods just over the squatty commercial strip.

TOP CHOICE **Paradise Cottages** HOTEL $$
(☎08 5831 4228; www.paradisecottagekohchang.com; r 700-1200B; ❄📶) A whole lot of chillin'-out happens at this mellow flashpacker spot. Dining hammocks hang over the water for guests to savour a meal with a view. The usual concrete huts are dressed up with style and function. Though it is oceanfront, the beach is too muddy and rocky for swimming.

Oasis Bungalows GUEST HOUSE $
(☎08 1721 2547; www.oasis-khochang.com; r from 350B; 📶) Sitting at the end of an interior soi, Oasis has basic wooden bungalows in a pretty fruit and flower garden. The hillside restaurant peeks at the ocean above the tree tops and is a pleasant place for traveller camaraderie. You'll have to walk through the village and down the main road to get to the beach. If Oasis is full, this soi is filled with comparable options.

Warapura Resort HOTEL $$
(☎08 3987 4777; www.warapuraresort.com; r 2000-3500B; ❄@≋) Chic for relatively cheap, Warapura has a collection of adorable cottages tucked in between the village and a mangrove beach. The oceanfront pool is perfect for people who would rather gaze at the ocean than frolic in it.

Kachapura GUEST HOUSE $
(☎08 60500754; www.kachapura.com; r 500-1800B; ❄📶) Warapura's modest sister, Kachapura does budget with care. Wooden walkways navigate a shady garden to clean and tidy bungalows that are basic but not busted up. It sits right in the middle of the village; no direct beach access.

Mangrove HOTEL $
(☎08 1949 7888; r 1000B) South of Lonely Beach is the real deal when it comes to an eco-lodge committed to a smaller footprint. Cascading down a forested hill to a private beach, Mangrove has beautiful yet simple bungalows purposefully designed with accordion-style doors that open to the views and the breezes (a natural air-con). The ambience is a pleasing combo of private rustic-chic.

BAN BANG BAO

Despite its touristy veneer, Ban Bang Bao is still a charming place to stay for folks who prefer scenery to swimming. Accommodation is mainly converted pier houses overlooking the sea with easy access to departing inter-island ferries. Daytime transport to a swimmable beach is regular thanks to the steady arrival and departure of day trippers. Night owls should either hire a motorbike or stay elsewhere as *sŏrng·tăa·ou* become rare and expensive after dinnertime.

TOP CHOICE **Bang Bao Sea Hut** HOTEL $$
(☎08 1285 0570; r 2500B; ❄) With individual bungalows built on the edge of Bang Bao's pier, this is one of Ko Chang's most unusual places to stay. Each 'hut' (actually much flasher than it sounds) is surrounded by a private deck where breakfast is served, with wooden shutters opening to the sea breeze.

Bang Bao Cliff Cottage GUEST HOUSE $
(☎08 5904 6706; www.cliff-cottage.com; r 350-700B) Partially hidden on a verdant hillside west of the pier are a few dozen simple thatch huts overlooking a rocky cove. Most have sea views and a couple offer spectacular vistas. There's easy-access snorkelling down below.

Ocean Blue GUEST HOUSE $

(☎08 1889 2348; www.oceanbluethailand.com; r 800B) Simple fan rooms line a long, polished-wood hallway at this traditional pier house. Toilets are the bucket variety, and showers are cold, but the rooms are clean and you can hear the ocean slosh beneath you. The crew running the place are quirky and funny.

Nirvana HOTEL $$$

(☎0 3955 8061; www.nirvanakohchang.com; r 3500-7000B;) Ko Chang's premium resort is its own private universe hidden away on a rocky, jungle-filled peninsula. Come to get away from it all, including everything else on the island, and to enjoy the stunning sea views from the comfort of the individually decorated Balinese-style bungalows. The adjacent beach is scenic but not swimmable.

NORTHERN INTERIOR & EAST COAST

The northern and eastern part of the island is less developed than the west coast and feels more isolated. You'll need your own transport and maybe even a posse not to feel lonely out here, but you'll be rewarded with a quieter, calmer experience.

Jungle Way GUEST HOUSE $

(☎08 9247 3161; www.jungleway.com; Khlong Son Valley; r 200-400B) Ko Chang's un-sung attribute is its jungle interior and the English-speaking guides who grew up playing in it. Lek, a local guide, and his family run this friendly guest house, deep in the woods and beside a babbling brook. Bungalows are simple but adequate and the on-site restaurant will keep you well fed. Free pier pick-up.

Amber Sands HOTEL $$

(☎0 3958 6177, www.ambersandsbeachresort.com; Ao Dan Kao; r 2000-2700B;) Sandwiched between mangroves and a quiet red sand beach, Amber Sands has eight comfortable bungalows with picture windows facing a high-definition sea view. South Africans Cheryl and Julian run the place with a professional and family touch. The location feels a world away but it is only 15 minutes from the pier.

The Souk GUEST HOUSE $

(☎08 1553 3194; Ao Dan Kao; r 700B;) Next door to Amber Sands, this funky spot has seven pop-art cool (fan only) bungalows at a pleasant price. There are lots of chill-out spaces and an urban vibe in the open-deck restaurant and cocktail bar. Young couples and long-stay visitors rave about this low-key find. Easy access to the ferry pier.

Salak Phet Homestay HOMESTAY $

(☎08 1294 1650; Ban Salak Phet; r incl meals 300B) Part of a village ecotour program, accommodation is provided in one of several pier homes in the fishing village of Salak Phet. Expect simple lodgings: a bedroll on the floor of a small room, and shared, basic bathrooms. You'll dine with the family and knowing some Thai is helpful. The **Salak Phet Kayak Station** (☎08 7834 9489) can help arrange the stay for you.

Treehouse Lodge GUEST HOUSE $

(☎08 1847 8215; Hat Yao; r 300B) The original Treehouse Lodge on Lonely Beach created the initial buzz about Ko Chang as a laid-back paradise. But civilisation arrived and the original owners defected to Ko Pha Ngan in 2009. Adopting the name and the ambience, the new Treehouse moved to remote Hat Yao (Long Beach), on the far southeastern peninsula. Basic huts (with basic bathrooms) chill along a hillside, looking down to a softly sanded slice of beach. The road to Hat Yao is well-sealed to the lookout point but poorly maintained past that, so plan on staying awhile. Inquire in Trat about a taxi service that goes all the way to Long Beach.

The Spa Koh Chang Resort HOTEL $$

(☎0 3955 3091; www.thespakohchang.com; Ao Salak Kok; r 1200-3000B;) In a lush garden setting embraced by the bay's mangrove forests, this spa resort specialises in all the popular health treatments (yoga, meditation, fasting etc) that burned-out professionals need. Elegantly decorated bungalows scramble up a flower-filled hillside providing a peaceful getaway for some quality 'me' time. No beach access.

Eating & Drinking

Virtually all of the island's accommodation has attached restaurants with adequate but not outstanding fare. Parties abound on the beaches and range from the older and surlier scene on Hat Sai Khao to the younger and sloppier on Lonely Beach.

WEST COAST

Oodie's Place INTERNATIONAL $$

(☎0 3955 1193; Hat Sai Khao; dishes 150-280B; lunch & dinner) Local musician Oodie runs a nicely diverse operation with excellent French food, tasty Thai specialities and live music from 10pm. After all these years, it is still beloved by expats.

Norng Bua THAI $$
(Hat Sai Khao; dishes 80-200B; ⏲breakfast, lunch & dinner) This popular stir-fry hut makes everything fast and fresh and with chillies and fish sauce (praise the culinary gods).

Invito Al Cibo ITALIAN $$$
(☎0 3955 1326; Koh Chang Hut, Hat Sai Khao; dishes 250-550B; ⏲lunch & dinner) Upscale Invito is no more but the executive chef has migrated to this start-up with a lovely sea view.

Saffron on the Sea THAI $$
(☎0 3955 1253; Hat Kai Mook; dishes 150-350B; ⏲breakfast, lunch & dinner) Owned by an arty escapee from Bangkok, this friendly boutique hotel has a generous portion of oceanfront dining and a relaxed, romantic atmosphere. All the Thai dishes are prepared in the island-style, more sweet than spicy.

KaTi Culinary THAI $
(☎08 1903 0408; Khlong Prao; dishes 80-150B; ⏲lunch & dinner) This popular Thai cooking school is equally popular for its attached restaurant. Apart from Thai dishes, on the menu are also creative smoothies, such as lychee, lemon and peppermint.

Iyara Seafood SEAFOOD $$
(☎0 3955 1353; Khlong Prao; dishes 150-300B; ⏲lunch & dinner) Iyara isn't your standard island seafood warehouse: after dining in the lovely bamboo pavilion, guests are invited to kayak along the nearby estuary.

Nid's Kitchen THAI $
(Hat Kaibae; dishes 30-80B; ⏲lunch & dinner) A sweaty little restaurant north of GajaPuri Resort, Auntie Nid's does all the Thai standards like a wok wizard. Plus the beers are cold.

Porn's Bungalows Restaurant THAI $
(Hat Kaibae; dishes 40-150B; ⏲lunch & dinner) This wooden tree-house restaurant affiliated with a Rasta-style guest house is the quintessential beachside lounge. Feel free to have your drinks outsize your meal and don't worry about dressing for dinner.

TOP CHOICE **Barrio Bonito** MEXICAN $$
(☎08 0092 8208; Lonely Beach; dishes 150-250B; ⏲breakfast, lunch & dinner) This breezy, hip place has all the island raving about its seriously good Mexican fare. A French-Mexican couple runs the place with flair and there's a plunge pool should the salsa induce sweating.

Magic Garden THAI $
(☎0 3955 8027; Lonely Beach; dishes 60-120B; ⏲dinner) Magic Garden is a pagoda to Lonely Beach's special variety of chill-laxin'. Grab some grub, polish off some Beer Changs, watch a movie and then wander down to the beach for some DJ beats.

Bailan Bay Resort Restaurant THAI $$
(Ao Bailan; dishes 150-250B; ⏲lunch & dinner) Our taxi driver recommended this hilltop restaurant south of Lonely Beach that serves spicy *sôm·đam* with a view.

Ruan Thai SEAFOOD $$
(Ban Bang Bao; dishes 100-300B; ⏲lunch & dinner) It's about as fresh as it gets (note your future dinner greeting you in tanks as you enter) and the portions are large. The doting service is beyond excellent – they'll even help you crack your crabs.

Buddha View Restaurant INTERNATIONAL $$
(☎0 3955 8157; Ban Bang Bao; dishes 250-350B; ⏲breakfast, lunch & dinner) Dangle your toes within teasing distance from the nibbling fish at the creative pier-side seating of this new addition to Bang Bao's restaurant scene. The view is nearly panoramic and the fare is mainly steak and pastas with Thai seafood as well.

NORTHERN INTERIOR & EAST COAST

Blues Blues Restaurant THAI $
(☎08 5839 3524; Ban Khlong Son; dishes 50-100B; ⏲lunch & dinner) Through the green screen of tropical plants is an arty stir-fry hut that is beloved for expertise, efficiency and economy. The owner's delicate watercolour paintings are on display too. The restaurant is about 600m from the turn-off to Ban Kwan Chang.

Jungle Way Restaurant THAI $
(☎08 9247 3161; Ban Khlong Son; dishes 60-70B; ⏲breakfast, lunch & dinner; 🖉) Enjoy the natural setting and home-style cooking of this guest house restaurant. Meal preparation takes a leisurely pace so climb up to the elevated wildlife-viewing platform to spot some jungle creatures while the wok is sizzling.

Paradise Behind the Sea Restaurant THAI $$
(☎08 1900 2388; Ban Hat Sai Daeng; dishes 110-280B; ⏲breakfast, lunch & dinner) If you're cruising the east coast for scenery, stop in for a

view and a meal at this cliffside restaurant. Vietnamese and Thai dishes crowd the tables and cool breezes provide refreshment. In Thai, this is called 'Lang Talay'.

Information

Dangers & Annoyances

It is not recommended to drive between Ban Khlong Son south to Hat Sai Khao as the road is steep and treacherous with several hairpin turns. There are mudslides and poor conditions during storms. If you do rent a motorbike, stick to the west coast beaches and take care when travelling between Hat Kaibae and Lonely Beach. Wear protective clothing when riding or driving a motorcycle to reduce injury if you do have an accident.

The police conduct regular drug raids on the island's accommodation. If you get caught with narcotics, you could face heavy fines or imprisonment.

Be aware of the cheap minibus tickets from Siem Reap to Ko Chang; these usually involve some sort of time- and money-wasting commission scam.

Ko Chang is considered a low-risk malarial zone, meaning that liberal use of mosquito repellent is probably an adequate precaution.

Emergency

Police station (0 3958 6191; Ban Dan Mai)

Tourist police office (1155) Based north of Ban Khlong Prao. Also has smaller police boxes in Hat Sai Khao and Hat Kaibae.

Internet Access

Internet access is easy to find all the way down the west coast and most guest houses have free wi-fi.

Medical Services

Bang Bao Health Centre (0 3955 8088; Ban Bang Bao; 8.30am-6pm) For the basics.

Ko Chang Hospital (0 3952 1657; Ban Dan Mai) Public hospital with a good reputation and affordably priced care; south of the ferry terminal.

Ko Chang International Clinic (0 3955 1151; Hat Sai Khao; 24hr) Related to the Bangkok Hospital Group; accepts most health insurances and has expensive rates.

Money

There are banks with ATMs and exchange facilities along all the west coast beaches.

Post

Ko Chang post office (0 3955 1240; Hat Sai Khao) At the far southern end of Hat Sai Khao.

Tourist Information

The free magazine *Koh Chang Guide* (www.whitesandsthailand.com) is widely available on the island and has handy beach maps.

The comprehensive website I Am Koh Chang (www.iamkohchang.com) is a labour of love from an irreverent Brit living on the island. His 'KC Essentials A-Z' section is jam-packed with opinion and information.

Getting There & Away

Whether originating from Bangkok or Cambodia, it is an all-day haul to reach Ko Chang.

TO/FROM MAINLAND: Ko Chang-bound boats depart from the mainland piers collectively referred to as Laem Ngop (see p122 for more information), southwest of Trat. You'll arrive in Ko Chang at either Tha Sapparot or Tha Centrepoint, depending on which pier and boat company you used on the mainland.

Tha Sapparot is the closest to the west coast beaches and receives vehicle ferries from the mainland pier of Tha Thammachat. **Koh Chang Ferry** (0 3955 5188) runs this service (one way 80B, 30 minutes, hourly 6.30am to 7pm).

At the time of writing, the car ferry associated with Tha Centrepoint was competing aggressively for business by offering cheaper prices, more commissions and a Bangkok–Laem Ngop bus service. You cut out some of the land transfers with the new bus service but Tha Centrepoint (on Ko Chang) is further from the west coast beaches, so the time-saving is negligible. **Centrepoint Ferry** (0 3953 8196) runs this service (one way/round-trip 80/100B, 45 minutes, hourly 6am to 7.30pm). Weekend service in high season runs until 9pm.

There is also a new bus route directly from Bangkok's Suvarnabhumi (airport) station to Ko Chang (308B, six hours) via the car ferry with stops on the mainland at Trat and Chanthaburi. The bus leaves Suvarnabhumi at 7.30am and departs Ko Chang at 1.30pm. On Ko Chang, the bus arrives and departs from Khlong Son. Another option is a minivan service from Bangkok's Victory Monument that goes all the way to Ko Chang's Tha Sapparot (one way 300B, four hours, hourly departures).

TO/FROM NEIGHBOURING ISLANDS: Tha Bang Bao in the southern part of the island is the pier used for boat trips to neighbouring islands. There is a daily inter-island ferry (known conflictingly as 'express' or 'slow' boat) operated by **Bang Bao Boats** (www.bangbaoboat.com) that does a loop to Ko Wai, Ko Mak, Ko Kut and back. Faster and more frequent speedboat departures do the same circuit. The slow boat is the smartest option when seas are rough and for ocean sightseeing as the speedboat ride is like a James Bond martini: shaken not stirred.

See the respective islands for getting there and away information.

Getting Around

Shared *sŏrng·tăa·ou* meet arriving boats to shuttle passengers to the various beaches (Hat Sai Khao 50B, Khlong Prao 60B and Lonely Beach 100B). Compared to other islands, *sŏrng·tăa·ou* drivers are almost invariably honest and reliable in their pricing, especially during the day when demand is high. Most hops between neighbouring west coast beaches should cost around 40B to 50B.

Businesses along the west coast charge 150B to 200B per day for motorbike hire. Ko Chang's hilly and winding roads are quite dangerous (see p227 for road safety considerations); make sure the bike is in good working order.

Ko Wai

เกาะหวาย

Stunning Ko Wai is teensy and primitive, but endowed with gin-clear waters, excellent coral reefs for snorkelling and a handsome view across to Ko Chang. Expect to share the bulk of your afternoons with day trippers but have the remainder of your time in peace.

Most bungalows close during the May-to-September low season when seas are rough and flooding is common.

Sleeping

Ko Wai Paradise GUEST HOUSE **$**
(r 300-500B) Simple wooden bungalows (some with shared bathroom) on a postcard-perfect beach. You'll share the coral out front with day trippers.

Good Feeling GUEST HOUSE **$**
(☎08 8503 3410; r 300-500B) Wooden huts (some with shared bathroom) spread out along a rocky headland interspersed with private sandy coves.

Grandma Hut GUEST HOUSE **$**
(☎08 1841 3011; r 250-500B) On the rocky northeastern tip of the island is this simple and remote place; speedboat operators know it by the nearby bay of Ao Yai Ma.

Ko Wai Pakarang GUEST HOUSE **$$**
(☎08 4113 8946; www.kohwaipakarang.com; r 600-2500B; ❄@) The closest Ko Wai comes to modernity with concrete air-con bungalows and lots of day trippers milling about.

Getting There & Around

Boats will drop you off at the nearest pier to your guest house; otherwise you'll have to walk 15 to 30 minutes along a narrow forest trail.

Bang Bao Boat (www.bangbaoboat.com) is the archipelago's inter-island ferry running a daily loop from Ko Chang to Ko Kut. Boats depart Ko Chang at 9am and arrive at Ko Wai (one way 300B, one hour) and continue on to Ko Mak (one way 300B, one hour) and Ko Kut (500B, three hours). You can return to Ko Chang at 1pm.

Several speedboat companies run from Ko Wai to the following destinations:

Ko Chang (one way 400B, 15 minutes, two daily departures)

Ko Mak (one way 350B, 30 minutes, two daily departures)

Ko Kut (one way 700B, one hour, two daily departures)

Laem Ngop (450B, two to three hours, one daily departure)

Ko Mak

เกาะหมาก

Little Ko Mak is only 16 sq km and doesn't have speeding traffic, wall-to-wall development, noisy beer bars or crowded beaches. The palm-fringed bays are bathed by gently lapping water and there's an overall relaxed island vibe. But Ko Mak is not destined for island super-stardom as the interior is a utilitarian landscape of coconut and rubber plantations and reports of sand flies make visitors a little nervous.

Visiting the island is easier in the high season; during the low season (May to September) many boats stop running and bungalow operations wind down. Storms also deposit uninvited litter on the exposed southern beaches.

Activities

Swimming and beach strolling are best on the northwestern bay of **Ao Suan Yai**, which is a wide arc of sand and looking-glass clear water; it is easily accessible by bicycle or motorbike if you stay elsewhere on the island. Offshore is **Ko Kham**, a private island that sold in 2008 for a reported 200 million baht. It used to be a popular day-trippers' beach but is currently under construction for its next incarnation as a super-luxury resort.

Koh Mak Divers (☎08 3297 7723; www.kohmakdivers.com; dive trips 2200-3000B) runs dive trips to the Mu Ko Chang National Marine Park, about 45 minutes away.

Sleeping & Eating

Most budget guest houses are located on Ao Khao, a decent strip of sand on the southwestern side of the island, while the resorts sprawl on the more scenic northwestern bay of Ao Suan Yai.

There is a handful of homey stir-fry shacks on the main road between Monkey Island and Makathanee Resort. And if you feel like a journey, use a meal or a sundowner as an excuse to explore different bays.

Monkey Island GUEST HOUSE **$$**
(☎08 9501 6030; www.monkeyislandkohmak.com; Ao Khao; r 350-3000B; ❄@) The troop leader of guest houses, Monkey Island has earthen or wooden bungalows in three creatively named models – Baboon, Chimpanzee and Gorilla – with various amenities (shared or private bathroom or private deck). All have fun design touches and the hip restaurant does respectable Thai cuisine in a leisurely fashion. In true Thai beach style, the affiliated bar rouses the dead with its nightly parties.

Baan Koh Mak GUEST HOUSE **$$**
(☎08 9895 7592; www.baan-koh-mak.com; Ao Khao; r from 1200B; ❄) Bright and funky, Baan Koh Mak provides a respectable flashpacker abode with colourful paint jobs and soft mattresses.

Island Huts GUEST HOUSE **$**
(☎08 7139 5537; Ao Khao; r 350-450B) Rickety shacks camp out on the beach with all the bare necessities: beach, bathroom and mattress.

Ao Kao Resort GUEST HOUSE **$$**
(☎08 3152 6564; www.aokaoresort.com; r 1200-2500; ❄) In a pretty crook of the bay, Ao Kao has an assortment of stylish and basic bungalows. Opt for a traditional Thai-style house complete with carved wood flourishes and handsome balconies. Families congregate here as there is front-yard swimming and the rocky headland harbours sea creatures.

Lazy Day Resort GUEST HOUSE **$$**
(☎08 1882 4002; www.kohmaklazyday.com; r 2250- 2700B; ❄) Next door to Ao Kao Resort this professionally run operation has picture-window bungalows posing in a grassy garden; rates include breakfast.

Koh Mak Resort HOTEL **$$**
(☎0 3950 1013; www.kohmakresort.com; Ao Suan Yai; r 1700-5400B; ❄≋) Though it isn't the island's best value, you can cut out your commute to the prettiest beach without much financial sacrifice.

SEARCHING FOR MR(S) RIGHT?

Still can't seem to find your island idyll? Give Ko Rayang a try. It is a private island with one tiny resort. **Rayang Island Resort** (☎0 3950 1000; www.rayang-island.com; r 2500-3800B) has 15 simple one- and two-bedroom bungalows (no air-con, no hot-water showers) with limited electricity and snorkelling outside your door. You can catch a speedboat shuttle (170B) from Ko Mak's Tha Makathanee and check it out if you're commitment shy.

Information

There are no banks or ATMs on the island, so stock up on cash before visiting. Speedboats arrive at Koh Mak Resort pier on Ao Suan Yai. The main cargo pier is at Ao Nid, on the eastern side of the island.

Ball's Cafe (☎08 1925 6591; Ao Nid Pier; ⏲9am-6pm) Has internet access, travel agent and coffee shop. Khun Ball is an active island promoter and runs www.kohmak.com as well as environmental initiatives.

Ko Mak Health Centre (☎08 9403 5986; ⏲8.30am-4.30pm) Can handle basic first-aid emergencies and illnesses. It's on the cross-island road near Ao Nid Pier.

Police (☎0 3952 5741) Near the health centre.

Getting There & Around

There are different piers used by different companies on the island but you don't have to worry about sorting it out; pier transfers are usually handled by guest houses and hotels free-of-charge.

A slow ferry leaves Ko Mak for Laem Ngop (mainland pier; one way 200B, three hours, one morning departure on certain days); on alternate days it departs from the mainland. Check with an agent about departure days and times, which are subject to change.

Ao Thai Marine Express (☎08 1863 3525; www.kohkoodspeedboat.com) runs speedboats from the mainland pier of Tha Dan Kao, 5km east of Trat, to Ko Mak (450B). Departure times are dependent upon demand.

Bang Bao Boat (www.bangbaoboat.com) is the archipelago's inter-island ferry running a daily loop from Ko Chang to Ko Kut. Boats depart Ko Chang at 9am and arrive at Ko Mak (one way

400B, 1½ to two hours) and continue on to Ko Kut (one way 300B, one to two hours, departs 1pm). In the opposite direction, you can catch it to Ko Wai (one way 300B, 45 minutes) and Ko Chang (400B, 2½ hours).

Several speedboat companies run from Ko Mak to the following destinations:

Ko Chang (one way 550B, 45 minutes, three daily departures)

Ko Kut (one way 400B, 45 minutes, two daily departures)

Laem Ngop (mainland pier; one way 450B, one hour, four daily departures)

Ko Wai (one way 350B, 30 minutes, two daily departures)

Once on the island, you can pedal (40B per hour) or motorbike (200B per day) your way around.

Ko Kut

เกาะกูด

All the paradise descriptions apply to Ko Kut: the beaches are graceful arcs of sand, the water is gin clear, coconut palms outnumber buildings, and a secluded, unhurried atmosphere embraces you upon arrival. There's nothing in the form of nightlife or even dining, really, but those are the reasons for visiting.

Half as big as Ko Chang and the fourth-largest island in Thailand, Ko Kut has long been the domain of package-tour resorts and a seclusion-seeking elite. The most recent news on the island was that the Beckhams had bought a vacation home here. Even more noteworthy is Six Senses' new Soneva Kiri resort, which is accessible by private plane and has base rates starting at US$2000 per night. But the island is becoming more egalitarian and independent travellers, especially families and couples, will find home sweet home here.

Sights & Activities

Beaches BEACHES

Blonde beaches with gorgeous aquamarine water are along the western side of the island. **Hat Khlong Chao** is one of the island's best and could easily compete with Samui's Hat Chaweng in a beach beauty contest; the clear water is shallow and bathtub smooth. **Ao Noi** is a pretty boulder-strewn beach with a steep drop-off and steady waves for strong swimmers. **Ao Prao** is another lovely sweep of sand. There is no public transport on Ko Kut but you can rent motorbikes for exploring the west coast beaches as traffic is minimal and the road is paved from Khlong Hin in the southwest to Ao Noi in the northeast.

With its quiet rocky coves and mangrove estuaries, Ko Kut is great for **snorkelling** and **kayaking**. Most resorts have equipment on offer.

Nam Tok Khlong Chao WATERFALL

Two waterfalls on the island make good short hiking destinations. The larger and more popular Nam Tok Khlong Chao is wide and pretty with a massive plunge pool. Expect to share it with dozens of other visitors, especially on weekends. It's a quick jungle walk to the base, or you can kayak up Khlong Chao. Further north is **Nam Tok Khlong Yai Ki**, which is smaller but also has a large pool to cool off in.

Sleeping

During low season (May to September) many boats stop running and bungalow operations wind down. On weekends and holidays during the high season, vacationing Thais fill the resorts. Call ahead during busy periods so you can be dropped off at the appropriate pier by the speedboat operators.

You can scrimp your way into the neighbourhood of beautiful Hat Khlong Chao by staying at one of the village guest houses, which are a five- to 15-minute walk to the beach. Families might like the midrange and budget options on Ao Ngam Kho, which has a small sandy section in the far northern corner of the bay, though the rest is an old coral reef and very rocky. Bring swim shoes.

Ao Bang Bao is another popular spot for independent travellers though the beach is mediocre and so is the accommodation.

If you're itching to splurge, Ko Kut is the place to do it.

TOP CHOICE **Bann Makok** HOTEL $$

(☎08 1934 5713; Khlong Yai Ki; r 2500-3000B; ❄@) Be the envy of the speedboat patrons when you get dropped off at this boutique hotel tucked into the mangroves. Recycled timbers painted in vintage colours have been constructed into a maze of eight rooms designed to look like a traditional pier fishing village. Common decks and reading nooks provide a peaceful space to listen to birdsong or get lost in a book.

Tinkerbell Resort HOTEL $$$

(☎08 1813 0058; www.tinkerbellresort.com; Hat Khlong Chao; r incl meals from 7900B; ❄@≋) Natural materials, like towering bamboo

WORTH A TRIP

CAMBODIA'S SOUTH COAST *MAHER SATTAR*

With casinos outlawed in Thailand, the less-than-holy trifecta of gambling, brothels and smuggling tends to be the dominating feature of the towns across the Thai–Cambodian border crossings. For instance, the nondescript border town of Poipet is one of the biggest gambling hubs in Southeast Asia.

Cambodia's southern coast has managed to steer relatively clear of this path – for now. The region's premier seaside resort, **Sihanoukville**, has attracted the attentions of builders aware of the location's potential, but it's still a long way from the overdevelopment found on most of Thailand's coasts. Easily accessed from Trat in Thailand via the border crossing at Hat Lek (p123), Sihanoukville aims to please the masses, offering up four beaches with four distinct identities.

The unpronounceable – and almost un-spellable – Occheuteal Beach is the most popular and the most cosmopolitan. Its clientele includes hippies, backpackers, cons, package tourists, locals and Phnom Penh escapees. Just south of Occheuteal, Otres Beach is a rare deserted-island beach on the mainland, although thanks to round after round of bulldozing and changing development plans, most of the accommodation is no longer on the beach itself. Victory Beach, the one-time backpacker mainstay, is now a seedy and depressing hub of poverty and exploitation reminiscent of Thailand's Pattaya. Sokha Beach is universally acknowledged as the prettiest one, but part of the reason for that might be that it is almost completely a private beach owned by Sokha Beach Resort, which takes good care of it. Still, part of Sokha remains open to the public and this is where local families hang out. A worthwhile option might also be to purchase the US$10 day pass to treat yourself to one of the nicest beaches in Cambodia. Although word is that if you're not a local it's easy enough to wander in without a pass.

However, the islands off the coast of Sihanoukville are the real draw. Paradise is a word thrown around frequently when describing tropical islands, but the long stretches of white sand on **Koh Rong** come close to doing the description justice. Both Koh Rong and nearby **Koh Rong Saloem** offer snorkelling, night-swimming and diving opportunities. Both are expected to have major development projects transform them soon, but at the moment they make Ko Chang look like Phuket.

If you want a break from beach hopping, a conventional detour is actually not a detour at all. Getting to Sihanoukville's resorts along the NH48 highway means passing through the **Koh Kong Conservation Corridor**, which encompasses mangrove forests and parts of the majestic Cardamom Mountains, home to at least 62 endangered species. Plenty of buses will drop you off or pick you up from stops on the NH48. Although as is the case elsewhere in Cambodia, minibuses or share taxis might be the best mode of transportation to Sihanoukville.

There's also tiny **Krong Koh Kong**, which until recently would have been a typical border-crossing town awash with gamblers, pimps, and prostitutes with their tricks. But with the Trat-to-Sihanoukville passage gaining in popularity among backpackers, the place has cleaned up its act a bit. Bona-fide tourist attractions are hard to come by, but Koh Kong has its own lazy charm. There are plenty of bars to grab a drink at, and wandering around what was one of the Khmer Rouge's last strongholds can be an interesting way to do some beach detoxing before heading on to more sun and sand.

For those crossing over to Cambodia seeking something truly different, the answer lies almost at your doorstep once you're on the other side of the border. The largest island in Cambodia is a two-hour boat ride (full day per person including lunch and snorkelling equipment US$25, or overnight for US$55) from Koh Kong town. **Koh Kong Island** doesn't just give you the deserted island feel, it practically is a deserted island, with no accommodation and only one small settlement on the southeast coast. For the day-tripper or adventurous camper, Koh Kong Island is all yours.

privacy fences and thatched roof villas, sew this resort seamlessly into the landscape. The rooms are bright and airy and smack dab on the prettiest beach you've ever seen.

Mangrove Bungalows GUEST HOUSE $$
(☎08 5279 0278; Ban Khlong Chao; r 600-1200B; ❄) Lounging pleasantly along mangrove-forested Khlong Chao, this place has large bungalows sporting polished wood floors and hot-water showers. A restaurant hangs above the lazy canal, and it is a 10-minute walk to the beach.

Mark House Bungalows GUEST HOUSE $$
(☎08 6133 0402; www.markhousebungalow.com; Ban Khlong Chao; r 800-1200B; ❄) Right behind the beachside resorts, Mark House is the closest cheapie to the beach. The bungalows sit beside the canal and the ambience feels like you're halfway through a nap.

Koh Kood Ngamkho Resort GUEST HOUSE $
(☎08 1825 7076; www.kohkood-ngamkho.com; Ao Ngam Kho; r 650B; @) Uncle Joe along with his niece and nephew run one the best budget options around. Rustic huts outfitted with new linens, creatively decorated bathrooms and accordion-style front doors perch on a forested hillside. The restaurant is fabulous (fresh coconut milk curries, spicy stir-fries). At the time of writing, Uncle Joe was looking to sell the land, and we selfishly hope that he reconsiders.

Dusita HOTEL $$
(☎08 1523 7369; Ao Ngam Kho; r 700-1200B; ❄) Solid bungalows spaciously occupy a shady oceanfront garden ideally suited for families who need running space for young ones.

Ao Noi Resort GUEST HOUSE $$
(☎0 3952 4979; www.kohkoodaonoi.com; Ao Noi; r 1200-2000B; ❄) This village of thatched-roof huts is adequate yet unremarkable. In return for lacklustre lodging you get a semi-private palm-fringed beach with vigorous surf. Skip the overpriced fan ones, though.

The Beach Natural Resort HOTEL $$
(☎08 6009 9420; www.thebeachkohkood.com; Ao Bang Bao; r incl breakfast 1200-2600B; ❄@) Bungalows sit among a shady garden on a rocky stretch of beach. The customer service is beyond Thai-friendly. Thais pack this place for karaoke-fuelled fun at the weekend, so opt for a weekday.

Siam Beach GUEST HOUSE $$
(☎08 4332 0788; Ao Bang Bao; r incl breakfast 1200-2000B; ❄@) With a monopoly on the sandiest part of the beach, Siam Beach hasn't put much effort into its bungalows. But location is what you get.

ℹ Information

There are no banks or ATMs, though major resorts can exchange money. A small **hospital** (☎0 3952 5748; ⏲8.30am-4.30pm) can handle minor emergencies and is located inland at Ban Khlong Hin Dam. The **police station** (☎0 3952 5741) is nearby. Internet access is still a bit spotty, though many resorts have at least a common terminal.

ℹ Getting There & Around

Ko Kut is accessible from the mainland pier of Laem Sok, 22km southeast of Trat, the nearest bus transfer point.

Ninmoungkorn Boat (☎08 6126 7860) runs an air-con boat (one way 350B, two hours, one daily departure) that docks at Ao Salad, in the northeastern corner of the island; free land transfer (about 45 minutes each way) is available on each side of the journey.

Speedboats also make the crossing to/from Laem Sok (one way 450B to 600B, 1½ hours, three daily departures), and will drop you off at your hotel's pier.

Bang Bao Boat (www.bangbaoboat.com) is the archipelago's inter-island ferry running a daily loop from Ko Chang, departing at 9am, to Ko Kut (one way 700B, five to six hours). In the opposite direction, you can catch it to Ko Mak (one way 300B, one to two hours) and Ko Wai (one way 400B, 2½ hours).

Several speedboat companies run from Ko Kut to Ko Chang (one way 900B, 45 minutes, three daily departures) with stops in Ko Mak and Ko Wai.

To get around, you should rent a motorbike (300B per day) or mountain bike (100B to 150B per day).

Hua Hin & the Southern Gulf

Includes »

Best Places to Eat

» Rang Yen Garden, Cha-am (p147)

» Night Market, Hua Hin (p147)

» Sang Thai Restaurant, Hua Hin (p155)

» Rim Lom, Prachuap Khiri Khan (p165)

Best Places to Stay

» Baan Bayan, Hua Hin (p155)

» Away Hua Hin, Pranburi (p159)

» Brassiere Beach, Pranburi (p159)

» Aow Noi Sea View, Prachuap Khiri Khan (p164)

» Proud Thai Beach Resort, Ban Krut (p166)

Why Go?

Known as the 'royal' coast, the upper southern gulf has long been the favoured retreat of the Bangkok monarchy and elite. Each Thai king, dating from Rama IV, has found an agreeable spot to build a royal getaway. Today domestic tourists flock to this coast in the same pursuit of leisure as well as to pay homage to the revered kings whose palaces-away-from-palace are now open to the public. Rarely does culture and coast meet with such proximity and collaboration.

Indeed this is the country's surf-and-turf destination offering historic sites, pleasant provincial life, jungle-filled parks and long sandy beaches all within an easy commute from Bangkok. That most backpackers suffer a gruelling trip further south to the built-up Samui islands is a great mystery to anyone who has walked for kilometres along Hua Hin's powdery white sands. The one blemish is that there are few reefs (so little to no diving and snorkelling) and as a result the water takes more of an Atlantic greyish hue than a tropical azure.

When to Go

The best time to visit is during the hot and dry season (February to June). From July to October (southwest monsoon) and October to January (northeast monsoon) there is occasional rain and strong winds; but the region tends to stay drier than the rest of the country during the monsoon period because of a geographic anomaly.

During stormy periods, stinging jellyfish are often carried close to shore making swimming hazardous. Thais get around this by swimming fully clothed.

Hua Hin & the Southern Gulf Highlights

1. Exploring the hilltop palace and underground caves of **Phetchaburi** (p141)
2. Strolling the long blonde coastline of **Hua Hin** (p148) dotted with wave-jumping kiteboarders.
3. Eating and shopping (and eating some more) at Hua Hin's **Night Market** (p155)
4. Escaping into the wild depths of **Kaeng Krachan National Park** (p145) and spotting gibbons and wild elephants.
5. Letting the kids run around all day in their bathing suits at **Dolphin Bay** (p159)
6. Making the popular pilgrimage to **Khao Sam Roi Yot National Park** (p160) to see the illuminated cave shrine of Tham Phraya Nakhon.
7. Motorcycling between curvaceous bays and limestone peaks in **Prachuap Khiri Khan** (p162)
8. Being a beach bum on kicked-back **Hat Bang Saphan Yai** (p166)

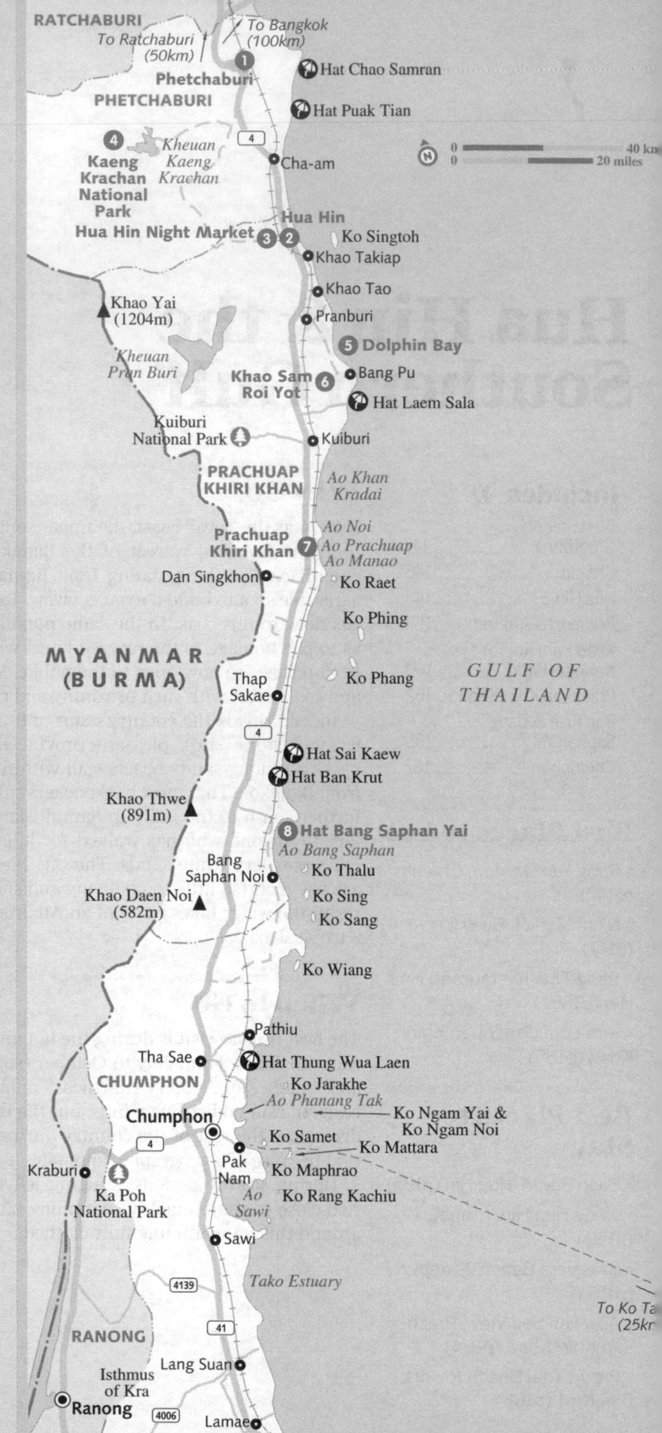

Phetchaburi (Phetburi)

เพชรบุรี

POP 46,600

An easy escape from Bangkok, Phetchaburi should be on every cultural traveller's itinerary. It has temples and palaces like Ayuthaya, outlying jungles and cave shrines like Kanchanaburi and access to the coast (unlike either of the two). The town offers a delightful slice of provincial life with busy markets, old teak shophouses and visiting groups of Thai students who work up the courage to say 'hello' to the few foreigners in town.

Historically Phetchaburi is a visible timeline of kingdoms that have migrated across Southeast Asia. During the 11th century, the Khmer empire settled in, though their control was relatively short-lived. As Khmer power diminished, Phetchaburi became a strategic royal fort during the Thai-based Sukhothai and Ayuthaya kingdoms. During the stability of the Ayuthaya kingdom, the upper peninsula flourished and Phetchaburi thrived as a 17th-century trading post between Burma and Ayuthaya. The town is often referred to as a 'Living Ayuthaya', since the equivalent of the many relics that were destroyed in the former kingdom's capital are still intact here.

Sights & Activities

For such a small town, Phetchaburi has a number of historic temples that keep Thai tourists busy for the day. The most noteworthy are included below.

Phra Nakhon Khiri Historical Park HISTORIC SITE

(อุทยานประวัติศาสตร์พระนครคีรี; ☎0 3240 1006; admission 150B; ⊙8.30am-5pm) This national historical park sits regally atop Khao Wang (Palace Hill) surveying the city with subdued opulence. Rama IV (King Mongkut) built the palace and surrounding temples in 1859 to be used as a retreat from Bangkok. The hilltop location allowed the king to pursue his interest in astronomy and stargazing.

The palace was built in a mix of European and Chinese styles and each breezy hall is furnished with royal belongings. Cobblestone paths lead from the palace through the forested hill to three summits, each topped by a chedi. The white spire of **Phra That Chom Phet** skewers the sky and can be spotted from the city below.

There are two entrances to the site. The front entrance is across from Th Ratwithi and involves a strenuous footpath that passes a troop of unpredictable monkeys. The back entrance is on the opposite side of the hill and has a **tram** (one way adult/child 40B/free; ⊙8.30am-5.30pm) that glides up and down the summit. This place is a popular school-group outing and you'll be as much of a photo-op as the historic buildings.

A **Monday night market** lines the street in front of Khao Wang with the usual food and clothing stalls.

Wat Mahathat Worawihan TEMPLE

(วัดมหาธาตุวรวิหาร; Th Damnoen Krasem) Centrally located, gleaming white Wat Mahathat is a lovely example of an everyday temple with as much hustle and bustle as the busy commercial district around it. The showpiece is a five-tiered Khmer-style *prang* (Khmer-style stupa) decorated in stucco relief, a speciality of Phetchaburi's local artisans. Inside the main *wí·hăhn* (shrine hall or sanctuary) are contemporary murals, another example of the province's thriving temple craftsmanship. The tempo of the temple is further heightened with the steady beat from traditional musicians and dancers who perform for merit-making services.

After visiting the temple, follow Th Suwanmunee through the old teak house district filled with the smells of incense from religious paraphernalia shops.

Wat Kamphaeng Laeng TEMPLE

(วัดกำแพงแลง; Th Phokarang) Back before Siam had defined itself as an independent entity, the Angkor (Khmer) kingdom stretched from present-day Cambodia all the way to the Malay peninsula. To mark their frontier conquests, the Khmers built ornate temples in a signature style that has been copied throughout Thai history. This Khmer remnant is believed to date back to the 12th century and was originally Hindu before the region's conversion to Buddhism. There is one intact sanctuary flanked by two smaller shrines and deteriorating sandstone walls. Though it isn't the most remarkable example of Khmer architecture, it is a peaceful place to snap a few arty pictures.

Tham Khao Luang CAVE

(ถ้ำเขาหลวง; ⊙8am-6pm) About 4km north of town is Tham Khao Luang, a dramatic stalactite-filled chamber that is one of Thailand's most impressive cave shrines and a favourite of Rama IV. The cave is accessed

Phetchaburi (Phetburi)

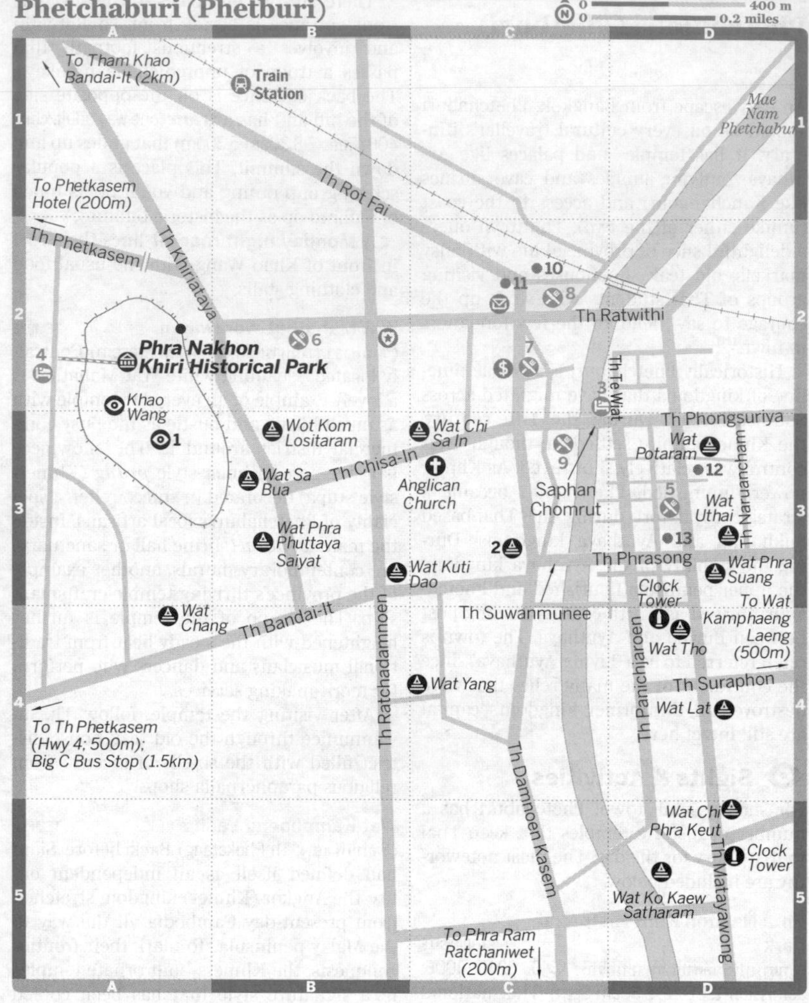

through a steep set of stairs. It's central Buddha figure is often illuminated with a heavenly glow when sunlight filters in through the heart-shaped skylight. On the opposite end of the chamber is a row of sitting Buddhas casting repetitive shadows on the undulating cavern wall.

According to the guides, Rama IV built the stone gate that separates the main chamber from a second chamber as a security measure for a couple who once lived in the cave. A figure of a prostrate body in the third chamber is said to represent the cycle of life and death but it hasn't experienced a peaceful resting place as bandits destroyed much of it in search of hidden treasures. Deeper in the cave is supposedly a rock formation that looks like Christ on the cross but our literal eyes couldn't spot it. (Thais are especially imaginative at spotting familiar forms in cave stalactites.)

Around the entrance to the cave you'll meet brazen monkeys looking for handouts. Guides are available for hire near the car park though they aren't always forthcoming about their fees (usually 100B per person).

You'll need to arrange transport here from town (around 150B roundtrip).

Phetchaburi (Phetburi)

Top Sights
Phra Nakhon Khiri Historical Park........A2

Sights
1 Phra That Chom Phet........A3
Rabieng Rim Nam........(see 9)
2 Wat Mahathat Worawihan........C3

Sleeping
3 Jomklow Hotel........C2
4 Sun Hotel........A2

Eating
5 Day Market........D3
6 Jek Meng........B2
Khon Toy Restaurant........(see 4)
7 Na & Nan........C2
8 Night Market........C2
9 Rabieng Rim Nam........C3

Transport
10 Air-con Buses to Bangkok........C2
11 Minivans to Bangkok........C2
12 Ordinary Buses to Cha-am & Hua Hin........D3
13 Sŏrng·tăa·ou to Ban Kaeng Krachan........D3

Tham Khao Bandai-It CAVE
(ถ้ำเขาบันไดอิฐ; donation appreciated; 9am-4pm) This hillside monastery, 2km west of town, sprawls through several large caverns converted into simple Buddha shrines and hermit meditation rooms. English-speaking guides (tip appreciated) lead tours through the caves, mainly as a safety precaution from the monkeys. One cavern contains a significant population of bats, and guides will instruct you not to look up with your mouth open (a good rule for everyday life).

Phra Ram Ratchaniwet HISTORIC SITE
(พระรามราชนิเวศน์; Ban Peun Palace; 0 3242 8083; admission 50B; 8am-4pm Mon-Fri). An incredible art deco creation 1km south of town, construction of this royal summer palace began in 1910 at the behest of Rama V (who died just after the project was started). It was designed by German architects, who used the opportunity to showcase contemporary innovations in construction and interior design. The structure is typical of the early 20th century, a period that saw a Thai passion for erecting European-style buildings in an effort to keep up with the 'modern' architecture of its colonised neighbours.

The outside of the two-storey palace is not too exciting, but inside there are spacious sun-drenched rooms decorated with exquisite glazed tiles, stained glass, parquet floors and plenty of wrought-iron details. The double-spiral staircase provides a debutante's debut and the king's personal bathroom was state-of-the-art.

Hat Puak Tian BEACH
(หาดปึกเตียน) Locals come to this dark-sands beach, 20km southeast of Phetchaburi, on weekends to eat seafood and frolic in the surf. Another modest attraction is the literary role this beach played in the Thai epic poem *Phra Aphaimani,* written by Sunthorn Phu. A partially submerged statue of a giant woman standing offshore with an outstretched hand and a forlorn expression depicts a character from the poem who disguised herself as a beautiful temptress to win the love of the hero and imprison him on this beach. But he discovers her treachery (and her true ugliness) and with the help of a mermaid escapes to Ko Samet (a nicer beach so maybe he was on to something).

You'll need private transport to reach this beach.

Festivals & Events

Phra Nakhon Khiri Fair CULTURAL
Centred on Khao Wang, this provincial-style celebration takes place in early April and lasts nine days. Phra Nakhon Khiri is festooned with lights, there are traditional dance performances, craft and food displays and a beauty contest.

Sleeping

Phetchaburi is seriously lacking in accommodation, especially in the budget range, since most people visit as a daytrip from Hua Hin or Cha-am. Pity that there isn't more of a guest-house scene here since it is an ideal place for cultural tourists overwhelmed by Bangkok.

Sun Hotel HOTEL $$
(0 3240 0000; www.sunhotelthailand.com; 43/33 Soi Phetkasem; r 800-1500B;) The best of an uninspiring bunch, the Sun Hotel

PHETCHABURI SIGHTSEEING

Some of the city's best sights are outside of town but don't let the distance deter you. Hire a *sŏrng·tăa·ou* (passenger pick-up truck) for the day (usually around 400B) to hit all the highlights. **Rabieng Rim Nam** (☎0 3242 5707; 1 Th Chisa-In; 950B per person for 4 people), a guest house and restaurant, also runs day tours with an English-speaking guide.

sits opposite the back entrance to Phra Nakhon Khiri. It has large, comfortable rooms with functional bathrooms and professional staff. There's a pleasant cafe downstairs; internet and wi-fi are available for a fee.

Jomklow Hotel HOTEL $
(☎0 3242 5398; 1 Th Te Wiat; r 180B) A multistorey hotel in need of a serious makeover has very, very basic jail-cell style rooms.

Phetkasem Hotel HOTEL $
(☎0 3242 5581; 86/1 Th Phetkasem; r 200-400B; ❄) Another candidate for an extreme makeover, the Phetkasem has rundown rooms with broken down furniture but at least there is a roof over your head.

Eating

Surrounded by palm sugar plantations, Phetchaburi is famous for Thai sweets, including *kà·nŏm môr gaang* (egg custard) and the various 'golden' desserts made from egg yolks to portend good fortune. Nearby fruit orchards produce refreshingly aromatic *chom·pôo Phet* (Phetchaburi rose apple), pineapples and golden bananas.

Day Market MARKET $
A good spot for people-watching and local noshing, the day market, north of the clock tower, has food stalls on the perimeter serving the usual noodle dishes as well as specialities such as *kà·nŏm jeen tôrt man* (thin noodles with fried spicy fishcake) and the hot-season favourite *kôw châa pét·bù·ree* (moist chilled rice served with sweetmeats).

Rabieng Rim Nam INTERNATIONAL $
(☎0 3242 5707; 1 Th Chisa-In; dishes 40-180B; ⊙breakfast, lunch & dinner) This riverside restaurant serves up terrific food and a lot of tourist information in English – a rarity in this town – and organises tours. Sadly the affiliated guest house is just too decrepit to recommend.

Khon Toy Restaurant THAI $
(soi behind Sun Hotel; dishes from 35B; ⊙lunch & dinner) This open-air restaurant is shielded from the street by a screen of greenery. Inside is a simple but busy kitchen that does a brisk business in evening takeaway meals. Everything is stir-fried and tasty.

Jek Meng THAI $
(85 Th Ratwithi; dishes 50-80B; ⊙lunch & dinner) Dishes up big, piping-hot bowls of noodles and fried rice. Look for the black-and-white chequered tablecloths.

Na & Nan THAI $
(Th Damnoen Kasem; dishes 40-60B; ⊙lunch & dinner) Another friendly noodle place along a strip of casual restaurants in the centre of town. Their *gŏo·ay đĕe·o gài* (chicken noodles) comes southern style with a whole chicken drumstick.

Information

There's no formal information source in town, but Rabieng Rim Nam is a great resource for both Phetchaburi and Kaeng Krachan National Park. The Sun Hotel has wi-fi and one terminal (per hr 100B).

Main post office (cnr Th Ratwithi & Th Damnoen Kasem)

Police station (☎0 3242 5500; Th Ratwithi) Near the intersection of Th Ratchadamnoen.

Siam Commercial Bank (2 Th Damnoen Kasem) Other nearby banks also offer foreign exchange and ATMs.

Telephone office (cnr Th Ratwithi & Th Damnoen Kasem; ⊙7am-10pm) Upstairs at the post office.

Getting There & Away

The stop for buses to Bangkok is beside the night market. There are services to/from Bangkok's Southern (Sai Tai Mai) station (120B, two hours; hourly morning departures). Across the street is a minivan stop with services to Bangkok's Victory Monument (80B) and Southern station (100B).

Ordinary buses to Cha-am (40B) and Hua Hin (50B) stop in town near Th Matayawong.

Most southbound air-conditioned buses and minivans stop out of town on Th Phetkasem in front of the Big C department store. Destinations include Cha-am (50B, 40 minutes, frequent departures) and Hua Hin (50B, two hours). Motorcycle taxis await and can take you into town for around 50B.

WORTH A TRIP

KAENG KRACHAN NATIONAL PARK อุทยานแห่งชาติแก่งกระจาน

Wake to the eerie symphony of gibbon calls as the early morning mist hangs limply above the forest canopy. Hike through lush forests to spot elephant herds and other wildlife at the communal watering holes. Or sweat through your clothes as you summit the park's highest peak. At 3000 sq km, Thailand's largest **national park** (☎0 3245 9293; www.dnp.go.th; admission 200B; ⏲visitors centre 8.30am-4.30pm) is surprisingly close to civilization but shelters an intense tangle of wilderness that sees few tourists. Two rivers (Mae Nam Phetchaburi and Mae Nam Pranburi), a large lake and abundant rainfall keep the place green year-round. Animal life is abundant and includes wild elephants, deer, gibbons, boars, dusky langurs and wild cattle.

This park also occupies an interesting overlapping biozone for birds as the southernmost spot for the northern species and the northernmost for the southern species. There are about 400 species of birds, including hornbills as well as pheasants and other ground-dwellers.

Activities

Hiking is the best way to explore the park. Most of the trails are signed and branch off of the main road. The **Nam Tok Tho Thip** trail starts at the Km36 marker and continues for 4km to an 18-tiered waterfall. **Phanoen Thung** is the park's highest point and can be summited via a 6km hike that starts at the Km27 marker. Note that some trails, including the one to Phanoen Thung, are closed during the rainy season (August to October).

The twin waterfalls of **Pa La-U Yai** and **Pa La-U Noi** in the southern section of the park are popular for daytrippers on minivan tours from Hua Hin. It's also possible to organise mountain biking in the park from Hua Hin.

Tourist infrastructure in Kaeng Krachan is somewhat limited and the roads can be rough. The park rangers can help arrange camping-gear rental, food and transport. There are crowds on weekends and holidays but weekdays should be people free. The best months to visit are between November and April. **Rabieng Rim Nam** (☎0 3242 5707; 1 Th Chisa-In, Phetchaburi; from 1950B per person for 4 people) arranges trekking and birding tours that range from one day to multiple days if you don't want to figure out the logistics yourself.

Sleeping & Eating

There are various **bungalows** (☎0 2562 0760; www.dnp.go.th/parkreserve; bungalows from 1200B) within the park, mainly near the reservoir. These sleep from four to six people and are simple affairs with fans and fridges. There are also **camp sites** (per person 60-90B), including a pleasant grassy one near the reservoir at the visitors centre and a modest restaurant. Tents can be rented at the visitors centre.

On the road leading to the park entrance are several simple resorts and bungalows. About 3.5km before reaching the visitors centre, **A&B Bungalows** (☎08 9891 2328; r from 700B) is scenic and popular with bird-watching groups. There is a good restaurant here that can provide you with a packed lunch.

Getting There & Away

Kaeng Krachan is 52km southwest of Phetchaburi, with the southern edge of the park 35km from Hua Hin. If you have your own vehicle, drive 20km south from Phetchaburi on Hwy 4 to the town of Tha Yang. Turn right (west) and after 38km, you'll reach the visitors centre. You use the same access road from Tha Tang if coming south from Hua Hin.

You can also reach the park by **minivan** (☎08 9231 5810; one-way 100B) from Phetchaburi; they don't travel to a fixed schedule so have your hotel call to make arrangements. Alternatively you can catch a *sŏrng·tăa·ou* (pick-up trucks; 80B, 1½ hours, 6am to 2pm) from Phetchaburi (near the clock tower) to the village of Ban Kaeng Krachan, 4km before the park. From the village, you can charter transport to the park. You can also charter your own *sŏrng·tăa·ou* all the way to the park but you'll need to haggle.

Minivan tours also operate from Hua Hin.

Frequent rail services run to/from Bangkok's Hua Lamphong station. Fares vary depending on the train and class (3rd class 84B to 144B, 2nd class 188B to 358B, three hours).

Getting Around

Motorcycle taxis go anywhere in the town centre for 40B to 50B. *Sŏrng·tăa·ou* cost about the same. It's a 20-minute walk (1km) from the train station to the town centre.

Rabieng Rim Nam (p144) hires out bicycles (120B per day) and motorbikes (250B per day).

Cha-am

ชะอำ

POP 72,341

At weekends and on public holidays, Cha-am is a beach getaway for working-class families and Bangkok students. Neon-painted buses (called '*chor ching cha*') deliver young holidaymakers, firmly in party mode, fuelled by thumping techno music. It is a 100% Thai-style beach party with eating and drinking marathons held around umbrella-shaded beach chairs and tables. Entertainment is provided by the banana boats that zip back and forth eventually making a final jack-knife turn that throws the passengers into the sea. Applause and giggles usually follow from the beachside audience.

Cha-am sees only a few foreigners, usually older Europeans who winter here instead of more expensive Hua Hin. And the beach sees even fewer bathing suits since most Thais frolic in the ocean fully clothed. This isn't the spot to meet a lot of young travellers or even a good option for families of young children who might be overwhelmed by paparazzi-like Thais in holiday mode. But for everyone else, Cha-am's beach is wide and sandy, the grey-blue water is clean and calm, the people-watching is superb and the prices are some of the most affordable anywhere on the coast.

Festivals & Events

Crab Festival FOOD

In February, Cha-am celebrates one of its local marine delicacies: blue crabs. Food stalls, concerts, and lots of neon turn the beachfront into a pedestrian party.

Gin Hoy, Do Nok, Tuk Meuk FOOD

You really can do it all at this annual festival held in September. The English translation means 'Eat Shellfish, Watch Birds, Catch Squid' and is a catchy slogan for all of Cha-am's local attractions and fishing traditions. Mainly it is a food festival showcasing a variety of shellfish but there are also bird-watching events at nearby sanctuaries and squid-fishing demonstrations.

ANIMAL ENCOUNTERS

Modern sensibilities have turned away from circus-like animal attractions but many well-intentioned animal lovers curious to see Thailand's iconic creatures (such as elephants, monkeys and tigers) unwittingly contribute to an industry that is poorly regulated and exploitative. Animals are often illegally captured from the wild and disfigured to be less dangerous (tigers often have their claws and teeth removed), they are acquired as pets and then neglected or inhumanely confined, or they are abandoned when they are too sick or infirm to work.

Wildlife Friends Foundation Thailand runs a **wildlife rescue centre** (☎0 3245 8135; www.wfft.org; Wat Khao Luk Chang, 35km northwest of Cha-am) that adopts and cares for abused and abandoned animals. Most of these animals are wild creatures that can't return to the wild due to injuries or lack of survival skills. The centre cares for 400 animals, including bears, tigers, gibbons, macaques, loris and birds. There is also an affiliated elephant rescue program that buys and shelters animals being used as street beggars.

The centre offers a **full access tour** (5000B for six people) that introduces the animals and discusses their rescue histories. The tour includes a visit with the elephants (but no rides are offered) and hotel transfer from Hua Hin or Cha-am.

Those looking for a more intimate connection with the animals can volunteer to help at the centre. An average day could involve chopping fruits and vegetables to feed sun bears, cleaning enclosures and rowing out to the gibbon islands with a daily meal. Volunteers are required to stay a minimum of two weeks and work a full (usually 6.30am to 6.30pm) six days a week. Contact the centre or visit the **volunteer website** (www.wildlifevolunteer.org) for prices and details.

Sleeping

Cha-am has two basic types of accommodation: apartment-style hotels along the beach road (Th Ruamjit) and more expensive 'condotel' developments (condominiums with a kitchen and operating under a rental program). Expect a discount on posted rates for weekday stays.

The northern end of the beach (known as Long Beach) has a wider, blonder strip of sand and sees more foreign tourists, while the southern end is more Thai. Th Narathip divides the beach into north and south and the beach road (Th Ruamjit) soi are numbered in ascending order in both directions from this intersection.

Charlie House GUEST HOUSE $$
(☎0 3243 3799; 241/60-61, Soi 1 North, Th Ruamjit; r 650-800B; ❄📶) This cheery place boasts a lime-green lobby and colourful rooms that are fun to return to after a day of people watching. Don't confuse it with institutional Charlie Place or Charlie TV on the same soi.

Cha-am Mathong Guesthouse GUEST HOUSE $$
(☎08 1550 2947; www.chaammathongcom; cnr Th Ruamjit & Soi 3 South; r 600-800B; ❄) Clean and convenient with all the mod cons, Mathong won't win any awards for hand-holding but you get a lot of bang for your baht.

Dee Lek GUEST HOUSE $$
(☎0 3247 0396; www.deelek.com; 225/30-33 Soi Long Beach, Th Ruamjit; r 1200-1500B; ❄📶) Popular with Scandinavians, Dee Lek has roomy rooms with spacious bathrooms and upholstered European-style furniture.

Casa Papaya HOTEL $$$
(☎0 3247 0678; www.casapapayathai.com; 810/4 Th Phetkasem; r 3000-5000B; ❄🏊) This quirky spot is right on the beach in between Cha-am and Hua Hin and garners fans with its homely and hospitable atmosphere. The beachfront and sea-view bungalows have rooftop decks to enjoy the sunlight (or the moonlight), and inside there are king-size beds and bathrooms in wonderfully brave colours.

Eating

From your beach chair you can wave down the itinerant vendors selling barbecued and fried seafood or order from a menu of nearby beachfront restaurants. At the far northern end of the beach, seafood restaurants with reasonable prices can be found at the fishing pier.

TOP CHOICE **Rang Yen Garden** THAI $
(☎0 3247 1267; 259/40 Th Ruamjit; dishes 60-180B; ⏲lunch & dinner Nov-Apr) This lush garden restaurant is a cosy and friendly spot to feel at home after a day of feeling like a foreigner. It serves up Thai favourites and is only open in the high season.

Bella Pizza ITALIAN $$
(Soi Bus Station, Th Ruamjit; dishes 150-200B; ⏲lunch & dinner) There are enough foreigners in town to warrant a pizza restaurant and this pie shop makes everyone happy. Plus there's a curious international pedigree: the Thai owner worked in Sweden at a pizza restaurant.

Poom Restaurant SEAFOOD $$
(☎0 3247 1036; 274/1 Th Ruamjit; dishes 120-250B; ⏲lunch & dinner) Slightly more expensive than other nearby beach restaurants, but worth it for the fresh seafood served under tall sugar palms. It appears to be the restaurant of choice for weekending Thais – always a good sign.

Pla Too Restaurant SEAFOOD $$
(☎032 508175; dishes 150-250B; ⏲lunch & dinner) Thanks to the smells from the kitchen, you'll be hungry just walking from the car park to the sprawling beachfront restaurant, beloved by Thais and foreigners alike. It is near the Courtyard Marriott in between Cha-am and Hua Hin.

Information

Phetkasem Hwy runs through Cha-am's busy town centre, which is about 1km away from the beach. The town centre is where you'll find the main bus stop, banks, the main post office, an outdoor market and the train station.

You'll find plenty of banks along Th Ruamjit with ATMs and exchange services.

Only Chaam (www.onlychaam.com) is an online blog and website about visiting Cha-am.

Communications Authority of Thailand (CAT; Th Narathip) For international phone calls.

Post office (Th Ruamjit) On the main beach strip.

Tourism Authority of Thailand (TAT; ☎0 3247 1005; tatphet@tat.or.th; 500/51 Th Phetkasem; ⏲8.30am-4.30pm) On Phetkasem Hwy, 500m south of town. The staff speak good English.

Getting There & Away

Buses stop on Phetkasem Hwy near the 7-Eleven store at the intersection of Th Narathip. Frequent bus services operating to/from Cha-am include the following:

Bangkok's Southern (Sai Tai Mai) station (150B, three hours)

Phetchaburi (50B, 40 minutes)

Hua Hin (50B, 30 minutes).

Minivans to Bangkok's Victory Monument (160B, 2½ hours, hourly 7am to 5.30pm) leave from Soi Bus Station, in between Th Ruamjit and Th Chao Lay. Other minivan destinations include Hua Hin (120B) and Phetchaburi (100B). A private taxi to Hua Hin will cost 500B.

The **train station** (Th Narathip) is west of Phetkasem Hwy. From Bangkok's Hua Lamphong station five daily trains go to Cha-am (40B to 150B, four hours) and continue on to Hua Hin. Cha-am is listed in the timetable only in Thai as 'Ban Cha-am'.

Getting Around

From the city centre to the beach it's a quick motorcycle (30B) or *sŏrng·tăa·ou* (40B) ride. Some drivers will try to take you to hotels that offer commissions instead of the one you requested.

You can hire motorcycles for 300B per day all along Th Ruamjit. Cruisy bicycles are available everywhere for 20B per hour or 100B per day, and are a good way to get around.

Hua Hin

หัวหิน

POP 98,896

Thailand's original beach resort is no palm-fringed castaway island and arguably it is all the better for it. Instead it is a delightful mix of city and sea with a cosmopolitan ambience, lively markets, tasty street eats, long wide beaches and fully functional city services (meaning no septic streams bisect the beach like those *other* places).

Hua Hin traces its aristocratic roots to the 1920s when Rama VI (King Vajiravudh) and Rama VII (King Prajadhipok) built summer residences here to escape Bangkok's stifling climate. The most famous of the two is **Phra Ratchawang Klai Kangwon** (Far from Worries Palace), 3km north of town and which is still a royal residence today and so poetically named that Thais often invoke it as a city slogan. Rama VII's endorsement of Hua Hin and the construction of the southern railway made the town *the* place to be for Thai nobility who built their own summer residences beside the sea.

In the 1980s the luxury-hotel group Sofitel renovated the town's grand dame hotel that in turn sparked overseas tourism. Today all the international hotel chains have properties in Hua Hin, and a growing number of wealthy expats retire to the nearby housing estates and condominiums. Middle-class and high-society Thais from Bangkok swoop into town on weekends, making parts of the city look a lot like upper Sukhumvit.

There's a lot of money swirling around, which unnecessarily scares off baht-minded backpackers. Because this is a bustling Thai town, seafood is plentiful and affordable, there's cheap public transport for beach hopping and it takes a lot less time and effort (and money) to get here from Bangkok than to the southern islands. So quit wasting your time everywhere else and hurry up to Hua Hin beach.

Sights

The city's beaches are numerous, wide and long; swimming is safe, and Hua Hin continues to enjoy some of the peninsula's driest weather. During stormy weather, watch out for jellyfish.

HUA HIN TOWN

เมืองหัวหิน

A former fishing village, Hua Hin town retains its roots with an old teak shophouse district bisected by narrow soi, pier houses that have been converted into restaurants or guest houses and a busy fishing pier still in use today. South of the harbour is a rocky headland that inspired the name 'Hua Hin', meaning 'Stone Head'. In the commercial heart are busy markets and all the modern conveniences you forgot to pack.

Hat Hua Hin BEACH

(หาดหัวหิน; public access via eastern end of Th Damnoen Kasem) When viewed from the main public entrance, Hua Hin's beach might seem like a lot of hype. Initially you meet a pleasant but not stunning stretch of sand punctuated by round, smooth boulders and bordered here by the Sofitel resort, which nearly kisses the high tide mark. Don't be dismayed; this is the people-watching spot. Visiting Thais come here to photograph their friends wading ankle-deep in the sea and pony rides are offered to anyone standing still.

But if you're after swimming and sunbathing continue south to where the 5km-long beach stretches into a Buddha-adorned headland (Khao Takiab). The sand is a fine white powder that is wide and long and the sea is a calm grey-green. Instead of coconut trees, resort towers line the interior of the beach but this is a minor distraction for long uninterrupted walks. Access roads lead to Th Phetkasem, where you can catch a green *sŏrng·tăa·ou* back to town.

Hua Hin Train Station HISTORIC SITE
(สถานีรถไฟหัวหิน; Th Liab Tang Rot Fai) An iconic piece of local architecture, the red-and-white pavilion that sits beside Hua Hin's train station once served as the royal waiting room during the reign of Rama VI. It was the railway that made Hua Hin's emergence as a tourist destination possible for the Bangkok-based monarchy and the city's elite. In the early 20th century, the four-hour journey between Hua Hin and Bangkok was a transportation revolution. That was before the emergence of speeding minivan drivers fuelled by energy drinks.

NORTH HUA HIN

The summer residences of the royal family and minor nobility dot the coast northward from Hua Hin's fishing pier toward Cha-am.

Hat Hua Hin Neua BEACH
(หาดหัวหินเหนือ; North Hua Hin Beach; public access paths off of Th Naebkehardt) Genteel but modest Thai-Victorian garden estates bestowed with ocean-inspired names, such as 'Listening to the Sea House', line this end of the coast. The current monarchy's palace lies about 3km north of town but visitors are only allowed on the **grounds** (⌚5.30-7.30am & 4-7pm; ID required). On weekends, Th Naebkehardt is the preferred getaway for Bangkok Thais, some of whom still summer in the old-fashioned residences while others come to supper in the houses that have been converted into restaurants.

FREE **Plearn Wan** NOTABLE BUILDING
(เพลินวาน; ☎0 3252 0311; www.plearnwan.com; Th Phetkasem btw Soi 38 & 40) More of an art installation than a commercial enterprise, Plearn Wan is a vintage village containing stylized versions of old-fashioned shophouses that once occupied the Thai-Chinese districts of Bangkok and Hua Hin. There's a pharmacy selling (well actually displaying) roots, powders and other concoctions that Thai grandmothers once used; a music store specialising in the crooner era of the 1950s and 1960s; and other bygone shops and attractions that pre-date the arrival of 7-Eleven. It would be a tourist trap if it

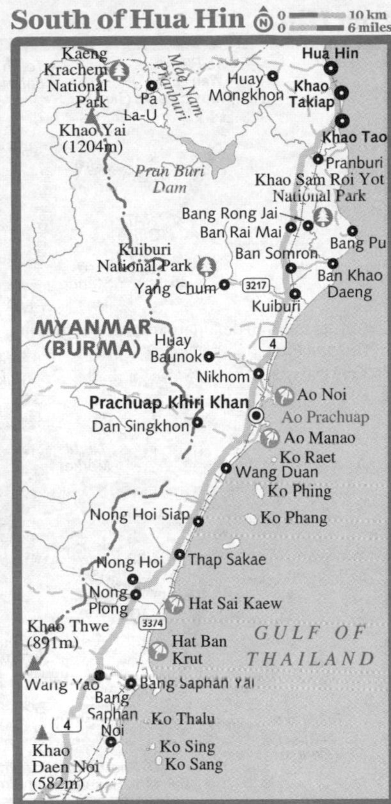

charged an admission fee but most visitors just wander the grounds snapping photos without making any impulse purchases. If you want to support this bit of nostalgia, there are retro souvenirs and snack shops.

Phra Ratchaniwet Mrigadayavan HISTORIC SITE
(พระราชนิเวศน์มฤคทายวัน; ☎0 3250 8443; admission 30B; ⌚9am-4.30pm) With a breezy seaside location 10km north of Hua Hin, this summer palace was built during the reign of Rama VI (King Vajiravudh) in 1923 as a health-promoting retreat for the king who suffered from rheumatoid arthritis. The court's Italian architect built the palace to maximise air circulation and admire the sea. The result is a series of interlinked teak houses with tall shuttered windows and patterned fretwork built upon stilts forming a shaded ground-level boardwalk. It is functional and elegant without excessive opulence. Surrounding the palace is a beautiful

Hua Hin

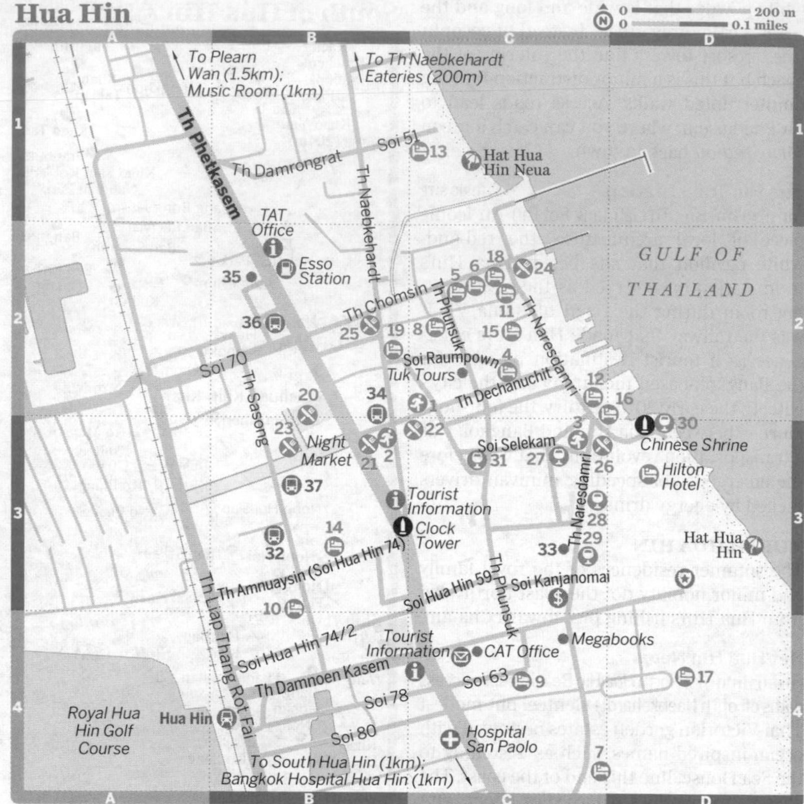

garden with statuesque trees, some nearing a century old. A traditional Thai orchestra helps transport visitors' imaginations backwards in time.

The palace is located within the grounds of Camp Rama VI, a military post, and you need to check in at the gate. It is easiest to come via private transport but you can also catch a Hua Hin to Cha-am bus and ask to be dropped off at the turn-off to the palace. There are often motorcycle taxis waiting that will take you the remaining 2km.

INLAND OF HUA HIN

Baan Silapin ART GALLERY

(บ้านศิลปิน; ☎032534830; www.huahinartistvillage.com; Th Hua Hin-Pa Lu-U; ⊙10am-5pm Tue-Sun) Local painter Tawee Kase-ngam established this artist collective in a shady grove 4km west of Th Phetkasem. The galleries and studio spaces highlight the works of 21 artists, many of whom opted out of Bangkok's fast-paced art world in favour of Hua Hin's more relaxed atmosphere and its scenic landscape of mountains and sea. Outlying clay huts shelter the playful sculptures of Nai Dee and Mae A-Ngoon. Khun Nang, a skilful and charismatic teacher, leads **art classes** (9.30am-11.30am; 300/200B adult/child) for adults on Tuesday and Thursday and for children on Saturday.

Hua Hin Hills Vineyard VINEYARD

(ไร่องุ่นหัวหินฮิลล์ วินยาร์ด; ☎08 1701 8874; www.huahinhillsvineyard.com; Th Hua Hin-Pa Lu-U; ⊙10am-6pm) Part of the New Latitudes wine movement (see the boxed text, p152), this vineyard is nestled in a scenic mountain valley 45km west of Hua Hin. The loamy sand and slate soil feeds several Rhone grape varieties that are used in their Monsoon Valley wine label.

You can spend the day here learning about viticulture in a tropical climate on a **vineyard tour** (free; ⊙1 & 4pm), doing a **wine**

Hua Hin

Activities, Courses & Tours
1 Buchabun Art & Crafts Collection ... C2
2 Hua Hin Adventure Tour ... B3
3 Hua Hin Golf Centre ... C3

Sleeping
4 All Nations Guest House ... C2
5 Araya Residence ... C2
6 Baan Chalelarn Hotel ... C2
7 Baan Laksasubha ... C4
Baan Oum-or Hotel ... (see 9)
8 Baan Tawee Suk ... C2
9 Ban Somboon ... C4
10 Euro-Hua Hin City Hotel (YHA) ... B3
11 Fat Cat Guesthouse ... C2
12 Fulay Guesthouse ... C2
13 Green Gallery Bed and Breakfast ... C1
14 My Place Hua Hin ... B3
15 Pattana Guest House ... C2
16 Sirima ... D2
17 Sofitel Centara Grand Resort and Villas ... D4
18 Supasuda Guest House ... C2
19 Tong-Mee House ... B2

Eating
20 Chatchai Market ... B2
21 Hua Hin Koti ... B3
22 Jek Pia Coffeeshop ... C3
23 Night Market ... B3
24 Sang Thai Restaurant ... C2
Sofitel Cafe & Tea Corner ... (see 17)
25 Th Chomsin Food Stalls ... B2
26 World News Coffee ... C3

Drinking
27 el Murphy's Mexican Grill & Steakhouse ... C3
28 Hua Hin Brewing Company ... C3
29 Mai Tai Cocktail & Beer Garden ... C3
30 No Name Bar ... D3
31 O'Neill's Irish Pub ... C3

Transport
32 Air-con Buses to Bangkok ... B3
33 Lomphraya Office ... C3
34 Minivans to Bangkok ... B2
35 Minivans to Bangkok's Victory Monument ... B2
36 Ordinary Buses to Phetchaburi & Cha-am ... B2
37 Sŏrng•tăa•ou to Khao Takiab; bus to Pranburi ... B3

tasting (290B for 3 samples) or eating at the picturesque **Sala Wine Bar & Bistro** (dishes 200-500B). There is also a pétanque course, mountain-biking trails and elephant riding.

A vineyard shuttle leaves the affiliated **Hua Hin Hills Wine Cellar store** (☎0 3252 6 351, Market Village, Th Phetkasem, South Hua Hin) at 10.30am and 3pm and returns at 1.30pm and 6pm; return ticket is 200B.

KHAO TAKIAB เขาตะเกียบ

About 7km south of Hua Hin, Monumental Chopstick Mountain guards the southern end of Hua Hin beach and is adorned with a giant standing Buddha. Atop the 272m mountain is a Thai-Chinese temple (**Wat Khao Lat**) and many resident monkeys who are not to be trusted – but the views are great. On the southern side of Khao Takiab is **Suan Son Pradipath** (Sea Pine Garden), a muddy beach maintained by the army and popular with weekending Thais. Green *sŏrng·tăa·ou* go all the way from Hua Hin to Khao Takiab village, where you'll find loads of simple Thai eateries.

The new and stylish **Cicada Market** (Th Phetkasem; ⏰4-11pm Fri & Sat, 4-10pm Sun) is an outdoor market still moulting in the food and shopping category, but it has found its niche on Friday nights when live bands hit the stage and the vibe is mellow and arty. You can catch a green *sŏrng·tăa·ou* (20B; from 6am to 9pm) from Hua Hin Night Market; a hired túk-túk will cost 150B one-way.

Activities

There are many travel agencies in town offering day trips to nearby national parks. Unless you're in a group, you may have to wait until enough people sign up for the trip of your choice.

Hua Hin Adventure Tour (☎0 3253 0314; www.huahinadventuretour.com; Th Naebkehardt) offers more somewhat active excursions including kayaking trips in the Khao Sam Roi Yot National Park and mountain biking in Kaeng Krachan National Park.

NEW ATTITUDES TOWARDS WINE

Common wisdom would tell you that tasty wine grapes don't grow alongside coconut trees. But advances in plant sciences and a global palette for wines has changed all of that and ushered in the geographic experiment dubbed New Latitude Wines, produced from grapes grown outside the traditional 30- to 50-degree parallels.

The New Latitudes' main challenge is to replicate the wine-producing grapes preferred climate as best as possible. That means introducing a false dormancy or winter period through pruning, regulated irrigation and companion planting of grasses to prevent soil loss during the rainy season. If you're familiar with viticulture in the Old World, you'll be shocked to see all the cultivation rules Thai vineyards successfully break.

Wine experts have yet to crown a New Latitude that surpasses the grand dames but they do fill a local niche. Siam Winery, the parent company of Hua Hin Hills Vineyard (see p150), aims to produce wines that pair with the complex flavours of Thai food. The vineyard grows columbard, chenin blanc, muscat, shiraz and sangiovese grapes, among others, and typically the citrus-leaning whites are a refreshing complement to the fireworks of most Thai dishes.

Because of the hot climate, a wine drinker's palette is often altered. The thinner wines produced in Thailand tend to have a more satisfying effect than the bold chewy reds that pair well with a chilly spring day. Drinking red wine in Thailand has always been a challenge because the heat turns otherwise leathery notes straight into vinegar. To counteract the tropical factor, break yet another wine rule and chill reds in the refrigerator to replicate 'cellar' temperature as close as possible.

Kiteboarding

Adding to the beauty of Hua Hin beach are the airborne kites (attached to a wave board) that seem to sail among the puffy clouds. Hua Hin is an ideal kiteboarding spot: it has a long, consistent windy season. Winds blow from the northeast from October to December and from the southeast from January to March. In 2010 Hua Hin hosted the Kiteboarding World Cup.

Kiteboarding Asia KITEBOARDING
(☎08 8230 0016; www.kiteboardingasia.com; South Hua Hin; beginner courses 11,000B) This 10-year old company operates four beachside shops that rent equipment and teach lessons. The three-day introductory course teaches beginners the physical mechanics of the sport, and the instructor recommends newbies come when the winds are blowing from the southeast (January to March) and the sea is less choppy.

Golf

Home to the country's first golf course, Hua Hin continues to be an international and domestic golfing destination.

Hua Hin Golf Centre GOLF
(☎0 3253 0476; www.huahingolf.com; Th Selakam; ⏲noon-10pm) The friendly staff at this pro shop can steer you to the most affordable, well-maintained courses where the monkeys won't try to run off with your balls. The company also organises golf tours and rents equipment.

Black Mountain Golf Course GOLF
(☎0 3261 8666; www.bmghuahin.com; green fees 2500B) The city's newest course is currently everyone's favourite. About 10km west of Hua Hin, the 18-hole course was carved out of jungle and an old pineapple plantation and it retains some natural creeks used as water hazards. The 2009 and 2010 Asian PGA tour was held here.

Cycling

Cycling is a scenic and affordable option for touring Hua Hin's outlying attractions, especially since hiring a taxi to cover the same ground is ridiculously expensive. Don't be spooked by the busy thoroughfares; there are plenty of quiet byways where you can enjoy the scenery.

Hua Hin Bike Tours CYCLING
(☎08 1173 4469; www.huahinbiketours.com; 4/34 Soi Hua Hin 96/1, Th Phetkasem, South Hua Hin; tours 1500-2500B) A husband-and-wife team (see the boxed text, p154) operates this cycling company that leads half-, full-, and multi-day tours to a variety of attractions in and around Hua Hin. Pedal to the Hua Hin Hills Vineyard (p150) for some well-earned refreshment, tour the coastal byways south

of Hua Hin, or ride among the limestone mountains of Khao Sam Roi Yot National Park (p160). They also rent premium bicycles (500B per day) for independent cyclists and can recommend routes. The same couple also leads long-distance charity and corporate bike tours across Thailand; visit the parent company **Tour de Asia** (www.tourdeasa.org) for more information.

Courses

Buchabun Art & Crafts Collection COOKING
(08 1572 3805; www.thai-cookingcourse.com; 22 Th Dechanuchit; courses 1500B) Aspiring chefs should sign up for a half-day Thai cooking class that includes a market visit and recipe book. They only run it if several people are interested.

Festivals & Events

King's Cup Elephant Polo Tournament ELEPHANT RACING
Polo with a Thai twist, this annual tournament involving elephant mounts instead of horses takes place on the scenic grounds of the Anantara Hua Hin resort in September. It might not be as fast-paced as its British cousin but it is a charitable event that raises money for elephant-welfare issues.

Hua Hin Jazz Festival JAZZ
In honour of the king's personal interest in the genre, the city that hosts royal getaways also hosts an annual jazz festival featuring Thai and international performers. All events are free and usually occur in June.

Fringe Festival THEATRE
Organised by the Patravadi Theatre, a renowned avant-garde performance space in Bangkok, this modern arts festival is held at its sister location, **Vic Hua Hin** (0 3282 7814; www.vichuahin.com; 62/70 Soi Hua Na Nong Khae, South Hua Hin). Running from January to March, there are a host of dance, music and comedy performances from local and international artists as well as multinational collaborations.

Sleeping

Most budget and midrange options are in town occupying multistorey buildings in the old shophouse district. It is an atmospheric setting with cheap tasty food nearby but you'll have to 'commute' to the beach, either by walking to north Hua Hin beach (best at low tide) or catching a *sŏrng·tăa·ou* to the southern end of Hua Hin beach.

The top end options are beachfront resorts sprawling south from the Sofitel. All the international brands have a presence in Hua Hin but we've only listed unique and local options for a more intimate experience.

HUA HIN TOWN

Pattana Guest House GUEST HOUSE $
(0 3251 3393; 52 Th Naresdamri; r 350-550B;) Tucked away down a soi, this simple teak house has a lovely garden filled with little reading nooks. The rooms are small and basic but adequate and the family who runs it is friendly and artistic.

Tong-Mee House GUEST HOUSE $
(0 3253 0725; 1 Soi Raumpown, Th Naebkehardt; r 450-550B;) Hidden away in a quiet residential soi, this smart guest house is the best value in town. The rooms are small but well kept and have balconies.

Supasuda Guest House GUEST HOUSE $
(0 3251 3618; www.spghouse.com; 1/8 Th Chomsin; r 800-1000B;) Large rooms come with mermaid murals and hot showers. The more expensive ones have verandahs and a bit of road noise. Guests have access to the common terrace.

Ban Somboon GUEST HOUSE $
(0 3251 1538; 13/4 Soi Hua Hin 63, Th Phetkasem; r 950-1200B;) With family photos decorating the walls and a compact garden, this place is like staying at your favourite Thai auntie's house. This is a very quiet, centrally located soi with several other good-value guest houses.

Baan Tawee Suk GUEST HOUSE $
(0 89459 2618; 43/8 Th Poonsuk; r 800B;) This new multistorey guest house is fresh and clean with all the mod cons. Rooms are a little cramped so leave the super-sized luggage at home.

Sirima GUEST HOUSE $
(0 3251 1060; Th Naresdamri; r 550B;) The best of the old-style pier guest houses, Sirima has a pretty exterior with stained glass and polished wood. A long hallway leads to a common deck overlooking the water. Rooms come in various degrees of quality but the tile-floored ones are better.

My Place Hua Hin HOTEL $$
(0 32514 1112; www.myplacehuahin.com; 17 Th Amnuaysin, Th Phetkasem; r 1850-2200B;) A small well-maintained hotel in the heart of the city – it might sound commonplace but

My Place actually delivers on what turns out to be a tall order.

Euro-Hua Hin City Hotel YHA HOSTEL $
(☎0 3251 3130; 5/15 Th Sasong; r 250-800B; ❄) Just like any large hostel back home, this place feels both comfortable and institutional. All rooms have air-con, even the somewhat cramped dorms. There are also single and double private rooms and all accommodation includes breakfast. Add 50B to these prices if you don't belong to HI.

Baan Chalelarn Hotel HOTEL $$
(☎0 3253 1288; www.chalelarnhuahin.com; 11 Th Chomsin; r 1200-1300B; ❄@) Chalelarn has a beautiful lobby with wooden floors, while the big rooms are equipped with king-size beds. Verandahs and breakfast are all part of the perks.

Araya Residence HOTEL $$
(☎0 3253 1130; www.araya-residence.com; 15/1 Th Chomsin; r 1500-2000B; ❄@) Wood and concrete are combined to create a rustic yet modern feel at this pseudo-stylish hotel. The rooms are spacious and comfortable though the hotel is a little tatty around the edges.

Also recommended:

Fat Cat Guesthouse GUEST HOUSE $
(☎08 6206 2455; 8/3 Th Naresdamri; r 300-900B; ❄) The rooms with fan occupy a separate building down a residential soi and some have fantastic views of the city.

Fulay Guesthouse GUEST HOUSE $
(☎0 3251 3145; www.fulayhuahin.net; 110/1 Th Naresdamri; r 430-980B; ❄📶) An old-style pier guest house, with good beds, newish bathrooms and flowering plants in the common area.

Baan Oum-or Hotel HOTEL $$
(☎0 3251 5151; 77/18-19 Soi 63, Th Phetkasem; r 1000-1500B; ❄) The rooms are big and bright and there are only seven of them so book ahead.

LOCAL KNOWLEDGE

SIRANEE (GAE) MEESITH, CO-OWNER HUA HIN BIKE TOURS

I am from a very small village surrounded by rice farms, water buffalos and such. It is a bit boring sometimes but Bangkok, where I went to university, is extreme. Hua Hin is in between. It is a relaxing little town but still has places to go: peaceful beaches, mountains, caves and activities (biking, kiteboarding or swimming in the ocean). There are also shopping, bakeries, cafes and loads of good seafood restaurants.

BEST BEACH

Hua Hin beach is beautiful with white sand from the Hilton Hotel, south all the way to Khao Takiap.

BEST BIKE RIDE

I enjoy cycling outside of the centre of Hua Hin where there are so many small roads and dirt trails with beaches to visit, mountain viewpoints, clean air and plenty of sunshine. You can't see all this by car and cycling is also good exercise and environmentally friendly to help keep Hua Hin beautiful and clean.

FAVOURITE OUTING FOR OUT-OF-TOWNERS

Tham Phraya Nakhon is an amazing cave in Khao Sam Roi Yot National Park that has a Thai-style pavilion inside with a statue of Rama V. Three of Thailand's kings have visited this cave and two have signed the wall of the cave. Getting to the cave is also part of the attraction because it is inside a mountain that requires trekking up a 430m jungle trail reached by taking a boat from a nearby beach or hiking over another small mountain. Plus there are nearby inexpensive and excellent Thai seafood restaurants too.

SECRET SPOT

Eighteen Below Ice Cream (Th Naebkehardt, North Hua Hin) is owned by a young couple: the wife used to be a Thai actress and the husband is a Belgian pastry chef who makes amazing ice cream and pastries. They started out just selling to the finer hotels in Hua Hin but later decided to turn their home into a lovely garden cafe. Many Thai people from Bangkok go there on weekends but most foreigners have no idea the place exists.

All Nations Guest House GUEST HOUSE $
(☎0 3251 2747; 10-10/1 Th Dechanuchit; r 500-800B; ❄) Has slightly dingy rooms but at a decent price with enough noise protection.

HUA HIN BEACHES

TOP CHOICE **Baan Bayan** HOTEL $$$
(☎0 3253 3540; www.baanbayan.com; 119 Th Phetkasem, South Hua Hin; r 4000-11,000B; ❄🏊) A colonial beach house built in the early 20th century, Baan Bayan is perfect for travellers seeking a luxury experience without the overkill of a big resort. The airy, high-ceilinged rooms are painted a relaxing buttery yellow, the staff are attentive and the location is absolute beachfront.

Green Gallery Bed & Breakfast HOTEL $$
(☎0 3253 0487; www.greenhuahin.com; 3/1 Soi Hua Hin 51, Th Naebkehardt, North Hua Hin; r 1200B; ❄📶) Just as cute as candy, this small hotel occupies a converted colonial-style beach house. Individually decorated rooms reflect a hip artiness that defines urban Thai style. You're also a short walk to north Hua Hin beach.

Rahmahyah Hotel GUEST HOUSE $$
(☎0 3253 2106; 113/10 Soi Hua Hin 67, Th Phetkasem, South Hua Hin; r from 1000B; ❄🏊📶) Across the street from Market Village, about 1km south of town, is a small guest house enclave tucked between the high-end resorts, with beach access. The Rahmahyah is the best of the bunch with professional staff and clean functional rooms. The front rooms get a lot of highway noise.

Baan Laksasubha HOTEL $$$
(☎032514525; www.baanlaksasubha.com; Th 53/7 Naresdamri; r 4200-7900B; ❄🏊📶) Next door to the Sofitel, this petite resort, owned by a Bangkok aristocrat, specialises in family-friendly cottages. The decor is so crisp and subdued that it is almost plain, meandering garden paths lead past the pool to the beach and there's a dedicated kid's room with toys and books. The taxi drivers will understand you better if you say 'baan lak-su-pah'.

Veranda Lodge HOTEL $$$
(☎032533678; 113 Soi Hua Hin 67, Th Phetkasem, South Hua Hin; www.verandalodge.com; r 3000-5000B; ❄🏊📶) Beachfront without the whopping price tag, this top-end hotel has a variety of options, from modern hotel rooms to luxurious garden bungalows.

Sofitel Centara Grand Resort and Villas HOTEL $$$
(☎0 3251 2021; www.sofitel.com; 1 Th Damnoen Kasem; r from 5500B; ❄@🏊) The historic Railway Hotel, Hua Hin's first seaside hotel, was restored to suit modern beachgoers with expansive grounds, a spa and sporting facilities and colonial or new world rooms.

Anantara Resort & Spa HOTEL $$$
(☎0 3252 0205; www.huahin.anantara.com; r from 7500B; Th Phetkasem; ❄🏊📶) Anantara's self-contained resort, 4.5km north of Hua Hin, is designed to invoke a traditional Thai village with a low-key but luxurious ambience. An experiential resort, there are spa facilities, water sports and cultural activities.

Chiva-Som International Health Resort HOTEL $$$
(☎0 3253 6536; www.chivasom.com; 74/4 Th Phetkasem, South Hua Hin; 3-night packages from 68,310B; ❄🏊) When a getaway isn't enough, there's Chiva-Som, for overworked, overstressed (and just maybe overpaid) business folk and celebrities. Health and wellness services include nutrition consultation, yoga and fitness classes, massage of every variety as well as detox programs.

Eating

Night Market SEAFOOD $
(Th Dechanuchit btw Th Phetkasem & Th Sasong; dishes from 60B; ⏰5pm-midnight) An attraction that rivals the beach, Hua Hin's night market tops locals' lists of favourite spots to eat. Ice-packed displays of spiny lobsters and king prawns appeal to the big spenders but the simple stir-fry stalls are just as tasty. Try *pàt pǒng gà·rèe Ъoo* (crab curry), *gûng tôrt* (fried shrimp) and *hǒy tôrt* (fried mussel omelette). In between, souvenir stalls cater to Thai's favourite digestive activity: shopping.

Sang Thai Restaurant THAI $
(Th Naresdamri; dishes 120-350B; ⏰lunch & dinner) One of many beloved pier-side restaurants, Sang Thai soaks in the view and specialises in whole steamed fish that arrives still sizzling to your table.

Jek Pia Coffeeshop SEAFOOD $
(51/6 Th Dechanuchit; dishes 80-160B; ⏰lunch & dinner) More than just a coffee shop, this 50-year-old restaurant is another culinary destination specialising in an extensive array of stir-fried seafood dishes. If it is too full to get a seat, you can order from the same

menu at the sukiyaki restaurant further south on Th Naebkehardt.

Hua Hin Koti SEAFOOD $$
(☎0 3251 1252; 16/1 Th Dechanuchit; dishes 80-250B; ⊙lunch & dinner) Across from the Night Market, this Thai-Chinese restaurant is a national culinary luminary. Thais adore the fried crab balls, while foreigners swoon over *đôm yam gûng* (shrimp soup with lemongrass). And everyone loves the spicy seafood salad *(yam tá-lair)* and deep-fried fish with ginger.

Th Chomsin Food Stalls THAI $
(cnr Th Chomsin & Th Naebkhardt; dishes from 30B; ⊙lunch & dinner) If you're after 100% authentic eats, check out the food stalls that congregate at this popular lunch corner. Though the setting is humble, Thais are fastidious eaters and use a fork (or their fingers with a pinch of *kôw nĕe·o*) to remove the meat from the bones of *gài tôrt* (fried chicken) rather than putting teeth directly to flesh.

Sofitel Cafe & Tea Corner CAFE $$
(1 Th Damnoen Kasem; dishes 80-150B; ⊙breakfast & lunch) It is customary to pay homage to a city's grand dame hotel with a spot of tea and the Sofitel obliges with this refined tea room occupying the grounds of the former Railway Hotel. The cafe is serenaded by classical music and cooled by sea breezes, perfect for thumbing the newspaper and sipping your stimulants with an aristocratic air. There are also a few historic photos and memorabilia earning it the unlikely designation of 'museum'. The real draw, though, is the hotel's topiary garden filled with gigantic clipped shrubs depicting elephants, giraffes and geese.

Chatchai Market THAI $
(Th Phetkasem; ⊙daylight hours; dishes from 30B) The city's day market resides in an historic building built in 1926 with a distinctive seven-eaved roof in honour of Rama VII. There are the usual market refreshments: morning vendors selling *ɓah·tôrng·gŏh* (Chinese-style doughnuts) and *gah·faa boh·rahn* (ancient-style coffee spiked with sweetened condensed milk); as well as all-day noodles with freshly made wontons; and the full assortment of fresh tropical fruit.

World News Coffee CAFE $
(130/2 Th Naresdamri; dishes 70-150B; ⊙breakfast, lunch & dinner; @) This Starbucks-esque cafe serves baked goods and lots of different coffees. You can surf the web for 50B per hour and there are magazines and newspapers to complement your first cup of the day.

Drinking & Entertainment

Drinking in Hua Hin is still stuck in the '90s: sports bars or hostess bars – and sometimes you can't tell the difference. But the onslaught of weekending Bangkok Thais has kicked up the sophistication factor. Apart from these, also consider Cicada Market in Khao Takiab (see p151).

No Name Bar BAR
(Th Naresdamri) Past the Chinese shrine that sits on the rocky headland is this cliffside restaurant and bar that drinks in the ocean along with all the alcoholic adult beverages.

Hua Hin Brewing Company BAR
(33 Th Naresdamri) Though there's no longer any beer brewed here, the spacious outdoor deck is a mature spot to watch the passing parade on Th Naresdamri.

Mai Tai Cocktail & Beer Garden BAR
(33/12 Th Naresdamri) Recession-era prices are on tap at this convivial outdoor terrace made for people-watching and beer-drinking.

O'Neill's Irish Pub IRISH BAR
(5 Th Phunsuk) Pretty authentic for being so far from the Blarney Stone, O'Neill's does cheap draught specials and live sports on several tellies.

El Murphy's Mexican Grill & Steakhouse BAR
(25 Soi Selakam, Th Phunsuk) Every sports bar has an international gimmick and this comfy spot marries Mexico and Ireland. Come in to enjoy a tall one, the live band and an unlikely assortment of tourists and expats.

Music Room LIVE MUSIC
(Soi Hua Hin 32, Th Phetkasem, North Hua Hin) The place to be for weekending Thais, the Music Room features live bands of every imaginable genre as well as theme parties and a local collection of celebrities.

Information

Emergency

Tourist police (☎0 3251 5995; Th Damnoen Kasem)

Internet Access

Internet access is available all over Hua Hin, in guest houses and cafes.

KEEPING UP WITH THE BANGKOK THAIS

On weekends, a different kind of tidal system occurs in Hua Hin. Bangkok professionals flow in, filling up hotels and restaurants on Th Naebkehardt, washing over the night market or crowding into nightclubs. And then come Sunday they clog the roadways heading north, obeying the pull of the upcoming work week.

Their presence is so pronounced that there is an irresistible urge to join them. And because of restaurant features on Thai TV or food magazines, everyone goes to the same places. So don your designer sunglasses and elbow your way to a table at one of these popular spots in North Hua Hin:

Sôm·đam Stand FOOD STALL
(Th Naebkehardt; dishes 50-80B; ⌚lunch) Across from Iammeuang Hotel is a *sôm·đam* stand that easily wipes out the country's supply of green papayas in one weekend. We couldn't even elbow our way to a seat before they packed up for the day.

Eighteen Below Ice Cream ICE CREAM
(Th Naebkehardt; dishes 160B; closed Wed) At the end of the road behind Baan Talay Chine Hotel, this gourmet ice cream shop is run by a trained chef and specialises in rich and creamy flavours.

Baan Itsara SEAFOOD
(Th Naebkehardt; dishes from 160B; ⌚lunch & dinner) Overpriced in our opinion, Baan Itsara is a must-be-seen spot that does 'inter' versions of Thai seafood dishes. Squid with basil comes with pine nuts so it is more like a pesto than the traditionally spicy Thai version.

Jae Siam NOODLES
(Th Naebkehardt; dishes 30-50B; ⌚lunch & dinner) If you've lost track of the days of the week, cruise by this open-air noodle shop, next to Evergreen Hotel, where Hua Hin civil servants pack in on weekdays and Bangkok Thais come on weekends. The shop is famous for *gŏo·ay đěe·o mŏo đŭn* (stewed pork noodles) and *gŏo·ay đěe·o gài đŭn* (stewed chicken noodles).

Internet Resources

Tourism Hua Hin (www.tourismhuahin.com) A cursory intro to the site with a good run-down on the outlying area.

Hua Hin Observer (www.observergroup.net) An expat-published magazine available online.

Medical Services

Hospital San Paolo (☎0 3253 2576; 222 Th Phetkasem) Just south of town with emergency facilities.

Bangkok Hospital Hua Hin (☎0 3261 6800; www.bangkokhospital.com/huahin; Th Phetkasem btw Soi Hua Hin 94 & 106;) The latest outpost of the luxury hospital chain; it's in South Hua Hin.

Money

There are exchange booths and ATMs on Th Naresdamri and banks on Th Phetkasem.

Post & Telephone

Main post office (Th Damnoen Kasem) Includes the CAT office for international phone calls.

Tourist Information

TAT office (☎0 3251 3885; 39/4 Th Phetkasem; ⌚8.30am-4.30pm) Staff here speak English and are quite helpful; the office is north of town near Soi Hua Hin 70.

Municipal Tourist Information Office (☎0 3251 1047; cnr Th Phetkasem & Th Damnoen Kasem; ⌚8.30am-4.30pm Mon-Fri) Provides maps and information about Hua Hin. There's another branch (☎0 3252 2797; Th Naebkehardt; 9am-7.30pm Mon-Fri, 9.30am-5pm Sat & Sun) near the clock tower.

Travel Agencies

Tuk Tours (☎0 3251 4281; www.tuktours.com; 33/5 Th Phunsuk) Helpful, no-pressure place that can book activities and transport all around Thailand.

 Getting There & Away

Air

The **airport** (www.huahinairport.com) is 6km north of town but only has charter services through **Nok Mini** (☎0 2641 4190; www.nokmini.com).

Bus

Hua Hin's long-distance **bus station** (Th Phetkasem btw Soi Hua Hin 94 & 98) is south of town and serves the following destinations:

Chiang Mai (785B, 12 hours, three daily departures)

Prachuap Khiri Khan (65B, 1½ hours)

Phuket (856B, nine hours, one nightly departure)

Surat Thani (480B, seven hours, two daily departures)

Ubon Ratchathani (1200B, 13 hours, one daily departure)

Buses to Bangkok (160B, three hours, every two hours from 8am to 9pm) also leave from a bus company's in-town **office** (Th Sasong), near the Night Market.

Ordinary buses depart from a **station** (cnr Th Phetkasem & Th Chomsin), north of the market, and destinations include **Cha-am** (50B, 30 minutes) and **Phetchaburi** (50B, 1½ hours).

Lomprayah (☎0 3253 3739; Th Narasdamri) offers a bus-boat combination from Hua Hin to Ko Tao (1000B, 8½ hours; one morning and one night departure).

Minivans

Minivans to Bangkok's Sai Tai Mai (Southern) bus station and Victory Monument (180B, three hours, every 30 minutes from 4am to 8pm) leave from an office on Th Naebkehardt. A direct service to Victory Monument leaves from an office on the corner of Th Phetkasem and Th Chomsin.

Train

There are frequent trains running to/from Bangkok's Hualamphong station (2nd class 212-302B, 3rd class 94-154B, four hours) and other stations on the southern railway line.

🛈 Getting Around

Green *sŏrng·tăa·ou* depart from the corner of Th Sasong & Th Dechanuchit, near the Night Market and travel south on Th Phetkasem to Khao Takiab (20B). Pranburi-bound buses depart from the same stop.

Túk-túk fares in Hua Hin are outrageous and start at a whopping 100B and barely budge from there. Motorcycle taxis are much more reasonable (40B to 50B) for short hops.

Motorcycles (250B to 500B per day) can be hired from shops on Th Damnoen Kasem. **Thai Rent A Car** (☎0 2737 8888; www.thairentacar.com) is a professional car-rental agency with competitive prices, a well-maintained fleet and hotel drop-offs.

Hua Hin to Pranburi

South of Hua Hin are a series of beaches framed by dramatic headlands that make great daytrips when Hua Hin beach feels too urban.

HAT KHAO TAO หาดเขาเต่า

About 13km south of Hua Hin, a barely inhabited beach stretches several kilometres south from Khao Takiab to Khao Tao (Turtle Mountain). It is blissfully free of civilization: there are no high rises, no beach chairs, no sarong sellers and no horseback riders.

The mountain has a sprawling temple dedicated to almost every imaginable deity: Buddha, Khun Yin (Chinese goddess of Mercy), Vishnu and even the Thai kings. Follow the trail toward the oceanfront to hike up to the Buddha on the hill.

To get here take a Pranburi bus from Hua Hin and ask to be dropped off at the turn-off for Khao Tao (20B); a motorcycle taxi can take you to the temple (20B). Getting back to the highway might be tricky as return transport is rare; you can always walk or flag down a ride as people are usually coming and going from the temple.

HAT SAI NOI หาดทรายน้อย

About 20km south of Hua Hin, a scenic cove, Hat Sai Noi, drops off quickly into the sea providing a rare opportunity for deep-water swimming. Nearby are all the amenities: simple seafood restaurants and even small guest houses. For ideal seclusion, come on a weekday. The beach is south of Khao Tao on a lovely road that passes a reservoir and is lined with bougainvillea and limestone cliffs. To get here follow the same directions for Khao Tao but instruct the motorcycle taxi to take you to Hat Sai Noi (60B); getting back to the highway will be difficult but inquire at one of the restaurants for assistance.

Pranburi & Around

POP 75,571

Continuing along the highway south from Hua Hin leads to the country 'suburb' of Pranburi district, which has become the *in-the-know* coastal alternative for Bangkok Thais. Some even go so far as to call it the 'Thai Riveria'. Yet locally the fishing village and nearby beaches are known by a more humble name: **Pak Nam Pran** (mouth of the Pranburi River), designating only its geographic location.

A coastal road separates a string of small villa-style resorts from the beach and with each successive rainy season the ocean claims more sand than its fair share requiring the installation of a bulkhead along parts of the long coastline. Since the primary clientele are Thai, the disappearing beach is of minor consequence. Instead most domestic tourists come for sea views and the village's primary product: dried squid. In the mornings the squid boats dock in the river, unloading their catch and beginning the process of sun-drying. It is a pungent but interesting affair with large drying racks spread out across town.

Bordering the river is an extensive mangrove forest, protected by the **Pranburi Forest Park** (☎0 3262 1608; admission free). Within the park is a wooden walkway that explores the mangroves from the perspective of a a mud-dweller, a sea-pine lined beach and accommodation facilities. The park also offers boat trips along the river and small canals.

The coastal road provides a pleasant trip to **Khao Kalok** (Skull Mountain), a mammoth headland that shelters a beautiful bay on the southern side. This southern beach is wide and sandy and far removed from the hubbub of Hua Hin and even from Pak Nam Pran for that matter, though it does get busy on weekends. Lazying along this stretch are several secluded boutique resorts that would be ideal for honeymooners or folks looking to 'get away from it all' without having to go too far.

The next southern bay is often called **Dolphin Bay**, because of the seasonal visit from bottlenose dolphins and finless porpoise from February to May. Sculpted, jungle-covered islands sit scenically off-shore and the beach is wide and unhindered. This area is a family favourite because the resorts are value-oriented, traffic is minimal and nightlife is non-existent. You're also a few kilometres from the northern entrance to Khao Sam Roi Yot National Park (see p160 for more information).

Sleeping & Eating

It is mainly high, high-end here but not all of the beach resorts sufficiently earn the price tag so be discerning when making online reservations for places not listed here. That said, this area has some of the best seaside boutiques in Thailand that wholeheartedly deserve a splash-out occasion.

TOP CHOICE Away Hua Hin HOTEL $$$
(☎0891446833; www.away-huahin.com; south of Khao Kalok; r from 5000B;) A boutique resort without pretence, Away has reconstructed seven antique teak houses, many from northern Thailand, to this coastal patch of paradise and outfitted them with large cosy beds and stylish bathrooms. The affable owners, a Thai–Australian family, set a homey mood where breakfast is enjoyed at a common table in the 'big' house providing instant camaraderie with worldly friends. Some villas provide extreme privacy while others accommodate families.

La a natu Bed & Bakery HOTEL $$$
(☎0 3268 9941; www.laanatu.com; south of Khao Kalok; r from 5000B;) Turning the humble Thai rice village into a luxury experience is all the rage in the boutique hotel world but La a natu does it with a little more panache than most. The thatched roof villas growing on stilts from cultivated rice paddies have rounded modern corners and a Flintstone-esque playfulness to their design. Each villa is extremely private but evocative of traditional rustic lifestyles with living quarters on the ground floor and often steep, ladder-like stairs leading to the sleeping area. And then there's the semiprivate beach right at your doorstep.

Dolphin Bay Resort HOTEL $$
(☎0 3255 9333; www.dolphinbayresort.com; Dolphin Bay; r from 1500B;) The resort that defined Dolphin Bay as a family-friendly retreat offers a low-key holiday camp ambience with a variety of standard issue, value-oriented bungalows and apartments. The grounds are large enough for kids to roam safely, there are two large pools and the nice sandy beach is just across the street. The gang will love it.

Brassiere Beach HOTEL $$$
(☎0 3263 0555; www.brassierebeach.com; Dolphin Bay; r from 5000B;) A delicious combination of privacy and personality, these nine stucco villas abut the mountains of Khao Sam Roi Yot National Park and face a secluded beach, 100m from the nearest paved road. The rooms have an uncluttered Mexican-villa style, some with roof decks and most with open-air showers. Though the prude in you might mispronounce it, Brassiere Beach deserves your support.

Khao Kalok Restaurant THAI $
(dishes 60-150B; ⌚lunch & dinner) At the southern base of the mountain, this open-air restaurant provides a front-row view of the moored fishing boats. Tasty dishes, like *gaang kĕe·o wăhn* (green curry), *Ƀlah mèuk gà·prow* (squid stir-fried with basil) and even the standard *pàt pàk roo·am* (stir-fried vegetables) arrive at a leisurely pace.

Also recommended:

Pranburi Forest Park CAMPING GROUND $
(☎0 32621608, Pak Nam Pran; tent site & gear rental 300B) A popular spot for 'freshy' (university freshmen) parties, the forest park has a shaded oceanfront camping ground, basic bungalows (1000/2000B for 6/12 people) and a restaurant. No fires allowed.

Pineapple Resort GUEST HOUSE $
(☎0 81933 9930; Pak Nam Pran; r 500-600B; ❄) A little dishevelled, Pineapple's basic concrete bungalows sit about 50m from the beach but provides a cheap retreat in the land of luxury.

Palm Beach Pranburi HOTEL $$
(☎0 3263 1966; www.palmbeachpranburi.com; Pak Nam Pran; r from 1500B; ❄≋) A solid midranger surrounded by neighbours who think they're boutique.

The Beach House GUEST HOUSE $
(☎08 7164 6307; Pak Nam Pran; r 500-800B; ❄⌔) One of the cheapest options around, this guest house caters to young kite-boarders who allot their funds toward the sport instead of lodging.

ℹ Getting There & Around

Pranburi is about 35km south of Hua Hin and accessible by ordinary bus from Hua Hin's Night Market (20B). You'll be dropped off on the highway where you can catch a *sŏrng·tăa·ou* to Pak Nam Pran. There is also a minivan service from Bangkok's Victory Monument to Pranburi (180B); if you're going to Dolphin Bay (sometimes referred to as Khao Sam Roi Yot Beach), you'll have to negotiate an additional fare with the driver (usually 100B).

If you want to explore the area, you'll need to rent a motorbike as public transport isn't an option.

Khao Sam Roi Yot National Park

อุทยานแห่งชาติเขาสามร้อยยอด

Towering limestone outcrops form a rocky jigsaw-puzzled landscape at this 98-sq-km **park** (☎0 3282 1568; adult/child 200/100B), which means Three Hundred Mountain Peaks. There are also caves, beaches and coastal marshlands to explore for outdoor enthusiast and bird-watchers. With its proximity to Hua Hin, the park is well travelled by daytrippers and contains a mix of public conservation land and private shrimp farms, so don't come expecting remote virgin territory.

Rama IV and a large entourage of Thai and European guests came here on 18 August 1868 to see a total solar eclipse (apparently predicted by the monarch himself) and to enjoy a feast prepared by a French chef. Two months later the king died from malaria, contracted from mosquito bites inflicted here. Today the risk of malaria in the park is low, but the mosquitoes can be pesky.

The **Khao Daeng Visitors Centre** in the southern end of the park has the largest collection of tourist information and English-speaking rangers. Maps are handed out at the entrance gates.

Travel agencies in Hua Hin run daytrips. **Hua Hin Bike Tours** (☎08 1173 4469; www.huahinbiketours.com; tours 1500-2500B) offers cycling and hiking tours.

Sights & Activities

The following are listed in geographic order north to south because the maps provided at the park checkpoints are often in Thai.

Tham Kaew CAVE
(ถ้ำแก้ว) Not a popular daytrippers' stop, Tham Kaew is a series of underground chambers and narrow passageways accessed by a steep scramble 128m up the mountain. Stalactites and limestone formations here glitter with calcite crystals (hence the cave's name, 'Jewel Cave') are plentiful. You can hire lamps from the booth at the footpath's entrance, and exercise caution as the path can be slippery and dangerous.

Tham Phraya Nakhon & Hat Laem Sala CAVE
(ถ้ำพระยานคร/หาดแหลมศาลา) The park's most popular attraction is this revered cave sheltering a royal *săh·lah* (meeting hall; often spelled *sala*) built for Rama V in 1890 that is often bathed in streams of light.

BIRDS OF A FEATHER

Because the park is at the intersection of the East Asian and Australian migration routes, as many as 300 migratory and resident bird species have been recorded at Khao Sam Roi Yot National Park, including yellow bitterns, cinnamon bitterns, purple swamphens, water rails, ruddy-breasted crakes, bronze-winged jacanas, grey herons, painted storks, whistling ducks, spotted eagles and black-headed ibises. Thung Sam Roi Yot is one of only two places in the country where the purple heron breeds.

Waterfowl are most commonly seen in the cool season. November to March are the best waterfowl-watching months. The birds come from as far as Siberia, China and northern Europe to winter here. Common places for bird-watchers are the Mangrove Centre, Khlong Khao Daeng and even some of the beaches.

Thai Birding (www.thaibirding.com) provides more in-depth information about the park's bird species and where to spot them.

The cave is accessed by a walking trail from picturesque **Hat Laem Sala**, a sandy beach flanked on three sides by limestone hills and casuarinas. The beach hosts a small visitors centre, restaurant, bungalows and camp sites. The cave trail is 450m long and is steep, rocky and at times slick so don't wear your ballet flats. Once there you'll find two large caverns with sinkholes – the meeting hall is the second of the two.

Reaching Laem Sala requires alternative travel since there is no road connection. It is reached by boat from Bang Pu (300B return), which sits beachfront from the turn-off from Tham Kaew. Alternatively you can follow the steep footpath from Bang Pu for a 20-minute hike to the beach.

Tham Sai CAVE

(ถ้ำไทร) This cave sits at the end of a 280m hillside trail and features a large single cavern filled with stalactites and stalagmites. Be careful of steep drop-offs inside and slippery footings. Usually only the more adventurous types undertake this one. Villagers rent out lamps near the cave mouth. It is just north of Hat Sam Phraya.

Hat Sam Phraya BEACH

(หาดสามพระยา) This shady casuarina-lined beach is about 1km long and is a pleasant stop for a swim after a sweaty hike. There is a restaurant and toilets.

Khao Daeng HIKING

(เขาแดง) The turn-off to the trail winds through towering mountains promising a rewarding hike. The 30-minute step trail that leads to the top of Khao Daeng delivers spectacular views of limestone cliffs against a jagged coastline.

Khlong Khao Daeng BIRDING

(คลองเขาแดง) You can hire a boat at Wat Khao Daeng for a cruise (400B, 45 minutes) along the canal in the morning or afternoon. Before heading out, chat with your prospective guide to see how well they speak English. Better guides will know the English names of common waterfowl and point them out to you.

Mangrove Walk NATURE TRAIL

Located behind the visitors centre in the southern end of the park is a wooden boardwalk that circumnavigates a mangrove swamp popular for bird-watching and crab spotting. There are guides available for hire from the centre depending on availability and English-language ability.

Thung Sam Roi Yot BIRDING

(ทุ่งสามร้อยยอด) The country's largest freshwater marsh is recognized as a natural treasure and provides an important habitat for songbirds and water birds, amphibians and other wetland species. It sits in the western corner of the park accessible from Hwy 4 (Th Phetkasem) at the Km275.6 marker; hold on to your entrance fee ticket to avoid having to pay again.

Sleeping & Eating

The **National parks department** (☎0 2562 0760; www.dnp.go.th/parkreserve; tent site 60-90B, bungalows 1200-1400B) hires out bungalows (sleeping up to six people) at Hat Laem Sala and at the visitors centre; advance reservations required. You can pitch a tent at campsites near the Khao Daeng viewpoint, Hat Laem Sala or Hat Sam Phraya. There are basic restaurants at all these locations.

WORTH A TRIP

WHERE THE ELEPHANTS ARE

Want to see herds of wild elephants enjoying an evening bath surrounded by the sounds of the jungle? Though urbanised Thailand seems hundreds of kilometres away from such a natural state, **Kuiburi National Park** (☎0 3264 6292; Hwy 3217; adult/child 200/100B), southwest of Khao Sam Roi Yot National Park, shelters one of the country's largest herds of wild elephants (estimated at over 140 animals). The park provides an important habitat link between the rugged Myanmar (Burma) border and Kaeng Krachan National Park, forming one of the largest intact forest tracts in Southeast Asia. The herds can frequently be found bathing at the watering ponds near the Pa Yang substation, which is equipped with wildlife-viewing platforms.

Trekking and elephant-spotting tours include English-speaking guides and transport and can be arranged through the park headquarters.

Bungalow **accommodation** (www.dnp.th.go/parkreserve; bungalows 1800B) is available for overnight stays with advance reservations.

There are also private resorts within 4km of the park at Dolphin Bay; see Pranburi & Around (p164) for more information.

Getting There & Away

The park is about 40km south of Hua Hin, and best visited by vehicle. There are two main entrances into the park. The turn-off for the northern entrance is at Km256 marker on Hwy 4 (Th Phetkasem). The southern entrance is off the Km286.5 marker.

If you don't have your own wheels and don't want to take a tour from Hua Hin, you can get a minivan from Bangkok's Victory Monument to Pranburi (180B) and then hire a motorcycle to tour the park independently. You can also negotiate with the minivan driver to drop you off at the entrance to the park but then you won't have transport into the park.

Prachuap Khiri Khan

ประจวบคีรีขันธ์

POP 86,870

A sleepy seaside town, Prachuap Khiri Khan feels like you've finally arrived in southern Thailand. The pace is supremely relaxed, Muslim headscarves are common and the broad bay is a tropical blue punctuated by bobbing fishing boats. Usually you have to travel to the southern Andaman to find the honeycombed limestone mountains that saddle Prachuap's scenic bays. All in all it is a slice of everything nice – pretty coastal scenery and laid-back provincial-style living.

In recent years, more and more expats have been defecting to Prachuap from the overbuilt Samui archipelago bringing with them the travellers' amenities that the town was lacking. Now it is a lot less lonely but just as enjoyable. Attractions, with a small 'a', include climbing to a hill-top temple, taking a leisurely motorbike ride to the excellent beaches north and south of town, or just enjoying some of Thailand's freshest (and cheapest) seafood.

Prachuap Khiri Khan, and specifically Ao Manao, was one of seven points on the gulf coast where Japanese troops landed on 8 December 1941 during their invasion of Thailand. Several street names around town commemorate the skirmish that ensued afterwards: Phithak Chat (Defend Country), Salachip (Sacrifice Life) and Suseuk (Fight Battle).

Sights & Activities

Khao Chong Krajok VIEWPOINT

(เขาช่องกระจก) At the northern end of town, Khao Chong Krajok ('Mirror Tunnel Mountain', so named for the mountain-side hole that seemingly reflects the sky) provides a beloved Prachuap tradition: climbing to the top, dodging ill-behaved monkeys and enjoying a cascading view of a curlicue coastline. A long flight of stairs soiled by the partly wild monkeys leads to a mountain-top **temple** established by Rama VI. From here there are perfect views of the town and the bay and even the border with Myanmar, just 11km away. Don't bring food, drink or plastic bags with you as the monkeys will assume it is a prize worth nipping.

Ao Prachuap BAY

(อ่าวประจวบ) The town's crowning feature is Ao Prachuap (Prachuap Bay), a gracefully curving bay outlined by an oceanfront esplanade. In the cool hours of the morning and evening, locals run, shuffle or promenade along this route enjoying the ocean breezes and sea music. On Friday and Saturday evenings, the esplanade hosts a **Walking Street market** (Th Chai Thaleh; ⏲from 5pm), selling food, souvenirs and clothes.

North of Khao Chong Krajok, just over the bridge, the bay stretches peacefully to a toothy mountain scraper with less commercial activity than its in-town counterpart. There is a nice sandy beach here though it does lack in privacy due to its proximity to passing motorists. Nonetheless, weekending Thais often visit because there is no bulkhead and it is a pleasant beachcombing spot. At the far northern end is a traditional fishing village decorated with colourful wooden trawlers and a visible sense of hard work and a hand-made life.

Wat Ao Noi TEMPLE

(วัดอ่าวน้อย) From Ao Prachuap, follow the coastal road 8km north as it skirts through the fishing village and flower-filled lanes to reach this beautiful teak temple that straddles two bays (Ao Noi and Ao Khan Kradai). Limestone mountains pose photogenically in the background, while a dramatic nine-headed naga protects the temple's exterior. Inside are unique bas-relief murals depicting the *jataka* stories (Buddha's previous lives).

The temple grounds are forested with a variety of fruit trees (jackfruit, pomegranate, mango and rose apple) and a lotus pond filled with ravenous fish, eager to be feed by merit-makers. You'll catch an unpleasant odour nearby indicating that the temple is in the business of raising swiftlets for the profitable edible bird's nest industry; don't try to steal any nests or eggs as the fine and punishment (five years' imprisonment and 500,000B) are severe.

A craggy limestone mountain (Khao Khan Kradai) shelters the temple from the coast and contains a locally famous cave temple, known as **Tham Phra Nawn** (Sleeping Buddha Cave). The cave is accessible via a concrete trail that leads up and around the side of the hill providing scenic views of Ao Khan Kradai and the foothills beyond. It is blissfully quiet and the forested hill is dotted with blooming cactus clinging to the craggy rocks. Inside the cave is a small cavern leading to a larger one that contains the eponymous reclining Buddha. If you have a torch (flashlight) you can proceed to a larger second chamber also containing Buddha images.

Prachuap Khiri Khan

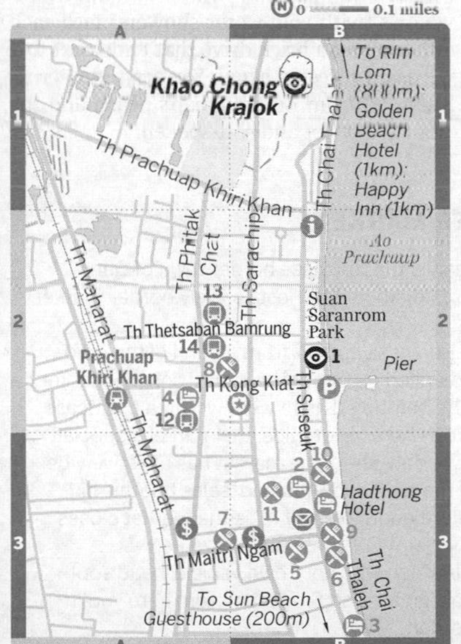

Prachuap Khiri Khan

Top Sights

Khao Chong Krajok B1

Sights

1 Weekend Walking Street/Market B2

Sleeping

2 Maggie's Homestay B3
3 Prachuap Beach Hotel B3
4 Yuttichai Hotel A2

Eating

5 Day Market B3
6 Ma Prow B3
7 Muslim Chicken Stall A3
8 Night Market A2
9 Ning's Guesthouse Restaurant B3
10 Phloen Samut B3
11 Suan Krua B3

Transport

12 Air-con Buses to Hua Hin, Cha-am, Phetchaburi & Bangkok A2
13 Minivans to Ban Krut, Bang Saphan Yai & Chumphon A2
14 Minivans to Hua Hin & Bangkok A2

Ao Manao SWIMMING

(อ่าวมะนาว) On weekends, locals head to Ao Manao, 4km south of town, an island-dotted bay ringed by a clean sandy beach. It is within Wing 5 of a Thai air-force base and each and every week the beach is given a military-grade clean up. There are the usual beach amenities: a restaurant and rentable beach chairs, umbrellas and inner tubes. En route to the beach you'll pass Thailand's Top Guns relaxing on a nearby golf course and driving range. You enter the base through a checkpoint on Th Suseuk from town; you may need to show your passport. The beach closes at 8pm.

Sleeping

You can always find a cosy place to stay near the sea as many of the oceanfront residences rent out rooms. Just cruise down Th Chai Thaleh and see who has a vacancy sign out. In recent years, Prachuap has even gained a few full-fledged guest houses.

IN TOWN

Maggie's Homestay GUEST HOUSE $

(08 7597 9720; 5 Soi Tampramuk; r 150-600B;) In the old-fashioned backpacker tradition, lovely owner Maggie oversees an eclectic collection of travellers who call her house home. Simple rooms occupy a converted house with a shady garden and shared kitchen facilities.

Yuttichai Hotel GUEST HOUSE $

(0 3261 1055; 115 Th Kong Kiat; r 160-400B;) One of Prachuap's original guest houses, Yuttichai has simple budget rooms (with cold water showers) close to the train station. The cheapest rooms share bathrooms. If you don't stay here, at least stop by their old-style Thai-Chinese cafe popular with the 'men in brown' (police).

Sun Beach Guesthouse GUEST HOUSE $$

(0 3260 4770; www.sunbeach-guesthouse.com; 160 Th Chai Thaleh; r 700-1000B;) With hotel amenities and guest-house hospitality, Sun Beach is a superb midranger. Its neoclassical styling and bright-yellow paint liven things up, while the rooms are super-clean and come with large verandahs.

Prachuap Beach Hotel HOTEL $$

(0 3260 1288; 123 Th Suseuk; r 650-1100B;) Crisp white linens and splashy accent walls add a bit of flair to this multistorey number. One side has fabulous sea views, while the other has decent, though not exciting, mountain views.

OUT OF TOWN

TOP CHOICE **Aow Noi Sea View** HOTEL $$

(0 3260 4440; www.aownoiseaview.com; Ao Noi; r 600-800B;) North of town, this three-storey hotel is Prachuap's best beachfront option. With pretty Ao Noi beach at your doorstep, you'll enjoy sea breezes, rooms with large bathrooms and a homey ambience complete with linen drying on the line outside.

Happy Inn GUEST HOUSE $

(0 3260 2082; 149-151 Th Suanson; r 250-500B) About 1km north of town, these simple bungalows (with cold-water showers) face each other along a brick drive that ends next to a pleasant forested canal. You are right across the road from Ao Prachuap's beach and the staff are sweet and soft-spoken.

DETOUR: DAN SINGKHON BORDER MARKET

A mere 12km southwest of Prachuap Khiri Khan is the Burmese border town of Dan Singkhon. Once a strategic military point, Dan Singkhon now hosts a lively border market beloved by locals for its many bargains.

Beginning at dawn on Saturday mornings, Burmese appear from a bend in the road just beyond the checkpoint, pushing handcarts piled high with the usual trinkets, market goods and plants. Short-term tourists might be befuddled as to what will fit in a suitcase but locals and expats make frequent buying trips here for orchids, the market's specialty, and hardwood furniture. Even if you come to window-shop, the market has a festive vibe, with music blaring, colourful umbrellas lining the road and thatched 'sales booths' hidden under palms. You'll need to arrive well before noon to enjoy it, as the market closes at midday.

To get to Dan Singkhon from Prachuap Khiri Khan with your own vehicle, head south on Hwy 4. After several kilometres you'll see a sign for Dan Singkhon; from here you'll head west about 15km before reaching the border.

Golden Beach Hotel HOTEL $$
(☎0 3260 1626; www.goldenbeachprachuap.com; 113-115 Th Suanson; r 500-1200B; ❄📶) Near Happy Inn, Golden Beach is a comfortable midrange option across from Ao Prachuap's beach. Some rooms have generous picture windows providing a marine sleeping companion.

Eating

Restaurants in Prachuap are cheap and tasty and Western food is popping up at little restaurants on Th Chai Thaleh. The **day market** (Th Maitri Ngam; ⏲daylight hours) is the place to get pineapples fresh from the orchards; ask the vendor to cut it for you. Across the street is a **Muslim chicken stall** (Th Maitri Ngam; dishes 40-60B; ⏲dinner) that does some of the crispiest fried chicken in the country. The **night market** (Th Kong Kiat; ⏲5-9pm) is small and has the usual stir-fry stalls.

TOP CHOICE **Rim Lom** SEAFOOD $$
(5 Th Suanson; dishes 120-220B; ⏲lunch & dinner) We still dream about this meal on a bright sunny day surrounded by lunching civil servants. The *pàt pŏng gà·rèe Ъoo* (crab curry) comes with big chunks of sweet crab meat and the *yam ta-lair* (seafood salad) is spicy, zesty and festooned with seafood.

Phloen Samut SEAFOOD $$
(44 Th Chai Thaleh; dishes 80-200B; ⏲lunch & dinner) One of a few seafood restaurants along the promenade, Phloen Samut is conveniently located in town though locals complain that the food needs improvement.

Ma Prow INTERNATIONAL $$
(48 Th Chai Thaleh; dishes 80-200B; ⏲lunch & dinner) An airy wooden pavilion across from the beach, Ma Prow cooks up excellent *Ъlah săm·lee dàat dee·o* (a local specialty of whole sun-dried cotton fish that is fried and served with mango salad). The tamarind fish dish is another favourite with foreigners and locals.

Ning's Guesthouse Restaurant INTERNATIONAL $
(Th Chai Thaleh; dishes 40-120B; ⏲breakfast, lunch & dinner) Decorated in a playful Rasta-style mood, Ning is an early riser serving Western breakfasts before anyone else is awake. She continues cooking through the day too.

Suan Krua VEGETARIAN $
(Soi Tampramuk; dishes 30-60B; ⏲lunch) Next door to Maggie's Homestay, this vegetarian restaurant cooks fast and furiously for a limited time only and then it closes until the next day. Be here promptly and hungrily.

Information

Bangkok Bank (cnr Th Maitri Ngam & Th Sarachip)

Police station (Th Kong Kiat) Just west of Th Sarachip.

Post office (cnr Th Maitri Ngam & Th Suseuk)

Thai Farmers Bank (Th Phitak Chat) Just north of Th Maitri Ngam.

Tourist office (☎0 3261 1491; Th Chai Thaleh; ⏲8.30am-4.30pm) At the northern end of town. The staff speak English and are very helpful.

Getting There & Away

There are hourly air-conditioned buses that leave from Th Phitak Chat to the following destinations:

Bangkok (170B, five hours)
Cha-am (100B, two hours)
Hua Hin (100B, 1½ hours)
Phetchaburi (140B, three hours)

Minivans leave from the corner of Th Thetsaban Bamrung and Th Phitak Chat to the following destinations:

Bangkok (250B)
Ban Krut (70B, one hour)
Bang Saphan Yai (80B, 1½ hours)
Chumphon (180B, 3½ hours)
Hua Hin (80B)

Long-distance buses to southern destinations (such as Phuket and Krabi) stop at the new bus station, 2km northwest of town on the main highway; motorcycle taxis will take you for 40B to 50B.

The train station is on Th Maharat; there are frequent services to/from Bangkok (1st class 768B, 2nd class 210-425B, 3rd class 168B; six hours).

Getting Around

Prachuap is small enough to get around on foot, but you can hop on a motorcycle taxi around town for 20B to 30B. To reach outlying destinations, Ao Noi and Ao Manao it is 100B to 150B.

You can hire motorbikes for 250B per day. The roads in the area are very good and it's a great way to see the surrounding beaches.

Ban Krut & Bang Saphan Yai บ้านกรูด/บางสะพานใหญ่

POP 4275/ 68,344

What a nice surprise to find these lovely low-key beaches (80km to 100km south of Prachuap Khiri Khan, respectively) so close to civilization but so bucolic. Dusk falls softly through the coconut trees and the sea is a crystalline blue lapping at a long sandy coastline. No high-rises, no late-night discos, and no speeding traffic to distract you from a serious regimen of reading, swimming, eating and biking.

Though both beaches are pleasantly subdued, they are also well known by Thais and Ban Krut, in particular, hosts bus tours as well as weekending families. During the week you'll have the beaches largely to yourself and a few long-tail boats.

Check out the websites **Ban Krut Info** (www.bankrutinfo.com) and **Bang Saphan Guide** (www.bangsaphanguide.com) for local information on the area.

Ban Krut is a divided into two beaches by a temple-topped headland. To the north is **Hat Sai Kaew**, which is remote and private with only a few resorts in between a lot of jungle. To the south is **Hat Ban Krut**, with a beachfront road and a string of bungalow-style resorts and restaurants on the interior side of the road. Both are golden-sand beaches with clear, calm water but Hat Ban Krut is slightly more social and easier to get around without private transport.

Bang Saphan Yai, 20km south of Ban Krut, fits that most famous beach cliché: It is Thailand 15 years ago before pool villas and package tourists pushed out all the beach bums. Once you settle into a simple beachfront hut, you probably won't need shoes and the days will just melt away. Islands off the coast, including **Ko Thalu** and **Ko Sing**, offer good snorkelling and diving from the end of January to mid-May.

Sleeping & Eating

BAN KRUT

You'll struggle to find true budget options here, but if you visit on a weekday you should secure a discount. In Hat Ban Krut, bicycles (100B per day) and motorcycles (300B per day) can be hired to run errands in town, and most accommodation options arrange snorkelling trips to nearby islands. If you stay in Hat Sai Kaew you'll need private transport.

TOP CHOICE Proud Thai Beach Resort GUEST HOUSE $$
(08 9682 4484; www.proudthairesort.com; Hat Ban Krut; r 700-1200B;) Well-maintained bungalows in a flower-filled garden come with porches and morning coffee delivered by the affable owner.

NaNa Chart Baan Kruit HOTEL $$
(0 3269 5525; www.thailandbeach.com; Hat Sai Kaew; dm 490B, r 800-2600B;) Technically it is a hostel, but NaNa Chart easily qualifies as a resort with a variety of bungalows on a barely inhabited beach. The cheapest are wooden huts with shared bathroom, and the ritzy beachfront ones have most of the mod-cons. The resort caters to large groups so expect some company. Hostel members (200B for three-year membership) receive discounted rates.

Bayview Beach Resort HOTEL $$$
(0 3269 5566; www.bayviewbeachresort.com; Hat Sai Keaw; r 1700-4800B;) A great choice for families, Bayview has handsome bungalows with large verandahs amid shady grounds. There's a beachside pool and a kid-friendly wading pool as well as a small playground. The resort also has meeting facilities for groups and conventions.

Kasama's Pizza PIZZARIA $$
(Hat Ban Krut; dishes from 150B; lunch & dinner) An expats' favourite, this open-air spot near the main road to town does praiseworthy New York–style pizzas in coconut territory.

BANG SAPHAN YAI

The beach is 6km south of the town of Bang Saphan Yai. Accommodation is a mix of high-end pool villas on the south side of Why Not Bar and basic beach huts to the north.

Roytawan GUEST HOUSE $
(r from 300B,) Smack dab on the beach, this bare-bones operation is run by a sweet local family. The bungalows provide basic shelter and the resident roosters kindly sleep until daybreak. The restaurant is fab too. If you continue north from here you'll find similar set-ups.

Patty Hut GUEST HOUSE $
(08 6171 1907; r 300-700B;) This funky spot behind the Coral Hotel is 300m from the beach. It is a collection of wooden bungalows ranging from simple to simpler.

Suan Luang Resort GUEST HOUSE $
(☎0 3281 7031; www.suanluang.com; bungalows 480-680B; ❄) The most professional of the guest houses, Suan Luang is run by a friendly family and has wooden bungalows around an interior garden. You're 700m from the beach, though. The excellent restaurant serves Thai and French food, and there are day trips to waterfalls and parks on offer.

Coral Hotel HOTEL $$
(☎0 3281 7121; www.coral-hotel.com; r 1525-5580B; ❄@≋) This upmarket hotel is right on the beach and has all the resort amenities, including organised diving and snorkelling tours. The rooms probably don't deserve to be priced this high but competition in this category is low.

Getting There & Around

Because public transport around here is either nonexistent or limited; be sure to take a bus that stops in town instead of on the highway, an inconvenient and expensive distance from the beaches. When booking transport, don't confuse Bang Saphan Yai with Bang Saphan Noi, which is a fisherman's village 15km further south.

From Bangkok's Southern (Sai Tai Mai) station buses go to Ban Krut (275B, departs 12.30pm, six hours) and Bang Saphan Yai (275B, hourly, six hours); in Bangkok, use **Dangsaphan Tour** (☎08 7829 7752).

Frequent minivans run from Prachuap Khiri Khan to Ban Krut (70B) and Bang Saphan Yai (80B).

Many seasoned visitors prefer to take the train for closer proximity to the beaches. There are several daily options but the sprinter train (special express No 43) is one of the fastest. It leaves Bangkok's Hua Lamphong station at 8am and arrives in Ban Krut (445B) at 12.45pm and Bang Saphan Yai (450B) at 1pm. You can also hop on an afternoon train to Chumphon with plenty of time to spare before the ferry to Ko Tao.

A motorcycle taxi from town to the beaches should cost 40B to 70B. Talk to your hotel or guest house about arranging transport back to town for your onward travel.

Chumphon ชุมพร

POP 55,835

Chumphon is a transit town funnelling travellers to and from Ko Tao or westward to Ranong or Phuket.

While there's not a lot to do while you wait, the surrounding beaches are good places to step off the backpacker bandwagon for a few days. **Hat Thung Wua Laen** (15km north of town) is a pretty beach with easy public transport to Chumphon and plenty of traveller amenities.

For a transit hub, Chumphon is surprisingly unconsolidated. You'll need to rely on the travel agencies (p169) to book tickets, provide timetables and point you to the right bus stop; fortunately agents in Chumphon are a dedicated lot.

Festivals & Events

Chumphon Marine Festival CULTURAL
From mid-March to the end of April, Hat Thung Wua Laen hosts a variety of events including folk-art exhibits, shadow-puppet performances and a food display.

Chumphon Traditional Boat Race CULTURAL
To mark the end of Buddhist Lent in October (Ork Phansaa), traditional long-tail boats race each other on the Mae Nam Lang Suan (Lang Suan River), about 60km south of Chumphon. Other merit-making activities coincide with the festival.

Sleeping

Since most people overnighting in Chumphon are backpackers, accommodation is priced accordingly.

IN TOWN

TOP CHOICE **Suda Guest House** GUEST HOUSE $
(☎0 7750 4366; 8 Soi Bangkok Bank; r 230-500B; ❄) Suda, the friendly English-speaking owner, maintains her impeccable standards in six rooms with wooden floors and a few nice touches that you wouldn't expect for the price. It's very popular so phone ahead.

San Tavee New Rest House GUEST HOUSE $
(☎0 7750 2147; 4 Soi Bangkok Bank; r 200-300B) If Suda's, two doors down is full, check the four rooms here. They're small but clean, and have fans and shared bathroom.

Farang Bar GUEST HOUSE $
(☎0 7750 1003; 69/36 Th Tha Taphao; r 150-300B; @) A backpacker dive, Farang Bar has ramshackle rooms next door to its bar (naturally) catering mainly to travellers who get deposited here by buses from Bangkok's Th Khao San. Day-use showers (20B) decorated in round pebbles give an unexpected (and unintentional, we're sure) spa-like feel. The restaurant isn't worth bothering about, though.

Chumphon

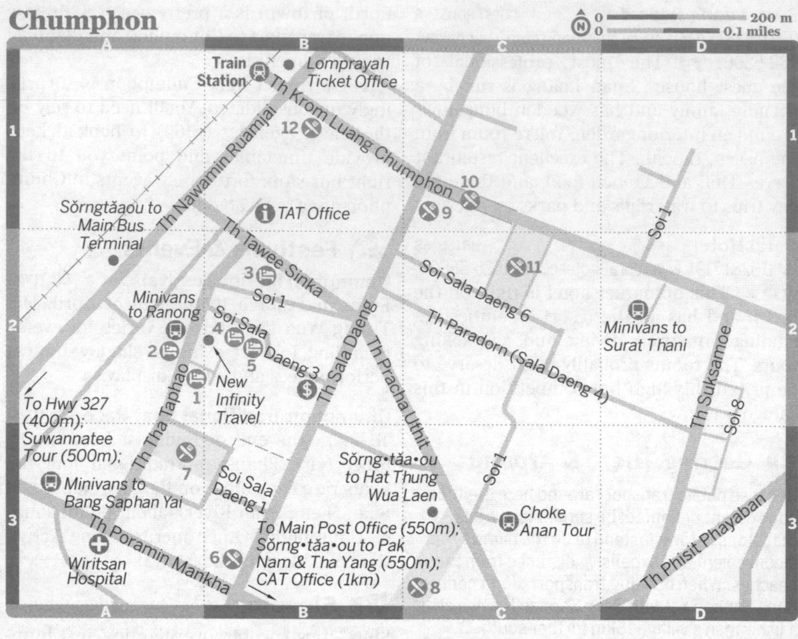

Chumphon

Sleeping

1 Chumphon Gardens Hotel A2
2 Farang Bar A2
3 Morakot Hotel B2
4 San Tavee New Rest House B2
5 Suda Guest House B2

Eating

6 Ban Yang Na B3
7 Day Market A3
8 Day Market C3
9 Fame Restaurant C1
Khanom Jeen Restaurant .... (see 9)
10 Night Market C1
11 Ocean Shopping Mall C2
12 Papa Seafood B1

Morakot Hotel HOTEL **$$**
(☎0 7750 2999; 102-112 Th Tawee Sinka; r 800-950B; ❄) The multistorey lime-green building has recently received a fresh upgrade making it a solid midrange choice for provincial VIPs.

Chumphon Gardens Hotel HOTEL **$**
(☎0 7750 6888; 66/1 Th Tha Taphao; r 500B; ❄) Spacious rooms including cable TV are a great distraction while you hang around and wait.

OUT OF TOWN

Chumphon Cabana Resort & Diving Centre HOTEL **$$$**
(☎0 7756 0245; www.cabana.co.th; Hat Thung Wua Laen; r 1800-2700B; ❄) Though the rooms are in need of an upgrade, Chumphon Cabana has done a great job upgrading its environmental profile. Inspired by the King's environmental sustainability speech, the owner reconfigured the resort to look to the past for instructions on how to be green. The grounds are devoted to raising the resort's own food with rice fields, hydroponic vegetable gardens and a chicken farm. Waste water is recycled through water-hyacinth ponds. And their efforts are used to instruct others.

If you don't stay here, at least enjoy some homegrown food at **Rabieng Talay**, the resort's affiliated restaurant.

View Resort BUNGALOWS
(Hat Thung Wua Laen, r 650-1000B; ❄) The nicest of a few simple bungalow operations on Hat Thung Wua Laen.

MT Resort HOTEL $$
(☎0 7755 8153; www.mtresort-chumphon.com; Hat Tummakam Noi; r 950-1500B; ❄) This friendly spot on a quiet beach beside the Lomprayah ferry pier is a good place to break your journey before or after Ko Tao. Free kayaks are provided to explore offshore islands and the mangroves of the nearby Mu Ko Chumphon National Park. Call to organise a transfer from Chumphon.

Eating & Drinking

Chumphon's **night market** (Th Krom Luang Chumphon) is excellent, with a huge variety of food options and good people-watching. There are two **day markets** (Th Tha Taphao & Th Pracha Uthit).

Khanom Jeen Restaurant THAI $
(Th Sala Daeng; dishes 60B; ⊙breakfast & lunch) Next to Fame Restaurant, this hole-in-the-wall eatery is locally famous for its spicy bowls of *kà·nŏm jeen* (rice noodles served with a spicy fish sauce). Add your own touch with condiments of holy basil, sliced cucumber and pickled vegetables.

Ban Yang Na CAFE $
(Th Sala Daeng; dishes from 40B; ⊙breakfast & lunch; ❄) This air-conditioned cafe provides a nice retreat from the heat plus the usual caffeine and bakery treats.

Papa Seafood SEAFOOD $$
(2-2/1 Th Krom Luang Chumphon; dishes 80-200B; ⊙lunch & dinner) The food (mainly seafood, obviously) is good, without being exceptional, but it's a popular local hang-out. Next door is Papa 2000 where you can dance off dinner.

Fame Restaurant INTERNATIONAL $
(188/20 Th Sala Daeng; dishes 80-220B; ⊙breakfast, lunch & dinner) A farang (foreigner) depot, Fame does a little bit of everything; cooks up Western breakfasts and Thai stir-fries, books ferry tickets and rents out day-use showers. It's open from before the crack of dawn until late at night.

Ocean Shopping Mall INTERNATIONAL $$
(off of Th Sala Daeng; dishes 150-250B; ⊙lunch & dinner) It isn't a culinary destination but Chumphon's shopping mall has air-con and chain restaurants for cool and convenient layover noshing.

Information

There are banks along Th Sala Daeng with exchange facilities and ATMs.

Bangkok Bank (Th Sala Daeng) Has an ATM.

CAT office (Th Poramin Mankha) About 1km east of the post office.

Main post office (Th Poramin Mankha) In the southeastern part of town.

New Infinity Travel (☎0 7757 0176; 68/2 Th Tha Taphao; ⊙8am-10pm; @) A great travel agency with knowledgeable and friendly staff; they'll also sell you paperbacks and rent you one of four rooms.

TAT (☎0 7750 1831; 111/11-12 Th Tawee Sinkha; ⊙9am-4.30pm) Hands-out maps and brochures but not always up-to-date on transport information.

Wiratsin Hospital (☎0 7750 3238; Th Poramin Mankha) Privately owned; handles emergencies.

Getting There & Away

Air

Solar Air (☎0 7755 8212; www.solarair.co.th) flies to Bangkok (once daily, one hour, 2900B).

Boat

You have many boat options for getting to Ko Tao (p207), though departure times are limited to mainly morning and night. Most ticket prices include pier transfer. If you buy a combination ticket, make sure you have a ticket for both the bus and the boat.

Slow boat (250B, six hours, midnight) – the cheapest, slowest and most scenic option as everyone stretches out on the open deck of the fishing boat with the stars twinkling overhead. This boat doesn't run in rough seas or inclement weather.

Car ferry (350B, six hours, 11pm Mon-Sun) – a more comfortable ride with bunk or mattress options available on board.

Songserm express boat (450B, three hours, 7am) – faster, morning option leaving from Tha Talaysub, about 10km from town.

Lomprayah catamaran (600B, 1¾ hours, 7am & 1pm) – a popular bus-boat combination that leaves from Tha Tummakam, 25km from town; the ticket office is beside Chumphon train station.

Bus

The main bus terminal is on the highway, an inconvenient 16km from Chumphon. To get there you can catch a *sŏrng·tăa·ou* (50B) from Th Nawamin Ruamjai. You'll have to haggle with the opportunistic taxi drivers for night transit to/from the station; no matter what they tell you, it shouldn't cost more than 200B.

There are several in-town bus stops to save you a trip out to the main bus station. **Choke Anan Tour** (☎0 7751 1757; soi off of Th Pracha Uthit), in the centre of town, has daily departures to the following destinations:

Bangkok's Southern (Sai Tai Mai) station (375B to 550B, eight hours, five departures)

Hat Yai (370B; seven hours; four departures)

Phuket (320B; 3½ hours; four departures)

Ranong (320B; two hours; four departures)

Suwannatee Tour (☎0 7750 4901), 700m southeast of train station road, serves the following destinations:

Bangkok's Southern (Sai Tai Mai) station (270B to 405B 2nd class-VIP buses, three departures)

Cha-am (175B)

Hua Hin (170B)

Phetchaburi (205B)

Prachuap Khiri Khan (120B)

Minivan companies are numerous and depart from individual offices throughout town (see the Chumphon map):

Surat Thani (170B, three hours, every hour) Departs from an unnamed soi on Th Krom Luang Chumphon; the soi is east of an optical shop.

Bang Saphan Yai (120B, two hours, two afternoon departures) Leaves from Th Poramin Mankha, near the hospital.

Ranong (120B, 2½ hours, every hour 7am to 3pm) Departs from Th Tha Taphao; arrives at Ranong bus station (not in the town).

Train

There are frequent services to/from Bangkok (2nd class 292B to 382B, 3rd class 235B, 7½ hours). Overnight sleepers range from 440B to 770B.

Southbound rapid and express trains – the only trains with 1st and 2nd class – are less frequent and can be difficult to book out of Chumphon from November to February.

Getting Around

Sŏrng·tăa·ou and motorcycle taxis around town cost 40B and 20B respectively per trip. *Sŏrng·tăa·ou* to Hat Thung Wua Laen cost 30B.

Motorcycles can be rented at travel agencies and guest houses for 200B to 250B per day. Car hire costs around 1500B per day from travel agencies.

Ko Samui & the Lower Gulf

Includes »

Best Places to Eat

» Dining On The Rocks (p186)
» Five Islands (p187)
» The Whitening (p218)

Best Places to Stay

» Six Senses Samui (p182)
» Anantara Bo Phut (p183)
» L'Hacienda (p183)
» Sarikantang (p196)
» The Sanctuary (p202)

Why Go?

The Lower Gulf features Thailand's ultimate island trifecta: Ko Samui, Ko Pha-Ngan and Ko Tao. This family of spectacular islands lures millions of tourists every year with their powder-soft sands and emerald waters. Ko Samui is the oldest brother, with a business-minded attitude towards vacation. High-class resorts operate with Swiss efficiency as uniformed butlers cater to every whim. Ko Pha-Ngan is the slacker middle child with tangled dreadlocks and a penchant for hammock-lazing and all-night parties. Baby Ko Tao has plenty of spirit and spunk – offering high-adrenaline activities, including world-class diving and snorkelling.

Travellers seeking something a bit more off the radar than these island brethren will find a thin archipelago of pin-sized islets just beyond. Known as Ang Thong Marine National Park, this ethereal realm of greens and blues offers some of the most picture-perfect moments in the entire kingdom.

When To Go

From February to April celebrate endless sunshine after the monsoon rains have cleared. From June to August – which conveniently coincides with the Northern Hemisphere's summer holidays – are some of the most inviting months in the region, with relatively short drizzle spells.

From October to December torrential monsoon rains rattle hot-tin roofs like anxious fingernails, as room rates drop significantly to lure a few optimistic beach-goers

Ko Samui & the Lower Gulf Highlights

1. Find Nemo in the technicolour kingdom off the coast of **Ko Tao** (p207).
2. Dimple virgin sands on the hidden bleach-blonde beaches of **Ang Thong Marine National Park** (p222).
3. String up a cotton hammock and toe the curline tide along a secluded beach on **Ko Pha-Ngan** (p192)
4. Purr like a kitten during a five-star massage session on **Ko Samui** (p174)
5. Join the masses of party pilgrims and trance the night away at the **Full Moon Party** (see boxed text, p194) in Hat Rin on Ko Pha-Ngan

6 Savour steaming street-stall seafood on the sands of **Songkhla** (p229)

7 Spot elusive pink dolphins gliding along the shores of **Ao Khanom** (p225)

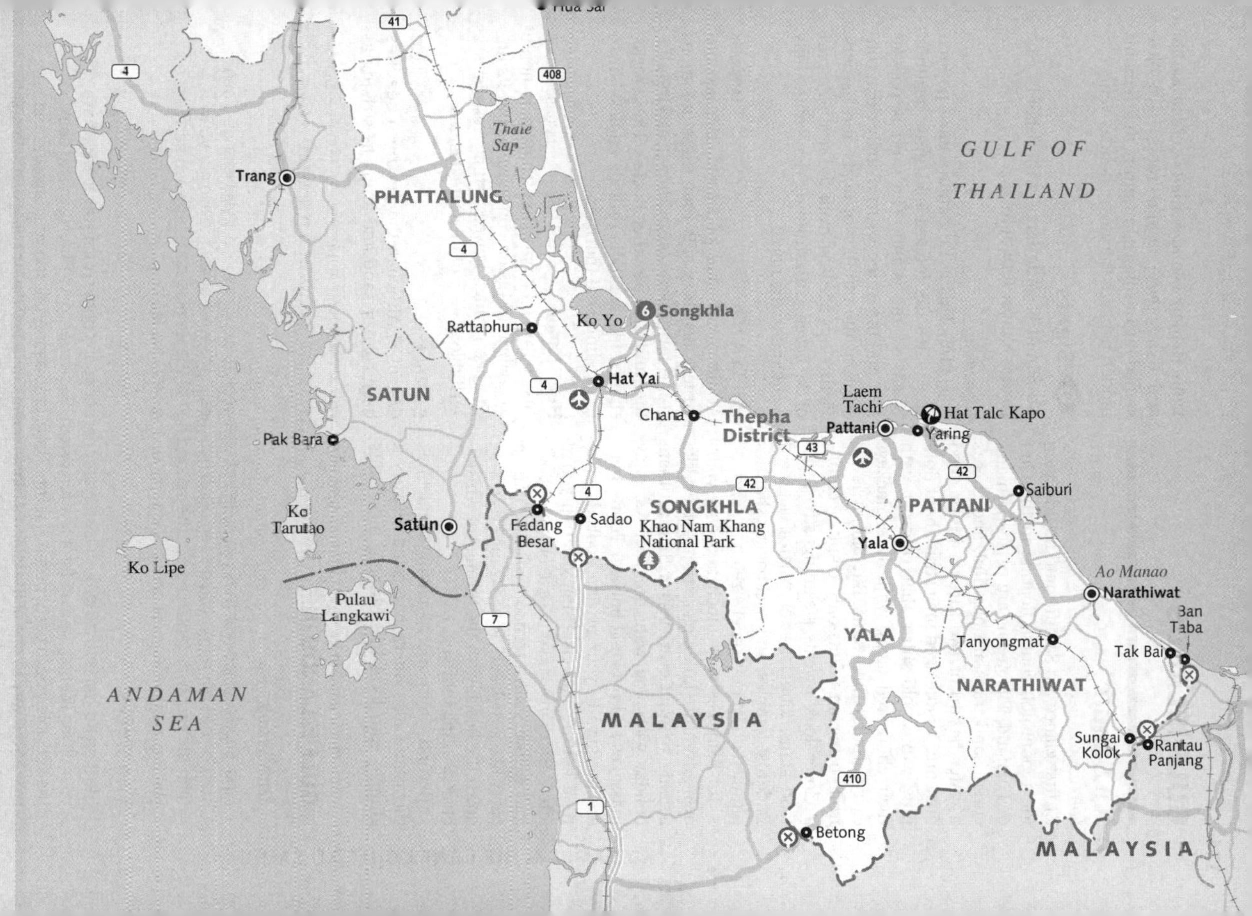

GULF OF THAILAND

ANDAMAN SEA

PHATTALUNG

SATUN

SONGKHLA

PATTANI

YALA

NARATHIWAT

MALAYSIA

MALAYSIA

Thale Sap

Trang

Rattaphum

Ko Yo

Songkhla

Hat Yai

Chana

Thepha District

Laem Tachi

Pattani

Hat Talo Kapo

Yaring

Saiburi

Pak Bara

Ko Tarutao

Ko Lipe

Satun

Padang Besar

Sadao

Khao Nam Khang National Park

Yala

Ao Manao

Narathiwat

Ban Taba

Tak Bai

Tanyongmat

Sungai Kolok

Rantau Panjang

Betong

Pulau Langkawi

41

4

408

4

4

4

43

42

42

7

410

1

GULF ISLANDS

Ko Samui เกาะสมุย

POP 40,230

At first glance, Ko Samui could be mistaken for a giant golf course floating in the Gulf of Thailand. The greens are perfectly manicured, sand traps are plentiful, and there's a water hazard or two thrown in for good measure. Middle-aged men strut about donning white polo shirts that contrast with their cherry-red faces, while hired lackeys carry around their stuff. But Samui is far from being an adults-only country club – a closer look reveals steaming street-side food stalls, 2am jetsetter parties, secreted Buddhist temples, and backpacker shanties plunked down on a quiet stretch of sand.

Ko Samui is very much a choose-your-own-adventure kinda place that strives, like a genie, to grant every visitor their ultimate holiday wish. You want ocean views, daily massages and personal butlers? Poof – here are the keys to your private poolside villa. It's a holistic aura-cleansing vacation you're after? Shazam – take a seat on your yoga mat before your afternoon colonic. Wanna party like a rockstar? Pow – trance your way down the beach with the throngs of whisky-bucket-toting tourists.

Beyond the merry-making machine, the island also offers interested visitors a glimpse into local life. Chinese merchants from Hainan Island initially settled Samui and today these unique roots have blossomed into a small community that remains hidden beneath the glossy holiday veneer.

Sights

Ko Samui is quite large – the island's ring road is almost 100km total.

Chaweng BEACH

(Map p176) This is Ko Samui's most popular spot – it's the longest and most beautiful beach on the island. The sand is powder soft, and the water is surprisingly clear, considering the number of boats and bathers. Picture ops are best from the southern part of the beach, with stunning views of the hilly headland to the north.

Hin-Ta & Hin-Yai LANDMARK

At the south end of **Lamai**, the second-largest beach, you'll find these infamous stone formations (also known as Grandfather and Grandmother Rocks). These rocks, shaped like genitalia provide endless mirth to giggling Thai tourists.

Hua Thanon NEIGHBOURHOOD

Just beyond Lamai, Hua Thanon is home to a vibrant Muslim community, and its anchorage of high-bowed fishing vessels is a veritable gallery of intricate designs.

Bo Phut NEIGHBOURHOOD

(Map p178) Although the **northern beaches** have coarser sand and aren't as striking as

GULF ISLANDS IN...

One Week

First, shed a single tear that you have but one week to explore these idyllic islands. Then start on one of Ko Pha-Ngan's secluded beaches in the west or east to live out your ultimate castaway fantasies. For the second half of the week choose between partying in Hat Rin, pampering over on Ko Samui, or diving on li'l Ko Tao.

Two Weeks

Start on Ko Tao with a 3½-day Open Water certification course (or, if you already have your diving licence, sign up for a few fun dives). Slide over to Ko Pha-Ngan and soak up the sociable vibe in party-prone Hat Rin. Then, grab a long-tail and your luggage and make your way to one of the island's hidden coves for a few days of detoxing and quiet contemplation. Ko Samui is next on the agenda. Try Bo Phut for boutique sleeps, or live it up like a rock star on Chaweng or Choeng Mon beach. And, if you have time, do a day trip to Ang Thong Marine National Park.

One Month

Follow the two-week itinerary at a more relaxed pace, infusing many extra beach-book-and-blanket days on all three islands. Be sure to plan your schedule around the Full Moon Party, which takes place at Hat Rin's Sunrise Beach on Ko Pha-Ngan.

Ko Samui

the beaches in the east, they have a laid-back vibe and stellar views of Ko Pha-Ngan. Bo Phut stands out with its charming Fisherman's Village; a collection of narrow Chinese shophouses that have been transformed into trendy resorts and boutique hotels.

Nam Tok Na Muang WATERFALL
(Map p175) At 30m, this is the tallest waterfall on Samui and lies in the centre of the island about 12km from Na Thon. The water cascades over ethereal purple rocks, and there's a great pool for swimming at the base. This is the most scenic – and somewhat less frequented – of Samui's falls. There are two other waterfalls in the vicinity: a smaller waterfall called **Na Muang 2**, and, thanks to recently, improved road conditions, the high drop at **Nam Tok Wang Saotong** (Map p175). These chutes are situated just north of the ring road near Hua Thanon.

Wat Hin Lat TEMPLE
(Map p175; ☎0 7742 3146) On the western part of Samui, near the waterfalls of the same name, is a meditation temple that teaches daily *vipassana* courses.

Nam Tok Hin Lat WATERFALL
(Map p175) Near Na Thon, this is worth visiting if you have an afternoon to kill before taking a boat back to the mainland. After a mildly strenuous hike over streams and boulders, reward yourself with a dip in the pool at the bottom of the falls. Keep an eye out for the Buddhist temple that posts signs with spiritual words of moral guidance and enlightenment. Sturdy shoes are recommended.

Wat Laem Saw TEMPLE
(Map p175) For temple enthusiasts, Wat Laem Saw, at the southern end of Samui near Ban Phang Ka, has an interesting, highly venerated old Srivijaya-style stupa.

Hat Chaweng

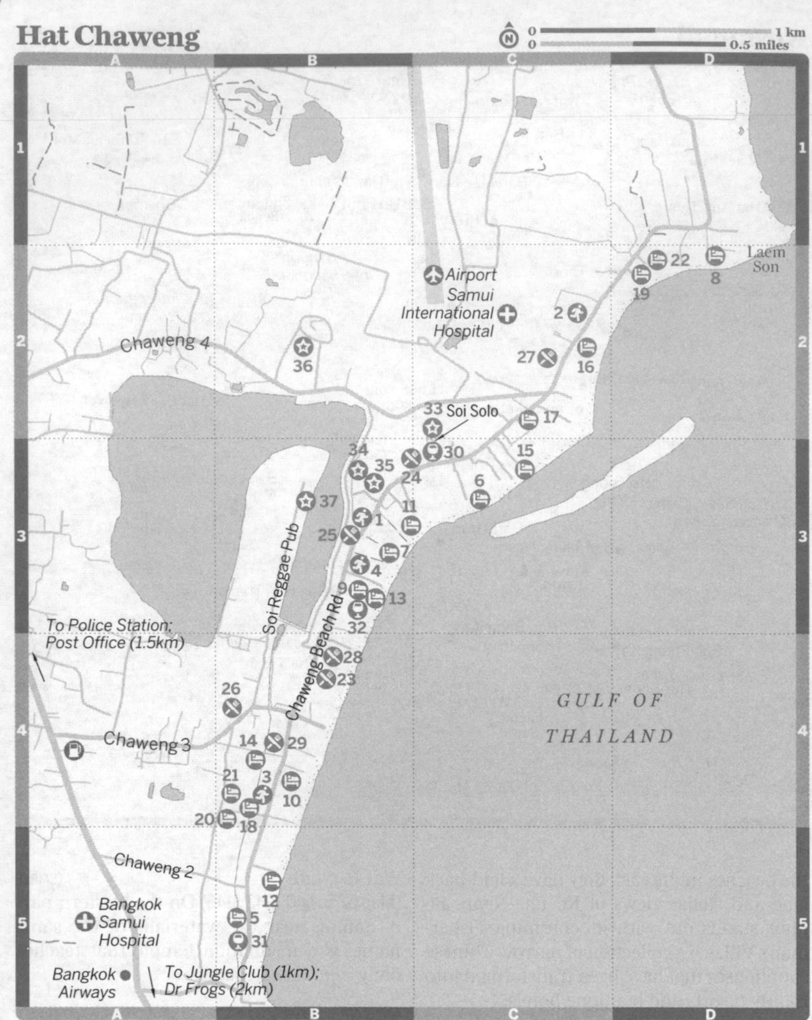

Wat Phra Yai TEMPLE

(Temple of the Big Buddha; Map p175) At Samui's northern end, on a small rocky island linked by a causeway, is Wat Phra Yai. Erected in 1972, the modern Buddha (sitting in the Mara posture) stands 15m high and makes an alluring silhouette against the tropical sky and sea. Nearby, a new temple, **Wat Plai Laem** (Map p175), features an enormous 18-armed Buddha.

Wat Khunaram TEMPLE

(Map p175) Several temples have the mummified remains of pious monks, including Wak Khunaram, which is south of Rte 4169 between Th Ban Thurian and Th Ban Hua. Its monk, Luang Phaw Daeng, has been dead for over two decades but his corpse is preserved sitting in a meditative pose and sporting a pair of sunglasses.

Wat Samret TEMPLE

(Map p175) At Wat Samret, near Th Ban Hua, you can see a typical Mandalay sitting Buddha carved from solid marble – a common sight in India and northern Thailand, but not so common in the south.

Hat Chaweng

Activities, Courses & Tours
- 1 Blue Stars B3
- 2 Diveversity C2
- 3 Samui Institute of Thai Culinary Arts B4
- 4 Samui Planet Scuba B3

Sleeping
- 5 Akwa B5
- 6 Ark Bar C3
- 7 Baan Chaweng Beach Resort B3
- 8 Baan Haad Ngam D2
- 9 Baan Samui B3
- 10 Centara Grand B4
- 11 Chaweng Garden Beach B3
- 12 Kirikayan Boutique Resort B5
- 13 Library B3
- 14 Loft Samui B4
- 15 Lucky Mother C3
- 16 Muang Kulay Pan Hotel C2
- 17 Nora Chaweng C2
- 18 P Chaweng B4
- 19 Pandora Boutique Hotel D2
- 20 Queen Boutique Resort B4
- 21 Samui Hostel B4
- 22 Tango Beach Resort D2

Eating
- 23 Betelnut@Buri Rasa B4
- 24 Gringo's Cantina B3
- 25 Khaosan Restaurant & Bakery B3
- 26 Laem Din Market B4
- Page .... (see 13)
- 27 Prego C2
- Samui Institute of Thai Culinary Arts .... (see 3)
- 28 Wave Samui B4
- 29 Zico's B4

Drinking
- Ark Bar .... (see 6)
- 30 Bar Solo C3
- 31 Good Karma B5
- 32 Tropical Murphy's B3

Entertainment
- 33 Christy's Cabaret C2
- 34 Green Mango B3
- 35 Mint B3
- 36 Q-Bar B2
- 37 Reggae Pub B3

Activities

Diving

If you're serious about diving, head to Ko Tao and base yourself there for the duration of your diving adventure. If you're short on time and don't want to leave Samui, there are plenty of operators who will take you to the same dive sites (at a greater fee, of course). Try to book with a company that has its own boat (or leases a boat) – it's slightly more expensive, but you'll be glad you did it. Companies without boats often shuttle divers on the passenger catamaran to Ko Tao, where you board a second boat to reach your dive site. These trips are arduous, meal-less and rather impersonal.

Certification courses tend to be twice as expensive on Ko Samui as they are on Ko Tao, this is largely due to use of extra petrol, since tiny Tao is significantly closer to the preferred diving locations. You'll drop between 16,000B and 22,000B on an Open Water certification, and figure between 3200B and 6200B for a diving day trip depending on the location of the site.

Ko Samui's hyperbaric chamber is at Big Buddha Beach (Hat Bang Rak).

100 Degrees East DIVING
(☎0 7742 5936; www.100degreeseast.com; Bang Rak) Highly recommended.

Diveversity DIVING
(Map p176; ☎0 7741 3196; www.diveversity.nl; Hat Chaweng) Based at the Amari Hotel.

Samui Planet Scuba DIVING
(SIDS; Map p176; ☎0 7723 1606; samuiplanetscuba@planetscuba.net; Hat Chaweng)

Other Activities

Blue Stars KAYAKING, SNORKELLING
(Map p176; ☎0 7741 3231; www.bluestars.info; trips 2600B) For those interested in snorkelling and kayaking, book a day trip to the stunning Ang Thong Marine Park. Blue Stars, based in Hat Chaweng on Ko Samui, offers guided sea-kayak trips in the park.

Football Golf SPORT
(☎08 9771 7498; ☉9am-6.30pm) At Choeng Mon there's a strange combustion called 'football golf' where you 'putt' your football

Bo Phut

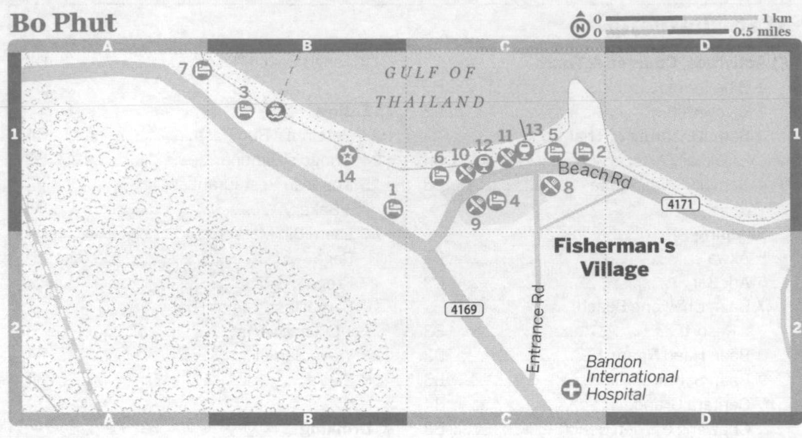

Bo Phut

Sleeping

1	Anantara	B1
2	B1 Villa Spa	C1
3	Ibis Bo Phut	B1
4	Khuntai	C1
5	L'Hacienda	C1
6	Lodge	C1
7	Zazen	A1

Eating

8	Karma Sutra	C1
9	Shack Bar & Grill	C1
10	Starfish & Coffee	C1
11	Villa Bianca	C1
	Zazen	(see 7)

Drinking

12	Billabong Surf Club	C1
13	Pier	C1

Entertainment

14	Gecko Village	B1

into a rubbish-bin-sized hole. It's great for the kids and each game (300B) comes with a complimentary soft drink. It's a par 66.

Namuang Safari Park THEME PARK
(Map p175; ☎0 7742 4098) Located near Na Muang Falls, Namuang has safari options and packages galore. Adventure tours (from 900B) vary in length and can include elephant trekking, monkey shows, 4WD rides and even a visit to a rubber plantation to drain the trees (now that's excitement). Prices include hotel transfer.

Samui Aquarium & Tiger Zoo THEME PARK
(Map p175; ☎0 7742 4017; adult/child 750/450B; 9am-6pm) The Samui Aquarium & Tiger Zoo features the standard array aquariums and tigers, as well as a large aviary. It's a pleasant diversion for the kids, though some of the cages and tanks are noticeably rundown. The tiger show is at 2.30pm and the sea lion spectacle starts at 1.30pm. The admission includes the use of the large on-site swimming pool.

Spas & Yoga

Competition for Samui's five-star accommodation is fierce, which means that the spas are of the highest calibre. For top-notch pampering, try the spa at Anantara Bo Phut, or the Hideaway Spa at the Six Senses Samui. The Spa Resort in Lamai is the island's original health destination, and is still known for its effective 'clean me out' fasting regime.

Yoga Thailand YOGA & SPA
(☎0 7792 0090; www.yoga-thailand.com; Phang Ka; retreats from €680;) Secreted away along the southern shores, Yoga Thailand is ushering in a new era of therapeutic holidaying with its state-of-the-art facilities and dedicated team of trainers. Accommodation is located in a comfy apartment block up the street while yoga studios, wellness centres and a breezy cafe sit calmly along the shore.

Tamarind Retreat THAI MASSAGE
(☎0 7723 0571; www.tamarindretreat.com) Tucked far away from the beach within a silent coconut-palm plantation, Tamarind's small collection of villas and massage studios is seamlessly incorporated into nature: some have granite boulders built into walls and floors, others offer private ponds or creative outdoor baths.

Health Oasis Resort YOGA & SPA
(☎0 7742 0124; www.healthoasisresort.com) If you're lookin' to get 'cleansed', whether it's your aura or your colon, then you've happened upon the right place. New Age is all the rage at the Health Oasis. Guests can choose from a variety of healing packages involving everything from meditation to fasting. Bungalows are modern and receive plenty of sunshine. There's also a vegetarian restaurant on site, of course.

Absolute Sanctuary YOGA & SPA
(☎0 7760 1190; www.absoluteyogasamui.com) What was once a friendly yoga studio has blossomed into a gargantuan wellness complex featuring plenty of accommodation and an exhaustive menu of detox and wellness programs.

Courses

Samui Institute of Thai Culinary Arts COOKING
(SITCA; Map p176; ☎0 7741 3434; www.sitca.net; Hat Chaweng) If you're contemplating a Thai cooking course, SITCA is the place to do it. It has daily Thai-cooking classes and courses in the aristocratic Thai art of carving fruits and vegetables into intricate floral designs. Lunchtime classes begin at 11am, while dinner starts at 4pm (both cost 1950B for a three-hour course with three or more dishes). Included is an excellent tutorial about procuring ingredients in your home country. Of course you get to eat your projects, and even invite a friend along for the meal. Complimentary DVDs with Thai cooking instruction are also available so you can practise at home.

Sleeping

'Superior', 'standard', 'deluxe', 'standard deluxe', 'deluxe superior', 'superior standard' – what does it all mean? Trying to decode Samui's obnoxious hotel lingo is like trying to decipher the ancient Maya language. The island's array of sleeping options is overwhelming – we've compiled a list of our favourites, but the following inventory is by no means exhaustive.

If you're looking to splurge, there is definitely no shortage of top-end resorts sporting extravagant bungalows, charming spas, private infinity pools, and first-class dining. Bo Phut, on the island's northern coast, has a charming collection of boutique lodging – the perfect choice for midrange travellers. Backpack-toting tourists will have to look a little harder, but budget digs do pop up once in a while along all of the island's beaches.

Private villa services have become quite popular in recent years. Rental companies often advertise in the various tourist booklets that circulate on the island.

This large section is organised as follows: we start on the popular east coast with Chaweng and Lamai, then move anticlockwise around the island covering the smaller beaches.

CHAWENG

TOP CHOICE **Jungle Club** BUNGALOWS $$
(Map p176; ☎08 1894 2327; www.jungleclubsamui.com; bungalows 800-4500B;) The perilous drive up the slithering dirt road is totally worthwhile once you get a load of the incredible views from the top. This isolated mountain getaway is a huge hit among locals and tourists alike. There's a relaxed back-to-nature vibe – guests chill around the stunning horizon pool or tuck themselves away for a catnap under the canopied roofs of an open-air *săh·lah* (hall; often spelled *sala*). Call ahead for a pick-up – you don't want to spend your precious jungle vacation in a body cast. Taxis from the main road cost 50B; it's 100B from central Chaweng.

TOP CHOICE **Library** RESORT $$$
(Map p176; ☎0 7742 2767; www.thelibrary.name; r from 13,300B;) This place is too cool for school, which is ironic since it's called 'The Library'. The entire resort is a sparkling white mirage accented with black trimming and slatted curtains. Besides the futuristic iMac computer in each page (rooms are called 'pages' here), our favourite feature is the large monochromatic wall art – it glows brightly in the evening and you can adjust the colour depending on your mood. Lifesize statues are engaged in the act of reading, and if you too feel inclined to pick up a book, the on-site library houses an impressive assortment of colourful art and design books. The large rectangular pool is not to

be missed – it's tiled in piercing shades of red, making the term 'bloodbath' suddenly seem appealing.

Tango Beach Resort RESORT $$
(Map p176; ☎0 7742 2470; www.tangobeachsamui.com; r 1600-4600B;) A midrange all-star, Tango features a string of bungalows arranged along a teak boardwalk that meanders away from the beach.

Centara Grand RESORT $$$
(Map p176; ☎0 7723 0500; www.centralhotelsresorts.com; r 8900-19,500B;) Centara is a massive, manicured compound in the heart of Chaweng, but the palm-filled property is so large that you can safely escape the streetside bustle. Rooms are found in a hotel-like building that is conspicuously Western in theme and decor. Grown-ups can escape to the spa, or one of the four restaurants, and leave the children at the labyrinth of swimming pools under the watchful eye of an in-house babysitter.

Baan Chaweng Beach Resort RESORT $$$
(Map p176; ☎0 7742 2403; www.baanchawengbeachresort.com; bungalows 3500-7000B;) A pleasant option for those who want top-end luxury without the hefty bill, Baan Chaweng is one of the new kids on the block and is keeping the prices relatively low. The immaculate rooms are painted in various shades of peach and pear, with teak furnishings that feel both modern and traditional.

Muang Kulay Pan Hotel RESORT $$$
(Map p176; ☎0 7723 0849-51; www.kulaypan.com; r 4200-15,000B;) No, that's not a rip in the wallpaper – it's all part of the design concept. The architect cites a fusion between Zen and Thai concepts, but we think the decor is completely random. The seaside grounds have been purposefully neglected to lend an additional sense of chaos to this unique resort.

Baan Haad Ngam RESORT $$$
(Map p176; ☎0 7723 1500; www.baanhaadngam.com; bungalows 6400-14,000B;) Vibrant Baan Haad Ngam shuns the usual teak and tan – every exterior is painted an interesting shade of green – like radioactive celery. It's sassy, classy and a great choice if you've got the dime.

Pandora Boutique Hotel RESORT $$
(Map p176; ☎0 7741 3801; www.pandora-samui.com; r 2700-4900B;) As adorable as it is memorable, Pandora looks like it just fell out of a comic book – maybe *Tintin and the Mystery of Surprisingly Cheap Accommodation in Chaweng*? Rooms are outfitted with cheerful pastels, wooden moulding, and the occasional stone feature.

Kirikayan Boutique Resort RESORT $$$
(☎0 7733 2299; www.kirikayan.com; r from 5295B;) Simple whites, lacquered teak and blazing red accents set the colour scheme at this hip address along Chaweng's southern sands. Wander past thick palm trunks and sky-scraping foliage to find the relaxing pool deck at the back.

Ark Bar RESORT $$
(Map p176; ☎0 7742 2047; www.ark-bar.com; bungalows 1500B;) You'll find two of every creature at Ark Bar – hardcore partiers, chilled out hippies, teenagers, forty-somethings, even Canadians. Lately, the perennially popular resort has started to shift gears – higher-end digs is now the name of the game.

Chaweng Garden Beach RESORT $$
(Map p176; ☎0 7796 0394; www.chaweng garden.com; r from 1850-8500B;) A popular 'flashpacker' choice, this campus of accommodation has a large variety of room types serviced by an extra-smiley staff.

Nora Chaweng HOTEL $$
(Map p176; ☎0 7791 3666; www.norachawenghotel.com; r from 2100B;) Nora Chaweng is not on the beach, but this newer addition to the Chaweng bustle has swankily designed rooms, an inviting on-site pool and a relaxing spa studio.

Loft Samui HOSTEL $
(Map p176; ☎0 7741 3420; www.theloftsmaui.com; r from 590B;) A newer budget operation in Chaweng, the Loft is giving has-beens such as the Wave a run for their money with cheap digs furnished by a couple of quirky details – adobe styling and savvy built-ins. It seems to be quite popular with travelling Israelis.

Akwa GUEST HOUSE $
(Map p176; ☎08 4660 0551; www.akwaguesthouse.com; r from 700B;) A charming B&B-style sleeping spot, Akwa has a few funky rooms decorated with bright colours. Expect teddy bears adorning each bed, quirky bookshelves stocked with DVDs and cartoon paintings all over.

Queen Boutique Resort HOTEL $
(Map p176; ☎0 7741 3148; queensamui@yahoo.com; r from 800-1200B; ❄@📶) Despite the less-than-friendly staff, Queen offers up boutique sleeps for backpacker prices. Make sure, however, that you get a room with tiled floors; the ones with scuffed linoleum are far less appealing.

Baan Samui RESORT $$
(Map p176; ☎0 7723 0965; www.see2sea.com; r from 8240B; ❄@📶🏊) In sharp contrast to the austere Library next door, Baan Samui is a campus of colourful beachside units. If the Flintstones had a holiday ranch house, it would probably look something like this.

Samui Hostel HOSTEL $
(Map p176; ☎08 9874 3737; dm 180B; ❄@) It doesn't look like much from the front, but the dorm rooms here are surprisingly spic and span. It's a great place for solo travellers on a tight budget, although couples should know that a private double room can be scouted in Chaweng for around 400B.

P Chaweng HOTEL $
(Map p176; ☎0 7723 0684; r 400-600B, ste 1000B; ❄@) This vine-covered cheapie doesn't even pretend to be close to the beach, but the pink-tiled rooms are spacious and squeaky clean (minus a couple of bumps and bruises on the wooden furniture). Pick a room facing away from the street – it seems a tad too easy for someone to slip through an open window and pilfer your stuff.

LAMAI

TOP CHOICE **Rocky Resort** RESORT $$$
(☎0 7741 8367; www.rockyresort.com; Hua Thanon; r 4890-17,000B; ❄📶🏊) Our favourite spot in Lamai (well, actually just south of Lamai), Rocky finds the right balance between an upmarket ambience and an unpretentious, sociable atmosphere. During the quieter months the prices are a steal, since ocean views abound, and each room has been furnished with beautiful Thai-inspired furniture that seamlessly incorporates a modern twist. The pool has been carved in between a collection of boulders mimicking the rocky beach nearby (hence the name).

Banyan Tree Koh Samui RESORT $$$
(☎0 7791 5333; www.banyantree.com/en/samui/overview; villas from 23,000B; ❄@📶🏊) Phuket's most prestigious address has set up a sister property along the secluded northern sands of Lamai. Occupying an entire bay, this sprawling homage to over-the-top luxury sports dozens of villas hoisted above the foliage by spider-like stilts. Golf carts zip around the grounds carrying jetsetters between the myriad dining venues and the gargantuan spa (which sports a relaxing rainforest simulator, no less).

Samui Jasmine Resort RESORT $$$
(☎0 7723 2446; 131/8 Moo 3; r & bungalows 3800-5000B; ❄📶🏊) Smack dab in the middle of Lamai beach, pleasant Samui Jasmine is a great deal. Go for the lower-priced rooms – most have excellent views of the ocean and the crystal-coloured lap pool. The design scheme features plenty of varnished teak and also frilly accessories such as lavender pillows.

Spa Resort BUNGALOWS $$
(☎0 7723 0855; www.spasamui.com; Lamai North; bungalows 800-2800B; ❄📶) This health spa has a bevy of therapeutic programs on offer, and no one seems to mind that the lodging is cheap by Lamai's standards. Programs include colonics, massage, aqua detox, hypnotherapy and yoga, just to name a few. The bathrooms leave a bit to be desired, but who needs a toilet when you're doing a week-long fast? Accommodation tends to book up quickly, so it's best to reserve in advance (via email). Nonguests are welcome to partake in the programs.

iBed HOSTEL $
(☎0 7745 8760; www.ibedsamui.com; dm/s 550/1100B) The sleekest hostel on the island (if not all of Thailand), iBed has all the accoutrements of an Apple-sponsored space station: personal TVs at each bed, smooth coats of paint, bleach-white linens, and plenty of polished concrete. The wide verandahs, ample common space and mod kitchen foster a sociable vibe during the busier months.

Lamai Wanta RESORT $$
(☎0 7742 4550, 0 7742 4218; www.lamaiwanta.com; r & bungalows 1954-4800B; ❄@📶🏊) The pool area feels a bit retro, with its swatch book of beige- and blue-toned tiles, but in the back there are modern motel rooms and bungalows that have fresh coats of white paint. On the inside, rooms tread a fine line between being minimal and sparse. Lamai Wanta is located towards the south end of Lamai – be on the look out for the resort's small sign; it's located down a small beachside soi.

Amarina Residence GUEST HOUSE **$**
(www.amarinaresidence.com; r 900-1200B) Although the lobby is unusually dark compared to most tropical foyers, the rooms upstairs are sun-drenched and sport tasteful light-wood furnishing.

Beer's House BUNGALOWS **$**
(☎0 7723 0467; 161/4 Moo 4 Lamai North; bungalows 200-550B) These tiny shade-covered bungalows are lined up right along the sand. Some huts have a communal toilet, but all have plenty of room to sling a hammock and laze the day away.

New Hut BUNGALOWS **$**
(☎0 7723 0437; newhut@hotmail.com; Lamai North; huts 200-500B) New Hut is a rare beachfront cheapie with tiny-but-charming A-frame huts.

NORTHERN BEACHES

Ko Samui's northern beaches have the largest range of accommodation. Choeng Mon has some of the most opulent resorts in the world, while Mae Nam and Bang Po cling to their backpacker roots despite the recent construction of several flash pads. Bo Phut, in the middle, is the shining star in Samui's constellation of beaches.

CHOENG MON

TOP CHOICE **Six Senses Samui** RESORT **$$$**
(☎0 7724 5678; www.sixsenses.com/hideaway-samui/index.php; bungalows from 18,000B; ❄@📶🏊) This hidden bamboo paradise is worth the once-in-a-lifetime splurge. Set along a rugged promontory, Six Senses strikes the perfect balance between opulence and rustic charm, and defines the term 'barefoot elegance'. Most of the villas have stunning concrete plunge pools and offer magnificent views of the silent bay below. The regal, semi-outdoor bathrooms give the phrase 'royal flush' a whole new meaning. Beige golf buggies move guests between their hidden cottages and the stunning amenities strewn around the property – including a world-class spa and two excellent restaurants.

Tongsai Bay RESORT **$$$**
(☎0 7724 5480-5500; www.tongsaibay.co.th; ste 11,000-30,000B; ❄📶🏊) For serious pampering, head to this secluded luxury gem. Expansive and impeccably maintained, the hilly grounds make the cluster of bungalows look more like a small village. Golf carts whiz around the vast landscape transporting guests to various activities (such as massages) or dinner. All the extra-swanky split-level suites have day-bed rest areas, gorgeous romantic decor, stunning views, large terraces and creatively placed bathtubs (you'll see). Facilities include salt- and freshwater pools, a tennis court, the requisite spa, a dessert shop and also several restaurants.

Sala Samui RESORT **$$$**
(☎0 7724 5888; www.salasamui.com; bungalows US$360-1100; ❄@📶🏊) Look out folks, these guys mean business – they quote their room rates in US dollars instead of baht. Is the hefty price tag worth it? Definitely. The design scheme is undeniably exquisite – regal whites and lacquered teaks are generously lavished throughout, while subtle turquoise accents draw on the colour of each villa's private plunge pool.

Imperial Boat House Hotel RESORT **$$$**
(☎0 7742 5041-52; www.imperialhotels.com; Hat Choeng Mon; r 4000-5500B, boat ste 6000-6700B; ❄📶🏊) This sophisticated retreat has a three-storey hotel and several free-standing bungalows made from imported-teak rice barges whose bows have been transformed into stunning patios. Oxidised copper cannons blast streams of water into the boat-shaped swimming pool.

Ô Soleil BUNGALOWS **$**
(☎0 7742 5232; r & bungalows from 400B; ❄) One of the cheaper beachfront properties on the island, old Ô Soleil offers a scatter of bungalows and semidetached rooms extending inland from the sand. It's a very casual affair, so be sure to safely store your valuables.

BIG BUDDHA BEACH (BANG RAK)

This area gets its moniker from the huge golden Buddha that acts as overlord from the small nearby quasi-island of Ko Fan. Its proximity to the airport means lower prices at the resorts.

Samui Mermaid RESORT **$**
(☎0 7742 7547; www.samui-mermaid.info; r 400-2500B; ❄@📶🏊) Samui Mermaid is a great choice in the budget category because it feels like a full-fledged resort. There are two large swimming pools, copious beach chairs, two lively restaurants and every room has cable TV. The landing strip at Samui's airport is only a couple of kilometres away, so sometimes there's noise, but free airport transfers sweeten the deal.

Shambala BUNGALOWS $

(0 7742 5330; www.samui-shambala.com; bungalows 600-1000B;) While surrounding establishments answer the call of upmarket travellers, this laid-back, English-run place is a backpacking stalwart with a subtle hippy feel. There's plenty of communal cushion seating, a great wooden sun-deck, and the bungalows are bright and roomy. Staff doles out travel tips and smiles in equal measure.

Ocean 11 GUEST HOUSE $$

(0 7741 7118; www.o11s.com; bungalows 1900-3200B;) A little slice of luxury at a very reasonable price, Ocean 11's apartments are a steal (get it?!). Silly film references aside, this mellow spot with cottagey, Med-style decor is a great midrange getaway along a relatively quiet patch of sand.

BO PHUT

The beach isn't breathtaking, but Bo Phut has the most dynamic lodging in all of Samui. A string of vibrant boutique cottages starts deep within the clutter of Fisherman's Village and radiates outward along the sand.

TOP CHOICE **Anantara** RESORT $$$

(Map p178; 0 7742 8300; www.anantara.com; r 4000-18,000B;) Anantara's stunning palanquin entrance satisfies every fantasy of a far-flung oriental kingdom. Low-slung torches spurt plumes of unwavering fire, and the residual smoke creates a light fog around the fanned palm fronds higher up. Clay and copper statues of grimacing jungle creatures abound on the property's wild acreage, while guests savour wild teas in an open-air pagoda, swim in the lagoon-like infinity-edged swimming pool, or indulge in a relaxing spa treatment. The new wing of adjacent white-washed villas brings the resort up to another level of opulence.

TOP CHOICE **L'Hacienda** GUEST HOUSE $$

(Map p178; 0 7724 5943; www.samui-hacienda.com; r 1400-3500B;) Polished terracotta and rounded archways give the entrance a Spanish mission motif. Similar decor permeates the eight adorable rooms, which sport loads of personal touches such as pebbled bathroom walls and translucent bamboo lamps. There's a charming surprise waiting for you on the roof, and we're pretty sure you'll love it as much as we did.

Zazen RESORT $$$

(Map p178; 0 7742 5085; www.samuizazen.com; r 6010-17,200B;) What was once a simple place has now transformed into the boutique-iest boutique resort on Samui – every inch of this charming getaway has been thoughtfully and creatively designed. It's 'Asian minimalism meets modern Rococo' with a scarlet accent wall, terracotta goddesses, a dash of feng shui, and a generous smattering of good taste. Guests relax poolside on comfy beach chairs gently shaded by canvas parasols. The walk-in prices are scary, so it's best to book in advance.

Lodge HOTEL $$

(Map p178; 0 7742 5337; www.apartmentsamui.com; r 1400-2500B;) Another great choice in Bo Phut, the Lodge feels like a colonial hunting chalet with pale walls and dark wooden beams jutting across the ceiling. Every room has scores of wall hangings and a private balcony overlooking the beach. The 'pent-huts' on the top floor are very spacious. Reservations are a must – this place always seems to be full.

Ibis Bo Phut HOTEL $$

(Map p178; 0 7791 4800; www.ibishotel.com/thailand; r from 1600B;) The biggest resort on the island, the brand new Ibis still has that new car smell in its shiny, efficient rooms. Families will love the children's bunk beds and the grassy grounds perfect for a game of tag. If you're looking for a resort with traces of Thai character, this is not the place for you.

B1 Villa Spa APARTMENTS $$$

(Map p178; 0 7742 7268, www.b1villa.com; ste 2800-7000B;) There's a refreshing burst of character at this inn-style option along the beach in Fisherman's Village. Each room displays a unique collection of wall art, and has been given a special moniker – the 2nd-storey spaces are named after the stars in Orion's belt. Oh, and it's B1 as in 'B1 with yourself', get it?

Khuntai GUEST HOUSE $

(Map p178; 0 7724 5118; r 400-850B;) This clunky orange guest house is as cheap as decent rooms get on Samui. A block away from the beach, on the outskirts of Fisherman's Village, Khuntai's 2nd-floor rooms are drenched in afternoon sunshine and feature outdoor lounging spots.

MAE NAM & BANG PO

W Retreat Koh Samui RESORT $$$

(☎0 7791 5999; www.starwoodhotels.com/whotels; r from 23,000B; ❄@📶🏊) A bejewelled 'W' welcomes guests as they drive up the curling road to the lobby, and upon arrival jaws immediate drop whilst staring out over the glittering infinity pools and endless horizon. The trademark 'W glam' is palpable throughout the resort, which does its darnedest to fuse an urban vibe with tropical serenity. It'll be a while before this new resort finds its groove, so until then we recommend coming by for the Sunday brunch (2500B) or a sunset cocktail at Woo Bar.

Napasai By Orient Express RESORT $$$

(☎0 7742 9200; www.napasai.com; r from 9200B; ❄@📶🏊) Gorgeously manicured grounds welcome weary travellers as they glide past grazing water buffalo and groundsmen donning cream-coloured pith helmets. A generous smattering of villas dot the expansive landscape – all sport traditional Thai-style decorations, from the intricately carved wooden ornamentation to streamers of luscious local silks.

Maenam Resort BUNGALOWS $$

(☎0 7742 5116; www.maenamresort.com; bungalows 1400-3000B; ❄@📶) Palm-bark cottages are set in several rows amid a private, jungle-like garden. They're decked out in a mix of wicker and wooden furnishings, and vary in price according to their distance from the beach. Suites are a steal for families.

Harry's BUNGALOWS $$

(☎0 7742 5447; www.harrys-samui.com; bungalows 1200-3000B; ❄🏊) Arriving at Harry's feels like entering sacred temple grounds. Polished teak wood abounds in the lobby and the classic pitched roofing reaches skyward. The concrete bungalows, stashed in a verdant garden, do not retain the flamboyant architectural theme out front, but they're cute and comfortable nonetheless.

Coco Palm Resort BUNGALOWS $$

(☎0 7742 5095; bungalows 1200B; ❄🏊) The bungalows at Coco Palm have been crafted with tonnes of rattan. A rectangular pool is the centrepiece along the beach – and the price is right for a resort-like atmosphere.

Shangrilah BUNGALOWS $

(☎0 7742 5189; bungalows 300-2000B; ❄) A backpacker's Shangri La indeed – these are some of the cheapest huts around and they're in decent condition.

WEST COAST

Largely the domain of Thai tourists, Samui's west coast doesn't have the most picturesque beaches, but it's a welcome escape from the east-side bustle.

InterContinental Samui Baan Taling Ngam Resort RESORT $$$

(☎0 7742 9100; www.ichotelsgroup.com/intercontinental; r from 6300B; ❄@📶🏊) Unlike most of Samui's five-star digs, Baan Taling Ngam has been designed in a 'classic Thai' theme. Luxuriously appointed guest accommodation contains custom-made Thai-style furnishings and the service here is impeccable. As it's not right on the beach, a shuttle service transports guests back and forth; airport and ferry transfers are also provided.

Am Samui BUNGALOWS $$

(☎0 7723 5165; www.amsamuiresort.com; bungalows from 1100B; ❄📶🏊) Cast modesty aside, spread your curtains wide, and welcome sunshine and sea views in through your floor-to-ceiling windows. Lounge-worthy porch furniture further contributes to the comfy, casual vibe established at the open-air restaurant and pool.

SOUTH COAST

The southern end of Ko Samui is spotted with rocky headlands and smaller sandy coves. The following options are all well worth the baht, in fact, these resorts represent some of our favourite places to stay on the island.

Easy Time BUNGALOWS $$

(☎0 7792 0110; www.easytimesamui.com; Phang Ka; r from 1950B; ❄@📶🏊) Safely tucked away from the throngs of tourists, this little haven – nestled inland around a serene swimming pool – is a great place to unwind. Duplex villa units and a chic dining space create an elegant mood that is refreshingly unpretentious.

Elements RESORT $$$

(☎0 7791 4678; www.elements-koh-samui.com; Phang Ka; r 5540-21,500B; ❄@📶🏊) A refreshing twist on the modern boutique sleep, Elements occupies a lonely strand of palm-studded sand. Rooms are arranged in condo-like blocks, each one featuring an eye-pleasing blend of Thai and West styling. Hidden villas dot the path down to the fire-coloured restaurant and ocean-side lounge area.

Eating

If you thought it was hard to pick a place to sleep, the island has even more options when it comes to dining. From roasted crickets to beluga caviar – Samui's got it and is not afraid to flaunt it.

Influenced by the mainland, Samui is peppered with *kôw gaang* (rice and curry) shops, usually just a wooden shack displaying large metal pots of southern Thai-style curries. Folks pull up on their motorcycles, lift up the lids to survey the vibrantly coloured contents, and pick one for lunch. *Kôw gaang* shops are easily found along the Ring Rd (Rte 4169) and sell out of the good stuff by 1pm. Any build-up of local motorcycles is usually a sign of a good meal in progress.

The upmarket choices are even more numerous and although Samui's swank dining scene is laden with Italian options, visitors will have no problem finding flavours from around the globe. Lured by high salaries and spectacular weather, world-class chefs regularly make an appearance on the island.

CHAWENG

Dozens of the restaurants on the 'strip' serve a mixed bag of local bites, international cuisine, and greasy fast food. For the best ambience, get off the road and head to the beach, where many bungalow operators set up tables on the sand and have glittery fairy lights at night.

TOP CHOICE Samui Institute of Thai Culinary Arts THAI $$$
(SITCA; Map p176; ☎0 7741 3434; course 1950B; ⏲lunch & dinner Mon-Sat) Go one better than savouring a traditional Thai meal: cook it yourself!

Laem Din Market MARKET $
(Map p176; dishes from 30B; ⏲4am-6pm, night market 6pm-2am) A busy day market, Laem Din is packed with stalls that sell fresh fruits, vegetables and meats and stock local Thai kitchens. Pick up a kilo of sweet green oranges or wander the stalls trying to spot the ingredients in last night's curry. For dinner, come to the adjacent night market and sample the tasty southern-style fried chicken and curries.

Gringo's Cantina MEXICAN $$
(Map p176; dishes 140-280B; ⏲dinner) Wash down a Tex-Mex classic with a jug of sangria or a frozen margarita. We liked the *chimichangas* (mostly because we like saying *chimichanga*). There are burgers, pizzas and vegie options too, for those who don't want to go 'south of the border'.

Page ASIAN FUSION $$$
(Map p176; dishes 180-850B; ⏲breakfast, lunch & dinner) If you can't afford to stay at the ultra-swanky Library, have a meal at its beachside restaurant. The food is expensive (of course) but you'll receive glances from the beach bums on the beach as they try to figure out if you're a jetsetter or movie star. Lunch is a bit more casual and affordable, but you'll miss the designer lighting effects in the evening.

Prego ITALIAN $$$
(Map p176; www.prego-samui.com; mains 200-700B; ⏲dinner) This smart ministry of culinary style serves up fine Italian cuisine in a barely-there dining room of cool marble and modern geometry. Reservations are accepted for seatings at 7pm and 9pm.

Dr Frogs STEAKHOUSE $$$
(off Map p176; mains 380-790B; ⏲lunch & dinner) Perched atop a rocky overlook, Dr Frogs combines incredible ocean vistas with delicious international flavours (namely Italian and Thai favourites). Delectable steaks and crab cakes, and friendly owners, put this spot near the top of our dining list.

Betelnut@Buri Rasa ASIAN FUSION $$$
(Map p176; mains 600-800B; ⏲dinner) Fusion can be confusing, and often disappointing, but Betelnut will set you straight. Chef Jeffrey Lords claims an American upbringing and European culinary training, but most importantly he spent time in San Francisco, where all good food is born. The menu is a pan-Pacific mix of curries and chowder, papaya and pancetta.

Zico's BRAZILIAN $$$
(Map p176; menu 790B; ⏲dinner) This palatial *churrascaria* puts the *carne* in Carnival. Vegetarians beware – Zico's is an all-you-can-eat Brazilian meat-fest complete with saucy dancers sporting peacock-like outfits.

Khaosan Restaurant & Bakery INTERNATIONAL $
(Map p176; dishes from 60B; ⏲breakfast, lunch & dinner) From *filet mignon* to flapjacks and everything in between, this chow house is popular with those looking for a cheap nosh. Hang around after your meal and catch a newly released movie on the big TV. It's everything you'd expect from a place called 'Khaosan'.

Wave Samui INTERNATIONAL $
(Map p176; dishes from 60B; ⊙breakfast, lunch & dinner) Everyone says that Samui is going upmarket, but the most crowded restaurants at dinnertime are still the old-fashioned budget spots, like this one. This jack-of-all trades (guest house-bar-restaurant) serves honest food at honest prices and fosters a travellers' ambience with an in-house library and a popular happy hour (3pm to 7pm).

LAMAI

As Samui's second-most populated beach, Lamai has a surprisingly limited assortment of decent eateries when compared to Chaweng next door. The Tesco Lotus is a great place to pick up snacks for a beachside picnic. Most visitors, however, dine wherever they're staying.

Rocky's INTERNATIONAL $$$
(dishes 300-800B; ⊙lunch & dinner) Easily the top dining spot on Lamai, Rocky's gourmet dishes are actually a bargain when you convert the baht into your native currency. Try the signature beef tenderloin with blue cheese – it's like sending your tastebuds on a Parisian vacation. On Tuesday evenings, diners enjoy a special Thai-themed evening with a prepared menu of local delicacies. Rocky's is located at the like-named resort just south of Lamai.

Lamai Day Market MARKET $
(dishes from 30B; ⊙6am-8pm) The Thai equivalent of a grocery store, Lamai's market is a hive of activity, selling food necessities and takeaway food. Visit the covered area to pick up fresh fruit or to see vendors shredding coconuts to make coconut milk. Or hunt down the ice-cream seller for homemade coconut ice cream. It's next door to a petrol station.

Hua Thanon Market MARKET $
(dishes from 30B; ⊙6am-6pm) Slip into the rhythm of this village market slightly south of Lamai; a window into the food ways of southern Thailand. Vendors shoo away the flies from the freshly butchered meat and housewives load bundles of vegetables into their baby-filled motorcycle baskets. Follow the market road to the row of food shops delivering edible Muslim culture: chicken biryani, fiery curries or toasted rice with coconut, bean sprouts, lemongrass and dried shrimp.

NORTHERN BEACHES

Some of Samui's finest establishments are located on the northern coast. Boho Bo Phut has several trendy eateries to match the string of yuppie boutique hotels.

CHOENG MON & BIG BUDDHA BEACH (BANG RAK)

TOP CHOICE **Dining On The Rocks** ASIAN FUSION $$$
(☎0 7724 5678; reservations-samui@sixsenses.com; Choeng Mon; menus from 2200B; ⊙dinner) Samui's ultimate dining experience takes place on nine cantilevered verandahs of weathered teak and bamboo that yawn over the gulf. After sunset (and a glass of wine), guests feel like they're dining on a wooden barge set adrift on a starlit sea. Each dish on the six-course prix-fixe menu is the brainchild of the experimental cooks who regularly experiment with taste, texture and temperature. If you're celebrating a special occasion, you'll have to book well in advance if you want to sit at 'table 99' – the honeymooners' table – positioned on a private terrace. Dining On The Rocks is located at the isolated Six Senses Samui.

BBC INTERNATIONAL $$
(Big Buddha Beach; dishes 60-200B; ⊙breakfast, lunch & dinner) No, this place has nothing to do with *Dr Who* – BBC stands for Big Buddha Café. It's popular with the local expats, the international menu is large, and there are exquisite ocean views from the patio.

Antica Locanda ITALIAN $$
(www.anticasamui.com; dishes 170-280B; ⊙dinner) This friendly trattoria has pressed white tablecloths and caskets of Italian wine. Try the *vongole alla marinara* (clams in white wine) and don't forget to check out the succulent specials of the day.

If you're waiting for a ferry in Bang Rak consider stopping by one of the following:

Catcantoo BBQ $$
(http://catcantoo.net; mains 90-350B; ⊙breakfast, lunch & dinner) Enjoy bargain-basement breakfast (99B) in the morning, succulent ribs at noon, or shooting some pool later in the day.

Pae Chuan Chim THAI $
(mains 30-40B; ⊙breakfast & lunch) Without an ounce of atmosphere to speak of, this open-air noodle-scooping haunt is popular with locals who break for lunch to reenergise. Located next to the hyperbaric chamber.

BO PHUT

Shack Bar & Grill STEAKHOUSE **$$$**

(Map p178; www.theshackgrillsamui.com; mains 480-780B; ⏰dinner) With hands down the best steaks on the island, the Shack imports the finest cuts of meat from Australia and slathers them in a rainbow of tasty sauces from red wine to blue cheese. Booth seating and jazz over the speakers give the joint a distinctly Western vibe, though you'll find all types of diners come here to splurge.

Zazen ASIAN FUSION **$$$**

(Map p178; dishes 550-850B, set menu from 1300B; ⏰lunch & dinner) The chef describes the food as 'organic and orgasmic', and the ambient 'yums' from elated diners definitely confirm the latter. This romantic dining experience comes complete with ocean views, dim candle lighting and soft music. Reservations recommended.

Starfish & Coffee THAI **$$**

(Map p178; mains 130-180B; ⏰breakfast, lunch & dinner) This streamer-clad eatery was probably named after the Prince song, since we couldn't find any starfish on the menu (there's loads of coffee though). Evenings feature standard Thai fare and sunset views of rugged Ko Pha-Ngan.

Villa Bianca ITALIAN **$$**

(Map p178; dishes from 200B; ⏰lunch & dinner) Another fantastic Italian spot on Samui, Villa Bianca is a sea of crisp white tablecloths and woven lounge chairs. Who knew wicker could be so sexy?

Karma Sutra INTERNATIONAL **$$**

(Map p178; mains 130-260B; ⏰breakfast, lunch & dinner) A haze of purples and pillows, this charming chow spot in the heart of Bo Phut's Fisherman's Village serves up international and Thai eats listed on colourful chalkboards. Karma Sutra doubles as a clothing boutique.

MAE NAM & BANG PO

Angela's Bakery BAKERY, INTERNATIONAL **$$**

(Mae Nam; dishes 80-200B; ⏰breakfast & lunch) Duck through the screen of hanging plants into this beloved bakery, smelling of fresh bread and hospitality. Angela's sandwiches and cakes have kept many Western expats from wasting away in the land of rice.

Bang Po Seafood SEAFOOD **$$**

(Bang Po; dishes from 100B; ⏰dinner) A meal at Bang Po Seafood is a test for the tastebuds. It's one of the only restaurants that serves traditional Ko Samui fare (think of it as island roadkill, well, actually it's more like local sea-kill): recipes call for ingredients such as raw sea urchin roe, baby octopus, sea water, coconut, and local turmeric.

WEST COAST

The quiet west coast features some of the best seafood on Samui. Na Thon has a giant **day market** on Th Thawi Ratchaphakdi – it's worth stopping by to grab some snacks before your ferry ride.

TOP CHOICE **Five Islands** SEAFOOD **$$$**

(www.thefiveislands.com; Taling Ngam; dishes 150-500B, tours 3000-6500B; ⏰lunch & dinner) Five Islands defines the term 'destination dining' and offers the most unique eating experience on the island. Before your meal, a traditional longtail boat will take you out into the turquoise sea to visit the haunting Five Sister Islands where you'll learn about the ancient and little-known art of harvesting bird nests to make bird's-nest soup, a Chinese delicacy. This perilous task is rewarded with large sums of cash – a kilo of nests is usually sold for 100,000B to restaurants in Hong Kong (yup, that's five zeros). The lunch tour departs around 10am, and the dinner program leaves around 3pm. Customers are also welcome to dine without going on the tour and vice versa.

About Art & Craft Café VEGETARIAN **$$**

(Na Thon; dishes 80 180B; ⏰breakfast & lunch) An artistic oasis in the midst of hurried Na Thon, this cafe serves an eclectic assortment of healthy and wholesome food, gourmet coffee and, as the name states, art and craft, made by the owner and her friends. Relaxed and friendly, this is also a gathering place for Samui's dwindling population of bohemians and artists.

Drinking & Entertainment

Samui's biggest party spot is, without a doubt, noisy Chaweng. Lamai and Bo Phut come in second and third respectively, while the rest of the island is generally quiet, as the drinking is usually focused around self-contained resort bars.

CHAWENG & LAMAI

Making merry in Chaweng is a piece of cake. Most places are open until 2am and there are a few places that go strong all night long. Soi Green Mango has loads of girly bars. Soi Colibri and Soi Reggae Pub are raucous as well.

POP'S CULTURE: LIFE AS A LADYBOY

Pop, age 45, is what Thais call a *gà·teu·i*, usually referred to as a 'ladyboy' in English. Thailand's transgender population is the subject of many debates and conversations, especially among tourists. Although tolerance is widespread in Buddhist Thailand, concealed homophobia prevails – for *gà·teu·i*, this can be a challenging life, with the entertainment and sex industries the only lucrative career avenues open. We spent the day with Pop and got the skinny on what life was really like as a member of Thailand's oft-talked-about 'third sex'.

LET'S START WITH A QUESTION THAT MANY TOURISTS IN THAILAND WOULD LIKE TO ASK: WHY DOES THERE SEEM TO BE SO MANY GA-TEU-I IN THAILAND?

Well, that's like asking me why I am a ladyboy! I have no idea. I didn't ask to have these feelings. I think the more important thing to notice is why there are so many ladyboys in the cabaret or sex industry. First, however, let me start by staying that the word *gà·teu·i* is the informal way of saying 'person with two sexes'; the term *pôo yĭng kâhm pêt* is generally more polite. Also, *gà·teu·i* is strictly reserved for people who still have male body parts but dress as female, so I am not technically *gà·teu·i* anymore.

Most tourists think that there are tonnes of ladyboys in Thailand because they are in places that many tourists visit. Yes, some ladyboys want to be cabaret dancers, just like some women want to be cabaret dancers, but most of them don't. These types of jobs are the only ones available to ladyboys, and the pay is lousy. Life is not as 'Hollywood' for a ladyboy as it may seem on stage. Most ladyboys don't have the chance to have a job that is respected by the community. We are not allowed to become doctors or psychologists and most corporations do not allow ladyboy employees because they don't want *gà·teu·i* to be associated with their company's image. Since many of us cannot have proper jobs, many ladyboys drop out of school at a young age , and lately this educational gap in the culture has become huge. Ladyboys work in the sex industry because they aren't given the opportunity to make a lot of money doing something else. I feel like a second-class citizen; we are not allowed to use male *or* female bathrooms! I used to have to climb 14 flights of stairs to use the special ladyboys' bathroom at my old job! Also, Thai law states that my ID cards and passport must always have an 'M' for male because the definition of a female in Thailand is someone who can bear children. It's hard for me to leave the country because my passport says 'male' but I look like a female. They will never let me through security because it looks like a fraudulent passport.

WHEN DID YOU FIRST REALISE THAT YOU MIGHT BE A TRANSGENDER PERSON?

I realised that I was different when I was about six years old. I always wanted to dress up like my sister and would get upset when my parents dressed me in boy's clothing. It felt wrong being in boy's clothes. I felt good in my sister's outfits.

HOW DOES ONE TELL THE DIFFERENCE BETWEEN A LADYBOY AND A WOMAN ON THE STREET?

Sometimes it's really hard to tell...sometimes a ladyboy can be more beautiful than a woman! There is no set way to figure it out, unless you ask them for their ID card. These days, doctors are really starting to perfect the operations, and the operations are expensive – mine was 150,000B! I had the 'snip', then I had breast implants, my Adam's apple was shaved off, and I also had a nose job (I didn't like my old nose anyways). Other operations available include silicone implants in the hips, jaw narrowing, cheekbone shaving and chin sculpting – to make it rounder. But before anyone can have an operation, you have to have a psych evaluation. The operation was extremely painful. I spent seven days in the hospital

Beach Republic LOUNGE
(www.beachrepublic.com; 176/34 Moo 4 Hat Lamai) Recognised by its yawning thatch-patched awnings, Beach Republic would be the perfect spot to shoot one of those MTV Spring Break episodes. There's an inviting wading pool, comfy lounge chairs and an endless cocktail list.

Q-Bar LOUNGE
(Map p176; www.qbarsamui.com; Hat Chaweng) Overlooking Chaweng Lake, Q-Bar is a little piece of Bangkok nightlife planted among the

and it took me about two months to fully recover. Younger patients tend to heal faster – I was about 40 years old when I had the operation.

WHY DIDN'T YOU HAVE THE OPERATION EARLIER? AND HOW HAVE YOUR HANDLED THE TRANSITION?

I didn't 'change' earlier because I didn't want to give up my job, and I knew that after the operation I would be forced to quit. I was working as a software instructor at a university, and university teachers are not allowed to be transgender. I also waited until my father passed away so that it would be easier on my family when I made the transition.

Well, contrary to what some tourists believe, no family particularly *wants* a transgender child, even a family with only boys. Some of my close friends no longer speak to their families. My mother was always very comforting. A month before my operation she told me 'you will always be my child, but never lie to anyone about who you are – accept who you are'. I have two adopted sons who are now quite grown-up, and after I made the change, they bought me presents on Mother's Day instead of Father's Day – I thought that was very sweet. My father, on the other hand, was never very supportive. When he found I was sleeping with men, he...well...let's put it this way, he practised his *moo·ay thai* [also spelled *muay thai*] boxing on me.

HOW DID YOU FEEL WHEN YOU WOKE UP AFTER THE OPERATION? HOW HAS LIFE BEEN SINCE THE OPERATION?

I woke up with a big smile. Life is great. I am happy that I can be on the outside what I am on the inside – I can stop feeling sad every time I look down! Finding a job after my surgery was hard. I wrote on my CV 'transgender post-op' so that there would be no surprises in the interview, but I never heard back from any companies. Oh, actually one company asked me to come for an interview, but they spent the meeting asking me inappropriate questions about my personal life. It was very disheartening. I finally found a queer-friendly company, where I am employed as a hospitality software implementer, meaning that I go around to hotels around Thailand and teach front desk staff how to use the hotel's computer system. I adore my job.

Now that my surgery is far behind me, I have to take female hormones regularly until I die. I take a pill twice per week, but some male-to-females take one injection per month (I hate needles). Some people have a bad reaction to the medication at first. I have had friends that got a lot of pimples and got really fat. Sometimes it takes a while before you find the right amount of hormones. Besides the hormones, there is a certain amount of... maintenance...that needs to take place in order to keep my new parts working. Put it this way, when you get your ears pierced, if you don't regularly wear earrings...well... Anyways, my aunt, who moved to the United States, asked me if I wanted to move too, but I am happy in Thailand. Even though transgender individuals don't have a lot of rights, I'm not convinced that it is that much better anywhere else.

AND FINALLY, WHAT DO YOU FEEL IS THE BIGGEST MISCONCEPTION ABOUT GÀ·TEU·I IN THAILAND?

This is an easy question. The biggest misconception is that we are all promiscuous whores and liars. Like any human being, we are just looking for love. It is true that many ladyboys do try to trick the people around them, but this is because they are afraid of being rejected for who they really are. Also, many of them lie because they desperately want to be real women, but they will never be real women. I know that – that's why I always show the real me – I am comfortable with who I am. I wish everyone else would be too.

As told to Brandon Presser.

coconut trees. The upstairs lounge opens just before sunset, treating cocktail connoisseurs to various highbrow tipples and a drinkable view of southern Chaweng – mountains, sea and sky. After 10pm, the night-crawlers descend upon the downstairs club where DJs spin the crowd into a techno amoeba. A taxi there will cost between 200B and 300B.

Ark Bar BAR

(Map p176; www.ark-bar.com; Hat Chaweng) The 'it' destination for a Wednesday-night romp on Samui. Drinks are dispensed from the multicoloured bar draped in paper lanterns, and guests lounge on pyramidal pillows strewn down the beach. The party usually starts around 4pm.

Christy's Cabaret CABARET
(Map p176; Hat Chaweng) This flashy joint offers free *gà·teu·i* (ladyboys; also spelled *kàthoey*) cabaret every night at 11pm and attracts a mixed clientele of both sexes. Other ladyboys loiter out front and try to drag customers in, so to speak.

Good Karma BAR
(Map p176; Hat Chaweng) Open all day, this snazzy lounge lures the hip 'hi-so' (Thai high society) crowd with canopied daybeds and a hidden pond.

Bar Solo BAR
(Map p176; Hat Chaweng) A sign of things to come, Bar Solo has future-fitted Chaweng's outdoor beer halls into an urban setting with sleek cubist decor and a cocktail list that doesn't scream holiday hayseed. The evening drink specials lure in the front-loaders preparing for a late, late night at the dance clubs on Soi Solo and Soi Green Mango.

Tropical Murphy's IRISH BAR
(Map p176; Hat Chaweng) A popular *fa·ràng* (foreigner) joint, Tropical Murphy's dishes out steak-and-kidney pie, fish and chips, lamb chops and Irish stew (mains 50B to 300B). Come night-time, the live music kicks on and this place turns into the most popular Irish bar on Samui (yes, there are a few).

Green Mango BAR
(Map p176; Hat Chaweng) This place is so popular it has an entire soi named after it. Samui's favourite power drinking house is very big, very loud and very faràng. Green Mango has blazing lights, expensive drinks and masses of sweaty bodies swaying to dance music.

Reggae Pub BAR
(Map p176; Hat Chaweng) This fortress of fun sports an open-air dance floor with music spun by foreign DJs. It's a towering two-storey affair with long bars, pool tables and a live-music stage. The whole place doubles as a shrine to Bob Marley.

Mint BAR
(Map p176; Hat Chaweng) The scene on Green Mango Soi is too entertaining to keep the crowds corralled in this stylish club on ordinary nights. But the Mint is able to lure a few DJ heavyweights for a Samui spin on extraordinary nights. Watch the entertainment listings for special events.

NORTHERN & WEST COAST BEACHES

Woo Bar LOUNGE
(Mae Nam) The W Retreat's signature lobby bar gives the word 'swish' a whole new meaning with cushion-clad pods of seating plunked in the middle of an expansive infinity pool that stretches out over the infinite horizon. This is, without a doubt, the best place on Samui for a sunset cocktail.

Nikki Beach LOUNGE
(www.nikkibeach.com/kohsamui; Lipa Noi) The acclaimed luxury brand has brought its international *savoir faire* to the secluded west coast of Ko Samui. Expect everything you would from a chic address in St Barts or St Tropez: haute cuisine, chic decor and gaggles of jetsetters. Themed brunch and dinner specials keep the masses coming throughout the week, and sleek bungalow accommodation is also on offer.

Pier LOUNGE
(Map p178; Bo Phut) This sleek black box sticks out among Bo Phut's narrow Chinese tenements. It's the hippest address in Fisherman's Village, sporting multilevel terraces, a lively bar, and plenty of wide furniture to lounge around on and watch the rickety fishing vessels pull into the harbour.

Gecko Village CLUB
(Map p178; Bo Phut) For electronica fans, Gecko Village is the original maven of beats. It's a beachfront bar and resort that has used its London connections to lure international DJs to Samui paradise. The New Year's Eve parties and Sunday sessions are now legendary thanks to the big names that grace the turntables.

Billabong Surf Club BAR
(Map p178; Bo Phut) Billabong's all about Aussie Rules football – it's playing on the TV and the walls are smothered with memorabilia from Down Undah. There are great views of Ko Pha-Ngan and hearty portions of ribs and chops to go with your draught beer.

ℹ Information

Dangers & Annoyances

As on Phuket, the rate of road accident fatalities on Samui is quite high. This is mainly due to the large number of tourists who rent motorcycles only to find out that the winding roads, sudden tropical rains and frenzied traffic can be lethal. If you decide to rent a motorcycle, protect yourself by wearing a helmet, and ask for one that has a plastic visor. Even if you escape unscathed from a riding experience, we've heard reports that some shops will claim that you damaged your rental and will try to extort you for some serious cash.

Beach vendors are registered with the government and should all be wearing a numbered jacket. No peddler should cause an incessant disturbance – seek assistance if this occurs.

Emergency

Tourist police (Map p175; ☎0 7742 1281, emergency 1155) Based at the south of Na Thon.

Immigration Offices & Visas

Located about 2km south of Na Thon is Ko Samui's **Immigration Office** (Map p175; ☎0 7742 1069; ⊙8.30am-noon & 1-4.30pm Mon-Fri). Officials here tend to issue the minimum rather than maximum visa extensions. During our visits here we've watched dozens of tourists wait through exhausting lines only to get curtly denied an extension for no particular reason. On a particularly bad day expect extensions to take the entire afternoon. See p406 for more details on visas.

Internet Access

There are countless places all over the island for internet access, even at the less popular beaches. Prices range from 1B to 2B per minute. Keep an eye out for restaurants that offer complimentary wi-fi service. Most accommodation offers a wi-fi connection; ironically you'll pay extra for it at high-end hotels.

Media & Maps

The Siam Map Company puts out quarterly booklets including a *Spa Guide, Dining Guide*, and an annual directory, which lists thousands of companies and hotels on the island. Its *Siam Map Company Samui Guide Map* is fantastic, free, and easily found throughout the island. Also worth a look is the *Samui Navigator* pamphlet. **Essential** (www.essential-samui) is a pocket-sized pamphlet focused on promoting Samui's diverse activities. *Samui Guide* looks more like a magazine and features mostly restaurants and attractions.

Medical Services

Ko Samui has four private hospitals, all near Chaweng's Tesco-Lotus supermarket on the east coast (where most of the tourists tend to gather). The government hospital in Na Thon has seen significant improvements in the last couple of years but the service is still a bit grim because funding is based on the number of Samui's legal residents (which doesn't take into account the many illegal Burmese workers).

Bandon International Hospital (Map p178; ☎0 7742 5840, emergency 0 7742 5748)

Bangkok Samui Hospital (Map p176; ☎0 7742 9500, emergency 0 7742 9555) Your best bet for just about any medical problem.

Hyperbaric Chamber (Map p175; ☎0 7742 7427; Big Buddha Beach) The island's dive medicine specialists.

Samui International Hospital (Map p176; ☎0 7742 2272; www.sih.co.th; Hat Chaweng) Emergency ambulance service is available 24 hours and credit cards are accepted. Near the Amari Resort in Chaweng.

Money

Changing money isn't a problem on the east and north coasts, and in Na Thon. Multiple banks and foreign-exchange booths offer daily services and there's an ATM every couple of hundred metres. You should not have to pay credit card fees as you do on neighbouring Ko Tao.

Post

In several parts of the island there are privately run post-office branches charging a small commission. You can almost always leave your stamped mail with your accommodation.

Main post office (Map p175; Na Thon) Near the TAT office; not always reliable.

Tourist information

Essential (www.essential-samui) A pocket-sized pamphlet focused on promoting Samui's diverse activities.

Samui Guide (www.samuiguide.com) This guide looks more like a magazine and features mostly restaurants and attractions.

Samui Navigator (www.samuinavigaot.com) This pamphlet is also worth a look.

Siam Map Company (www.siammap.com) Puts out quarterly booklets including guides to spas and dining spots, and an annual directory, which lists thousands of companies and hotels on the island. Its *Siam Map Company Samui Guide Map* is fantastic, free and easily found throughout the island.

TAT office (Map p175; ☎0 7742 0504; Na Thon; ⊙8.30am-4.30pm) At the northern end of Na Thon; this office is friendly, helpful and has handy brochures and maps – although travel agents throughout the island can provide similar information.

Getting There & Away

Air

Samui's airport is located in the northeast of the island near Big Buddha Beach. **Bangkok**

Airways (www.bangkokair.com) operates flights roughly every 30 minutes between Samui and Bangkok's Suvarnabhumi Airport (50 minutes). Bangkok Air also flies direct from Samui to Phuket, Pattaya, Chiang Mai, Singapore and Hong Kong. **Firefly** (www.fireflyz.com.my) operates direct flights from Samui to Kuala Lumpur's Subang airport.

There is a **Bangkok Airways Office** (Map p176; ☎0 7742 0512-9) in Chaweng and another at the **airport** (☎0 7742 5011). The first (at 6am) and last (10pm) flights of the day are always the cheapest.

During the high season, make your flight reservations far in advance as seats often sell out. If the Samui flights are full, try flying into Surat Thani from Bangkok and taking a short ferry ride to Samui instead. Flights to Surat Thani are generally cheaper than a direct flight to the island, although they are much more of a hassle.

Boat

To reach Samui, the four main piers on the mainland are Ao Ban Don, Tha Thong, Don Sak and Khanom – Tha Thong (in central Surat) and Don Sak being the most common. On Samui, the three oft-used ports are Na Thon, Mae Nam and Big Buddha. Expect complimentary taxi transfers with high-speed ferry services.

There are frequent boat departures between Samui and Surat Thani. The hourly Seatran ferry is a common option. Ferries take one to five hours, depending on the boat. A couple of these departures can connect with the train station in Phun Phin (for a nominal extra fee). The slow night boat to Samui leaves from central Surat Thani each night at 11pm, reaching Na Thon around 5am. It returns from Na Thon at 9pm, arriving at around 3am. Watch your bags on this boat.

There are almost a dozen daily departures between Samui and Ko Pha-Ngan. These leave from the Na Thon, Mae Nam or Big Buddha pier and take from 20 minutes to one hour. The boats departing from Big Buddha service Hat Rin, and the other boats alight at Thong Sala. From the same piers, there are also around six daily departures between Samui and Ko Tao. These take 1¼ to 2½ hours.

Bus & Train

A bus-ferry combo is more convenient than a train-ferry package for getting to Ko Samui because you don't have to switch transportation in Phun Phin. However, the trains are much more comfortable and spacious – especially at night. If you prefer the train, you can get off at Chumphon and catch the Lomprayah catamaran service the rest of the way.

Getting Around

Motorbikes You can rent motorcycles (and bicycles) from almost every resort on the island. The going rate is 200B per day, but for longer periods try to negotiate a better rate.

Sŏrng·tăa·ou Drivers of *sŏrng·tăa·ou* love to try to overcharge you, so it's always best to ask a third party for current rates, as they can change with the season. These vehicles run regularly during daylight hours. It's about 50B to travel between beaches, and no more than 100B to travel halfway across the island. Figure about 20B for a five-minute ride on a motorcycle taxi.

Taxis On Samui service is quite chaotic due to the plethora of cabs. In the past taxi fares were unwieldy; these days prices are more standardised across the islands (though fares are still ridiculously inflated compared to Bangkok). Taxis typically charge around 500B for an airport transfer. Some Chaweng travel agencies can arrange minibus taxis for less.

Ko Pha-Ngan

เกาะพงัน

POP 11,000

In the family of southern Gulf islands, Ko Pha-Ngan sits in the crystal sea between Ko Samui, its business-savvy older brother, and little Ko Tao, the spunky younger brother full of dive-centric energy. Ko Pha-Ngan is a chilled out middle child who is a beach bum with tattered dreadlocks, a tattoo of a Chinese serenity symbol, and a penchant for white nights and bikini-clad pool parties.

The scenic cape of Hat Rin has long been the darling destination of this laid-back paradise. Sunrise Beach started hosting the world-famous Full Moon Parties long before Alex Garland's *The Beach* inspired many to strap on a rucksack. Today, thousands of visitors still flock to the island's sands for an epic trance-a-thon fuelled by adrenaline and a couple of other substances...

But like any textbook teenager, this angst-ridden island can't decide what it wants to be when it grows up. Should the party personality persist or will the stunning and secluded northern beaches finally come out from under Hat Rin's shadow?

While Pha-Ngan's slacker vibe and reputation will no doubt dominate for years to come, the island is secretly starting to creep upmarket. Every year, tired old shacks are being replaced by crisp modern abodes. In Hat Rin, you will be hard-pressed to find a room on Sunrise Beach for less than 1000B. Soon, the phrase 'private infinity pool' and 'personal butler' will find a permanent place

in the island's lexicon, replacing 'pass the dutch' and 'another whiskey bucket please'. But don't fret just yet – the vast inland jungle continues to feel undiscovered, and there are still plenty of secluded bays in which you can string up a hammock and watch the tide roll in.

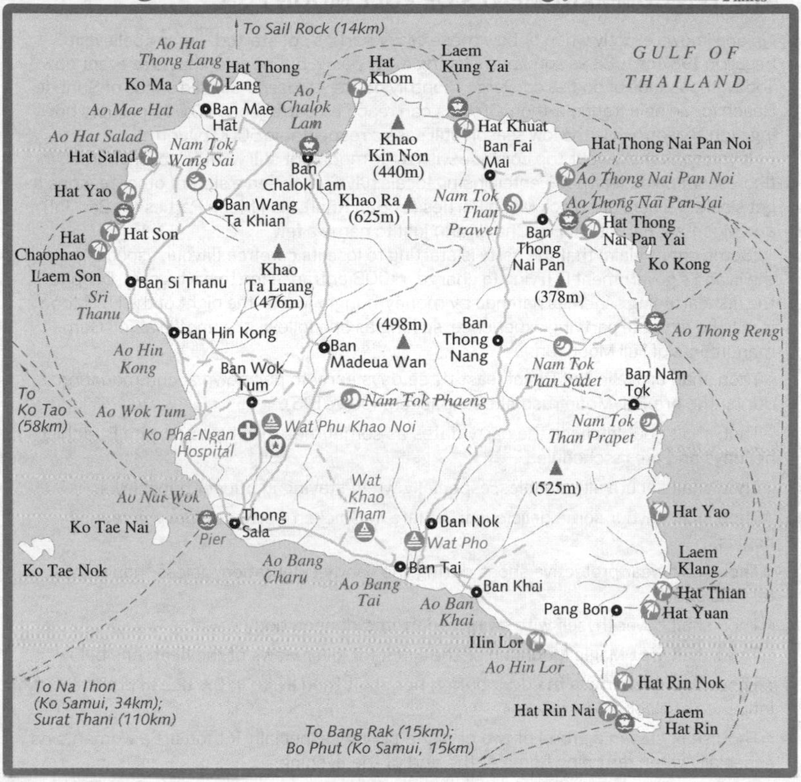

Sights

For those who tire of beach-bumming, this large jungle island has many natural features to explore including mountains, waterfalls and, most importantly, some of the most spectacular beaches in all of Thailand.

Beaches & Waterfalls

There are many waterfalls throughout the island's interior, four of which gush throughout the year.

Nam Tok Than Sadet WATERFALL

These falls feature boulders carved with the royal insignia of Rama V, Rama VII and Rama IX. King Rama V enjoyed this hidden spot so much that he returned over a dozen times between 1888 and 1909. The river waters of Khlong Than Sadet are now considered sacred and used in royal ceremonies. Also near the eastern coast, **Than Prawet** is a series of chutes that snake inland for approximately 2km.

Nam Tok Phaeng WATERFALL

In the centre of the island, Nam Tok Phaeng is protected by a national park; this waterfall is a pleasant reward after a short, but rough, hike. Continue the adventure and head up to **Khao Ra**, the highest mountain on the island at 625m. Those with eagle-eyes will spot wild crocodiles, monkeys, snakes, deer and boar along the way, and the **viewpoint** from the top is spectacular – on a clear day you can see Ko Tao. Although the trek isn't arduous, it is very easy to lose one's way, and we *highly* recommend hiring an escort in Ban

THE TEN COMMANDMENTS OF FULL MOON FUN

No one knows exactly when or how these crazy parties got started – many believe it began in 1987 or 1988 as someone's 'going away party', but none of that is relevant now. Today, thousands of bodies converge monthly on the kerosene-soaked sands of Sunrise Beach for an epic trance-a-thon. Crowds can reach an outrageous 40,000 partiers during high season, while the low season still sees a respectable 5000 pilgrims.

If you can't make your trip coincide with a full moon but still want to cover yourself in fluorescent paint, fear not – enterprising locals have organised a slew of other reasons to get sloshed. There are Black Moon Parties (at Ban Khai), Half Moon Parties (at Ban Tai) and Moon-set Parties (at Hat Chaophao) just to name a few.

Some critics claim that the party is starting to lose its carefree flavour, especially since the island's government is trying to charge a 100B entrance fee to partygoers. Despite the disheartening schemes hatched by money-hungry locals, the night of the Full Moon is still the ultimate partying experience, so long as one follows the unofficial Ten Commandments of Full Moon fun:

» Thou shalt arrive in Hat Rin at least three days early to nail down accommodation during the pre-Full Moon rush of backpackers (see p196).

» Thou shalt double-check the party dates as sometimes they coincide with Buddhist holidays and are rescheduled.

» Thou shalt secure all valuables, especially when staying in budget bungalows.

» Thou shalt savour some delicious fried fare in Chicken Corner before the revelry begins.

» Thou shalt wear protective shoes during the sandy celebration, unless thou want a tetanus shot.

» Thou shalt cover thyself with swirling patterns of neon body paint.

» Thou shalt visit Magic Mountain or the Rock for killer views of the heathens below.

» Thou shalt not sample the drug buffet, nor shalt thou swim in the ocean under the influence of alcohol.

» Thou shalt stay in a group of two or more people, especially if thou art a woman, and especially when returning home at the end of the evening.

» Thou shalt party until the sun comes up and have a great time.

Madeua Wan (near the falls). The local guides have crude signs posted in front of their homes, and, if they're around, they'll take you up to the top for 500B. Most of them only speak Thai.

Hat Khuat BEACH

Also called Bottle Beach, Hat Khuat is a classic fave. Visitors flock to this shore for a relaxing day of swimming and snorkelling – some opt to stay the night at one of the several bungalow operations along the beach. For additional seclusion, try the isolated beaches on the east coast, which include **Than Sadet**, **Hat Yuan**, **Hat Thian** and the teeny **Ao Thong Reng**. For additional enchanting beaches, consider doing a day trip to the stunning **Ang Thong Marine National Park** (p222).

Wát

Remember to change out of your beach clothes when visiting one of the 20 wát on Ko Pha-Ngan. Most temples are open during daylight hours.

The oldest temple on the island is **Wat Phu Khao Noi**, near the hospital in Thong Sala. While the site is open to visitors throughout the day, the monks are only around in the morning. **Wat Pho**, near Ban Tai, has a **herbal sauna** (admission 50B; ⌚3-6pm) accented with natural lemongrass. The **Chinese Temple** is believed to give visitors good luck. It was constructed about 20 years ago after a visiting woman had a vision of the Chinese Buddha, who instructed her to build a fire-light for the island. **Wat Khao Tham**, also near Ban Tai, sits high on a hill and has resident female monks. At the temple there is a bulletin board detailing a meditation retreat taught by an American-Australian couple. For additional information, write in advance to Wat Khao Tham, PO Box 8, Ko Pha-Ngan, Surat Thani 84280.

Activities

Diving & Snorkelling

With Ko Tao, the high-energy diving behemoth, just a few kilometres away, Ko Pha-Ngan enjoys a much quieter, more laid-back diving scene focused on fun diving rather than certifications. A recent drop in Open Water certification prices has made local prices competitive with Ko Tao next door. Group sizes tend to be smaller on Ko Pha-Ngan since the island has less divers in general.

Like the other islands in the Samui Archipelago, Pha-Ngan has several small reefs dispersed around the island. The clear favourite snorkelling spot is **Ko Ma**, a small island in the northwest connected to Ko Pha-Ngan by a charming sandbar. There are also some rock reefs of interest on the eastern side of the island.

A major perk of diving from Ko Pha-Ngan is the proximity to **Sail Rock** (Hin Bai), the best dive site in the Gulf of Thailand and a veritable beacon for whale sharks. This large pinnacle lies about 14km north of the island. An abundance of corals and large tropical fish can be seen at depths of 10m to 30m, and there's a rocky vertical swim-through called 'The Chimney'.

Dive shops on Ko Tao sometimes visit Sail Rock, however the focus tends to be more on swallow reefs (for newbie divers) and the shark-infested waters at Chumphon Pinnacle. The most popular trips departing from Ko Pha-Ngan are three-site day trips which stop at **Chumphon Pinnacle**, Sail Rock and one of the other premiere sites in the area (see boxed text p209). These three-stop trips cost from around 3650B to 3800B and include a full lunch. Two-dive trips to Sail Rock will set you back around 2350B to 2500B.

The following list includes the main operators on the island with a solid reputation.

Reefers DIVING
(☎08 6471 4045; www.reefersdiving.com) Based at Shiralea (p200), this is one of the newer outfits on the island. Vic, the owner, and his gaggle of instructors are chilled and professional. Recommended.

Lotus Diving DIVING
(☎0 7737 4142; www.lotusdiving.net) This dive centre has top-notch instructors, and owns not one, but two beautiful boats (that's two more vessels than most of the other operations on Ko Pha-Ngan). Trips can be booked at their office in Chalok Lam, or at the Backpackers Information Centre (p570). Recommended.

Haad Yao Divers DIVING
(☎08 6279 3085; www.haadyaodivers.com) Established in 1997, this dive operator has garnered a strong reputation by maintaining European standards of safety and customer service.

Other Activities

Hiking and snorkelling day trips to **Ang Thong Marine National Park** (p222) generally depart from Ko Samui, but recently tour operators are starting to shuttle tourists from Ko Pha-Ngan as well. Ask at your accommodation for details about boat trips as companies often come and go due to unstable petrol prices.

Many of the larger accommodation options can hook you up with a variety of aquatic equipment such as jet skis and kayaks, and the friendly staff at Backpackers Information Centre (p570) can attend to any of your other water-sports needs.

Wake Up WAKEBOARDING
(☎08 7283 6755; www.wakeupwakeboarding.com; ⊙Jan-Oct) Jamie passes along his infinite wakeboarding wisdom to eager wannabes at his small water sports school in Chalok Lam. Fifteen minutes of 'air time' will set you back 1500B (2500B for 30 minutes), which is excellent value considering you get one-on-one instruction. Kite-boarding, wake-skating and waterskiing sessions are also available, as are round-the-island day trips (2000B per person; a six-person quorum needed).

Eco Nature Tour TOUR
(☎08 4850 6273) This exceedingly popular oufit offers a 'best of' island trip, which includes elephant trekking, snorkelling and a visit to the Chinese temple, a stunning viewpoint and Phang waterfall. The day trip, which costs 1500B, departs at 9am and returns around 3pm. Bookings can be made at its office in Thong Sala or at the Backpackers Information Centre. **Pha-Ngan Safari** (☎0 7737 4159, 08 1895 3783) offers a similar trip for 1900B.

Sleeping

Ko Pha-Ngan's legendary history of laid-back revelry has solidified its reputation as *the* stomping ground for the gritty backpacker lifestyle. Recently, however, the island is starting to see a shift towards a more upmarket clientele. Many local mainstays have collapsed their bamboo huts and constructed newer, sleeker accommodation aimed at the ever-growing legion of 'flashpackers'.

On other parts of the island, new tracts of land are being cleared for Samui-esque five-star resorts. But backpackers fear not; it'll still be many years before the castaway lifestyle goes the way of the dodo. For now, Ko Pha-Ngan can revel in its three distinct classes of lodging: pinch-a-penny shacks, trendy midrange hang-outs, and blow-the-bank luxury.

Hat Rin sees a huge number of visitors compared to the rest of the island. Party pilgrims flock to this picturesque peninsula for the legendary festivities, and although most of them sleep through the daylight hours, the setting remains quite picturesque despite the errant beer bottle in the sand. The southern part of Sunrise Beach is starting to reek of kerosene due to the nightly fire-related shenanigans at Drop-In Bar – needless to say it's best to sunbathe at the quieter northern part of the sand.

Pha-Ngan also caters to a subculture of seclusion-seekers who crave a deserted slice of sand. The northern and eastern coasts offer just that – a place to escape.

The following sleeping options are organised into five sections: we start in Hat Rin, move along the southern coast, head up the west side, across the northern beaches and down the quiet eastern shore.

HAT RIN

The thin peninsula of Hat Rin features three separate beaches. Hat Rin Nok (Sunrise Beach) is the epicentre of Full Moon tomfoolery, Hat Rin Nai (Sunset Beach) is the less impressive stretch of sand on the far side of the tiny promontory, and Hat Seekantang (also known as Hat Leela), just south of Hat Rin Nai, is a smaller, more private beach. The three beaches are linked by Ban Hat Rin (Hat Rin Town) – a small inland collection of restaurants and bars.

Needless to say, the prices listed here are meaningless during periods of maximum lunar orbicularity. Also, during Full Moon events, bungalow operations expect you to stay for a minimum number of days (around four or five). If you plan to arrive the day of the party (or even the day before), we strongly suggest booking a room in advance, or else you'll probably have to sleep on the beach (which you might end up doing anyway). Full Mooners can also stay on Samui and take one of the hourly speedboat shuttles (from 550B) to access the festivities.

TOP CHOICE Sarikantang RESORT **$$$**
(Map p197; ☎0 7737 5055; www.sarikantang.com; Hat Seekantang; bungalows 1400-6200B; ❄📶🏊) Don't get too strung out over trying to pronounce the resort's name – you can simply call this place 'heaven'. Cream-coloured cabins, framed with teak posts and lintels, are sprinkled among swaying palms and crumbling winged statuettes. Inside, the rooms look like the set of a photo shoot for an interior design magazine.

Pha-Ngan Bayshore Resort RESORT **$$**
(Map p197; ☎0 7737 5227; www.phanganbayshore.com; Hat Rin Nok; r 1700-3200B; ❄@📶🏊) After a much-needed overhaul in 2009, this hotel-style operation has primed itself for the ever-increasing influx of flashpackers in Hat Rin. Sweeping beach views and a giant swimming pool make Pha-Ngan Bayshore one of the top addresses on Sunrise Beach.

Seaview Sunrise BUNGALOWS **$**
(Map p197; www.seaviewsunrise.com; Hat Rin Nok; r 500-800; ❄📶) As far as budget digs are concerned, this is the only solid option for Full Moon revellers who want a sleeping spot within inches of the tide. Huts are sturdy and perfectly utilitarian. The polished wooden interiors are splashed with the occasional burst of neon paint from the ghosts of parties past. Try for a bungalow away from the small canal to avoid the mosquitos.

Palita Lodge BUNGALOWS **$$**
(Map p197; ☎0 7737 5172; www.palitalodge.com; Hat Rin Nok; bungalows 1800-5900B; ❄📶🏊) Smack in the heart of the action, Palita is a tribute to the never-ending party that is Hat Rin's Sunrise Beach. Spacious concrete bungalows, with wooden accents and modern design elements, are neatly pressed together on this beachy wedge of sand and shrubs. Week-long bookings are a must during Full Moon revelry.

Delight GUEST HOUSE **$**
(Map p197; ☎0 7737 5527; www.delightresort.com; Ban Hat Rin; r 700-2200B; ❄📶🏊) Tucked behind the bright yellow Kodak sign in

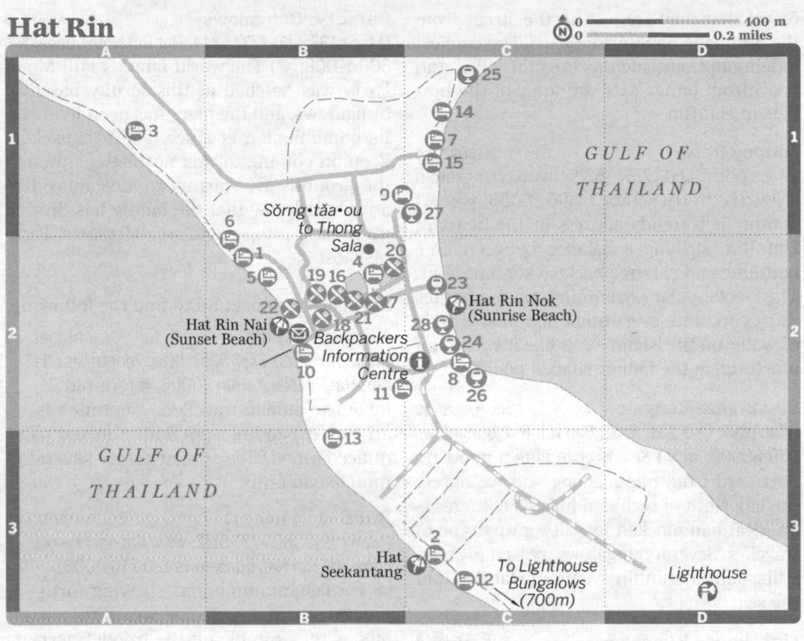

Hat Rin

Sleeping

1 Blue Marine B2
2 Cocohut Village C3
3 Coral Bungalows A1
4 Delight B2
5 Friendly Resort B2
6 Neptune's Villa B2
7 Palita Lodge C1
8 Paradise Bungalows C2
9 Pha-Ngan Bayshore Resort B1
10 Rin Beach Resort B2
11 Same Same B2
12 Sarikantang C3
13 Sea Breeze Bungalow B3
14 Seaview Sunrise C1
15 Tommy Resort C1

Eating

16 Lazy House B2
17 Little Home B2
18 Lucky Crab B2
Mama Schnitzel .... (see 20)
19 Monna Lisa B2
20 Mr K B2
21 Nic's B2
22 Om Ganesh B2
Same Same Burger .... (see 11)

Drinking

23 Cactus Bar C2
24 Drop-In Bar C2
25 Mellow Mountain C1
26 Rock C2
27 Sunrise C1
28 Zoom/Vinyl C2

Entertainment

Club Paradise .... (see 8)
Tommy .... (see 15)

the centre of Hat Rin, Delight offers some of the best lodging around. Spic-and-span hotel rooms come with subtle designer details (such as peacock murals) and are sandwiched between an inviting swimming pool and a lazy lagoon peppered with lily pads.

Cocohut Village RESORT $$$
(Map p197; ☎0 7737 5368; www.cocohut.com; Hat Seekantang; bungalows 2800-12,000B; ❄@🛜🏊) This super-social place is the unofficial gathering spot for vacationing Israelis. In fact, Cocohut is so happenin' that guests might

forget that they are just up the street from the brouhaha on Sunrise Beach. The priciest lodging options, such as the cliff villas and beachfront bungalows, are some of the best bets in Hat Rin.

Tommy Resort RESORT **$$**
(Map p197; ☎0 7737 5215; www.phangantommyresort.com; Hat Rin Nok; r 1490-8000B; ❄@≋) Tommy is a trendy address in the heart of Hat Rin, striking a balance between chic boutique and carefree backpacker hang-out. The rectangular swimming pool charges things up, since every other man-made body of water on the island looks like it was manufactured at the kidney-shaped pool factory.

Sea Breeze Bungalow BUNGALOWS **$$**
(Map p197; ☎0 7737 5162; Ban Hat Rin; bungalows 500-8000B; ❄≋) Sea Breeze gets a good report card from our readers, and we agree; the labyrinth of secluded hillside cottages is an ideal hammocked retreat for any type of traveller. Several bungalows, poised high on stilts, deliver stunning views of Hat Rin and the sea.

Lighthouse Bungalows BUNGALOWS **$**
(off Map p197; ☎0 7737 5075; www.lighthousebungalows.com; Hat Seekantang; bungalows 300-1200B) Hidden at the far end of Hat Rin, this low-key collection of humble huts gathers along a sloping terrain punctuated by towering palms. To access this secluded resort, walk through Leela Beach Bungalows (don't bother stopping) and follow the wooden boardwalk as it curves to the left (southeast) around the sea-swept boulders.

Coral Bungalows RESORT **$**
(Map p197; ☎0 7737 5023; www.coralhaadrin.com; Hat Rin Nai; bungalows 500-1000B;❄@≋) This party-centric paradise has firmly planted its flag in 'Backpackerland' as the go-to spot for a booze-addled rompfest. By day, sun-worshippers straddle beachside chaises. Then, by night, like a vampire, Coral transforms into a sinister pool-party machine fuelled by one too many vodka Red Bulls.

Same Same GUEST HOUSE **$**
(Map p197; ☎0 7737 5200; www.same-same.com; Ban Hat Rin; r 500-800B;❄📶) Although still a super-sociable spot for Scandinavians during the Full Moon madness, Same Same is but a faint flicker of what it used to be – especially during the quieter parts of the month.

Paradise Bungalows BUNGALOWS **$**
(Map p197; ☎0 7737 5244; Hat Rin Nok; bungalows 300-1200B; ❄) The world-famous Full Moon Party was hatched at this scruffy batch of bungalows, and the place has been living on its name fame ever since. The backpackers keep on coming to wax nostalgic, although the grounds are starting to look more like a junkyard now that the family has divvied up to land into several small 'resorts'. Paradise lost.

Stroll down Sunset Rd to find the following:

Neptune's Villa RESORT **$$**
(Map p197; ☎0 7737 5251; http://neptunesvilla.net; Hat Rin Nai; r from 2000B;❄) An old favourite among travellers, Neptune's is an ever-expanding spot with a mixed bag of accommodation spread across several motel-style units.

Rin Beach Resort RESORT **$$**
(Map p197; ☎0 7737 5112; www.rinbeachresort.com; Hat Rin Nai; bungalows 1200-10,000B; ❄📶≋) Giant amphorae, spewing forth gushes of water, welcome weary travellers as they tumble off the wooden ferry. Cottages are bright and airy with dark cherry-wood accents and colourful sutra paintings.

Friendly Resort RESORT **$$**
(Map p197; ☎0 7737 5167; friendly_resort@hotmail.com; Hat Rin Nai; r from 1000B; ❄📶≋) Looking out over the pier, Friendly has a tangle of accommodation wrapped around a small central pool.

Blue Marine BUNGALOWS **$**
(Map p197; ☎0 7737 5079; www.bluemarinephangan.com; Hat Rin Nai; bungalows 600-1200B; ❄📶) Prim concrete bungalows topped by shimmering blue-tiled roofs.

SOUTHERN BEACHES

The accommodation along the southern coast is the best bang for your baht on Ko Pha-Ngan. There are fleeting views of the islands in the Ang Thong Marine National Park; however, the southern beaches don't have the postcard-worthy turquoise waters you might be longing for. This section starts at the port in Thong Sala and follows the coast east towards Hat Rin.

BAN TAI

The waters at Ban Tai tend to be shallow and opaque, especially during low season, but lodging options are well-priced compared to other parts of the island, and you're not too far from Hat Rin.

TOP CHOICE **Coco Garden** BUNGALOWS $
(☎0 7737 7721, 08 6073 1147; www.cocogardens.com; bungalows 450-1250B; ❄📶) The best budget spot along the southern coast, Coco Garden one-ups the nearby resorts with well-manicured grounds and sparkling bungalows that are almost pathologically clean.

B52 BUNGALOWS $$
(www.b52-beach-resort-phangan.info; bungalows 1650-4000B; ❄📶🏊) Find your very own love shack at B52's campus of Thai-styled bungalows sporting plenty of thatch, polished concrete floors and rustic tropical tree trunks.

Milky Bay Resort RESORT $$$
(☎0 7723 8566; http://milkybaythailand.com; bungalows 2300-13,200B; ❄@📶🏊) Milky white walls, which permeate the grounds, are peppered with large black stones resembling the spots on a cow. These bovine bulwarks snake through the resort linking the airy, thatched bungalows to the sea.

BAN KHAI

Like Ban Tai, the beaches aren't the most stunning, but the accommodation is cheap and there are beautiful views of Ang Thong Marine National Park in the distance.

Boom's Cafe Bungalows BUNGALOWS $
(☎0 7723 8318; www.boomscafe.com; bungalows 400-1000B;❄) Staying at Boom's is like visiting the Thai family you never knew you had. The friendly owners lovingly tend their sandy acreage and dote on the contented clientele. No one seems to mind that there's no swimming pool, since the curling tide rolls right up to your doorstep. Boom's is located at the far eastern corner of Ban Khai, near Hat Rin.

Mac Bay BUNGALOWS $
(☎0 7723 8443; bungalows 500-1500B; ❄🏊) Home to the Black Moon Party (another lunar excuse for Ko Pha-Ngan to go wild), Mac Bay is a sandy slice of Ban Khai where even the cheaper bungalows are spic and span. At beer o'clock, grab a shaded spot on the sand and watch the sun dance amorphous shadows over the distant islands of Ang Thong Marine Park.

Morning Star BUNGALOWS $$
(☎0 7737 7756; www.morningstar-resort.info; bungalows 1600-5390B; ❄📶🏊) This collection of wooden and concrete jungle cottages has spotless interiors; some rooms are furnished with noticeably ornate dressers and vanities, others have subtle dark-wood trimming. A dozen white wooden beach chairs orbit the adorable kidney-bean-shaped pool.

WEST COAST BEACHES

Now that there are two smooth roads between Thong Sala and Chalok Lam, the west coast has seen a lot of development. The atmosphere is a pleasant mix between the east coast's quiet seclusion and Hat Rin's sociable vibe, although some of the beaches along the western shores (particularly towards the south) aren't as picturesque as the other parts of the island.

AO NAI WOK TO SI THANU

Close to Thong Sala, the resorts peppered along this breezy strip mingle with patches of gnarled mangroves. Despite the lack of appealing beaches, the prices are cheap and the sunsets are memorable.

TOP CHOICE **Chills Resort** RESORT $$
(☎08 9875 2100; www.chillsresort.com; Ao Srithanu; r from 1200B; ❄📶🏊) Set along a stunning and secluded stretch of stony outcrops, Chills' cluster of delightfully simple-but-modern rooms all have peaceful ocean views letting in plenty of sunlight and sea breezes. The natural rock-pool perched along the breakers is the perfect place to swig an afternoon cocktail while watching the sunset.

TOP CHOICE **Shambhala Bungalow Village** BUNGALOWS $
(☎08 9875 2100; www.shambhala-phangan.com; Ao Nai Wok; bungalows 600-1200B; ❄📶) Rather than bulldozing tired old beachside bungalows, the owners of Shambhala have lovingly restored a batch of huts and added loads of personal touches that make this not only a memorable place to stay, but also a very comfortable one for those with small coffers. Expect fresh linen, carved wood, artistic lighting and neatly designed bathrooms.

Loy Fa BUNGALOWS $
(☎0 7737 7319; loyfabungalow@yahoo.com; Ao Srithanu; bungalows 300-800B; ❄) Loy Fa scores high marks for its friendly, French-speaking Thai staff, charming gardens and sturdy huts guarding sweeping ocean views. Modern bungalows tumble down the promontory onto an uberprivate sliver of ash-coloured sand.

Grand Sea Resort RESORT $$
(0 7737 7777; www.grandsearesort.com; Ao Nai Wok; bungalows 1200-3000B;) A good choice for those wanting a bit of sand close to Thong Sala, Grand Sea feels like a collection of wooden Thai spirit houses.

HAT CHAOPHAO

Like Hat Yao up the coast, this rounded beach is lined with a variety of bungalow operations. There's an inland lake further south, and a 7-Eleven to cure your midnight munchies.

Sunset Cove BUNGALOWS $$
(0 7734 9211; www.thaisunsetcove.com; bungalows 1200-3580B;) There's a feeling of Zen symmetry among the forested assortment of boutique bungalows; the towering bamboo shoots are evenly spaced along the cobbled paths weaving through brush and boulders. The beachside abodes are particularly elegant, sporting slatted rectangular windows and barrel-basined bathtubs.

Pha-Ngan Paragon BUNGALOWS $$$
(08 4728 6064; www.phanganparagon.com; bungalows 2250-13,100B;) A tiny hideaway with seven rooms, the Paragon has decor that incorporates stylistic elements from ancient Khmer, India and Thailand, without forfeiting any modern amenities. The 'royal bedroom' deserves a special mention – apparently the canopied bed has been imported from Kashmir.

HAT YAO & HAT SON

One of the busier beaches along the west coast, Hat Yao sports a swimmable beach, numerous resorts and a few extra services such as ATMs and convenience stores.

Shiralea BUNGALOWS $
(08 0719 9256; www.shiralea.com; Hat Yao; bungalows 500B;) Although this batch of fresh-faced poolside bungalows is not right on the beach (about 100m away), you'll be hard-pressed to find a better deal on the island. Reefers, the on-site dive outfit offers world-class diving at your doorstep, and don't forget to ask the friendly owner where the name Shiralea comes from – we're pretty sure you'll be quite surprised.

Haad Yao Bay View Resort RESORT $$$
(0 7734 9193; www.haadyao-bayviewresort.com; Hat Yao; r & bungalows 1500-7000B;) Still sparkling after a facelift in 2008, this conglomeration of bungalows and hotel-style accommodation looks like a tropical mirage on Hat Yao's northern headland. Vacationers, in various states of undress, linger around the large turquoise swimming pool catching rays and Zs. Others nest in their private suites amid polished hardwood floors and wicker daybeds.

Haad Son Resort RESORT $$
(0 7734 9104; www.haadson.info; Hat Son; bungalows 1000-8000B;) The word 'complex' has a double meaning at this vast resort; we suggest leaving a trail of breadcrumbs along the serpentine paths if you ever want to find the way back to your room. The poshest rooms aren't worth the baht, so go for the budget digs; they're simple, but you'll have access to all of the on-site amenities.

Tantawan Bungalows BUNGALOWS $
(0 7734 9108; www.tantawanbungalow.com; Hat Son; bungalows 450-550B;) This charming teak nest, tucked among jungle fronds, is dripping with clinking chandeliers made from peach coral and khaki-coloured seashells. Guests can take a dip in the trapezoidal swimming pool or enjoy the sunrise on their small bamboo porches. Don't forget to try the tasty on-site restaurant. Diners sit in a sea of geometric cushions while gobbling up some of the tastiest Thai and French-inspired dishes on the island.

High Life BUNGALOWS $
(0 7734 9114; www.highlifebungalow.com; Hat Yao; bungalows 500-2000B;) We can't decide what's more conspicuous: the dramatic ocean views from the infinity-edged swimming pool, or the blatant double entendre in the resort's name. True to its moniker, the 25 bungalows, of various shapes and sizes, sit on a palmed outcropping of granite soaring high above the cerulean sea. Advance bookings will set you back an extra 200B.

Haad Yao See Through Boutique Resort HOTEL $$
(0 7734 9315; www.haadyao.net; Hat Yao; r from 1750B;) After a slice of Hat Yao beach was cut up among brothers, 'See Through' came into existence along a thin tract of land. Rooms are decorated with a vibrant swatchbook of yellows, greens and reds, however the exterior – an imposing block of polished concrete – looks more construction site than boutique chic.

HAT SALAD

Hat Salad is our favourite beach on the west coast, and it isn't short on quality digs set along the inviting sand.

Cookies Salad RESORT **$$**
(0 7734 9125, 08 3181 7125; www.cookies-phangan.com; bungalows 1500-3000B;) The resort with a tasty name has delicious Balinese-styled bungalows orbiting a two-tiered lap pool tiled in various shades of blue. Shaggy thatching and dense tropical foliage gives the realm a certain rustic quality, although you won't want for creature comforts.

Green Papaya BUNGALOWS **$$$**
(0 7737 4182; www.greenpapayaresort.com; bungalows 3600-8500B;) The polished wooden bungalows at Green Papaya are a clear standout along the lovely beach at Hat Salad, however they come at quite a hefty price.

Salad Hut BUNGALOWS **$$**
(0 7734 9246; www.saladhut.com; bungalows 1400-4000B;) Wholly unpretentious yet sharing a beach with some distinctly upscale options, this small clutch of Thai-style bungalows sits but a stone's throw from the rolling tide. Watch the sun gently set below the waves from your lacquered teak porch.

Salad Beach Resort BUNGALOWS **$$**
(0 7734 9149; www.phangan-saladbeachresort.com; bungalows 1900-4900B;) A full-service retreat along the sands of Salad. Room decor employs an unusual palette of colours, but the grounds are tasteful and understated – especially around the pool.

AO MAE HAT

The northwest tip of the island has excellent ocean vistas, and little Ko Ma is connected to Pha-Ngan by a stunning sandbar.

Royal Orchid BUNGALOWS **$**
(0 7737 4182; royal_orchid_maehaad@hotmail.com; bungalows 300-800B;) Handsome backpacker bungalows are arranged like a zipper along a slender garden path – most have fleeting views of the serene beach and idyllic sandbar that extends to scenic Ko Ma offshore.

NORTHERN BEACHES

Stretching from Chalok Lam to Thong Nai Pan, the dramatic northern coast is a wild jungle with several stunning and secluded beaches – it's the most scenic coast on the island.

CHALOK LAM (CHALOKLUM) & HAT KHOM

The cramped fishing village at Chalok Lam is like no other place on Ko Pha-Ngan. The conglomeration of teak shanties and huts is a palpable reminder that the wide-reaching hand of globalisation has yet to touch some parts of the world. *Sŏrng·tăa·ou* ply the route from here to Thong Sala for around 100B per person. There's a dirt road leading from Chalok Lam to Hat Khom, and water taxis are available as well (50B to 100B).

Malibu BUNGALOWS **$**
(0 7737 4013; Chalok Lam; bungalows 300-1300B;) The casual vibe around the large backyard beach (over the lagoon bridge) sets Malibu apart from the other budget bungalows around Chalok Lam. A drink-wielding hut, stationed on the private sandbar, lures guests of every ilk. The cheapest huts are a bit rough around the edges, although the new round bungalow-like concoctions are overpriced.

Mandalai HOTEL **$$$**
(0 7737 4316; www.mymandalai.com; Chalok Lam; r 2750-5600B;) Like an ash-white Riyadh from a distant Arabian land, this small boutique hotel quietly towers over the surrounding shantytown of fishermen's huts. Floor-to-ceiling windows command views of tangerine-coloured fishing boats in the bay, and there's an intimate wading pool hidden in the inner cloister.

BOTTLE BEACH (HAT KHUAT)

This isolated dune has garnered a reputation as a low key getaway, and has thus become quite popular. During high season, places can fill up fast so it's best to try to arrive early. Grab a long-tail taxi boat from Chalok Lam for 50B to 120B (depending on the boat's occupancy).

Bottle Beach II BUNGALOWS **$**
(0 7744 5156; bungalows 350-500B) At the far eastern corner of the beach, this is the spot where penny pinchers can live out their castaway fantasies.

Smile BUNGALOWS **$**
(08 1956 3133; smilebeach@hotmail.com; bungalows 400-700B) At the far western corner of the beach, Smile features an assortment of wooden huts that climb up a forested hill. The two-storey bungalows (700B) are our favourite.

THONG NAI PAN

The pair of rounded bays at Thong Nai Pan looks a bit like buttocks; Ao Thong Nai Pan Yai (*yai* means 'big') is the southern half, and Ao Thong Nai Pan Noi (*noi* means 'little') curves just above. These beaches have been increasing in popularity over the last few years, as bamboo bungalows are being razed to make room for elaborate resorts.

Anantara Rasananda RESORT **$$$**
(☎0 7723 9555; www.rasananda.com; villas from 5000B; ❄@📶🏊) Rasananda represents the future of Ko Pha-Ngan. This attempt at five-star luxury is a sweeping sand-side property with a smattering of semi-detached villas – many bedecked with private plunge pools. A savvy mix of modern and traditional *săh·lah* styling prevails, and new Anantara management means that this high-end stalwart is here to stay.

Dolphin BUNGALOWS **$**
(bungalows 500-1400B;❄📶) This hidden retreat gives yuppie travellers a chance to rough it in style, while granola-types will soak up every inch of the laid-back charm. Quiet afternoons are spent lounging on the comfy cushions in one of the small pagodas hidden throughout the jungle. Lodging is only available on a first-come basis.

Longtail Beach Resort BUNGALOWS **$**
(☎0 7744 5018; www.longtailbeachresort.com; bungalows 390-1150B; ❄📶) Effortlessly adorable, and one of the last remaining batches of beach bungalows in the area, Longtail offers backpackers a taste of Pha-Ngan's past with its charming thatch-and-bamboo abodes.

EAST COAST BEACHES

Robinson Crusoe, eat your heart out. The east coast is the ultimate hermit hang-out. For the most part you'll have to hire a boat to get to these beaches, but water taxis are available in Thong Sala and Hat Rin.

THAN SADET & THONG RENG

Mai Pen Rai BUNGALOWS **$**
(☎0 7744 5090; www.thansadet.com; bungalows 600B; @) *Mai pen rai* is the Thai equivalent of 'don't worry, be happy', which isn't too surprising since this bay elicits nothing but sedate smiles. Bungalows mingle with Plaa's next door on the hilly headland, and sport panels of straw weaving with gabled roofs.

Treehouse BUNGALOWS **$**
(treehouse.kp@googlemail.com; bungalows from 200B) The legendary backpacker hang-out of Ko Chang (the big Ko Chang) has recently set up shop along the secluded waters of Thong Reng. Follow the cheery plastic flowers over the hill from Than Sadet to find uberbasic digs drenched in bright shades of paint.

HAT THIAN

TOP CHOICE **The Sanctuary** BUNGALOWS **$$**
(☎08 1271 3614; www.thesanctuarythailand.com; dm 200B, bungalows 450-5450B) If you're looking for Alex Garland's mythical beach, this is about as close as it gets. A friendly enclave promoting relaxation, the Sanctuary is an inviting haven offering splendid lodgings while also functioning as a holistic retreat (think yoga classes and detox sessions). Accommodation, in various manifestations of twigs, is scattered around the resort, married to the natural surroundings. You'll want to Nama-stay forever.

Beam Bungalows BUNGALOWS **$**
(☎0 7927 2854; bungalows 300-700B) Beam is set back from the beach and tucked behind a coconut palm grove. Charming wooden huts have dangling hammocks out front, and big bay windows face the ocean through the swaying palms.

HAT YUAN

Hat Yuan has a few bungalow operations, and is quite secluded as there are no roads connecting this little beach to Hat Rin down the coast.

Barcelona BUNGALOWS **$**
(☎0 7737 5113; bungalows 300-700B) Solid wood huts come in two shades: natural wood or creamy white. They climb up the hill on stilts behind a palm garden and have good vistas and jovial staff.

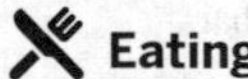

Eating

Ko Pha-Ngan is no culinary capital, especially since most visitors quickly absorb the lazy lifestyle and wind up eating at their accommodation. Those with an adventurous appetite should check out the island's centre of local commerce, Thong Sala.

HAT RIN

This bustling 'burb has the largest conglomeration of restaurants and bars on the island, yet most of them are pretty lousy. The infamous Chicken Corner is a popular intersection stocked with several faves such as **Mr K Thai Food** (Map p197; Ban Hat Rin; dishes 30-80B) and **Mama Schnitzel** (Map p197;

Ban Hat Rin; dishes 40-100B), which promise to cure any case of the munchies, be it noon or midnight.

Lazy House INTERNATIONAL $$
(Map p197; Hat Rin Nai; dishes 90-270B; ⏲lunch & dinner) Back in the day, this joint was the owner's apartment – everyone liked his cooking so much that he decided to turn the place into a restaurant and hang-out spot. Today, Lazy House is easily one of Hat Rin's best places to veg out in front of a movie with a scrumptious shepherd's pie.

Little Home THAI $
(Map p197; Ban Hat Rin; mains from 40B; ⏲breakfast, lunch & dinner) With no design aesthetic whatsoever, Little Home woos the masses with cheap, flavourful Thai grub that's gobbled up with alacrity among wooden tables and flimsy plastic chairs.

Monna Lisa ITALIAN $$
(Map p197; Hat Rin Nai; pizza & pasta from 200B; ⏲breakfast, lunch & dinner) The best spot in Hat Rin for a pizza, Monna Lisa is a relatively new operation run by a team of friendly Italians. The mushroom and ham pizza practically knocked our socks off – as did the homemade truffle pasta.

Nic's INTERNATIONAL $$
(Map p197; Ban Hat Rin; mains 80-280B; ⏲dinner) A dizzying realm of polished concrete and coloured pillows, Nic's – at the back of Hat Rin's lake – slings tasty pizzas and tapas every evening. Slurp a Singha during the 6pm-to-8pm happy hour.

Lucky Crab SEAFOOD $$
(Map p197; Hat Rin Nai; dishes 100-400B; ⏲lunch & dinner) Lucky Crab is your best bet for seafood in Hat Rin. Rows of freshly caught creatures are presented nightly atop miniature longtail boats loaded with ice. Once you've picked your prey, grab a table inside amid dangling plants and charming stone furnishings.

Om Ganesh INDIAN $$
(Map p197; Hat Rin Nai; dishes 70-190B; ⏲breakfast, lunch & dinner) Customers meditate over curries, biryani rice, roti and lassis though the local expats joke that every dish tastes the same. Platters start at 350B.

Same Same Burger BURGER $$
(Map p197; www.same-same.com; Hat Rin Nai; burgers 180-230B; ⏲lunch & dinner) Owned by the folks who run the backpacker digs with the *same same* name, this bright-red burger joint is the *same same* as McDonald's (except pricier).

SOUTHERN BEACHES

On Saturday evenings from 4pm to 10pm, a side street in the eastern part of Thong Sala becomes **Walking Street** – a bustling pedestrian zone mostly filled with locals hawking their wares to other islanders. There's plenty on offer, from clothing to food. Be sure to try the delicious red prok with gravy (40B) at Lang Tang – you'll find it in glass cases next to a large English sign saying 'Numpanich'.

Night Market MARKET $
(Thong Sala; dishes 25-180B; ⏲dinner) A heady mix of steam and snacking locals, Thong Sala's night market is a must for those looking for a dose of culture while nibbling on a low-priced snack. The best place to grab some cheap grub is the stall in the far right corner with a large white banner. Hit up the vendor next door for tasty seafood platters, such as red snapper served over a bed of thick noodles. Banana pancakes and fruit smoothies abound for dessert.

Kaito JAPANESE $$
(Thong Sala; dishes from 130B; ⏲dinner Thu-Mon) Authentic Japanese imports are the speciality here – slurp an Asahi while savouring your tangy seaweed salad and *tonkatsu* (pork cutlet). The upstairs level has cosy cushion seating while the main sitting area is flanked with *manga* and pocket-sized Japanese novels.

Mason's Arms BRITISH $$
(Thong Sala; mains 160-350B; ⏲lunch & dinner) Suddenly, a clunky structure emerges from the swaying palms; it's a Tudor style manse, plucked directly from Stratford-upon-Avon and plunked down in the steamy jungle. This lodge like lair is one blood pudding away from being an official British colony. The fish 'n' chips is a local favourite.

Pizza Chiara ITALIAN $$
(Thong Sala; pizzas 180-320B; ⏲lunch & dinner) The quintessential chequered tablecloths confirm it (in case you didn't guess from the name): Pizza Chiara is all about tasty Italian fare. Go for the Pizza Cecco smothered with prosciutto, salami, mushrooms and *cotto* cheese.

Ando Loco MEXICAN $
(Ban Tai; mains from 59B; ⏲dinner) This outdoor Mexican hang-out looks like an animation

cell from a vintage Hanna-Barbera cartoon, with assorted kitschy accoutrements such as papier-mâché cacti. Down a super-sized margarita and show your skills on the beach volleyball court. Ando Loco closes during low season (around September to December).

OTHER BEACHES

TOP CHOICE Sanctuary HEALTH FOOD $$
(Hat Thian; mains from 130B) Forget what you know about health food: the Sanctuary's restaurant proves that wholesome eats can also be delicious. Enjoy a tasty parade of plates – from Indian pakoras to crunchy Vietnamese spring rolls – as an endless playlist of music (undoubtedly the island's best) wafts overhead. Don't forget to wash it all down with a shot of neon-green wheatgrass. Yum!

Cucina Italiana ITALIAN $$
(Jenny's; Chalok Lam; pizza 180B; ⌚dinner) Cucina Italiana has a cult following on Ko Pha-Ngan. The friendly Italian chef is passionate about his food, and creates all of his dishes from scratch. On Thursday and Sunday you can order unlimited toppings on your oven-roasted pizza for only 180B.

Peppercorn STEAKHOUSE $$
(www.peppercornphangan.com; Sri Thanu; mains 160-400; ⌚2-10pm Mon-Sat) Escargot and succulent steaks in a rickety jungle cottage? You bet. Peppercorn may be tucked in the brush away from the sea, but that shouldn't detract foodies from seeking out one of Pha-Ngan's best attempts at highbrow international cuisine.

Cookies Salad THAI $$
(Hat Salad; mains from 100B; ⌚breakfast, lunch & dinner) Worth tracking down if you're staying on the west coast, this casual restaurant, perched atop a cliff on the south side of Hat Salad, offers a stunning assortment of Thai treats (don't miss the Penang curry) and unique smoothies (including a rich nutella swirl). Sadly cookie salads are not on offer.

Drinking

Every month, on the night of the full moon, pilgrims pay tribute to the party gods with trance-like dancing, wild screaming and glow-in-the-dark body paint. The throngs of bucket-sippers and fire twirlers gather on the infamous Sunrise Beach (Hat Rin Nok) and party until the sun replaces the moon in the sky.

A few other noteworthy spots can be found around the island for those seeking something a bit mellower.

HAT RIN

Hat Rin is the beating heart of the legendary Full Moon fun, and the area can get pretty wound up even without the influence of lunar phases. When the moon isn't lighting up the night sky, partygoers flock to other spots on the island's south side. See the boxed text on p194 for details. The following party venues flank Hat Rin's infamous Sunrise Beach from south to north.

Rock BAR, CLUB
(Map p197) Great views of the party from the elevated terrace on the far south side of the beach.

Club Paradise BAR, CLUB
(Map p197) Paradise basks in its celebrity status as the genesis of the lunar *loco*-motion.

Drop-In Bar BAR, CLUB
(Map p197) This dance shack blasts the chart toppers that we all secretly love. The other nights of the year are equally as boisterous.

Zoom/Vinyl BAR, CLUB
(Map p197) An ear-popping trance venue.

Cactus Bar BAR, CLUB
(Map p197) Smack in the centre of Hat Rin Nok, Cactus pumps out a healthy mix of old school tunes, hip-hop and R&B.

Sunrise BAR, CLUB
(Map p197) A newer spot on the sand where trance beats shake the graffiti-ed walls.

Tommy BAR, CLUB
(Map p197) One of Hat Rin's largest venues lures the masses with black lights and trance music blaring on the sound system. Drinks are dispensed from a large ark-like bar.

Mellow Mountain BAR, CLUB
(Map p197) Also called 'Mushy Mountain' (you'll know why when you get there), this trippy hang-out sits at the northern edge of Hat Rin Nok delivering stellar views of the shenanigans below.

OTHER BEACHES

Eagle Pub BAR
(Hat Yao) At the southern end of Hat Yao, this drink-dealing shack, built right into the rock face, is tattooed with the neon graffiti of virtually every person who's passed out on the

lime green patio furniture after too many *caipirinhas*.

Jam BAR

(Hin Wong; www.thejamphangan.com) It's DIY live music at this friendly nightspot on the west coast. Saturday nights are open mic, and the rest of the week you'll usually catch a few locals jamming on their guitars.

Pirates Bar BAR

(Hat Chaophao) This wacky drinkery is a replica of a pirate ship built into the cliffs. When you're sitting on the deck and the tide is high (and you've had a couple drinks), you can almost believe you're out at sea. These guys host the well-attended Moon Set parties, three days before Hat Rin gets pumpin' for the Full Moon fun.

Sheesha Bar BAR

(Chalok Lam) The antithesis of grungy Hat Rin, Sheesha Bar swaps buckets of Samsung for designer drinks. The enticing patchwork of beige sandstone and horizontal slats of mahogany fit right in with the arabesque Mandalai Hotel across the street (owned by the same family).

Flip Flop Pharmacy BAR

(Thong Nai Pan) This open-air bar on the sands of Thong Nai Pan is the area's preferred hang-out spot.

Amsterdam BAR

(Ao Plaay Laem) Near Hat Chaophao on the west coast, Amsterdam attracts tourists and locals from all over the island, who are looking for a chill spot to watch the sunset.

Information

Dangers & Annoyances

Some of your fondest vacation memories may be forged on Ko Pha-Ngan; just be mindful of the following situations that can seriously tarnish your experience on this hot-blooded jungle island.

DRUGS You're relaxing on the beach when suddenly a local walks up and offers you some local herb at a ridiculously low price. 'No thanks,' you say, knowing that the penalties for drug use in Thailand are fierce. But the vendor drops his price even more and practically offers you the weed for free. Too good to be true? Obviously. As soon as you take a toke, the seller rats you out to the cops and you're whisked away to the local prison where you must pay a wallet-busting fine. This type of scenario happens all the time on Ko Pha-Ngan so it's best to avoid the call of the ganja.

Here's another important thing to remember: your travel insurance does not cover any drug-related injury or treatment. Drug-related freak-outs *do* happen – we've heard first-hand accounts of partiers slipping into extended periods of delirium. Suan Saranrom (Garden of Joys) Psychiatric Hospital in Surat Thani has to take on extra staff during full-moon periods to handle the number of *fa·ràng* who freak out on magic mushrooms, acid or other abundantly available hallucinogens.

WOMEN TRAVELLERS Female travellers should be extra careful when partying on the island. We've received many reports about drug- and alcohol-related rape (and these situations are not limited to Full Moon Parties). Another disturbing problem is the unscrupulous behaviour of some of the local motorcycle taxi drivers. Several complaints have been filed about drivers groping female passengers; there are even reports of severe sexual assaults.

MOTORCYCLES Ko Pha-Ngan has more motorcycle accidents than injuries incurred from Full Moon tomfoolery. Nowadays there's a system of paved roads, but much of it is a labyrinth of rutty dirt-and-mud paths. The island is also very hilly, and even if the road is paved, it can be too difficult for most to take on. The *very* steep road to Hat Rin is a perfect case in point. The island now has a special ambulance that trolls the island helping injured bikers.

Emergency

Main police station (Map p193; ☎0 7737 7114, 191) Located about 2km north of Thong Sala. The police station in Hat Rin (near Hat Rin school) will not let you file a report; to do so you must go to Thong Sala. Local police have been known to charge 200B to file a report. Do not pay this – it should be free. Note that if you are arrested you do have the right to an embassy phone call; you do not have to agree to accept the 'interpreter' you are offered.

Internet Access

Hat Rin and Thong Sala are the main centres of internet activity, but every beach with development now offers access. Rates are generally 2B per minute, with a 10B to 20B minimum and discounts if you stay on for more than an hour. Places offering a rate of 1B per minute usually have turtle-speed connections.

Laundry

If you got fluorescent body paint on your clothes during your full-moon romp, don't bother sending them to the cleaners – the paint will never come out. Trust us, we tried. For your other washing needs, there are heaps of places that will gladly wash your clothes. Prices hover around 40B per kilo, and express cleanings shouldn't be more than 60B per kilo.

Medical Services

Medical services can be a little crooked in Ko Pha-Ngan – expect unstable prices and underqualified doctors. Many clinics charge a 3000B entrance fee before treatment. Serious medical issues should be dealt with on nearby Ko Samui.

Ko Pha-Ngan Hospital (Map p193; ☎0 7737 7034; Thong Sala; ⊙24hr) About 2.5km north of Thong Sala; offers 24-hour emergency services.

Money

Thong Sala, Ko Pha-Ngan's financial 'capital', has plenty of banks, currency converters and several Western Union offices. Hat Rin has numerous ATMs and a couple of banks at the pier. There are also ATMs in Hat Yao, Chaloklum and Thong Nai Pan.

Post

Main post office (Map p197; ⊙8.30am-4.30pm Mon-Fri, 9am-noon Sat) In Thong Sala; there's a smaller office right near the pier in Hat Rin.

Tourist information

There are no government-run Tourist Authority of Thailand (TAT) offices on Ko Pha-Ngan, instead tourists get their information from local travel agencies and brochures. Most agencies are clumped around Hat Rin and Thong Sala. Agents take a small commission on each sale, but collusion keeps prices relatively stable and standardised. Choose an agent you trust if you are spending a lot of money – faulty bookings do happen on Ko Pha-Ngan, especially since the island does not have a unit of tourist police.

Several mini-magazines also offer comprehensive information about the island's accommodation, restaurants, activities and Full Moon Parties. Our favourite option is the pocket-sized **Phangan Info** (www.phangan.info).

Backpackers Information Centre (Map p197; ☎0 7737 5535; www.backpackersthailand.com; Hat Rin) A must for travellers looking to book high-quality tours (diving, live-aboards, jungle safaris etc) and transport. Not just for backpackers, it's an expat-run travel agency that offers peace of mind with every purchase – travellers are provided with the mobile phone number of the owners should any problems arise. It also runs the Crystal Dive shop next door.

Websites

Backpackers Thailand (www.backpackersthailand.com) Everything you need to know about Ko Pha-Ngan, from booking accommodation to finding out the Full Moon schedule. Doubles as a vast resource for the whole country as well.

Getting There & Away

As always, the cost and departure times are subject to change. Rough waves are known to cancel ferries between the months of October and December.

Bangkok, Hua Hin & Chumphon

The Lomprayah and Seatran Discovery service has bus-boat combination packages that depart from Bangkok and pass through Hua Hin and Chumphon. It is also quite hassle-free to take the train from Bangkok to Chumphon and switch to a ferry service (it works out to be about the same price and the train is comfier if you get a couchette). Travellers can also opt for the slightly cheaper government bus to Bangkok. For additional information about travelling through Chumphon see p169.

Ko Samui

There are around a dozen daily departures between Ko Pha-Ngan and Ko Samui. These boats leave throughout the day from 7am to 6pm and take from 20 minutes to an hour. All leave from either Thong Sala or Hat Rin on Ko Pha-Ngan. The *Haad Rin Queen* goes back and forth between Hat Rin and Big Buddha Beach on Samui.

Ko Tao

Ko Tao-bound Lomprayah ferries depart from Thong Sala on Ko Pha-Ngan at 8.30am and 1pm and arrive at 9.45am and 2.15pm. The Seatran service departs from Thong Sala at 8.30am and 2pm daily. Taxis depart Hat Rin for Thong Sala one hour before the boat departure. The cheaper-but-slower Songserm leaves Ko Pha-Ngan at 12.30pm and alights at 2.30pm.

Surat Thani & the Andaman Coast

Combination boat-bus tickets are available at any travel agency. Simply tell them your desired destination and they will sell you the necessary links in the transport chain. Most travellers will pass through Surat Thani as they swap coasts. There are approximately six daily departures between Ko Pha-Ngan and Krabi on the Raja Car Ferry, Songserm or Seatran. These boats leave from Thong Sala throughout the day from 7am to 8pm. Every night, depending on the weather, a night boat runs from Surat, departing at 11pm. Boats in the opposite direction leave Ko Pha-Ngan at 10pm. Visit **Backpackers Thailand** (www.backpackersthailand.com) to get detailed departure times for additional Andaman destinations.

Getting Around

Motorbikes You can rent motorcycles all over the island for 150B to 250B per day. Always wear a helmet – it's the law on Ko Pha-Ngan, and local policemen are starting to enforce it. If you plan on riding over dirt tracks it is imperative that you rent a bike comparable to a Honda MTX125 – gearless scooters cannot make the journey. Bicycle rentals are discouraged unless you're fit enough to take on Lance Armstrong.

Sŏrng·tăa·ou Pick-up trucks and *sŏrng·tăa·ou* chug along the island's major roads and the riding rates double after sunset. Ask your accommodation about free or discount transfers when you leave the island. The trip from Thong Sala to Hat Rin is 100B; further beaches will set you back around 150B.

Water taxi Long-tail boats depart from Thong Sala, Chalok Lam and Hat Rin, heading to a variety of far-flung destinations such as Hat Khuat (Bottle Beach) and Ao Thong Nai Pan. Expect to pay anywhere from 50B for a short trip, and up to 300B for a lengthier journey. You can charter a private boat ride from beach to beach for about 150B per 15 minutes of travel.

Ko Tao เกาะเต่า

POP 1382

First there was Ko Samui, then Ko Pha-Ngan; now, the cult of Ko Tao ('Ko Taoism' perhaps?) has emerged along Thailand's crystalline gulf coast. Today, thousands of visitors come to worship the turquoise waters offshore, and quite often they stay. The secret to Ko Tao's undeniable appeal? Simple: although the island is only 21 sq km, tiny Tao sure knows how to pack it in – there's something for everyone, and nothing is in moderation. Diving enthusiasts cavort with sharks and rays in a playground of tangled neon coral. Hikers and hermits can re-enact an episode from *Lost* in the dripping coastal jungles. And when you're Robinson Crusoe-ed out, hit the pumpin' bar scene that rages on until dawn.

Many years have passed since the first backpacker came to the scrubby island and planted a flag in the name of self-respecting shoestring travellers everywhere (hello pizza parlours and ladyboy shows), but fret not, there's still plenty of time to join the tribe. Ko Tao has several years to go before corporate resort owners bulldoze the remaining rustic cottages, and visitors start discussing stockholdings rather than sea creatures spotted on their latest dive.

Activities

Diving

Never been diving before? Ko Tao is *the* place to lose your scuba virginity. The island issues more scuba certifications than any-

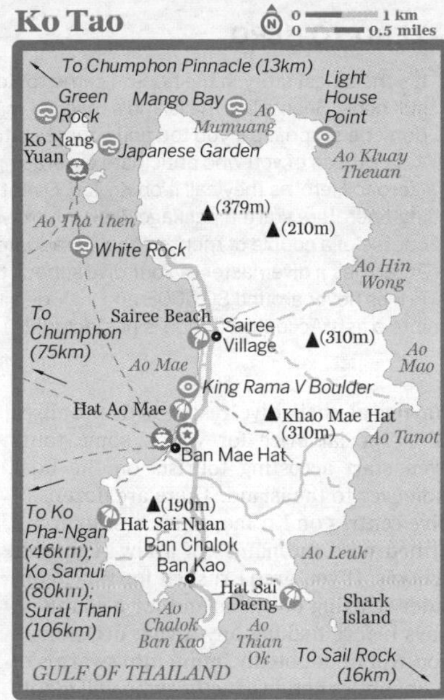

where else in the world. The shallow bays scalloping the island are the perfect spot for newbie divers to take their first stab at scuba. On shore, over 40 dive centres are ready to saddle you up with some gear and teach you the ropes in a three-and-a-half-day Open Water certification course. We know, we know, homework on a holiday sucks, but the intense competition among scuba schools means that certification prices are unbeatably low, and the standards of service are top notch, as dozens of dive shops vie for your baht.

It's no surprise that this underwater playground has become exceptionally popular with beginners; the waters are crystal clear, there are loads of neon reefs, and temperatures feel like bathwater. The best dive sites are found at offshore pinnacles within a 20km radius of the island (see the boxed text p209), but seasoned scubaholics almost always prefer the top-notch sites along the Andaman coast. The local marine wildlife includes groupers, moray eels, batfish, bannerfish, barracudas, titan triggerfish, angelfish, clownfish (Nemos), stingrays, reef sharks, and frequent visits by almighty whale sharks.

When you alight at the pier in Mae Hat, swarms of touts will try to coax you into

ZERO TO HERO

It's the oldest story in the book: 'I came to Ko Tao on vacation and six months later I'm still here!' Seems like the island's magical magnetic energy catches hold of everyone, so don't be surprised if you too find yourself altering plane tickets.

For those of you who anticipate embracing the castaway lifestyle, consider going from 'Zero to Hero' as they call it on Ko Tao. Over the last few years, several of the savvier diving operators started package deals where you can go from scuba newbie to pro over the course of a couple of months. You'll graduate through four levels of diving certifications, 'intern' as a divemaster at your dive school, then take a stab at the instructor program. Prices hover around 80,000B and include all the bells and whistles necessary to turn you into a fish. Accommodation is not included.

staying at their dive resort with promises of a 'special price for you' – some touts even start accosting tourists on the boat ride over to the island. There are dozens of dive centres on Ko Tao, so it's best to arrive armed with the names of a few reputable schools. If you aren't rushed for time, consider relaxing on the island for a couple of days before making any diving decisions – you will undoubtedly bump into swarms of scubaphiles and instructors who will gladly offer their advice and opinions. Remember: the success of your diving experience (especially if you are learning how to dive) will largely depend on how much you like your instructor. There are other factors to consider as well, like the size of your diving group, the condition of your equipment, and the condition of the dive sites, to name a few.

For the most part, diving prices are somewhat standardised across the island, so there's no need to spend your time hunting around for the best deal. A **PADI** (www.padi.com) Open Water certification course costs 9800B; an **SSI** (www.ssithailand.com) Open Water certificate is slightly less (9000B) because you do not have to pay for instructional materials. An Advanced Open Water certification course will set you back 8500B, a rescue course is 9500B and the Divemaster program costs a cool 25,000B. Fun divers should expect to pay roughly 1000B per dive, or around 7000B for a 10-dive package. These rates include all dive gear, boat, instructors/guides and snacks. Discounts are usually given if you bring your own equipment. Be wary of dive centres that offer too many price cuts – safety is paramount, and a shop giving out unusually good deals is probably cutting too many corners.

Most dive schools will hook you up with cheap – or even free – accommodation. Almost all scuba centres offer gratis fan rooms for anyone doing beginner coursework.

Expect large crowds and booked-out beds throughout the months of December, January, June, July and August, and a monthly glut of wannabe divers after every Full Moon Party on Ko Pha-Ngan next door. If you are planning to do 'diving detox' after a Full Moon romp, make sure you purchase your ferry tickets at least two days before the eve of the lunar lunacy – boats sell out quickly.

The following dive schools are among the best operators on the island; they all do their bit to help keep Ko Tao a pristine place.

Ban's Diving School DIVING
(Map p210; ☎0 7745 6466; www.amazingkohtao.com; Sairee Beach) A well-oiled diving machine and relentlessly expanding conglomerate, Ban's certifies more divers per year than any other scuba school in the world and refurbishments in 2009 have given it a five-star feel. Classroom sessions tend to be conducted in large groups, but there's a reasonable amount of individual attention in the water. A breadth of international instructors means that students can learn to dive in their native tongue. The affiliated resort (p213) is quite popular with party-seekers.

Big Blue Diving DIVING
(Map p210; ☎0 7745 6415, 0 7745 6772; www.bigbluediving.com; Sairee Beach) If Goldilocks were picking a dive school, she'd probably pick Big Blue – this midsize operation (not too big, not too small) gets props for fostering a sociable vibe while maintaining a high standard of service. Divers of every

ilk can score dirt-cheap accommodation at their resort (p214).

Buddha View DIVING
(☎0 7745 6074; www.buddhaview-diving.com; Chalok Ban Kao) Another big dive operation on Ko Tao, Buddha View offers the standard fare of certification and special programs for technical diving (venturing beyond the usual parameters of recreational underwater exploration). Discounted accommodation is available at its friendly resort (p215).

Crystal Dive DIVING
(Map p210; ☎0 7745 6107; www.crystaldive.com; Mae Hat) Crystal is the Meryl Streep of diving operators, winning all the awards for best performance year after year. It's one of the largest schools on the island (and around the world), although high-quality instructors and intimate classes keep the school feeling quite personal. Multilingual staff members, air-conditioned classes and two on-site swimming pools sweeten the deal. Highly recommended.

New Heaven DIVING
(☎0 7745 6587; www.newheavendiveschool.com; Chalok Ban Kao) The owners of this small diving operation dedicate a lot of their time to preserving the natural beauty of Ko Tao's underwater sites by conducting regular reef checks and contributing to reef restoration efforts. A special CPAD research diver certification program is available in addition to the regular order of programs and fun dives.

Scuba Junction DIVING
(Scuba J; Map p210; ☎0 7745 6164; www.scuba-junction.com; Sairee Beach) A groovy new storefront and a team of outgoing instructors lure travellers looking for a more intimate dive experience. Scuba Junction guarantees a maximum of four people per diving group.

Snorkelling

Snorkelling is a popular alternative to diving, although scuba snobs will tell you that

DIVE SITES AT A GLANCE

In general, divers don't have a choice as to which sites they explore. Each dive school chooses a smattering of sites for the day depending on weather and ocean conditions. Deeper dive sites such as Chumphon Pinnacle are usually visited in the morning. Afternoon boats tour the shallower sites such as Japanese Gardens. Recently, two large vessels have been sunk off the coast, providing scubaphiles two new wreck dives. Divers hoping to spend some quality time searching for whale sharks at Sail Rock should join one of the dive trips departing daily from Ko Pha-Ngan.

» **Chumphon Pinnacle** (36m maximum depth), 13km west of Ko Tao, has a colourful assortment of sea anemones along the four interconnected pinnacles. The site plays host to schools of giant trevally, tuna and large grey reef sharks. Whale sharks are known to pop up once in a while.

» **Green Rock** (25m maximum depth) is an underwater jungle gym featuring caverns, caves and small swim-throughs. Rays, grouper and triggerfish are known to hang around. It's a great place for a night dive.

» **Japanese Gardens** (12m maximum depth), between Ko Tao and Ko Nang Yuan, is a low-stress dive site perfect for beginners. There's plenty of colourful coral, and turtles, stingray and pufferfish often pass by.

» **Mango Bay** (16m maximum depth) might be your first dive site if you are putting on a tank for the first time. Lazy reef fish swim around as newbies practice their skills on the sandy bottom.

» **Sail Rock** (34m maximum depth), best accessed by Ko Pha-Ngan, features a massive rock chimney with a vertical swim-through, and large pelagics like barracuda and kingfish. This is one of the top spots in southeast Asia to see whale sharks.

» **Southwest Pinnacle** (33m maximum depth) offers divers a small collection of pinnacles that are home to giant groupers and barracudas. Whale sharks and leopard sharks are sometimes spotted (pun partially intended).

» **White Rock** (29m maximum depth) is home to colourful corals, angelfish, clown fish and territorial triggerfish. Another popular spot for night divers.

Mae Hat & Sairee Beach

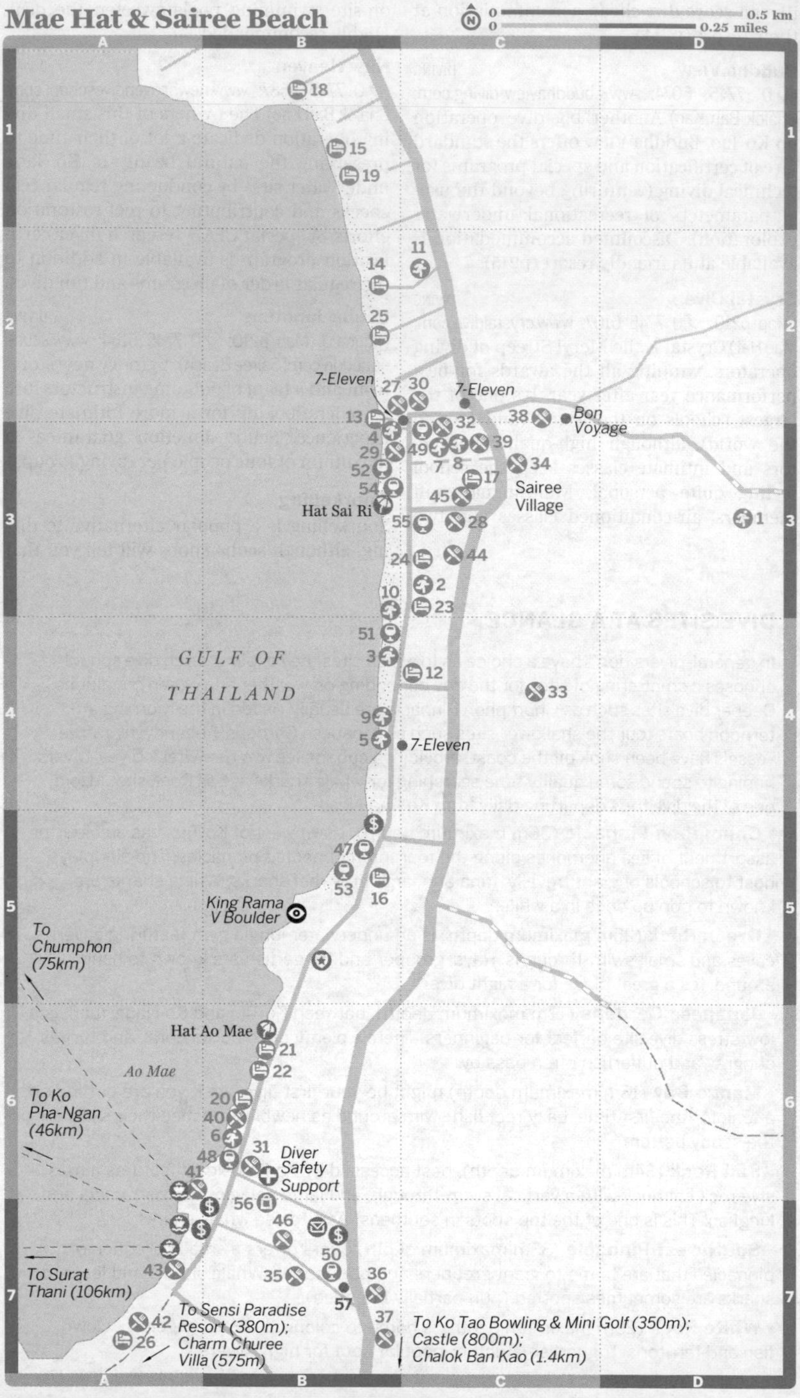

0 — 0.5 km
0 — 0.25 miles

GULF OF THAILAND

7-Eleven
7-Eleven
7-Eleven
Bon Voyage
Sairee Village
Hat Sai Ri
King Rama V Boulder
Hat Ao Mae
Ao Mae
Diver Safety Support
To Chumphon (75km)
To Ko Pha-Ngan (46km)
To Surat Thani (106km)
To Sensi Paradise Resort (380m); Charm Churee Villa (575m)
To Ko Tao Bowling & Mini Golf (350m); Castle (800m); Chalok Ban Kao (1.4km)

Mae Hat & Sairee Beach

Activities, Courses & Tours
1 ACE Marine Images D3
2 Apnea Total C3
3 Ban's Diving School B4
4 Big Blue Diving B3
5 Blue Immersion B4
6 Crystal Dive B6
7 Davy Jones' Locker C3
8 Flying Trapeze Adventures C3
9 Goodtime Adventures B4
10 Scuba Junction B3
11 Shambhala C2

Sleeping
12 Ban's Diving Resort C4
13 Big Blue Resort B2
14 Blue Wind B2
15 Bow Thong B1
Crystal Dive Resort (see 6)
16 In Touch B5
17 Koh Tao Backpackers C3
18 Koh Tao Cabana B1
19 Koh Tao Coral Grand Resort B1
20 Montra Resort & Spa B6
21 Mr J Bungalow B6
22 Regal Resort B6
23 Sairee Cottage C3
24 Seashell Resort C3
25 Sunset Buri Resort B2
26 Utopia Suites A7

Eating
27 Ally The Pancake Man B2
28 Barracuda Restaurant & Bar C3
29 Big Blue East B3
Blue Wind Bakery (see 14)
30 Café Corner C2
31 Café del Sol B6
32 Chopper's Bar & Grill C3
33 Darawan C4
34 El Gringo C3
35 Farango's B7
36 Food Centre B7
37 Greasy Spoon B7
38 Kanya C2
39 Krua Thai C3
40 Pranee's Kitchen B6
41 Safety Stop Pub A6
42 Tattoo Bar & Restaurant A7
43 Whitening A7
44 ZanziBar C3
45 Zest Coffee Lounge C3
46 Zest Coffee Lounge B7

Drinking
47 AC Party Pub B5
48 Crystal Bar B6
49 Diza C3
50 Dragon Bar B7
51 Fish Bowl B4
52 Fizz B3
53 In Touch B5
54 Lotus Bar B3
Maya Bar (see 47)
55 Office Bar C3

Shopping
56 Avalon B7

Transport
57 Lederhosenbikes B7

strapping on a snorkel instead of an air tank is like eating spray cheese when there's Camembert on the table. Orchestrating your own snorkelling adventure is simple, since the bays on the east coast have small bungalow operations offering equipment rental for between 100B and 200B per day.

Most snorkel enthusiasts opt for the do-it-yourself approach on Ko Tao, which involves swimming out into the offshore bays or hiring a longtail boat to putter around further out. Guided tours are also available and can be booked at any local travel agency. Tours range from 500B to 700B (usually including gear, lunch and a guide/boat captain) and stop at various snorkelling hotspots around the island. **Laem Thian** is popular for its small sharks, **Shark Island** has loads of fish (and ironically no sharks), **Hin Wong** is known for its crystalline waters, and **Light House Point**, in the north, offers a dazzling array of colourful sea anemones. Dive schools will usually allow snorkellers on their vessels for a comparable price – but it's only worth snorkelling at the shallower sites such as Japanese Gardens. Note that dive boats visit the shallower sites in the afternoons.

Freediving

Over the last couple of years freediving (exploring the sea using breath-holding techniques rather than scuba gear) has grown rapidly in popularity. Several small schools have opened up across the island. We recommend the capable staff at **Apnea Total** (Map p210; ☎08 7183 2321; www.apnea-total.com; Sairee Beach) who have earned several awards in the freediving world and possess a special knack for easing newbies into this heart-pounding sport. The student-teacher ratio of three to one also ensures plenty of attention to safety. Also worth a special mention is **Blue Immersion** (Map p210; ☎08 7682 1886; www.blue-immersion.com; Sairee Beach) run by friendly Akim, a martial arts expert and a freediving pro – he is one of the first people in the world to freedive below 100m. Freediving prices are standardised across the island as well – a 2½-day SSI beginner course will set you back 5500B.

Technical Diving & Cave Diving

Well-seasoned divers and hardcore Jacques Cousteaus should contact **Tech Thailand** (www.techthailand.com) if they want to take their underwater exploration to the next level and try a technical dive. According to PADI, tec diving, as it's often known, is 'diving other than conventional commercial or recreational diving that takes divers beyond recreational diving limits'. Technical diving exceeds depths of 40m and requires stage decompressions, and a variety of gas mixtures are often used in a single dive.

Several years ago, Tech Thailand's old boat, MS *Trident,* made a name for itself in the diving community after successfully locating dozens of previously undiscovered wrecks in the Gulf of Thailand. Its most famous discovery was the USS *Lagarto,* an American naval vessel that sank during WWII. The gulf has long been an important trading route and new wrecks are being discovered all the time, from old Chinese pottery wrecks to Japanese *marus* (merchant ships). In 2011 the *Trident* was purposefully sunk off the coast of Ko Tao to create an artificial reef. A miscalculation with the explosives has left the wreck a bit too deep for beginners.

Recently, cave diving has taken Ko Tao by storm, and the most intrepid scuba buffs are lining up to make the half-day trek over to Khao Sok National Park (p288). Beneath the park's main lake lurks an astonishing submarine world filled with hidden grottos, limestone crags and skulking catfish. In certain areas divers can swim near submerged villages that were flooded in order to create a reservoir and dam. Most cave-diving trips depart from Ko Tao on the afternoon boat service and return to the island on the afternoon boat service of the following day. Overnight stays are arranged in or near the park.

Stop by Buddha View (p209) on Saturdays for a free introduction into the world of technical diving, or hit the waters with the Tech Thailand team on 'wreck Wednesdays'. If you aren't diving with Buddha View or Master Divers, your dive school of choice can easily help you get sorted.

Underwater Photography & Videography

If your wallet is already full of PADI certification cards, consider renting an underwater camera or enrolling in a marine videography course. Many scuba schools hire professional videographers to film Open Water certifications, and if this piques your interests, you could potentially earn a few bucks after completing a video internship. Your dive operator can put you in touch with any of the half-dozen videography crews on the island. We recommend **ACE Marine Images** (Map p210; ☎0 7745 7054; www.acemarineimages.com; Sairee Beach), one of Thailand's leading underwater videography studios. Their interactive eight-dive course (30,000B) includes an independent diver certification and one-on-one instruction in the editing room. **Deep Down Productions** (☎08 7133 4102; www.deepdown-productions.com) and **Oceans Below** (☎08 6060 1863; www.oceansbelow.net) offer videography courses and internships that are a bit easier on the pocketbook.

Other Activities

TOP CHOICE Flying Trapeze Adventures ACROBATICS

(FTA; Map p210; ☎08 0696 9269; www.flyingtrapezeadventures.com; Sairee Beach; ⌚4-8pm, lessons at 4pm, 5pm & 6pm) Find out if you're a great catch while donning a pair of hot pink tights during a one-hour group trapeze lesson (950B). Courses are taught by super-friendly Gemma and her posse of limber sidekicks, who take you from circus neophyte to soaring savant in four jumps or less. Bookings are best done over the phone, or you can show up at one of the nightly demos, which start at 7.30pm. Participants must be at least six years old.

Goodtime Adventures TOURS

(Map p210; ☎08 7275 3604; www.gtadventures.com; Sairee Beach; ⌚noon-late) Although most activities on Ko Tao revolve around the sea, the friendly crew at Goodtime Adventures offer a wide variety of land-based activities to get the adrenaline pumping. Hike through the island's jungly interior, swing from rock to rock during a climbing and abseiling session (from 2000B), or unleash your inner daredevil during an afternoon of cliff jumping. Goodtime also offers accredited boating certifications, and at the time of research they were setting up a groovy zipline course on neighbouring Ko Nang Yuan. The Goodtime office, along the Sairee sands, doubles as a friendly cafe serving an assortment of international nibbles (including dip coffee!)

Shambhala YOGA
(Map p210; ☎08 4440 6755; Sairee Beach) Ko Tao's only full-time yoga centre is housed in beautiful wooden *săh·lah* located on the forested grounds of Blue Wind (see p213) in Sairee Beach. The two-hour classes, led by Kester, the energetic yogi, cost 300B.

Ko Tao Bowling & Mini Golf BOWLING, MINIGOLF
(off Map p210; ☎0 7745 6316; ⏲noon-midnight) Located on the main road between Mae Hat and Chalok Ban Kao, Ko Tao Bowling & Mini Golf has several homemade bowling lanes where the employees reset the pins after every frame (300B per hour). The 18-hole minigolf course has a landmark theme – putt your ball through Stonehenge or across the Golden Gate Bridge.

Sleeping

If you are planning to dive while visiting Ko Tao, your scuba operator will probably offer you free or discounted accommodation to sweeten the deal. Some schools have on-site lodging, while others have deals with nearby bungalows. It's important to note that you only receive your scuba-related discount on the days you dive. So, for example, if you buy a 10-dive package, and decide to take a day off in the middle, your room rate will not be discounted on that evening. Also, a restful sleep is important before diving, so scope out these 'great room deals' before saying yes – some of them are one 'roach away from being condemned.

There are also many sleeping options that have absolutely nothing to do with the island's diving culture. Ko Tao's secluded eastern coves are dotted with stunning retreats that still offer a true getaway experience, but these can be difficult to reach due to the island's dismal network of roads. You can often call ahead of time and arrange to be picked up from the pier in Mae Hat.

Note that Ko Tao is not Ko Samui – if you are looking for impeccable service and perfect five-star standards you will not find it here...yet.

SAIREE BEACH

Giant Sairee is the longest and most developed strip on the island, with a string of dive operations, bungalows, travel agencies, minimarkets and internet cafes. The narrow 'yellow brick road' stretches the entire length of the beach (but watch out for motorcycles).

Blue Wind BUNGALOWS $
(Map p210; ☎0 7745 6116; bluewind_wa@yahoo.com; bungalows 300-1000B; ❄📶) Hidden within a clump of bodacious lodging options, Blue Wind offers a breath of fresh air from the high-intensity dive resorts strung along Sairee Beach. Sturdy bamboo huts are peppered along a dirt trail behind the beachside bakery. Large, tiled air-conditioned cabins are also available, boasting hot showers and TVs.

Ban's Diving Resort RESORT $$
(Map p210; ☎0 7745 6466; www.amazingkohtao.com; r 500-2500B; ❄@📶🏊) This dive-centric party palace offers a wide range of quality accommodation from basic backpacker digs to sleek hillside villas. Post-scuba chill sessions happen on Ban's prime slice of beach, or at one of the two swimming pools tucked within the strip of jungle between the two motel-like structures. Evenings are spent at the Fish Bowl bar downing international cuisine and 'buckets' in equal measure.

Place VILLA $$$
(www.theplacekohtao.com; villas 4000-7000B) Honeymooners will delight in this unique option – two private luxury villas nestled in the leaf-clad hills with sweeping ocean views down below. A private plunge pool comes standard – naturally – and private chef services are available for those who choose to remain in their love nest instead of sliding down to Sairee for restaurant eats.

Ko Tao Cabana BUNGALOWS $$$
(Map p210; ☎0 7745 6250; www.kohtaocabana.com; bungalows 2600-11,800B; ❄@📶🏊) This prime piece of beachside property offers timber-framed villas and crinkled white adobe huts dotted along the boulder-strewn beach. Bric-a-brac cheers the colourful bungalows – stone gnomes greet you with a naughty smirk as you shower in the roofless bathrooms. The newly constructed private

villas are one of the more upscale options on the island, though they're a bit rough around the edges compared to the five-star behemoths on Ko Samui.

Big Blue Resort BUNGALOWS $
(Map p210; ☎0 7745 6050; www.bigbluediving.com; r 400-1000B; ❄@) This scuba-centric resort has a summer camp vibe – diving classes dominate the daytime, while evenings are spent en masse, grabbing dinner or watching fire twirling. Both the basic fan bungalows and motel-style air-con rooms offer little when it comes to views, but who has the time to relax when there's an ocean out there to explore?

Sairee Cottage BUNGALOWS $$
(Map p210; ☎0 7745 6126; saireecottage@hotmail.com; bungalows 400-1500B; ❄) The air-con bungalows are hard to miss since they've been painted in various hues of fuchsia. Low prices mean low vacancy rates – so arrive early to score one of the brick huts facing out onto a grassy knoll.

Bow Thong BUNGALOWS $
(Map p210; ☎0 7745 6266; bungalows from 600B; ❄ 📶 ≋) A member of the quieter northern section of silky Sairee Beach, Bow Thong has a cluster of comfortable bungalows, if you're looking to be near the waves and aren't affiliated with a dive school.

Sunset Buri Resort BUNGALOWS $$
(Map p210; ☎0 7745 6266; bungalows 700-2500B; ❄@📶≋) A long beach-bound path is studded with beautiful white bungalows featuring enormous windows and flamboyant temple-like roofing. The kidney-shaped pool is a big hit, as are the large beach recliners sprinkled around the resort.

Koh Tao Coral Grand Resort BUNGALOWS $$$
(Map p210; ☎0 7745 6431; www.kohtaocoral.com; bungalows 3350-6950B; ❄📶≋) The plethora of pink facades at this family-friendly option feels a bit like Barbie's dream Thai beach-house. Cottage interiors are coated in cheery primary colours framed by white truncated beams while pricier digs have a more distinctive Thai flavour, boasting dark lacquered mouldings and gold-foiled art.

Seashell Resort BUNGALOWS $$
(Map p210; ☎0 7745 6299; www.seashell-resort.com; bungalows 450-3800B; ❄📶) Several bungalows have ocean views from their porches (a rarity in Sairee), while others sit in a well-maintained garden of colourful vegetation and thin palm trunks. Seashell welcomes divers and nondivers alike.

In Touch Resort BUNGALOWS $$
(Map p210; ☎0 7745 6514; bungalows 500-1200B; ❄📶) Older bungalows are a mishmash of bamboo and dark wood, while several rounded air-con rooms have a cave theme – it's all very *Flintstones,* except the shower nozzle hasn't been replaced with the trunk of an elephant.

Koh Tao Backpackers HOSTEL $
(Map p210; ☎08 8447 7921; www.kohtaobackpackers.com; dm 300B; ❄📶) No-frills bunk beds for serious penny pinchers.

MAE HAT

All ferry arrivals pull into the pier at the busy village of Mae Hat. Accommodation is spread throughout, but the more charming options extend in both directions along the sandy beach.

NORTH OF THE PIER

Regal Resort RESORT $$
(Map p210; ☎0 7745 6007; www.kohtaoregal.com; r 1500-4900B; ❄@📶≋) Home to the most inviting swimming pool on the island, sparkling white Regal proudly sits along the sands of Mae Hat. Set slightly away from the pier, this is a solid option for travellers seeking a sprinkle of air-con and ocean views from their balcony.

Crystal Dive Resort BUNGALOWS $$
(Map p210; ☎0 7745 6107; www.crystaldive.com; bungalows 800-1500B; ❄≋) The bungalow and motel-style accommodation at Crystal is reserved for its divers, and prices drop significantly for those taking courses. Guests can take a dip in the refreshing pool when it isn't overflowing with bubble-blowing newbie divers.

Montra Resort & Spa RESORT $$$
(Map p210; ☎0 7745 7057; www.kohtaomontra.com; r 4000-12,800B; ❄@📶≋) A newer address virtually at the Mae Hat pier, Montra is an upmarket affair with all the modern bells and whistles. The hotel structure is rather imposing when compared to the scatter of humble bungalows next door.

Mr J Bungalow BUNGALOWS $
(Map p210; ☎0 7745 6066; bungalows 250-1000B) Even though Mr J tried to charge us 50B for his business card, we still think he's well worth the visit. The eccentric owner entangles guests in a philosophical web while

tending to his flock of decent bungalows. Ask him about reincarnation if you want to hear some particularly twisted conjectures.

SOUTH OF THE PIER

Charm Churee Villa RESORT $$$
(off Map p210; ☎0 7745 6393; www.charmchureevilla.com; bungalows 3700-18,700B; ❄@≋) Tucked gently under sky-scraping palms, the luxuriant villas of Charm Churee are dedicated to the flamboyant spoils of the Far East. Gold-foiled oriental demigods pose in arabesque positions, with bejewelled eyes frozen in a Zen-like trance. Staircases, chiselled into the rock face, dribble down a palmed slope revealing teak huts strewn across smoky boulders. The villas' unobstructed views of the swishing indigo waters are charming.

Sensi Paradise Resort RESORT $$$
(Map p210; ☎0 7745 6244; www.sensiparadise.com; bungalows 2100-700B; ❄☰≋) There are one too many geckos in the bathroom to call this place 'natural chic', but if you like to be at one with nature then you'll appreciate that these rustic cottages are somehow simultaneously upscale. Friendly caretakers and several airy teak *săh·lah* add an extra element of charm.

Utopia Suites APARTMENTS $$
(Map p210; ☎0 7745 6729; r/ste from 600/2000B, monthly from 20,000B) Utopia is located in the charming fishing village, just a stone's throw from the pier. The beachside apartment-style accommodation is perfect for families and small groups. Ask about discounts for extended stays.

The following sleeping spots are located further south and can be accessed by a quick ride in a boat taxi:

Sai Thong Resort BUNGALOWS $$
(☎0 7745 6868; Hat Sai Nuan; bungalows 400-900B; ❄) As the rush of Mae Hat dwindles away along the island's southwest shore, Sai Thong emerges along sandy Hat Sai Nuan. Bungalows, in various incarnations of weaving and wood, have colourful porch hammocks and palm-filled vistas. Guests frequent the restaurant's relaxing sun deck – a favourite spot for locals too.

Tao Thong Villa BUNGALOWS $
(☎0 7745 6078; Ao Sai Nuan; bungalows from 500B) Very popular with long-termers seeking peace and quiet, these funky, no-frills bungalows have killer views. Tao Thong actually straddles two tiny beaches on a craggy cape about halfway between Mae Hat and Chalok Ban Kao.

CHALOK BAN KAO

Ao Chalok, about 1.7km south of Mae Hat by road, is the third-largest concentration of accommodation on Ko Tao, but can feel a lot more crowded because the beach is significantly smaller than Sairee and Mae Hat. The beach itself isn't tops as low tides are often muddy.

Ko Tao Resort RESORT $$$
(☎0 7745 6133; www.kotaoresort.com; r & bungalows from 2500B; ❄@☰≋) The entrance is a throwback to the days when taste and architecture weren't particularly synonymous (the '70s perhaps?), but inside everything's thoroughly modern and the facilities themselves fit the true definition of a resort. Rooms are split between 'pool side' and 'paradise zone' – all are well stocked, water sports equipment is on offer, and there are several bars primed to serve an assortment of fruity cocktails. 'Chalok Harbour', a new addition, features an extra dining option and additional chaise seating along a spacious pier.

Chintakiri Resort RESORT $$$
(☎0 7745 6133; www.chintakiri.com; r & bungalows 2900-4000B; ❄@≋) Perched high over the gulf waters overlooking Chalok Ban Kao, Chintakiri is one of Ko Tao's newer luxury additions as the island furtively creeps upmarket. Rooms are spread around the inland jungle, and sport crisp white walls with lacquered finishing.

Buddha View Dive Resort BUNGALOWS $$
(☎0 7745 6074; www.buddhaview-diving.com; r 300-1500B; ❄) Like the other large diving operations on the island, Buddha View offers its divers discounted on-site digs in a super-social atmosphere. If you plan on staying a while, ask about the 'Divers Village' across the street, which offers basic accommodation from around 4000B per month.

New Heaven Resort BUNGALOWS $$
(☎0 7745 6422; newheavenresort@yahoo.co.th; r & bungalows 1200-3900B) Just beyond the clutter of Chalok Ban Kao, New Heaven delivers colourful huts perched over impossibly clear waters. A steep path of chiselled stone tumbles down the shrubby rock face revealing views ripped straight from the pages of *National Geographic*.

Freedom Beach BUNGALOWS $

(☎0 7745 6596; bungalows 400-1500B; ❄) On its own secluded beach at the eastern end of Ao Chalok, Freedom feels like a classic backpacker haunt, although there's a variety of accommodation to suit various humble budgets. The string of bungalows (from wooden shacks to sturdier huts with air-con) links the breezy seaside bar to the resort's restaurant high on the cliff.

Viewpoint Resort BUNGALOWS $$

(☎0 7745 6666; www.kohtaoviewpoint.com; bungalows 800-1300B) A hot-shot architect from Bangkok allegedly designed this friendly, family-run retreat at the end of civilisation. Cottages are spartan but airy and well maintained. Some have partial sea views; others quietly sit in a gorgeous hillside garden that thrums with cicadas at night.

Also worth a look:

Tropicana GUEST HOUSE $

(☎0 7745 6167; www.koh-tao-tropicana-resort.com; r from 400) Low-rise hotel units peppered across a garden campus that provide fleeting glimpses of the ocean between fanned fronds and spiky palms.

JP Resort GUEST HOUSE $

(☎0 7745 6099; r from 400B) A colourful menagerie of prim motel-style rooms stacked on a small scrap of jungle across the street from the sea.

EAST COAST BEACHES

The serene eastern coast is, without a doubt, one of the best places in the region to live out your island paradise fantasies. The views are stunning; beaches are silent, yet all of your creature comforts are 10 minutes away. Accommodation along this coast is organised from north to south.

HIN WONG

A sandy beach has been swapped for a boulder-strewn coast, but the water is crystal clear. The road to Hin Wong is paved in parts, but sudden sand pits and steep hills can toss you off your motorbike.

Hin Wong Bungalows BUNGALOWS $

(☎0 7745 6006; bungalows from 300B) Pleasant wooden huts are scattered across vast expanses of untamed tropical terrain – it all feels a bit like *Gilligan's Island* (minus the millionaire castaways). A rickety dock, jutting out just beyond the breezy restaurant, is the perfect place to dangle your legs and watch schools of black sardines slide through the cerulean water.

View Rock BUNGALOWS $

(☎0 7745 6548/9; viewrock@hotmail.com; bungalows 300-400B) When coming down the dirt road into Hin Wong, follow the signs as they lead you north of Hin Wong Bungalows. View Rock is precisely that: views and rocks; the hodgepodge of wooden huts, which looks like a secluded fishing village, is built into the steep crags offering stunning views of the bay.

TANOTE BAY (AO TANOT)

Tanote Bay is more populated than some of the other eastern coves, but it's still rather quiet and picturesque. It is the only bay on the east coast that is accessible by a decent road. Discounted taxis (around 100B) bounce back and forth between Tanote Bay and Mae Hat; ask at your resort for a timetable.

Poseidon BUNGALOWS $

(☎0 7745 6735; poseidonkohtao@hotmail.com; bungalows from 300B) Poseidon keeps the tradition of the budget bamboo bungalow alive with a dozen basic-but-sleepable huts scattered near the sand.

Family Tanote BUNGALOWS $$

(☎0 7745 6757; bungalows 700-3500) As the name suggests, this scatter of hillside bungalows is run by a local family who take pride in providing comfy digs to solitude seekers. Strap on a snorkel mask and swim around with the fish at your doorstep, or climb up to the restaurant for a tasty meal and pleasant views of the bay.

AO LEUK & AO THIAN OK

Jamahkiri Resort & Spa RESORT $$$

(☎0 7745 6400; www.jamahkiri.com; bungalows 6900-13,900B) The flamboyant decor at this whitewashed estate is decidedly focused around tribal imagery. Wooden gargoyle masks and stone fertility goddesses abound amid swirling mosaics and multi-armed statues. Feral hoots of distant monkeys confirm the overarching jungle theme, as do the thatched roofs and tiki-torched soirees. The resort's seemingly infinite number of stone stairways can be a pain, so it's a good thing Ko Tao's most luxurious spa is located on the premises.

KO NANG YUAN

Photogenic Ko Nang Yuan, just off the coast of Ko Tao, is easily accessible by the Lomprayah catamaran, and by water taxis that depart from Mae Hat and Sairee.

Ko Nangyuan Dive Resort BUNGALOWS $$$

(☎0 7745 6088; www.nangyuan.com; bungalows 1200-9000B; ❄📶) Although the obligatory 100B tax to access the island is a bit off-putting (as is the 100B water taxi ride each way), Nangyuan Dive Resort is nonetheless a charming place to stay. The rugged collection of wood and aluminium bungalows winds its way across three coolie-hat-like conical islands connected by an idyllic beige sandbar. The resort also boasts the best restaurant on the island, but then again, it's the only place to eat...

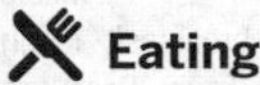

Eating

With super-sized Samui lurking on the horizon, it's hard to believe that quaint little Ko Tao holds its own in the gastronomy category. Most resorts and dive operators offer on-site dining, and stand-alone establishments are multiplying at lightning speed in Sairee Beach and Mae Hat. The diverse population of divers has spawned a broad range of international cuisine, including Mexican, French, Italian, Indian and Japanese. On our quest to find the tastiest Thai fare on the island, we discovered, not surprisingly, that our favourite local meals were being dished out at small, unnamed restaurants on the side of the road.

SAIREE BEACH

Darawan INTERNATIONAL $$

(Map p210; mains 160-400B; ⏲lunch & dinner) Like a top-end dining venue plucked from the posh shores of Samui nearby, regal Darawan is the island's newest place to take a date. Perched atop the trees at the back of Ban's sprawling resort, the yawning outdoor balcony offers beautiful views of the setting sun (come around 6pm). Designer lighting, efficient waiters and a tasty 'wagyu' burger seal the deal.

Barracuda Restaurant & Bar ASIAN FUSION $$

(Map p210; mains 180-380B; ⏲dinner) A wonderful addition to Ko Tao's ever-expanding dining scene, Barracuda offers a refined selection of seafood and gourmet bites. The owner, a masterful chef with many years in the biz, makes an earnest attempt to use only locally sourced ingredients to enhance his fusion faves. The seafood platter is a steal at 395B – wash down your meal with a mojito and head next door to watch the owner's boyfriend perform in the ladyboy cabaret.

ZanziBar SANDWICHES $

(Map p210; sandwiches 90-140B; ⏲breakfast, lunch & dinner) The island's outpost of sandwich yuppie-dom slathers a mix of unpronounceable condiments betwixt two slices of whole-grain bread.

Blue Wind Bakery INTERNATIONAL $

(Map p210; mains 50-120B; ⏲breakfast, lunch & dinner) This beachside shanty dishes out Thai favourites, Western confections and freshly blended fruit juices. Enjoy your thick fruit smoothie and flaky pastry while reclining on tattered triangular pillows.

Chopper's Bar & Grill INTERNATIONAL $$

(Map p210; dishes 60-200B; ⏲breakfast, lunch & dinner) So popular that it's become a local landmark, Chopper's is a two-storey hang-out where divers and travellers can widen their beer belly. There's live music, sports on the big-screen TVs, billiards and a cinema room. Friday nights are particularly popular; the drinks are 'two for one', and dishes are half-priced as well. Cheers for scored goals are interspersed with exaggerated chatter about creatures seen on the day's dive.

Kanya THAI $

(Map p210; mains 60-130B; ⏲breakfast, lunch & dinner) Tucked at the back of Sairee Village on the road to Hin Wong, four-table Kanya serves an assortment of international dishes, but you'll be missing out if you stray from the delectable array of home-cooked Thai classics – the *đôm yam Ƀlah* is divine.

Café Corner CAFE $$

(Map p210; snacks & mains 30-120B; ⏲breakfast & lunch) Prime real estate, mod furnishings, and tasty iced coffees have made Café Corner a Sairee staple over the last few years. Swing by at 5pm to stock up for tomorrow morning's breakfast; the scrumptious baked breads are buy-one-get-one-free before being tossed at sunset.

Big Blue East THAI, INTERNATIONAL $$

(Map p210; dishes 70-250B; ⏲breakfast, lunch & dinner) Big Blue Resort's busy chow house, located about 2m from the crashing tide, dispatches an assortment of Thai and international eats, including tasty individual pizzas. The joint fills up around sunset with divers chuckling at the daily dive bloopers shown on the big-screen TV.

Ally the Pancake Man CREPES $
(Map p210; pancakes from 20-40B; ⏰lunch & dinner) Stop by the 7-Eleven beside Big Blue Resort to check out Ally The Pancake Man as he dances around – like an Italian chef making pizza – while cooking your tasty snack. The 'banana Nutella' is a fave.

Krua Thai THAI $
(Map p210; dishes 50-120B; ⏰lunch & dinner) Popular with the tourists who want their food 'faráng spicy' rather than 'Thai spicy', Krua Thai offers a large assortment of classic favourites served in a well-maintained storefront.

El Gringo MEXICAN $$
(Map p210; dishes 80-150B; ⏰breakfast, lunch & dinner) As if there aren't already enough nicknames for white people in Thailand. The self-proclaimed 'funky Mexican joint' slings burritos of questionable authenticity in both Sairee Beach and Mae Hat. Delivery available.

MAE HAT

TOP CHOICE **Whitening** INTERNATIONAL $$
(Map p210; dishes 160-300B; ⏰dinner) Although it looks like a pile of forgotten driftwood during the day, this beachy spot falls somewhere between being a restaurant and being a chic seaside bar – foodies will appreciate the tasty twists on indigenous and international dishes while beertotalers will love the beachy, bleached-white atmosphere that hums with gentle lounge music. Dine amid dangling white Christmas lights while keeping your bare feet tucked into the sand. This is the top spot on the island for a celebratory dinner. And the best part? It's comparatively easy on the wallet.

Café del Sol INTERNATIONAL $$
(Map p210; dishes 70-320B; ⏰breakfast, lunch & dinner; @📶) Even the pickiest eater will be satisfied with the menu's expansive selection of 'world cuisine'. Located just steps away from the pier, this is our favourite breakfast spot on the island – go for the 'Del Sol breakfast' (delicious fruit salad, yoghurt and coffee) with a scrumptious spinach omelette on the side. Lunch and dinner dishes range from hearty pepper hamburgers to homemade pasta, though prices tend to be quite inflated.

Zest Coffee Lounge CAFE $
(Map p210; dishes 70-190B; ⏰breakfast & lunch; 📶) Indulge in the street-cafe lifestyle at Zest – home to the best cup of joe on the island. Idlers can nibble on *ciabatta* sandwiches or sticky confections while nursing their creamy caffe latte. There's a second branch in Sairee, although we prefer this location.

Safety Stop Pub INTERNATIONAL $
(Map p210; mains 60-250B; ⏰breakfast, lunch & dinner; 📶) A haven for homesick Brits, this pier-side restaurant and bar feels like a tropical beer garden. Stop by on Sundays to stuff your face with an endless supply of barbecued goodness, and surprisingly the Thai dishes aren't half bad!

Pranee's Kitchen THAI $
(Map p210; dishes 50-120B; ⏰breakfast, lunch & dinner; 📶) An old Mae Hat fave, Pranee's serves scrumptious curries and other Thai treats in an open-air pavilion sprinkled with lounging pillows, wooden tables and TVs. English movies (with hilariously incorrect subtitles) are shown nightly at 6pm.

Food Centre THAI $
(Map p210; mains from 30B; ⏰breakfast, lunch & dinner) An unceremonious gathering of hot tin food stalls, Food Centre – as it's come to be known – lures lunching locals with veritable smoke signals rising up from the concrete parking lot abutting Mae Hat's petrol station. You'll find some of the island's best papaya salad here.

Greasy Spoon BREAKFAST $
(Map p210; English breakfast 120B; ⏰breakfast & lunch) Although completely devoid of character, Greasy Spoon stays true to its name offering a variety of heart-clogging breakfast treats: eggs, sausage, stewed vegies and chips (their speciality) that'll bring a tear to any Brit's eye.

Tattoo Bar & Restaurant BURGERS $$
(Map p210; mains 150B) Just 30m south of the Whitening (at the edge of the fishing village), Tattoo is a casual affair with a cosy area for TV watching. If you're hungry, try the massive Aussie burger, homemade meat pies and sausage rolls.

Farango's PIZZA $$
(Map p210; dishes 80-230B; ⏰lunch & dinner) Ko Tao's first faràng restaurant spins tasty pizzas and other signature Italian fare. Free delivery. There's a second location on the outskirts of Sairee Village.

LEARNING THE LOCAL LINGO

Due to the steady influx of international visitors, English is spoken just about everywhere; however, the locals on this scuba-savvy island regularly incorporate diving sign-language symbols into common parlance – especially at the bars.

Here are a few gestures to get you started:

» **I'm OK** Make a fist and tap the top of your head twice

» **Cool** Bring together the tips of your index finger and thumb forming an 'O'

» **I'm finished/I'm ready to go** Hold your hand tight like a karate chop and quickly swing it back and forth perpendicular to your neck

CHALOK BAN KAO

Long Pae STEAKHOUSE **$$$**

(mains 100-430B; ⏲dinner) Situated off the radar from most of the island's tourist traffic, 'Uncle Pae' sits on a scruffy patch of hilly jungle with distant views of the sea down below. The speciality here is steak, which goes oh-so well with a generous smattering of pan-Asian appetisers.

New Heaven Restaurant INTERNATIONAL **$$**

(mains 60-350B; ⏲lunch & dinner) The best part about New Heaven Restaurant is the awe-inducing view of Shark Bay (Ao Thian Ok) under the lazy afternoon moon. The turquoise waters below are so translucent that the curving reef is easily visible from your seat. The menu is largely international, and there are nap-worthy cushions tucked under each low-rise table.

Koppee CAFE **$$**

(mains 60-180B; ⏲breakfast, lunch & dinner) A clone of some of the sleeker cafes in Mae Hat and Sairee, white-washed Koppee serves scrumptious international fare including a variety of home-baked desserts.

Drinking & Entertainment

After diving, Ko Tao's favourite pastime is drinking, and there's definitely no shortage of places to get tanked. In fact, the island's three biggest dive centres each have bumpin' bars – **Fish Bowl** (Map p210), **Crystal Bar** (Map p210) and **Buddha On The Beach** in Chalok Bak Kao – that attract swarms of travellers and expats alike. It's well worth stopping by even if you aren't a diver. Fliers detailing upcoming parties are posted on various trees and walls along the island's west coast (check the two 7-Elevens in Sairee). Also keep an eye out for posters touting 'jungle parties' held on nondescript patches of scrubby jungle in the centre of the island.

In addition to the following options, several places already reviewed (p217), such as Choppers and Safety Stop Pub, double as great hang-out joints for a well-deserved post-dive beer.

Just remember: don't drink and dive.

Castle CLUB

(off Map p210; www.thecastlekohtao.com; Mae Hat) Located along the main road between Mae Hat and Chalok Ban Kao, the Castle has quickly positioned itself as the most loved party venue on the island, luring an array of local and international DJs to its triad of parties each month.

Fizz BAR

(Map p210; Sairee Beach) Recline on mattress-sized pillows and enjoy designer cocktails while listening to Moby, or Enya, mixed with hypnotic gushes of the rolling tide.

Lotus Bar BAR

(Map p210; Sairee Beach) Lotus is the de facto late-night hang-out spot along the northern end of Sairee. Muscular fire twirlers toss around flaming batons, and the drinks are so large there should be a lifeguard on duty.

Dragon Bar LOUNGE

(Map p210; Mae Hat) This bar caters to those seeking snazzy, cutting-edge surroundings. There is a happening 'communist chic' retro styling throughout, and everything's dimly lit, moody and relaxing. Dragon Bar is rumoured to have the best cocktails on the island.

Office Bar BAR

(Map p210; Sairee Beach) With graffiti proudly boasting 'No Gaga, and no Black Eyed F*^#*# Peas', this hexagonal hut lures regulars with grunge beats and rickety wooden seats.

Diza BAR

(Map p210; Sairee Beach) Once a tatty shack that blasted music as it sold pirated DVDs, Diza has evolved into a casual hang-out at the crossroads of Sairee Village. Locals lounge on plastic chairs as they slurp their beer and people-watch.

Clumped at the southern end of Sairee Beach, **AC Party Pub** (Map p210), **In Touch** (Map p210) and **Maya Bar** (Map p210) take turns reeling in the partiers throughout the week.

Shopping

Although most items are cheap when compared to prices back home, diving equipment is a big exception to the rule. On Ko Tao you'll be paying Western prices plus shipping plus commission on each item (even with 'discounts') so it's better to do your scuba shopping at home or on your computer.

If you're having trouble scrubbing the sea salt out of your hair, stop by **Avalon** (Map p210; Mae Hat; ⌚10am-7pm Mon-Sat) for some locally made (and ecofriendly) body and hair care products.

Information

The ubiquitous *Koh Tao Info* booklet lists loads of businesses on the island and goes into some detail about the island's history, culture and social issues.

Dangers & Annoyances

There's nothing more annoying than enrolling in a diving course with your friends and then having to drop out because you scraped your knee in a motorcycle accident. The roads on Ko Tao are horrendous, save the main drag connecting Sairee Beach to Chalok Ban Kao. While hiring a moped is extremely convenient, this is not the place to learn how to drive. The island is rife with abrupt hills and sudden sand pits along gravel trails. Even if you escape unscathed from a riding experience, scamming bike shops may claim that you damaged your rental and will try to extort you for some serious cash.

Travellers should also be aware that mosquito-borne dengue fever (and a similar but less-severe cousin) is a real and serious threat. The virus can spread quickly due to tightly packed tourist areas and the small size of the island.

Emergency

Police station (Map p210; ☎0 7745 6631) Between Mae Hat and Sairee Beach along the rutty portion of the beachside road.

Internet Access

Rates are generally 2B per minute, with a 20B minimum and discounts if you log on for one hour or longer. You may find, however, that certain useful tourism websites have been firewalled at internet cafes affiliated with travel agencies. The larger dive schools on the island usually have a wireless connection available for laptop-toting travellers.

Medical Services

All divers are required to sign a medical waiver before exploring the sea. If you have any medical condition that might hinder your ability to dive (including mild asthma), you will be asked to get medical clearance from a doctor on Ko Tao. If you're unsure about whether or not you are fit to dive, consider seeing a doctor before your trip as there are no official hospitals on the island, and the number of qualified medical professionals is limited. Also, make sure your traveller's insurance covers scuba diving. On-island medical 'consultations' (and we use that term very lightly) cost 300B. There are several walk-in clinics and mini-hospitals scattered around Mae Hat and Sairee. All serious medical needs should be dealt with on Ko Samui. If you are diving, ask your outfitter to point you in the proper direction of medical advice.

Diver Safety Support (Map p210; ☎08 1083 0533; kohtao@sssnetwork.com; Mae Hat; ⌚on call 24hr) Has a temporary hyperbaric chamber and offers emergency evacuation services.

Money

There are 24-hour ATMs at the island's 7-Elevens. There's also a cluster of ATMs orbiting the ferry docks at Mae Hat. There is a money exchange window at Mae Hat's pier and a second location near Choppers in Sairee. There are several banks near the post office in Mae Hat, at the far end of town along the island's main inland road. They are usually open from 9am to 4pm on weekdays. Almost all dive schools accept credit cards, however there is usually a 3% or 4% handling fee.

Post

Post office (Map p210; ☎0 7745 6170; ⌚9am-5pm Mon-Fri, 9am-noon Sat) A 10- to 15-minute walk from the pier; at the corner of Ko Tao's main inner-island road and Mae Hat's 'down road'.

Tourist Information

There's no government-run TAT office on Ko Tao. Transportation and accommodation bookings can be made at most dive shops or at any of the numerous travel agencies, all of which take a small commission on services rendered.

Bon Voyage (Sairee Beach) Run by the kind Ms Jai, a Ko Tao native, this is a great place to make your transport connections and update your blog beneath cool blasts of air-con. It's located along the road connecting Sairee Beach and Hin Wong.

Websites

Koh Tao Online (www.kohtaoonline.com) An online version of the handy *Koh Tao Info* booklet.

 Getting There & Away

As always, the cost and departure times are subject to change. Rough waves are known to cancel ferries between the months of October and December. When the waters are choppy we recommend taking the Seatran rather than the Lomprayah catamaran if you are prone to seasickness. The catamarans ride the swell, whereas the Seatran cuts through the currents as it crosses the sea. Note that we highly advise purchasing your boat tickets *several* days in advance if you are accessing Ko Tao from Ko Pha-Ngan after the Full Moon Party.

Bangkok, Hua Hin & Chumphon

Lomprayah's new air service, **Solar Air** (www.lomprayah.com), jets passengers from Bangkok's Don Muang airport to Chumphon once daily in each direction from Monday to Saturday. Upon arriving in Chumphon, travellers can make a seamless transfer to the catamaran service bound for Ko Tao.

Bus-boat package tickets from Bangkok are available from travel agencies all over Bangkok and the south. Buses switch to boats in Chumphon and Bangkok-bound passengers can choose to disembark in Hua Hin (for the same price as the Ko Tao–Bangkok ticket).

If you are planning to travel through the night, the train's couchettes are a much more comfortable option than the bus. Travellers can plan their own journey by taking a boat to Chumphon, then making their way to Chumphon's town centre to catch a train up to Bangkok (or any town along the upper southern gulf); likewise in the opposite direction.

From Ko Tao, the high-speed catamaran departs for Chumphon at 10.15am and 2.45pm (1½ hours), the Seatran leaves the island at 4pm (two hours), and a Songserm fast boat makes the same journey at 2.30pm (three hours). There may be fewer departures if the swells are high.

There's also a midnight boat from Chumphon arriving early in the morning. It returns from Ko Tao at 11pm.

Ko Pha-Ngan

The Lomprayah catamaran offers a twice-daily service, leaving Ko Tao at 9.30am and 3pm and arriving on Ko Pha-Ngan around 10.50am and 4.10pm. The Seatran Discovery Ferry offers an identical service. The Songserm Express Boat departs daily at 10am and arrives on Ko Pan-Ngan at 11.30am. Hotel pick-ups are included in the price.

Ko Samui

The Lomprayah catamaran offers a twice-daily service, leaving Ko Tao at 9.30am and 3pm and arriving on Samui around 11.30am and 4.40pm. The Seatran Discovery Ferry offers an identical service. The Songserm Express Boat departs daily at 10am and arrives on Samui at 12.45pm. Hotel pick-ups are included in the price.

Surat Thani & the Andaman Coast

If you are heading to the Andaman coast and do not want to stop on Ko Pha-Ngan or Ko Samui along the way, there are two routes you can take. The first, and more common, approach is through Surat Thani. First, board a Surat-bound boat (the Songserm or the night ferry, unless you want to change ships) then transfer to a bus upon arrival. The night boat leaves Ko Tao at 8.30pm. Daily buses to the Songserm Express Boat depart from Surat Thani at 8am and arrive at 2.30pm. Return passengers leave Ko Tao at 10am and arrive in Surat Thani at 4.30pm.

The second option is to take a ferry to Chumphon on the mainland and then switch to a bus or train bound for the provinces further south.

 Getting Around

Sŏrng·tăa·ou In Mae Hat *sŏrng·tăa·ou*, pick-up trucks and motorbikes crowd around the pier as passengers alight. If you're a solo traveller, you will pay 100B to get to Sairee Beach or Chalok Ban Kao. Groups of two or more will pay 50B each. Rides from Sairee to Chalok Ban Kao cost 80B per person, or 150B for solo tourists. These prices are rarely negotiable, and passengers will be expected to wait until their taxi is full unless they want to pay an additional 200B to 300B. Prices double for trips to the east coast, and the drivers will raise the prices when rain makes the roads harder to negotiate. If you know where you intend to stay, we highly recommend calling ahead to arrange a pick up. Many dive schools offer free pick-ups and transfers as well.

Motorbikes Renting a motorcycle is a dangerous endeavour (see Dangers & Annoyances, opposite) if you're not sticking to the main, well-paved roads. Daily rental rates begin at 150B for a scooter. Larger bikes start at 350B. Discounts are available for weekly and monthly rentals. Try **Lederhosenbikes** (Map p210; ☎08 1752 8994; www.lederhosenbikes.com; Mae Hat; ⊙8.30am-6pm Mon-Sat). Do not rent all-terrain-vehicles (ATVs) or jet skis – they are unsafe.

Water taxis Boat taxis depart from Mae Hat, Chalok Ban Kao and the northern part of Sairee Beach (near Vibe Bar). Boat rides to Ko Nang Yuan will set you back at least 100B. Long-tail boats can be chartered for around 1500B per day, depending on the number of passengers carried.

Ang Thong Marine National Park อุทยานแห่งชาติหมู่เกาะอ่างทอง

The 40-some jagged jungle islands of Ang Thong Marine National Park stretch across the cerulean sea like a shattered emerald necklace – each piece a virgin realm featuring sheer limestone cliffs, hidden lagoons and perfect peach-coloured sands. These dream-inducing islets inspired Alex Garland's cult classic *The Beach,* about dope-dabbling backpackers.

February, March and April are the best months to visit this ethereal preserve of greens and blues; crashing monsoon waves means that the park is almost always closed during November and December.

Sights

Every tour stops at the park's head office on **Ko Wua Talap**, the largest island in the archipelago. The island's **viewpoint** might just be the most stunning vista in all of Thailand. From the top, visitors will have sweeping views of the jagged islands nearby as they burst through the placid turquoise water in easily anthropomorphised formations. The trek to the lookout is an arduous 450m trail that takes roughly an hour to complete. Hikers should wear sturdy shoes and walk slowly on the sharp outcrops of limestone. A second trail leads to **Tham Bua Bok**, a cavern with lotus-shaped stalagmites and stalactites.

The **Emerald Sea** (also called the Inner Sea) on **Ko Mae Ko** is another popular destination. This large lake in the middle of the island spans an impressive 250m by 350m and has an ethereal minty tint. You can look but you can't touch; the lagoon is strictly off-limits to the unclean human body. A second dramatic **viewpoint** can be found at the top of a series of staircases nearby.

The naturally occurring stone arches on **Ko Samsao** and **Ko Tai Plao** are visible during seasonal tides and weather conditions. Because the sea is quite shallow around the island chain, reaching a maximum depth of 10m, extensive coral reefs have not developed, except in a few protected pockets on the southwest and northeast sides. There's a shallow coral reef near Ko Tai Plao and Ko Samsao that has decent but not excellent snorkelling. There are also several novice dives for exploring shallow caves and colourful coral gardens and spotting banded sea snakes and turtles. Soft powder beaches line **Ko Tai Plao**, **Ko Wuakantang** and **Ko Hintap**.

Tours

The best way to experience Ang Thong is by taking one of many guided tours departing from Ko Samui and Ko Pha-Ngan. The tours usually include lunch, snorkelling equipment, hotel transfers and (with fingers crossed) a knowledgeable guide. If you're staying in luxury accommodation, there's a good chance that your resort has a private boat for providing group tours. Some midrange and budget places also have their own boats, and if not, they can easily set you up with a general tour operator. Dive centres on Ko Samui and Ko Pha-Ngan offer scuba trips to the park, although Ang Thong doesn't offer the world-class diving that can be found around Ko Tao and Ko Pha-Ngan.

Due to the tumultuous petrol prices, tour companies tend to come and go like the wind. Ask at your accommodation for a list of current operators.

Sleeping

Ang Thong does not have any resorts; however, on Ko Wua Talap the national park has set up five bungalows, each housing between two and eight guests. Campers are also allowed to pitch a tent in certain designated zones. Advance reservations can be made with the **National Parks Services** (☎0 7728 6025; www.dnp.go.th; bungalows 500-1400B). Online bookings are possible, although customers must forward a bank deposit within two days of making the reservation.

Getting There & Around

The best way to reach the park is to catch a private day-tour from Ko Samui or Ko Pha-Ngan (located 28km and 32km away, respectively). The islands sit between Samui and the main pier at Don Sak; however, there are no ferries that stop off along the way.

The park officially has an admission fee (adult/child 400/200B), although it should be included in the price of every tour (ask your operator if you are unsure). Private boat charters are also another possibility, although high petrol prices will make the trip quite expensive.

SURAT THANI PROVINCE

Surat Thani อำเภอเมืองสุราษฎร์ธานี

POP 128,990

Known in Thai as 'City of Good People', Surat Thani was once the seat of the ancient Srivijaya empire. Today, this busy junction has become a transport hub that indiscriminately moves cargo and people around the country. Travellers rarely linger here as they make their way to the deservedly popular islands of Ko Samui, Ko Pha-Ngan and Ko Tao.

Sleeping

For a comfy night in Surat, escape the grimy city centre and hop on a *sŏrng·tăa·ou* heading towards the Phang-Nga district. When you climb aboard, tell the driver 'Tesco-Lotus', and you'll be taken about 2km to 3km out of town to a large, box-like shopping centre. A handful of hotel options orbit the mall and have reasonable prices and refreshingly modern amenities.

Options in the downtown area are cheaper, but they tend to offer 'by the hour' service, so things can get a bit noisy as clients come and go. If you're on a very tight budg et, consider zipping straight through town and taking the night ferry to reach your island destination.

100 Islands Resort & Spa RESORT $
(0 7720 1150; www.roikoh.com; 19/6 Moo 3, Bypass Rd; r 590-1200B;) Across the street from the suburban Tesco-Lotus, 100 Islands is as good as it gets in Thailand for under 600B. This teak palace looks out of place along the highway, but inside, the immaculate rooms surround an overgrown garden and lagoon-like swimming pool.

Wangtai Hotel HOTEL $$
(0 7728 3020; www.wangtaisurat.com; 1 Th Talad Mai; r 790-2000B;) Across the river from the TAT office, Wangtai tries its best to provide a corporate hotel atmosphere. Polite receptionists and tux-clad bellboys bounce around the vast lobby, and upstairs, rooms have unmemorable furnishings, but there are good views of the city.

Eating

For foodstuffs, go to the **night market** (Sarn Chao Ma; Th Ton Pho) to enjoy fried, steamed, grilled or sautéed delicacies. There are additional evening food stalls near the departure docks for the daily night boats to the islands, a seafood market at Pak Nam Tapi, and an afternoon **Sunday market** (4-9pm) near the TAT office. During the day many food stalls near the downtown bus terminal sell *kôw gài òp* (marinated baked chicken on rice).

Crossroads Restaurant INTERNATIONAL $$
(Bypass Rd; dishes 50-200B; lunch & dinner) Located southwest of Surat across from the Tesco-Lotus mall, Crossroads has a quaint bluesy vibe enhanced by dim lighting and live music. Try the oysters – Surat Thani is famous for its giant molluscs, and the prices are unbeatable.

Information

Th Na Meuang has a bank on virtually every corner in the heart of downtown. If you're staying near the 'suburbs', the Tesco-Lotus has ATMs as well.

Boss Computer (per hr 20B; 9am-midnight) The cheapest internet connection around. Located near the post office.

Post office (0 7727 2013, 0 7728 1966; Th Talat Mai; 8.30am-4.30pm Mon-Fri, 8.30am-12.30pm Sat) Across from Wat Thammabucha. The local One Tambon One People (OTOP) craft house is located inside.

Siam City Bank (Th Chonkasem) Has a Western Union office.

Taksin Hospital (0 7727 3239; Th Talat Mai) The most professional of Surat's three hospitals. Just beyond the Talat Mai Market in the northeast part of downtown.

TAT office (0 7728 8817; tatsurat@samart.co.th; 5 Th Talat Mai; 8.30am-4.30pm) Friendly office southwest of town. Distributes plenty of useful brochures and maps, and staff speak English very well.

Getting There & Away

In general, if you are departing Bangkok or Hua Hin for Ko Pha-Ngan or Ko Tao, consider taking the train or a bus-boat package that goes through Chumphon rather than Surat. You'll save time, and the journey will be more comfortable. Travellers heading to/from Ko Samui will most likely pass through. If you require any travel services, try **Holiday Travel** (Th Na Meuang) or **Pranthip Co** (Th Talat Mai) – both are reliable and English is spoken.

Air

Although flights from Bangkok to Surat Thani are cheaper than the flights to Samui, it takes quite a bit of time to reach the gulf islands from the airport. In fact, if you are attempting to fly back

Surat Thani

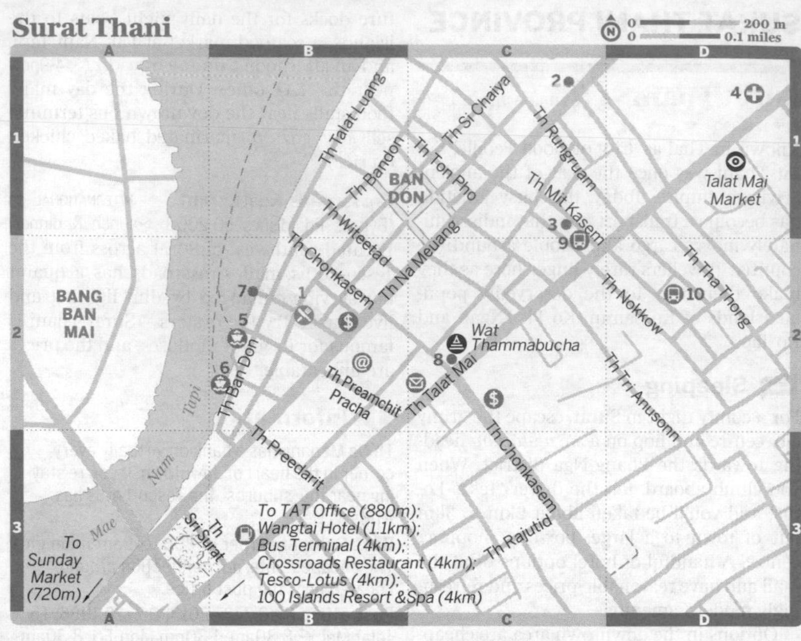

Surat Thani

Eating
1 Night Market.......B2

Information
2 Holiday Travel.......C1
3 Pranthip Company.......C1
4 Taksin Hospital.......D1

Transport
5 Ko Tao Night Ferry Pier.......B2
Lomprayah.......(see 7)
6 Night Boat to Ko Pha-Ngan.......B2
7 Seatran Discovery.......B2
8 Seatran Office.......C2
Songserm.......(see 7)
9 Talat Kaset 1 Bus Terminal.......C2
10 Talat Kaset 2 Bus Terminal.......D2

to Bangkok from the gulf islands, you'll probably have to leave your beachside bungalow the evening before your flight and spend the night in Surat. Not ideal. If you want to fly through Surat, there are daily shuttles to Bangkok on **Thai Airways International** (THAI; ☎0 7727 2610; 3/27-28 Th Karunarat).

Boat

In the high season travellers can usually find bus-boat services to Ko Samui and Ko Pha-Ngan directly from the Phun Phin train station (which is 14km west of Surat). These services don't cost any more than those booked in Surat Thani and can save you some serious waiting time. There are also several ferry and speedboat operators that connect Surat Thani to Ko Tao, Ko Pha-Ngan and Ko Samui. Most boats – such as the Raja and Seatran services – leave from Don Sak (about one hour from Surat; bus transfers are included in the ferry ticket) although the Songserm leaves from the heart of Surat town. Be warned that the Raja service can be a very frustrating experience, especially for travellers who are tight on time. The boat trip usually takes around 90 minutes to Ko Samui and 2½ hours to Ko Pha-Ngan, although oftentimes the captain will cut the engines to half propulsion, which means that the journey can take up to five hours.

From the centre of Surat there are nightly ferries to Ko Tao (eight hours, departs at 10pm), Ko Pha-Ngan (seven hours, departs at 10pm) and Ko Samui (six hours, departs at 11pm). These are cargo ships, not luxury boats, so bring food and water and watch your bags.

Bus & Minivan

The most convenient way to travel around the south, frequent buses and minivans depart from two main locations in town known as Talat Kaset 1 and Talat Kaset 2. Talat Kaset 1, on the north side of Th Talat Mai (the city's main drag) offers speedy service to Nakhon. This is also the location of Pranthip Co, one of the more trustworthy agencies in town. Buses to Phun Phin also leave from Talat Kaset 1. At Talat Kaset 2, on the south side of Th Talat Mai, you'll find frequent transportation to Hat Yai and minibuses to Nakhon, Trang, Khanom and Krabi. Andaman-bound buses (usually destined for Phuket) depart every hour from 7am to 3.30pm, stopping at Takua Pa for those who want to access Khao Sok National Park. The 'new' bus terminal (which is actually a few years old now, but still referred to as new by the locals) is located 7km south of town on the way to Phun Phin. This hub services traffic to and from Bangkok.

Train

When arriving by train you'll actually pull into Phun Phin, a cruddy town 14km west of Surat. From Phun Phin, there are buses to Phuket, Phang-Nga and Krabi – some via Takua Pa, a junction city further west and the stopping point for Khao Sok National Park. Transport from Surat moves with greater frequency, but it's worth checking the schedule in Phun Phin first – you might luck out and save yourself a slow ride between towns.

If you plan on travelling during the day, go for the express railcars. Night travellers should opt for the air-con couchettes. Odd-numbered trains are travelling from Bangkok south – even-numbered trains are travelling in the opposite direction. Trains passing through Surat stop in Chumphon and Hua Hin on their way up to the capital, and in the other direction you'll call at Trang, Hat Yai and Sungai Kolok before hopping the border. The train station at Phun Phin has a 24-hour left-luggage room that charges around 20B a day. The advance ticket office is open from 6am to 6pm daily (with a nebulous one-hour lunch break somewhere between 11am and 1.30pm).

Getting Around

Air-conditioned vans to/from Surat Thani airport cost around 70B per person and they'll drop you off at your hotel.

To travel around town, *sŏrng·tăa·ou* cost 10B to 30B (it's 15B to reach Tesco-Lotus from the city centre), while săhm·lór (three-wheeled vehicles; also spelled săamláw) charge between 20B and 40B.

Fan-cooled Orange buses run from Phun Phin train station to Surat Thani every 10 minutes (15B, 25 minutes). For this ride, taxis charge a cool 200B for a maximum of four people, while share-taxis charge 100B per person. Other taxi rates are posted just north of the train station (at the metal pedestrian bridge).

NAKHON SI THAMMARAT PROVINCE

Ao Khanom อ่าวขนอม

Little Khanom, halfway between Surat Thani and Nakhon Si Thammarat, quietly sits along the blue gulf waters. Overlooked by tourists who flock to the jungle-islands nearby, this pristine region, simply called Khanom, is a worthy choice for those seeking a serene beach setting unmarred by enterprising corporations.

Sights

The most unique feature in Khanom are the **pink dolphins** – a rare albino breed with a stunning pink hue. They are regularly seen from the old ferry pier and the electric plant pier around dawn and dusk.

WORTH A TRIP

WÁT SUAN MOKKHAPHALARAM

Surrounded by lush forest, **Wát Suan Mokkhaphalaram** (Wat Suanmokkh; www.suanmokkh.org), whose name means 'Garden of Liberation', charges 2000B for a 10-day program that includes food, lodging and instruction (although technically the 'teaching' is free). English retreats, run by the International Dhamma Hermitage, begin on the first day of every month and registration takes place the afternoon before. Founded by Ajan Buddhadasa Bhikkhu, arguably Thailand's most famous monk, the temple's philosophical teachings are ecumenical in nature, comprising Zen, Taoist and Christian elements, as well as the traditional Theravada schemata.

For details on reaching the temple, located 7km outside of Chaiya, check out www.suanmokkh-idh.org/idh-travel.html.

The area is also home to a variety of pristine geological features including **waterfalls** and **caves**. The largest of the falls, known as **Samet Chun**, has tepid pools for cooling off, and great views of the coast. To reach the falls, head south from Ban Khanom and turn left at the blue Samet Chun sign. Follow the road for about 2km and after crossing a small stream, take the next right and hike up into the mountain following the dirt road. After about a 15-minute walk, listen for the waterfall and look for a small trail on the right. The scenic **Hin Lat Falls** is the smallest cascade, but it's also the easiest to reach. There are pools for swimming and several huts providing shade. It's located south of Nai Phlao.

There are also two beautiful caves along the main road (Hwy 4014) between Khanom and Don Sak. **Khao Wang Thong** has a string of lights guiding visitors through the network of caverns and narrow passages. A metal gate covers the entrance; stop at the house at the base of the hill to retrieve the key (and leave a small donation). Turn right off the main highway at Rd 4142 to find **Khao Krot Cave**, which has two large caverns, but you'll have to bring a torch (flashlight).

For a postcard-worthy vista of the undulating coastline, head to **Dat Fa Mountain**, located about 5km west of the coast along Hwy 4014. The hillside is usually deserted, making it easy to stop along the way to snap some photos.

Sleeping & Eating

In the last few years, there has been talk of further developing Khanom's beaches into a more laid-back alterative to the islands nearby. The area is still far from booming, but large-scale development is on the cards. A recent surge in gulf oil rigging has meant that developers are eyeing Khanom as a potential holiday destination for the nearby workers.

There are enough options here that prebooking isn't a must – in fact we advise checking out a few places before picking a spot to crash. Many of the resorts see very few customers and the constant disuse (not regularly flushing the toilets etc) means that some rooms are dank as the relentless jungle reclaims them. It's best to stay away from the large hotels and stick to beachside bungalow operations.

For some cheap eats, head to **Kho Khao Beach** at the end of Rd 4232. You'll find a steamy jumble of BBQ stands offering some tasty favourites such as *mŏo nám đòk* (spicy pork salad) and *sôm đam* (spicy green papaya salad). On Wednesday and Sunday there are markets further inland near the police station.

JATUKHAM RAMMATHEP

If you've spent more than 24 hours in Thailand, you've probably seen a Jatukham Rammathep dangling around someone's neck – these round amulets are everywhere.

The bearers of the Jatukham Rammathep are supposed to have good fortune and protection from any harm. The origin of the amulet's name remains a mystery, although a popular theory suggests that Jatukham and Rammathep were the aliases of two Srivajayan princes who buried relics under Nakhon's Wat Phra Mahathat some 1000 years ago.

A notorious Thai police detective first wore the precious icon, and firmly believed that the guardian spirits helped him solve a particularly difficult murder case. He tried to popularise the amulet, but it wasn't a market success until his death in 2006. Thousands of people attended his funeral, including the crown prince, and the Jatukham Rammathep took off.

The talismans are commissioned at the Mahathat temple, and in the last several years, southern Thailand has seen a spike in economic activity. The first amulet was sold in 1987 for 39B, and today, over 100 million baht are spent on the town's amulets every *week*. The desire for these round icons has become so frenzied that a woman was crushed to death on the temple grounds during a widely publicised discount sale (she was not wearing her talisman).

Every day, trucks drive along Nakhon's main roads blaring loud music to promote new shipments. These thumping beats have started to shake the ground beneath the temple, and the repeated hammering has, in an ironic metaphor, bent the main spire of Wat Mahathat.

Racha Kiri RESORT $$$

(☎0 7530 0245; www.rachakiri.com; bungalows 3500-12,500B; ❄📶🏊) Khanom's upscale retreat is a beautiful campus of rambling villas. The big price tag means no crowds, which can be nice, although the resort feels like a white elephant when the property isn't being used as a corporate retreat.

Talkoo Beach Resort BUNGALOWS $$

(☎0 7552 8397; bungalows 1470B; ❄🏊) This charming operation has dozens of snazzy white cottages featuring quirky fixtures such as sinks made from hollowed-out tree trunks. This is the best lodging option in the vicinity.

Suchada Villa BUNGALOWS $

(☎0 7552 8459; bungalows 800B; ❄) Right along the main road, Suchada is recognisable by its cache of brightly coloured bungalows. Rooms are cute and clean with quirky designer details such as strings of shells dangling in front of the bathroom doors.

Information

The police station and hospital are located just south of Ban Khanom at the junction leading to Kho Khao Beach. There's a 7-Eleven (with an ATM) in the heart of Ban Khanom.

Getting There & Away

From Surat Thani, you can catch any Nakhon-bound bus and ask to be let off at the junction for Khanom. Catch a motorcycle taxi (70B) the rest of the way. You can get a share taxi from Nakhon Si Thammarat's share-taxi terminal to Khanom town for 85B.

From Khanom town you can hire motorcycle taxis out to the beaches for about 60B. There are three separate bus stops in the vicinity. Ask your driver to stop near the fruit market or the hospital, as these are the closest stops to the beach.

Nakhon Si Thammarat

อำเภอเมืองนครศรีธรรมราช

POP 117,100

The bustling city of Nakhon Si Thammarat (usually shortened to 'Nakhon') won't win any beauty pageants. However, travellers who stop in this historic town will enjoy a decidedly cultural experience amid some of the most important wát in the kingdom.

Hundreds of years ago, an overland route between the western port of Trang and the eastern port of Nakhon Si Thammarat functioned as a major trade link between Thailand and the rest of the world. This ancient influx of cosmopolitan conceits is still palpable today, and can be found in the recipes of local cuisine, or housed in the city's temples and museums.

Sights

Most of Nakhon's commercial activity (hotels, banks and restaurants) takes place in the northern part of the downtown. South of the clock tower, visitors will find the city's historic quarter with the oft-visited Wat Mahathat. Th Ratchadamnoen is the main thoroughfare and teems with cheap *sŏrng·tăa·ou* heading in both directions.

Wat Phra Mahathat Woramahawihaan TEMPLE

(Th Si Thamasok) The most important wát in southern Thailand, Wat Phra Mahathat Woramahawihaan (simply known as Mahathat) is a stunning campus boasting 77 *chedi* (stupa) and an imposing 77m *chedi* crowned by a gold spire. According to legend, Queen Hem Chala and Prince Thanakuman brought relics to Nakhon over 1000 years ago, and built a small pagoda to house the precious icons. The temple has since grown into a rambling site, and today, crowds gather daily to purchase the popular Jatukham amulets (see opposite). Don't miss the modest ceramics museum inside.

Shadow Puppets MUSEUM

(Th Si Thamasok Soi 3) Traditionally, there are two styles of local shadow puppet: *năng đà·lung* and *năng yài*. At just under 1m tall, the former feature movable appendages and parts (including genitalia); the latter are nearly life-sized, and lack moving parts. Both are intricately carved from cow hide. Suchart Subsin's puppet house has a small museum where staff can demonstrate the cutting process. Short shows can be performed for visitors for a nominal fee.

National Museum MUSEUM

(Th Ratchadamnoen; admission 30B; ⌚9am-4pm Wed-Sun) When the Tampaling (also known as Tambralinga) kingdom traded with merchants from Indian, Arabic, Dvaravati and Champa states, the region around Nakhon became a melting pot of crafts and art. Today, many of these relics are on display behind the run-down facade of the national museum.

DON'T MISS

KHAO LUANG NATIONAL PARK

Known for its beautiful mountain and forest walks, cool streams, waterfalls and orchards, **Khao Luang National Park** (อุทยานแห่งชาติเขาหลวง; ☎0 7530 9644-7; adult/child 400/200B) surrounds the 1835m peak of Khao Luang. This soaring mountain range reaches up to 1800m, and is covered in virgin forest. An ideal source for streams and rivers, the mountains show off impressive waterfalls and provide a habitat for a plethora of bird species – this place is a good spot for any budding ornithologist. Fans of flora will also get their kicks here; there are over 300 species of orchid in the park, some of which are found nowhere else on earth.

Park bungalows can be rented for between 600B and 1000B per night, and sleep six to 12 people. **Camping** is permitted along the trail to the summit. To reach the park, take a *sŏrng·tăa·ou* (around 25B) from Nakhon Si Thammarat to the village of Khiriwong, at the base of Khao Luang. The entrance to the park and the offices of the Royal Forest Department are 33km from the centre of Nakhon on Rte 4015, an asphalt road that climbs almost 400m in 2.5km to the office and a further 450m to the car park.

Sleeping & Eating

Nakhon is a great place to sample cuisine with a distinctive southern twist. In the evening, Muslim food stands sell delicious *kôw mòk gài* (chicken biryani), *má·đà·bà* (*murdabag;* Indian pancake stuffed with chicken or vegetables) and roti. Several tasty options cluster around Bovorn Bazaar on Th Ratchadamnoen.

Nakorn Garden Inn GUEST HOUSE $
(☎0 7532 3777; 1/4 Th Pak Nakhon; r 445B; ❄) The motel-style Nakorn Garden Inn offers a pleasant alternative to the usual cement cube. Rooms are encased in exposed crimson brick and set around a sandy garden. Each unit is identical, sporting a TV and fridge; try to score a room that gets plenty of sunlight.

Twin Lotus Hotel HOTEL $$
(☎0 7532 3777; www.twinlotushotel.net; 97/8 Th Phattanakan Khukhwang; r 1400-1600B; ❄📶🏊) Its age is starting to show, but Twin Lotus is still a nice spot for a little pampering while visiting Nakhon. This 16-storey behemoth sits a couple of kilometres southeast of the city centre.

Khrua Nakhon THAI $$
(Bovorn Bazaar; dishes 60-200B; ⊙breakfast & lunch) This joint has a great selection of traditional Nakhon cuisine. Order a sharing platter, which comes with five types of curry (including an unpalatable spicy fish sauce), or try the *kôw yam* (southern-style rice salad). There's one at a second location in Robinson Ocean Mall.

Rock 99 INTERNATIONAL $
(1180/807 Bavorn Bazaar; dishes 40-130B; ⊙dinner) The choice *fa·ràng* hang-out in Nakhon, Rock 99 has a good selection of international fare – from taco salads to pizzas (avoid the Thai fare though). There's live music on Wednesday, Friday and Saturday nights, but expect to bump into friendly expats almost all the time.

Information

Several banks and ATMs hug Th Ratchadamnoen in the northern end of downtown. There is an English-language bookstore on the 3rd floor of Robinson Ocean shopping mall.

Bovorn Bazaar (Th Ratchadamnoen) A mall housing a few internet cafes.

Police station (☎1155; Th Ratchadamnoen) Opposite the post office.

Post office (Th Ratchadamnoen; ⊙8.30am-4.30pm)

TAT office (☎0 7534 6515) Housed in a 1926-vintage building in the northern end of the Sanam Na Meuang (City Park). Has some useful brochures in English. The local OTOP craft house is just a block away on the west side of Sanam Na Meuang Park.

Getting There & Away

Air Several small carriers such as Nok Air, Air Asia and Orient Thai Airlines (plus Thai Airways) fly from Bangkok to Nakhon everyday. There are about six daily one-hour flights.

Trains There are two daily train departures from Bangkok to Nakhon (stopping through Hua Hin, Chumphon and Surat Thani along the way). They are both 12-hour night trains leaving at 5.35pm and 7.15pm. These trains continue on to Hat Yai and Sungai Kolok.

Bus Buses from Bangkok depart either between 6am and 8am, or between 5.30pm and 10pm. There are about seven daily departures. Ordinary buses to Bangkok leave from the bus terminal, but a couple of private buses leave from booking offices on Th Jamroenwithi, where you can also buy tickets. The journey takes 12 hours.

When looking for minivan stops to leave Nakhon, keep an eye out for small desks along the side of the downtown roads (minivans and waiting passengers may or may not be present nearby). It's best to ask around as each destination has a different departure point. Krabi and Don Sak minivans are grouped together – just make sure you don't get on the wrong one. Stops are scattered around Th Jamroenwithi, Th Wakhit and Th Yommarat.

Getting Around

Sŏrng·tăa·ou run north–south along Th Ratchadamnoen and Th Si Thammasok for 10B (a bit more at night). Motorcycle-taxi rides start at 20B and cost up to 50B for longer distances.

SONGKHLA PROVINCE

Songkhla's postal code is 90210, but this ain't no Beverly Hills! The province's two main commercial centres, Hat Yai and Songkhla, are not usually affected by the political turmoil plaguing the cities further south. Intrepid travellers will be able to count the number of other tourists on one hand as they wander through local markets, savour Muslim-Thai fusion cuisine and relax on breezy beaches.

Songkhla & Around สงขลา

POP 90,780

'The great city on two seas' lends itself perfectly to the click of a visitor's camera; however, slow-paced Songkhla doesn't see much in the way of foreign tourist traffic. Although the town hasn't experienced any of the Muslim separatist violence plaguing the provinces further south, it's still catching the same bad press. This is a darn shame, since it's the last safe city where travellers can experience the unique flavour of Thailand's predominately Muslim deep south.

The population is a mix of Thais, Chinese and Malays, and the local architecture and cuisine reflect this fusion at every turn.

Sights

National Museum MUSEUM

(พิพิธภัณฑสถานแห่งชาติสงขลา; Th Wichianchom; admission 150B; 9am-4pm Wed-Sun, closed public holidays) The 1878 building that now houses the **national museum** was originally built in a Chinese architectural style as the residence of a luminary. This museum is easily the most picturesque national museum in Thailand and contains exhibits from all Thai art-style periods, particularly the Srivijaya. Also on display are Thai and Chinese ceramics and sumptuous Chinese furniture owned by the local Chinese aristocracy.

Hat Samila BEACH

(หาดสมิหลา) If museums aren't your style, head to the beach. The residents have begun taking better care of the strip of white sand along Hat Samila, and it is now quite pleasant for strolling or flying a kite (a local obsession). A bronze **Mermaid sculpture**, depicted squeezing water from her long hair in tribute to Mae Thorani (the Hindu-Buddhist earth goddess), sits atop some rocks at the northern end of the beach. Locals treat the figure like a shrine, tying the waist with coloured cloth and rubbing the breasts for good luck. Next to that are the **Cat and Rat sculptures**, named for the Cat and Rat Islands (Ko Yo and Ko Losin). Fragments of a dragon statue are sliced up and placed around the city. The **Nag Head** (dragon head), which shoots water into the ocean, is said to bring prosperity and fresh water – it's a popular meeting spot for locals.

Ko Yo ISLAND

(เกาะยอ) A popular day trip from Songkhla, this island in the middle of Thale Sap is actually connected to the mainland by bridges and is famous for its cotton-weaving industry. There's a roadside market selling cloth and ready-made clothes at excellent prices.

If you visit Ko Yo, don't miss **Wat Phrahorn Laemphor**, with its giant reclining Buddha, and check out the **Thaksin Folklore Museum** (0 7459 1618; admission 100B; 8.30am-4.30pm), which actively aims to promote and preserve the culture of the region, and is a must-see. The pavilions here are reproductions of southern Thai–style houses and contain folk art, handicrafts and traditional household implements.

If you have kids in tow, try the following:

Songkhla Zoo ZOO
(สวนสัตว์สงขลา; Khao Rup Chang; adult/child 30/5B; ⏲9am-6pm) Enjoy cuddling with baby tigers.

Songkhla Aquarium AQUARIUM
(สงขลาอะควาเรียม; www.songkhlaaquarium.com; adult/child 150/80B; ⏲9am-5pm Wed-Mon) Point at clownfish at this flashy new attraction.

Sleeping & Eating

Songkhla's hotels tend to be lower priced than other areas in the gulf, which makes going up a budget level a relatively cheap splurge.

For quality seafood, head to the street in front of the BP Samila Beach Hotel – the best spot is the restaurant directly in the roundabout. If market munching is your game, you'll find a place to sample street food every day of the week. On Sundays try the bustling market that encircles the Pavilion Hotel. Monday, Tuesday and Wednesday feature a night market (which closes around 9pm) near the local fish plant and bus station, and the Friday-morning market sits diagonally opposite the City Hall.

BP Samila Beach Hotel HOTEL $$
(☎0 7444 0222; www.bphotelsgroup.com; 8 Th Ratchadamnoen; r 1680-2500B; ❄@≋) A landmark in quaint Songkhla, the city's poshest address is actually a really good deal – you'd pay nearly double for the same amenities on the islands. The beachfront establishment offers large rooms with fridges, satellite TVs and a choice of sea or mountain views (both are pretty darn good).

Green World Palace Hotel HOTEL $$
(☎0 7443 7900-8; 99 Th Samakisukson; r 1000-1200B; ❄@⊜≋) When expats say that sleeping in Songkhla is a steal, they're not lying – Green World is the proof. This classy affair boasts chandeliers, a spiralling staircase in the lobby and a 5th-floor swimming pool with views. Rooms are immaculate and filled with all the mod cons of a hotel twice the price.

Khao Noy CURRY SHOP $
(☎0 7431 1805; 14/22 Th Wichianchom; dishes 30-50B; ⏲breakfast & lunch Thu-Tue) Songkhla's most lauded *ráhn kôw gaang* (curry shop) serves up an amazing variety of authentic southern-style curries, soups, stir-fries and salads. Look for the glass case holding several stainless-steel trays of food just south of the sky-blue Chokdee Inn.

Information

Banks can be found all over town.

Indonesian Consulate (☎0 7431 1544; Th Sadao)

Malaysian Consulate (☎0 7431 1062; 4 Th Sukhum)

Police station (☎0 7432 1868; Th Laeng Phra Ram) North of the town centre.

Post office (Th Wichianchom) Opposite the market; international calls can be made upstairs.

Getting There & Around

Trains From Songkhla you'll have to go to Hat Yai to reach most long-distance destinations in the south (trains no longer pass through town).

Buses The government bus station is located a few hundred metres south of the Viva Hotel. Three 2nd-class buses go daily to Bangkok, stopping in Chumphon, Nakhon Si Thammarat and Surat Thani, among other places. For Hat Yai, buses and minivans take around 40 minutes, and leave from Th Ramwithi. *Sŏrng·tăa·ou* also leave from here for Ko Yo.

Hat Yai หาดใหญ่

POP 157,400

Welcome to backcountry Thailand's version of big city livin'. Songkhla Province's liveliest town has long been a favourite stop for Malaysian men on their weekend hooker tours. These days Hat Yai gladly shakes hands with globalisation – Western-style shopping malls stretch across the city, providing local teenagers with a spot to loiter and middle-aged ladies with a place to do their cardio.

Tourists usually only get a glimpse of the city's winking commercial lights from the window of their train carriage as they connect the dots along the peninsula, but those who decide to explore will be rewarded with excellent local cuisine (the city has hundreds of restaurants), shopping (DVDs anyone?) and an evening bar scene that brilliantly mixes cosy pubs and bouncing discotheques.

Sleeping & Eating

Hat Yai has dozens of hotels within walking distance of the train station. The city is the unofficial capital of southern Thailand's cuisine, offering Muslim roti and curries, Chinese noodles and dim sum, and fresh Thai-style seafood from both the gulf and Andaman coasts. On Th Niyomrat, between Niphat Uthit 1 and 2, starting at Tamrab

Muslim, is a string of casual and inexpensive Muslim restaurants open from about 7am to 9pm daily. Meals at these places cost between 20B to 60B.

The **night market** (Th Montri 1) boasts heaps of local eats including several stalls selling the famous Hat Yai-style deep-fried chicken and *kà·nŏm jeen* (fresh rice noodles served with curry), as well as a couple of stalls peddling grilled seafood.

Regency Hotel HOTEL **$$**
(☎0 7435 3333-47; www.theregencyhatyai.com; 23 Th Prachathipat; r 798-5680B; ❄@≋) This beautiful hotel has that grand old-world charm that's so very rare nowadays. Rooms in the old wing are smaller (and cheaper) and feature attractive wood furnishings, while the new wing boasts amazing views.

Sor Hueng 3 THAI **$**
(☎08 1896 3455; 79/16 Th Tharnnoonvithi; dishes 30-120B; ⊙dinner) This popular local legend with branches all over town prepares heaps of delicious Thai-Chinese and southern Thai faves. Simply point to whatever looks good or order something freshly wok-fried from the extensive menu.

ℹ Information

Immigration Office (Th Phetkasem) Near the railway bridge, it handles visa extensions.

TAT Office (tatsgkhla@tat.or.th; 1/1 Soi 2, Th Niphat Uthit 3) Very helpful staff here speak excellent English and have loads of info on the entire region.

Tourist police (Th Niphat Uthit 3; ⊙24hr) Near the TAT office.

ℹ Getting There & Away

Air

Thai Airways International (THAI; 182 Th Niphat Uthit 1) operates eight flights daily between Hat Yai and Bangkok.

Nearly all of the low-cost airlines now operate flights to and from Bangkok:

Air Asia (www.airasia.com) Daily flights from Hat Yai to Bangkok and Kuala Lumpar.

Nok Air (www.nokair.com) Daily flights between Hat Yai and Bangkok's Don Muang Airport.

Bus

Most interprovincial buses and south-bound minivans leave from the bus terminal 2km southeast of the town centre, while most north-bound minivans now leave from a minivan terminal 5km west of town at Talat Kaset, a 60B túk-túk ride from the centre of town. Buses link Hat Yai to almost any location in southern Thailand.

Prasert Tour (Th Niphat Uthit 1) conducts minibuses to Surat Thani (4½ hours, 8am to 5pm), and **Cathay Tour** (93/1 Th Niphat Uthit 2) can also arrange minivans to many destinations in the south.

Train

There are four overnight trains to/from Bangkok each day, and the trip takes at least 16 hours. There are also seven trains daily that run along the east coast to Sungai Kolok and two daily trains running west to Butterworth and Padang Besar, both in Malaysia.

There is an advance booking office and left-luggage office at the train station; both are open 7am to 5pm daily.

ℹ Getting Around

An **Airport Taxi Service** (☎0 7423 8452; 182 Th Niphat Uthit 1) makes the run to the airport four times daily (80B per person, 6.45am, 9.30am, 1.45pm and 6pm). A private taxi for this run costs 280B.

Sŏrng·tăa·ou run along Th Phetkasem (10B per person). Túk-túk and motorcycle taxis around town cost 20B to 40B per person.

DEEP SOUTH

Yala ยะลา

POP 65,000

Landlocked Yala feels quite different from the neighbouring towns. The city's gaping boulevards and well-organised street grid feels distinctly Western, especially since Yala is predominantly a university town.

Yala's biggest attraction is **Wat Kuha Pi Muk** (also called Wat Na Tham or Cave-front Temple), 8km west of town on the road connecting Yala to Hat Yai (Rte 409). This Srivijaya-period cave temple features a reclining Buddha that dates back to AD 757. A statue of a giant guards the temple's entrance, and inside small natural openings in the cave's roof let in the sun's rays to illuminate a variety of ancient Buddhist cave drawings. Wat Kuha Pi Muk is one of the most important pilgrimage points in southern Thailand.

Take a breather from wát ogling and check out what is known as the largest mail box in Thailand, built in the township of Betong in 1924. Betong also functions as a legal, but inconvenient, border crossing to

TROUBLE IN THE DEEP SOUTH

Background

Thailand's southernmost frontier is lush, green and prone to violence. Though the three provinces in Thailand's deep south were conquered by the Siamese kingdom more than 100 years ago, a regional insurgency still kicks and screams for independence.

Armed separatists dream of reclaiming 'Patani', a Qatar-sized Muslim sultanate that perished long before today's insurgents were even born. Along with much of the Malay-Indonesian archipelago, the region absorbed Islamic beliefs from 13th-century Arab traders. The kingdom existed for about 500 years until 1902, when it was seized by Buddhist Siam and carved into three provinces: Yala, Narathiwat, Pattani and parts of neighbouring Satun.

But the deep south has never truly assimilated with Thailand. After a relative lull of violence in the 1980s and '90s, the independence struggle is now raging harder than ever.

Deaths have reached 4600 since 2004, a year marking the revival of violent struggle. Despite separatists' semi-secret peace talks with the Royal Thai Army, few expect the low-grade civil war to end anytime soon.

Killings occur at a daily clip. Shock tactics rival those of insurgents in Iraq or Pakistan. Beheadings of monks and kids are recurrent. Teachers, seen as agents of cultural assimilation, are shot dead en route to morning lessons. Rubber farmers are gunned down with AK-47 fire simply for having good relations with Buddhist neighbours.

The separatists are also growing more sophisticated and savvy. Their roadside bombs were once built from Tupperware, C-4 and rusty nails. They have since graduated to radio-control detonators and complex attacks, which first wipe out unlucky civilians and then responding bomb squads with secondary bombs planted nearby.

What compels insurgents to such extremes? According to separatists, they must resist 'Siamese Infidels' forcing Buddhist culture down their throats. As far back as 1939, the Thai state shut down the region's Islamic schools and Qu'ranic sharia law courts. The local Yawi dialect was forbidden in government offices.

Locals still bemoan the indignity of visiting government bureaus where imported officials can't speak their local tongue. The army also enforces a 'state of emergency' – essentially martial law – that limits the rights of those arrested. Muslim groups complain that men are falsely accused and never come home. Powerful positions, from army officers to police chiefs to mayors, are typically held by Thai Buddhists and not local Muslims.

Two army scandals have helped galvanise disdain for the Thai state: the Tak Bai and Krue Sae events of 2004. The former saw roughly 80 Muslim protesters in the town of Tak Bai, Narathiwat, stacked in a truck's sweltering cargo hold until they suffocated. In the latter incident, troops stormed a mosque called Krue Sae in Pattani and gunned down more than 30 suspected insurgents. The alleged separatists were armed with knives and a single gun. The army insists both incidents were accidental.

Perhaps the separatists' most unique feature is their ironclad code of silence. Thai soldiers say combating the insurgency is akin to fighting ghosts. The self-proclaimed 'Patani Mujahedin' run what one academic calls a network without a core: a patchwork of village-based cells operating independently.

The various resistance groups share common ideals but no common leader. Accounts vary, but the various networks are believed to control roughly 8000 separatists. Unlike al-Qaeda or the Taliban, they seldom claim responsibility for attacks, preferring silence to glory.

Leaflets scattered around victims' corpses are the insurgents' preferred method of communication. One typical screed reads: 'Make violence brutally. Attack the Buddhist Thais. We know that the Buddhist Thais do not like violence and love peace. When the Buddhist Thais cannot stand, they will surrender.'

As intended, killings have stoked Buddhist flight en masse. In parts of the army's so-called 'red zone', vestiges of the Thai state control, such as schools and even postal routes, are few and far between. Monks dare not go on alms runs without M-16-gripping soldiers at their sides. At times, according to some experts, as many as 25% of the deep south's villages have at some point fallen under de facto insurgency control.

The insurgency is noted for its reluctance to attack targets outside the deep south, which is likely the reason the conflict attracts scant global interest. The greater region offers targets that, if attacked, would deal great damage to the psyche of Thailand and its tourists.

But separatists have left alone the backpacker beaches of Krabi, Phuket's resorts and even Bangkok, the heart of the Thai authority. Likewise, insurgents appear uninterested in joining forces with al-Qaeda or Islamic terror groups in Pakistan or Indonesia.

One senior member of the oldest insurgent group, the Patani United Liberation Organization, has insisted the insurgency will never solicit outside help. Though speaking only for one of several factions, he claims post-revolution Patani will warmly welcome Western tourists to its pristine beachfront.

But for now, the violence has strangled regional tourism. Even if separatists are only out to harm Thai Buddhists and Muslim collaborators, marketplace bombs kill indiscriminately. Hotels classy enough to satisfy tourists have also come under attack; these are the same hotels favoured by high-ranking officers.

The only reliable stream of tourism comes from Malaysian men travelling north for booze and rented female company. Still, given a spate of explosions outside dodgy nightclubs, they do so at a pronounced risk.

But no matter how much blood the 'Patani Mujahedin' spill, they are unlikely to secure their stated goal: an independent Islamic state.

Though most Thais view the deep south as a different planet, heavy nationalism imbued in Thai schools has bred a population incapable of stomaching territorial loss. An authority figure who backed ceding Thai soil would risk political suicide. And though the Bangkok press chronicles daily killings in detail, the insurgency remains an afterthought to voters convinced terror will never creep outside the deep south.

Instead of Thai surrender, some version of autonomy is a more reasonable, but still distant, hope for insurgents and their sympathisers. Sporadic talks between Thai military officials and separatists in exile have taken place since the late 2000s. However, the army's faith is shaken each time insurgency heads try to prove their authority through ceasefires that are ignored by rebels on the ground.

So a vexing question remains for Thailand's military: how do you negotiate with a network with no core?

Patrick Winn is the Southeast Asia correspondent for the Global Post foreign news agency

Should You Go?

Although it's possible to visit the region, the insurgency has stifled tourism in the deep south to the extent that tourist infrastructure – hotels, restaurants, transportation and activities – is minimal. And the threat of violence means that exploring the area's largely pristine and uninhabited beaches – ostensibly most travellers' reason for visiting the region – can't generally be recommended.

To date, tourists have not been targeted, but the haphazard nature of the insurgency makes it difficult to predict which way the situation will turn (and bombs kill indiscriminately). If you plan to visit the region and want to know the situation on the ground, the authorities suggest contacting the local Tourist Police or TAT, but you'll have to be prepared for pessimistic spiel. Generally speaking, travel in Pattani and Narathiwat in the early morning and late evening is discouraged, and independent travel via rented motorcycle carries considerable risk. While in urban areas, it's probably also a good idea not to linger around parked motorcycles, as they have been used to carry remote-controlled bombs.

Austin Bush, author of the Deep South section of this chapter

Malaysia; contact Yala's **immigration office** (☎0 7323 1292) or see the boxed text, p236 for details.

Sleeping & Eating

The lack of tourism means great bargains for a comfy bed.

Chang Lee Hotel HOTEL $
(☎0 7324 4600; www.yalasirichot.4t.com; 318 Th Sirirot; s & d 400-460B; ❄) A 15-minute walk from the train station, the Chang Lee has plush rooms that cater to business travellers. Facilities include a karaoke nightclub and coffeeshop.

Although inland, Yala has several excellent seafood restaurants – there's a cluster around Th Pitipakdee and Th Sribumrung. Rice and noodle stalls abound near the train station.

Getting There & Around

Buses to Hat Yai (150B, 2½ hours) stop several time a day on Th Sirirot, outside the Prudential TS Life office. Across the street is the stop for other short- to medium-distance buses north. Yala's train station has four daily departures for Bangkok (193B to 1675B, 18 to 22 hours) and seven for Sungai Kolok (41B to 917, two to three hours).

Pattani ปัตตานี

POP 118,000

Like a rebellious child that can never get along with his stepmother, Pattani has never quite adjusted to Thai rule. It was once the heart and soul of a large Muslim principality that included the nearby provinces of Yala and Narathiwat. Although today's political situation has stunted the area's development, Pattani has a 500-year history of trading with the world's most notorious imperial powerhouses. The Portuguese established a trading post here in 1516, the Japanese passed through in 1605, the Dutch in 1609, and the British flexed their colonial muscle in 1612.

Yet despite the city's interesting past, there's little of interest in Pattani except its access to some decent nearby beaches. Unfortunately, the ongoing insurgency (see the boxed text, p232) has made all but a handful of these sandy destinations unsafe for the independent traveller.

Sights

The Mae Nam Pattani (Pattani River) acts as a divider between the older town to the east and the newer town to the west. Along Th Ruedi you can see what is left of old Pattani architecture – the Sino-Portuguese style that was once so prevalent in this part of southern Thailand. On Th Arnoaru there are several very old, but still quite intact, Chinese-style homes.

Thailand's second-largest mosque is the **Matsayit Klang** (Th Naklua Yarang), a traditional structure with a green hue that is probably still the south's most important mosque. It was built in the 1960s.

If it weren't for the political unrest, Pattani could be one of the better beach destinations in the region. Unfortunately, exploring much of the area independently is not a safe option at this time, and there are plenty of pretty beaches further north that are perfectly safe.

Locals frequent **Laem Tachi**, a sandy cape that juts out over the northern end of Ao Pattani. It can be reached by boat taxi from Pattani pier. **Hat Talo Kapo**, 14km east of Pattani near Yaring Amphoe, is another hot spot. And although it's technically in Songkhla Province, **Thepha district**, 35km northwest of Pattani, is the most developed beach destination in the area. There you'll find a few slightly aged resorts that cater mostly to middle-class Thais. At **Hat Soi Sawan**, near the Songkhla–Pattani border, several families have set up informal beachfront restaurants that are popular with weekend visitors. To reach Thepha, hop on any Songkhla-bound bus from Pattani (or vice versa); mention the name of your resort and you'll be deposited at the side of the road for the brief walk to the beach.

Sleeping & Eating

PATTANI TOWN

CS Pattani Hotel HOTEL $$
(☎0 7333 5093; www.cspattanihotel.com; 299 Moo 4, Th Nong Jik; r/ste incl breakfast 1000-1500/2500-3500B; ❄@🛜🏊) If you are spending the night in Pattani, you might as well enjoy it. The CS Pattani features a gorgeous colonial lobby, two pools, an excellent restaurant, a sauna and steam room…the list goes on. It's located about 2km west of the centre of town.

Palace Hotel HOTEL $
(☎0 7334 9171; 10-12 Pipit Soi Talattewiwat 2; r 200-700B; ❄) Despite its location in a grubby soi near the town market, the rooms here, in particular those with air-con on the lower floors, are neat and comfortable.

Satay Jao Kao MUSLIM-THAI $
(37/20 Th Udomwithi; dishes 20-30B; ⌚10am-6pm) This well-respected open-air restaurant serves beef satay local style with cubes of rice and a sweet dipping sauce. Several other restaurants along Th Udomwithi come highly recommended by Pattani's Muslim foodies.

THEPHA DISTRICT

Sakom Cabana RESORT $$
(☎0 7431 8065; 136 Moo 4, Tambon Sakom; r 600-800B; ❄) Located about 40km from Pattani town, this basic resort features a clean compound with several attractive wooden duplex bungalows a short walk from the beach.

Information

There are several banks along the southeastern end of Th Pipit, near the Th Naklua Yarang intersection.

Internet cafe (cnr Th Peeda Talattewiwat 2 & Th Pipit; per hr 20B) Near Palace Hotel.

Pattani Hospital (☎0 7332 3411-14; Th Nong Jik)

Police station (☎0 7334 9018; Th Pattani Phirom)

Getting There & Around

Minivans are the region's most popular mode of transport and there are frequent daytime departures to Hat Yai (100B, 1½ hours), Narathiwat (100B, two hours), Songkhla (90B, 1½ hours) and Sungai Kolok (130B, 2½ hours) at various terminals around Pattani town. Ask at your hotel for the departure points. Buses to Bangkok (594B to 1187B, 15 to 16 hours) depart from the station near the CS Pattani Hotel. Local taxis can take you anywhere in town for 10B per person.

Narathiwat

นราธิวาส

POP 109,000

Sitting on the banks of the Bang Nara River, Narathiwat is probably the most Muslim large city in Thailand. Some of the Sino-Portuguese buildings lining the riverfront are over a century old, and some pleasant beaches are just outside town. Unfortunately the security situation in this part of the country (see the boxed text, p232) has suffocated the little tourism that this region used to see. Be sure to check the latest situation before travelling to Narathiwat.

Sights

Towards the southern end of Th Pichitbamrung stands **Matsayit Klang**, a wooden mosque built in the Sumatran style. It was reputedly built by a prince of the former kingdom of Pattani over a hundred years ago.

Just north of town is **Hat Narathat**, a 5km-long sandy beach fronted by towering pines, which serves as a veritable public park for locals. The beach is only 2km from the town centre – you can easily walk there or take a săhm·lór.

Five kilometres south of town, **Ao Manao** used to be a popular sun and sand destination, but today it's increasingly the stomping ground of local fishermen.

The tallest seated-Buddha image in southern Thailand is at **Wat Khao Kong**, 6km southwest on the way to the train station in Tanyongmat. The image is 17m long and 24m high, and made of reinforced concrete covered with tiny gold coloured mosaic tiles that glint magically in the sun.

Sleeping & Eating

Most of the town's accommodation is located on and around Th Puphapugdee along the Bang Nara River.

Tanyong Hotel HOTEL $$
(☎0 7351 1477; 16/1 Th Sophaphisai; r incl breakfast 900-1700B; ❄📶) A few decades ago this was undoubtedly Narathiwat's most upscale hotel, but the passing of time has rendered it a convenient and competent, although slightly overpriced, choice.

Ocean Blue Mansion HOTEL $
(☎0 7351 1109; 297 Th Puphapugdee; r 350-1500B; ❄) This hotel/apartment is the only one in town to really take advantage of the riverfront view. Rooms include a huge fridge and cable TV.

Jay Sani MUSLIM-THAI $
(50/1 Th Sophaphisai; dishes 30-60B) This is where locals go for excellent Thai-Muslim food. Point to whatever curry or stir-fry looks good, but be sure not to miss the sublime beef soup.

Ang Mo CHINESE, THAI $
(cnr Th Puphapugdee & Th Chamroonnara; dishes 30-80B; ⌚lunch & dinner) This exceedingly popular Chinese restaurant is both cheap and tasty, and has even fed the likes of members of the Thai royal family.

BORDER CROSSING: SUNGAI KOLOK TO RANTAU PANJANG

The Thai **border** (⏲5am-9pm) is about 1km from the centre of Sungai Kolok or the train station. After completing border formalities, cross the bridge to the Malaysian border post, and then to an informal transport centre, where a share taxi to Kota Bharu, the capital of Malaysia's Kelantan State, will cost about RM$8 per person (about 80B) or about RM$40 to charter the whole car yourself. The ride takes around 40 minutes. There are also buses to Kota Bharu for RM$4.50, taking about an hour.

It's possible to continue south by the so-called 'jungle train', but the closest station is at Pasir Mas, located along taxi/bus routes to Kota Bharu.

Tak Bai, also in Narathiwat, and Betong, further south in Yala, are also legal crossing points for foreign tourists, but the abundance of transport and other infrastructure makes Sungai Kolok–Rantau Panjang the area's most convenient crossing point.

Information

The **Tourism Authority of Thailand office** (TAT; ☎nationwide call centre 1672, Narathiwat 0 7352 2411) is inconveniently located a few kilometres south of town, just across the bridge on the road to Tak Bai.

Getting There & Around

Air Asia (☎nationwide call centre 02 515 9999; www.airasia.com; Narathiwat Airport) and **Nok Air** (☎nationwide call centre 1318; www.nokair.co.th; Narathiwat Airport) each operate a daily flight to and from Bangkok (from 1790B, 90 minutes).

Air-con buses to Bangkok and Phuket and most minivans leave from the **bus terminal** (☎0 7351 1552) 2km south of town on Th Rangae Munka. Buses to Phuket (530B, 12 hours), which originate in Sungai Kolok, pass Narathiwat three times daily at 7am, 9am and 6.30pm, and continue via Pattani, Hat Yai, Songkhla, Trang, Krabi and Phang-Nga. Buses to Bangkok (669B to 1296B, 15 hours) depart several times during the day.

Minivans heading to Hat Yai (150B, three hours), Pattani (100B, two hours), Songkhla (150B, two hours), Sungai Kolok (70B, one hour) and Yala (100B, 1½ hours) generally leave on an hourly basis from 5am to 5pm.

Narathiwat is small enough to navigate by foot, although motorcycle taxis only charge 20B to get around.

Sungai Kolok สุไหงโกลก

POP 70,000

Although Narathiwat is officially the provincial capital, it's a skinny wimp compared to its bigger and brasher sibling, Sungai Kolok. This soulless border town is the main southern coastal gateway between Malaysia and Thailand, and the primary industries here revolve around border trade and catering to weekending Malaysian men who are often looking for sex. Every night Soi Phuthon and the small strip behind the Marina Hotel come alive with booming bars that make Pattaya or Patong look sedate in comparison.

Sleeping & Eating

If you must stay the night in Sungai Kolok, there's a large assortment of hotels to choose from – most cater to the 'by-the-hour' clientele.

Unfortunately, despite the mix of cultures and emphasis on tourism, Sungai Kolok is definitely not a culinary destination. A small **night market** unfolds next to the immigration office – exceptionally good and cheap eats can be got at the stall in the centre that only has Chinese writing.

Genting Hotel HOTEL $$
(☎0 7361 3231; 250 Th Asia 18; r 620-720B, ste 1520B; ❄📶🏊) Geared towards the conference trade, the Genting comes equipped with a pub and a karaoke lounge. There are some good, only slightly scuffed, midrange rooms, and it's away from the seedier areas.

Merlin Hotel HOTEL $
(☎0 7361 8111; 68 Th Charoenkhet; r 480-700B; ❄) Don't let the lobby fool you – the rooms here are very plain indeed, but the Merlin's a good choice if you need a cheap room with a view.

Information

In addition to the one at the border, there is an **immigration office** (☎0 7361 1231; Th Charoenkhet; ⏲8.30am-4.30pm Mon-Fri) across from the Merlin Hotel. A tourist police office sits at the border. There are plenty of banks with

ATMs in town as well as foreign-exchange booths, which are open during border-crossing hours.

CS Internet (Th Asia 18; internet per hr 20B; ⌚10am-9pm) Across from the Genting Hotel.

Getting There & Away

Bus & Minivan

The long-distance **bus station** (☎0 7361 2045) is located east of downtown, from where there are three daily air-con buses for the 18-hour trip to Bangkok (720B to 1400B) between 9pm and 10pm. There are two early-morning buses that head to Phuket (580B), stopping in Krabi (460B) along the way. Minivans to Narathiwat (80B, one hour) depart on the half-hour from across from the train station. Minivans heading to Pattani (130B, 2½ hours), Yala (90B) and Hat Yai (180B, four hours) depart hourly during daylight hours, from in front of the Genting Hotel.

Train

Two daily trains connect Sungai Kolok to Bangkok (200B to 1753B, about 20 hours, departures at 11.30am and 2.20pm). Local trains also make stops in Surat Thani, Nakhon Si Thammarat and Hat Yai; to check timetables and prices for other destinations contact the **State Railway of Thailand** (☎nationwide call centre 1690; www.railway.co.th) or look at their website.

Getting Around

Motorcycle taxis zoom around town – it'll cost you around 30B to make the ride between the city centre and the border.

Phuket & the Northern Andaman Coast

Includes »

Best Places to Eat

» Rum Jungle (p253)
» Ka Jok See (p249)
» Tatonka (p268)
» Mama's Restaurant (p292)
» Cook (p249)

Best Places to Stay

» Six Senses Hideaway (p298)
» Mom Tri's Villa Royale (p255)
» Twin Palms (p266)
» Phuket 346 (p248)
» Nangthong Beach Resort (p292)

Why Go?

Whether you've got designer-villa wishes, bamboo-hut desires or something in between, the northern Andaman coast serves it up hot with a shot of turquoise ocean to wash it down. Phuket, on the southern extremity, is the audacious starlet of the region, flaunting glitzy five-star hotels that grace ultrawhite beaches. Here sleep is an afterthought to parties, water sports and spa pampering. Ranong, to the far north, is a mix of Burmese and Thais who eke out a living in a dusty frontier removed from the tourist industry. Travel the 300km between Ranong and Phuket, and you'll see it all: Muslim and Moken stilt villages and vertical limestone karsts, resorts out of the pages of *Architectural Digest* and bays abuzz with jet skis, tangled mangrove swamps and skittish clouds of swallows.

When to Go

May to October is the rainy season. At this time, the sea swells kick up surf, many resorts close and others slash their prices. The Vegetarian Festival is held in late September or October and involves parades of pierced-face worshippers, endless firecrackers and great meatless food.

December to January is the high season for tourism. Prices soar, and accommodation and transport need to be booked in advance.

PHUKET PROVINCE

The island of Phuket has long been misunderstood. Firstly, the 'h' is silent. Ahem. And secondly, Phuket doesn't feel like an island at all. It's so huge (the biggest in Thailand) that you rarely get the sense that you're surrounded by water, which is probably the reason why the 'Ko' (meaning 'island') was dropped from its name. Dubbed the 'pearl of the Andaman' by marketing execs, this is Thailand's original flavour of tailor-made fun in the sun.

The island's 'sin city' of Patong is the biggest town and busiest beach. It's the ultimate gong show where podgy beach-aholics sizzle off their hangovers and go-go girls play ping-pong...without paddles. But ultimately the island's affinity for luxury far outshines its other stereotypes. Jet-setters come through in droves, getting pummelled during swanky spa sessions and swigging sundowners at one of the many fashion-forward nightspots. And you don't have to be an heiress to tap into Phuket's trendy to-do list. There's deep-sea diving, high-end dining, and white beaches that beckon you and your book – whatever your heart desires.

Activities

Diving & Snorkelling

Phuket enjoys an enviable central location relative to the Andaman's top diving destinations. The much-talked-about Similan Islands sit to the north, while dozens of dive sites orbit Ko Phi-Phi (p317) and Ko Lanta (p325) to the south. Of course, this means that trips from Phuket to these awesome destinations cost slightly more than from places closer to the sites since you'll be forking over extra dough for your boat's petrol. Most operators on Phuket take divers to the nine decent sites orbiting the island, like Ko Raya Noi and Ko Raya Yai (also called Ko Racha Noi and Ko Racha Yai), but these spots rank lower on the wow-o-meter. The reef off the southern tip of Raya Noi is the best spot, particularly good for experienced divers, with soft corals and pelagic fish species aplenty. Manta and marble rays are also frequently glimpsed here and, if you're lucky, you might even see a whale shark.

Typical one-day dive trips to nearby sites cost around 3500B, including two dives and equipment. Nondivers (and snorkellers) are permitted to join these trips for a significant discount. PADI Open Water certification courses cost around 15,000B for three days of instruction and equipment hire.

Snorkelling is best along Phuket's western coast, particularly at the rocky headlands between beaches. Mask, snorkel and fins can be rented for around 250B a day. As with scuba diving, you'll find better snorkelling, with greater visibility and variety of marine life, along the shores of small outlying islands such as Ko Raya Yai and Ko Raya Noi.

As is the case elsewhere in the Andaman Sea, the best diving months are December to May when the weather is good and the sea is smooth and clear.

Recommended diving and snorkelling centres on Phuket include the following:

Sea Fun Divers DIVING
(off Map p260; ☎0 7634 0480; www.seafundivers.com; 29 Soi Karon Nui, Patong) An outstanding and very professional diving operation. Standards are extremely high and service is impeccable. There's an office at Le Meridien resort in Patong, and a second location at Katathani Resort (p255) in Kata Noi.

Offspray Leisure DIVING, SNORKELLING
(☎08 1894 1274; www.offsprayleisure.com; 43/87 Chalong Plaza, Chalong; trips from 2950B) A dive and snorkelling excursion company specialising in small-load, intimate trips to the reefs around Ko Phi-Phi.

Oi's Longtail SNORKELLING
(☎08 1978 5728; 66 Moo 3, Hat Nai Yang; tours 1600B) Oi specialises in two-hour snorkelling tours of the reefs around Ko Waeo. Located at Bank Restaurant, opposite the long-tail boat harbour.

Dive Asia DIVING
(Map p256; ☎0 7633 0598; www.diveasia.com; 24 Th Karon, Kata) There is a second location at 623 Th Karon near Hat Karon.

Adrenalin Sports

Cable Jungle Adventures ADVENTURE SPORTS
(Map p242; ☎08 1977 4904; 232/17 Moo 8, Th Bansuanneramit; per person 1600B; ⏰9am-6pm) Tucked into the hills behind a quilt of pineapple fields, rubber plantations and mango groves is this maze of eight zip lines linking cliffs to ancient ficus trees. The zips range from 6m to 23m above the ground and the longest run is 100m long. Closed-toe shoes are a must.

Jungle Bungy Jump ADVENTURE SPORTS
(Map p242; ☎0 7632 1351; www.phuketbungy.com; 61/3 Moo 6, Kathu; jump 1600B) In operation

Phuket & the Northern Andaman Coast Highlights

1. Staying at an over-the-top luxury spa resort on **Phuket** (p239)
2. Enjoying unmentionably wild nights in **Patong** (p262)
3. Searching for monkeys in the Jurassic Park of **Khao Sok** (p288)
4. Kayaking the surreal green waters of **Ao Phang-Nga** (p295) to empty coves
5. Catching up on your reading on a quiet **Ko Phayam** (p273) beach
6. Exploring the enchanting Sino-Portuguese architecture of the newly restored cafes, shops and galleries around **Phuket Town** (p248)
7. Snorkelling, diving or simply exploring the psychedelically green and blue **Surin** (p278) and **Similan Islands** (p293)
8. Learning first hand about fishing-village culture during a homestay with a community-based tourism project like **Andaman Discoveries** (p278)
9. Beach-bumming, cycling and relaxing to the max without all the tourist hype on **Ko Yao Noi** (p297)

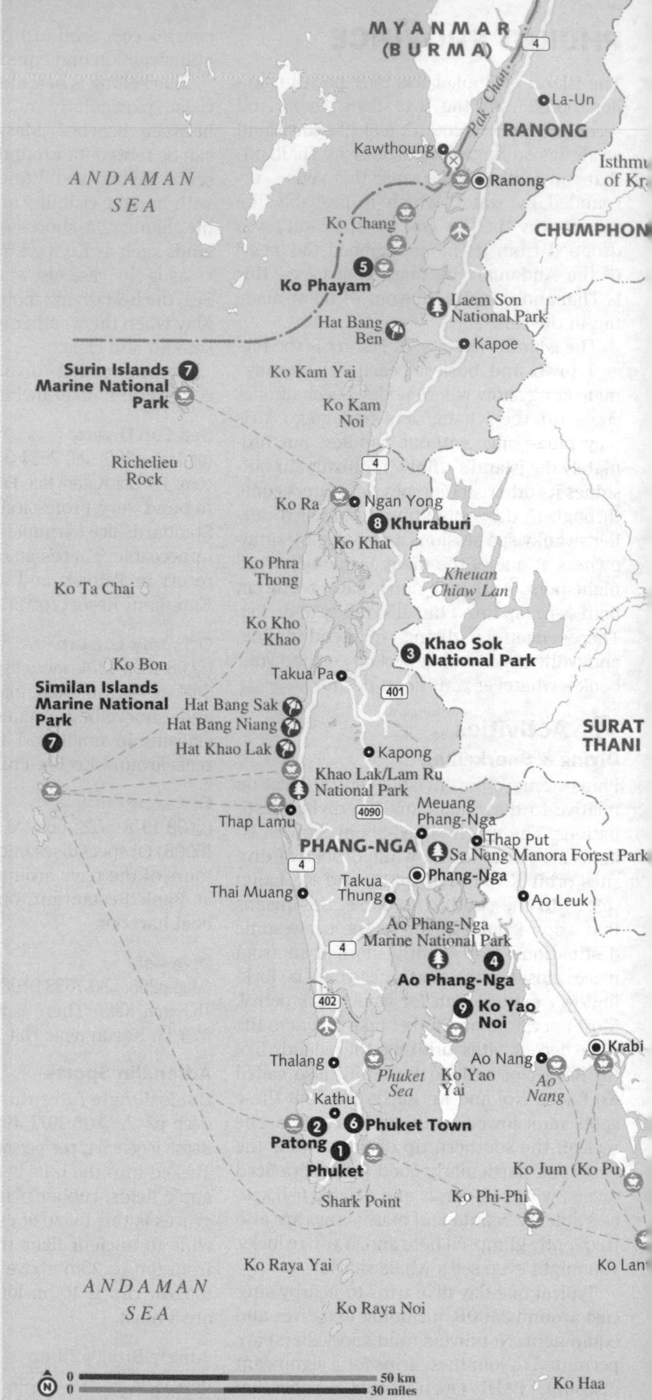

PHUKET FOR CHILDREN

There's plenty for kids to do on Phuket. And while the seedier face of the sex industry is on full show in Patong (we wouldn't bring our kids there, although many people do), the rest of the island is fairly G-rated.

Elephant treks are always a big hit with kids, with the best options available on the Kata-Hat Nai Han road. **Phuket Aquarium** (p252) and a visit to the tiny **Phuket Gibbon Rehabilitation Centre** (p270) are also terrific animal-themed activities that are sure to please.

The main family-flogged feature of Phuket is **Phuket Fantasea** (p264), which is a pricey extravaganza of animals, costumes, song, special effects, pyrotechnics and a lousy dinner.

Other fun activities include the following:

Splash Jungle (Map p242; ☎0 7637 2111; www.splashjunglewaterpark.com; Mai Khao; adult/5-12yr/under 5yr 1500/750B/free) The biggest water park in Thailand has a wave pool, a play pool with tipping buckets and water cannons, 12 very cool water slides for all ages, and a sauna and bar for mum and dad. The price includes pick-up at your resort.

Dino Park (Map p256; ☎0 7633 0625; www.dinopark.com; Th Patak West, Karon; adult/child 240/180B; ⏲10am-midnight) Jurassic Park meets minigolf at this bizarre park on the southern edge of Hat Karon. It's a maze of caves, lagoons, leafy gardens, dinosaur statues and, of course, putting greens.

since 1992, this 20-storey bungy jump inland from Patong is built and operated to Kiwi standards. Jumpers have the option to dunk in the water, leap in pairs or experience the Rocket Man, where you'll be shot 50m into the air, then do the bungy thing on the way down.

Horse Riding

Phuket Riding Club (Map p242; ☎0 7628 8213; www.phuketridingclub.com; 95 Th Viset, Rawai) offers one-hour (per person 800B) and two-hour (1500B) rides in the jungle around Rawai and along nearby beaches.

Sea Kayaking

Several companies based on Phuket offer canoe tours of scenic Ao Phang-Nga (see p294). Kayaks can enter semisubmerged caves inaccessible to long-tail boats. A day paddle costs from 3950B per person including meals, equipment and transfer. Many outfits also run all-inclusive, three-day (from 13,700B) or six-day (from 27,100B) kayak/camping trips.

TOP CHOICE **John Gray's Seacanoe** KAYAKING
(off Map p247; ☎0 7625 4505-7; www.johngray-seacanoe.com; 124 Soi 1, Th Yaowarat) The original, still the most reputable and by far the most ecologically sensitive company on the island. Like any good brand in Thailand, John Gray's 'Seacanoe' name and itineraries have been frequently copied. Located north of Phuket Town.

Paddle Asia KAYAKING
(☎0 7621 6145; www.paddleasia.com; 9/71 Moo 3, Th Rasdanusorn, Ban Kuku) Another popular company that caters to small groups, Paddle Asia offers several day and multi-day trips to Ao Phang-Nga and Khao Sok National Park on classic kayaks rather than sit-on-tops or inflatables.

Surfing

Phuket is an undercover surf destination. Once the monsoons bring their midyear swell, glassy seas fold into barrels. The best waves arrive between June and September, when annual competitions are held in Kata and Kalim. **Phuket Surf** (www.phuketsurf.com) is based in Kata, at the south end of the bay near the best break, which typically tops out at 2m. Hat Nai Han can get bigger waves (up to 3m) near the yacht club. Be warned: both Kata and Nai Han have vicious undertows that can claim lives.

Hat Kalim, just north of Patong, is sheltered and has a consistent break that also gets up to 3m. This is a hollow wave, and is considered the best break on the island. The **Phuket Boardriders Club** (www.phuketboardriders.com) sponsors an August contest here. Kamala's northernmost beach has a nice 3m beach break, and Laem Singh, just up the

Phuket

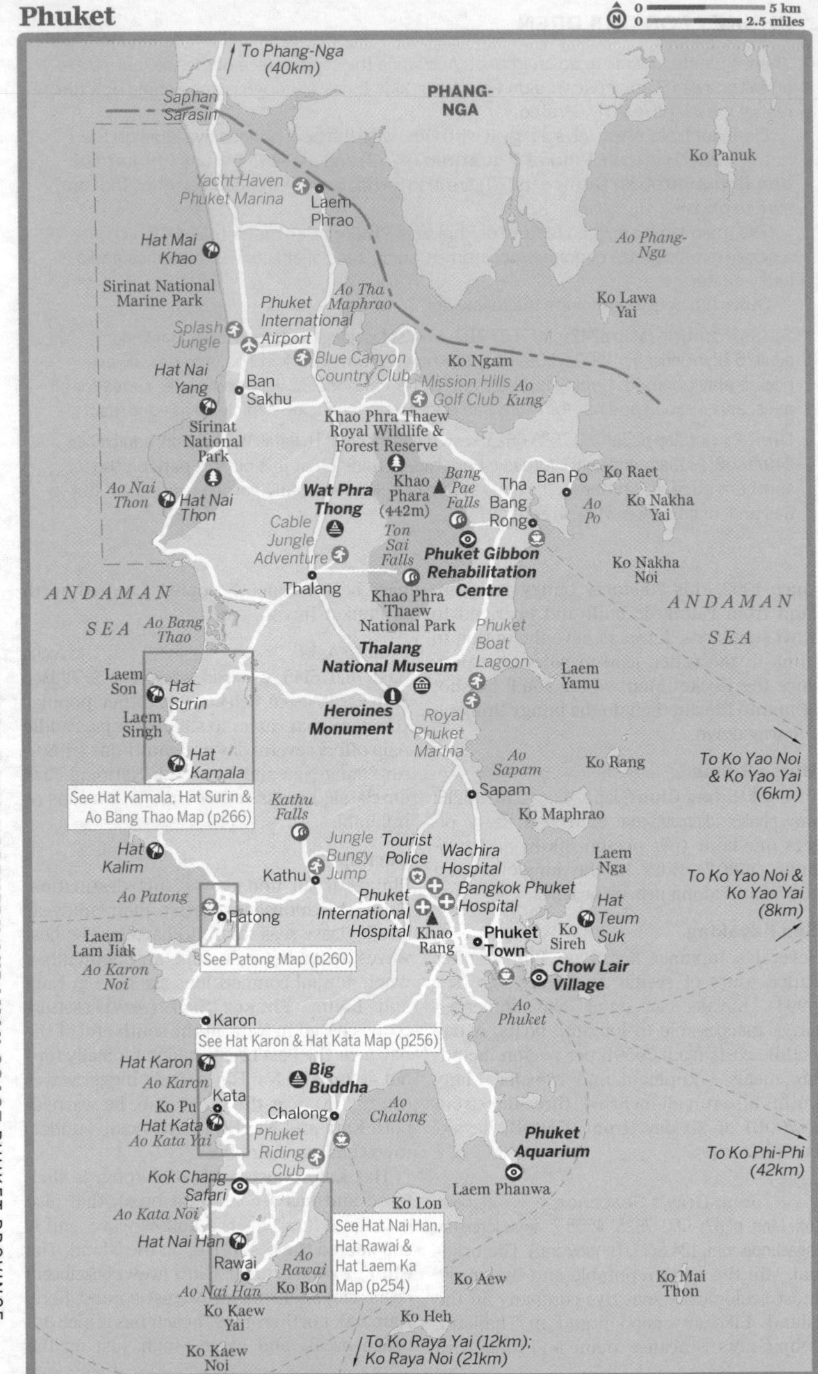
0 5 km
0 2.5 miles
To Phang-Nga (40km)
PHANG-NGA
Saphan Sarasin
Ko Panuk
Yacht Haven Phuket Marina
Laem Phrao
Hat Mai Khao
Ao Phang-Nga
Sirinat National Marine Park
Phuket International Airport
Ao Tha Maphrao
Ko Lawa Yai
Splash Jungle
Blue Canyon Country Club
Ko Ngam
Hat Nai Yang
Ban Sakhu
Mission Hills Golf Club
Ao Kung
Sirinat National Park
Khao Phra Thaew Royal Wildlife & Forest Reserve
Ban Po
Ko Raet
Ao Nai Thon
Hat Nai Thon
Wat Phra Thong
Khao Phara (442m)
Bang Pae Falls
Tha Bang Rong
Ao Po
Ko Nakha Yai
Cable Jungle Adventure
Ton Sai Falls
Phuket Gibbon Rehabilitation Centre
Ko Nakha Noi
Thalang
Khao Phra Thaew National Park
ANDAMAN SEA
Ao Bang Thao
Phuket Boat Lagoon
ANDAMAN SEA
Thalang National Museum
Laem Yamu
Laem Son
Hat Surin
Laem Singh
Heroines Monument
Royal Phuket Marina
Hat Kamala
Ao Sapam
Ko Rang
To Ko Yao Noi & Ko Yao Yai (6km)
Sapam
See Hat Kamala, Hat Surin & Ao Bang Thao Map (p266)
Kathu Falls
Ko Maphrao
Hat Kalim
Jungle Bungy Jump
Tourist Police
Wachira Hospital
Laem Nga
Kathu
To Ko Yao Noi & Ko Yao Yai (8km)
Ao Patong
Phuket International Hospital
Bangkok Phuket Hospital
Hat Teum Suk
Patong
Khao Rang
Phuket Town
Ko Sireh
Laem Lam Jiak
See Patong Map (p260)
Chow Lair Village
Ao Karon Noi
Ao Phuket
Karon
See Hat Karon & Hat Kata Map (p256)
Hat Karon
Ao Karon
Big Buddha
Kata
Ko Pu
Ao Chalong
Chalong
Hat Kata
Ao Kata Yai
Phuket Riding Club
Phuket Aquarium
To Ko Phi-Phi (42km)
Kok Chang Safari
Laem Phanwa
Ao Kata Noi
Ko Lon
See Hat Nai Han, Hat Rawai & Hat Laem Ka Map (p254)
Hat Nai Han
Rawai
Ao Rawai
Ko Aew
Ko Mai Thon
Ao Nai Han
Ko Bon
Ko Kaew Yai
Ko Heh
To Ko Raya Yai (12km); Ko Raya Noi (21km)
Ko Kaew Noi

TOP FIVE PHUKET SPAS

There seems to be a massage shop on every corner on Phuket. Most are low-key family affairs where traditional Thai massage goes for about 250B per hour, and a basic mani-pedi costs around 150B – a real steal. The quality of service at these places varies, and changes rapidly as staff turnover is high. Go with your gut instinct or ask fellow travellers or your hotel staff for recommendations. No matter where you choose, it's still a massage and likely to be extremely pleasant and relaxing – especially if it's sporting a wood-fired herbal sauna on the premises..

If you're looking for a more Western spa experience, head to one of Phuket's plentiful spa resorts. These places are often affiliated with a ritzy hotel (but nearly all are open to nonguests). They are *haute couture* affairs with sumptuous Zen designs and huge treatment menus. Prices vary depending on location, but treatments generally start at around 1000B.

Here are our top five Phuket spa picks:

Bua Luang Spa This spa at the Anantara Phuket (p269) combines the best of Thai and Ayurvedic healing traditions. Why not follow that Turmeric Body Scrub with a Thai Herbal Compress Massage?

Six Senses Spa Sublimely back-to-nature in setting, yet cutting-edge as far as treatments are concerned, is this spa based at the Evason Phuket Resort (p253). Try the Energising Journey (three hours, 7600B), which includes a body toner, an energiser massage and foot acupressure.

Sala Resort & Spa Get wrapped in Asian White Clay (2000B) or detoxifying seaweed (2500B) and follow it with a Tri Phase Stone Therapy Massage (2900B) at the Sala Resort & Spa (p269).

Hideaway Day Spa One of Phuket's first spas, the Hideaway (p267) still enjoys an excellent reputation. More reasonably priced than many hotel counterparts, it offers treatments in a tranquil setting by a lagoon.

Raintree Spa Another reasonably good, refreshing choice is located at Sino House (p248) in Phuket Town. When locals crave spa therapy (massages 500B to 1000B) they come here.

coast in front of the Amanpuri, gets very big and fast, plus it's sheltered from wind by the massive headland.

Hat Nai Yang has a consistent if soft wave that breaks more than 200m offshore. Swells get up to 3m high and there is no undertow.

There are a few surf shops with boards for rent:

Phuket Surf SURFING

(Map p256; ☎08 7889 7308, 08 1684 8902; www.phuketsurf.com) On Hat Kata Yai's southern cove; offers surf lessons starting at 1500B for a half-day, as well as board rentals for 100/300B per hour/day. Check its website for more info about local surf breaks.

Phuket Surfing SURFING

(Map p256; ☎0 7628 4183; www.phuketsurfing.com) Just in front of Phuket Surf and sharing a roof with Nautilus dive, it rents boards by the hour for 100B to 150B.

Kiteboarding

One of the world's fastest growing sports is also one of Phuket's latest fads. The three best spots are Hat Nai Yang, Karon (in the low season) and Rawai (ideal conditions for beginners in the high season). Phuket's two kiteboarding outfitters are both affiliated with the International Kiteboarding Organization (think: PADI for kites).

Kiteboarding Asia WATER SPORTS

(Map p256; ☎08 1591 4594; www.kiteboardingasia.com; lessons from 4000B) Its main office is on Hat Nai Yang, but it has a kiosk on the south end of Hat Karon that's open in the low season. It also offers lessons off Rawai's Friendship Beach.

Kite Zone WATER SPORTS

(Map p254; ☎08 3395 2005; www.kitesurfingphuket.com; beginner lessons from 1100B) With locations in Nai Yang and Rawai, it is the younger, hipper of the two schools, with a tremendous perch on Friendship Beach.

PHUKET'S MOO·AY TAI EXPLOSION *ADAM SKOLNICK*

Over the past few years, spurred in no small part by the increasing global presence and popularity of mixed martial arts, several *moo·ay tai* (Thai boxing; also spelled *muay thai*) gyms catering to international male and female athletes have sprouted off the beach in Phuket. Based on the original *moo·ay tai* camp concept, fighters live and train on site with seasoned *moo·ay tai* professionals.

The whole thing started with Pricha 'Tuk' Chokkuea and his gym, **Rawai Muay Thai** (Map p254; ☎08 1476 9377; www.rawaimuaythai.com; 43/42 Moo 7, Th Sai Yuan). He and former business partner Danny Avison, a Phuket-based triathlete, decided to train tourists as a fundraising mechanism so Tuk could also train impoverished, up-and-coming Thai fighters, without dipping deeply into their fight purse (the traditional *moo·ay tai* business model, and something Tuk always resented). For years his was the only gym around, but in Rawai alone there are now more than half-a-dozen gyms. The best new gym is Avison's **Promthep Muay Thai Camp** (☎08 5786 2414; www.promthepmuaythai.com; 91 Moo 6, Soi Yanui). In addition to training fighters, Avison has a tremendous multisport cross-training weight-loss program. Wherever you enter the ring, be warned: this is no wussie watered-down-for-Westerners theme-park ride. Prepare to sweat, cringe, grapple and bleed. If you're the real deal, maybe you'll even win a fight under the Bang-la Stadium lights?

Courses range in length from an hour to five days.

Yachting

Phuket is one of Southeast Asia's main yachting destinations, and you'll find all manner of crafts anchored along its shores – from 80-year-old wooden sloops to the latest in hi-tech motor cruisers.

Marina-style facilities with year-round anchorage are presently available at a few locations:

Phuket Boat Lagoon BOATING
(Map p242; ☎0 7623 9055, fax 0 7623 9056) Located at Ao Sapam on the eastern shore, about 10km north of Phuket Town. It offers an enclosed marina with tidal channel access, serviced pontoon berths, 60- and 120-tonne travel lifts, a hard-stand area, plus a resort hotel, laundry, coffee shop, fuel, water, repairs and maintenance services.

Royal Phuket Marina BOATING
(Map p242; ☎0 7637 9397; www.royalphuketmarina.com) The US$25 million Royal Phuket Marina is located just south of Phuket Boat Lagoon. It's more luxurious with shiny new townhouses, upscale restaurants and a convention centre overlooking 190 berths.

Yacht Haven Phuket Marina BOATING
(Map p242; ☎0 7620 6704; www.yacht-haven-phuket.com) This marina is at Laem Phrao on the northeastern tip. The Yacht Haven boasts 130 berths with deep-water access and a scenic restaurant. It also does yacht maintenance.

Port clearance is rather complicated; the marinas will take care of the paperwork (for a fee, of course) if notified of your arrival in advance. Expect to pay from 17,000B per day for a high-season, bareboat charter.

For information on yacht charters (both bareboat and crewed), contact the following:

Asia Marine (www.asia-marine.net; Yacht Haven Phuket Marina)

Tawan Cruises (☎08 8194 3234; www.tawancruises.com)

If you're interested in a more affordable sailing trip, seek out **Phuket Sail Tours** (☎08 7897 0492; www.phuketsailtours.com; Ao Por). Its day trips through Ao Phang-Nga (3000B all-inclusive) come highly recommended.

Golf

Blue Canyon Country Club GOLF
(Map p242; ☎0 7632 8088; www.bluecanyonclub.com; 165 Moo 1, Th Thepkasatri; 18 holes 5300B) A luxury country club with two championship golf courses that have hosted two dramatic (and one record-setting) Tiger Woods tournament wins. There is also a full-service spa, two restaurants and luxury apartments on the property. The facilities are showing their age, but you'll come for the golf course.

Mission Hills Golf Club GOLF
(Map p242; ☎0 7631 0888; www.missionhillsphuket.com; 195 Moo 4, Pla Khlok; 18 holes 3800B)

Twenty-seven more holes of tournament-calibre golf can be found at this Jack Nicklaus-designed course near the east coast. It, too, has a spa and hotel rooms and two swimming pools.

Volunteering

Soi Dog Foundation (☎08 7050 8688; www.soidog.org) is a well-organised unit aimed at sterilising, providing medical care for and feeding stray dogs. Check the website for updates and details, or turn to p406 for more information about volunteering.

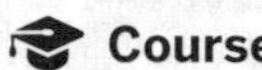

Courses

Mom Tri's Boathouse COOKING
(☎0 7633 0015; www.boathousephuket.com; 2/2 Th Kata (Patak West), Hat Kata) Offers a fantastic weekend Thai cooking class (per person one day/weekend 2200/3500B) with its renowned chef, Rattana. See also p255.

Blue Elephant Restaurant & Cookery School COOKING
(Map p247; ☎0 7635 4355; www.blueelephant.com; 96 Th Krabi, Phuket Town; half-day classes 2800B) Phuket's newest cookery school is in the stunning restored 1903 Sino-Portuguese style Phra Phitak Chyn Pracha Mansion (see p248). There are a variety of options from short group lessons to five day private training (78,000B). Morning classes include a market visit.

Phuket Thai Cookery School COOKING
(☎0 7625 2354; www.phuketthaicookeryschool.com; Ko Sireh; ⏲8.30am-5pm) Get intimate with aromatic Thai spices at this popular cooking school set on a quiet seafront plot on Ko Sireh's east coast. Courses (per day 2500B to 2900B) can last up to six hours. It provides hotel pick-ups, market tours and a cookbook.

Pum Thai Cooking School COOKING
(Map p260; ☎0 7634 6269; www.pumthaifoodchain.com; 204/32 Tha Rat Uthit, Hat Patong) This restaurant chain (with three locations in Thailand and two in France) holds several daily one- to six-hour classes (per person 4650B). Longer classes begin with a market tour and end with a meal.

Tours

It's not hard to find elephant rides and 4WD tours of the island's interior, though none of those will win their way into the hearts of animal-rights activists or environmentalists. So why not take a bike ride? **Amazing Bike Tours** (☎0 7628 3436; www.amazingbiketoursthailand.asia; 32/4 Moo 9, Th Chaofa, Chalong; day trips from 1600B), Phuket's best new adventure outfitter, leads small groups on half-day bicycle tours through the Khao Phra Thaew Royal Wildlife & Forest Reserve, and offers terrific day trips around Ko Yao Noi and the gorgeous beaches and waterfalls of Thai Muang in nearby Phang-Nga province.

Information

Dangers & Annoyances

During the May to October monsoon, large waves and fierce undertows sometimes make it too dangerous to swim. Dozens of drownings occur every year on Phuket's beaches, especially on Laem Singh, Kamala and Karon. Red flags are posted to warn bathers of serious rip tides.

Keep an eye out for jet skis when you are in the water. Although the Phuket governor declared jet skis illegal in 1997, enforcement of the ban is another issue.

Renting a motorcycle or motorbike can be a high-risk proposition. Thousands of people are injured or killed every year on Phuket's highways. If you must rent one, make sure you at least know the basics and wear a helmet.

There have been recent late-night motorbike muggings and stabbings on the road leading from Patong to Hat Karon, and on the road between Kata and the Rawai–Hat Nai Han area. There have also been a few recent random sexual assaults on women. Women should think twice before sunbathing topless (a big no-no in Thailand anyway) or alone, especially on an isolated beach. It can also be dangerous to run alone at night or early in the morning.

Medical Services

Local hospitals are equipped with modern facilities, emergency rooms and outpatient-care clinics. Both of the following have hyperbaric chambers:

Bangkok Phuket Hospital (Map p242; ☎0 7625 4425; www.phukethospital.com; Th Yongyok Uthit) Reputedly the favourite with locals.

Phuket International Hospital (Map p242; ☎0 7624 9400; www.phuketinternationalhospital.com; Th Chalermprakiat) International doctors rate this hospital as the best on the island.

Tourist Information

The weekly English-language *Phuket Gazette* publishes information on activities, events, dining and entertainment around the island, as well as the latest scandals. It can be accessed online at www.phuketgazette.net.

Websites

Jamie's Phuket (www.jamie-monk.com) A fun insider's blog written by a long-time Phuket expat resident with excellent photos and travel tips.

One Stop Phuket (www.1stopphuket.com) A user-friendly travel guide and internet booking referral service.

Phuket Dot Com (www.phuket.com) Offers a sophisticated compendium of many kinds of information, including accommodation on the island.

 Getting There & Away

Air

Phuket International Airport (☎0 7632 7230) is 30km northwest of Phuket Town and it takes around 45 minutes to an hour to reach the southern beaches from here.

Some regional airline carriers:

Air Asia (www.airasia.com) Serves Phuket beautifully. In addition to several daily Bangkok flights (around 1480B), it also flies direct to Hong Kong (5000B), Chiang Mai (1600B), Singapore (1400B), Bali (2730B) and more.

Bangkok Airways (off Map p247; ☎0 7622 5033; www.bangkokair.com; 58/2-3 Th Yaowarat) Has daily flights to Ko Samui (2380B), Bangkok (1725B) and more.

Nok Air (www.nokair.com) Links Phuket with Bangkok.

Thai Airways International (THAI; Map p247; ☎0 7621 1195; www.thaiairways.com; 78/1 Th Ranong, Phuket Town) Operates around seven daily flights to Bangkok (from around 3000B) with connections to/from several other cities in Thailand, as well as international destinations.

Several international airlines fly to Phuket and have offices in Phuket Town, including the following:

Dragonair (Map p247; ☎0 7621 5734; Th Phang-Nga, Phuket Town)

Malaysia Airlines (off Map p247; ☎0 7621 6675; 1/8-9 Th Thungkha, Phuket Town)

Silk Air (Map p247; ☎0 7621 3891; www.silkair.com; 183/103 Th Phang-Nga, Phuket Town)

Ferry & Speedboat

Phuket's Tha Rasada, north of Phuket Town, is the main pier for boats to Ko Phi-Phi (for more info see p323), connecting onward to Krabi, Ko Lanta, the Trang Islands, Ko Lipe and even as far as Langkawi Island in Malaysia (where there are further ferry connections to Penang). For quicker service to Krabi and Ao Nang via the Ko Yao Islands, boats leave from Tha Bang Bong north of Tha Rasada; see p310 for more details.

METERED TAXIS

To escape Phuket's 'taxi mafia' (an organisation of overpriced chartered cars that are often the only means of transport in the beach areas) get the phone number of a metered taxi and use the same driver throughout your stay in Phuket. The easiest way to do this is to take a metered taxi from the airport (one of the only places where you'll find them) when you arrive, then take down your driver's phone number. Metered taxis are found about 50m to the right as you exit the arrivals hall.

Minivan

Phuket travel agencies all around the island sell tickets (including ferry fare) for air-con minivans down to Ko Samui and Ko Pha-Ngan. Air-con minivan services to Krabi, Ranong, Trang, Surat Thani and several other locations are also available. Prices are slightly more than the buses, which all stop in Phuket Town (see p251).

 Getting Around

Local Phuket transport is terrible. The systems in place make tourists either stay on their chosen beach, rent a car or motorbike (which can be hazardous) or take overpriced private car 'taxis' or túk-túk (pronounced *dúk dúk*). There are sŏrng·tăa·ou (passenger pick-up trucks) which run to the beaches from Phuket Town but often you'll have to go via Phuket Town to get from one beach to another (say Hat Surin to Hat Patong), which can take hours. See the Getting Around sections of individual beaches for taxi and sŏrng·tăa·ou details.

Phuket Town

เมืองภูเก็ต

POP 94,325

Long before tourist T-shirts or flip-flops, Phuket was an island of rubber trees, tin mines and cash-hungry merchants. Attracting entrepreneurs from as far away as the Arabian Peninsula, China, India and Portugal, Phuket Town was a colourful blend of cultural influences, cobbled together by tentative compromise and cooperation. Today the city is proof of the island's historical soul. Wander down streets clogged with Sino-Portuguese architecture housing arty coffee shops, galleries, wonderful inexpensive restaurants and hip little guest houses;

Phuket Town

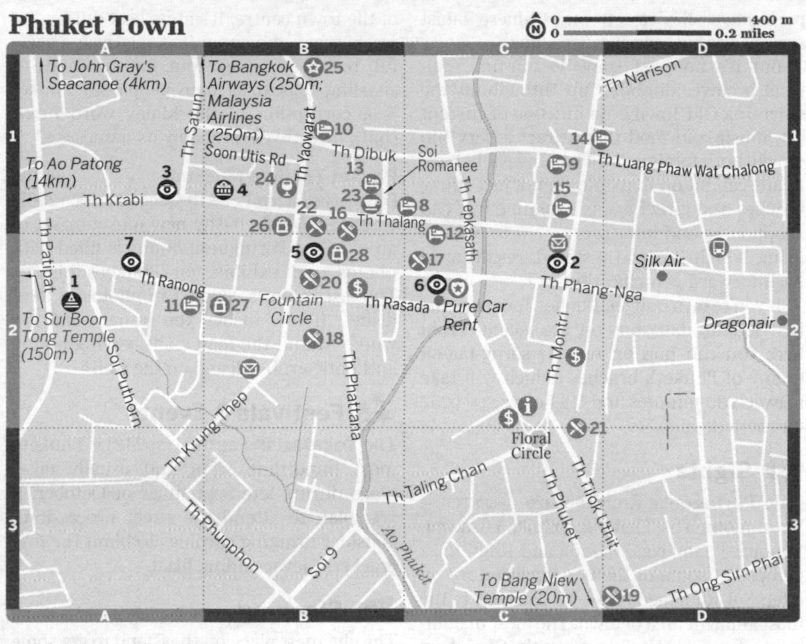

Phuket Town

Sights

1 Jui Tui Temple........A2
2 Old Post Office Building........C2
3 Phra Phitak Chyn Pracha Mansion........A1
Phuket Philatelic Museum........(see 2)
4 Phuket Thaihua Museum........B1
5 Shrine of the Serene Light........B2
6 Standard Chartered Bank........C2
7 THAI Office........A2

Activities, Courses & Tours

Blue Elephant Restaurant & Cookery School........(see 3)
Raintree Spa........(see 14)

Sleeping

8 99 Old Town Boutique Guesthouse........C1
9 Baan Suwantawe........C1
10 Casa 104........B1
11 Chinotel........A2
12 D's Corner & Guesthouse........C2
13 Phuket 346........B1
14 Sino House........C1
15 Sleep Sheep Phuket Hostel........C1

Eating

16 China Inn........B1
17 Cook........C2
18 Ka Jok See........B2
19 La Gaetana........D3
20 Siam Indigo........B2
21 Uptown Restaurant........C3
22 Wilai........B1

Drinking

23 Bo(ok)hemian........B1
24 Saneha........B1

Entertainment

25 Timber Hut........B1

Shopping

26 Ban Boran Textiles........B1
27 Day Market........B2
28 Southwind Books........B2

peek down alleyways to find Chinese Taoist shrines shrouded in incense smoke.

But it's not just some lost-in-time cultural archive. Bubbling up throughout the emerging Old Town is an infusion of current art, music and food that attract a very hip crowd, both foreign and Thai. Investors have finally caught on that culture, not just slinky beaches and girly bars, is a commodity. Old shophouses and homes, once left to rot, are being bought up and restored, resulting in flash-forward gentrification.

If you're on a budget, Phuket Town has the best lodging bargains on the island. From here you can hop on regular sŏrng·tăa·ou to any of Phuket's beaches (which will take between 30 minutes and 1½ hours; see p252 for more details).

Sights

Sino-Portuguese Architecture ARCHITECTURE
Stroll along Ths Thalang, Dibuk, Yaowarat, Ranong, Phang-Nga, Rasada and Krabi for a glimpse of some of the best architecture on offer. Soi Romanee off of Th Thalang is the most ambient area of town. The most magnificent examples of buildings are the **Standard Chartered Bank** (Th Phang-Nga), Thailand's oldest foreign bank; the **THAI office** (Th Ranong); and the **old post office building**, which now houses the **Phuket Philatelic Museum** (Th Montri; admission free; ⏲9.30am-5.30pm), a first stop for stamp boffins. The best-restored residential properties are found along Th Dibuk and Th Thalang. The fabulous **Phra Phitak Chyn Pracha Mansion** (9 Th Krabi) has been restored and turned into a branch of the upscale Blue Elephant restaurant chain and a cookery school (see p245).

Shrine of the Serene Light SHRINE
(ศาลเจ้าแสงธรรม; Map p247; Saan Jao Sang Tham; ⏲8.30am-noon & 1.30-5.30pm) A handful of Chinese temples inject some colour into the area but the Shrine of the Serene Light, tucked away at the end of a 50m alley near the Bangkok Bank of Commerce on Th Phang-Nga, is a cut above the rest. You'll see Taoist etchings on the walls and the vaulted ceiling stained from incense plumes. The altar is always alive with fresh flowers and burning candles. The shrine, which has been restored, is said to have been built by a local family in the mid-1880s.

Khao Rang VIEWPOINT
(เขารัง; Phuket Hill) For a bird's-eye view of the city, climb up pretty Khao Rang, northwest of the town centre. It's at its best during the week, when the summit is relatively peaceful, but keep an eye out for the mobs of snarling dogs. If, as many people say, Phuket is a corruption of the Malay word *bukit* (hill), then this is probably its namesake.

Phuket Thaihua Museum MUSEUM
(พิพิธภัณฑ์ภูเก็ตไทยหัว; 28 Th Krabi; admission 200B; ⏲9am-5pm) This flashy new museum, set in an old Sino-Portuguese home, is filled with photos and exhibits on Phuket's history. The last room is covered in photos of local dishes. If this makes you hungry, info on where to find the food stalls serving up the authentic grub is listed on the wall.

Festivals & Events

The **Vegetarian Festival** (sp248) is Phuket's most important event and usually takes place during late September or October. If you plan to attend the street processions, consider bringing earplugs to blunt the firecrackers' never-ending blast.

Sleeping

The cheapest place on the island to get some zzz's, Phuket Town is a treasure trove of budget lodging. Head out to the beaches for more midrange and top-end options.

Sino House HOTEL $$
(☎0 7623 2494; www.sinohousephuket.com; 1 Th Montri; r 2000-2500B; ❄@) Shanghai style meets *Mad Men* chic at this impressive Old Town offering. Rooms are massive with mod furnishings, fantastic handmade ceramic basins and quarter-moon shower tubs in the bathrooms. There's an on-site Raintree Spa and long-term rates (18,000B per month) are available.

TOP CHOICE **Phuket 346** GUEST HOUSE $$
(☎08 7281 1898; www.phuket346.com; 15 Soi Romanee; r 1200B; ❄) On charming Soi Romanee, this romantic old shophouse has been exquisitely restored to look like a cosy art gallery. Rooms have white patterned wallpaper and the occasional brightly coloured wall decorated with modern art. Downstairs are fish ponds and a street-side cafe playing sultry jazz tunes.

Casa 104 GUEST HOUSE $$
(☎0 7622 1268; 104 Th Yaowarat; r from 1000B; ❄📶) A stunning renovation of a 100-year-old shophouse with burgundy walls, dangling chandeliers, bouquets of bamboo and peacock

WORTH A TRIP

BIG BUDDHA

Set on a hilltop just northwest of Chalong circle and visible from almost half of the island, the Big Buddha (Map p242) sits at the best viewpoint on Phuket. To get here you'll follow the red signs from the main highway (Hwy 402) and wind up a country road, passing terraced banana groves and tangles of jungle. Once you're on top, pay your respects at the tented golden shrine, then step up to Big Buddha's glorious plateau where you can peer into Kata's perfect bay, glimpse the shimmering Karon strand and, on the other side, survey the serene Chalong harbour where the channel islands look like pebbles.

Of course, you'll be forgiven if you disregard the view for a few minutes to watch local craftsmen put the finishing touches on their 60-million-baht Buddha, dressed in Burmese alabaster. Over the last 20 years construction on Phuket hasn't stopped, so it means something when locals refer to the Big Buddha project as Phuket's most important development in the last 100 years.

feathers, and early days' swing on the sound system. And that's just the lobby bar. Guests' rooms are more spare and windowless, but still elegant with white concrete floors, rain showers and original art nouveau fixtures.

Baan Suwantawe HOTEL $$
(☎0 7621 2879; www.baansuwantawe.co.th; 1/10 Th Dibuk; r from 1200B; ❄@≋) With Zen art, hardwood floors, good-sized bathrooms and comfy lounge areas, these studio-style rooms are a steal. Higher-priced rooms have terraces overlooking the blue-tiled pool and lily pond, and the whole place smells like lemongrass.

99 Old Town Boutique Guesthouse GUEST HOUSE $
(☎08 4059 0010, 0 7622 3800; 99oldtown@hotmail.co.th; 99 Th Thalang; r 790-990B; ❄) Another shophouse-turned-B&B that's unpretentious at first glance but has surprisingly glamorous rooms with four-poster curtain-draped beds and large attached polished cement bathrooms. It's run by a lovely family, and a fountain gurgles in the communal back courtyard.

Chinotel HOTEL $$
(☎0 7621 4455; www.chinotelphuket.com; 133-135 Th Ranong; r 1380-1780B; ❄@?) Supercomfortable, clean, new and compact rooms with style – there's a bit of brick, a dash of bamboo and a brightly painted wall or two. Add a TV, fridge, hot-water bathroom and central location, and you have a real gem.

Sleep Sheep Phuket Hostel HOSTEL $
(☎0 7621 6464; www.sleepsheepphuket.com; 243-245 Soi Dtac Shop; r 650B; ❄@?) In an alleyway off Th Thalang, this relatively modern place has big, brightly painted rooms with hot-water bathrooms and uncommonly friendly staff; plus it smells like freshly laundered sheets.

D's Corner & Guesthouse GUEST HOUSE $
(☎08 3590 4828; 132 Th Thalang; r 380-700B; ❄@) Huge, airy and clean rooms in this spacious guest house are hidden off the road down an unlikely hallway. The welcome is mediocre but it's great value. Skip your free toast and eat breakfast at the Malaysian roti cafe next door.

Eating

There's good food in Phuket Town, and meals here cost a lot less than those at the beach.

TOP CHOICE **Ka Jok See** THAI, INTERNATIONAL $$$
(☎0 7621 7903; kajoksee@hotmail.com; 26 Th Takua Pa; dishes 180-480B; ⊙dinner Tue-Sun) Dining here is reason enough to come to town. Dripping Old Phuket charm and creaking under the weight of the owner's fabulous trinket collection, this atmospheric little eatery offers great food, top-notch music and – if you're lucky – some sensationally camp cabaret.

TOP CHOICE **Cook** INTERNATIONAL-THAI $
(☎0 7625 8375; 101 Th Phang-Nga; dishes 60-120B; ⊙lunch & dinner) The Thai owner-chef used to cook Italian at a megaresort, so when he opened this ludicrously inexpensive Old Town cafe he fused the two cultures. So, order the sensational green curry pizza with chicken, or the pork curry coconut milk pizza, and fall in love.

Wilai THAI $
(☎0 7622 2875; 14 Th Thalang; dishes from 65B; ⊙breakfast & lunch) Phuket soul food. It does Phuketian *pàt tai* with some kick to it, and

a fantastic *mee sua;* think noodles sautéed with egg, greens, prawns, chunks of sea bass, and squid. Wash it down with fresh chrysanthemum juice.

La Gaetana INTERNATIONAL **$$$**
(☎0 7625 0523; 352 Th Phuket; dishes 200-450B; ⏲lunch Mon, Tue & Fri, dinner Tue-Sun) An irresistibly intimate five-table restaurant, La Gaetana has black concrete floors, colourful walls and stemware, an open kitchen in the courtyard, and a superb Italian menu. Think duck breast carpaccio followed by osso bucco.

China Inn INTERNATIONAL-THAI **$$**
(☎0 7635 6239; Th Thalang; dishes 80-250B; ⏲breakfast & lunch daily, dinner Thu, Fri & Sat; ✍)

VEGETARIAN FESTIVAL

Loud popping sounds like machine-gun fire fill the streets, the air is nearly opaque with grey-brown smoke and men and women traipse along blocked-off city roads, their cheeks pierced with skewers and knives or, more surprisingly, lamps and tree branches. Some of the flock have blood streaming down their fronts or open lashes across their backs. No this isn't a war zone, this is the **Vegetarian Festival**, one of Phuket's most important festivals, centred in Phuket Town.

The festival, which takes place during the first nine days of the ninth lunar month of the Chinese calendar – usually late September or October – celebrates the beginning of 'Taoist Lent', when devout Chinese abstain from eating meat. But more obvious to outsiders are the daily processions winding their way through town with floats of ornately dressed children and ladyboys, near armies of flag-bearing colour-coordinated young people and, most noticeably, men and women engaged in outrageous acts of self-mortification. Shop owners along Phuket's central streets set up altars in front of their shopfronts offering nine tiny cups of tea, incense, fruit, firecrackers, candles and flowers to the nine emperor gods invoked by the festival.

Those participating as mediums bring the nine deities to earth by entering into a trance state, piercing their cheeks with an impressive variety of objects, sawing their tongues or flagellating themselves with spiky metal balls. Whatever form the self-flagellation takes, the mediums (primarily men) walk in procession, stopping at shop-front altars, where they picked up the offered fruit. They also drink one of the nine cups of tea, grab some flowers to stick in their waistbands or set strings of firecrackers alight. The shop owners and their families stand by with their palms together in a *wâi* gesture out of respect for these mediums who are temporarily possessed by deities. Surreal and overwhelming hardly describes it.

In Phuket Town, the festival activities are centred around five Chinese temples, with the **Jui Tui** temple on Th Ranong the most important, followed by **Bang Niew** and **Sui Boon Tong** temples. There are also events at temples in the nearby towns of Kathu (where the festival originated) and Ban Tha Reua. If you stop by the procession's starting point early enough in the morning, you may see a surprisingly professional, latex-glove-clad crew piercing the devotees' cheeks – not for the faint-hearted. Other ceremonies occur throughout the festival at the temples and can include firewalking and knife-ladder climbing. Beyond the headlining gore, fabulous vegetarian food stalls line the side streets offering a perfect opportunity to sample cheap local treats and strike up interesting conversations with the locals.

The TAT office in Phuket prints a helpful schedule of events for the Vegetarian Festival each year. The festival also takes place in Trang, Krabi and other southern Thai towns.

Oddly enough, there is no record of these sorts of acts of devotion associated with Taoist Lent in China. The local Chinese claim the festival was started by a theatre troupe from China that stopped off in nearby Kathu around 150 years ago. The story goes that the troupe was struck seriously ill because the members had failed to propitiate the nine emperor gods of Taoism. The nine-day penance they performed included self-piercing, meditation and a strict vegetarian diet.

For more info, visit www.phuketvegetarian.com.

The organics movement meets Phuket cuisine at this turn-of-the-20th-century shophouse. There's red curry with crab, a host of veggie options, tremendous homemade yoghurt and fruit smoothies flavoured with organic honey.

Uptown Restaurant THAI $
(☎0 7621 5359; Th Tilok Uthit; dishes 30-60B; ⊙10am-9pm) This classic, breezy Chinese-style cafe may not look fancy, but look around and you'll notice mounted photos of Thai celebrities who have stopped by Uptown to slurp the spectacular noodles.

Siam Indigo INTERNATIONAL-THAI $$
(☎0 7625 6697; www.siamindigo.com; 8 Th Phang-Nga; dishes 130-290B; ⊙lunch & dinner Wed-Mon) One of Phuket's most stylish gems is set in an 80-year-old Sino-Portuguese relic and specialises in Thai cuisine with a French-International twist.

Drinking & Entertainment

This is where you can party like a local. Bars buzz until late, patronised almost exclusively by Thais and local expats. If you're tired of the sleazy, resort party scene, the vibe here will feel like a fresh ocean breeze, even if it is another sweaty, windless night in Old Town.

TOP CHOICE **Saneha** BAR
(☎08 1892 1001; Th Yaowarat; ⊙6pm-late) A fun upscale bohemian joint lit by seashell chandeliers, with plenty of dark corners where you can sip, snuggle, snack and dig that soulful acoustic crooner on stage.

Bo(ok)hemian CAFE
(☎0 7625 2854; 61 Th Thalang; ⊙9am-10pm; wi-fi) Every town should have a coffee house this cool. The split-level open design feels both warm and cutting-edge. It has wi-fi, used books for sale, gourmet coffee and tea, and damn good chocolate cake.

Timber Hut NIGHTCLUB
(☎0 7621 1839; 118/1 Th Yaowarat; admission free; ⊙6pm-2am) Thai and expat locals have been filling this old clubhouse every night for nearly 20 years. They gather at long wooden tables on two floors, converge around thick timber columns, swill whiskey, and sway to live bands that swing from hard rock to funk to hip-hop with aplomb.

Shopping

There are some fabulous bohemian-chic boutiques scattered throughout Old Town selling jewellery, women's fashions, fabrics and souvenirs. Whimsical art galleries tucked behind charming Chinese shopfronts are mostly found on Th Yaowarat.

Ban Boran Textiles TEXTILES
(☎0 7621 1563; 51 Th Yaowarat; ⊙10am-7pm) Simply put, this dusty hole-in-the-wall is the best shop on the island for silk, raw silk, cotton textiles and sarongs.

Day Market MARKET
(Th Ranong) This market near the town centre traces its history back to the days when pirates, Indians, Chinese, Malays and Europeans traded in Phuket. You might still find some fabrics from Southeast Asia, though it mostly sells food now.

Southwind Books BOOKSTORE
(☎08 9724 2136; 1/2/5 Th Phang-Nga; ⊙9am-7pm Mon-Sat, 10am-3pm Sun) Peruse these dusty secondhand stacks. There are titles in 18 languages, including Polish.

Information

There are numerous internet cafes and ATMs around Th Phuket, Th Ranong, Th Montri and Th Phang-Nga.

Main post office (Th Montri; ⊙8.30am-4pm Mon-Fri, 9am-noon Sat)

Police (☎191, 0 7622 3555; cnr Th Phang-Nga & Th Phuket)

TAT office (☎0 7621 2213; www.tat.or.th; 73-75 Th Phuket; ⊙8.30am-4.30pm) Has maps, information brochures, a list of standard sŏrng·tăa·ou fares out to the various beaches, and the recommended charter costs for a vehicle.

Getting There & Around

To/From the Airport

Despite what airport taxi touts would like you to believe, a bright orange **government airport bus** (www.airportbusphuket.com; tickets 85B) runs between the airport and Phuket Town via the Heroines Monument about every hour between 6am and 7pm. There's also a minibus service at the airport that will take you into Phuket Town for 150B per person; Patong, Kata and Karon beaches cost 180B if there are enough passengers. Chartered cars between the airport and Phuket Town cost 500B; between the airport and beaches is 700B to 1000B. Metered taxis should cost no more than 550B (including airport tax) to anywhere around the island.

Bus

You'll find the **bus terminal** (☎0 7621 1977) just to the east of the town centre, within walking distance of the many hotels. Services from here are listed in the following table.

DESTINATION	BUS TYPE	FARE (B)	DURATION (HR)
Bangkok	2nd class	487	15
	air-con	626	13-14
	VIP	974	13
Hat Yai	air-con	556	6-7
Ko Samui	air-con	430	8 (bus/boat)
Krabi	ordinary	95	4
	air-con	145	3½
Phang-Nga	ordinary	120	2½
Ranong	ordinary	209	6
	air-con	270	5
Surat Thani	ordinary	195	6
	air-con	240	5
Trang	air-con	240	5

Car

There are cheap car-rental agencies on Th Rasada near **Pure Car Rent** (☎0 7621 1002; www.purecarrent.com; 75 Th Rasada), a good choice in the centre of town. Suzuki jeeps go for about 1200B per day (including insurance), though in the low season the rates can go down to 750B. And if you rent for a week or more, you should get a discount.

The rates are always better at local places than at the better-known internationals, though you may be able to get deals with the familiar companies if you reserve in advance.

Motorcycle

You can rent motorcycles on Th Rasada near Pure Car Rent, or from various places at the beaches. Costs are anywhere from 200B to 300B per day, and can vary depending on the season. Bigger bikes (over 125cc) can be rented at shops in Patong, Kata, Rawai and Karon.

Sŏrng·tăa ou & Túk-túk

Large bus-sized sŏrng·tăa·ou run regularly from Th Ranong near the market to the various Phuket beaches (25B to 40B per person) – see the respective destinations for details. These run from around 7am to 5pm; outside these times you have to charter a túk-túk to the beaches, which will set you back 500B to Patong, 500B to Karon and Kata, 400B to 340B to Rawai and 600B to Kamala. You'll have to bargain. Beware of tales about the tourist office being 5km away, or that the only way to reach the beaches is by taxi, or even that you'll need a taxi to get from the bus terminal to the town centre (it is more or less in the town centre). For a ride around town, túk-túk drivers should charge 100B to 200B.

Motorcycle taxis around town cost 30B.

Ko Sireh เกาะสิเหร่

This tiny island, 4km east of the district capital and connected to the main island by a bridge, is known for its *chow lair* (sea gypsies; also spelled *chao leh*) village and a hilltop reclining Buddha at **Wat Sireh**.

The largest settlement of *chow lair* in Thailand is little more than a poverty-stricken cluster of tin shacks on stilts, plus one seafood restaurant. The Urak Lawoi, the most sedentary of the three *chow lair* groups, are found only between the Mergui archipelago and the Tarutao-Langkawi archipelago, and speak a creolised mixture of Malay and Mon-Khmer.

A single road loops the island, passing a few residences, prawn farms, lots of rubber plantations and a bit of untouched forest. On the east coast there's a public beach called **Hat Teum Suk**, as well as a terrific cooking school on a quiet seafront plot, the **Phuket Thai Cookery School** (p245).

Laem Phanwa แหลมพันวา

Laem Phanwa is a gorgeous, wooded, elongated cape, jutting into the sea south of Phuket. At the tip of the cape, **Phuket Aquarium** (Map p242; ☎0 7639 1126; www.phuketaquarium.org; adult/child 100/50B; ⏲8.30am-4.30pm) displays a varied collection of tropical fish and other marine life. Experience it with a stroll along the walk-through tunnel.

The beaches and coves are rustic and protected by rocky headlands and mangroves. The sinuous coastal road is magic. If you just can't leave, check into the recently renovated **Cape Panwa Hotel** (☎0 7639 1123; www.capepanwa.com; 27 Moo 8, Th Sakdidej; r from 6100B; ❄📶🏊👪), a four-star, family-friendly stunner perched on 400m of secluded white sand.

The seafood restaurants along the Laem Phanwa waterfront are a great place to hang out and watch the pleasure skiffs and painted fishing boats passing by.

To get to the cape, take Rte 4021 south and then turn down Rte 4023 just outside Phuket Town.

Rawai ราไวย์

Now this is a place to live, which is exactly why Phuket's rapidly developing south coast is teeming with retirees, Thai and expat entrepreneurs, and a service sector that, for the most part, moved here from somewhere else.

The region is not just defined by its beaches but also by the lush coastal hills that rise steeply and tumble into the Andaman Sea, forming **Laem Promthep**, Phuket's southernmost point. These hills are home to pocket neighbourhoods and cul-de-sacs that are knitted together by just a few roads. So even with the growth you can feel nature, especially when you hit the beach.

Hat Nai Han, with its crescent of white sand backed by casuarinas, bobbing yachts, seafront temple Wat Nai Han and a monsoon-season surf break, is the best beach in the area, but there are smaller, hidden beaches that are just as beautiful. **Hat Rawai** lacks Nai Han's good looks. It's just a rocky longtail and speedboat harbour, which makes it the perfect place to open up a seafood grill. There is a string of them here. All are locally owned and serve equally delicious fare.

Sleeping

All the lodgings in lovely Hat Nai Han are reached via a skinny, rutted paved road that begins from the Phuket Yacht Club parking lot (yes, you can drive past the guard) – or charter a long-tail from Rawai for 500B.

Evason Phuket Resort HOTEL **$$$**
(0 7638 1010; www.sixsenses.com; 100 Th Viset, Hat Rawai; r 4992-12,935B;) This spa-hotel extraordinaire offers copious amounts of luxury. And while the Six Senses Spa experience (see p243) is usually rather indulgent and expensive, the prices at this four-star offering are downright reasonable. The resort also encompasses private Bon Island.

Vijitt HOTEL **$$$**
(0 7636 3600; www.vijittresort.com; 16 Moo 2, Th Viset, Hat Rawai; villas from 7800B;) Arguably the area's most elegant property, Vijitt is sprinkled with deluxe villas that boast limestone floors, large bathtubs, outdoor showers and gorgeous sea views from private terraces. Its stunning, black-bottom infinity pool overlooks Friendship Beach.

Royal Phuket Yacht Club HOTEL **$$$**
(0 7638 0200; www.royalphuketyachtclub.com; 23/3 Moo 1, Th Vises, Hat Nai Han; r from 6800B;) Still a destination for many a transcontinental yachty, Royal Phuket Yacht Club has an air of old-world elegance, especially in its fabulous lobby-bar spinning with ceiling fans. Rooms feature large terraces – and stunning bay views – and there's every creature comfort you could imagine somewhere on site.

Ao Sane Bungalows HOTEL **$**
(0 7628 8306, 08 1326 1687; 11/2 Moo 1, Th Vises, Hat Nai Han; bungalows 600-850B;) Rickety cold-water, fan-cooled wooden bungalows sit on a secluded beach, with million-dollar views of Ao Sane and Ao Nai Han. There's a beachside restaurant, dive centre and an old-hippy vibe.

Eating & Drinking

Besides the restaurants listed here, there are a dozen tasty seafood grills roasting fresh catch along the roadside near Hat Rawai.

TOP CHOICE **Rum Jungle** INTERNATIONAL **$$$**
(0 7638 8153; 69/8 Th Sai Yuan; meals 300-500B; dinner, closed Sun) The best restaurant in the area and one of the best in all of Phuket is family-run and spearheaded by a terrific Aussie chef. The New Zealand lamb shank is divine, as are the steamed clams, and the pasta sauces are all made from scratch. Everything – including the Pampero rocks – is served under a thatched roof to an exceptional world-beat soundtrack.

Nikita's BAR
(0 7628 8703; Hat Rawai; 11am-late) Overlooking the sea on Phuket's south coast, Nikita's is a pleasant open-air hangout, with coffee drinks, green teas, a nice selection of shakes, and cocktails. If you're hungry you can order from the attached restaurant, Baan Rimlay (wood-fired pizzas from 200B).

Getting There & Away

Rawai is about 18km from Phuket Town. Sŏrng·tăa·ou (30B) run from Phuket's fountain circle at Th Ranong – some continue to Hat Nai Han, but not all of them, so ask first. The túk-túk trip from Rawai to Nai Han is a hefty 200B.

You can hire taxis (which are actually just chartered cars) from Rawai and Hat Nai Han to the airport (700B), Patong (500B) and Phuket Town (500B).

Long-tail and speedboat charters are available from Hat Rawai. Destinations include Ko Bon (long-tail/speedboat 800/2000B), Coral Island

Hat Nai Han, Hat Rawai & Hat Laem Ka

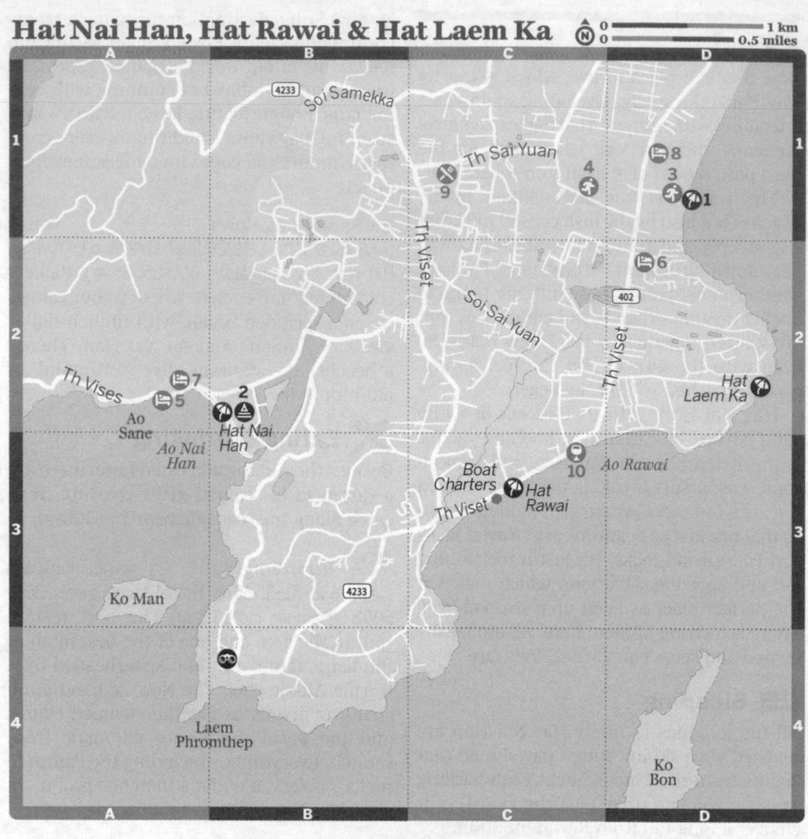

Hat Nai Han, Hat Rawai & Hat Laem Ka

Sights
1 Friendship Beach....D1
2 Wat Nai Han....B2

Activities, Courses & Tours
3 Kite Zone....D1
4 Rawai Muay Thai....C1

Sleeping
5 Ao Sane Bungalows....A2
6 Evason Phuket Resort....D2
7 Royal Phuket Yacht Club....A2
8 Vijitt....D1

Eating
9 Rum Jungle....C1

Drinking
10 Nikita's....C3

(long-tail/speedboat 1200/3000B) and Ko Kai (long-tail/speedboat 4000/8000B). Maximum six passengers.

Hat Kata หาดกะตะ

Kata attracts travellers of all ages with its shopping, surfing and lively beach, and without the seedy hustle endemic to Patong up the coast. While you might not find a secluded strip of sand, you will find lots to do and plenty of easy-going folks to clink beers with.

There's surfing in the shoulder and wet seasons, some terrific day spas and fantastic food. The beach is actually divided in two by a rocky headland, and the road between them is home to Phuket's original millionaire's row. Hat Kata Yai is on the north end, while the more secluded Hat Kata Noi unfurls to the south. Both offer soft golden sand and attract a bohemian crowd.

The main commercial street of Th Thai Na is perpendicular to the shore and has most of its restaurants and shops, along with some cheaper places to stay.

Sights & Activities

The small island of **Ko Pu** is within swimming distance of the shore (if you're a strong swimmer); on the way are some OK coral reefs. Be careful of rip tides, heed the red flags and don't go past the breakers. Both Hat Kata Yai and Hat Kata Noi offer decent surfing from April to November. Board rental costs 100B to 150B for one hour or 300B to 600B for the whole day.

Crave more heat? Consider a class at **Kata Hot Yoga** (Map p256; ☎0 7660 5950; www.katahotyoga.com; 217 Th Khoktanod; per class 420B). Classes are held three times per day.

Sleeping

These are average prices for the high season (May to October). Like Patong, it's getting harder and harder to find anything under 1000B during the high season, but prices drop radically when tourism is down.

TOP CHOICE Mom Tri's Villa Royale HOTEL $$$
(Map p256; ☎0 7633 3568; www.villaroyalephuket.com; ste incl breakfast from 12,500B;) Tucked away in a secluded Kata Noi location with the grandest of views, Villa Royale is a supremely romantic place with fabulous food. Unwind in beautiful rooms straight out of the pages of *Architectural Digest* and indulge in guilt-free pleasures, including an attached spa and a saltwater pool – if you prefer a tamer version of the real thing – which is just steps away.

TOP CHOICE Caffe@Caffe GUEST HOUSE $$
(Map p256; ☎0 7628 4005; www.caffeatcaffe.com; 100/60-61 Th Kata; r 1800B;) Tiled rooms with gold wallpaper alternating with white-painted walls, striped duvets, mini-balconies, fridges and TVs make this place as comfy as it is hip. It's in a three-storey building with a modern cafe downstairs.

Sawasdee Village HOTEL $$$
(Map p256; ☎0 7633 0979; www.phuketsawasdee.com; 38 Th Ked Kwan; bungalows 6500-8500B;) A boutique resort with a lush, opulent, but compact footprint built in classic Thai style. Ornate, peaked-roof bungalows have wooden floors, beamed ceilings and open on to a thick tropical landscape laced with *koi* (carp) canals and gushing with waterfalls. Not to mention those Buddhist art installations. Throw in its quality spa and this place is unique and inviting in every way, but it will cost you in the high season.

Mom Tri's Boathouse HOTEL $$$
(Map p256; ☎0 7633 0015; www.boathousephuket.com; 2/2 Th Kata (Patak West); r 9600-25,000B;) For Thai politicos, pop stars, artists and celebrity authors, the intimate boutique Boathouse is still the only place to stay on Phuket. Rooms are spacious and gorgeous, some sporting large breezy verandas. Critics complain that the Boathouse is a bit stiff-lipped and old-fashioned for this century, but no-one can deny that the main reason to stay here is for the food. The on-site restaurant, Boathouse Wine & Grill (p256), is among the best on the island. The Boathouse also provides cooking courses, see p255.

Fantasy Hill Bungalow HOTEL $
(Map p256; ☎0 7633 0106; fantasyhill@hotmail.com; 8/1 Th Patak; r with fan/air-con 450/800B;) Sitting in a lush garden on a hill, the older but well-maintained bungalows here are great value. It's peaceful but central and the staff is super sweet. Angle for a corner air-con room with a view.

Katathani Resort & Spa HOTEL $$$
(Map p256; ☎0 7633 0124; www.katathani.com; 14 Th Kata Noi; r from 7800B;) Taking over a huge portion of lush, relatively quiet Hat Kata Noi, this glitzy spa resort offers all the usual trimmings in stylish surrounds. It features a spa, a handful of pools, a beauty salon and heaps of space. Excellent low-season deals are often available.

Sugar Palm Resort HOTEL $$$
(Map p256; ☎0 7628 4404; www.sugarpalmphuket.com; 20/10 Th Kata; r incl breakfast 3700-5200B;) It's a 'chic chill-out world' at the Sugar Palm, as this Miami-meets-Thailand resort claims. Rooms, decorated in urban whites, blacks and lavender, are exceptional value and sublimely comfy, and all surround a black-bottomed, U-shaped pool. You feel a bit on stage going for a swim here, but the beach isn't far and you're in the heart of Kata's lively shopping and restaurant strip.

Kata Palm Resort HOTEL $$$
(Map p256; ☎0 7628 4334; www.katapalmresort.com; 60 Th Kata; r from 5500B; ❄📶🏊) Given the abundance of ever-creeping modernism, it's nice to see some classic Thai kitsch at this old standby. Expect Thai art on the walls, silks on the beds, fine wood furnishings, and handpainted columns in the lobby. Great deals are frequently available through its website.

Honey Resort HOTEL $$
(Map p256; ☎0 7633 0938; www.honeyresort.com; 100/69 Th Kata; r 3400-3900B; ❄📶) Spacious new rooms with (tasteful!) wood panelling to spare. All rooms have daybeds, built-in dressers, desks, bathtubs and marble washbasins. There's free wi-fi and flat-screen TVs, too. Promotional rates (699B) were absurdly low at research time, but rack rates are affordable year-round.

Baan Thai Homestay GUEST HOUSE $
(Map p256; ☎0 7633 0655; www.baanthaihomestay.com; 23 Th Ketkwan; r from 1000B; ❄📶) In a quirky, antique-looking building, common areas are decorated with carved wooden arches, stone work, ox cart wheels, plants and vines. Rooms are dark but clean and comfy with air-con, hot water and good beds.

Kata Country Resort HOTEL $$
(Map p256; ☎0 7633 3210; www.katacountryhouse.com; 82 Th Kata; r 1600-2600B; ❄🏊) We can't tell if the retro '60s/'70s kitsch is intentional here or if it's just a lovely accident. Expect wagon-wheel railings on the terraces, waterlily ponds and a Tiki-style (Polynesian) lounge. It's nothing luxurious but we give it five stars for character.

✕ Eating

There's some surprisingly classy food in Kata, though you'll be paying for it. For cheaper eats, head to Th Thai Na and to the cluster of affordable, casual seafood restaurants on Th Kata (Patak West) near the shore.

TOP CHOICE **Boathouse Wine & Grill** MEDITERRANEAN $$$
(Map p256; ☎0 7633 0015; www.boathousephuket.com; Th Kotanod; mains 450-950B; ⊙breakfast, lunch & dinner) The perfect place to wow a fussy date, the Boathouse is the pick of the bunch for most local foodies. The atmosphere can be a little stuffy – this is the closest Phuket gets to old-school dining – but the Mediterranean fusion food is fabulous, the wine list expansive and the sea views sublime.

Hat Karon & Hat Kata

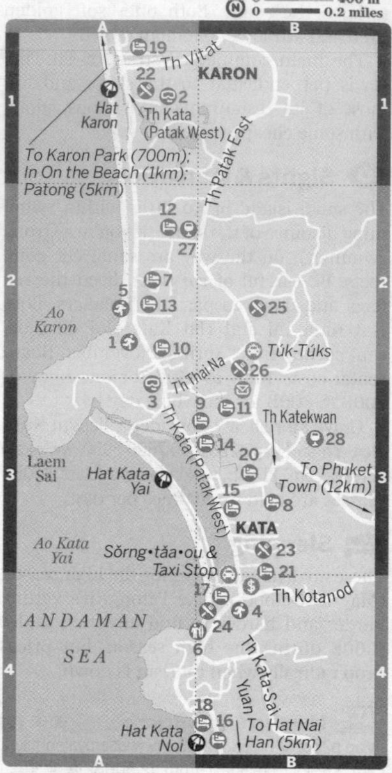

TOP CHOICE **Capannina** ITALIAN $$
(Map p256; ☎0 7628 4318; capannina@fastmail.fm; 30/9 Moo 2, Th Kata; mains 200-700B) Everything here – from the pastas to the sauces – is made fresh and you can taste it. The ravioli and gnocchi are memorably fantastic, the risotto comes highly recommended, and it has great pizzas, calzones and veal Milanese, too. It gets crowded during the high season, so you may want to reserve ahead.

Oasis FUSION $$$
(Map p256; ☎0 7633 3423; Th Kotanod; meals 350-600B) Two restaurants in one. The top level is an Asian-fusion tapas bar blessed with live jazz. The lower level is a candlelit fine-dining patio restaurant where you can sample fresh

Hat Karon & Hat Kata

Activities, Courses & Tours
1 Dino Park A2
2 Dive Asia A1
3 Dive Asia A3
4 Kata Hot Yoga B4
5 Kiteboarding Asia A2
Mom Tri's Boathouse .... (see 17)
6 Phuket Surf B4
Phuket Surfing .... (see 6)
Sea Fun Divers .... (see 16)

Sleeping
7 Andaman Seaview Hotel A2
8 Baan Thai Homestay B3
9 Caffe@Caffe B3
10 Fantasy Hill Bungalow A2
11 Honey Resort B3
12 Kangaroo Guesthouse A2
13 Karon Beach Resort A2
14 Kata Country Resort B3
15 Kata Palm Resort B3
16 Katathani Resort & Spa B4
17 Mom Tri's Boathouse B4
18 Mom Tri's Villa Royale B4
19 Mövenpick A1
20 Sawasdee Village B3
21 Sugar Palm Resort B3

Eating
22 Bai Toey A1
Boathouse Wine & Grill .... (see 17)
23 Capannina B3
24 Oasis B4
25 Pad Thai Shop B2
26 Thai Kitchen B2

Drinking
27 Nakannoi A2
28 Ratri Jazztaurant B3
Ska Bar .... (see 6)

barracuda fillet with a sun-dried herb crust while you watch the oblong paper lanterns swing in the trees.

Thai Kitchen THAI $
(Map p256; Th Thai Na; meals 80B; breakfast, lunch & dinner) Good rule of thumb: if a humble, roadside cafe is packed with Thai people, you can be certain that the food will rock. Its green curry (warning: your nose will run) and glass-noodle dishes are superb. It's just down the road from, ahem, 'Pussy Bar'.

Drinking

Kata's nightlife tends to be pretty mellow.

Ska Bar BAR
(Map p256; to late) At Kata's southernmost cove, tucked into the rocks and seemingly intertwined with the trunk of a grand old banyan tree, Ska is our choice for oceanside sundowners. The Thai bartenders add to the funky Rasta vibe, and the canopy dangles with buoys, paper lanterns and the flags of 10 countries.

Ratri Jazztaurant BAR
(Map p256; 0 7633 3538; Kata Hill; dishes 145-345B; 6pm-midnight) Hang out on the hillside terrace, listen to live jazz, watch the sun go down and enjoy delicious Thai food. Now *this* is a vacation.

Information

There are plenty of ATMs along Kata's main drag.

Post office (Map p256; 9am-4.30pm Mon-Fri, to noon Sat) On Rte 4028, at the end of Th Thai Na.

Getting There & Around

Sŏrng·tăa·ou to both Kata and Karon (per person 25B) leave frequently from the day market on Th Ranong in Phuket Town from 7am to 5pm. The main sŏrng·tăa·ou stop is in front of Kata Beach Resort.

Taxis from Kata go to Phuket Town (600B), Patong (600B) and Karon (200B).

Motorbike rentals (per day 300B) are widely available.

Hat Karon หาดกะรน

Hat Karon is like Hat Patong and Hat Kata's love child: It's chilled-out, a touch glamorous and a tad cheesy with some sleazy corners. There are two megaresorts and package tourists aplenty here but there's still more sand space per capita than at either Patong or Kata. The further north you go the more chic and beautiful the beach gets, culminating at the northernmost edge, accessible from a rutted road that extends past the vendors and food stalls, where the water is like turquoise glass. Within the inland network of streets and plazas you'll find a blend of good local food, more Scandinavian signage than seems reasonable, low-key girly bars, T-shirt vendors and lovely Karon Park, with its artificial lake and mountain backdrop. Fronting the whole mess is a fine stretch of sand.

Sleeping

Mövenpick HOTEL $$$
(Map p256; ☎0 7639 6139; www.moevenpick-hotels.com; 509 Th Kata (Patak West); r from 5900B, villas from 7000B;) Grab a secluded villa and choose from a private plunge pool or outdoor rainforest shower. Alternatively, chill in the cubelike rooms with huge floor-to-ceiling glass windows in the swank ultramodern hotel. Besides a prime location across the street from a pretty stretch of the beach, the Mövenpick offers artistic decor, top-end linen, a big pool with swim-up bar, a spa, and an alfresco restaurant and bar with a giant selection of wood-fired pizzas.

Karon Beach Resort HOTEL $$$
(Map p256; ☎0 7633 0006; www.katagroup.com; 51 Th Kata (Patak West); r from 7500B;) Perched on the south end of Hat Karon, there are some elegant touches here. From the Buddhist sculpture in the jasmine-scented halls to the crown mouldings, wood furnishings, ceramic tiles and cushy duvets in the rooms, to those luscious sea views from the balcony.

Andaman Seaview Hotel HOTEL $$$
(Map p256; ☎0 7639 8111; www.andamanphuket.com; 1 Soi Karon, Th Kata (Patak West); r from 4800B;) The design here is a sort of Cape Cod meets the colonial South Pacific with sky-blue-and-white exterior and chequerboard marble floors in the lobby; it's got a breezy plantation feel and a family vibe. Rooms have a turn-of-the-20th-century Americana theme with marble tables, antiquated ceiling fans, art deco–ish bathroom tiles and white-shutter cabinet doors. There's a bubbling kid's pool and an adult pool.

In On the Beach HOTEL $$
(off Map p256; ☎0 7639 8220; www.karon-inonthebeach.com; 695-697 Moo 1, Th Patak; r from 3500B;) A sweet, tasteful inn on Karon Park. The location is sublime, and the rooms – think marble floors, wi-fi, air-con and ceiling fans – horseshoe the pool and come with sea views. With substantial low-season discounts, this is the perfect surf lair.

Kangaroo Guesthouse GUEST HOUSE $
(Map p256; ☎0 7639 6517; 269/6-9 Karon Plaza; r 800B;) Basic, but very clean, sunny tiled rooms with hot water, air-con, a cute breakfast nook, and balconies overlooking a narrow, slightly seedy soi.

Eating & Drinking

There are a few cheap Thai and seafood places off the roundabout (including a number of beachside seafood houses under one louvred roof 100m north of it) and a similar group on the main road near the southern end of Hat Karon.

Bai Toey THAI $$
(Map p256; ☎08 1691 6202; Soi Old Phuket; meals 200B-250B) A charming Thai bistro with shaded outdoor patio and indoor seating. It has the traditional curry, stir-fry and noodle dishes, but you'd do well to sample its Thai-style grilled beef. It's a sliced fillet brushed in oyster sauce, served with sticky rice (200B).

Pad Thai Shop THAI $
(Map p256; Th Patak East; dishes 40B; ⊙breakfast, lunch & dinner) On the busy main road behind Karon, just north of the tacky Ping Pong Bar, is this glorified food stand where you can find rich and savoury chicken stew (worthy of rave reviews in its own right), and the best *pàt tai* on planet earth. Spicy and sweet, packed with prawns, tofu, egg and peanuts, and wrapped in a fresh banana leaf, you will be grateful. It closes at around 7pm.

Nakannoi BAR
(Map p256; ☎08 7898 5450; Karon Plaza; ⊙5pm-1am) A boho arthouse hideaway with original canvasses on the walls, found art decor (including antique motorcycles and bicycles), a concrete island bar and a permanent bandstand, where the owner jams with his mates almost every night after 8pm.

Getting There & Away

For details on transport to Karon, see p257.

Hat Patong หาดป่าตอง

Sun-seared Scandinavians in bad knock-off T-shirts, beach-buzzing wave runners, a complete disregard for managed development and a knack for turning the midlife crisis into a full-scale industry (sorry, Viagra, Patong was here first) make Patong rampant with unintentional comedy. But for all the concrete and silicon, and moral and gender bending, there's something honest about this place.

Patong is a free-for-all. Anything, from a Starbucks 'venti latte' to an, ahem, companion for the evening is available for the right price. And while that's true of dozens of other, phonier destinations, Patong doesn't try to hide it. Patong is what it is. And that's refreshing.

Of course, that doesn't mean you're going to like it. But when you arrive you'll take one look at the wide, white-sand beach and its magnificent crescent bay, and you'll understand how all this started. Today this town is much more of a city than Phuket Town and it's the centre of Phuket's action.

Diving and spa options abound, as well as upscale dining, street-side fish grills, campy cabaret, Thai boxing, dusty antique shops and one of Asia's coolest shopping malls.

Sleeping

It's getting pretty difficult to find anything in Patong under 1000B between approximately November and April (the period that corresponds to the prices listed in this book), but outside this time rates drop by 40% to 60%.

BYD Lofts HOTEL $$$
(☎0 7634 3024; www.bydlofts.com; 5/28 Th Rat Uthit; apt 4900-11,500B; ❄@📶≋) If style and comfort are more important to you than beachfront (although it's only a minute's walk to the beach), look no further. Urban-style apartments with lots of white (floors, walls, blinds) and sharp lines feel angelic compared to the seedy world of Patong on the streets below. There's a day spa, a rooftop pool and an excellent restaurant on the premises.

TOP CHOICE **Burasari** HOTEL $$$
(☎0 7629 2929; www.burasari.com; 18/110 Th Ruamchai; r 2700-9300B; ❄📶≋) A lovely maze of swimming pools and waterfalls, etched columns, cushion-strewn lounges and bars. Rooms are simple but chic with flat-screen TVs, queen-sized beds and bamboo accents. The **Naughty Radish** cafe here serves outrageous customizable salads (from 180B) and the best smoothies (120B) on Phuket.

La Flora HOTEL $$$
(☎0 7634 4241; www.laflorapatong.com; 39 Th Thawiwong; r from 9500B; ❄📶≋) Here's where clean lines and minimalist decor spill onto Patong beach. Rooms are large with wooden furnishings (check out that floating desk), flat-screen TV and DVD player, bathtub and shower. The minibar is stocked with complimentary soft drinks, and there's a huge lap pool.

TOP CHOICE **Baipho, Baithong & Sala Dee** GUEST HOUSE $$
(☎0 7629 2074, 0 7629 2738; www.baipho.com, www.baithong.com, www.saladee.com; 205/12-13 & 205/14-15 Th Rat Uthit 200 Pee; r 1800-3300B; ❄📶) These three outrageously arty guest houses are all on the same little soi under the same friendly and organised management. Rooms and common areas are filled with Buddha imagery and Zen spa-type trimmings mingling with modern art and urban touches. The dimly lit, nest-like rooms are all unique, so ask to see a few if possible. 'The Lounge' downstairs at Baithong, serves cocktails and very good Italian and Thai food as well as gourmet snacks. Guests can use the pool at the unsightly Montana Grand Phuket next door.

Newspaper HOTEL $$
(☎0 7634 6276; www.newspaperphuket.com; 125/4-5 Th Paradise; r 2500-5000B; ❄📶) One of Patong's classiest three-star inns is easily the most stylish and sophisticated on this gay-friendly block of bars and cafes. Rooms have upscale tile floors, bedside lanterns, dark-wood furnishings and understated feature walls. It's frequently fully booked, so reserve ahead.

Belle Resort HOTEL $$
(☎0 7629 2782; www.thebelleresort.com; 104/31-33 Soi Prisanee; r from 1800B; ❄📶≋) Simple, upscale Zen design, dimly lit rooms with wooden floors, lots of glass and soft beds make this a stylish choice. It's on a quiet street of Italian restaurants near the beach and in the heart of the action.

Baan Pronphateep HOTEL $$
(☎0 7634 3037; www.baanpronphateep.com; 168/1 Th Thawiwong; r 1600-2100B; ❄) Banyan tree-shaded and nestled down a secluded little soi, this is a quiet and simple three-star choice. Rooms are spacious and come with a full-sized fridge and a private patio.

Yorkshire Inn HOTEL $$
(☎0 7634 0904; www.theyorkshirehotel.com; 169/16 Soi Saen Sabai; r 1800-2300; ❄@📶) About as Thai as a plate of Yorkshire pud,

Patong

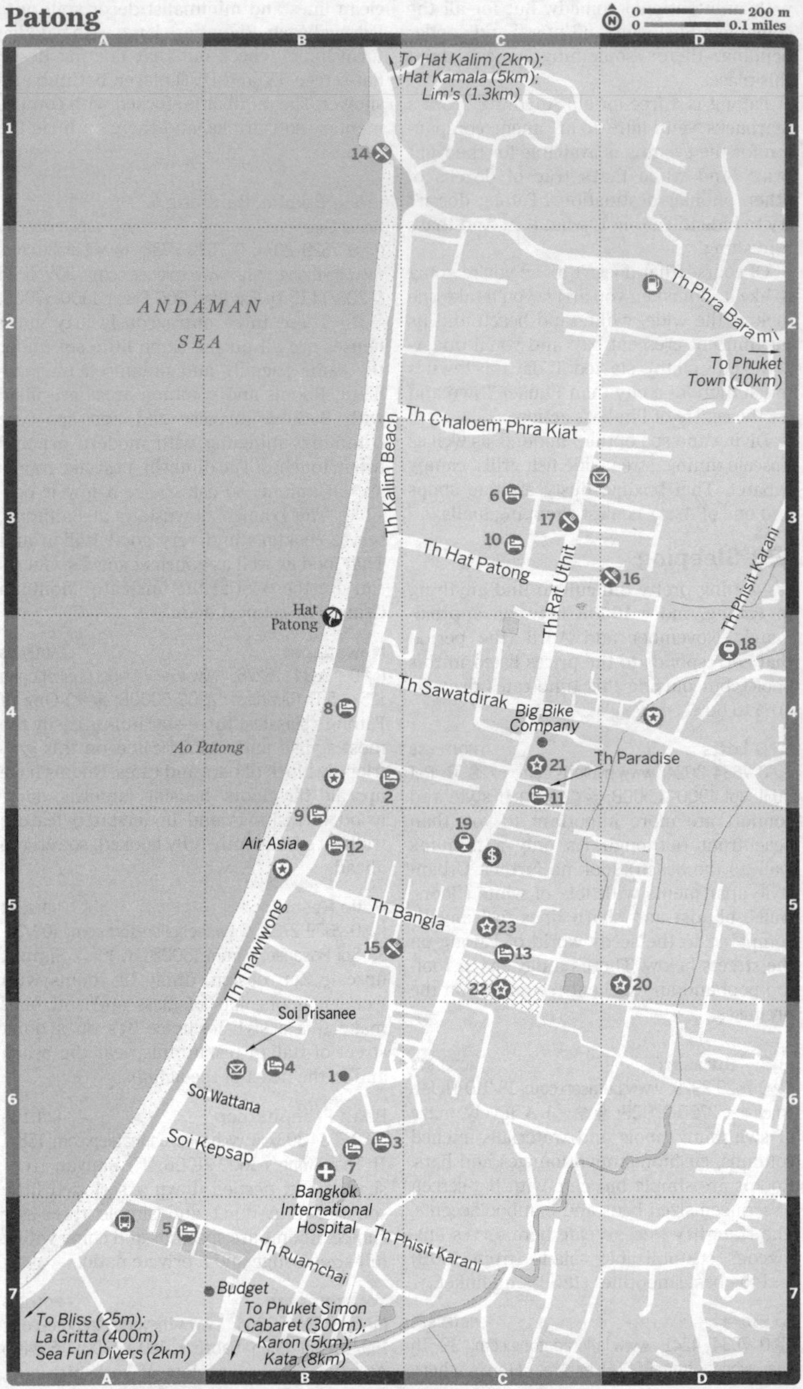

0 200 m
0 0.1 miles

ANDAMAN SEA

To Hat Kalim (2km); Hat Kamala (5km); Lim's (1.3km)

Th Phra Barami

To Phuket Town (10km)

Th Chaloem Phra Kiat

Th Kalim Beach

Th Hat Patong

Th Rat Uthit

Th Phisit Karani

Hat Patong

Th Sawatdirak

Big Bike Company

Ao Patong

Th Paradise

Air Asia

Th Bangla

Th Thawiwong

Soi Prisanee

Soi Wattana

Soi Kepsap

Bangkok International Hospital

Th Phisit Karani

Th Ruamchai

Budget

To Bliss (25m); La Gritta (400m) Sea Fun Divers (2km)

To Phuket Simon Cabaret (300m); Karon (5km); Kata (8km)

Patong

this British outfit courts visitors who insist on putting home in their comforts. There's a flicker of B&B charm here, it's very well managed and can put together a mean fry-up. The rooms are sleek, spotless and come with cable TV.

Merrison Inn HOTEL $$
(☎0 7634 0383; www.merrisoninn.com; 5/35 Th Hat Patong; r 1300B; ❄📶) Polished concrete floors, terrazzo bathrooms, wall-mounted flat-screen TVs, queen sized beds and more than a little Asian kitsch make this place a real bargain.

Casa Jip GUEST HOUSE $
(☎0 7634 3019; www.casajip.com; 207/10 Th Rat Uthit; r from 700B; ❄) Italian-run and great value, this place has very big, if simple, rooms with comfy beds and a taste of Thai style. You get cable TV and there's even a breakfast room service.

Patong Backpacker Hostel HOSTEL $
(☎0 7625 6680; www.phuketbackpacker.com; 167 Th Ranong; dm 300-450B, r 1200B; ❄📶) This has a great location near the beach and the owner offers info on all the best, cheapest places to eat in town. Dorm prices vary depending on the number of beds in the room (three to 10). The top floor is the brightest but dorm rooms on the lower floors each have their own attached bathrooms. Skip the overpriced room in favour of the better-value dorms.

Bliss HOTEL $$$
(☎0 7629 2098; www.theblissphuket.com; 40 Th Thawiwong; ste from 15,000B; ❄📶🏊) A sleek, new all-suite resort. Suites are 90 sq m with a full-sized living room and master bedroom with wooden floors, two flat-screen TVs, a lap pool, a Jacuzzi and a blooming garden on the terrace. Low-season discounts make it worth the splurge.

Impiana Phuket Cabana HOTEL $$$
(☎0 7634 0138; www.impiana.com; 41 Th Thawiwong; r from 7000B; ❄📶🏊) Cabana-style and plumb on the best part of the beach, the rooms here are laden with chic creature comforts, and are close to all the action.

Eating

Patong has stacks of restaurants and the trick is to steer around the watered-down Thai and poorly executed Western food clogging most main drags. The most glamorous restaurants are in a little huddle above the cliffs on the northern edge of town.

Bargain seafood and noodle stalls pop up across town at night – try the lanes on and around Th Bangla, or venture over to the **Patong Food Park** (Th Rat Uthit; ⌚4pm-midnight) once the sun drops.

Baan Rim Pa THAI $$$
(☎0 7634 4079; Th Kalim Beach; dishes 215-475B) Stunning Thai food is served with a side order of spectacular views at this institution. Standards are high, with prices to match, but romance is in the air, with candlelight and piano music aplenty. Book ahead and tuck in your shirt.

Lim's THAI $$$
(☎0 7634 4834; www.lim-thailand.com; 28 Th Phrabaramee, Soi 7; meals 300-600B; ⌚6pm-midnight) Lim's is 500m uphill from the coast road to Kamala. It's a modern, moulded-concrete dining room and lounge serving upscale Thai cuisine. When celebrities land in Phuket, most spend at least one evening here.

Mengrai Seafood SEAFOOD $$
(☎08 7263 7070; Soi Tun; meals 120-300B) Located down a sweaty, dark soi off Th Bangla, Mengrai is a wonderful food court serving fresh, local food. The stalls towards the end serve daily curries that local expats swear by. This restaurant specialises in (very) fresh fish, prawns and mussels.

Chicken Rice Briley THAI $
(☎0 7634 4079; Patong Food Park, Th Rat Uthit; meals 35-45B; ⌚breakfast & lunch) The only diner in the Patong Food Park to offer sustenance when the sun shines. Steamed chicken breast is served on a bed of rice with a bowl of chicken broth with crumbled bits of meat and bone, and roast pork. Dip in the fantastic chilli sauce. There's a reason it's forever packed with locals.

Ninth Floor INTERNATIONAL $$$
(☎0 7634 4311; www.the9thfloor.com; 47 Th Rat Uthit; mains 290-1990B; ⌚dinner) Come on up to the 9th floor of the Sky Inn Condotel building where you can watch the sea of lights spread through sliding floor-to-ceiling glass doors. This is the highest open-air restaurant on the island, but its ridiculously tender, perfectly prepared steaks and chops are what made it a Patong institution.

Drinking

Some visitors may find that Patong's bar scene is enough to put them off their *pàt tai,* but if you're in the mood for plenty of beer, winking neon and short skirts, it is certainly worth sampling.

Th Bangla is Patong's beer and bar-girl mecca and features a number of spectacular go-go extravaganzas, where you can expect the usual mix of gyrating Thai girls and often red-faced Western men. The music is loud (expect techno), the clothes are all but nonexistent and the decor is typically slapstick with plenty of phallic imagery. That said, the atmosphere is more carnival than carnage and you'll find plenty of Western women pushing their way through the throng to the bar.

Two Black Sheep PUB
(☎08 9592 1735; www.twoblacksheep.net; 172 Th Rat Uthit; ⌚11am-2am) Owned by a fun Aussie couple (he's a musician, she's a chef), this old-school pub is a great find. It has good grub and live music nightly. From 8pm to 10pm there's an acoustic set, then Chilli Jam, the house band, gets up and rocks till last call. And it bans bar girls, which keeps everything PG-13.

JP's Restaurant & Bar BAR
(☎0 7634 3024; www.bydlofts.com; 5/28 Th Hat Patong; ⌚10.30am-11.30pm) This hipster indoor-outdoor lounge definitely brings a touch of style and panache to Patong. There's a low-slung bar, the outdoor sofa booths are cushy, happy hour (with free tapas) starts at 10pm and there are weekly DJ parties.

La Gritta BAR
(☎0 7634 0106; www.amari.com; 2 Th Meunngern; ⌚10.30am-11.30pm) A spectacular, modern restaurant that doesn't fit in with the ageing bones of this once-great property, but who cares? With tiered booths, massive yet muted light boxes and a deck that is just centimetres above the boulder-strewn shore, there is no better place for a sunset cocktail.

Monte's BAR
(Th Phisit Karani; ⌚11am-midnight) Now this, my friends, is a tropical pub. There's a thatched roof, a natural-wood bar, dozens of orchids and a flat-screen TV for sport. The barflies swarm on Fridays for Monte's famous Belgian-style mussels, and on the weekends he fires up the grill.

☆ Entertainment

Once you've done the go-go, there's plenty more to see. Cabaret and Thai boxing, in particular, are something of a speciality here.

Phuket Simon Cabaret CABARET
(☎0 7634 2011; www.phuket-simoncabaret.com; Th Sirirach; admission 700-800B; ⌚performances

GAY PRIDE IN PHUKET

Although there are big gay pride celebrations in Bangkok and Pattaya, the **Phuket Gay Pride Festival** is considered by many to be the best in Thailand, maybe even Southeast Asia. The date has changed several times, but it usually lands between February and April. Whenever it blooms, the whole island – but the town of Patong specifically – is packed with (mostly male) revellers from all over the world.

The main events of the four-day weekend party are a huge beach volleyball tournament and, of course, the Grand Parade, featuring floats, cheering crowds and beautiful costumes in the streets of Patong. In recent years, the festival has also included social-responsibility campaigns against child prostitution and substance abuse, and for HIV awareness.

Any other time of year, the network of streets that link the Royal Paradise Hotel with Th Rat Uthit in Patong is where you'll find Phuket's gay pulse. The **Boat Bar** (☎0 7634 2206; www.boatbar.com; 125/20 Th Rat Uthit), Phuket's original gay nightspot and still its only disco, is usually jumping with a lively, mostly gay crowd. Make sure to arrive before the midnight cabaret! For updates on future festivals or for more information about the scene in general, go to www.gaypatong.com.

7.30pm & 9.30pm nightly) About 300m south of town, this cabaret offers entertaining transvestite shows. The 600-seat theatre is grand, the costumes are gorgeous and the ladyboys are convincing. The house is often full – book ahead.

Sound Phuket NIGHTCLUB
(☎0 7636 6163; www.soundphuket.com; Jung Ceylon, Unit 2303, 193 Th Rat Uthit; admission varies; ⌚10pm-4am) When internationally renowned DJs come to Phuket these days, they are usually gigging amid the rounded, futuristic environs of Patong's hottest (and least sleazy) nightclub. If top-shelf DJs are on the decks, expect to pay up to 300B entry fee.

Rock City NIGHTCLUB
(Th Rat Uthit; www.rockcityphuket.com; ⌚9pm-late) Let the grunge begin! This dark den of rock lives on the glory of AC/DC, Metallica and Guns N' Roses tribute bands. On Tuesdays, Fridays and Sundays, rockers channel the Red Hot Chili Peppers, the Rolling Stones, U2 and Bon Jovi in one International Rock City Party (1000B) with free cocktails and beer before 11pm, so get there early and keep it rockin'.

Bangla Boxing Stadium THAI BOXING
(☎0 7282 2348; Th Phisit Karani; admission 1000-1500B; ⌚9-11.30pm Tue, Wed, Fri & Sun) Old name, new stadium, same game: a packed line-up of competitive *moo·ay tai* (Thai boxing) bouts.

Jung Ceylon CINEMA $
(Th Rat Uthit) You can catch new Hollywood releases in pristine, amphitheatre-style cinemas at the shopping mall.

Information

There are internet cafes, and banks with ATM and currency-exchange facilities across town.

Post office (Th Thawiwong; ⌚9am-4.30pm Mon-Fri, to noon Sat)

Tourist police (☎1699; Th Thawiwong)

Getting There & Around

Air Asia (☎0 7634 1792; www.airasia.com; 39 Th Thawiwong; ⌚9am-9pm) has an office in town.

Túk-túks circulate around Patong for 50B to 100B per ride. There are numerous places to rent 125cc motorbikes and jeeps. **Big Bike Company** (☎0 7634 5100; 106 Th Rat Uthit) rents proper motorcycles (500B to 1000B per day). Keep in mind that the mandatory helmet law is strictly enforced in Patong, where roadblocks/checkpoints can spring up at a moment's notice. **Budget** (☎0 7629 2389; 44 Th Thawiwong; ⌚9am-4pm) has an office in the Patong Merlin Hotel.

Sŏrng·tăa·ou to Patong from Phuket Town leave from Th Ranong, near the day market and fountain circle; the fare is 25B. The after-hours charter fare is 500B. Sŏrng·tăa·ou then drop off and pick up passengers at the southern end of Patong beach. From here you can hop on a motorbike taxi (20B to 30B per ride), flag down a túk-túk (prices vary widely) or walk till your feet hurt.

Hat Kamala

หาดกมลา

A chilled-out hybrid of Hat Karon and Hat Surin, calm but fun Kamala tends to lure a mixture of longer-term, lower-key partying guests, a regular crop of Scandinavian families, and young couples. The bay is magnificent, turquoise and serene with shore breakers that lull you to sleep. Palms and pines mingle on the leafy and rocky northern end where the water is a rich emerald green and the snorkelling around the rock reef is pleasant, while new resorts are ploughed into the southern bluffs above the gathering longtails. The entire beach is backed with lush rolling hills, which one can only hope are left alone…forever. And it's the only beach with a walking path lined with this many restaurants, resorts and shops. Ditch the motorbike and step into Kamala bliss.

Sights & Activities

Local beach boffins will tell you that **Laem Singh**, just north of Kamala, is one of the best capes on the island. Walled in by cliffs, there is no road access so you have to park your car on the headland and clamber down a narrow path, or you could charter a long-tail (1000B) from Hat Kamala. It gets crowded.

Phuket Fantasea THEMED THEATRE $$
(Map p265; ☎0 7638 5000; www.phuket-fantasea.com; admission with/without dinner 1900/1500B; 6-11.30pm Fri-Wed) A US$60 million 'cultural theme park' located just east of Hat Kamala. Despite the billing, there aren't any rides, but there is a show that takes the colour and pageantry of Thai dance and combines this with state-of-the-art light-and-sound techniques that rival anything found in Las Vegas (think 30 elephants). All of this takes place on a stage dominated by a full-scale replica of a Khmer temple. Kids especially will be captivated by the spectacle but it is over-the-top cheesy, and cameras are forbidden.

Sleeping & Eating

Layalina Hotel HOTEL $$$
(Map p265; ☎0 7638 5942; www.layalinahotel.com; r incl breakfast 5500-7700B;) Nab one of the split-level suites with very private rooftop terraces at this small boutique hotel for romantic sunset views over white sand and blue sea. The decor is simple, Thai and chic, with fluffy white duvets and honey-toned wooden furniture. Room rates include a one-hour couple's massage at the on-site spa. The pool is ridiculously small – but that turquoise ocean *is* only steps away.

Cape Sienna Hotel HOTEL $$$
(Map p265; ☎0 7633 7300; www.capesienna.com; r 8500-10,130B, bungalows 4350-5600B;) This flashy, romantic hotel dominates the southern headland and offers magnificent azure bay views from the lobby, the pool and every single room. Rooms are modern, with plenty of clean, fresh lines and all the amenities. No kids allowed.

Clear House HOTEL $$
(Map p265; ☎0 7638 5401; www.clearhousephuket.com; r 1300B;) Shabby chic with a mod twist, white-washed rooms have pink feature walls, plush duvets, flat-screen TVs, wi-fi and huge pebbled baths. This place just feels good.

Beach Restaurants THAI, INTERNATIONAL $
(Map p265; Hat Kamala; dishes 50-250B; lunch & dinner) One of Kamala's highlights is its long stretch of eateries where you can dine in a swimsuit with your feet in the sand. There's everything from Thai to pizza, and plenty of cold beer. **Ma Ma Fati Ma** at the far northern part of the beach is our favourite.

Rockfish FUSION $$
(Map p265; ☎0 7627 9732; www.rockfishrestaurant.com; 33/6 Th Kamala Beach; dishes 150-1000B; breakfast, lunch & dinner) Perched above the river mouth and the bobbing long-tails, with beach, bay and mountain views, is Kamala's best dining room. It rolls out gems like braised duck breast with kale, and prosciutto-wrapped scallops.

Getting There & Away

To catch a regular sŏrng·tăa·ou from Kamala to Patong costs 50B per person, while a sŏrng·tăa·ou charter (starting in the evenings) costs 250B.

Hat Surin

หาดสุรินทร์

Like that hot boy or girl in school who also happens to have style, soul, a fun personality and wealthy parents, Surin beach is the kind of place that can inspire (travel) lust in anyone who meets him or her. With a wide, blonde beach, water that blends from pale turquoise in the shallows to a deep blue on the horizon and two lush, boulder-strewn headlands, Surin could easily attract tourists on looks alone. Ah, but there are stunning galleries, five-star spa resorts and wonderful beachfront dining options, too. So by the time you're done swimming, sunbathing, snacking at local fish grills and sipping cocktails at barefoot-chic beach clubs, don't be surprised if you've fallen in love.

Sleeping

Hat Surin is home to some of Phuket's classiest resorts but there's little available for small budgets.

TOP CHOICE Surin Phuket HOTEL $$$
(Map p265; ☎0 7662 1579; www.thesurinphuket.com; r 17,000-58,000B; ❄☎☒) Almost any place located on a private beach this quiet and stunning would have be a top pick. But the Surin's (previously 'The Chedi') bungalows, with naturalistic wooden exteriors that hide beneath the hillside foliage, and earthy, luxurious interiors, make the site that much better. The restaurant has a dreamy *Robinson Crusoe* feel and looks out over the water and an unexpectedly modern six-sided pool. You'll have to be in decent shape for walking around the resort, since it can be quite a hoof up hills and over wooden walkways to get to many of the bungalows. It received an extensive renovation mid-2011 so should be even better by the time you get there.

TOP CHOICE Twin Palms HOTEL $$$
(Map p265; ☎0 7631 6500; www.twinpalms-phuket.com; r 6100-38,800B; ❄@☎☒) This is the Audrey Hepburn of Phuket's hotels – it's classic yet completely contemporary. There's a pervasive feeling of space with minimalist, artsy swimming pools everywhere that are fringed by delicate white frangipani. Even the simplest rooms are extra spacious and have oversized bathrooms, sublimely comfortable beds and a supreme sense of calm. It's a few minutes' walk to the beach. Expats from all over Phuket can be found eating the island's most popular **brunch** (⊙noon-2pm; buffet 1300B) here on Sundays.

Chava HOTEL $$$
(Map p265; ☎0 7637 2600; www.thechavaresort.com; apt 14,000-18,000B; ❄@☒) Draped in flowering vines and blessed with gurgling fountains and shimmering reflection pools, this place is part hotel, part condo development and completely stylish. The massive two-, three- and four-bedroom apartments have fully stocked stylish, stainless-steel fridges in the kitchen, complete entertainment systems in the living room and another flat-screen TV in the master bedroom. It's privately owned and available for rent by the night, week and month. Bring a group and it can be terrific value.

Benyada Lodge HOTEL $$
(Map p265; ☎0 7627 1261; www.benyadalodge-phuket.com; r 2800-3500B; ❄@☎☒) Chic, modern rooms – with black louvred closets, terracotta-tiled bathrooms and silk, pastel-coloured throw pillows scattered in the lounging corner – are a great bargain for this area. Service is stellar. Admire in the sunset and have a dip in the pool at the rooftop bar or take the short walk to the beach.

Capri Hotel HOTEL $$
(Map p265; ☎0 7627 0597; www.phukethotelcapri.com; r 900-1500B; ❄☎) Here's your slice of Italy with pillars everywhere and Mediterranean-style painted archways over the bathrooms in the cute, bright rooms. The best nests have pink-painted wrought-iron balconies overlooking a not-very-European, but quiet street. Add the Italian bistro downstairs and it's a fantastic bargain.

Amanpuri Resort HOTEL $$$
(Map p265; ☎0 7632 4333; www.amanresorts.com; villas US$925-8050; ❄@☒) Over-the-top and luxurious, the Amanpuri is one of Phuket's most exclusive hotels (and a celebrity magnet).

Eating & Drinking

There are plenty of excellent restaurants in and around Surin. For cheap seafood, your first stop should be the numerous, fun and delicious seafront dining rooms.

TOP CHOICE Taste FUSION $$
(Map p265; ☎08 7886 6401; www.tastesurinbeach.com; tapas 160-225B) The best of a new breed of urban-meets-surf eateries along the beach. Dine indoors or alfresco on meal-sized salads, perfectly cooked fillet mignon or a variety of Thai-Mediterranean starters and mains. Service is outstanding and there's an enticing attached gallery selling Tibetan, Nepali and local jewellery and art.

Catch FUSION $$$
(Map p265; ☎0 7631 6500; mains 250-450B) Slip on your breeziest linen to dine at this draped, cabana-style eatery right on the beach. It's part of Twin Palms, even though

it's not attached, and has all the same classy attributes as the hotel in both ambience and cuisine.

Stereo Lab BAR, NIGHTCLUB
(Map p265; ☎08 9218 0162; www.stereolabphuket.com; ⏰11am-2am) A bar, dance floor and unbroken sea views. Special events feature known international DJs.

Information

There is an ATM at Surin Plaza, just east of the beach on Rte 4025. Internet access is available at most hotels for 1B per minute.

Getting There & Away

A regular sŏrng·tăa·ou from Phuket Town's Th Ranong to Hat Surin costs 35B per person, and túk-túk or sŏrng·tăa·ou charters cost 450B.

Rent cars from **Andaman Car Rental** (Map p265; ☎0 7662 1600; www.andamancarrent.com; ⏰9am-9pm), opposite the entrance to Twin Palms. Vehicles can be rented from 1400B per day.

Ao Bang Thao อ่าวบางเทา

Almost as large and even more beautiful than Ao Patong, the stunning, 8km-long white-sand sweep of Ao Bang Thao is the

Hat Kamala, Hat Surin & Ao Bang Thao

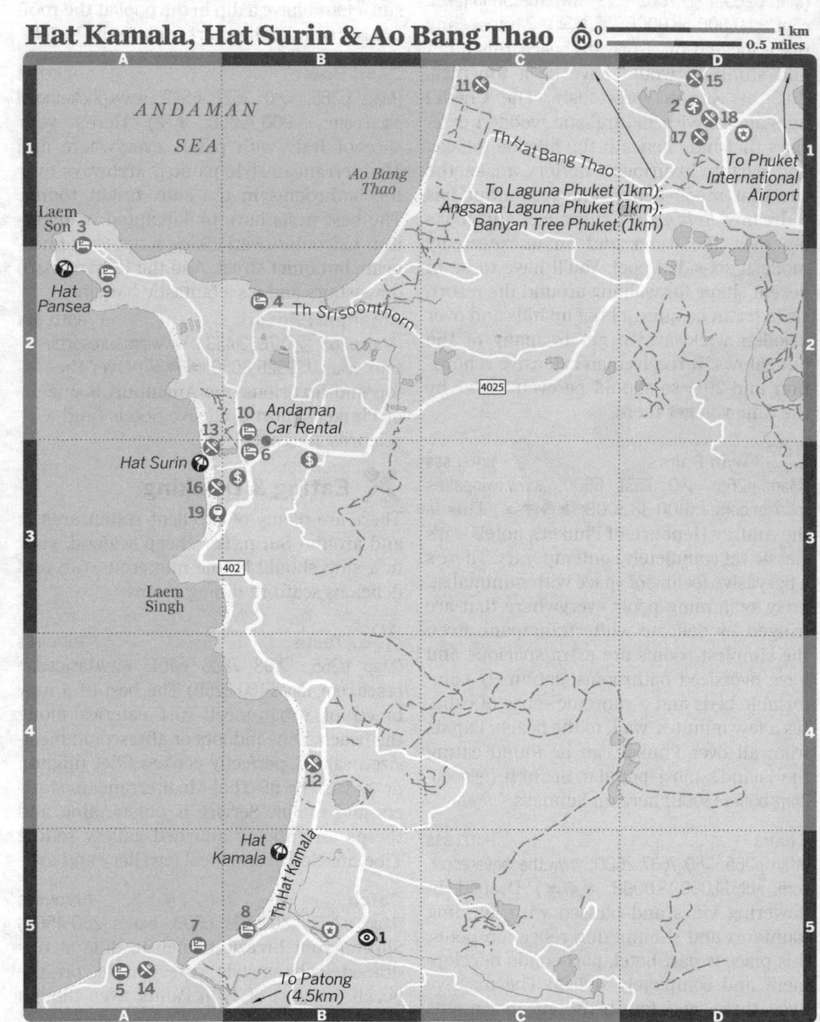

glue that binds the region's disparate elements. The southern half is home to a sprinkling of three-star bungalow resorts. Further inland you'll find an old fishing village laced with canals along with a number of upstart villa subdivisions. Don't be alarmed if you see a herd of water buffalo grazing just 100m from a gigantic construction site. That's how fast Bang Thao is changing.

Smack in the centre of it all is the somewhat absurd Laguna Phuket complex – a network of five four- and five-star resort properties and an ageing shopping mall knitted together by an artificial lake, patrolled by tourist shuttle boats, and a paved nature trail. But in the north Mother Nature asserts herself once more, and a lonely stretch of powder-white sand and tropical blue sea extends past all the bustle and change, and delivers the kind of peace you imagined when you booked your trip.

The **Hideaway Day Spa** (Map p265) has an excellent reputation. It offers traditional Thai massage, sauna and mud body wraps in a tranquil wooded setting at the edge of a lagoon. Treatments start at 1500B. The Hideaway also has its own line of spa products. See also p243.

Sleeping

Laguna Phuket is home to five luxury resorts, an 18-hole golf course and 30 restaurants (the gargantuan Sheraton Grande alone has eight restaurants). Guests at any one of the resorts can use the dining and recreation facilities at all of them. Frequent shuttle buses make the rounds of all the hotels, as do pontoon boats (via the linked lagoons).

TOP CHOICE **Banyan Tree Phuket** HOTEL $$$
(Map p265; 0 7632 4374; www.banyantree.com; villas from 25,000B;) One of Phuket's finest hotels, and the first to introduce bungalows with their own private pool, the Banyan Tree Phuket (in Laguna Phuket) is an oasis of sedate, understated luxury. Accommodation is in villas – and, as long as you're here, the on-site spa should not be missed.

Angsana Laguna Phuket HOTEL $$$
(Map p265; www.angsana.com; d from 8310B;) Gated away in Laguna Phuket, the Angsana Laguna Phuket is a remodel of the older Sheraton Grande Laguna. The gigantic hotel reopened in late 2011 and will appeal to a lively, active crowd. It features a gigantic 323m-long pool, water-sports facilities galore and well over 400 rooms.

Andaman Bangtao Bay Resort HOTEL $$$
(Map p265; 0 7627 0246; www.andamanbangtaobayresort.com; bungalows 3900-5900B;) Every bungalow has a sea view and there's a summer-camp vibe at this pleasant little resort. The design is very Thai, with woodcarvings on the walls and coconuts hanging from the eaves of the roofs, but for this price we expected a little more luxury.

Eating

Many of Phuket's finest eateries are found just outside Laguna's main gate, and there

Hat Kamala, Hat Surin & Ao Bang Thao

Sights
1 Phuket Fantasea B5

Activities, Courses & Tours
2 Hideaway Day Spa D1

Sleeping
3 Amanpuri Resort A1
4 Andaman Bangtao Bay Resort B2
Benyada Lodge .... (see 6)
5 Cape Sienna Hotel A5
6 Capri Hotel B3
Chava .... (see 10)
7 Clear House A5
8 Layalina Hotel B5
9 Surin Phuket A2
10 Twin Palms B2

Eating
11 Babylon Beach Club C1
12 Beach Restaurants B4
13 Catch A3
Chaba .... (see 18)
14 Rockfish A5
15 Siam Supper Club D1
16 Taste A3
17 Tatonka D1
18 Tawai Restaurant D1

Drinking
19 Stereo Lab A3

are even more at the seafood-oriented beach cafes south of the Banyan Tree Phuket.

Tatonka INTERNATIONAL $$$
(Map p265; ☎0 7632 4349; Th Srisoonthorn; dishes 250-300B; ⏲dinner Thu-Tue) This is the home of 'globetrotter cuisine', which owner-chef Harold Schwarz developed by taking fresh local products and combining them with cooking and presentation techniques learned in Europe, Colorado and Hawaii. The eclectic, tapas-style selection includes creative vegetarian and seafood dishes and such delights as Peking duck pizza (220B). There's also a tasting menu (750B per person, minimum two people), which lets you try a little of everything. Call ahead during the high season.

Siam Supper Club INTERNATIONAL $$$
(Map p265; ☎0 7627 0936; Hat Bang Thao; dishes 180-450B) One of the hippest spots on Phuket where the 'infamous' come to sip cocktails, listen to breezy jazz and eat an excellent meal. The menu is predominantly Western with gourmet pizzas, seafood *cioppino* (Italian style seafood stew) and hearty mains such as veal tenderloin with wild mushrooms on truffle mash. Don't miss the insane cheesecake.

Babylon Beach Club ITALIAN, THAI $$$
(Map p265; ☎08 1970 5302; Hat Bang Thao; dishes 120-850B; 👪) Accessible by dirt road are the seaside, polished, whitewashed environs of the Babylon Beach Club. Under new Italian management, lunch is more casual 'beach fare' such as burgers and salads while dinner gets more lavish with mains like prawn and asparagus risotto.

Tawai Restaurant THAI $$$
(Map p265; ☎0 7632 5381; Moo 1, Laguna Resort Entrance; mains 180-300B) Set in a lovely old house decorated with traditional art is this gem of a Thai kitchen, serving classics like roast duck curry and pork *lâhp*. Free shuttle service is available to and from the Laguna hotels.

Chaba THAI $$$
(Map p265; ☎0 7627 1580; Moo 1, Laguna Resort Entrance; meals 400-800B) Upscale Thai served with flair on the lagoon just outside the Laguna gates. Just point and the restaurant will steam, grill or fry it.

Getting There & Away

A sŏrng·tăa·ou between Ao Bang Thao and Phuket Town's Th Ranong costs 25B per person. Túk-túk charters are 700B.

Sirinat National Park

อุทยานแห่งชาติสิรินาถ

Comprising the beaches of Nai Thon, Nai Yang and Mai Khao, as well as the former Nai Yang National Park and Mai Khao wildlife reserve, **Sirinat National Park** (☎0 7632 8226; www.dnp.go.th; admission 200B; ⏲8am-5pm) encompasses 22 sq km of coastal land, plus 68 sq km of sea.

The whole area is 15 minutes or less from Phuket International Airport, which makes it particularly convenient for a first stop after a long trip.

Sleeping

HAT NAI THON

หาดในทอน

If you're after a lovely arc of fine golden sand, away from the buzz of Phuket busyness, **Hat Nai Thon** is it. Swimming is quite good here except at the height of the monsoon, and there is some coral near the headlands at either end of the bay.

Naithonburi HOTEL $$$
(☎0 7620 5500; www.naithonburi.com; Moo 4, Th Hat Nai Thon; r 3500-4500B; ❄📶@🏊👪) A mellow megaresort if ever there was one. Yes, it has 222 rooms, but it rarely feels too crowded. Rooms are spacious with terracotta tile floors, Thai silks on the bed and private balconies. The enormous pool is lined with lounges and daybeds. Its **Chao Lay Bistro** (mains from 180B) is as swank as Nai Thon gets.

Naithon Beach Resort HOTEL $$$
(☎0 7620 5379; www.phuket-naithon.com; 23/31 Moo 4, Th Hat Nai Thon; cottages 3300B; ⏲Nov-May; ❄) Aka Woody's Paradise. Small polished wood chalets with slate bathrooms are tucked into the south end of Hat Nai Thon, 10 steps from the sand.

HAT NAI YANG & HAT MAI KHAO

หาดในยาง/หาดไม้ขาว

Hat Nai Yang's bay is sheltered by a reef that slopes 20m below the surface – which makes for both good snorkelling in the dry season and fantastic surfing in the monsoon season. Along the dirt road at the very southern end is a seemingly endless strip of seafood restaurants, beach bars and, oddly enough, tailor shops. It's all refreshingly rough around the edges.

About 5km north of Hat Nai Yang is **Hat Mai Khao**, Phuket's longest beach. Sea turtles lay their eggs here between November and February. Take care when swimming, as there's a strong year-round undertow. Except on weekends and holidays you'll have this place almost to yourself.

Anantara Phuket HOTEL **$$$**
(☎0 7633 6100; www.phuket.anantara.com; 888 Moo 3, Tumbon Mai Khao; villas from 35,000B;) This all-villa property opens onto a serene lotus-filled lagoon that extends to the beach. Luxurious, classic Thai pool villas are connected to the lobby, bars and restaurants, and to the beach by old timber boardwalks that wind beneath swaying palms. It also offers the **Bua Luang Spa** (see p243) and its **Sea Fire Salt Restaurant** is worth a romantic splurge even if you're not staying here.

TOP CHOICE **Indigo Pearl** HOTEL **$$$**
(☎0 7632 7006; www.indigo-pearl.com; r 6800-26,250B;) One of the most unique and hip of Phuket's high-end resorts takes its design cues from the island's tin-mining history. Although it sounds weird, this industrial theme melded with tropical luxe creates a spectacularly soothing place to stay. Hardware, such as vices, scales and other mining tools, is used in the decor to the tiniest detail – even the toilet-paper rolls are big bolts – and the common lounge areas are infused with indigo light. The gardens are modern and lush, and surround a pool that looks like an oasis with a big waterfall.

Sala Resort & Spa HOTEL **$$$**
(☎0 7633 8888; www.salaphuket.com; 333 Moo 3, Tambon Maikhao; r from 11,550B, villas from 15,750B;) This uberstylish, boutique property is a blend of Sino-Portuguese and art deco influences with mod flair. Even 2nd-floor rooms have outdoor bathrooms. The black-granite infinity pool at the beachfront is gorgeous, and the bar area includes cushy, circular sofa lounges. It's the kind of place that makes everyone feel like a celebrity. It also offers spa services (p243).

Nai Yang Beach Resort HOTEL **$$**
(☎0 7632 8300; www.naiyangbeachresort.com; 65/23-24 Th Hat Nai Yang; r from 3600B;) This workhorse of a midranger is as clean as it is busy and dominates casuarina-lined Hat Nai Yang. The lowest-end rooms are fan-cooled, while higher-end ones are decorated in modern Thai style and are quite chic.

JW Marriott Phuket Resort & Spa HOTEL **$$$**
(☎0 7633 8000; www.marriott.com; r from 6800B;) So big there's a free shuttle to get around it, the Marriott wends its way around swimming pools and lily ponds along a steep light-gold beach – at night it's lit by flaming torches. Rooms are elegant with big bathrooms, hardwoods and sea views.

Sirinat National Park CAMPING GROUND **$$**
(☎0 7632 7152; www.dnp.go.th/parkreserve/nature.asp?lg=2, reserve@dnp.go.th; campsites 30B, bungalows 1000-2000B) There are campsites (bring your own tent) and large, concrete bungalows at the park headquarters on a gorgeous, shady, white sand bluff. Check in at the visitors centre or book online or via email.

Rimlay Bungalows GUEST HOUSE **$**
(☎08 9646 0239; andaman-car@hotmail.com; 90 Moo 5 Nai Yang; bungalow 500B, r 800-1800B) Spread over two properties, bamboo bungalows are minuscule and basic while fan-cooled or air-con rooms are tiled, have attached hot-water bathrooms and are great value.

Getting There & Away

If you're coming from the airport, a taxi costs about 200B. There is no regular sŏrng·tăa·ou, but a túk-túk charter from Phuket Town costs about 800B.

Khao Phra Thaew Royal Wildlife & Forest Reserve

อุทยานสัตว์ป่าเขาพระแทว

It's not all sand and sea. In the north of the island, this park protects 23 sq km of virgin island rainforest (evergreen monsoon forest). There are some pleasant hikes over the hills and a couple of photogenic waterfalls: **Nam Tok Ton Sai** and **Nam Tok Bang Pae**. The falls are best seen in the rainy season between June and November; in the dry months they are less impressive. The highest point in the park is **Khao Phara** (442m). Because of its royal status, the reserve is better protected than the average national park in Thailand.

A German botanist discovered a rare and unique species of palm in Khao Phra Thaew about 50 years ago. Called the white-backed palm – or *langkow* palm – the fan-shaped plant stands 3m to 5m tall and is found only here and in Khao Sok National Park (p288).

Tigers, Malayan sun bears, rhinos and elephants once roamed the forest here, but nowadays resident mammals are limited to humans, pigs, monkeys, slow loris, langur, civets, flying foxes, squirrels, mousedeer and other smaller animals. Watch out for cobras and wild pigs.

The tiny **Phuket Gibbon Rehabilitation Centre** (Map p242; ☎0 7626 0492; www.gibbonproject.org; donations encouraged; ⏲9am-4pm), in the park near Nam Tok Bang Pae, is open to the public. Financed by donations (1500B will care for a gibbon for one year), the centre adopts gibbons that have been kept in captivity in the hopes they can be reintroduced to the wild.

Park rangers may act as guides for hikes in the park on request; payment for services is negotiable.

To get to Khao Phra Thaew from Phuket Town, take Th Thepkasatri north about 20km to Thalang District and turn right at the intersection for Nam Tok Ton Sai, which is 3km down the road.

Thalang District อำเภอถลาง

A few hundred metres northeast of the famous **Heroines Monument** (Map p242) in Thalang District on Rte 4027, and about 11km northwest of Phuket Town, is **Thalang National Museum** (Map p242; ☎0 7631 1426; admission 30B; ⏲8.30am-4pm). The museum contains five exhibition halls chronicling southern themes such as the history of Thalang-Phuket and the colonisation of the Andaman coast. The legend of the 'two heroines' (memorialised on the nearby monument), who supposedly drove off an 18th-century Burmese invasion force by convincing the island's women to dress as men, is also recounted in detail.

Also in Thalang District, just north of the crossroads near Thalang town, is **Wat Phra Thong** (Map p242; admission by donation; ⏲dawn-dusk), Phuket's 'Temple of the Gold Buddha'. The image is half buried so that only the head and shoulders are visible. According to local legend, those who have tried to excavate the image have become very ill or encountered serious accidents. The temple is particularly revered by Thai-Chinese, many of whom believe the image hails from China. During Chinese New Year pilgrims descend from Phang-Nga, Takua Pa and Krabi.

RANONG PROVINCE

Ranong ระนอง

POP 27,772

On the eastern bank of the Sompaen River's turbid, tea-brown estuary, the frontier town of Ranong is a short boat ride – or a filthy swim – from Myanmar. This border town par excellence (shabby, frenetic, slightly seedy) has a thriving Burmese population (keep an eye out for men wearing traditional *longyi*, Burmese sarongs), a clutch of hot springs and some tremendous street food.

Today the town is basking in transit tourism to Ko Phayam more than the visa runs it was once known for (visas given at the border are only two weeks now). Meanwhile, more and more dive operators specialising in live-aboard trips to the Surin Islands and Burma Banks are establishing themselves here, adding a pinch of an expat feel.

Activities

Rakswarin Hot Springs HOT SPRINGS
(Th Petchkasem; admission free; ⏲8am-5pm) Ranong lacks the sophistication of your standard spa town, but you can sample the waters near this sacred, outdoor hot spring where pools are hot enough to boil eggs (65°C); it's thought to possess miraculous healing powers.

Siam Hot Spa HOT SPRINGS
(☎0 7781 3551; www.siamhotsparanong.com; 73/3 Th Petchkasem) Opposite the public springs, this place offers a more sterilised mineral bath experience. You can dip into Jacuzzi (600B) or standard tubs (300B), and pair it with a salt scrub (550B) or a massage (200B).

Diving

Live-aboard diving trips to world-class bubble-blowing destinations, including the Burma Banks and the Surin and Similan Islands, are all the rage in Ranong. Try **A-One-Diving** (☎0 7783 2984; www.a-one-diving.com; 256 Th Ruangrat; 4-night packages from 15,900B) or **Andaman International Dive Center** (☎0 7783 4824; www.aidcdive.com; Th Petchkasem), located at the bus station.

Sleeping

Accommodation in town can help you arrange a visa run and transport to the islands.

The places on or near Th Petchkasem (Hwy 4) can be reached from town by sŏrng·tăa·ou 2.

Luang Poj GUEST HOUSE $
(☎0 7783 3377, 08 7266 6333; luangpoj@gmail.com; 225 Th Ruangrat; r 500B; ❄📶) This new and expanding place is a gorgeous remodel

Ranong

Ranong

Sights
Siam Hot Spa...........(see 3)

Activities, Courses & Tours
1 Andaman International Dive Center...........C4
2 A-One Diving...........B2
3 Rakswarin Hot Springs...........D3

Sleeping
4 Dhala House...........B2
5 Luang Poj...........B3
6 Springs Guest House...........D3
7 Suta House Bungalows...........B2

Eating
8 Appreski Resort...........D4
9 Day Market...........B3
10 Jammy Bar...........B2
11 Night Market...........D3
12 Sophon's Hideaway...........B1

RENEWING YOUR VISA AT VICTORIA POINT

The dusty, tumbledown port at the southernmost tip of mainland Myanmar was named Victoria Point by the British, but is known as Ko Song (Second Island) by the Thais. The Burmese appellation, Kawthoung, is most likely a corruption of the Thai name. Most travellers come here to renew their visas, but the place also makes an interesting day trip.

Fishing and trade with Thailand keep things ticking over, but Kawthoung also churns out some of Myanmar's best kickboxers. Nearby islands are inhabited by bands of nomadic *chow lair* (sea gypsies; also spelled *chao leh*).

The easiest way to renew your visa is to opt for one of the 'visa trips' (from 1000B per person including visa fees) offered by travel agencies in Ranong such as Pon's Place, but it's relatively easy to do the legwork yourself.

When the Thailand–Myanmar border is open, boats to Kawthoung leave from the pier at **Saphan Plaa** (off Map p271; Pla Bridge) about 5km from the centre of Ranong. Take sŏrng·tăa·ou (passenger pick-up truck) 2 from Ranong (20B) to the pier, where long-tail captains will lead you to the immigration window then to their boat (per person one-way/return 100/200B). When negotiating your price, confirm whether it is per person or per ride, and one way or return. At the checkpoint, you must inform the authorities that you're a day visitor – in which case you will pay a fee of US$10 (it must be a crisp bill, you can get one from harbour touts for 500B). The only big hassles come from 'helpers' on the Myanmar side who offer to do everything from carrying your day pack to collecting forms, then ask for hefty tips.

It's possible to stay overnight in one of Victoria Point's dingy, overpriced hotels but take note that this is a rough town and lone women in particular may not feel safe. If you have a valid Myanmar visa in your passport, you'll be permitted to stay for up to 28 days.

If you're just coming to renew your Thai visa, the whole process will take a minimum of two hours. Bear in mind when you are returning to Thailand that Myanmar's time is 30 minutes behind Thailand's. This has caused problems in the past for returning visitors who got through Burmese immigration before its closing time only to find the **Thai Immigration office** (⌚8.30am-4.30pm) closed. It's a good idea to double-check Thai immigration closing hours when leaving the country – if you don't get stamped in you'll have to return to Myanmar again the next day.

of a 1920s-era building that was once Ranong's first hotel. Rooms are windowless and share warm-water bathrooms but each is spotless, very comfy and decorated in a signature colour and modern flair: think Indian art, birdcages, one-of-a-kind light fixtures and retro photography.

Dhala House GUEST HOUSE $
(☎0 7781 2959; http://dahla.siam2web.com; 323/5 Th Ruangrat; r 400-500B; ❄📶) Cute, concrete bungalows with tiled floors and pebbled tile baths line a garden; set off the main drag. It's got the friendliest vibe in town and management will happily arrange a late check-out if you're on a visa run.

Suta House Bungalows GUEST HOUSE $
(☎0 7783 2707; Th Ruangrat; r 250-500B; ❄) Right in the town centre, this off-the-road, very popular place has a cluster of simple ageing bungalows – and plenty of flowers. Beds are hard but the showers are hot.

Springs Guest House GUEST HOUSE $
(☎0 7781 2818; Th Kamlangsap; r with shared bathroom 250B) This guest house has quirky retro-cool rooms with shared bathrooms at the mouth of Ranong canyon.

Eating & Drinking

Ranong has a lively, young and very local drinking scene involving lots of karaoke.

On Th Kamlangsap, not far from Hwy 4, there is a night market that sells great Thai dishes at low prices. The day market on Th Ruangrat offers inexpensive Thai and Burmese meals.

Appreski Resort SCANDINAVIAN $
(☎08 7817 7033; 129/6 Moo 1, Th Petchkasem; sandwiches 45B; ⌚breakfast, lunch & dinner) Built into Ranong canyon across the river from the hot springs, this eatery has cultivated a reputation for Danish-style open sandwiches piled with imported cheese, pork liver pâté or gravlax cured in-house.

Jammy Bar THAI, INTERNATIONAL **$$**
(Th Ruangrat; dishes from 69B; 📶) The indoor/outdoor garden with polished cement pillars and terracotta tiles is vaguely Balinese and is the best-looking dining area in town. Luckily the food is great, too: the Thai dishes are fantastic, as are the stranger choices including grilled ostrich (229B), crocodile (177B) or local beef (129B). There's live music on weekend nights.

Sophon's Hideaway THAI, INTERNATIONAL **$$**
(☎0 7783 2730; Th Ruangrat; mains 80-250B; ⏰10am-midnight; 📶) This expat favourite has everything, including internet access, a free pool table, a pizza oven, a full bar, water features and rattan furnishings aplenty.

Information

Internet can be found along Th Ruangrat for 20B per hour and there are a cluster of ATMs at the Th Tha Meuang and Th Ruangrat intersection.

Immigration Offices

The main Thai immigration office is on the road to Saphan Plaa, about halfway between town and the main piers, across from a branch of the Thai Farmer's Bank. If entering Thailand from Myanmar via Kawthoung, you'll have to visit this office to get your passport stamped with a visa on arrival, but you'll still only get 15 days.

There is also a smaller immigration post in the vicinity of Tha Saphan Plaa. If you're just going in and out of Myanmar's Kawthoung for the day, a visit to the small post will suffice.

Post

Main post office (Th Chonrau; ⏰9am-4pm Mon-Fri, to noon Sat)

Telephone

Communications Authority of Thailand (CAT; Th Tha Meuang; ⏰24hr)

Getting There & Away

Air

Ranong Air (☎0 7783 2222; www.ranongair.com) runs four flights per week between Ranong and Bangkok (one way 2800B), Phuket (one way 2300B) and Hat Yai (one way 2800B). Book flights at Pon's Place (see p273).

Bus

The bus terminal is on Th Petchkasem 1km from town, though some Bangkok-bound buses stop at the main market. Sŏrng·tăa·ou 2 (blue) passes the terminal.

DESTINATION	FARE (B)	DURATION (HR)
Bangkok	240-680	10
Chumphon	100	3
Hat Yai	410	5
Khao Lak	150	3½
Krabi	200-300	6
Phang-Nga	150	5
Phuket	240	5-6
Surat Thani	100-180	4-5

Minivans (Map p271) head to Surat Thani (250B, 3½ hours, four times daily) and Chumphon (120B, three hours, hourly from 6am to 5pm).

Getting Around

Motorcycle taxis will take you almost anywhere in town for 20B, to the hotels along Th Petchkasem for 25B and to the pier for boats to Ko Chang, Ko Phayam and Myanmar for 50B. Pon's Place can assist with motorcycle and car rentals and offers shuttle vans from its office to the ferry docks for 50B.

Ko Phayam

เกาะพยาม

Technically part of Laem Son National Park (p276), little Ko Phayam is a beautiful, beach-laden isle that – for now – is managing to go mainstream while still holding onto its soul. With spectacular beaches on the northwest and southwest coasts dotted with beach bungalows, breezy restaurants and bars, and a wooded interior laced with concrete streets, you can certainly understand the appeal. Fauna in the area includes wild pigs, monkeys and snakes, and there

PON'S PLACE: RANONG'S TOURISM EXPERT

Pon's Place (☎08 1597 4549; www.ponplace-ranong.com; Th Ruangrat; ⏰7.30am-midnight) has become the go-to spot in Ranong for everything from Western breakfasts (from 40B) to Ranong Air bookings and information about bus schedules. Pon himself is a high-energy, friendly guy with his phone essentially attached to his head as he micromanages his Ranong tourism empire. If you need help with anything, stop here first.

KO PHAYAM'S BEACHES

Ko Phayam is dotted with small beaches but these two long stretches of sandy bliss are where most folks end up:

Ao Khao Kwai (Buffalo Bay) A luscious cove with golden sand, jungled bluffs and a rock reef offshore – it's the most stunning location on the island. Lovers of peace and quiet head here along with some hippies and the occasional German package tourist. It's a terrific swimming beach, too, except at low tide when the sea recedes leaving mud flats at the southern end.

Ao Yai Long, wide and chilled out yet social, attracting everyone from gap-year backpackers to glam-packing couples to young families to retirees. Surf kicks up in the fringe and low seasons and you can rent boogie boards and surfboards at guest houses along the beach. At other times the swimming is great here and the island's best snorkelling (don't expect much) is found off Leam Rung, Ao Yai's northernmost point.

is tremendous bird life. Look for sea eagles, toucans and hornbills. The one 'village' on the island, where you will also find the main pier and a majestic golden Buddha at **Wat Phayam**, caters mostly to tourists but hit it during a festival (such as the Cashew Festival in April) and you'll see that islanders still have a firm grip on their homeland. Motorcycle pathways run down the middle of the island, feeding smaller concrete roadways and dirt trails, some of which can be rutted to the point of hazardous – drive slowly.

The main drawback of Ko Phayam is that the snorkelling isn't great. But the Surin Islands are closer to here than anywhere else and you can hop aboard live-aboard dive expeditions or speedboat transfers. For dive trips and PADI courses contact **Phayam Divers** (☎08 6995 2598; www.phayamlodge.com; Ao Yai).

Sleeping

Electricity is often only available from sunset to 10pm or 11pm. Most resorts are open year-round and have attached eateries serving Thai fare.

AO KHAO KWAI & AO HIN-KHOW

The only (very slow) internet on Ao Khao Kwai is at Mr Gao's for 2B per minute.

TOP CHOICE **PP Land** HOTEL $
(☎08 1678 4310; www.payampplandbeach.com; Ao Hin-Khow; bungalows 650B;) A stunning eco-lodge, north of the pier on the little-visited windward side of the island. The stylish concrete bungalows are powered by the wind and sun and have terraces that overlook the sea. The Belgian–Thai owners also preserved a vast tract of jungle south of the resort, and good birdwatching is available from the top floor of their restaurant. They have an organic garden, make their own all-natural laundry detergent and treat the sewage with a cutting-edge grey-water system. Some people talk green; these folks live it.

Chomjan Resort HOTEL $
(☎08 5678 4166; www.chomjanresort.com; Ao Khao Kwai; bungalows 500-800B) One of the most comfortable places on this beach, tidy concrete bungalow are perched on a beachside slope and have sea views through mature trees. All have terraces with lounging cushions and open-to-sky bathrooms but otherwise the decor is fairly bland. The restaurant here serves excellent Thai fare.

TOP CHOICE **Buffalo Bay Vacation Club** HOTEL $$
(☎08 5107 9473; www.buffalobayclub.com; Ao Khao Kwai; bungalows 600-1500B;) Run by Dimitri, a charming Russian world traveller, Buffalo's spotless, airtight, concrete bungalows with sliding glass doors, hot water and TVs are posh by Phayam standards and great value. Even better is the amazing restaurant – serving the best international food north of Phuket – that has a phenomenal menu including everything from (excellent) fajitas to authentic Thai curries.

Starlight Bungalows GUEST HOUSE $
(☎08 1978 5301; http://sites.google.com/site/starlightbungalows; Ao Khao Kwai; bungalows 500-650B) American–Thai run, choose from high-ceilinged spacious wooden huts or small bamboo ones farther back in the trees. The social vibe here is fab, as is the food – Pom, the cook, regularly wins local Thai food cook-offs.

Jansom Bungalows HOTEL $

(☎08 9587 8252; Ao Khao Kwai; bungalows 400-500B) The wooden bungalows here are basic but the view from the terraces over white sand, grey boulders and aqua sea is simply stunning. The landscaped gardens and stone pathways also make this place feel more upscale. It's right off the beach and the restaurant is reliably good.

Mr Gao HOTEL $

(☎0 7787 0222; www.mr-gao-phayam.com; Ao Khao Kwai; bungalows from 250B;) The varnished wood or bamboo bungalows are very popular with activity-oriented couples and families. It has 24-hour electricity and kayak rental, and arranges transport and multiday trips to the Surin Islands (p278).

AO YAI

A new upscale resort was under construction on Ao Yai when we passed and more are likely to follow. Most places have wi-fi or internet for 2B per minute.

Bamboo Bungalows GUEST HOUSE $$

(☎0 7782 0012; www.bamboo-bungalows.com; bungalows 550-1500B;) A very popular and social beachfront property. There's a lush garden and an attractive lounge-restaurant with hammocks and cool log swings out the front. Bungalows range from sagging bamboo jobs to fairly luxurious peaked-roof cottages that have tiled floors, ceiling fans and outdoor rain showers. There's 24-hour electricity and free kayaks.

Frog Beach House HOTEL $$

(☎08 3542 7559; frogbeach@gmail.com; bungalows 800-1000B) This is a lovely spot with traditional Thai-style hardwood chalets with wooden floors, outdoor bathrooms, glass-bowl sinks and mosquito nets, all lined up just off the beach next to a small stream. The beach is laid-back and gorgeous but management is rather strict, so mind your Ps and Qs.

Aow Yai Bungalows GUEST HOUSE $

(☎0 7787 0216, 08 9819 8782; bungalows 300-600B) The thatched bamboo bungalow pioneer that started it all 24 years ago. This French–Thai operation was Phayam's first and remains one of the island's best. Choose between small wooden and bamboo bungalows in the palm grove and a larger beachfront model on the southern end of Ao Yai. It rents snorkelling gear, kayaks and bodyboards, too.

Drinking

Hippy Bar BAR

(Ao Khao Kwai; ⏰11am-2am Nov-Apr) An amazing beach bar cobbled out of found driftwood, bottles, seashells and anything else that has happened to wash up on shore. The lounge resembles the bow of a pirate ship. There are orchids, waterfall fountains and dub tunes on the sound system.

River Bar BAR

(Ao Yai; ⏰11am-2am) A highly recommended watering hole that sits by the river mouth on Ao Yai. If it has a party going on, be there.

Getting There & Away

From Ranong, take a sŏrng·tăa·ou from Th Ruangrat Market (25B) or one of the many shuttles that service most guest houses (50B) to the Phayam Pier near Saphan Plaa. If you have three or more people in your group it makes better sense to hire a driver (100B).

There are daily ferries from here to Ko Phayam's main pier (150B, 1½ to two hours) at 9am and 2pm, and speedboats (350B, 45 minutes) at 10am and 2.30pm. From Ko Phayam back to Ranong the boats run at 9am and 1pm. Long-tail boat charters to Ko Chang are 1200B, or you can take the taxi boat (150B, one hour) that departs from the main pier on weekdays only at 4pm.

Getting Around

Motorcycle taxis provide transport around Ko Phayam; there are no cars. A motorcycle taxi from the pier to the main beaches costs 50B to 80B per person each way, depending on the beach. Walking is possible but distances are long – it's about 45 minutes from the pier to Ao Khao Kwai, the nearest bay. Motorbike and bicycle rentals are available in the village, and from most of the larger resorts.

Ko Chang เกาะช้าง

This little-visited rustic isle is a long way – in every respect – from its much more popular Trat Province namesake. Pass the time exploring the island's tiny village capital (where the boats dock during the dry season) or wend your way around the island on one of the dirt trails. Sea eagles, Andaman kites and hornbills all nest here and, if you're lucky, you'll catch sight of them floating above the mangroves and the jungled east coast. The wide, west-coast beach of **Ao Yai** has gorgeous marbled white and black sand in the south, which obscures the otherwise clear water. A short trail leads over the bluff to **Ao Tadeng**, another marbled beach strewn with boulders and the island's best sunset spot. White-sand snobs will be happiest on Ao Yai's north end.

There are no banks or cars on Ko Chang, but internet has arrived at **Cashew Resort** (Ao Yai; per min 2B).

Bungalow operations on the island can arrange **boat trips** to Ko Phayam and other nearby islands for around 200B per person (including lunch) in a group of six or more. Dive trips are also possible. **Aladdin Dive Safari** (☎0 7782 0472; www.aladdindivecruise.de) runs PADI courses and offers a range of live-aboard dive safaris. A five-day live-aboard trip to Myanmar costs 28,500B; a four-day trip visiting both the Surin and Similan Islands costs 20,400B.

Trails lead south from the village in the island's interior to the national park station on the east coast. That's where you'll find the island's best stretch of intact jungle. Elsewhere it's all been tamed into cashew orchards and rubber plantations.

Sleeping & Eating

Basic bamboo huts reign supreme on Ko Chang and, for the most part, they're only open from November to April. Electricity is limited and a few places have solar and wind power.

Ao Yai is the main beach where you'll find most lodging options and a few more places are tucked away on Ao Tadaeng, to the south, which is linked to Ao Yai via a short walking track. More isolated options can be found on the beaches to the north and far south of the island.

Crocodile Rock GUEST HOUSE $
(☎08 0533 4138; tonn1970@yahoo.com; Ao Yai; bungalows 250-450B) Outstanding bamboo bungalows perched on Ao Yai's serene southern headland. Although it's not 'on' the beach, it has superb bay views through gentle foliage. Its classy kitchen turns out homemade yoghurt, breads, cookies, good espresso, and a variety of veggie and seafood dishes. This place has its own pier, so ask to be dropped here by the long-tail.

Sawasdee GUEST HOUSE $
(☎08 6906 0900, 08 1803 0946; www.sawadeekohchang.com; Ao Yai; bungalows 350-600B) New-looking A-frame wooden bungalows have vented walls to keep things cool and every option has sunken bathrooms painted bright colours, and hammocks on the terraces. Its alfresco restaurant (think driftwood furniture spread beneath a massive tree dangling with lanterns) is as classy as it is delicious.

Sunset Bungalows GUEST HOUSE $
(☎08 4339 5224, 08 0693 8577; Ao Yai; bungalows 250-400B) Sweet wooden bungalows with bamboo decks and attached Thai-style bathrooms sit back in the trees lining Ao Yai's best stretch of beach. The restaurant is charming and offers a tasty menu, and the staff is as friendly and happy as they come.

Mama's GUEST HOUSE $
(☎0 7782 0180, 08 0530 7066; mamasbungalows@yahoo.com; Ao Tadaeng; huts 250-300B) One of three good choices on Ao Tadaeng, Mama's is tucked into a pretty corner on a rocky, hibiscus-laden hillside. The good-sized wooden huts here all have private bathrooms. Mama serves some of the best Thai food around.

Getting There & Away

From Ranong take a sŏrng·tăa·ou (25B) from the day market on Th Ruangrat to Tha Ko Phayam near Saphan Plaa. Alternatively, most Ranong guest houses will arrange for a taxi to shuttle you to the pier for 50 to 100B.

Two speedboats to Ao Yai (per person 350B, 45 minutes, 10am and 2.30pm) leave daily from late October to April. They return to Ranong at 9am and 1pm. It's cheaper and just as convenient to travel on one of three daily long-tail taxi boats (per person 150B, two hours, 9.30am, noon, 2pm). They stop at all the west-coast beaches. Taxi boats return at 7.30am and 1.30pm. During the monsoon months boats make the crossing three days a week, docking at the main pier on the northeast coast.

A taxi boat service connecting Ko Chang and Ko Phayam runs on weekdays only by Koh Chang Resort. Taxi boats (per person 150B each way, one hour) leave Ko Chang at 10am weekdays and return at 4pm. You can also charter a long-tail boat to Ko Phayam through Koh Chang Resort (1200B) or Mama's (800B).

Laem Son National Park

อุทยานแห่งชาติแหลมสน

This **national park** (☎0 7786 1431; www.dnp.go.th; adult/child 200/100B) covers 315 sq km, and includes about 100km of Andaman Sea coastline – the longest protected shore in the country – and over 20 islands. Much of the coast here is edged with mangroves and laced with tidal channels, home to various species of birds, fish, deer and monkeys. Sea turtles nest on Hat Praphat.

The most accessible beach is the gorgeous 3km white sweep of **Hat Bang Ben**, where the park headquarters are located. Look south and peninsulas jut out into the ocean like fingers hiding isolated coves accessible only by long-tail boat. All of the beaches are said to be safe for swimming year-round. From here you can also see several islands, including the nearby Ko Kam Yai, Ko Kam Noi, Mu Ko Yipun, Ko Khang Khao and, to the north, Ko Phayam. Park staff arrange boat trips to any of these islands for 1500B to 1800B depending upon the destination. If there is a prettier sunset picnic spot on the north Andaman coast, we missed it.

Sleeping & Eating

The following accommodation options are at Hat Bang Ben. Camping is allowed anywhere among the casuarinas for 80B per person (pay at the park office just inside the park entrance) or you can rent a tent from 150B per night.

Wasana Resort GUEST HOUSE $
(☎0 7786 1434; bungalows 400-750B; ❄📶) A family-run ring of cosy bungalows wrapping around the colourful on-site restaurant. The owners, a Dutch–Thai couple, have plenty of great ideas for exploring Laem Son (ask about the stunning 10km trek around the headland) and can take you on a day trip to the islands.

National Park Bungalows HOTEL $$
(☎0 2562 0760; reserve@dnp.go.th; bungalows with fan 1200B, houses with air-con 1600B; ❄) Choose from basic fan-cooled bungalows and bigger, air-conditioned houses. The on-site restaurant serves three meals per day.

Getting There & Away

The turn-off for Laem Son National Park is about 58km from Ranong down Hwy 4 (Petchkasem Hwy), between the Km 657 and Km 658 markers. Buses heading south from Ranong can drop you off here (ask for Hat Bang Ben). Once you're off the highway, however, you'll have to flag down a pickup truck going towards the park. If you can't get a ride all the way, it's a 10km walk from Hwy 4 to the park entrance. The road is paved, so if you're driving it's a breeze.

Boats out to other various islands can be chartered from the park's visitors centre; the cost is generally 1200B to 1500B per day.

PHANG-NGA PROVINCE

Khuraburi คุระบุรี

Blink and you'll miss it. But if you keep your eyes wide open you'll enjoy this soulful, dusty gateway to the Surin Islands (p278) and some of the south's best community-based tourism opportunities (p278). For locals it's a market town relied on by hundreds of squid fishermen who live in ramshackle stilted bamboo villages or new princess-sponsored subdivisions tucked away in the rolling jade hills.

For tourist information try **Tom & Am Tour** (☎08 6272 0588) across from the bus station.

Sleeping & Eating

Don't miss the **morning market** (⌚6-10am daily) across from Boon Piya Resort. It's biggest on Tuesdays.

Greenview Resort HOTEL $$
(☎0 7640 1400; www.kuraburigreenviewresort.com; 129 Moo 5 Bangwan; r incl breakfast 1500-4000B; ❄) A lovely landscaped jungle property with unique rooms and bungalows made from stone, wood or bamboo with high-end touches such as waterfall-style showers in outdoor bathrooms and Thai art on the walls. There's a shaded pool and a lake for canoeing.

Boon Piya Resort GUEST HOUSE $
(☎0 7649 1969, 08 1752 5457; 175/1 Th Pekasem; bungalows 600B; ❄) These spacious, sparkling, modern concrete bungalows with tiled floors and hot-water bathrooms, set in a garden compound off the main road are the best in town.

Getting There & Away

Any Ranong- or Phuket-bound bus will stop in Khuraburi. Take a Phuket-bound bus to Takua Pa, about 50km south of Khuraburi, to transfer to destinations such as Surat Thani (ordinary/air-con 80/100B, three hours), Krabi (ordinary 120B, four hours) and Khao Sok National Park (60B to 80B, one hour).

The pier for the Surin Islands is about 9km north of town. Whoever books your boat to the islands will arrange free transfer.

COMMUNITY-BASED TOURISM IN PHANG-NGA PROVINCE

Post-tsunami, Phang-Nga looks pretty much back to normal if you stay in tourist areas. What the majority of visitors don't know is that many fishing communities have had their way of life changed forever, either by the loss of key family members, the destruction of fishing equipment or relocation inland out of necessity or fear. Recovery nowadays is taking the form of community development and visitors can help by enjoying a glimpse of 'real life' on the Andaman coast via community tourism.

Andaman Discoveries (08 7917 7165; www.andamandiscoveries.com; Khuraburi), formerly Northern Andaman Tsunami Relief, runs highly recommended community-based tours of one to seven days, including to **Ban Talae Nok**, a historic nearby fishing village, surrounded by tropical forest and mangroves, just down the road from 6km of uninhabited beach. There's an award-winning homestay here featuring cultural and handicraft activities, and fishing and snorkelling trips to uninhabited islands. Pair it with a visit to **Laem Son** and its with warm-hearted residents, who also offer handicraft and sustainable agriculture demonstrations.

Andaman Discoveries also manages three community-service projects: a learning centre for children of Burmese migrant workers; an orphanage outside of Khao Lak; and a school for disabled children in Phuket. Volunteer placement is available. For more information about volunteering, see p406.

Surin Islands Marine National Park

อุทยานแห่งชาติหมู่เกาะสุรินทร์

The five gorgeous islands that make up the **Surin Islands Marine National Park** (www.dnp.go.th; admission 400B; mid-Nov–mid-May) sit 60km offshore, just 5km from the Thailand–Myanmar marine border. Healthy rainforest, pockets of white-sand beach in sheltered bays and rocky headlands that jut into the ocean characterise these granite-outcrop islands. The clearest of water makes for great marine life, with underwater visibility often up to 35m. The islands' sheltered waters also attract *chow lair* – sea gypsies – who live in a village onshore during the monsoon season from May to November. Around here they are known as Moken, from the local word *oken* meaning 'salt water'.

Ko Surin Neua (north) and Ko Surin Tai (south) are the two largest islands. Park headquarters and all visitor facilities are at Ao Chong Khad and Ao Mai Ngam on Ko Surin Neua, near the jetty. The setting of flaxen sand and sparkling blue-green bays is spectacular.

Khuraburi is the jumping-off point for the park. The pier is about 9km north of town, as is the mainland **national park office** (0 7649 1378; 8am-5pm), with good information, maps and helpful staff.

Sights & Activities

Ban Moken VILLAGE

Moken Village at Ao Bon on the south island welcomes visitors. Post-tsunami, Moken have settled in this one sheltered bay where a major ancestral worship ceremony (Loi Reua) takes place in April. The national park offers a **Moken Village Tour** (per person 300B). You'll stroll through the village where you should ask locals for permission to hike the 800m **Chok Madah trail** over the jungled hills to an empty beach. Tours depart at 9.15am and must be reserved the day before. You can also organise a ride from the park's HQ (per person 100B). Handicrafts are for sale to help support its economy and there's a clothing donation box at park headquarters for the Moken – this is a good, responsible place to lighten your load.

Diving & Snorkelling

Dive sites in the park include **Ko Surin Tai** and **HQ Channel** between the two main islands. **Richelieu Rock** (a seamount 14km southeast) is also technically in the park and happens to be one of the best, if not the best, dive sites on the Andaman coast. Whale sharks are sometimes spotted here during March and April. There's presently no dive facility in the park itself, so dive trips (four-day live-aboards around 20,000B) must be booked from the mainland; see Getting There & Away (p287), and the Khao Lak

(Continued on page 287)

Underwater Thailand

Diving in Thailand »
Top Dives »
Diving Itinerary »
Snorkelling »

Similan Islands Marine National Park (p293)

Diving in Thailand

Thailand's beaches are sharply split between two coasts – both, however, have dive sites that are worth exploring. The Andaman is best visited between December and March, when the visibility is high and wandering pelagics stop by to feed, clean and breed. Thailand's ultimate scuba experience is the multi-day live-aboard diving circuit that takes in the Surin and Similan Islands towards the Burmese border on the Andaman coast. Although some of the reefs have suffered serious coral bleaching, the northernmost sites – such as Richelieu Rock – still boast world-class fun.

Although the Andaman tends to have a better reputation in the scuba world, the gulf holds its own with a separate set of superlatives. Mantas tend to populate the Andaman waters, but the gulf boasts a higher (much higher!) percentage of whale shark viewings. Most of these gentle beasts congregate around Sail Rock, located halfway between Ko Tao and Ko Pha-Ngan. If you're hoping to dive Sail Rock several times during your trip, it is best to access the pinnacle from Ko Pha-Ngan, where there are daily departures. The diving around Ko Tao tends to focus on instruction rather than quality fun dives. The other advantage of the gulf is that the weather is less dramatic, meaning that it's generally possible to dive almost every month of the year.

Clockwise from top left

1. Diving with mantas, Thailand **2.** Whale shark, Richelieu Rock (p278) **3.** Coral and baitfish, Similan Islands Marine National Park (p293)

2

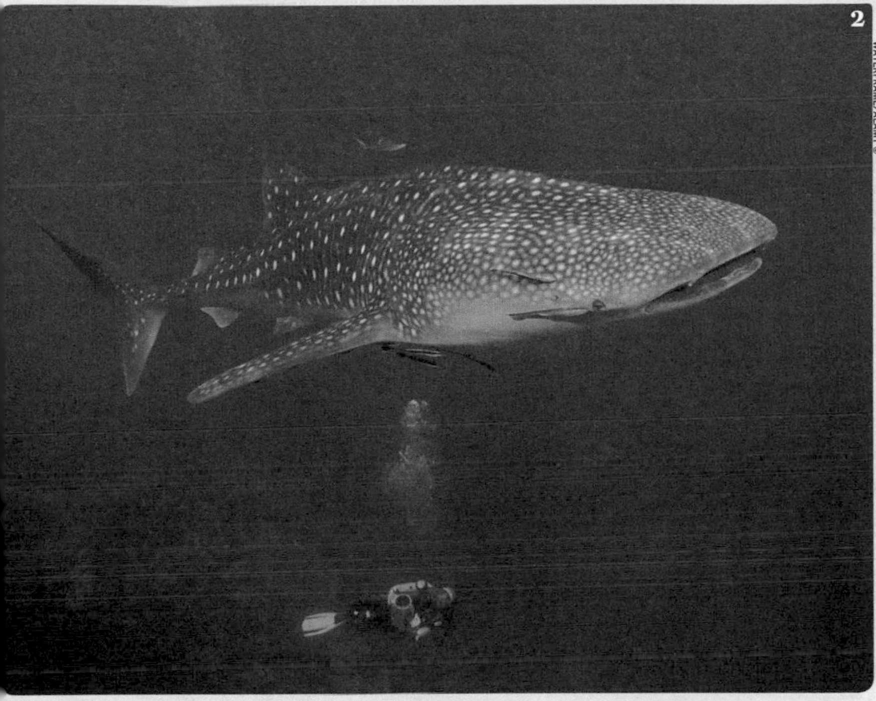

WATERFRAME/ALAMY ©

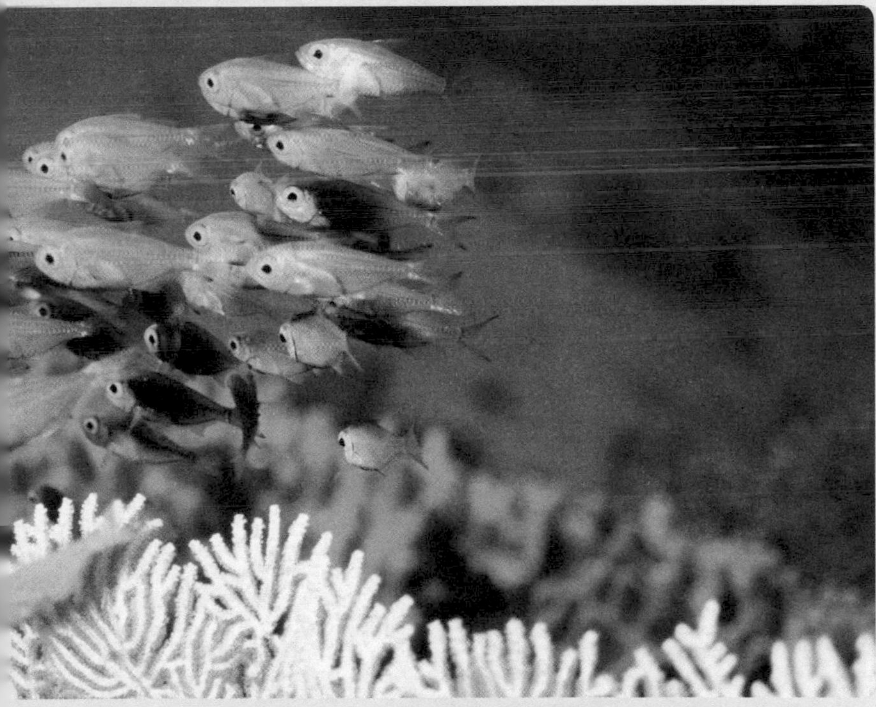

ERNEST MANEWAL/LONELY PLANET IMAGES ©

1

3

GZO /SHUTTERSTOCK ©

Top Dives

Quietly lurking off Thailand's crystal coastlines are some of the world's most dazzling playgrounds of neon coral. And, luckily, these submarine wonders are neatly spread out across the kingdom like a constellation of underwater supernovae, allowing divers to spread themselves out along the shoreline so that none of the best sites are horribly overrun.

Richelieu Rock

1 Marked on the ocean's surface by a tiny toothlike stone, Richelieu Rock (p278) reveals itself under the waves with its stone tower shaped like the horseshoe of a giant equine. Covered in thick strands of deep purple coral, Richelieu acts as a feeding station for wandering pelagics – from December to February you're almost guaranteed to see manta rays.

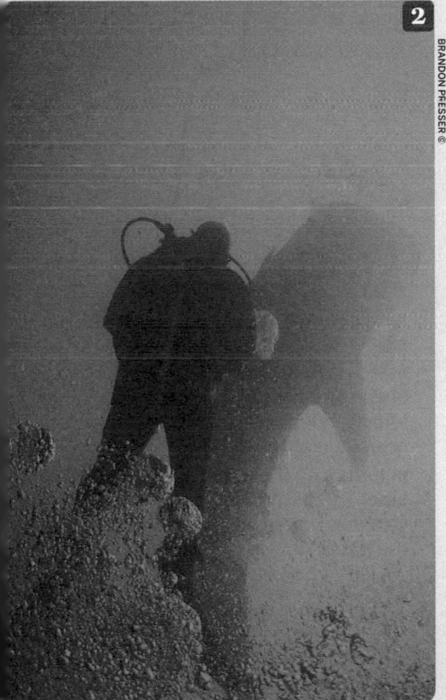
2
BRANDON PRESSER ©

Sail Rock

2 A lonely pinnacle hidden deep within the gulf, Sail Rock (p195) is Thailand's whale-shark all-star. With mellower shifts in winds and rains through the year, this is a great option for divers looking to explore the seas during the low or shoulder seasons.

Hin Daeng & Hin Muang

3 A boat ride away from the popular island of Ko Lanta, the twin undersea towers of Hin Daeng and Hin Muang (p325) – known as Red Rock and Purple Rock respectively – are the best scuba spots in the southern part of the Andaman. Join a submarine photography class and snap shots of the diverse marine life that calls these sites home.

Clockwise from top
1. Coral reef, Richelieu Rock (p278) **2.** Diver in Thailand **3.** Leopard shark

Diving Itinerary

A Three-Week Itinerary

Strap on a scuba mask and sample the best that southern Thailand has to offer on this all-encompassing overland adventure that takes in all of the region's highlights.

» Fly into **Ko Samui** for a couple of days of R&R before hitting the surf on the islands next door.

BEN PIPE PHOTOGRAPHY/GETTY IMAGES ©

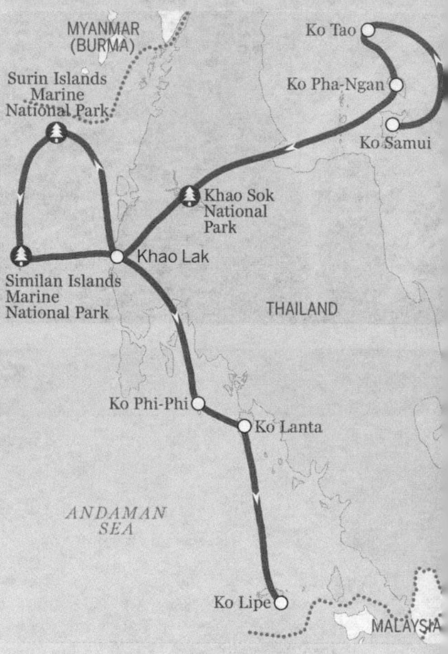

» Jump over to **Ko Tao** to lose your diving virginity at one of the myriad shallow dive sites that hug the tiny jungle island.

» After scoring your PADI Open Water certification, hop over to **Ko Pha-Ngan** and roll the dice for an opportunity to spot a whale shark at Sail Rock.

» As you cross over to the Andaman coast, stop in rugged **Khao Sok National Park** if you dare to try an advanced cave dive.

» Slide over to **Khao Lak** and hop on a live-aboard for a few days of quiet cruising around the Surin and Similan Islands Marine National Parks.

» Move south to **Ko Phi-Phi** and base yourself among the soaring limestone crags for a few days of mellowed-out diving with a side of snorkelling.

» It's on to **Ko Lanta** next to jet out to the deep sea pinnacles of Hin Daeng and Hin Muang, but don't miss the shallower reefs near snorkel-friendly Ko Haa.

» If the weather holds out, head down to **Ko Lipe**. The visibility can be variable, but on a clear day you're likely to be the only one in the water.

Clockwise from top left

1. Diver with Oriental sweetlips **2.** Khao Lak/Lam Ru National Park (p290) **3.** Ko Phi-Phi Don (p316) **4.** Khao Sok National Park (p288)

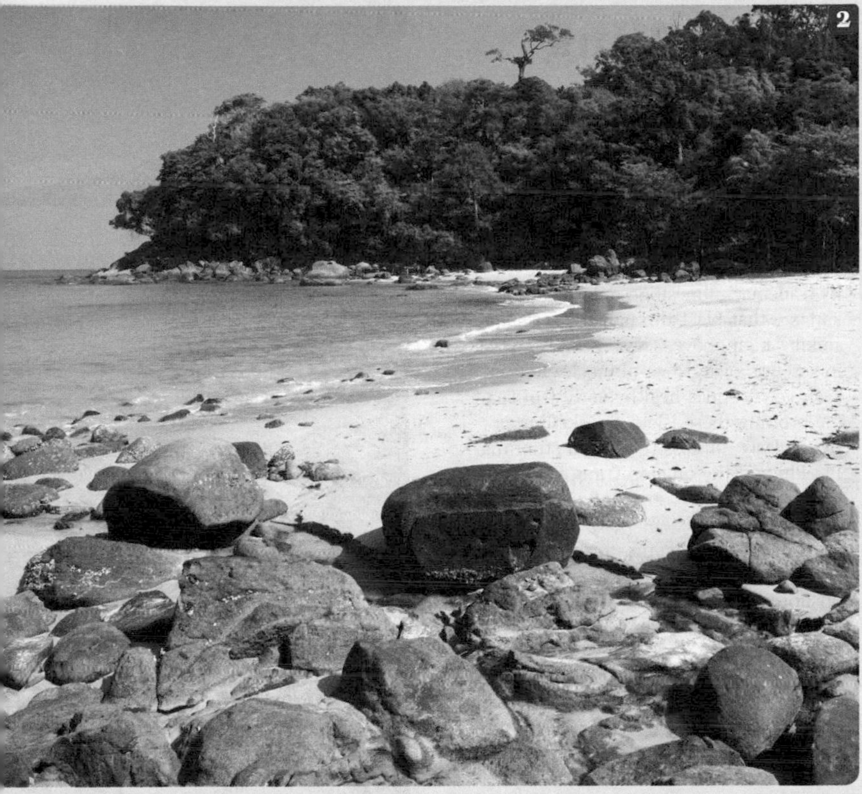

ANDREW BAIN/LONELY PLANET IMAGES ©

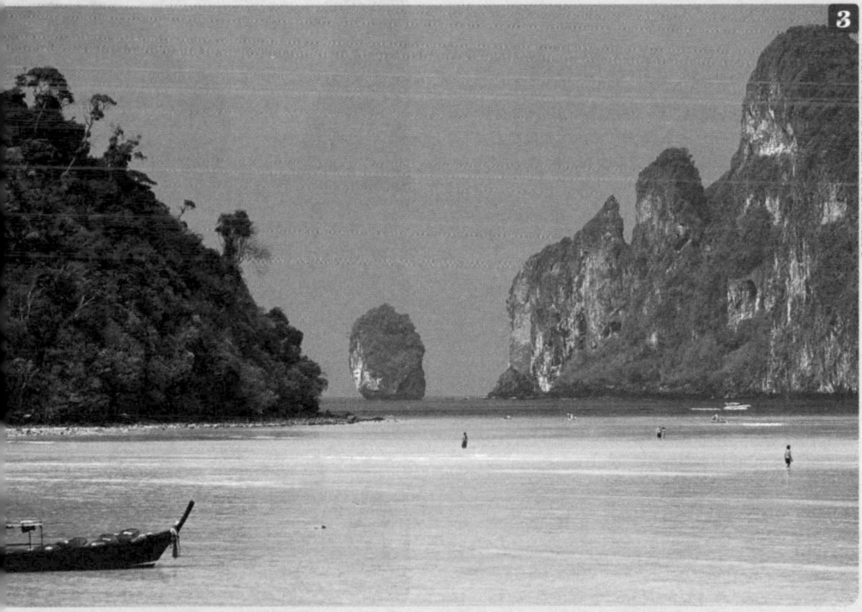

NOBORU KOMINE/LONELY PLANET IMAGES ©

Snorkelling

The swerving, scalloping bays of Thailand's islands and coasts make it one of the best places in the world to strap on a snorkel and explore. Both the gulf and the Andaman coast have their fair share of snorkelling hubs, but each region offers different types of bubble-blowing experiences. The Andaman coast features its trademark limestone outcrops – or karsts – that blast through the sea's surface spiking high above. These islands are, in essence, overgrown pinnacles and as such you'll find a healthy variety of sea life orbiting these islets. Snorkelling is particularly impressive around stunning Ko Phi-Phi and the quieter Trang Islands just south of Krabi.

The gulf islands emerge less suddenly from the ocean's depths, forming arcing, coolie-hat-like peaks. As a result, the offshore reefs tend to be shallower, hosting colourful coral and smaller creatures – great for beginners. The top spots to kick your fins include Ko Nang Yuan in the shallows of Ko Tao, the east coast of Ko Tao, and the northwest coast of Ko Pha-Ngan.

BEST SNORKELLING SPOTS

» **Trang Islands** Tiny islets sport charming house reefs where the coral barely stays tucked in the lapping shallow waters.

» **Ko Pha-Ngan** Strap on the fins and waddle around the offshore islet of Ko Ma in the northwest.

» **Ko Phi-Phi** Go one better than snorkelling with the Nemos and get up at dawn to kick around with a crew of local reef sharks.

» **Ko Tao** The west coast may be 'diver central' but the island's east side is scalloped with shallow bays that beckon the snorkel and mask.

Right

1. Snorkelling near Ko Butang, Ko Tarutao Marine National Park (p346) **2.** Ao Maya, Ko Phi-Phi Leh (p324)

(Continued from page 278)

(p291) and Ranong (p270) sections for more information.

Snorkelling isn't as good as it used to be due to recent bleaching of the hard corals but you'll still see fish and soft corals. Two-hour snorkelling trips (per person 80B, gear per day 150B) leave the park headquarters at 9am and 2pm daily. Expect to be in the company of mostly Thais, who swim fully clothed. If you'd like a more serene snorkelling experience, charter your own long-tail from the national park (half day 1000B) or, better yet, directly from the Moken themselves in **Ban Moken**. The best section of reef is between the white buoys along the northern peninsula. There are more fish off tiny **Ko Pajumba**, but the coral isn't in great shape.

Wildlife & Hiking

Around park headquarters you can explore the forest fringes, looking out for crab-eating macaques and some of the 57 resident bird species, which include the fabulous Nicobar pigeon, endemic to the Andaman islands. Along the coast you're likely to see the Brahminy kite soaring and reef herons on the rocks. Twelve species of bat live here, most noticeably the tree-dwelling fruit bats (also known as flying foxes).

A rough-and-ready **walking trail** winds 2km along the coast, through forest and back down to the beach at **Ao Mai Ngam**, which has camping facilities and its own canteen. At low tide it's easy to walk along the coast between the two campsites.

Sleeping & Eating

Park accommodation is decent, but because of the island's short, narrow beaches it can feel seriously crowded when full (around 300 people). Book online at www.dnp.go.th or with the mainland **national park office** (0 7649 1378; 8am-5pm) in Khuraburi. The clientele is mostly Thai, giving the place a lively holiday-camp feel. You can camp on both Ao Chong Khad and Ao Mae Ngam. The former has the more spectacular beach; the latter fills up last, is more secluded and, with its narrow white-sand shallow bay, feels a bit wilder.

Bungalows (2000B) on Ao Chong Khad have wooden floors and private terraces, as well as private terracotta bathrooms and fans that run all night. There are no bungalows on Ao Mae Ngam. **Tents** (2-/4-person 300/450B, bedding per person 60B) are available for rent at both beaches or you can pitch your own **tent** (per night 80B). There's generator power until 10pm.

A park **restaurant** (dishes from 80B, set menus 170-200B) serves decent Thai food.

Getting There & Away

Tour operators now use speedboats (return 1600B, one hour one way) exclusively. They leave around 9am and honour open tickets. Return whenever you please.

Several tour operators also run day tours (2900B including food and park lodging) to the park. The best in safety, service and value is **Greenview** (0 7640 1400; Khuraburi pier). Agencies in Hat Khao Lak (p293), Phuket (p239) and Ranong (p270) are the most convenient booking options for live-aboard dive trips. Transfers from the place of purchase are always included.

Ko Phra Thong & Ko Ra

เกาะพระทอง/เกาะระ

Legend has it that many centuries ago, pirates docked at Ko Phra Thong and buried a golden Buddha beneath the sands. The legendary statue was never found but the modern-day treasures at Ko Phra Thong (Golden Buddha Island) are its endless sandy beaches, mangroves, vast bird life and rare orchids.

The island is as quiet as a night on the open ocean and as flat as Kansas, and fishing (squid, prawns and jellyfish) remains its key industry. The local delicacy is pungent *gà·Ъì* (fermented prawn paste).

Nearby and even quieter is Ko Ra, encircled by golden beaches and mangroves. This small isle is a mountainous jungle with an impressive array of wildlife (including leopard cats, flying lemurs, scaly anteaters and slow loris) and has a welcoming local population of fisherfolk.

Sleeping

TOP CHOICE Golden Buddha Beach Resort HOTEL $$$

(08 1892 2208; www.goldenbuddharesort.com; Ko Phra Thong; bungalows 3100-14,000B) The area's most posh resort attracts a stream of yoga aficionados keen for a spiritual getaway. Accommodation is in naturalistic-chic privately owned wooden houses rented out short- or long-term. All have open-air bathrooms with views of the sea and the surrounding forest. There's also a dive centre.

Ko Ra Eco-Resort HOTEL $$
(☎08 9867 5288, 08 5280 5507; www.thaiecolodge.com; Ko Phra Thong; bungalows 1100-1900B) Nestled in the trees off its own small private beach, this older place is under new, activity-oriented management. Everything from meditation retreats to spectacular wildlife hikes and diving and snorkelling tours to the most pristine and secret coves – or to the relatively nearby Surin Islands – are available. Bungalows are dark and basic and the restaurant serves excellent local specialities.

Mr Chuoi's GUEST HOUSE $
(☎08 4855 9886, 08 7898 4636; www.mrchuoibarandhut.com; Ko Phra Thong; bungalows 500B) Simple stilted thatched huts look like hay bales and are enlivened by pony-tailed Mr. Chuoi's artistic style. Call and he'll arrange transport between Ko Phra Thong and Khuraburi for 1000B.

Getting There & Away

There are no regular boats to Ko Phra Thong, but you could theoretically charter a long-tail from the Khuraburi pier for around 1500B each way – boatmen are hard to find. It's far better and probably cheaper to contact your resort in advance to arrange transport.

Locals of Tung Dap village on the southern tip of Ko Phra Thong have requested that tourists not visit their area, so please be respectful and avoid this corner.

Khao Sok National Park อุทยานแห่งชาติเขาสก

If your leg muscles have atrophied after one too many days of beach-bumming, consider venturing inland to the wondrous Khao Sok National Park. Many believe this lowland jungle – the wettest spot in Thailand – to be over 160 million years old, making it one of the oldest rainforests on the globe. It features dramatic limestone formations and waterfalls that cascade through juicy thickets drenched with rains and morning dew. A network of dirt trails snakes through the quiet park, allowing visitors to spy on the exciting array of indigenous creatures.

The best time of year to visit is between December and April – the dry season. During the June to October wet season, trails can be extremely slippery, flash flooding is common and leeches come out in force. On the other hand, animals leave their hidden reservoirs throughout the wet months, so you're more likely to stumble across big fauna.

Sights & Activities

Khao Sok's vast terrain makes it one of the last viable habitats for large mammals. During the wetter months you may happen upon bear, boar, gaur, tapirs, gibbons, deer, wild elephants and perhaps even a tiger. There are more than 300 bird species, 38 bat varieties and one of the world's largest flowers, the rare *Rafflesia kerrii,* which, in Thailand, is found only in Khao Sok. These giant flowers can reach 80cm in diameter.

The stunning **Chiaw Lan** sits about an hour's drive (65km) east of the visitors centre. The lake was created in 1982 by an enormous shale-clay dam called Ratchaprapha (Kheuan Ratchaprapha or Chiaw Lan). The limestone outcrops protruding from the lake reach a height of 960m, over three times higher than the formations in the Phang-Nga area. Technical divers can drop into the emerald waters and glimpse ghostly stalagmites with the tech-diving team from **Big Blue** (☎0 7745 6415; www.bigbluekhaosok.com), which is based on the gulf island of Ko Tao.

Tham Nam Thalu cave contains striking limestone formations and subterranean streams, while **Tham Si Ru** features four converging passageways used as a hideout by communist insurgents between 1975 and 1982. The caves can be reached on foot from the southwestern shore of the lake. You can rent boats from local fishermen to explore the coves, canals, caves and cul-de-sacs along the lakeshore.

Elephant trekking, kayaking and rafting are popular park activities. The hiking is also excellent, and you can arrange park tours from any guest house – just be sure you get a certified guide (they wear an official badge). Various trails you can hike independently from the visitors centre lead to the waterfalls of **Sip-Et Chan** (4km), **Than Sawan** (9km) and **Than Kloy** (9km), among other destinations. The park office hands out free trail maps.

Sleeping

The road leading into the park is lined with simple, charming guest houses and all offer a variety of park tours and guide services. We recommend going on a two-day, one-night trip (2500B per person) to Chiaw

Lan where you sleep in floating huts on the lake and go on variety of canoe and hiking excursions.

Art's Riverview Jungle Lodge GUEST HOUSE $$
(☎08 6470 3234; http://krabidir.com/artsriverviewlodge; bungalows 650B) In a monkey-filled jungle bordering a clear river with a natural limestone cliff-framed swimming hole, this is the prettiest location in Khao Sok. Wooden bungalows are simple but big, all have river views and the charming restaurant overlooks the sublime swimming hole.

Cliff & River Jungle Resort HOTEL $$$
(☎08 7271 8787; www.thecliffandriver.com; bungalows incl breakfast 1800B; ❄🏊) This beautiful property with stilted bamboo bungalows is set below the jagged cliffs and is removed from Khao Sok's budget huddle. If you need air-con, come here. The food is terrific, too.

Morning Mist Resort HOTEL $$
(☎08 9971 8794; www.khaosokmorningmistresort.com; bungalows 650-1000B; 👪) One of the more comfortable choices. Clean, tiled, fan-cooled bungalows all have balconies and the most expensive overlook the river.

Jungle Huts GUEST HOUSE $
(☎0 7739 5160; www.khao-sok-junglehuts.com; huts 300-1200B) Basic but good-value huts sit in a forest of fruit trees near a river or high up on stilts connected by a vertiginous walkway.

Information

The **park headquarters** (☎0 7739 5025; www.khaosok.com; park admission 200B) and visitors centre are 1.8km off Rte 401, close to the Km 109 marker.

There's an ATM outside the Morning Mist Mini-Mart and internet is available near the park entrance for 2B per minute.

Getting There & Around

Minivans to Surat Thani (250B, one hour), Krabi (300B, two hours) and a handful of other destinations leave daily. Otherwise, from Surat catch a bus going towards Takua Pa and, on the Andaman coast, take a Surat Thani–bound bus. Buses drop you off along the highway (Rte 401), 1.8km from the visitors centre. If guest-house touts don't meet you, you'll have to walk to your chosen nest (from 50m to 2km).

To explore Chiaw Lan on your own, charter a long-tail (2000B per day) at the dam's entrance.

KHAO SOK TOURS

Tours in and around Khao Sok can be up to 50% cheaper when booked at guest houses or travel agents around the park itself. Tours booked from further-afield destinations such as Phuket or Khao Lak will include higher-priced transport and tour agent commissions.

Hat Pakarang & Hat Bang Sak หาดปะการัง/หาดบางสัก

Essentially one long, sleepy stretch of sand, the beaches at Pakarang and Bang Sak had been attracting an ever-growing number of tourists until the 2004 tsunami washed away scores of businesses and hotels in an instant. With thick mangroves, ample rolling pasture and rubber-tree plantations forming a wide buffer between the coast and highway, you really feel like you've escaped from it all when you land here.

If you've spent your life looking for a consistent, long wave on an empty beach with almost no surfers in the water, **Hat Pakarang** is your dream break. **Pakarang Surf Shop** (☎0 7648 5350; www.pakarangsurfshop.com; Th Petchkasem) in Khao Lak offers board rental (per hour 200B), lessons (1000B, 1½ hours) and local surf secrets.

Sleeping & Eating

There are just a few hotels along these pretty beaches, making them ideal romantic hideaways.

Sarojin HOTEL $$$
(☎0 7642 7900-4; www.sarojin.com; Hat Pakarang; r 12,500-22,250B; ❄@📶🏊) A quiet retreat with a Japanese-meets-modern-Thai style. Service here is stellar and the setting is elegant and intimate. The very private spa (treatments from 2300B), which takes in views of coconut groves, is one of the best on the Andaman coast. Cooking classes take place on the banks of the Takuapa river, where you can watch water buffalo stroll by. No kids allowed.

Le Meridian HOTEL $$$
(☎0 7642 7500; www.lemeridian.com; Hat Bang Sak; r from 5220B, villas from 11,200B; ❄@📶🏊) A four-star megaresort, its 243 rooms and 20 villas are the only nests on Hat Bang Sak. It lacks the boutique touch and five-star

service of the Sarojin, but it is slightly cheaper and is certainly majestic, sprawling nearly all the way from the highway to the sea.

White Sand Beach Bungalow HOTEL **$$**
(☎0 7648 7580; Hat Pakarang; cottages 1500B; ❄) Next door to the Sarojin are eight, simple, clean, air-conditioned cottages with queen-sized beds, hot water and a five-star slice of sand.

Getting There & Away

From Khao Lak catch a frequent public sŏrng·tăa·ou (60B) between 8.30am and 5pm. Buses running between Takua Pa and Phuket will also get you here, but the highway is a bit of a stroll from most resorts. Your best bet is to take public transport to Khao Lak and charter a sŏrng·tăa·ou (500B to 700B) from there.

Hat Khao Lak หาดเขาหลัก

Hat Khao Lak is a beach for folks who shun the glitz and cheesiness of Phuket's bigger resort towns, but still crave comfort, shopping and plenty of facilities. With long stretches of white sand backed by forested hills, warm waves to frolic in and easy day trips to the Similan and Surin Islands, Khao Sok and Khao Lak/Lam Ru National Parks or even Phuket, the area is a central and kicked-back base for exploring the northern Andaman. About 2.5km north of Hat Khao Lak, **Hat Bang Niang** is an even quieter version of sandy bliss with skinnier beaches but fewer people. Khao Lak proper (also called Khao Lak Town by locals) – a hodgepodge of restaurants, tourist markets and low-rise hotels along a grey highway – isn't exactly eye-catching, but it is convenient and you'll probably spend your days at the beach or further afield, anyway.

Internet is widely available and banks and ATMs are everywhere.

Sights

Khao Lak/Lam Ru National Park NATIONAL PARK
(อุทยานแห่งชาติเขาหลัก-ลำรู่; ☎0 7642 0243; www.dnp.go.th; adult/child 100/50B; ⏲8am-4.30pm) The area immediately south of Hat Khao Lak has been incorporated into the vast 125 sq km Khao Lak/Lam Ru National Park, a collage of sea cliffs, 1000m-high hills, beaches, estuaries, forested valleys and mangroves. Wildlife includes hornbills, drongos, tapirs, gibbons, monkeys and Asiatic black bears. The visitors centre, just off Hwy 4 between the Km 56 and Km 57 markers, has little in the way of maps or printed information, but there's a very nice open-air restaurant perched on a shady slope overlooking the sea. From the restaurant you can take a fairly easy 3km round-trip nature trail that heads along the cape and ends at often-deserted Hat Lek beach.

Khlong Thap Liang NATURE RESERVE
Guided hikes along the coast or inland can be arranged through many tour agencies in town, as can long-tail boat trips up the scenic Khlong Thap Liang estuary. The latter affords opportunities to view mangrove communities of crab-eating macaques. Between Khao Lak and Bang Sak is a network of sandy beach trails – some of which lead to deserted beaches – which are fun to explore on foot or by rented motorcycle. Most of the hotels in town rent out motorbikes for 250B per day.

TSUNAMI EARLY WARNING SYSTEM

On the morning of 26 December 2004, an earthquake off the coast of the Indonesian island of Sumatra sent enormous waves crashing against much of Thailand's Andaman coast, claiming around 8000 lives and causing millions of dollars of damage to homes and businesses. In 2005 Thailand officially inaugurated a national disaster warning system, which was created in response to the country's lack of preparedness in 2004. The Bangkok-based centre anticipates that a tsunami warning can be issued within 30 minutes of the event being detected by existing international systems.

The public will be warned via the nationwide radio network, Channel 5 army TV network, the state-operated TV pool and SMS messages. For non-Thai speakers, the centre has installed warning towers along the high-risk beachfront areas that will broadcast announcements in various languages accompanied by flashing lights. The **call centre** (☎1860) also handles questions and tips from the public regarding potential or unfolding disasters.

Khao Lak

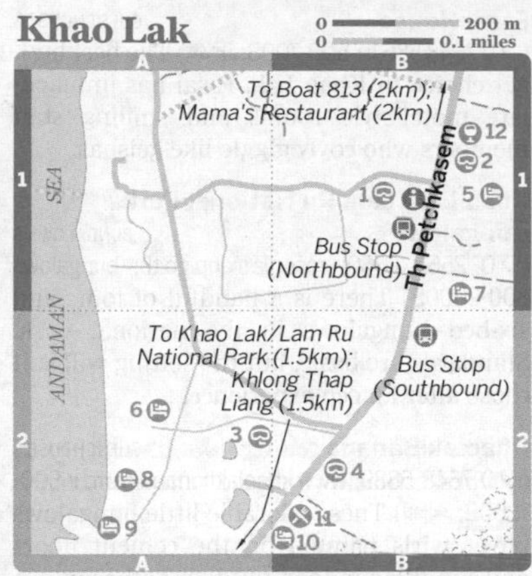

Khao Lak

Activities, Courses & Tours

1	Big Blue	B1
2	Sea Dragon Dive Center	B1
3	Similan Diving Safaris	A2
4	Wicked Diving	B2

Sleeping

5	Fasai House	B1
6	Greenbeach	A2
7	Khaolak Banana	B1
8	Nangthong Bay Resort	A2
9	Nangthong Beach Resort	A2
	Tiffy's Café	(see 2)
10	Walker's Inn	B2

Eating

11	Phu Khao Lak	B2

Drinking

12	Happy Snapper	B1

Boat 813 HISTORICAL SITE

Perched in an open field nearly 1km from shore, this boat was hurled to its current location by the powerful 2004 Boxing Day tsunami. More than five years later, it remains the region's most prominent reminder of the disaster. There's an information booth nearby with a tsunami timeline in both Thai and English, as well as some compelling photo books for sale. It's just a 50B sŏrng·tăa·ou between here and Khao Lak.

Activities

Diving or snorkelling day excursions to the Similan and Surin Islands are immensely popular but, if you can, opt for a live-aboard. Since the islands are around 60km from the mainland (about three hours by boat), you'll have a more relaxing trip and experience the islands sans day trippers. All dive shops offer live-aboard trips from around 17,000/29,000B for three-/five-day packages and day trips for 4900B to 6500B.

On these two-, three-, four- or five-day trips, you'll wake up with the dawn and slink below the ocean's surface up to four times per day in what's commonly considered to be one of the top 10 diving realms in the world. While both the Similan and Surin Islands have experienced vast coral bleaching recently, **Richelieu Rock** is still the crème de la crème of the region's sites and **Ko Bon** and **Ko Ta Chai** are two other good sites due to the traffic of giant manta rays.

Although geared towards divers, all dive shops welcome snorkellers who can hop on selected dive excursions or live-aboards for a discount of around 40%; otherwise, tour agencies all around town offer even cheaper snorkelling trips to the Similan Islands for around 2700B. PADI Open Water certification courses cost anywhere from 10,000B to 18,000B depending on where you dive. You can go on a 'discover scuba' day trip to the Similans for around 6000B to 6500B.

Recommended dive shops:

TOP CHOICE **Wicked Diving** DIVING

(0 7648 5868; www.wickeddiving.com) An exceptionally well-run and environmentally conscious outfit that runs diving and snorkelling overnight trips, as well as a range of live-aboards. Trips include Whale Sharks & Mantas, Turtle & Reefs and Sharks & Rays conservation trips that are run in conjunction with **Ecocean** (www.whaleshark.org). It does all the PADI courses, too.

Similan Diving Safaris DIVING

(0 7648 5470; www.similan-diving-safaris.com) The speciality here is the high-quality four-day live-aboard (18,800B all-inclusive) that regularly attracts return customers. Knowledgeable staff and amazing food sweeten the deal. As far as live-aboards are concerned, this is probably the best bang for your baht. Day trips are also available.

Big Blue DIVING

(0 7648 5544; www.bigbluekhaolak.com) Japanese- and Swedish-owned; its

speedboat, live-aboard trips and dive instructors are among the best in Khao Lak.

Sea Dragon Dive Center DIVING
(☎0 7648 5420; www.seadragondivecenter.com; Th Phetkasem) One of the older operations in Khao Lak, Sea Dragon has maintained high standards throughout the years.

Sleeping

Backpacker accommodation predominates in the congested centre of town, while three- and four-star resorts dominate the coast.

For the cheapest sleeps in town, head to Sea Dragon Dive Center
 and ask about the dorm beds at **Tiffy's Café**, which go for 180B per night.

La Flora Resort HOTEL $$$
(☎0 7642 8000; www.lafloraresort.com; r 5700-7700B, villas 9000-10,500B; ❄@📶🏊👪) On gorgeous Hat Bang Niang, this is resort exudes barefoot class; it's both elegant and supremely relaxing. Cabana-style villas are large and modern with sexy beachfront infinity pools, and there's a kid-friendly pool in the centre of things. Rooms have marble floors, ceramic sinks and striking modern art.

TOP CHOICE **Nangthong Beach Resort** HOTEL $$
(☎0 7648 5911; www.nangthong2.com; r 2000-2200B, bungalows 2500-3000B; ❄@📶🏊👪) The best choice in Khao Lak proper has large, well-appointed rooms, and even larger bungalows, with ceramic-tile floors, dark-wood furnishings, a bourgeoning garden, impeccable service and the best stretch of sand in town.

Nangthong Bay Resort HOTEL $$
(☎0 7648 5088; www.nangthong.com; r 2000-3000B; ❄@📶👪🏊) Until its sister property opened, this was the best midranger on the beach. Rooms are designed with a sparse black-and-white chic decor. The cheapest rooms are set back from the beach, but are fantastic value. Grounds are lush and service is excellent.

Greenbeach HOTEL $$
(☎0 7648 5845; greenbeach_th@yahoo.com; bungalows 1300-2300B; ❄) On an excellent stretch of beach and extending back into a garden, this place has a warm family-style soul. The wooden bungalows have glass doors, air-con and fan, shady terraces and views of a towering, ancient banyan tree. Even the cheapest rooms have sea views.

Fasai House GUEST HOUSE $
(☎0 7648 5867; r 500-700B; ❄@) The best budget choice in Khao Lak, Fasai has immaculate motel-style rooms and smiling staff members who coyly giggle like geishas.

Khao Lak/Lam Ru National Park Bungalows BUNGALOWS $
(☎0 2562 0760; reserve@dnp.go.th; bungalows 800-2000B) There is a handful of four- and six-bed bungalows in the national park. Standards are basic, but the setting will suit those after an eco-experience.

Khaolak Banana GUEST HOUSE $
(☎0 7648 5889; www.khaolakbanana.com; r 500-1200B; ❄🏊) These adorable little bungalows have swirls painted on the cement floors and sun-filled indoor–outdoor bathrooms. A cute pool with deckchairs sweetens the deal.

Walker's Inn GUEST HOUSE $
(☎0 7648 5668; Th Petchkasem; r 400-750B; ❄📶) Big but plain and ageing tiled rooms with air-con and hot showers sit above a pub. It's friendly and popular with backpackers.

Eating & Drinking

This is no culinary capital, but there are a few local haunts where tourists congregate to rehash the day's diving yarns. Early-morning divers will be hard-pressed to find a place to grab a bite before 8.30am.

TOP CHOICE **Mama's Restaurant** SEAFOOD $$
(☎08 4850 7417; Th Petchkasem; dishes 60-300B; ⏲lunch & dinner) Nobody, and we do mean nobody, does seafood better than Mama, who's set up across from Boat 813. Her fish cakes are insane, and so is the barracuda sautéed in yellow curry.

Phu Khao Lak INTERNATIONAL, THAI $$
(☎0 7648 5141; Th Petchkasem; dishes 80-240B; ⏲breakfast, lunch & dinner) With its clothed tables spilling to the edges of a lawn at the south end of the Khao Lak strip, it's hard to miss. And you shouldn't because there's a huge menu of Western and Thai dishes with ample descriptions, all cooked to perfection.

Happy Snapper BAR
(☎0 7648 5500; Th Petchkasem) Here's a bar stocked with good liquor, with a map of the world on the ceiling, the tree of life on the wall and a rockin' house band on stage six nights a week in the high season, led by the owner, a Bangkok-born bass legend.

Information

For diving-related emergencies, call the **SSS Ambulance** (08 1081 9444) emergency, which rushes injured persons down to Phuket for treatment. The ambulance can also be used for car or motorcycle accidents. There is also one nurse in Bang Niang who caters to diving-related injuries.

There are numerous travel agencies scattered about – the best is **Khao Lak Land Discoveries** (0 7648 5411; www.khaolaklanddicovery.com; Th Phetkasem) – that rent motorbikes for around 250B per day.

Getting There & Away

Any bus running along Hwy 4 between Takua Pa (50B, 45 minutes) and Phuket (100B, two hours) will stop at Hat Khao Lak if you ask the driver.

Khao Lak Land Discoveries runs hourly minibuses to Phuket International Airport (600B, one hour 15 minutes). Alternately you can take a taxi (1200B) or tell a Phuket-bound bus-driver to let you off at the 'airport' – you'll be let off at an intersection from which motorcycle taxis to the airport (10 minutes) cost 100B.

Similan Islands Marine National Park

อุทยานแห่งชาติหมู่เกาะสิมิลัน

Known to divers the world over, beautiful **Similan Islands Marine National Park** (www.dnp.go.th; admission 400B; Nov-May) is 60km offshore. Its smooth granite islands are as impressive above water as below, topped with rainforest, edged with white-sand beaches and fringed with coral reefs. Unfortunately recent coral bleaching has killed off many of the hard corals but soft corals are still intact, the fauna is there and it's still a lovely place to dive.

Two of the nine islands, Island 4 (Ko Miang) and Island 8 (Ko Similan), have ranger stations and accommodation; park headquarters and most visitor activity centres are on Island 4. 'Similan' comes from the Malay word *sembilan*, meaning 'nine', and while each island is named, they're more commonly known by their numbers. Recently, the park was expanded to included Ko Bon and Ko Tachai, and both have remained unscathed by coral bleaching making them some of the better diving and snorkelling areas.

Hat Khao Lak is the jumping-off point for the park. The pier is at Thap Lamu, about 10km south of town.

Sights & Activities

Diving & Snorkelling

The Similans offer diving for all levels of experience, at depths from 2m to 30m. There are rock reefs at **Ko Payu** (Island 7) and dive-throughs at **Hin Pousar** (Elephant Head), with marine life ranging from tiny plume worms and soft corals to schooling fish and whale sharks. There are dive sites at each of the six islands north of Ko Miang (Island 4); the southern part of the park (Islands 1, 2 and 3) is a turtle nesting ground and off-limits to divers. No facilities for divers exist in the national park itself, so you'll need to take a dive tour. Agencies in Hat Khao Lak (p291) and Phuket (p239) book dive trips (three-day live-aboards from around 14,500B).

You can hire snorkelling gear (per day 100B) from the park headquarters. Day-tour operators usually visit three or four different snorkelling sites. Plenty of tour agencies in Hat Khao Lak offer snorkelling-only day/overnight trips (from around 3000/5000B).

Wildlife & Hiking

The forest around the park headquarters on Ko Miang (Island 4) has a couple of walking trails and some great wildlife. The fabulous Nicobar pigeon, with its wild mane of grey-green feathers, is common here. Endemic to the islands of the Andaman Sea, it's one of some 39 bird species in the park. Hairy-legged land crabs and fruit bats (flying foxes) are relatively easily seen in the forest, as are flying squirrels.

A small **beach track**, with information panels, leads 400m to a tiny, pretty snorkelling bay. Detouring from the track, the **Viewpoint Trail** – 500m or so of steep scrambling – has panoramic vistas from the top. A 500m walk to **Sunset Point** takes you through forest to a smooth granite platform facing – obviously – west.

On Ko Similan (Island 8) there's a 2.5km forest hike to a **viewpoint**, and a shorter, steep scramble off the main beach to the top of **Sail Rock** (aka Balance Rock).

Sleeping & Eating

Accommodation in the park is available for all budgets. Book online at www.dnp.go.th or with the mainland **national park office** (0 7645 3272) at Hat Khao Lak. Tour agents in Hat Khao Lak also arrange overnight to multi-day trips that include transport, food and lodging at the park – these cost little more than it would to go solo.

Similan Islands

On Ko Miang (Island 4) there are sea-view **bungalows** (r 2000B; ❄) with balconies; two dark five-room wood-and-bamboo **longhouses** (r 1000B; ❄) with fans, and **tents** (2-/4-person 300/450B). There's electricity from 6pm to 6am.

Tents are also available on Ko Similan (Island 8). You can pitch your own **tent** (per night 80B) on either island.

A **restaurant** (dishes 100-150B) near the park headquarters serves simple Thai food.

Getting There & Away

There's no official public transport to the park, but theoretically independent travellers can book a speedboat transfer (return 1700B, 1½ hours one way) with a Hat Khao Lak snorkelling operator, though they much prefer that you join the snorkelling tour and generally discourage independent travel to the Similans. Most will collect you from Phuket or Hat Khao Lak, but if you book through national parks (which uses the same tour operators' boats anyway), be aware that you'll have to find your own way to their office and then wait for a transfer to the pier.

Agencies in Hat Khao Lak and Phuket book day/overnight tours (from around 3000/5000B) and dive trips (three-day live-aboards from around 14,500B). Generally these cost little more than what you'd pay trying to get to the islands independently when you factor in meals, bus tickets etc.

Ao Phang-Nga & Phang-Nga อ่าวพังงา

POP 11,000

With turquoise bays peppered with craggy limestone rock towers, brilliant-white beaches and tumbledown fishing villages, Ao Phang-Nga is one of the region's most spectacular landscapes. Little wonder then that it was here, among the towering cliffs and swifts' nests that James Bond's nemesis, Scaramanga *(The Man with the Golden Gun)*, chose to build his lair. Wanted assassins with goals of world domination would not be recommended to hide out here nowadays, since the area is swarming with tourists in motorboats and sea kayaks nearly year-round. Much of the bay, and some of the coastline, has now been incorporated into the Ao Phang-Nga National Marine Park.

Sights & Activities

Phang-Nga is a scruffy, luckless town backed up against sublime limestone cliffs. There isn't a whole lot to see or do unless you happen to be here during the annual **Vegetarian Festival** (p248) in late September or October.

About 8.5km south of the town centre is Tha Dan. From here, you can charter boats to see half-submerged **caves**, oddly shaped islands and **Ko Panyi**, a Muslim village on stilts. There are tours to the well-trodden **Ko Phing Kan** (James Bond Island) and **Ao Phang-Nga National Marine Park** (500B per person for a two- to three-hour tour). Takua Thung, another pier area about 10km further west of Tha Dan, also has private boats for hire at similar prices to tours. The park office, inside Ao Phang-Nga National Marine Park also offers boat tours.

Although it can be a pain to haggle with boatmen, it's nice to create your own itinerary. Of course, it's easier (and cheaper) to go with an organised tour through an agency in town. **Sayan Tours** (☎0 7643 0348; www.sayantour.com) has been doing tours of Ao Phang-Nga for many years, and continues to receive good reviews from travellers. Half-/full-day tours cost from 700/1000B per person and include **Tham Lawt** (a large water cave), Ko Phing Kan and Ko Panyi, among other destinations. For an extra 300B you can add a bit of kayaking. It also offers a **river rafting trip** (per person 1600B) to the Son Pat Waterfall 25km south of Phang-Nga, and tours to nearby destinations, including **Sa Nang Manora Forest Park**.

Ao Phang-Nga

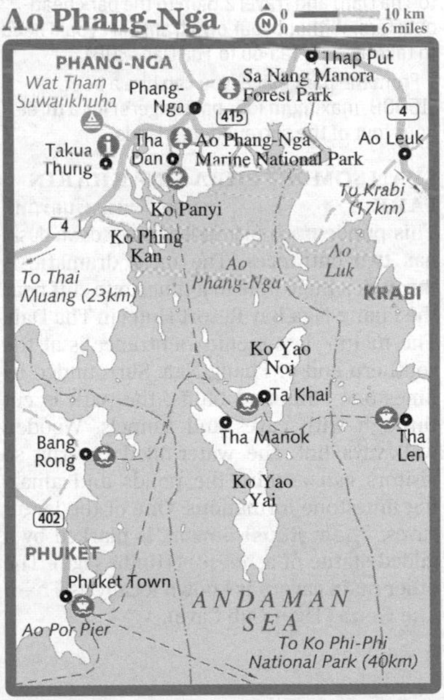

Sleeping & Eating

Phang-Nga doesn't have much in the way of quality sleeping and most folks choose to swing by on a day trip. Several food stalls on the main street of Phang-Nga sell delicious *kà·nŏm jeen* (thin wheat noodles) with chicken curry, *nám yah* (spicy ground-fish curry) or *nám prík* (spicy sauce). There's a morning market open from 5am to 10am daily and a small night market on Tuesday, Wednesday and Thursday evenings, located just south of Soi Lohakit.

Phang-Nga Inn HOTEL $$
(☎0 7641 1963; 2/2 Soi Lohakit, Phang-Nga; r 400-1500B; ❄) This converted residential villa is an absolute gem and features heavy wooden staircases, louvred cabinets and peaceful gardens. It's well furnished, there's a little eatery and the staff are gracious.

Phang-Nga Guest House GUEST HOUSE $
(☎0 7641 1358; Th Petchkasem, Phang-Nga; r 250-380B; ❄) Nothing fancy. Just a clean block of cheap and cherry-tiled rooms in the otherwise drab centre of town.

TOP CHOICE **Kror Son Thong** THAI $
(☎08 4182 4684; 29/1 Th Rongua, Phang-Nga; mains 70-200B; ⊙lunch & dinner) Overlooking the river, south of the commercial strip, is this kitchen, which verges on gourmet. Try the *pla tod kamin*, crab omelette or roast duck with kale. It's all excellent.

Around Phang-Nga

AO PHANG-NGA NATIONAL MARINE PARK อุทยานแห่งชาติอ่าวพังงา

Established in 1981 and covering an area of 400 sq km, **Ao Phang-Nga National Marine Park** (☎0 7641 1136; www.dnp.go.th;

BUSES TO PHANG-NGA

Phang-Nga's bus terminal is located just off the main street on Soi Bamrung Rat. Bangkok buses to/from Phang-Nga include VIP (912B, 12 hours, one daily), 1st class (552B, 12 to 13 hours, two daily) and 2nd class (441B, 12 hours, three to four daily).

There are several other bus services available:

DESTINATION	FARE (B)	DURATION (HR)	FREQUENCY
Hat Yai	300	6	2 daily
Krabi	74	1½	frequent
Phuket	85	1½	frequent
Ranong	170	5	4 daily
Surat Thani	150	3	frequent
Trang	240	3½	frequent

admission 200B; ⌚8am-4pm) is noted for its classic karst scenery. There are over 40 islands with huge vertical cliffs, some with caves that are accessible at low tide and lead into hidden *hôrngs* (lagoons surrounded by solid rock walls). The bay itself is composed of large and small tidal channels including Khlong Ko Phanyi, Khlong Phang-Nga, Khlong Bang Toi and Khlong Bo Saen. These channels run through vast mangroves in a north–south direction and today are used by fisher folk and island inhabitants as aquatic highways. They are the largest remaining primary mangrove forests in Thailand.

In the peak season the bay can become a package-tourist superhighway. But if you explore in the early morning (best done from Ko Yao Noi or Ko Yao Yai) or stay out a bit late, you'll find a slice of beach, sea and a limestone karst to call your own. The best way to experience the park is by kayak.

Sights & Activities

John Gray's Seacanoe KAYAKING
(☎0 7622 6077; www.johngray-seacanoe.com) John Gray was the first kayak outfitter in the bay and remains the most ecologically minded. He's constantly clamouring for more protection for his beloved *hôrngs* among local national park rangers and their supervisors in Bangkok. His **Hong by Starlight daytrip** (per person 3950B) dodges the crowds, involves plenty of sunset paddling and will introduce you to Ao Phang-Nga's famed bioluminescence once night falls. See also p241.

Ko Phing Kan ISLAND
The biggest tourist drawcard in the park is the so-called 'James Bond Island', known to Thais as Ko Phing Kan (literally 'Leaning on Itself Island'). Once used as a location setting for *The Man with the Golden Gun*, the island is now full of vendors hawking coral and shells that should have stayed in the sea. It's much wiser to venture further afield.

Getting There & Around

From the centre of Phang-Nga, drive about 6km south on Hwy 4, turn left onto Rte 4144 (the road to Tha Dan) and travel 2.6km to the park headquarters. Without your own transport you'll need to take a sŏrng·tăa·ou to Tha Dan (30B).

From the park office, you can hire a boat (1500B, maximum four passengers) for a three-hour tour of the surrounding islands.

SUAN SOMDET PHRA SINAKHARIN PARK สวนสมเด็จพระศรีนครินทร์

This public **park** (admission free; ⌚dawn-dusk) has two entrances. The most dramatic is through a huge hole in a limestone cliff near the Phang-Nga Bay Resort Hotel in Tha Dan. The main – less scenic – entrance is at the southern end of Phang-Nga. Surrounded by limestone cliffs and bluffs, the park is cut through with caves and tunnels. Wooden walkways link the water-filled caverns so visitors can admire the ponds and amazing limestone formations. One of the larger caves, **Tham Reusi Sawan**, is marked by a gilded statue of a *reu·sěe* (Hindu sage). The other main cavern is known locally as **Tham Luk Seua** (Tiger Cub Cave).

WAT THAM SUWANKHUHA วัดถ้ำสุวรรณคูหา

Wat Tham Suwankhuha (Heaven Grotto Temple; admission 20B; ⌚dawn-dusk) is a cave *wát* (temple) full of Buddha images. The shrine consists of two main caverns, the larger one containing a 15m-high reclining Buddha and tiled with *lai·krahm* and *benjarong* (two coloured patterns more common in pottery). The smaller cavern displays spirit flags and a *reu·sěe* statue. It's swarming with monkeys.

The wát is 10km southwest of Phang-Nga. To get here without your own transport, hop on any sŏrng·tăa·ou running between Phang-Nga and Takua Thung (90B). The wát is down a side road.

Ko Yao เกาะยาว

With mountainous backbones, unspoilt shorelines, a large variety of birdlife and a population of friendly Muslim fishermen and their families, **Ko Yao Yai** and **Ko Yao Noi** are laid-back vantage points for soaking up Ao Phang-Nga's beautiful scenery. The islands are part of the Ao Phang-Nga National Marine Park (p295) but are most easily accessed from Phuket.

Please remember to respect the beliefs of the local Muslim population and wear modest clothing when away from the beaches.

Sights & Activities

KO YAO NOI เกาะยาวน้อย

Despite being the relative pipsqueak of the Ko Yao Islands, Ko Yao Noi is the main population centre, with fishing, coconut farming and tourism sustaining its small, year-round population. Bays on the east coast recede to mud flats at low tides, and don't expect postcard-perfect white-sand beaches and turquoise lagoons even when the tide is high. That said, **Hat Pa Sai** and **Hat Paradise** are both gorgeous.

Biking

Bring along or rent (200B per day from most guest houses) a mountain bike if you want to explore the island's numerous dirt trails, or join up with Phuket's **Amazing Bike Tours** (☎08 7263 2031; www.amazingbiketoursthailand.com; day trip 2900B). If you like the idea of biking but think it's too darn hot, explore the island's paved roads with an eco-friendly electric bicycle (220B per day) from **Eco Island Vehicles** (☎08 6476 1143), who will pick you up at your hotel and take you to their rental office; they also rent mountain bikes (200B).

Diving & Snorkelling

Koh Yao Diver (☎08 7895 7551; www.kohyaodiver.com) leads dive trips around the bay and beyond. Half-day three-island snorkelling tours (1700B, maximum six passengers) through Ao Phang-Nga are easily organised from any guest house or with long-tail captains on the beach.

Rock Climbing

The Mountain Shop Adventures (☎08 9971 0380, 08 4841 1540; www.themountainshop.org; Tha Khao) offers full-day rock-climbing trips from 2500B, as well as fishing, snorkelling and kayaking trips. There are over 150 climbs on Ko Yao Noi and owner Mark has routed most of them himself – many trips involve boat travel to get to remote limestone cliff faces. Most climbs are equipped with titanium bolts and beginner to advanced trips are available.

KO YAO YAI เกาะยาวใหญ่

Ko Yao Yai is far less developed than Ko Yao Noi; it offers an even more remote and wild getaway. It's twice the size of Yao Noi with a fraction of the development, which is why villagers are still pleasantly surprised to see

ROCK ART IN AO PHANG-NGA

Many of the limestone islands in Ao Phang-Nga feature prehistoric rock art painted on or carved into the walls and ceilings of caves, rock shelters, cliffs and rock massifs. In particular you can see rock art on Khao Khian, Ko Panyi, Ko Raya, Tham Nak and Ko Phra At Thao. Khao Khian (Inscription Mountain) is probably the most visited of the sites. The images contain scenes of human figures, fish, crabs, prawns, bats, birds and elephants, as well as boats and fishing equipment, and seem to reference some sort of communal effort tied to the all-important sea harvest. The rock paintings don't fall on any one plane of reference; they may be placed right-side up, upside-down or sideways. Most of the paintings are monochrome, while some have been traced in orange-yellow, blue, grey and black.

tourists pedalling their bicycles or buzzing the concrete streets on rented motorbikes. If you explore some of the island's dirt trails that wind into the hills you may glimpse wild boar, monkeys, flying squirrels or small barking deer.

Hat Lo Pa Red and **Hat Tiikut** are two of the island's best beaches – the former lined with coconut palms, the latter with casuarina trees. But **Hat Chonglard**, best accessed from Thwison Beach Resort, trumps them both. The powder-white sand extends into a jutting palm-shaded peninsula to the north, and it's perfectly oriented to the limestone islands that layer the eastern horizon.

Ko Bele, a small island east of the twin Ko Yao islands, features a large tidal lagoon, three white-sand beaches, and easily accessible caves and coral reefs.

On Ko Yao Yai's west coast, **Elixir Divers** (☎08 7897 0076; www.elixirdivers.com) leads two-tank trips around Ao Phang-Nga and beyond. **Koh Yao Diver** (☎08 7895 7551; www.kohyaodiver.com) has a location here and on Ko Yao Noi.

Sleeping & Eating

KO YAO NOI

TOP CHOICE Six Senses Hideaway HOTEL $$$
(☎0 7641 8500; www.sixsenses.com/hideaway-yaonoi; r 32,000-40,000B; ❄@≋) This swanky five-star property – where 56 hillside pool villas (and their tremendous spa) have been built to resemble an old *chow lair* village – doesn't disappoint. Views of distant limestone are jaw-dropping, its Thai kitchen is tantalising, its loungy bar and white-sand beach are both worthy of the fashionistas that frequently fly in for photo shoots, and its commitment to sustainability is unparalleled among global five-star chains.

Koyao Island Resort HOTEL $$$
(☎0 1606 1517; www.koyao.com; villas 7000-13,200B; ❄@≋) Open-concept thatched bungalows offer serene views across a palm-shaded garden and infinity pool to a skinny white beach. We love the elegant, near safari-esque feel of the villas here with their fan-cooled patios and indoor/outdoor bathrooms. There's a posh restaurant bar and service is stellar.

Lom Lea GUEST HOUSE $$
(☎0 7659 7486; www.lomlae.com; bungalows 2000-5500B; 👪) Stylish, naturalist wooden bungalows are fronted by a stunning and secluded beach with views of Phang-Nga's signature karst islands. There's a dive centre, a good restaurant and plenty of activities on offer. We found the bungalows a bit rustic for the price, but the setting and service do merit extra baht.

Paradise Hotel HOTEL $$$
(☎08 1892 4878; www.theparadise.biz; Hat Paradise; r from 7500B) Tucked into a private cove on the far north, and accessible only by longtail or by a winding, rutted earthen road, stay here for the exceptionally beautiful and remote location. Older rooms and bungalows are built into a hillside and sprinkled throughout a blooming garden, and the restaurant and pool are nestled just behind an arc of golden sand that disappears into a turquoise lagoon.

Sabai Corner Bungalows GUEST HOUSE $
(☎0 7659 7497; www.sabaicornerbungalows.com; bungalows 500-2000B) Tucked into a rocky headland, the wooden and bamboo bungalows here are full of character and blessed with gorgeous views. The restaurant is also good and a great place to hang out.

Tha Khao Bungalow GUEST HOUSE $
(☎08 1676 7726; www.kohyaobungalow.com; bungalows 700B) The wooden bungalows are very basic but big with terraces that overlook a sublime stretch of Tha Khao Beach with endless karst formations in the distance. There's a very local vibe here and Ahn, the owner's outdoorsy nephew, offers lots of outings from climbing to kayaking or fishing.

Pasai Cottage GUEST HOUSE $
(☎08 7238 9389; pasaicottage@hotmail.com; Hat Pasai; bungalows 700-900B; @) A lively spot with a social cafe, lots of activities on offer, kayak and bike rentals, and skinny little Pasai beach with some local snack vendors across the street. The bamboo or wood bungalows are spacious and come with fan and mosquito nets.

Ko Yao Beach Bungalows GUEST HOUSE $$
(☎08 7896 3815; Hat Tha Khao; bungalows 1500B; ❄) Attractive, spacious, tiled bungalows with hot water and air-con across the road from a fantastic swimming beach. Great value.

KO YAO YAI

Thiwson Beach Resort GUEST HOUSE $$
(☎08 1737 4420; www.thiwsonbeach.com; bungalows 800-3000B; ❄👪) Easily the cleanest, and sweetest, of the island's bungalow properties. Here are proper wooden bungalows

with polished floors, outdoor baths, and wide patios facing the best beach on the island. Beachfront bungalows are the largest, but fan rooms are tremendous value.

Elixir HOTEL $$$

(☎08 7808 3838; www.elixirresort.com; bungalows 8000-25,500B; ❄@≋) The first of Yao Yai's two four-star resorts offers tasteful beachfront and hillside peaked-roof villas steeped in classic Thai style. It's set on a private beach, where you'll also find a common pool, a dive centre, massage pagodas and spectacular sunsets over Phuket.

Fa Sai Beach Bungalows GUEST HOUSE $

(☎08 1691 3616; bungalows 500B) Basic but clean cold-water bungalows are stilted in the mangroves south of Tha Lo Jak, and just back from a gorgeous strip of white sand.

Information

In **Ta Khai**, the largest settlement on Ko Yao Noi, there's a 7-Eleven with an attached ATM, and another ATM around the corner at Government Savings Bank.

On Ko Yao Yai, the only ATM is out of the way near the Klong Hia Pier, so you'd be wise to carry plenty of cash.

Getting There & Away

From Phuket

To get to Ko Yao Noi from Phuket, take a taxi (600B to 800B) to Tha Bang Rong. From here, there are hourly long-tails (150B, 20 minutes) or three daily speedboats (200B, 20 minutes) between 7.30am and 5.40pm. They all dock at Tha Klong Hia on Ko Yao Yai upon request before crossing to Ko Yao Noi. Boats begin returning to Phuket at 6.30am. Returning to Phuket from Ko Yao Noi, taxis run from Tha Bang Rong to the resort areas for 600B to 800B, or there's one sŏrng·tăa·ou (80B) to Phuket Town at 2.30pm daily.

The best way to reach Ko Yao Yai from Phuket is to catch a speedboat or ferry from Tha Rasada near Phuket Town. Ferries depart at 8.30am, 10.30am and 2pm (one hour, 100B). Speedboats (30 minutes, 150B) make the run at 4pm and 5pm. On Fridays the schedule shifts to accommodate prayer times.

From Krabi

There are four 'express' boats (450B, 1½ hours) and two speedboats (600B, 45 minutes) per day from Krabi's Tha Len pier to Ko Yao Noi piers at Tha Manok and Tha Khao.

From Phang-Nga

From Tha Sapan Yao in Phang-Nga there's a 7:30am ferry to Ko Yao Noi continuing to Ko Yao Yai (200B, two hours) that makes an excellent budget cruise of Ao Phang-Nga. It leaves Ko Yao Noi for the return trip at 1pm.

Getting Around

To get from Ko Yao Noi to Ko Yao Yai, catch a shuttle boat from Tha Manok (100B to 150B, 15 minutes) to Tha Klong Hia. On the islands, you can travel by túk-túk for about 150B per ride or rent a motorbike from most guest houses for around 250B per day. It's around 70B to 100B for túk-túk transport to the resorts.

Ko Phi-Phi & the Southern Andaman Coast

Includes »

Best Places to Eat

- » Trang Night Market (p334)
- » Krabi Night Market (p303)
- » Sukorn Beach Bungalows (p342)
- » Daya Resort (p351)
- » Lanta Seafood (p330)

Best Places to Stay

- » Rayavadee (p315)
- » Costa Lanta (p328)
- » Relax Beach Resort (p322)
- » Sukorn Beach Bungalows (p342)
- » Chan Cha Lay (p301)

Why Go?

Island hoppers, this is your dreamland. The south is the quieter half of the Andaman coast; even the regional star, Ko Phi-Phi, can't rival the glam and crowds of Phuket. Just slowly putter from white-sand isle to white-sand isle – and prepare for serious relaxation, outdoor fun and chummy nights at beachside bars.

Social seekers will love the developed beauties, such as Ko Phi-Phi and Ko Lanta, where you can party into the wee hours and meet plenty of fellow ramblers on the beach yet still find a peaceful strip of sand. And roads less travelled are just next door: head down through the lightly developed Trang islands to the even-less-visited Satun Province to find powder-white beaches, outrageous snorkelling and plenty of spicy southern Thai culture.

When to Go

The weather can be a big concern for travellers in this region. The Andaman coast receives more rain than the southern gulf provinces, with May to October being the months of heaviest rainfall. During this time passenger boats to some islands, such as Ko Tarutao, are suspended. If you find the weather on the Andaman coast unpleasant, you can easily travel to the southwestern gulf coast, where you're more likely to find the sun shining.

Top daytime temperatures average 32°C year-round with high humidity during the wet season.

KRABI PROVINCE

When travellers talk about the amazing Andaman, they are probably talking about Krabi, with its trademark karst formations curving along the coast like a giant limestone fortress. Rock climbers will find their nirvana in Railay, while castaway wannabes should head to Ko Lanta, Ko Phi-Phi or any of the other 150 islands swimming off the bleach-blonde shores.

Krabi กระบี่

POP 30,882

Krabi Town is majestically situated among impossibly angular limestone karsts jutting from the mangroves, but mid-city you're more likely to be awe-struck by the sheer volume of guest houses and travel agencies packed into this compact, quirky little town. Western restaurants are ubiquitous, as are gift shops that all sell the same old trinkets. Yet if you hang out awhile, you'll also see that there's a very real provincial scene going on in between the cracks.

Sights & Activities

For rock climbing (see p311), boats go from Krabi to Railay. For more activities in the area, see p307.

Khao Khanap Nam CLIFFS, CAVES

(ถ้ำเขาขนาบน้ำ) It's possible to climb one of these two limestone massifs, just north of the town centre. A number of human skeletons were found in the caves here, thought to be the remains of people trapped during an ancient flood. To get here, charter a longtail boat from Khong Kha pier for about 400B.

Sea Kayak Krabi KAYAKING

(☎0 7563 0270; www.seakayak-krabi.com; 40 Th Ruen Rudee) Offers a wide variety of sea-kayaking tours, including to Ao Thalane (half/full day 900/1500B), which has looming sea cliffs; Ko Hong (full day 1800B), famed for its emerald lagoon; and Ban Bho Tho (full day 1700B), which has sea caves with 2000- to 3000-year-old cave paintings. All rates include guides, lunch, fruit and drinking water.

Blue Juice Divers DIVING

(☎0 7563 0679; www.bluejuicedivers.com; Th Chao Fah) This place is in town and has two-dive packages to local islands (2900B). It also runs PADI Open Water courses (13,900B) and it has a guest house.

Tours

Various companies offer day trips to Khlong Thom, about 45km southeast of Krabi on Hwy 4, taking in some nearby hot springs and freshwater pools. Expect to pay around 1000B to 1200B, including transport, lunch and beverages; bring a swimsuit and good walking shoes. Various other 'jungle tour' itineraries are available.

Sleeping

Krabi has an exceptional and ever-improving guest-house scene. The midrange and top-end options leave much to be desired (go to Ao Nang if you crave luxury) but the area is developing fast, so more chic options may well open during the life of this book. In the low season, guest-house prices can plummet to as low as 150B.

TOP CHOICE **Chan Cha Lay** GUEST HOUSE $

(☎0 7562 0952; www.chanchalay.com; 55 Th Utarakit; r 200-650B; ❄) The en-suite rooms here, all decorated in gorgeous Mediterranean blues and whites with white-pebble and polished-concrete semi-outdoor bathrooms, are Krabi's most stylish and comfortable. Shared-bathroom, fan-only rooms are plain but spotless with firm beds.

Pak-up Hostel HOSTEL $

(☎0 7561 1955; www.pakuphostel.com; 87 Th Utarakit; dm 180-200B, d 600B; ❄📶) The snazziest hostel on the Andaman coast features several uber-hip polished-cement 10-bed dorm rooms with big wooden bunks built into the wall, each equipped with personal lockers. There's only one double room, and it's constructed in the same style. Massive, modern shared bathrooms have cold-water stalls as well as a few hot-water rain showers. There are two on-site bars (one with nightly live music) and a young, hip, club-like vibe.

K Guesthouse GUEST HOUSE $

(☎0 7562 3166; kguesthouse@yahoo.com; 15-25 Th Chao Fah; r 150-600B; ❄@📶) A Wild West–looking place with varnished wooden rooms that line a second-storey veranda that overlooks the street. Cow heads on the walls and easy socialising in the downstairs cafe add to the frontier appeal.

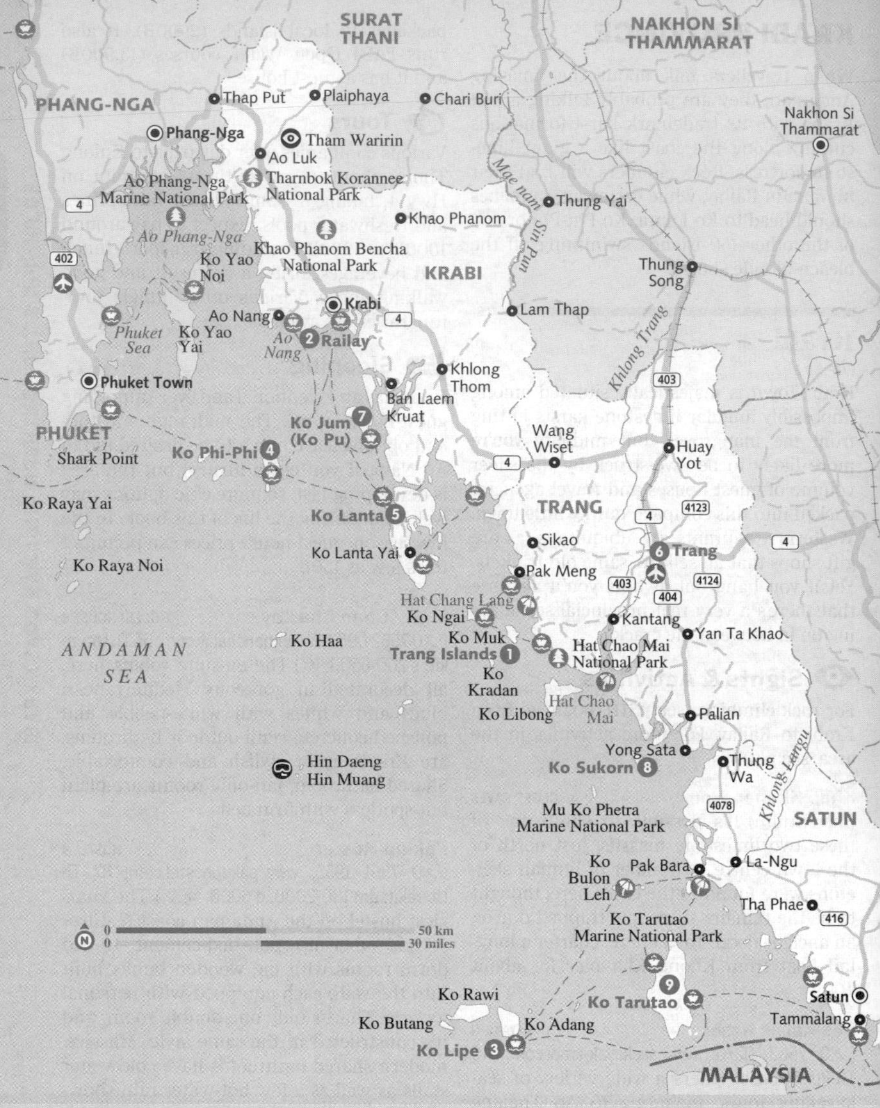

Ko Phi-Phi & the Southern Andaman Coast Highlights

1. Island hopping the serene **Trang Islands** (p335) by local long-tail
2. Climbing karst formations over seas of emerald glass in **Railay** (p311)
3. Gorging on seafood barbecue with on the soft, star-lit sands of **Ko Lipe** (p349)
4. Trying to decide if **Ko Phi-Phi** (p316) is more beautiful above or below water
5. Motorbiking along the wild jungle east coast of **Ko Lanta** (p324)
6. Trying everything from spicy seafood salads to fried grubs at the **Trang Night Market** (p334)
7. Having a stretch of grey-gold sand almost to yourself on jungle island **Ko Jum** (p332)
8. Listening to the mosque as you pedal past water buffalo on **Ko Sukorn** (p342)
9. Jungle trekking, exploring caves and cycling the forgotten roads on **Ko Tarutao** (p347)

NAVIGATING KRABI

Th Utarakit is the main road into and out of Krabi and most places of interest are on the soi (lanes) that branch off it. Ferries to Ko Phi-Phi, Ko Lanta and other islands leave from Khlong Chilat (Krabi passenger pier) about 4km southwest of town, while long-tail boats to Railay depart from Khong Kha (Chao Fa) pier on Th Khong Kha. The Krabi bus terminal is north of the town centre at Talat Kao, near the junction of Th Utarakit, while the airport is nearly 17km northeast on Hwy 4.

Krabi Maritime Park & Spa HOTEL $$$
(☎0 7562 0028; www.maritimeparkandspa.com; r from 4200B;) On lovely riverside grounds and framed by those signature limestone karsts, this run-down, once-glorious hotel is 2km from Krabi town proper. It sports a nightclub, pool, fitness centre, spa and even a lake on which you can pedal swan-shaped boats. There are free shuttle buses to Krabi town and Ao Nang, and shuttle boats to Railay.

Krabi River Hotel HOTEL $$
(☎0 7561 2321; krabiriver@hotmail.com; 73/1 Th Khong Kha; r 700-1000B;) Sure, it feels like a flashback from the early '80s, but rooms have newly tiled bathrooms and queen-sized beds, and offer terrific views of the dark river and misty mangroves. Quiet yet in town, it's a simple place in a five-star location.

Greenery Hotel HOTEL $$
(☎0 7562 3648; http://krabidir.com/thegreenery hotel/index.htm; 167/2 Th Maharat; r 600-800B;) Rooms here are modern with bright-coloured bedheads, cable TV and minifridges. The semi-outdoor hallways look out over the lush garden, which lends a peaceful feel to the place. It's about a five- to 10-minute walk from the town centre.

Eating

Night Market THAI $
(Th Khong Kha; meals 20-50B) The most popular and pleasant place for an evening meal is this market near the Khong Kha pier. The menus are in English but the food is authentic and excellent. Stalls here sell papaya salad, fried noodles, *dôm yam gûng* (prawn and lemon grass soup), grilled snapper, huge skillets of egg-battered and fried oysters, all things satay, plus sweet milky Thai desserts.

Day Market THAI $
(Th Sukhon; meals 20-60B) This market is even more authentic. Among the bouquets of flowers and weighty tropical-fruit stands are simmering curry pots and banquet trays of steaming noodles with fried squid, sautéed beef, devilled eggs, fried fish and boiled corn. Eat daringly. Though called the day market, it's open most nights too.

Good Steak House WESTERN $
(☎08 9724 7008; Th Utarakit; meals from 45B; ⊙breakfast, lunch & dinner) Airy and bright, with just a half-dozen tables and one large booth. The menu includes steaks and smoked sausage, but it's the wok stir-fried plates (from 45B) that merit mention here. Think sesame beef in oyster sauce, squid with hot basil, or prawns in chilli paste. Portions aren't huge, but at these prices who's complaining?

Cucina Italiana Viva ITALIAN $$
(☎0 7563 0517; 29 Th Phruksauthit; pizzas 200-260B) This is the place to sample tasty, thin-crust pizza, with a variety of cheeses and toppings to choose from. It has calzones, Italian wine, ice cream and coffee, and it delivers.

Information

Many of Krabi's guest houses and restaurants offer internet access for 40B to 60B per hour. There are numerous banks and ATMs.

Immigration office (☎0 7561 1350; Th Chamai Anuson; ⊙8.30am-4pm Mon-Fri) Handles visa extensions.

Krabi Hospital (☎0 7561 1210; Th Utarakit) North of town 1km.

Post office (Th Utarakit) Just south of the turn-off to Khong Kha pier.

Getting There & Away

Air

Most domestic carriers offer service between Bangkok and Krabi International Airport (one way around 4400B, 1¼ hours). **Bangkok Air** (www.bangkokair.com) has daily service to Ko Samui for around 3800B.

Boat

Boats to Ko Phi-Phi and Ko Lanta leave from the passenger pier at Khlong Chilat, about 4km southwest of Krabi. Travel agencies will arrange free transfers when you buy a boat ticket with them.

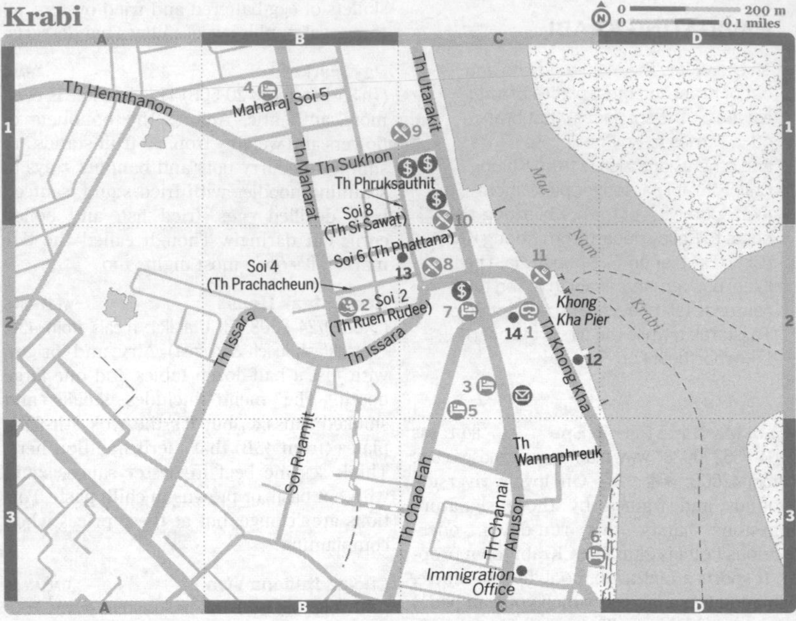

Krabi

Activities, Courses & Tours

1 Blue Juice Divers ... C2
2 Sea Kayak Krabi ... B2

Sleeping

3 Chan Cha Lay ... C2
4 Greenery Hotel ... B1
5 K Guesthouse ... C2
6 Krabi River Hotel ... C3
7 Pak-up Hostel ... C2

Eating

8 Cucina Italiana Viva ... C2
9 Day Market ... C1
10 Good Steak House ... C1
11 Night Market ... C2

Transport

12 PP Family Co ... C2
13 Sŏrng tăa ou ... C2
14 Yellow House ... C2

The largest boat operator is **PP Family Co** (☎0 7561 2463; www.phiphifamily.com; Th Khong Kha), which has a ticket office right beside the pier in town. In the high season there are boats to Ko Phi-Phi (300B, 1½ hours) at 9am, 10.30am, 1.30pm and 3pm while in low season the schedule is reduced to two boats per day.

From November to May, there is only one daily boat to Ko Lanta (350B, two hours) leaving Krabi at 11.30am. These can also stop at Ko Jum (one hour), where long-tails shuttle you to shore (though you'll pay the full 350B). During the wet season, you can only get to Ko Lanta by frequent air-con vans (300B, 2½ hours), which also run throughout the high season.

If you want to get to Railay, long-tail boats leave from Krabi's Khong Kha pier to Hat Railay East (150B, 45 minutes) from 7.45am to 6pm. The boatmen will wait until they can fill a boat with 10 people before they leave; if you're antsy to go before then, you can charter the whole boat for 1500B.

To get to Phuket or the Ko Yao Islands, the quickest route is with direct boats from the pier at Ao Nang (see p310). Sŏrng·tăa·ou run between the two piers for 50B, or a taxi costs 300B to 400B.

Minivan

Dozens of travel agencies in Krabi run air-con minivans and VIP buses to popular tourist centres throughout southern Thailand, but you may end up crammed cheek to jowl with other backpackers. Most travel agencies also offer

BUSES TO/FROM KRABI

Taking a government bus from the **Krabi bus terminal** (cnr Th Utarakit & Hwy 4) in nearby Talat Kao, about 4km from Krabi, is an altogether more relaxing option than taking a cramped minivan.

DESTINATION	FARE (B)	DURATION (HR)	FREQUENCY
Bangkok	720-1080	12	4 per day
Hat Yai	169	5	hourly
Phuket	145	3½	hourly
Ranong	200	6	2 per day
Surat Thani	140	1½B	frequent
Trang	90-115	2	frequent

combined minivan and boat tickets direct to Ko Samui (500B, 5½ hours) and Ko Pha-Ngan (550B, 7½ hours). Destinations from Krabi:

DESTINATION	FARE (B)	DURATION (HR)
Ao Luk	80	1
Hat Yai	350	3
Ko Lanta	350	1½
Phuket	350	2-3
Satun	550	5
Trang	350	2

Sŏrng·tăa·ou

Sŏrng·tăa·ou run from the bus station to central Krabi and on to Hat Noppharat Thara (40B), Ao Nang (60B) and the Shell Cemetery at Ao Nam Mao (80B). There are services from 6am to 6.30pm. In the high season there are less frequent services until 10pm for a 10B surcharge. For Ao Luk (80B, one hour) there are frequent sŏrng·tăa·ou from the corner of Th Phattana and Th Phruksauthit; the last service leaves at around 3pm.

Getting Around

Central Krabi is easy to explore on foot, but the bus terminal and airport are both a long way from the town centre. A taxi from the airport to town will cost 400B. In the reverse direction, taxis cost 350B, while motorcycle taxis cost 300B. Agencies in town can arrange seats on the airport bus for 120B. Sŏrng·tăa·ou between the bus terminal and central Krabi cost 40B.

Hiring a vehicle is an excellent way to explore the countryside around Krabi. Most of the travel agencies and guest houses in town can rent you a Yamaha motorbike for around 200B per day. **Yellow House** (☎0 7562 2809; Th Chao Fah) has a gleaming fleet of Yamahas and provides helmets. A few of the travel agencies along Th Utarakit rent out small 4WDs for 1200B to 1800B per day.

Wat Tham Seua วัดถ้ำเสือ

A sprawling hill and cave temple complex 8km northwest of Krabi, **Wat Tham Seua** (Tiger Cave Temple) is an easy and very worthwhile daytrip from Krabi Town. Although the main *wí·hăhn* (hall) is built into a long, shallow limestone cave at the wát's entrance, the best part of the temple grounds can be found by following a loop trail through a little forest valley behind the ridge where the *bòht* (central sanctuary) is located. You'll find several limestone caves hiding Buddha images, statues and altars as well as some of the monks' rustic jungle huts, behind which they hang out their saffron robes to dry. Troops of monkeys cackle from the trees.

Back near the park entrance again, you'll come to a gruellingly steep 1237 steps (you'll have the number memorised if you climb them) leading to a 600m karst peak. The fit and fearless are rewarded with a Buddha statue, a gilded stupa and spectacular views; on a clear day you can see well out to sea.

A huge new pagoda with even more stairs to climb was being built near the wát's parking lot when we passed.

Getting There & Away

A motorcycle taxi or túk-túk from Krabi to Wat Tham Seua costs 100B. By sŏrng·tăa·ou, get on at Krabi's Th Utarakit for 50B, and tell the driver 'Wat Tham Seua'. If no one else is going to the wát, the driver may ask an extra fee to drive you down the 300m lane from the main road to the wát's entrance. It's just as easy to get off at the

WHAT NOT TO WEAR AT THE WAT

Wat Tham Seua sees a large amount of Western visitors, many of whom unfortunately arrive in shorts, swimsuits and even shirtless as if they just stepped off the beach. Signs are posted around the wát asking visitors to dress respectfully but the monks themselves, as well as most Thais, are too polite to say anything to those disregarding their kind request. This is a sacred area of worship, so please be respectful and dress modestly: trousers or skirts past the knees, shirts covering the shoulders and nothing too tight.

road and walk. Motorcycle taxis and túk-túks hang out in the wát parking lot, or you could flag one down on the main road.

Tharnbok Korannee National Park

อุทยานแห่งชาติธารโบกขรณี

Close to the small town of Ao Luk, a stunning 46km drive northwest of Krabi, **Tharnbok Korannee National Park** (Than Bok; adult/child under 14yr 200/100B) protects a large area of islands, mangroves and limestone caves. The most important cave here is **Tham Pee Hua Toe** (Big-Headed Ghost Cave), reached by long-tail boat or sea kayak from the pier at Ban Bho Tho, 7km south of Ao Luk. Legend has it that a huge human skull was found in the cave, but the ghost story probably has more to do with the 2000- to 3000-year-old cave paintings that adorn the cave walls. Nearby **Tham Lot** (Tube Cave) can also be navigated by boat. Both caves are popular destinations for sea-kayaking tours from Krabi or Ao Nang, but you can also hire sea kayaks from local guides who grew up in the shadow of the Bho Tho pier. Long-tails are available for 400B.

There are at least seven other caves in the park, including **Tham Sa Yuan Thong** – a few kilometres southeast of Ao Luk – which has a natural spring bubbling into a pool. The national park also includes the uninhabited island of **Ko Hong**, which has fine beaches, jungle-cloaked cliffs and a scenic hidden lagoon. Sea-kayak and long-tail tours come here from Ao Nang.

Just to the south of Ao Luk, the park headquarters is a popular picnic spot. You'll find an 1800m nature trail that links a series of babbling brooks and shady emerald pools connected by little waterfalls. The usual vendors sell noodles, fried chicken and *sôm·đam* (spicy green papaya salad). There's also a small **visitors centre** (⏲6am-6pm; park admission 200B) that has displays in Thai and English.

Nearby Ao Them Lem is another stunning panorama of limestone and mangroves laced with concrete streets and sandy lanes. Day-trippers buzz in for long-tail trips to nearby *hôrng* (semisubmerged island caves) and lagoons, but otherwise this is a mellow, very local village with a few modest resorts.

Discovery Resort (☎08 1298 9533; 500 Moo 1 Kao Tong; bungalows 1300B; ❄) is the tightest operation. The owner-operator speaks English and her attractive peaked-roof bungalows have cable TV and are almost brand new. She offers kayak tours and rentals, with the mangroves and looming limestone karsts a short drive away. The Ramshackle **Coconut Bungalows** (☎08 1537 0247; bungalows 500B) are a bit yellow at the edges, but they are clean, spacious and set in a gorgeous coconut grove, steps from the sea with views of *hôrng* and islands on the horizon.

Getting There & Away

The park headquarters is about 1.5km south of Ao Luk town along Rte 4039. Buses and sŏrng·tăa·ou from Krabi stop on Hwy 4. Catch a government bus to Pha-Ngan or Phuket and ask to be let off at Ao Luk (80B, one hour), from where you can walk down to the park headquarters or take a motorcycle taxi for 15B. The easiest way to get to Tham Pee Hua Toe and Tham Lot is on a sea-kayaking tour from Krabi or Ao Nang.

To get to Ban Bho Tho from Ao Luk under your own steam, take a motorcycle taxi (70B) or a Laem Sak sŏrng·tăa·ou (30B) to the Tham Pee Hua Toe turn-off on Rte 4039. From the junction it's about 2km to Ban Bho Tho along the first signposted road on the left.

Sŏrng·tăa·ou from Krabi also travel directly to Ao Them Lem (60B).

Ao Nang

อ่าวนาง

POP 12,400

Granted, you're not breaking ground, but there's still plenty to like about Ao Nang, a beach town that's unabashedly devoted to tourism. It all starts with the beaches,

DETOUR: KHAO PHANOM BENCHA NATIONAL PARK

This 50-sq-km **park** (☎0 7566 0716; adult/child under 14yr 200/100B) protects a dramatic area of virgin rainforest along the spine of 1350m-high Khao Phanom Bencha, 20km north of Krabi. The park is full of well-signed trails to scenic waterfalls, including the 11-tiered **Huay To Falls**, 500m from the park headquarters. Nearby and almost as dramatic are Huay Sadeh Falls and Khlong Haeng Falls. On the way into the park you can visit **Tham Pheung**, a dramatic cave with shimmering mineral stalactites and stalagmites. The numerous trails that wend through the area are excellent for hiking.

The park is home to abundant wildlife – but only monkeys are commonly seen. Many bird-spotters come here to see white-crowned and helmeted hornbills, argus pheasants and the extremely rare Gurney's pitta. Local guides aren't absolutely necessary here, considering the well-marked trails. But visitors who hire guides tend to spot more wildlife, and have a deeper experience in general.

There is no public transport to the park, but it's easy to get here from Krabi by hired motorcycle; follow the sign-posted turn-off from Hwy 4. Park your motorcycle by the park headquarters and remember to apply the steering lock. Alternatively, you can hire a túk-túk (pronounced đúk đuk; motorised three-wheeled pedicab) for around 600B round-trip.

framed by limestone headlands tied together by narrow strips of golden sand. In the dry season the sea glows a lovely turquoise hue, in the wet season rip-tides stir up the mocha shallows. If you're hankering for a swim in crystalline climes at any time of year, you can easily book a trip to the local islands that dot the horizon.

Ao Nang is compact and easy to navigate, and with the onrush of attractive, midrange development, accommodation standards are especially high, with substantial discounts possible. It's not nearly as cheap (or as authentic) as Krabi town, but it's cleaner and sunnier; it's also much better value than what you'll find in Phuket. There's plenty to do (mangrove tours? snorkelling trips?), it's only 40 minutes away from the Krabi airport, and a smooth 20-minute long-tail boat ride from stunning Railay. It's no wonder this beach is increasingly popular with travellers of every ilk.

Activities

Loads of activities are possible at Ao Nang, and children under 12 typically get a 50% discount.

Kayaking

At least seven companies offer kayaking tours to mangroves and islands around Ao Nang. Popular destinations include the scenic sea lagoon at Ko Hong (1500B to 1800B) to view collection points for sea swallow nests (spurred by demand for bird's-nest soup). There are also trips to the lofty sea cliffs and wildlife-filled mangroves at Ao Thalane (half-/full day 500/800B) and to the sea caves and 2000- to 3000-year-old paintings at Ban Bho Tho (half-/full day 700/900B). Rates will vary slightly, but always include lunch, fruit, drinking water, sea kayaks and guides.

Diving & Snorkelling

Ao Nang has numerous dive schools offering trips to 15 local islands, including Ko Si, Ko Ha, Yava Bon and Yava Son. It costs about 3200B for two dives. Ko Mae Urai is one of the more unique local dives, with two submarine tunnels lined with soft and hard corals. Other trips run further afield to King Cruiser (three dives 4700B) and Ko Phi-Phi (two dives 3900B). A PADI Open Water course will set you back 14,900B to 16,000B. Reliable dive schools include **Ao Nang Divers** (☎0 7563 7244; www.aonang-divers.com) and **Poseidon Dive Center** (☎0 7563 7263; www.poseidon-diving.com). Most dive companies can also arrange snorkelling trips in the area.

Cycling

Take a Tour de Krabi by hooking up with **Krabi Eco Cycle** (☎0 7563 7250; www.krabiecocycle.com; 41/2 Muu 5; half-/full-day tour 800/1700B). The recommended full-day 15.5km pedal takes you through rubber plantations, small villages, hot springs and, finally, a cooler dip at the aptly named Emerald Pool. Lunch is included on all tours except the half-day bike-only tour.

Courses

Krabi Thai Cookery School COOKING
(☎0 7569 5133; www.thaicookeryschool.net; 269 Moo 2, Ao Nang, Rte 4204) About 10km from Ao Nang between Wat Sai Thai and Ao Nam Mao, this school offers one-day Thai-cooking courses from 1000B; transfers are included in the price.

Tours

Any agency worth its salt can book you on one of the popular four- or five-island tours for around 2200B. The **Ao Nang Long-tail Boat Service** ☎0 7569 5313; www.aonangboat co-op.com) offers private charters for up to six people to Hong Island (2500B) and Bamboo Island (3800B), and the standard five-island tour, of course. You can also book half-day trips to Poda and Chicken Islands (1700B, four hours) for up to four people.

Several tour agencies offer tours to **Khlong Thom**, including visits to freshwater pools, hot springs and the **Wat Khlong Thom Museum**; the price per adult/child is 1200/900B. So-called mystery tours visit local snake farms, rural villages, crystal pools and rubber, pineapple, banana and papaya plantations, and cost around 900/450B per adult/child. Tour agencies also offer trips to attractions around Ao Phang-Nga and to a number of dubious animal shows.

You can also arrange day tours to Ko Phi-Phi on the **Ao Nang Princess** (adult/child 1400/1000B). The boat leaves from the Hat Noppharat Thara National Park headquarters at 9am and visits Bamboo Island, Phi-Phi Don and Phi-Phi Leh. Free transfers from Ao Nang to Hat Noppharat Thara are included in the price.

Sleeping

Prices at all these places drop by 50% during the low season.

Golden Beach Resort HOTEL $$$
(☎0 7563 7870-74; www.goldenbeach-resort.com; r 3900-6100B, bungalows 5100-8100B;) This sprawling, unpretentious resort dominates the southernmost 400m of Ao Nang's beachfront – the best part of the beach. It's made up of large hotel blocks and stylish white cement, wood-trimmed bungalows arranged in garden foliage around a big pool. It's only verging on hip but it definitely feels good to be here. Check the website for specials.

Red Ginger Chic Resort HOTEL $$$
(☎0 7563 7777; www.redgingerkrabi.com; 88 Moo 3; r 6300-10,900B;) Fashionable and colourful with detailed tiles, large paper lanterns, and a frosted glass bar in the lobby. Large rooms feature elegant wallpaper, modern furnishings and large balconies overlooking an expansive pool.

Somkiet Buri Resort HOTEL $$
(☎0 7563 7320; www.somkietburi.com; r 3000-10,500B;) This place just might inspire you to slip into a yoga pose. The lush jungle grounds are filled with ferns and orchids, while lagoons, streams and meandering wooden walkways guide you to the 26 large and creatively designed rooms. A great swimming pool is set amid it all – balconies face either this pool or a peaceful pond. The service is first-rate.

Ao Nang Cliff Resort HOTEL $$$
(☎0 7562 6888; www.aonangcliffbeach.com; r 4500-7500B;) Think sunken bedrooms, daybeds, duvets and rain showers. The best-situated rooms have cliff and sea views, and the pool outside the lobby is stunning. If you come in the low season, you can grab a room for 2500B.

Ananta Burin HOTEL $$$
(☎0 7566 1551; www.anantaburinresort.com; 166 Moo 3; r 4500-5500B;) A new splashy boutique resort with an impressive vaulted roof lobby and hotel blocks that horseshoe around a pool. Rooms feature nice design elements, including built-in dark-wood furnishings. First-floor rooms spill directly into the pool.

Verandah HOTEL $$
(☎0 7563 7454; www.theverandahaonang.com; r incl breakfast 1700-2300B;) Solid value right in the middle of things. Rooms here are simple, spacious and immaculate, with tiled floors, minifridge, hot water, satellite TV and safety boxes. Guests are welcome to use the pool at nearby Peace Laguna Resort.

Apasari HOTEL $$
(☎0 7563 7188; www.apasari.com; r 1800-5800B;) One of a handful of stylish new midrangers on Ao Nang's newest boulevard. Rooms have high-end tiled floors, built-in desks and wardrobes, and flat-screen TVs. All rooms have balconies overlooking the lap pool. It's exceptional value in the low season.

Dream Garden HOTEL $
(☎0 7563 7338; r 950-1200B; ❄@) Walk through the entrance of a dingy travel agency, past a stylish polished-cement spa effusing lemongrass scent, to a two-storey block of plain – but clean and large – tiled rooms with hot water, wood furnishings and small terraces.

Phra Nang Inn HOTEL $$$
(☎0 7563 7130; www.phrananghotels.com; r incl breakfast 4000-9000B; ❄@≋) An artistic explosion of rustic coconut wood, bright orange and purple paint and plenty of elaborate Thai tiles. There are two pools, and a second, similarly designed branch is across the road from the original.

Aonang Villa Resort HOTEL $$$
(☎0 7563 7270; www.aonangvillaresort.com; r 3600-5400B; ❄≋) A pleasant, no-frills, family-oriented seaside joint nestled in the shadow of a towering limestone bluff. It's just across the street from an OK stretch of beach.

J Hotel HOTEL $
(☎0 7563 7878; j_hotelo@hotmail.com; r from 800B; ❄@) J Hotel is an old standby that caters well to backpackers. Large, bright rooms have new tiled floors, built-in desks, wardrobes and satellite TV, but some smell a bit musty. Sniff well before you commit.

Bernie's Place HOTEL $
(☎0 7563 7093; r 300-700B; ❄) The staff look and act like they're sleepwalking but rooms are big and bright with ceiling fans, and some have sea views from a common verandah. The dark downstairs bar offers protein-packed, backpacker-priced buffets (all you can eat for 250B).

Eating

Ao Nang is full of mediocre roadside restaurants serving Italian, Scandinavian, Indian, Thai and fast food. Prices are a bit inflated but you won't go hungry. For super-budget meals, a few stalls pop up at night on the road to Krabi (near McDonald's). You'll find *roti* (pancakes), *gài tôrt* (fried chicken), hamburgers and the like.

TOP CHOICE **Soi Sunset** SEAFOOD $$
(☎0 7569 5260; Soi Sunset; dishes 60-400B; ⏲lunch & dinner) At the western end of the beach is this narrow pedestrian-only alley housing several romantic seafood restaurants with gorgeous views of an island-dotted ocean. They all have model ice boats at the entrance showing off the day's catch and smiling staff to beckon you in to take a seat. One of the best (and most popular) is Krua Ao Nang at the end of the strip.

Bamboo Food Huts THAI $
(meals 35-90B) If you're in the mood for a ramshackle local food joint, walk a few minutes up the main road to Krabi from the beach to find a row of thatched beach-hut-style eateries. Ignore the Western dishes and dig into something tasty, spicy and authentic, like fried squid with hot basil, seafood *đôm yam* or massaman curry. There are plenty of vegie options too. **Lucky Yim Restaurant** is particularly good.

Coffee Arthit CAFE $
(☎0 7563 7847; set breakfasts from 120B; ⏲breakfast, lunch & dinner; 📶) An impressive menu including excellent all-day Western-style breakfasts (from continental to vegie and meaty fry-ups). It has tasty espresso, specialty teas, smoothies and protein shakes, too.

Jeanette's Restaurant SCANDINAVIAN, THAI $$
(☎08 9474 6178; www.jeanettekrabi.com; dishes 120-450B; ⏲breakfast, lunch & dinner) The most popular place in town thanks to its signature bench seating, inkblot art on the walls and traditional Thai menu augmented with Swedish hits (that apple pie does sound good).

Drinking & Entertainment

Last Café CAFE, BAR $
(⏲11am-7pm) At the far southern end of Hat Ao Nang is this barefoot beach cafe, with cold beer and cool breezes. Come here for a welcome blast of Ao Nang natural.

Amy's Bar BAR $
(⏲11am-2am) Give Amy's points for its floral retro hippy design, which comes with billiards, flat-screen TVs streaming live football games and ladies who love these pursuits. It's one of several pubs on this soi, which runs perpendicular to the cliff.

Aonang Krabi Muay Thai Stadium THAI BOXING $$
(☎0 7562 1042; admission 800B, ringside 1200B) If you get tired of the beach-bars and video movies on the strip, this place has boisterous *moo·ay tai* (Thai boxing; often spelled *muay thai*) bouts two days a week (check current schedules at any travel agent in town) from 8.45pm. A free sŏrng·tăa·ou runs

along the strip at Ao Nang, collecting punters before the bouts.

Information

All the information offices, including **Ao Nang Visitor Center** (☎0 7562 8221), on the strip, are private tour agencies, and most offer international calls and internet access for around 1B per minute. Several banks have ATMs and foreign-exchange windows (open from 10am to 8pm) on the main drag.

Getting There & Around

Boat

Boats to Railay's Hat Railay West are run by **Ao Nang Long-tail Boat Service** (☎0 7569 5313; www.aonangboatco-op.com) and rates are fixed at 80B per person from 7.30am to 6pm or 150B per person from 6pm to 6am. It's a 15-minute journey – boats leave when there are a minimum of six passengers or you can charter the whole boat by paying for the equivalent of six people. During rough seas, boats leave from a sheltered cove about 200m west of Ao Nang – you can get here from Ao Nang by motorcycle taxi (30B), sŏrng·tăa·ou (10B) or foot.

Ferries and speedboats leave from the nearby pier at Hat Noppharat Thara (see p310) to Ko Phi-Phi, Ko Lanta, Phuket and the Ko Yao Islands.

Car, Bus & Minivan

Ao Nang is served by regular sŏrng·tăa·ou from Krabi (50B, 20 minutes). These start at the Krabi bus terminal (add 10B to the fare) and then pass by the 7-Eleven on Th Maharat and the Khong Kha pier in Krabi, continuing on to Hat Noppharat Thara, Ao Nang and finally the Shell Cemetery. From Ao Nang to Hat Noppharat Thara or the Shell Cemetery it's 20B. Airport buses to and from Ao Nang cost 80B to 100B and leave throughout the day. Private taxis from the airport cost about 800B. Minibuses go to destinations all over the south including Phuket (350B to 400B, three to four hours), Pak Bara (300B; 3½ hours) and Koh Lanta (400B, two hours).

Dozens of places along the strip rent out small motorcycles for 150B to 200B. Budget Car Hire has desks at most of the big resort hotels and charges around 1600B per day for a dinky Suzuki micro-4WD.

Around Ao Nang

HAT NOPPHARAT THARA หาดนพรัตน์ธารา

North of Ao Nang, the golden beach goes a bit more *au naturel* as it curves around a headland for 4km with limited development, until the sea eventually spills into a natural lagoon at the Ko Phi-Phi Marine National Park headquarters. Here scores of long-tails mingle with fishing boats and speedboats against a stunning limestone backdrop. The small visitors centre has displays on coral reefs and mangrove ecology, labelled in Thai and English.

Several resorts advertise a 'central Ao Nang' location – so if you don't like reading fine print, you might end up sleeping out here (though you might prefer it anyway).

Sleeping & Eating

Sala Talay Resort & Spa HOTEL $$$
(☎0 7581 0888; www.salatalay.com; r 10,000-29,000B; ❄@≋) Just around the bluff from Ao Nang proper, this beautiful new hotel is all moulded concrete, wood and stone. Architectural features include arched walls and frosted-glass awnings, and the property abuts the mangroves. Rooms have polished concrete floors, walls and washbasins, DVD players and flat screen TVs. Online rates are significantly lower than our listed rack rates outside peak season.

Sabai Resort HOTEL $$
(☎0 7563 7791; www.sabairesort.com; bungalows 1300-2200B; ❄@≋) The most professionally run of the area's bungalow properties. The tiled-roof bungalows are fan cooled and have pebbled concrete patios overlooking a palm-shaded swimming pool, and a flower garden. It offers massage and accepts credit cards.

Government Bungalows BUNGALOWS $
(☎0 7563 7200; bungalows 800B-1000B) These wooden, fan-cooled bungalows across the street from the beach are rustic yet well maintained and a terrific budget choice. Prices don't go up in the high season, but you'd better book ahead. Check in at national park headquarters near the harbour. Meals are no longer served on-site.

Restaurants THAI, SEAFOOD
Around the national park headquarters there are several restaurants serving the usual Thai snacks, such as fried chicken and papaya salad, and there's a handful of dining stalls and seafood restaurants along the frontage road.

Getting There & Away

Sŏrng·tăa·ou between Krabi and Ao Nang stop in Hat Noppharat Thara; the fare is 40B from Krabi or 10B from Ao Nang.

From November to May the *Ao Nang Princess* runs between Ko Phi-Phi Marine National Park headquarters and Ko Phi-Phi (400B, two hours). The boat leaves from the national park jetty at 9am, returning from Ko Phi-Phi at 1.30pm. It also stops at Railay's Hat Railay West. This boat can also be used for day trips to Ko Phi-Phi. During the same high-season months, there's also a boat to Phuket (700B four hours), leaving from the same pier via Koh Lanta (470B, 1½ hours) at 10.30am and 3.30pm.

A faster alternative to Phuket is to take the *Green Planet* speedboat (950B, 75 minutes), which goes from Hat Noppharat Thara to Bang Rong Pier, north of Phuket Town via Ko Yao Noi and Koh Yao Yai (both 450B, 45 minutes). The boat leaves Hat Noppharat Thara at 11am and 4pm and transport to your Phuket accommodation is included in the fare.

WORTH A TRIP

SHELL CEMETERY

สุสานหอย

About 9km east of Ao Nang at the western end of Ao Nam Mao is the Shell Cemetery, also known as Gastropod Fossil or Su-San Hoi. Here you can see giant slabs formed from millions of tiny 75-million-year-old fossil shells. There's a small **visitors centre** (admission 50B; ⌚8.30am-4.30pm), with geological displays and various stalls selling snacks. Sŏrng·tăa·ou from Ao Nang cost 30B.

Railay

ไร่เล

Krabi's fairytale limestone crags come to a dramatic climax at Railay (also spelled Rai Leh), the ultimate jungle gym for rock-climbing fanatics. This quiet slice of paradise fills in the sandy gaps between each craggy flourish, and although it's just around the bend from chaotic tourist hustle in Ao Nang, the atmosphere here is nothing short of laid-back, Rasta-Thai heaven.

Sights

At the eastern end of Hat Phra Nang is **Tham Phra Nang** (Princess Cave), an important shrine for local fishers. Legend has it that a royal barge carrying an Indian princess foundered in a storm here during the 3rd century. The spirit of the drowned princess came to inhabit the cave, granting favours to all who paid their respects. Local fishermen – Muslim and Buddhist – still place carved wooden phalluses in the cave as offerings in the hope that the spirit will provide plenty of fish.

About halfway along the path from Hat Railay East to Hat Phra Nang, a crude path, with somewhat dodgy footing (especially after a rain), leads up the jungle-cloaked cliff wall to a murky hidden lagoon known as **Sa Phra Nang** (Holy Princess Pool). There's a dramatic viewpoint over the peninsula from the nearby cliff top. This is a strenuous, if brief, hike.

Above Hat Railay East is another large cave called **Tham Phra Nang Nai** (Inner Princess Cave; adult/child 40/20B; ⌚5am-8pm), also known as Diamond Cave. A wooden boardwalk leads through a series of caverns full of beautiful limestone formations but, with shifting rain patterns, the water is gone and with it the illuminati effects that won the diamond moniker. But even in monochrome conditions, it's still worth a stroll.

Activities

Rock Climbing

With nearly 500 bolted routes, ranging from beginner to challenging advanced climbs, all with unparalleled cliff-top vistas, it's no surprise that Railay is among the top climbing spots in the world. You could spend months climbing and exploring – and many people do. The newest buzz is deep-water soloing where climbers free-climb ledges over deep water – if you fall you will most likely just get wet, so even daring beginners can give this a try.

Most climbers start off at **Muay Thai Wall** and **One, Two, Three Wall**, at the southern end of Hat Railay East, which have at least 40 routes graded from 4b to 8b on the French system. The mighty **Thaiwand Wall** sits at the southern end of Hat Railay West and offers a sheer limestone cliff with some of the most challenging climbing routes.

Other top climbs include **Hidden World** (some classic routes for intermediate climbers), **Wee's Present Wall** (an overlooked 7c+ gem), **Diamond Cave** (another beginner-to-intermediate favourite) and **Ao Nang Tower** (a three-pitch climbing wall reached only by long-tail).

The going rate for climbing courses is 800B to 1000B for a half-day and 1500B to 2000B for a full day. Three-day courses (6000B) will involve lead climbing, where

Railay

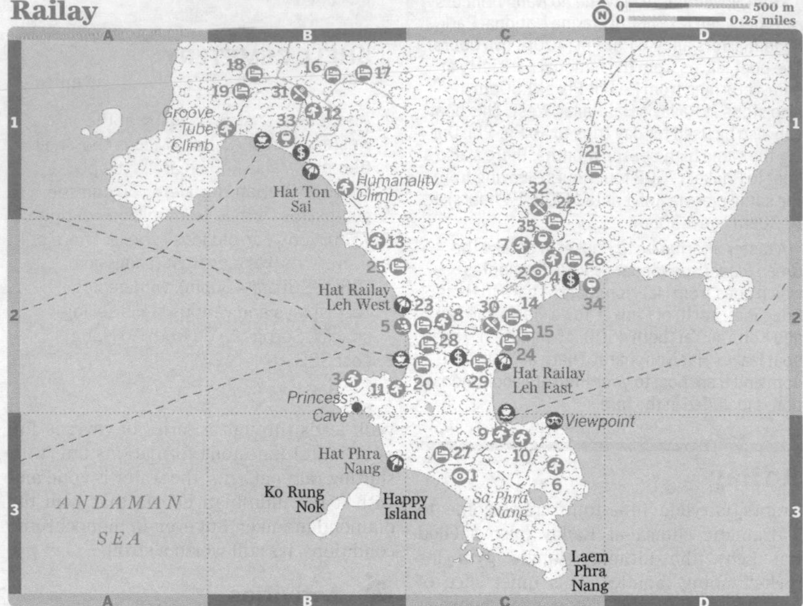

you clip into bolts on the rock face as you ascend. Experienced climbers can rent gear sets from any of the climbing schools for 800/1300B for a half-/full day – the standard set consists of a 60m rope, two climbing harnesses and climbing shoes. If you're planning to climb independently, you're best off bringing your own gear from home; be sure to bring plenty of slings and quickdraws, chalk (sweaty palms are inevitable in the tropics) and a small selection of nuts and cams as backup for thinly protected routes. If you forget anything, some climbing schools sell a small range of imported climbing gear but they might not have exactly what you need or the right size. A woven rattan mat (available locally for 100B to 150B) will help keep the sand out of your gear.

Several locally published books detail climbs in the area, but *Rock Climbing in Thailand* (US$40), by Elke Schmitz and Wee Changrua, is one of the more complete guides. Recommended climbing shops:

Highland Rock Climbing ROCK CLIMBING
(☎08 0693 0374; chaow_9@yahoo.com; Hat Railay East) If you're bunking on the mountain, this is the man to climb with.

Hot Rock ROCK CLIMBING
(☎0 7562 1771; www.railayadventure.com; Hat Railay West) Has a very good reputation and is owned by one of the granddaddies of Railay climbing.

King Climbers ROCK CLIMBING
(☎0 7563 7125; www.railay.com; Hat Railay East) One of the biggest, oldest, most reputable and commercial schools.

Wee's Climbing School ROCK CLIMBING
(☎08 1149 9745; www.tonsai basecamp; Hat Ton Sai) Arguably the most professional outfit in the area.

Water Sports

Several **dive** operations in Railay run trips out to Ko Poda and other dive sites. Two local dives at outlying islands costs about 2000B while a three- or four-day PADI Open Water dive course is 12,000B.

Full-day, multi-island **snorkelling** trips to Ko Poda, Chicken Island and beyond can be arranged through any of the resorts for about 1800B (maximum six people) or you can charter a long-tail (half/full-day 1700/2200B) from Hat Railay West beach. If you just want to snorkel off Railay, most resorts can rent you a mask set and fins for 100B to 150B each.

Flame Tree Restaurant (Hat Railay West) rents out **sea kayaks** for 200B per hour or 800B per day. Overnight trips to deserted islands can be arranged with local boat own-

Railay

Sights
1 Tham Phra Nang C3
2 Tham Phra Nang Nai C2

Activities, Courses & Tours
3 Ao Nang Tower B2
4 Diamond Cave C2
5 Flame Tree Restaurant B2
6 Hidden World C3
7 Highland Rock Climbing C2
8 Hot Rock C2
King Climbers .... (see 15)
9 Muay Thai Wall C3
10 One,Two,Three Wall C3
Railay Thai Cookery School .... (see 32)
11 Thaiwand Wall B2
12 Wee's Climbing School B1
13 Wee's Present Wall B2

Sleeping
14 Anyavee C2
15 Bhu Nga Thani C2
16 Countryside Resort B1
17 Forest Resort B1
18 Mountain View Resort B1
19 Paasook B1
20 Railay Bay Resort & Spa C2
21 Railay Cabana C1
22 Railay Phutawan Resort C2
23 Railay Village Resort & Spa C2
24 Railay Ya Ya Resort C2
25 Railei Beach Club B2
26 Rapala Rockwood Resort C2
27 Rayavadee C3
28 Sand Sea Resort C2
29 Sunrise Tropical Resort C2

Eating
30 Mangrove Restaurant C2
31 Pyramid Bar & Restaurant B1
32 Railay Phutawan Resort Restaurant C1

Drinking
33 Chillout Bar B1
34 Chok's Bar C2
Highland Rock Climbing .... (see 7)
35 Ya-ya Bar C2

Information
ATM .... (see 5)
Clinic .... (see 20)
Phra Nang Tours & Travel .... (see 14)

ers, but you'll need to bring your own camping gear and food.

Courses

Railay Thai Cookery School COOKING
(Railay Headlands; ☎08 1096 4994; courses 1200B) Right below Railay Phutawan Restaurant offers five-hour courses in a lovely semi-outdoor setting at 8.30am and 2.30pm daily.

Sleeping & Eating

HAT RAILAY WEST

It's all midrange and top-end options on this beach (where sunsets are fabulous), but rates often drop by 30% in the low season. All the resorts have decent restaurants.

Railay Bay Resort & Spa HOTEL $$$
(☎0 7562 2570-2; www.railaybayresort.com; bungalows 3700-17,800B; ❄@≋) The amoeba-shaped blue pool here faces onto the best bit of the beach, so you can switch between salt and fresh water. Elegant bungalows with big windows, white walls and rustic-chic timber terraces run right across the peninsula to Hat Railay East via gorgeously planted grounds and a second pool. Bungalows on the east side are older, with dark-tinted windows, and are the least expensive. The spa, which also overlooks the sea, offers a host of treatments at reasonable prices.

Railay Village Resort & Spa HOTEL $$$
(☎0 7563 7990; www.railayvillagekrabi.com; bungalows 7500-10,500B; ❄≋) A relatively new villa property featuring posh bungalows with private hot tubs spread throughout gardens of lily ponds, tall palms and gurgling fountains, and alongside two pools. The open-air restaurant serves excellent green curry and particularly convincing Western-style pastas that are a boon if you're travelling with children.

Railei Beach Club VILLA RENTAL $$
(☎08 6685 9359; www.raileibeachclub.com; houses from 2800B) Hidden in forested grounds at the northern end of the beach, this is a collection of Thai-style homes, each unique in size and design, rented out on behalf of foreign owners. They come with patios, kitchens and amenities to make extended

WHERE TO STAY IN RAILAY

There are four beaches around Railay, or you can choose to stay up on the headland. It's only about a five-minute walk between Hat Railay East, Hat Railay West, Hat Phra Nang and the headlands. Hat Ton Sai is more isolated, and to get to the other beaches you'll need to take a long-tail (50B) or hike – it takes about 20 minutes to scramble over the rocks from Hat Railay West.

Hat Railay East The most developed beach. The shallow, muddy bay lined with mangroves is not appetising for swimming, but the beach is lined with hotels and guest houses, and those headlands and limestone cliffs are miraculous.

Hat Railay West A near flawless, white wonder and the best place to swim, join an afternoon pick-up football game or just watch the sun go down. Tastefully designed midrange resorts are sprinkled throughout, and long-tail boats pick up and drop off here to/from nearby Ao Nang.

Hat Phra Nang Quite possibly one of the world's most beautiful beaches, with a crescent of pale, golden sand, framed by karst cliffs carved with caves. Those distant limestone islets peeking out of the cerulean sea are Chicken (Ko Hua Khwan) and Poda islands. Rayavadee, the peninsula's most exclusive resort, is the only one on this beach, but anyone can drop a beach towel.

Hat Ton Sai The grittier climbers' retreat. The beach here isn't spectacular, but with so many good climbs all around, most people don't mind. Bars and bungalows are nestled in the jungle behind the beach and it's a lively, fun scene.

Railay headlands Catch sea breezes and, since it's the most recent place to be developed, feels like a frontier with plantations, jungle and some very friendly locals. To get here, you'll have to walk about 500m from either Hat Railay West or East. From Hat Railay West follow 'Walking Street', veer left onto a dirt path then follow the signs to Ya-Ya Bar. From Hat Railay East turn right on the cement road accessible via the beachside Diamond Cave Restaurant.

stays very comfortable. Some sleep up to eight people. It's a superb deal and location, so book well in advance for the high season.

Sand Sea Resort HOTEL **$$**
(☎0 7562 2608; www.krabisandsea.com; bungalows incl breakfast 1950-5950B; ❄@≋) The lowest-priced resort on this beach offers everything from ageing fan-only bungalows to newly remodelled cottages with every amenity. The grounds aren't as swank as the neighbours, but rooms are comfy enough and there's a peaceful karst-view, foliage-enclosed pool – if you're able to tear yourself away from that sublime beach out the front, that is. The restaurant here does a full buffet breakfast.

HAT RAILAY EAST

Hat Railay East, also called Sunrise Beach, recedes to mud flats during low tide and can get steamy hot if the breezes aren't blowing your way. That said, this is where the cheaper restaurants and bars are concentrated, and it's only a five-minute walk to better beaches.

The following rates drop by half in the low season.

Sunrise Tropical Resort HOTEL **$$**
(☎0 7562 2599; www.sunrisetropical.com; bungalows incl breakfast 2500-5750B; ❄@≋) Bungalows here rival the better ones on Hat Railay West but are priced for Hat Railay East – so we think this is one of the best deals in Railay. Expect hardwood floors, Thai-style furniture, lush bathrooms with bright aqua tiles and private balconies or patios.

Bhu Nga Thani HOTEL **$$$**
(☎0 7581 9451; www.bhungathani.com; r from 7500B, villas 25,000B; ❄@≋) The newest, splashiest and easily the priciest spot on Railay East. The entry is elegant with louvred bridges over reflection pools. Rooms are exceptionally well built with high ceilings, limestone floors and all the amenities of a 4½-star joint, including wide terraces with magnificent karst views.

Anyavee HOTEL **$$**
(☎0 7581 9437; www.anyavee.com; bungalows 2800-7000B; ❄@≋) A quirky resort but one with more style than most on this beach. Bungalows here have lots of windows mak-

ing them bright but not private. Interiors are country chic, with cream-and-beige plaid duvets and plenty of hardwoods.

Rapala Rockwood Resort BUNGALOWS $
(☎08 4191 5326; bungalows 500-750B) Ramshackle bamboo bungalows have verandahs, bathrooms, mosquito nets and fans. The delightful location atop a hill means breezes and views of the sea (and your neighbours). The cushion-lined restaurant here is perfect for chilling – it serves Thai and Indian food and is run by a charming Thai grandma.

Railay Ya Ya Resort HOTEL $$
(☎0 7562 2593; www.railayyayaresort.com; r 1600-2000B; ❄@) The large wooden-panelled rooms are a bit dark, and some seem to shudder with every footstep, but the treehouse vibe works. Fan-cooled rooms are dingy but the air-con rooms are brightly painted, clean and good value. Its low-season discounts (rooms from 500B), which can extend into the fringe season, make this place a steal.

Mangrove Restaurant THAI $
(dishes from 50B) This humble, local-style place just off east beach turns out all your spicy Thai faves cheaply. It has fried rice and noodles, curries and *sôm đam*. Praise goes to the kitchen's matriarch. She means business, and her husband can turn a spoon just fine, too.

RAILAY HIGHLANDS

The resorts in the highlands above the beach are among the best-value lodging in the area.

TOP CHOICE **Railay Phutawan Resort** HOTEL $$
(☎08 4060 0550, 0 7581 9478; www.phuritvalley resort.com; bungalows 1140-1940B, r 1640B; @❄) This place doesn't really know its name yet (it's also called the Railay Phurit Valley Resort and the Highland Resort), so just call it a great place to stay. The best options are the super-spacious polished-cement bungalows highlighted with creamy yellow walls, big rain-shower bathrooms and all the trimmings of a high-end resort. Tiled rooms in an apartment-style block are a step down in luxury, but very comfortable and fan-cooled bungalows with bamboo ceilings are musty but good value. The staff is adorable.

Railay Cabana GUEST HOUSE $
(☎0 7562 1733, 08 4057 7167; bungalows 350-600B) Superbly located high in the hills in a bowl of karst cliffs, this is your hippy tropical mountain hideaway. Simple, clean thatched-bamboo bungalows are surrounded by mango, mangosteen, banana and guava groves. The only sounds are birds chirping and children laughing.

TOP CHOICE **Railay Phutawan Resort Restaurant** THAI, WESTERN $
(meals 80-180B; ⏲breakfast, lunch & dinner) Dine during the day to appreciate the views of dense jungle and karst cliffs. But the food (Thai and Western) is great any time. Try to get one of the intimate shaded booths at the jungle's edge.

HAT THAM PHRA NANG หาดถ้ำพระนาง

There's only one place to stay on this magnificent beach and it's a doozy.

TOP CHOICE **Rayavadee** HOTEL $$$
(☎0 7562 0740-3; www.rayavadee.com; pavilions 22,300-39,900B, villas 72,000-128,000B; 📶❄🏊) This exclusive resort has sprawling grounds that are filled with banyan trees and flowers, dotted with meandering ponds, and navigated by golf buggies. It's arguably one of the best hunks of beachfront property in Thailand. The two-storey, mushroom-domed pavilions are filled with antique furniture and every mod con – as well as the occasional private jacuzzi, swimming pool or butler service. There are yoga classes for guests, tours offered in luxury speedboats and a first-rate spa. Two restaurants grace Hat Tham Phra Nang (one is half inside an illuminated cave) and nonguests can stop in for pricey but divine Thai or Mediterranean meals.

HAT TON SAI หาดต้นไทร

There are plenty of backpacker options and this is the beach to go to if you're serious about climbing. For the best cheap eats go to the row of food shacks leading inland from the beach.

Countryside Resort HOTEL $
(☎08 5473 9648; countryside-resort.com; cabins 850B; ❄@📶) A UK-owned property with two rows of attractive, solar-powered cabins, which makes them the most ecologically sound in Railay. There are high ceilings, lace curtains and ceiling fans. Top-row nests have insane karst views, and you'll love Ewok-faced Ollie, the property mascot.

Paasook HOTEL $
(☎08 9645 3013; bungalows 300-800B) Definitely the most stylish budget establishment

on Ton Sai: wooden bungalows are huge, have elongated floor-to-ceiling windows and concrete floors. This place is at the far western end of the beach, right beneath Groove Tube. The gardens are lush, management is friendly and there's a rustic-chic outdoor restaurant, perfect for steamy evenings.

Mountain View Resort HOTEL **$$**
(☎0 7562 2610-3; bungalows 1300-1900B; ❄) Bright, cheery and immaculate with mint-green walls, tiled floors and crisp sheets in lodge-like environs. Some rooms are slightly musty, so sniff around.

Forest Resort HOTEL **$$**
(☎08 0143 8261; bungalows 1000B) A collection of large, basic, thatched bungalows perched on a flowery hillside with typically amazing limestone views. It also has a groovy restaurant, made from sculpted wood, serving Indian food among other dishes.

Pyramid Bar & Restaurant INTERNATIONAL **$**
(dishes from 60B, drinks from 30B) The most popular hangout in Ton Sai. It does fresh fruit lassis, shakes, ciabatta and baguette sandwiches with home-baked loaves, and tasty espresso drinks in thatched treehouse environs. Hit one of the hammocks or lounge on the floor cushions and stay a while.

Drinking & Entertainment

There's a bunch of places on the beaches where you can unwind and get nicely inebriated.

Chill Out Bar BAR **$**
(Hat Ton Sai) Right on the beach and with Thai lounging mats strewn over several levels of decks, this is where the bigger-name Thai and international bands play when they're in town. At other times, it's the ideal place to lounge with a beer.

Highland Rock Climbing CAFE **$**
(☎08 0693 0374; Railay Headlands) Part climbing school, part cafe cobbled from driftwood and dangling with orchids. The owner, Chaow, sources his beans from sustainable farms in Chiang Rai, and serves the best coffee on the peninsula.

Ya-ya Bar BAR **$**
(Railay Headlands) Ya-ya Bar has an awesome setting under a massive climbing wall. It's enveloped by jungle and has a drinking gazebo perched atop a boulder. Bob Marley looms like a patron saint. Mojitos (160B) are poured liberally. There's also a Thai boxing ring with courses on demand offered at 500B per hour.

Chok's Bar BAR **$**
(Hat Railay East; ⏲7pm-2am) A stylish, laid-back bamboo bar with live music almost nightly, decorated with bamboo mats and plenty of pillows to lean into. A popular hang-out when we came through.

Information

The website www.railay.com has lots of information about Railay. There are two ATMs along Hat Railay East. On Hat Ton Sai there is one ATM near the Ton Sai Bay Resort. Several of the bigger resorts can change cash and travellers cheques. For minor climbing injuries there's a small clinic at Railay Bay Resort & Spa (p313).

Wi-fi availability will depend on where you stay. If you lack the hardware, try **Phra Nang Tours & Travel** (internet per min 1B) on east beach.

Getting There & Around

Long-tail boats to Railay run from Khong Kha pier in Krabi and from the seafronts of Ao Nang and Ao Nam Mao. Boats between Krabi and Hat Railay East leave every 1½ hours from 7.45am to 6pm when they have six to 10 people (150B, 45 minutes). Chartering a special trip will set you back 1500B.

Boats to Hat Railay West or Hat Ton Sai from the eastern end of the promenade at Ao Nang costs 80B (15 minutes) from 7.30am to 6pm or 150B at other times; boats don't leave until six to eight people show up. Private charters cost 800B. If seas are rough, boats leave from a sheltered cove just west of Krabi Resort in Ao Nang. You can be dropped at Hat Phra Nang or Hat Ton Sai for the same fare.

During exceptionally high seas the boats from Ao Nang and Krabi stop running, but you may still be able to get from Hat Railay East to Ao Nam Mao (100B, 15 minutes), where you can pick up a sŏrng·tăa·ou to Krabi or Ao Nang.

From October to May the *Ao Nang Princess* runs from Hat Noppharat Thara National Park headquarters to Ko Phi-Phi with a stop at Hat Railay West. Long-tails run out to meet the boat at around 9.15am from in front of the Sand Sea Resort (p314). The fare to Ko Phi-Phi from Railay is 350B.

Ko Phi-Phi Don

เกาะพีพีดอน

Oh, how beauty can be a burden. Like Marilyn Monroe, Phi-Phi Don's stunning looks have become its own demise. Everyone wants a piece of her. Though not exactly Hollywood, this is Thailand's Shangri La: a hedonistic par-

Ko Phi-Phi Don

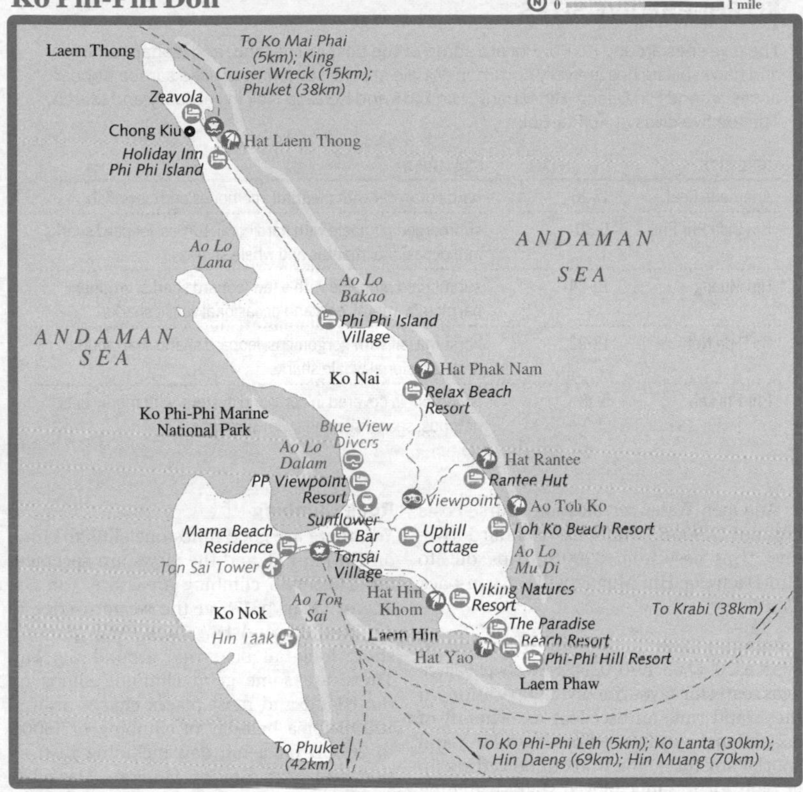

adise where tourists cavort in azure seas and snap pictures of long-tails puttering between craggy cliffs. With its flashy, curvy, blonde beaches and bodacious jungles, it's no wonder that Phi-Phi has become the darling of the Andaman coast. And, like any good starlet, this island can party hard all night and still look like a million bucks the next morning. Unfortunately, nothing can withstand this glamorous pace forever, and unless limits are set, Phi-Phi is in for an ecological crash.

Activities

The strenuous climb to the **Phi-Phi viewpoint** is a rewarding short hike. Follow the signs from the road heading east towards Ao Lo Dalam from the Tourist Village. The viewpoint is reached via a 300m vertical climb that includes hundreds of steep steps and narrow twisting paths. The views from the top are amazing – this is where you can see Phi-Phi's lush mountain butterfly brilliance in full bloom. From here you can head over the hill through the jungle to the peaceful eastern beaches for a DIY snorkelling tour.

Ao Lo Dalam is ripe for exploration. Stop at the **kayak rental stall** (Map p320; per hr 200B, full day 600B) on the sand in front of Slinky Bar, paddle out to the headland and dive in.

Diving

Crystal Andaman water and abundant marine life make the perfect recipe for top-notch scuba. Popular sights include the **King Cruiser Wreck**, sitting a mere 12m below the surface; **Anemone Reef**, teeming with hard corals and clownfish; **Hin Bida**, a submerged pinnacle attracting turtles and large pelagic fish; and **Ko Bida Nok**, with its signature karst massif luring leopard sharks. Hin Daeng and Hin Muang (p325), to the south, are expensive ventures from Ko Phi-Phi – it's cheaper to link up with a dive crew in Ko Lanta.

KO PHI-PHI DIVE SITES

The dive sites around Ko Phi-Phi are some of the best in Thailand, and leopard sharks and hawksbill turtles are very common. Whale sharks sometimes make cameo appearances around Hin Daeng, Hin Muang, Hin Bida and Ko Bida Nok in February and March. The top five dives at Ko Phi-Phi:

DIVE SITE	DEPTH (M)	FEATURES
Anemone Reef	17-26	hard coral reef with plentiful anemones and clownfish
Hin Bida Phi-Phi	5-30	submerged pinnacle with hard coral, turtles, leopard sharks and occasional mantas and whale sharks
Hin Muang	19-24	submerged pinnacle with a few leopard sharks, grouper, barracuda, moray eels and occasional whale sharks
Ko Bida Nok	18-22	karst massif with gorgonians, leopard sharks, barracuda and occasional whale sharks
Phi-Phi Leh	5-18	island rim is covered in coral and oysters, with moray eels, octopus, seahorses and swim-throughs

An Open Water certification course costs around 12,900B, while the standard two-dive trips cost from 3200B. Trips out to Hin Daeng or Hin Muang will set you back 5500B.

Adventure Club DIVING
(Map p320; ☎08 1970 0314; www.phi-phi-adventures.com) Our favourite diving operation on the island runs an excellent assortment of educational, eco-focused diving, hiking and snorkelling tours. You won't mind getting up at 6am for the much-loved shark-watching snorkel trips on which you're guaranteed to cavort with at least one reef shark.

Blue View Divers DIVING
(Map p317; ☎0 7581 9395; www.blueviewdivers.com) Focuses on community involvement and beach clean-ups (its latest cleared up 700 tonnes of rubbish) and is the only shop to offer dives from a long-tail.

Snorkelling

A popular snorkelling destination is **Ko Mai Phai** (Bamboo Island), north of Phi-Phi Don. There's a shallow area here where you may see small sharks. Snorkelling trips cost between 600B and 2400B, depending on whether you travel by long-tail or motorboat. On Ko Phi-Phi there is good snorkelling along the eastern coast of **Ko Nok**, near Ao Ton Sai, and along the eastern coast of **Ko Nai**. If you're going on your own, most bungalows and resorts rent out a snorkel, mask and fins for 150B to 200B per day.

Rock Climbing

Yes, there are good limestone cliffs to climb on Ko Phi-Phi, and the views are spectacular. The main climbing areas are **Ton Sai Tower** (Map p317), at the western edge of Ao Ton Sai, and **Hin Taak** (Map p317), a short long-tail boat ride around the bay. There are some good climbing shops on the island and most places charge around 1000B for a half-day of climbing or 1500B to 2000B for a full day, including instruction and gear. **Spider Monkey** (Map p320; ☎0 7581 9384; www.spidermonkeyclimbing.com) is run by Soley, one of the most impressive climbers on Phi-Phi. One of the bigger outfits around is **Cat's Climbing Shop** (Map p320; ☎08 1787 5101; www.catclimbingshop.com) in the Tourist Village. Cat's gets good reports for safety and service.

Courses

Pum Restaurant & Cooking School COOKING
(Map p320; ☎08 1521 8904; www.pumthaifoodchain.com; classes 450-4650B) Thai-food fans can take cooking courses here in the Tourist Village. You'll learn to make some of the excellent dishes that are served in its restaurant and go home with a great cookbook. Recommended.

Tours

Ever since Leo smoked a spliff in Alex Garland's *The Beach*, Phi-Phi Leh has become somewhat of a pilgrimage site. Aside from long-tail boat tours to Phi-Phi Leh and Ko

Mai Phai (Bamboo Island), tour agencies can arrange sunset tours to Monkey Bay and the beach at Wang Long, both on Phi-Phi Leh, for 600B. Adventure Club (see p318) is a good choice.

Sleeping

Finding accommodation on this ever-popular island has never been easy and you can expect serious room shortages at peak holiday times. Masses of touts meet incoming boats and, while often annoying, can make your life easier.

Be sure you lock the door while you sleep and close all the windows when you go out. Break-ins can be a problem.

AO TON SAI & AO LO DALAM อ่าวต้นไทร/อ่าวโละดาลัม

During high season the pedestrian-only streets in this area get so packed it's like moving through crowds at a rock concert. Euphemistically, central Tonsai is called the 'Tourist Village'.

The beach at Ao Dalam is the island's prettiest – a screensaver-worthy crescent of white sand backed by stunning karst cliffs. But it's clogged with people and long tail boats, and locals complain the water is polluted from the beach bar clientele's cigarette butts and day-visitors' sunscreen, urine and boat fuel.

The Ao Ton Sai coastline is even busier with the main ferry pier and a concrete ocean-front promenade, but peace can be found at the far western end, which has been roped off for swimming.

TOP CHOICE Mama Beach Residence HOTEL $$
(Map p317; 08 8443 1363, 0 7560 1365; www.mama-beach.com; r 2500-3800B;) Popular with French travellers, this is an uncommonly chic block-style hotel right on the best part of Ao Ton Sai beach. Mod-con-equipped rooms have large white tiled floors, sea-view terraces with relaxing wood deck furniture, and bathrooms with stone sinks and showers bordered with loose seashells. Seaside yoga classes (75-minute class 400B) are offered several nights a week at 6pm.

PP Viewpoint Resort HOTEL $$
(Map p317; 0 7560 1200, 0 7561 8111; www.phiphiviewpoint.com; bungalows 1700-3500B;) At the far northeastern end of Ao Lo Dalam, wooden bungalows sit high on stilts and enjoy awesome views. It has a small swimming pool that practically drops into the ocean below and a glass-walled tower with 360-degree views where you can pamper yourself with a Thai massage. The Ao Dalam party can be heard up here, so bring earplugs.

Chunut House GUEST HOUSE $$
(Map p320; 0 7560 1227; www.phiphichunuthouse.com; bungalows 2500-3500B;) On a quiet path away from the bazaar of the Tourist Village, this place is refreshingly tranquil. Spacious wooden and bamboo bungalows are dripping with naturalistic mobiles, planters and crafty touches, and have clean tiled bathrooms. Its rates have dramatically increased recently, making it only OK value.

SLEEPING (OR TRYING TO) ON KO PHI-PHI

Noise pollution on Phi-Phi is bad and centred around central Ao Ton Sai and Ao Dalam – although you shouldn't expect an early night on Hat Hin Khom either. At the time of writing bars had a 2am curfew in Ao Dalam and 1.30am in Ton Sai – which are more or less observed – but that doesn't stop inebriated revellers from making plenty of other noises (door slamming seems to be a late-night island pastime).

The most peaceful accommodation can be found on:

» Phi-Phi's east coast

» the back road that connects the southeast end of Ao Ton Sai with Ao Lo Dalam

» the hill near the road up to the viewpoint

» the far western section of Ao Ton Sai

» Hat Yao.

Of course, the best option may be to simply grab a bucket and join the scrum.

Tonsai Village

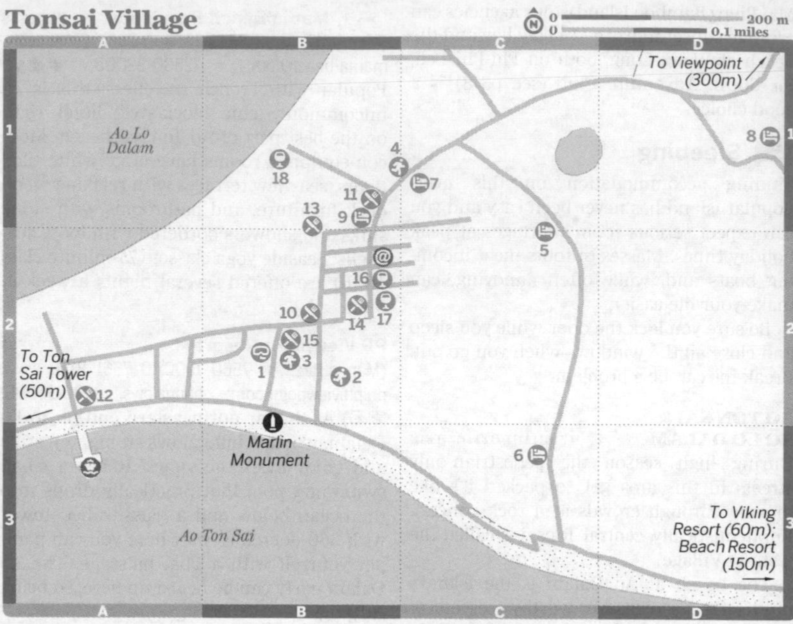

Tonsai Village

Activities, Courses & Tours

1 Adventure Club B2
2 Cat's Climbing Shop B2
Kayak Rental Stall .... (see 18)
3 Pum Restaurant & Cooking School B2
4 Spider Monkey B1

Sleeping

5 Chunut House C2
6 Oasis Guesthouse C3
7 Rock Backpackers C1
8 Uphill Cottage D1
9 White B1

Eating

10 Cosmic B2
11 Garlic Restaurant B1
12 Le Grand Bleu A2
13 Local Food Market B1
14 Papaya Restaurant B2
15 Unni's B2

Drinking

16 Breakers B2
17 Reggae Bar B2
18 Slinky Bar B1

White GUEST HOUSE $$
(Map p320; ☎0 7560 1300; www.whitephiphi.com; r 1500-1800B; ❄@📶) Geared towards the 'flashpacker' crowd, the White has two comfy and surprisingly quiet locations in Tonsai Village – the better being the White 2, which has a few rooftop suites with patios. Squeaky clean rooms, decked out with TVs and safes, are very white (of course), with hip touches like tiny black-and-white-tiled hot-water bathrooms.

Uphill Cottage GUEST HOUSE $
(Map p317; ☎0 7560 1124, 08 6553 2316; www.phiphiuphillcottage.com; r 700-1500B; ❄📶) Rooms are basic, but they're big and clean, and you can only faintly hear the noise from the tourist-centre party. Aptly named, this place is (surprise!) perched on a hill near the viewpoint path. Rooms have terraces with views over town and a hint of the sea.

Oasis Guesthouse GUEST HOUSE $
(Map p320; ☎0 7560 1207; r 900B; ❄) It's worth the walk up the side road east of the village

centre to find this cute guest house with wooden shutters surrounded by trees. The innkeeper can be surly, but freshly painted rooms have sparkling bathrooms. He won't take reservations. It's first come, first serve donly.

Rock Backpackers HOSTEL $
(Map p320; ☎08 1607 3897; dm 300B, r 400-600B) A proper hostel on the village hill, with clean dorms lined with bunk beds, tiny private rooms, an inviting restaurant-bar and a rugged, graffiti-scrawled exterior.

HAT HIN KHOM หาดหินคม

This area actually has a few small white-sand beaches in rocky coves, some of which are relatively quiet. It's about a 15-minute jungle walk from both Hat Yao and the Ao Ton Sai bustle, which unfortunately means you will hear whatever the DJs are spinning.

TOP CHOICE **Viking Natures Resort** HOTEL $$
(Map p317; ☎08 3649 9492; www.vikingnaturesresort.com; bungalows 1000-6500B; 📶) OK, it's funky (in all senses of the word) and not the place to stay if you're afraid of jungle insects and critters, but the wood, thatch and bamboo bungalows here are dreamily creative and stylish with lots of driftwood, shell mobiles and hammock-decked lounging spaces with outrageous views of Ko Phi-Phi Leh. All bungalows have mosquito nets and balconies, but the cheaper rooms don't have their own bathrooms. We say splurge for one of several wooden lodge rooms. They open onto inviting verandahs, are well lit with groovy lanterns and have huge bathrooms and high ceilings.

HAT YAO หาดยาว

You can either walk here in about 30 minutes from Tonsai via Hat Hin Khom or take a long-tail (100B to 150B) from Tonsai pier. This long stretch of pure-white beach is perfect for swimming and well worth the walk but don't expect to have it to yourself – it's popular with families and sporty types playing volleyball. A trail leads from here over to beautiful and secluded Ao Lo Mu Di.

Phi-Phi Hill Resort GUEST HOUSE $$
(Map p317; ☎0 7561 8203; www.phiphihill.com; bungalows 700-2000B; ❄@) High up in a very quiet plantation of banana, mango and plumeria, this simple resort spans the southern bluff of Ko Phi-Phi Don, so you can watch the sun rise on one side and set on the other. The best deals are the big, clean wooden fan-cooled cold-water bungalows on the sunset side. Every option has a life-altering view and there's a good restaurant perched on a breezy cliff. It closes from May to October.

Beach Resort HOTEL $$$
(Map p317; ☎0 7561 8268; phiphithebeach.com; bungalows 3450-5350B; ❄🏊) An expanding class act with a tiny pool and chic bar, this place swarms with package tourists looking for (and finding) comfort. The Thai-style teak bungalows are spacious and elegant, and built in an orderly fashion on a manicured jungle hillside with stunning views of Ko Phi-Phi Leh. It's by far the most attractive and stylish place on this beach.

The Paradise HOTEL $$
(Map p317; ☎08 1788 7868, 08 9077 7939; zer_zaa@hotmail.com, osopang@hotmail.com; bungalows from 1500B; ❄📶) This is the cutest place on Hat Yao and has comfy blue concrete bungalows in a flower-filled garden. It's not as big, flashy or expensive as the competition but the beach is the same and the rooms are a clean and air-conditioned standard.

HAT RANTEE & AO TOH KO หาดรันตี

Still fairly low-key, this series of small, remote eastern bays is home to a few modest family-run bungalows (some starting at 600B). The pretty beaches here are grey-gold and have rocky outcroppings and excellent snorkelling. You can either get here by long-tail from Ao Ton Sai pier (300B – although most resorts provide free pick up if you reserve and the return trip is 150B) or by making the strenuous 45-minute hike over the viewpoint.

TOP CHOICE **Toh Ko Beach Resort** GUEST HOUSE $$
(Map p317; ☎08 1537 0528; www.tohkobeachresort.com; bungalows 1000-2800B; @📶) All alone on white, mellow Ao Toh Ko, there's a summer-camp camaraderie here with several long-term guests and plenty of new ones who wish they were long term. Simple, wooden or bamboo fan-cooled bungalows are perched on a hill (think: hammock and sea view) and have stone baths and mosquito nets. There are also family rooms and a big, friendly restaurant right on the beach, where you'll find kayaks and snorkel gear for rent.

Rantee Hut GUEST HOUSE $
(Map p317; ☎08 9741 4846; bungalows 700-1000B) It's a little confusing where this place begins and ends, as its basic wood, cement or

bamboo huts perched on a hill are identical to those of the places (all named Rantee this or that) on either side. Rantee Hut stands out for its groovy seaview restaurant strewn with lounging cushions and seeping mellow reggae tunes. Snorkelling trips to Bamboo Island cost 600B.

HAT PHAK NAM อ่าวผักหนาม

This gorgeous white-sand beach is nestled on the same bay as a small fishing hamlet. To get here, you can either charter a long-tail from Ao Ton Sai for around 500B (150B by shared taxi boat upon your return), or make the very sweaty one-hour hike over the viewpoint.

TOP CHOICE Relax Beach Resort HOTEL $$

(Map p317; ☎08 1083 0194, 08 9475 6536; www.phiphirelaxresort.com; bungalows 1400-4400B; ❄@☒) There are 47 unpretentious but pretty Thai-style bungalows with wood floors, two-tiered terraces with lounging cushions and mosaic baths in the newest nests. All are rimmed by lush jungle – the resort has a good restaurant and breezy bar, and it's worked by incredibly charming staff who greet and treat you like family. It's one of the best choices on the island, so reserve ahead. You can walk to Hat Rantee at low tide.

AO LO BAKAO อ่าวโละบาเกา

This fine stretch of palm-backed sand ringed by dramatic hills is one of Phi-Phi's most lovely, with offshore views over aqua bliss to Bamboo and Mosquito Islands. Think of it as a cheaper version of Bora Bora. Phi-Phi Island Village arranges transfers for guests, but on your own a charter from Ao Ton Sai will cost 800B.

Phi-Phi Island Village HOTEL $$$

(Map p317; ☎0 7636 3700; www.ppisland.com; bungalows 7200-21,500B; ❄☞☒) This place really is a village unto itself: its whopping 100 bungalows take up much of the beachfront with palms swaying between them. Facilities vary from the family friendly and casual to romantic dining experiences and pampering spa treatments. It offers dozens of activities and excursions. The infinity pool blends seamlessly into the ocean, and fresh flowers are artfully arranged throughout the resort. Good living with a whiff of old-school luxury if you have the means.

HAT LAEM THONG หาดแหลมทอง

The beach here is long, white and sandy with a small, rubbish-strewn *chow lair* (sea gypsy) settlement of corrugated metal shacks at the north end. Despite the upmarket offerings, the beach is really busy and all the hotels are packed together. There are a few local-style seafood restaurants within the bustle that are worth a try. A long-tail charter from Ao Ton Sai costs 800B. Operators can also arrange transfers.

Zeavola HOTEL $$$

(Map p317; ☎0 7562 7000; www.zeavola.com; bungalows 9900-26,900B; ❄@☞☒) Hibiscus-lined pathways lead to shady teak bungalows with sleek, distinctly Asian indoor-outdoor floorplans. Each comes with glass walls on three sides (with remote-controlled bamboo shutters for privacy), beautiful 1940s fixtures and antique furniture, a patio and impeccable service. Some villas come with a private pool and there's a fabulous couples-oriented spa.

Holiday Inn Phi-Phi Island HOTEL $$$

(☎0 7562 7300; www.phiphi.holidayinn.com; bungalows 8297-10,400B; ❄☞☒) This is your standard Thailand-issue Holiday Inn – which means it's comfortable, white-concrete-with-dark-trim chic and filled with active types milling around the pool. You'll find tennis courts, beckoning hammocks, a spa and a dive centre. The restaurant has a gorgeous alfresco deck with sea views.

Eating

Most of the resorts, hotels and bungalows around the island have their own restaurants. Ao Ton Sai is home to some reasonably priced restaurants but don't expect haute cuisine.

Local Food Market THAI $

(Map p320; ⏲breakfast, lunch & dinner) The cheapest and most authentic eats are at the market. A handful of local stalls huddle on the narrowest sliver of the isthmus and serve up scrumptious *pàt tai,* fried rice, *som tam* and smoked cat fish. Walls are scrawled with the blessings of a thousand travellers.

Unni's WESTERN $$

(Map p320; mains around 120B; ⏲breakfast, lunch & dinner) Come here for lunch to dine on homemade bagels topped with everything from smoked salmon to meatballs. There are also massive salads, Mexican food, tapas, cocktails and more. It's a chic cafe lounge-style place with cooling overhead fans and jazzy mood music.

Garlic Restaurant THAI $
(Map p320; ☎08 3502 1426; dishes 45-95B; ⏰breakfast, lunch & dinner) A bright shack-like place that's always packed with happy travellers chowing terrific, not-too-spicy Thai food. It has all the usuals and an ice raft of fresh catch at supper.

Le Grand Bleu FUSION $$$
(Map p320; ☎08 1979 9739; mains 195-695B; ⏰lunch & dinner) Thai–Euro fusion set in a charming wooden house just off the main pier. It serves French and Aussie wines, and you can get your duck wok-fried with basil or oven-roasted and caramelised with mango. It closes between 2pm and 6.30pm.

Papaya Restaurant THAI $
(Map p320; ☎08 7280 1719; dishes 80-300B) Cheap, tasty and spicy. Here's some real-deal Thai food served in heaping portions. It has your basil and chilli, all the curries and *dôm yam,* too.

Cosmic WESTERN, THAI $$
(Map p320; pizzas from 160B; ⏰breakfast, lunch & dinner) This longstanding favourite still cranks out some of Phi-Phi's best pizzas as well as Western and Thai fare.

Drinking

A rowdy nightlife saturates Phi-Phi. Buckets of cheap whiskey and Red Bull, and sticky-sweet cocktails make this the domain for spring break wannabes and really bad hangovers. This is also the only place in Thailand where you're beckoned into bars by scantily clad *fa·ràng* (Western) girls, who are workin' it for free booze – yup, Phi-Phi is that kind of place. The truth is that if you're nesting within earshot of the wilds, you may as well enjoy the chaos.

TOP CHOICE **Sunflower Bar** BAR $
(Map p317; Ao Lo Dalam) Poetically ramshackle, this driftwood gem is still the chillest bar in Phi-Phi. Destroyed in the 2004 tsunami, the owner rebuilt it with reclaimed wood. The long-tail booths are named for the four loved ones he lost in the flood.

Reggae Bar BAR $$
(Map p320; Tourist Village) You haven't experienced Phi-Phi's nightlife until you've watched tourists (men and women) beat the crap out of each other in this rowdy bar's Thai boxing ring. Both contestants get a free bucket to ease the pain.

Slinky Bar CLUB $$
(Map p320; Ao Lo Dalam) This was the beach dancefloor of the moment when we visited. Expect the standard fire show, buckets of souped-up candy juice and throngs of Thais, local expats and tourists mingling, flirting and flailing to throbbing bass on the sand.

Breakers BAR $$
(Map p320; Tourist Village; burgers 200-240B; ⏰11am-2am; 📶) A sportsbar as good for TV football as it is for people-watching and great food. The burgers and steaks are awesome, and the starter plate sampler with a bit of everything from yummy buffalo wings to potato skins can feed a handful of pint swillers.

Information

ATMs and internet shops (per minute 2B) are spread thickly throughout the Tourist Village but aren't available on the more remote eastern beaches. Wi-fi is available at **D's Bookshop** (⏰7am-10pm) in the heart of the Tourist Village. It also sells new and used fiction, and pours a decent espresso (50B).

Getting There & Away

Ko Phi-Phi can be reached from Krabi, Phuket, Ao Nang, Railay and Ko Lanta Most boats moor at Ao Ton Sai, though a few from Phuket use the isolated northern pier at Laem Thong. The Phuket and Krabi boats operate year-round, while the Ko Lanta and Ao Nang boats only run in the October-to-April high season.

KO PHI-PHI Boats depart from Krabi for Ko Phi-Phi (300B, 1½ hours) at 9am and 3.30pm, and from Ao Nang (350B, 1½ hours) there's one boat per day at 3.30pm.

PHUKET From Phuket, boats leave at 9am, 2.30pm and 3pm and return from Ko Phi-Phi at 9am, 1.30pm and 3pm (400B, 1¾ to two hours).

KO LANTA To Ko Lanta, boats leave Phi-Phi at 11.30am and 2pm and return from Ko Lanta at 8am and 1pm (300B, 1½ hours).

RAILAY For Railay (350B, 1¼ hours) take the Ao Nang–bound ferry.

Getting Around

There are no roads on Phi-Phi Don, so transport on the island is mostly by foot, although long-tails can be chartered at Ao Ton Sai for short hops around Ko Phi-Phi Don and Ko Phi-Phi Leh.

Long-tails leave from the Ao Ton Sai pier to Hat Yao (100B to 150B), Laem Thong (800B), Hat Rantee (500B) and Viking Cave (500B). Chartering speedboats for six hours costs around 6500B, while chartering a long-tail boat costs 1200B for three hours or 2500B for the whole day.

Ko Phi-Phi Leh เกาะพีพีเล

Rugged Phi-Phi Leh is the smaller of the two islands and is protected on all sides by soaring cliffs. Coral reefs crawling with marine life lie beneath the crystal-clear waters and are hugely popular with day-tripping snorkellers. Two gorgeous lagoons await in the island's interior – **Pilah** on the eastern coast and **Ao Maya** on the western coast. In 1999 Ao Maya was controversially used as the setting for the filming of *The Beach,* based on the popular novel by Alex Garland. Visitor numbers soared in its wake.

At the northeastern tip of the island, **Viking Cave** (Tham Phaya Naak) is a big collection point for swifts' nests. Nimble collectors scamper up bamboo scaffolding to gather the nests. Before ascending, they pray and make offerings of tobacco, incense and liquor to the cavern spirits. This cave gets its misleading moniker from 400-year-old graffiti left by Chinese fishermen.

There are no places to stay on Phi-Phi Leh and most people come here on one of the ludicrously popular day trips out of Phi-Phi Don. Tours last about half a day and include snorkelling stops at various points around the island, with detours to Viking Cave and Ao Maya. Long-tail trips cost 800B; by motorboat you'll pay around 2400B. Expect to pay a 400B national park day-use fee upon landing.

It is possible to camp on Phi-Phi Leh through **Maya Bay Camping** (☎08 6944 1623; www.mayabaycamping.com; per person 2100B). It offers action-packed overnight trips that include kayaking, snorkelling, lunch, dinner, and sleeping bags under the stars.

Ko Lanta เกาะลันตา

POP 20,000

Long and thin, and covered in bleached-blonde tresses, Ko Lanta is Krabi's sexy beach babe. The largest of the 50-plus islands in the local archipelago, this relaxing paradise effortlessly caters to all budget types with its west-coast parade of peach sand – each beach better than the next. The northern beaches are busy but fun, and things get more and more mellow the further south you go.

Ko Lanta is relatively flat compared to the karst formations of its neighbours, so the island can be easily explored by motorbike. A quick drive around reveals a colourful crucible of cultures – fried-chicken stalls sit below slender minarets, creaking *chow lair* villages dangle off the island's side, and small Thai wát hide within green-brown tangles of curling mangroves.

Ko Lanta is technically called Ko Lanta Yai, the largest of 52 islands in an archipelago protected by the Mu Ko Lanta Marine National Park. Almost all boats pull into Ban Sala Dan, a dusty two-street town at the northern tip of the island.

Sights

Ban Ko Lanta TOWN

Halfway down the eastern coast, Ban Ko Lanta (Lanta Old Town) was the original port and commercial centre for the island, and provided a safe harbour for Arabic and Chinese trading vessels sailing between Phuket, Penang and Singapore. Some of the gracious and well-kept wooden stilt houses and shopfronts here are over 100 years old. Pier restaurants offer a fresh catch and have views over the sea. There's a small afternoon market on Sundays, and if you're looking for sturdy, attractive handmade leather goods, stop by **Lanta Leather** (☎08 5046 6410; ⏲8am-8pm); for quality hammocks don't miss **Hammock House** (☎0 4847 2012; www.jumbohammock.com; ⏲10am-5pm), where you can also pick up its fabulous *Lanta Biker's Map* full of off-the-beaten-path recommendations.

Chao Leh Museum MUSEUM

(พิพิธภัณฑ์ชาวเกาะลันตา; Ban Sanghka-U) If you crave information on culture, stop by this museum, where you'll find a complex of traditionally lashed bamboo homes, engaging oil canvases and exhibits detailing their myths, music and ceremonies. To find it, look for the houseboat jutting from the hillside across the road from the sea.

Mu Ko Lanta Marine National Park NATIONAL PARK

(อุทยานแห่งชาติเกาะลันตา; adult/child 400/200B) Established in 1990, this marine national park protects 15 islands in the Ko Lanta group, including the southern tip of Ko Lanta Yai. The park is increasingly threatened by the runaway development on the western coast of Ko Lanta Yai. The other islands in the group have fared slightly better – **Ko Rok Nai** is still very beautiful, with a crescent-shaped bay backed by cliffs, fine coral reefs and a sparkling white-sand beach. Camping is permitted on Ko Rok Nok and nearby **Ko Haa**, with permission from the national park headquarters. On the eastern side of Ko Lanta Yai, **Ko Talabeng** has some dramatic limestone caves that you can visit on sea-kayaking tours. The national-park fee applies if you visit any of these islands.

The **national park headquarters** is at Laem Tanod, on the southern tip of Ko Lanta Yai, reached by a steep and corrugated 7km dirt track from Hat Nui. There are some basic hiking trails and a **scenic lighthouse**, and you can hire long-tails here for island tours during the low season.

Tham Khao Maikaeo CAVE

(ถ้ำเขาไม้แก้ว) Monsoon rains – pounding away at limestone cracks and crevices for millions of years – have created this complex of forest caverns and tunnels. There are chambers as large as cathedrals, thick with stalactites and stalagmites, and tiny passages that you have to squeeze through on hands and knees. There's even a subterranean pool you can take a chilly swim in. Sensible shoes are essential, and total coverage in mud is almost guaranteed.

Tham Khao Maikaeo is reached via a guided trek through the jungle. A local family runs treks to the caves (with torches) for around 200B. The best way to get here is by rented motorcycle; alternatively most resorts can arrange transport.

Close by, but reached by a separate track from the dirt road leading to the marine national park headquarters, **Tham Seua** (Tiger Cave) also has interesting tunnels to explore; elephant treks run up here from Hat Nui.

Activities

Vacationers on Ko Lanta will be delighted to find that some of Thailand's top spots are within arm's reach. The best diving can be found at the undersea pinnacles called **Hin Muang** and **Hin Daeng**, about 45 minutes away. These world-class dive sites have lone coral outcrops in the middle of the sea, and act as important feeding stations for large pelagic fish such as sharks, tuna and occasionally whale sharks and manta rays. Hin Daeng is commonly considered to be Thailand's second-best dive site after Richelieu Rock (p278), near the Burmese border. The sites around **Ko Haa** have consistently good visibility, with depths of 18m to 34m, plenty of marine life and a cave known as 'the Cathedral'. Lanta dive outfitters also run trips up to the King Cruiser Wreck, Anemone Reef and Ko Phi-Phi.

Trips out to Hin Daeng and Hin Muang cost around 5000B to 6000B, while trips to Ko Haa tend to be around 3500B to 4500B. PADI Open Water courses will set you back around 14,000B to 17,000B.

Numerous tour agencies along the strip can organise snorkelling trips out to Ko Rok Nok, Ko Phi-Phi and other nearby islands.

Scubafish DIVING

(☎0 7566 5095; www.scuba-fish.com) One of the best dive operations on the island, located at Baan Laanta Resort (p329) on Ao Kantiang; there's also a small second office at the Narima resort (p329). Unlike some of the large and impersonal operators based in

LOCAL KNOWLEDGE

JUNIE KOVACS

Junie Kovacs is the founder of Lanta Animal Welfare, which rescues animals, organises sterilisation and vaccination campaigns, and offers local sensibility and education.

WHY ARE THERE SO MANY STRAYS?

Many guest houses get puppies or kittens for the tourist season because the guests like them. Once the season is over they'll abandon the animals on backroads.

HOW TO HELP

Volunteers are needed in the short or long term to walk dogs, help with fundraising campaigns, helping out volunteer vets, catching strays and so on. If you fall in love with an animal, we can help with the paperwork to bring it home with you! Soi Dog (see p245) on Phuket is another great place where you can help.

Ko Lanta

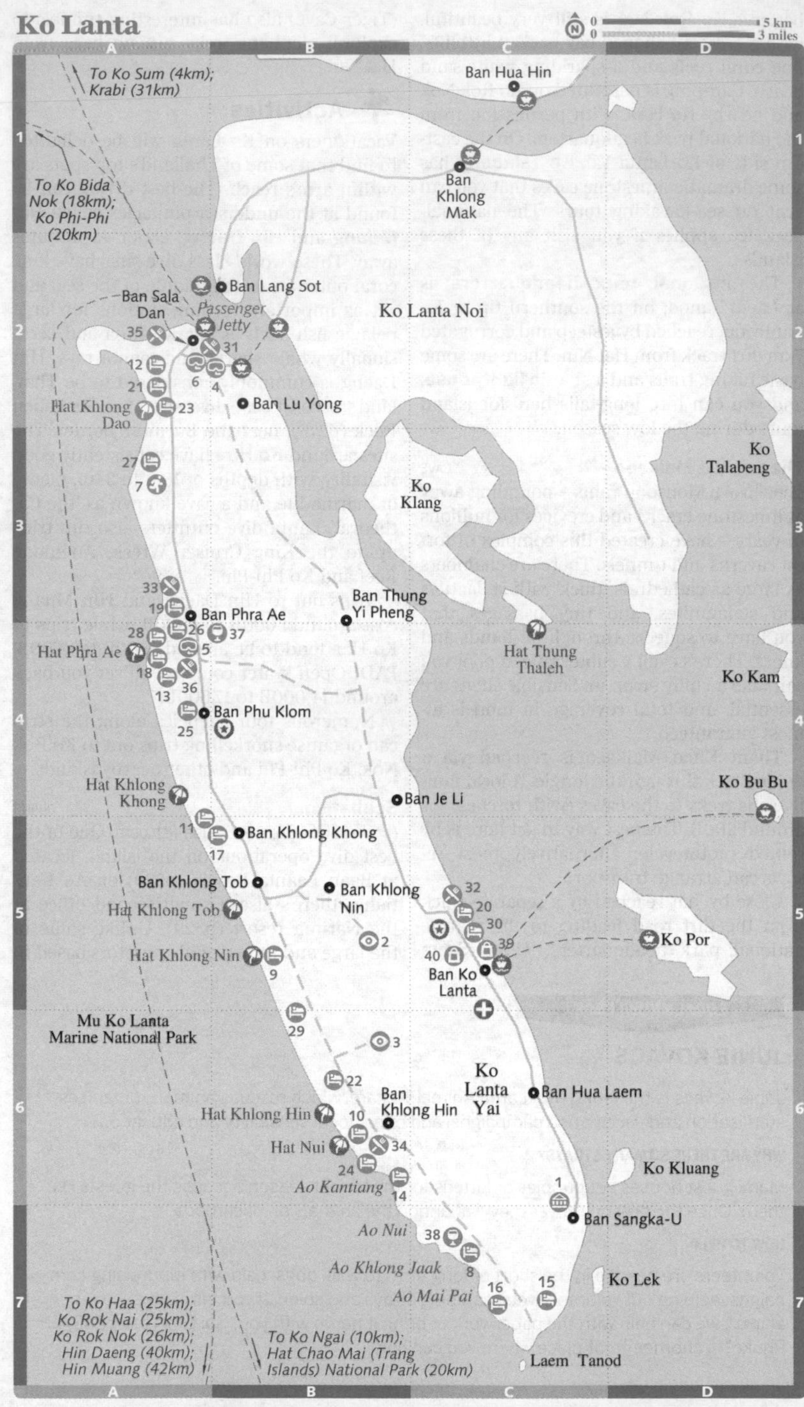
To Ko Sum (4km); Krabi (31km)
To Ko Bida Nok (18km); Ko Phi-Phi (20km)
Ban Hua Hin
Ban Khlong Mak
Ban Lang Sot
Ban Sala Dan
Passenger Jetty
Ko Lanta Noi
Ban Lu Yong
Hat Khlong Dao
Ko Talabeng
Ko Klang
Ban Thung Yi Pheng
Ban Phra Ae
Hat Phra Ae
Hat Thung Thaleh
Ko Kam
Ban Phu Klom
Hat Khlong Khong
Ko Bu Bu
Ban Je Li
Ban Khlong Khong
Ban Khlong Tob
Ban Khlong Nin
Hat Khlong Tob
Hat Khlong Nin
Ko Por
Ban Ko Lanta
Mu Ko Lanta Marine National Park
Ko Lanta Yai
Ban Hua Laem
Ban Khlong Hin
Hat Khlong Hin
Hat Nui
Ao Kantiang
Ko Kluang
Ban Sangka-U
Ao Nui
Ao Khlong Jaak
Ko Lek
Ao Mai Pai
To Ko Haa (25km); Ko Rok Nai (25km); Ko Rok Nok (26km); Hin Daeng (40km); Hin Muang (42km)
To Ko Ngai (10km); Hat Chao Mai (Trang Islands) National Park (20km)
Laem Tanod
5 km
3 miles

Ko Lanta

Sights

1 Chao Leh Museum C6
Liquid Lense .... (see 10)
2 Tham Khao Mai Kaeo B5
3 Tham Seua B6

Activities, Courses & Tours

4 Blue Planet Divers B2
5 Dive & Relax A4
6 Lanta Diver A2
Scubafish .... (see 10)
Scubafish .... (see 22)
7 Time for Lime A3

Sleeping

8 Andalanta Resort C7
9 Andalay Resort B5
10 Baan Laanta Resort & Spa B6
11 Bee Bee Bungalows A5
12 Costa Lanta A2
13 Hutyee Boat A4
14 Kantiang Bay View Resort B6
15 La Laanta C7
16 Lanta Darawadee B5
17 Lanta Marina A4
18 Layana Resort A3
19 Mango House C5
20 Maya Beach Resort A2
21 Mu Ko Lanta Marine National Park Headquarters C7
22 Narima B6
23 Ocean View Resort A2
24 Phra Nang Lanta B6
25 Relax Bay A4
26 Sanctuary A4
27 Slow Down Villas A3
28 Somewhere Else A4
29 Sri Lanta B6
30 Sriraya C5

Eating

31 Bai Fern B2
32 Beautiful Restaurant C5
33 Country Lao A3
34 Drunken Sailors B6
35 Lanta Seafood A2
36 Red Snapper A4

Drinking

Moonwalk .... (see 26)
37 Opium B4
38 Same Same But Different C7

Shopping

39 Hammock House C5
40 Lanta Leather C5

Ban Sala Dan, Scubafish runs personal and personable programs tailored to your needs, including the Liquid Lense underwater photography program. The three-day dive packages (9975B) are quite popular.

Other reliable dive companies include the following:

Blue Planet Divers DIVING
(☎0 7566 2724; www.blueplanetdivers.net; Ban Sala Dan) The only school that specialises in free-diving instruction.

Lanta Diver DIVING
(☎0 7568 4208; www.lantadiver.com; Ban Sala Dan)

Dive & Relax DIVING
(☎08 4842 2191; www.diveandrelax.com; Hat Phra Ae)

Courses

Time for Lime COOKING
(☎0 7568 4590; www.timeforlime.net) On Hat Khlong Dao, this place has a huge, hip and professional moulded-concrete kitchen with plenty of room to run amok. It offers excellent cooking courses with a slightly more exciting selection of dishes than most cookery schools in Thailand; five-hour courses cost 1800B with substantial discounts if you take more than one class. Profits from the school finance Lanta Animal Welfare (see p325).

Sleeping

Ko Lanta is home to many long stretches of good-looking beach packed with accommodation. Some resorts close for the May-to-October low season; others drop their rates by 50% or even more. Resorts usually have their own restaurants and tour-booking facilities, which can arrange island snorkelling, massages, tours and motorcycle rental.

HAT KHLONG DAO หาดคลองดาว

This is an outstanding 2km stretch of white sand with no rocks, which makes it perfect for swimming. Unfortunately garbage does accumulate when the tides shift. Locals say it comes from Phi-Phi. And they say it disdainfully.

TOP CHOICE **Costa Lanta** HOTEL $$$
(☎0 7566 8168; www.costalanta.com; r from 6200B; ❄@📶🏊) Incredibly Zen stand-alone abodes nestled in a garden shaded by coconut palms and laced with tidal canals at the north end of Hat Khlong Dao. Everything from the floors to the walls to the washbasins are polished concrete, and the barn doors of each cabana open on two sides to maximise air flow. The restaurant is stunning, as is the black spill-over pool on the edge of the sand. Discounts are available if booked through its website. Low-season rates are a steal.

Slow Down Villas VILLA RENTAL $$
(☎08 4999 6780; www.slowdownlanta.se, in Swedish; villas per week 25,000B; ❄@📶🏊👪) These nine mod, two- and three-bedroom wood-and-shingle villas are all about clean lines, open spaces, comfy beach living and family-style holidays. The website is only in Swedish but everyone's welcome. The villas are privately owned by expats but can be rented by the week and month.

Maya Beach Resort HOTEL $$$
(☎0 7568 4267; mayalanta.com; r 4300B; ❄@📶🏊) Ignore that Best Western affiliation if you can, because this place has attractive, large, Ikea-chic rooms on two floors. There are louvred railings on the terrace, Buddhist shrines on the sand and a pool that blends with the nearby sea.

Ocean View Resort HOTEL $$
(☎0 7568 4089; www.oceanviewlanta.com; bungalows 1300-2900B; ❄@🏊) Large, remotely stylish, tiled bungalows with queen-sized beds, cable TV, hammocks on the porch and a seaside pool. The fabulous Mrs Oh is here to help.

HAT PHRA AE หาดพระแอ

A large travellers' village has grown up along the extensive, sandy Hat Phra Ae (also called 'Long Beach'), with *fa·ràng*-oriented restaurants, beach bars, internet cafes and tour offices.

Relax Bay HOTEL $$
(☎0 7568 4194; www.relaxbay.com; bungalows 1200-2500B; ❄🏊) This gorgeous French-run place is spread out over a tree-covered headland by a small beach. Its wooden bungalows sit on stilts with large decks overlooking the bay and stunning sunsets. For a more unique experience sleep in a seaview luxury tent perched over the rocks on a wooden platform. And there's an incredibly stylish, open-air bar and restaurant.

Sanctuary GUEST HOUSE $
(☎08 1891 3055; sanctuary_93@yahoo.com; bungalows 600-1200B) The original Phra Ae resort is still a delightful place to stay. There are artistically designed wood-and-thatch bungalows with lots of grass and a hippyish atmosphere that's low-key and friendly. The restaurant offers Indian and vegetarian eats and the Thai usuals. It also holds yoga classes.

Hutyee Boat GUEST HOUSE $
(☎08 3633 9723; bungalows 350-400B) A hidden hippy paradise of big, solid bungalows with tiled bathrooms and minifridges in a forest of palms and bamboo. It's just back from the beach behind Nautilus. The robed and skull-capped owner is the happiest sultan on earth.

Layana Resort HOTEL $$$
(☎0 7560 7100; www.layanaresort.com; bungalows 11,900-17,700B; ❄) Yes, it's crowded with package tourists but the location between two un-built-up, natural parts of Long Beach and the fabulous palm-lined pool make them lucky to be here. Comfy and big hardwood rooms with soothing neutral decor make it that much nicer. Rack rates are steep but internet deals can make it a bargain.

Somewhere Else GUEST HOUSE $
(☎08 1536 0858; bungalows 400-1000B; 📶) Big octagonal bamboo huts grace a shady lawn right on a very social and lounge-worthy stretch of beach. Bathrooms are big and clean, as is the beachfront restaurant that serves Indian, Thai and European food. It's not private but is a lot of fun.

Lanta Marina GUEST HOUSE $
(☎0 7568 4168; www.lantamarina.com; bungalows 500-800B; ⏲Nov-Apr; 📶) For something really cool, try these giant bungalows, which almost look like towering hay bales with wide porches. It has a tribal feel and is on a nice quiet part of the beach.

HAT KHLONG KHONG หาดคลองโขง

This is thatched-roof, Rasta-bar bliss with plenty of beach volleyball games, moon parties and the occasional well-advertised mushroom shake. Still, it's all pretty low-key and all ages are present. The beach goes on forever in either direction.

TOP CHOICE **Bee Bee Bungalows** GUEST HOUSE $
(☎08 1537 9932; www.beebeebungalows; bungalows 400-800B; ❄@🏊) One of the best budget

spots on the island, Bee Bee's super-friendly staff care for a dozen creative bamboo cabins – every one is unique and a few are up on stilts in the trees. The on-site restaurant has a library of tattered paperbacks to keep you busy while you wait for your delicious Thai staples.

Lanta Darawadee HOTEL **$$**
(☎0 7566 7094; www.lantadarawadee.com; bungalows 1000-1600B; ❄📶🏊) If you dig the Hat Khlong Khong scene but can't live without air-con, here's a great-value option right on the beach. It's bland but the new, clean rooms have good beds, terraces, minifridges and TVs. Water is solar heated and rates include breakfast.

HAT KHLONG NIN หาดคลองนิน

After Hat Khlong Tob, the main road heading south forks: go left for the inland road, which runs to the east coast, go right for the country road hugs, which hugs the coastline for 14km to the tip of Ko Lanta. On the right fork the first beach is lovely, white Hat Khlong Nin. There are lots of small, inexpensive guest houses at the north end of the beach that are usually attached to restaurants – it's easy to get dropped off here, then shop around for a budget place to stay.

Sri Lanta HOTEL **$$**
(☎0 7566 2688; www.srilanta.com; cottages from 3000B; ❄@🏊) At the southern end of the beach, this decadent resort consists of minimalist, naturalistic wooden villas in wild gardens stretching from the beach to a landscaped jungle hillside. There's a very stylish beachside area with a restaurant, infinity pool and private drapery-swathed massage pavilions. The resort strives for low environmental impact by using biodegradable products and minimising energy use and waste.

Andalay Resort HOTEL **$$$**
(☎0 7566 2699; www.andalaylanta.com; bungalows 5400B; ❄📶🏊) Rooms here open onto porches perched above a lotus pond, which blends into the pool and sea. Inside find rose-coloured concrete floors, ceiling fan and air-con, built-in wood furnishings, satellite TV and wi-fi.

HAT NUI หาดนุ้ย

There are several small, rocky beaches around here with upmarket places to stay.

Narima HOTEL **$$**
(☎0 7566 2668; www.narima-lanta.com; bungalows 2300-3700B; ❄@🏊) A castaway-feeling place with ever-so-slightly upscale bamboo bungalows featuring wood floors, simple tiled baths and wide verandahs. The resort overlooks its own sheltered nugget of white sand but the bungalows lack the quality you'd expect from the price tag.

AO KANTIANG อ่าวกันเตียง

A superb sweep of sand backed by mountains is also its own self-contained village complete with mini-marts, internet cafes, motorbike rental and restaurants. Much of the beach here is undeveloped, although there are lots of sailboats and motorboats anchored in the bay. It's far from everything. If you land here, don't expect to move much.

TOP CHOICE **Phra Nang Lanta** HOTEL **$$$**
(☎0 7566 5025; lanta@vacation village.co.th; studios 6000B; ❄@📶🏊) Gorgeous Mexican-style adobe-looking concrete studios are huge and straight off the pages of an architectural mag. Interiors are decorated with clean lines, hardwoods and whites accented with bright colours. Outside, flowers and foliage climb over bamboo lattice sunshades, and the pool and lush restaurant-bar look over the beautiful beach.

Baan Laanta Resort & Spa HOTEL **$$$**
(☎0 7566 5091; www.baanlaanta.com; bungalows from 3500B; ❄@🏊) Landscaped grounds wind around stylish wooden bungalows and a pool that drops off to a stretch of white sandy beach. The bungalows' centrepiece is a futon-style bed on a raised wooden platform under a gauzy veil of mosquito netting.

Kantiang Bay View Resort HOTEL **$$**
(☎0 7566 5049; http://kantiangbay.net; bungalows 500-2000B; ❄@) Choose between the cheap, rickety, not-exactly-spotless wooden-and-bamboo bungalows or the more expensive, candy-coloured tiled rooms with minifridge. The bamboo-clad restaurant serves decent, *fa·ràng*-friendly Thai dishes.

AO KHLONG JAAK อ่าวคลองจาก

There's a splendid beach here. The namesake waterfall is further inland.

Andalanta Resort HOTEL **$$$**
(☎0 7566 5018; www.andalanta.com; bungalows 2600-6900B; ❄@📶) You'll find beach-style, modern air-con bungalows (some with loft) and simple fan-cooled ones, and they all face

the sea. The garden is a delight, there's an ambient restaurant and the waterfall is just a 30- to 40-minute walk away.

AO MAI PAI อ่าวไม้ไผ่

TOP CHOICE La Laanta HOTEL $$$
(0 7566 5066; www.lalaanta.com; bungalows 2800-6200B;) Barefoot elegance at its finest. Owned and operated by a young, hip, English-speaking Thai–Vietnamese couple, this is the grooviest spot on the entire island. Thatched bungalows have polished-concrete floors, platform beds, floral-design motifs and decks overlooking a pitch of sand, which blends into a rocky fishing beach. Set down a rutted dirt road, it's also the closest resort to the marine national park.

LAEM TANOD แหลมโตนด

The road to the marine national park headquarters fords the *klong* (canal), which can get quite deep in the wet season.

Mu Ko Lanta Marine National Park Headquarters (in Bangkok 0 2561 4292; camping with own tent per person 30B, with tent hire 300-400B) The secluded grounds of the national park headquarters are a wonderfully serene place to camp. The flat camping areas are covered in shade and sit in the wilds of the tropical jungle. Out the front lie craggy outcroppings and the sounds of the ocean lapping up the rocks. There are toilets and running water, but you should bring your own food. You can also get permission for camping on Ko Rok or Ko Ha here. National park entry fees apply (see p324).

BAN KO LANTA บ้านเกาะลันตา

There are a handful of inns open for business on Lanta's oft-ignored, wonderfully dated and incredibly rich Old Town.

Mango House GUEST HOUSE $$
(0 7569 7181; www.mangohouses.com; suites 2000B-2500B; Oct-Apr) These 100-year-old Chinese teak pole houses and former opium dens are stilted over the harbour. The original time-worn wood floors are still intact, ceilings soar and the house-sized rooms are decked out with satellite TVs, DVD players and ceiling fans. The restaurant is just as sea-shanty chic and serves Thai and Western dishes with panache.

Sriraya GUEST HOUSE $
(0 7569 7045; r 500B) Sleep in a simple but beautifully restored, thick-beamed Chinese shophouse. Walls are black, sheets are white and the bathrooms are shared. Angle for the street-front balcony room that overlooks the old town's ambient centre.

Eating

The best places to grab a bite are at the seafood restaurants along the northern edge of Ban Sala Dan. With tables on verandahs over water, they offer fresh seafood sold by weight (which includes cooking costs).

Beautiful Restaurant SEAFOOD $$
(0 7569 7062; Ban Ko Lanta; mains 100-200B) The best of Old Town's seafood houses. Tables are scattered on four piers that extend into the sea. Fish is fresh and exquisitely prepared.

Lanta Seafood SEAFOOD $$
(0 7566 8411; Ban Sala Dan) The best of the seafood-by-weight options. Order the *pla tod ka min* – it's white snapper rubbed with fresh, hand-ground turmeric and garlic then deep fried. It's not oily, but it is smoky, spicy and juicy. Its steamed mussels are also divine.

Country Lao THAI $
(08 5796 3024; Ban Phra Ae; mains 80-180B) A huddle of bamboo umbrellas and thatched pagodas on the main road. You'll endure the smooth jazz soundtrack for its house speciality: crispy papaya salad (150B). Green papaya shreds are battered and crispy fried. They're served in a heap alongside a bowl of lime dressing swimming with peanuts, green beans and juicy cherry tomatoes. Your job: combine, devour.

Red Snapper FUSION $$
(0 7885 6965; www.redsnapper-lanta.com; Ao Phra Ae; tapas/mains from 70/235B; dinner) A Dutch-run roadside tapas restaurant. The garden setting is romantic, and the duck breast with shitake mushrooms comes highly recommended.

Drunken Sailors FUSION $$
(0 7566 5076; dishes 100-200B; Hat Nui; breakfast, lunch & dinner) This hip, ultra-relaxed, octagonal pad is smothered with beanbags. The coffee drinks are top-notch and go well with interesting bites like the chicken green curry sandwich.

Bai Fern THAI $
(0 7566 8173; Ban Sala Dan; mains 40-100B; breakfast, lunch & dinner) Cheap, tasty and authentic Thai salads, noodles and curry

served over the water in a stilted dining room.

Drinking & Entertainment

During the high season Ko Lanta has some nightlife, but there are so many driftwood-style reggae bars along the west coast that it can become diluted. Low season is beyond mellow.

Same Same But Different BAR $$
(☎08 1787 8670; Ao Kantiang; cocktails 200B; ⊙8am-11pm) In a sweet seaside setting, you can sample tasty Thai cuisine and sip terrific cocktails beneath massive trees, thatched pagodas or in a bamboo chair sunk into the sand.

Moonwalk BAR $$
(Hat Phra Ae; cocktails 180B; ⊙7am-11pm) A sprawling, thatched bar and restaurant that brings a little Thai funk back to what is becoming an increasingly plotted, planned and international island. Expect tasty cocktails, Jack Johnson in stereo and seafood barbecue in the high season.

Opium NIGHTCLUB $$
(Hat Phra Ae; ⊙from 6pm) This chic club has live music some nights, guest DJs and a big dance floor. It's still the top party spot on Lanta.

Information

Ban Sala Dan has plenty of restaurants, minimarts, internet cafes (1B per minute), travel agencies, dive shops and motorcycle rentals. There are five 7-Elevens spread along the island's west coast – each one has an ATM.

Ko Lanta Hospital (☎0 7569 7085) The hospital is 1km south of Ban Ko Lanta (Old Town).

Police station (☎0 7569 7017)

Getting There & Away

Most people come to Ko Lanta by boat or air-con minivan. If you're coming under your own steam, you'll need to use the frequent **vehicle ferries** (motorcycle 20B, car/4WD 75/150B; ⊙7am-8pm) between Ban Hua Hin and Ban Khlong Mak (Ko Lanta Noi) and on to Ko Lanta Yai.

Boat

There are two piers at Ban Sala Dan. The passenger jetty is about 300m from the main strip of shops; vehicle ferries leave from a second jetty that's several kilometres further east.

There is one passenger ferry connecting Krabi's Khlong Chilat pier with Ko Lanta. It departs from Ko Lanta at 8am (400B, two hours) and returns from Krabi at 11am. It also stops at Ko Jum (for the full 400B fare).

Boats between Ko Lanta and Ko Phi-Phi technically run year-round, although service can peter out in the low season if there are too few passengers. Ferries usually leave Ko Lanta at 8am and 1pm (300B, 1½ hours); in the opposite direction boats leave Ko Phi-Phi at 11.30am and 2pm. From Ko Phi-Phi you can transfer to ferries to Phuket.

From around 21 October through May, you can join a four-island snorkelling tour to the Trang Islands and hop off with your bags at any destination you choose (350B) – bring your swimsuit. Boats stop on Ko Ngai (two hours), Ko Muk (three hours) and Ko Kradan (four hours).

There are also several speedboats boats that go from Ko Lanta to the Trang Islands, the fastest being the **Satun-Pak Bara Speedboat Club** (☎0 7475 0389, 08 2433 0114; www.tarutaolipeisland.com), which stops in Ko Ngai (650B, 30 minutes), Ko Muk (900B, one hour) and Ko Bulone Leh (1600B, two hours) then continues to Ko Lipe (1900B, three hours).

Tigerline (☎08 1092 8800; www.tigerlinetravel.com), a high-speed ferry, runs between Ban Sala Dan on Ko Lanta and Ko Lipe (1400B, four hours), stopping at Ko Ngai (500B, 30 minutes), Ko Kradan (750B, 1½ hours) and Ko Muk (750B, two hours). The service leaves at 1pm. The next day the same boat makes the return trip from Ko Lipe, departing at 9am and arriving in Ban Sala Dan at noon.

Minivan

Minivans run year-round and are your best option from the mainland. Daily minivans to Krabi airport (280B, 1½ hours) and Krabi Town (250B, 1½ hours) leave hourly between 7am and 3.30pm. From Krabi, minivans depart hourly from 8am till 4pm. Minivans to Phuket (350B, four hours) leave every two hours or so, but are more frequent in the high season. There are also several daily air-con minivans to Trang (250B, 2½ hours) and less frequent services to Khao Lak (650B, six hours), Ko Samui (650B including boat ticket) and other popular destinations.

Getting Around

Most resorts send vehicles to meet the ferries – a free ride to your resort. In the opposite direction expect to pay 80B to 250B. Alternatively, you can take a motorcycle taxi from opposite the 7-Eleven in Ban Sala Dan; fares vary from 50B to 250B, depending on distance.

Motorcycles (250B per day) can be rented all over. Unfortunately, very few places provide helmets and none provide insurance, so take extra care on the bumpy roads.

Several places rent out small 4WDs for around 1600B per day, including insurance.

Ko Jum & Ko Si Boya

เกาะจำ/เกาะศรีบอยา

Just north of Ko Lanta, Ko Jum and its neighbour Ko Si Boya have surprisingly little development; what's there is tucked away in the trees, making the islands look and feel nearly deserted. Although technically one island, the locals consider only the flatter southern part of Ko Jum to be Ko Jum; the northern hilly bit is called Ko Pu.

Ko Jum was once the exclusive domain of Lanta's *chow lair* people, but ethnic Chinese began arriving after Chairman Mao rose up in the 1950s. At the time there were no Thai people living here at all, but eventually the three cultures merged into one, which is best sampled amid the warm, early morning, ramshackle poetry of **Ban Ko Jum**, the island's fishing village. It has a few restaurants, an **internet cafe** (per min 3B) and a few dive shops, including **Blue Juice Divers** (in Krabi 0 7563 0679; www.bluejuicedivers.com).

Sleeping & Eating

KO JUM

Upwards of 20 properties are spread out along Ko Jum's west coast. Some places rent out sea kayaks, and most have a restaurant. Public transport to Ko Jum and Ko Si Boya is limited in the low season, so some resorts close between May and October.

TOP CHOICE **Koh Jum Beach Villas** VILLA RENTAL $$$
(08 6184 0505; www.kohjumbeachvillas.com; Hat Yao; villas 6000-16,000B;) Spacious wooden, tiled homes with plenty of living spaces, lush decks with cushioned seating and views of the sea are spread along a luscious white nub of Hat Yao. Houses are privately owned and rented out by the night, and the community is devoted to keeping the place as environmentally and socially responsible as possible (notice there's no air-con but the houses have been constructed to catch ocean breezes). The staff is delightful, the restaurant and bar scrumptious.

TOP CHOICE **Woodland Lodge** GUEST HOUSE $
(08 1893 5330; www.woodland-koh-jum.com; Hat Yao; bungalows 800-1000B) Tasteful, clean bamboo huts with proper thatched roofs, shiny, polished wood floors and verandahs. The exceptionally friendly British-Thai owners can organise boat trips and fishing and have an excellent, sociable restaurant. Great value and ambience.

Koh Jum Lodge HOTEL $$$
(0 7561 8275; www.kohjumlodge.com; Hat Yao; bungalows 4500-5500B;) An ecolodge with style: imagine lots of hardwoods and bamboo, gauzy mosquito netting, potted orchids, Thai carvings, manicured grounds and a hammock-strewn curve of white sand out the front. It strikes that hard-to-get-perfect balance of authenticity and comfort. Bliss.

Oon Lee Bungalows GUEST HOUSE $$
(08 7200 8053; www.koh-jum-resort.com; bungalows 500-3800B) This Crusoe-chic, Thai-French family-run resort is nestled on a deserted white beach on the Ko Pu part of Ko Jum. Wooden stilted bungalows are in a shady garden and plenty of activities, including some of the island's best hiking, are on offer. The fantastic fusion restaurant here is reason enough for a visit.

Koh Jum Resort HOTEL $$
(08 0221 4040; www.kohjumresort.com; Ko Pu; bungalows 1700-5500B;) Five stunning two-storey, ranch-style teak chalets are built with crooked, polished wood and designed with cylindrical turrets. Its five bamboo huts, attached to wide sun terraces stilted high above the sea, are rustic for the price but the excellent landscaping makes that easy to overlook.

Ting Rai Bay Resort HOTEL $$
(08 7277 7379; www.tingrai.com; Ko Pu; bungalows 600-2800B; May-Mar;) Next door to splashy Koh Jum Resort, this property is no slouch. Bungalows, which vary in size and comfort, are built in a horseshoe on a sloping landscaped hill, so they all have sea views.

Joy Bungalow GUEST HOUSE $
(0 7561 8199, 08 9875 2221; www.kohjum-joybungalow.com; Hat Yao; bungalows 500-2500B) On the southwestern coast of Ko Jum, Joy has some very attractive stilted, polished-wood cottages on a tremendous stretch of beach. The best are raised 2m high in the trees. This was the first resort on Ko Jum and it's still very popular.

Ko Jum Seafood SEAFOOD $$
(08 1893 6380; Ban Ko Jum; meals 100-400B) By all accounts the best fish kitchen on the island. Fresh catch is served on a stilted deck overlooking the narrow strait with a keyhole view of Ko Lanta.

KO SI BOYA

Low-lying, rural Ko Si Boya has yet to garner more than a trickle from the annual tourism stream, and that's just fine with repeat visitors – almost all of whom land at a single, exceptional bungalow compound.

Siboya Resort HOTEL $

(☎0 7561 8026, 08 1979 3344; www.siboyabungalows.com; bungalows 200-1200B; @📶) OK, the beach itself isn't spectacular. But the mangrove setting is wild, and full of life, and the wood bungalows are large, tasteful and affordable. The restaurant rocks and it's wired with high-speed internet. No wonder ever-smiling, secretive European and Canadian 50-somethings flock here like it's a more mature version of Alex Garland's *The Beach*.

Getting There & Around

From November to May, boats between Krabi and Ko Lanta can drop you at Ko Jum, but you'll pay full fare (400B, one hour) – see p303. In the fringe months of November and May only the early boat will drop you. There are also small boats to Ko Jum from Ban Laem Kruat, a village about 30km southeast of Krabi, at the end of Rte 4036, off Hwy 4. The boat (100B) leaves at 3pm and returns the following day at 7.45am.

If you plan to arrive in Ko Jum via Laem Kruat, your guest house can arrange transfers. A handful of places on the main road in Ban Ko Jum rent out bicycles (100B), mountain bikes (130B to 150B) and motorbikes (250B) at standard rates.

Boats to Ko Si Boya (50B) make the 10-minute hop from Laem Hin, just north of Ban Laem Kruat throughout the day. Private charters are 150B. Call Siboya Resort to arrange transfer from the pier.

TRANG PROVINCE

Lining the Andaman Sea south of Krabi, Trang Province has an impressive limestone-covered coast with several sublime islands. For the adventurous, there's also plenty of big nature to explore in the lush interior, including dozens of scenic waterfalls and limestone caves. And it's nowhere near as popular as Krabi, which means you're more likely to see tall rubber plantations here than rows of vendors selling 'same same but different' T-shirts. Transport links are improving every year, and during the high season, it's now possible to island hop all the way to Malaysia.

Trang ตรัง

POP 77,200

Most visitors to Trang are in transit to nearby islands, but if you're an aficionado of culture, Thai food or markets, plan to stay a day or more. It's an easy-to-manage town where you can get lost in wet markets by day and hawker markets and late-night Chinese coffee shops by night; at nearly any time of the year, there's likely to be some minor festival that oozes local colour.

Most of the tourist facilities lie along the main drag, Th Praram VI, between the clock tower and the train station.

Sights

Trang is more of a business centre than a tourist town. **Wat Tantayaphirom** (Th Tha Klang) has a huge white *chedi* (stupa) enshrining a footprint of the Buddha that's mildly interesting. The Chinese **Meunram Temple**, between Soi 1 and Soi 3, sometimes sponsors performances of southern Thai shadow theatre. It's also worth strolling around the large **wet & dry markets** on Th Ratchadamnoen and Th Sathani.

Activities

Tour agencies around the train station and along Th Praram VI offer various tours around Trang. **Boat trips** to Hat Chao Mai National Park and the Trang Islands start at 750B plus national park fees. There are also **sea-kayaking** tours to the gorgeous Tham Chao Mai mangrove forests (650B). **Snorkelling** trips on private long-tails to Ko Rok (3500B, maximum four people) and trips to local **caves and waterfalls** (1800B, maximum three people) by private car can also be arranged by most agencies. For a cultural fix you can spend a day **hiking** (2500B, maximum two people) in the Khao Banthat Mountains to visit villages of the Sa Kai mountain people.

Festivals & Events

Trang's Chinese population celebrates the wonderful **Vegetarian Festival** every October, coinciding with the similar festival in Phuket; for more about the latter festival, see p248.

Sleeping & Eating

Trang is famous for its *mŏo yâhng* (crispy barbecued pork) and *ráhn goh·Ƀêe* (coffee shops) that serve real filtered coffee. You can

Trang Province

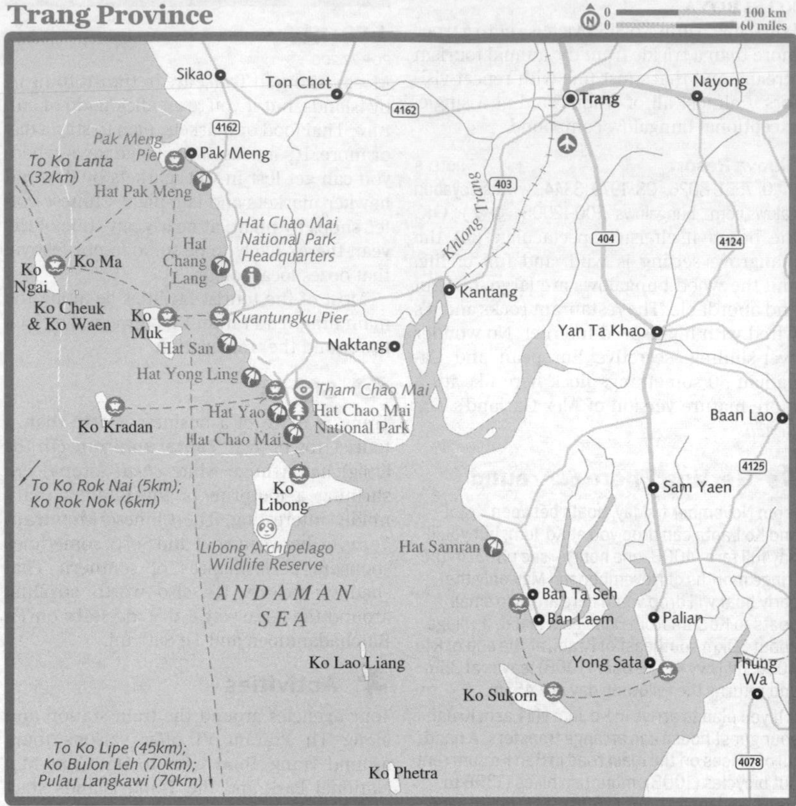

find *mŏo yâhng* in the mornings at some coffee shops or by weight at the wet market on Th Ratchadamnoen. To really get into the local scene, get to a dim sum depot early in the morning and stay out late at the coffee shops along Th Ratsada.

Sri Trang Hotel HOTEL $

(☎0 7521 8122; www.sritrang.com; 22-26 Th Praram VI; r 450-690B; ❄📶) There are a range of fan-cooled and air-con rooms in this renovated 60-year-old building with high ceilings, a winding wood staircase, groovy paint jobs, and wi-fi throughout. There's also a pleasant cafe-bar downstairs.

Rua Rasada Hotel HOTEL $$$

(☎0 7521 4230; www.ruarasadahotel.com; 188 Th Pattalung; r with breakfast from 2700B; ❄📶🏊) Trang's slickest choice is a 10-minute (25B) túk-túk ride from the train station. Chic rooms have large tiles, comfortable beds and a dusky blue, dark mauve and grey colour scheme. It's a five-minute walk to Robinson's Shopping Mall and Cinema City.

Koh Teng Hotel HOTEL $

(☎0 7521 8148; 77-79 Th Praram VI; r 180-380B; ❄) The undisputed king of backpacker digs in Trang. If you're feeling optimistic, the huge, window-lit rooms here have an adventuresome kind of shabby charm to them; if not, the grunge factor might get you down.

TOP CHOICE **Night Market** MARKET $

(btwn Th Praram VI & Th Ratchadamnoen; meals around 30B) The best night market on the Andaman coast will have you salivating over bubbling curries, fried chicken and fish, *pàt tai* and an array of Thai desserts. Go with an empty stomach and a sense of adventure. On Friday and Saturday nights there's a second night market right in front of the train station.

Asia Ocha THAI $

(Th Kantang; meals from 30B; ⏲breakfast, lunch & dinner) In business for 65 years, Asia Ocha serves filtered coffee to an all-Thai clientele who sit at vintage marble tables in an antiquated building. Don't miss the food either – the roast duck is delectable.

Information

You'll find several internet cafes and various banks with ATMs and foreign-exchange booths on Th Praram VI.

My Friend (☎0 7522 5984; 25/17-20 Th Sathani; per hr 30B) Has the best 24-hour internet cafe in town.

Post office (cnr Th Praram VI & Th Kantang) Also sells CAT cards for international phone calls.

Getting There & Away

Air

Nok Air (www.nokair.com) and **Orient Thai Airlines** (www.orient-thai.com) operate daily flights from Bangkok (Don Muang) to Trang (around 1500B one-way), but note that flights may be cancelled due to heavy rain. The airport is 4km south of Trang; minivans meet flights and charge 60B to town. In the reverse direction a taxi or túk-túk will cost 80B to 100B.

Minivan & Share Taxi

Hourly vans heading to Surat Thani (180B, 2½ hours), with connections to Ko Samui and Ko Pha-Ngan, leave from a **depot** (Th Tha Klang) just before Th Tha Klang crosses the railway tracks. Several daily air-con minivans between Trang and Ko Lanta (250B, 2½ hours) leave from the travel agents across from the train station. There are share taxis to Krabi (180B, two hours) and air-con minivans to Hat Yai (160B, two hours) from offices just west of the Trang bus terminal.

Local transport is mainly by air-con minivan rather than sŏrng·tăa·ou. Minivans leave regularly from the depot on Th Tha Klang for Pak Meng (70B, 45 minutes), Hat Chao Mai (80B, one hour) and Kuantungku pier (100B, one hour).

Train

Only two trains go all the way from Bangkok to Trang: the express 83 and the rapid 167, which both leave from Bangkok's Hualamphong station in the afternoon and arrive in Trang the next morning. From Trang, trains leave in the early and late afternoon. Fares are around 1480B/831B for a 1st-/2nd-class air-con sleeper and 285B for 3rd class.

Getting Around

Túk-túk mill around near the train station and should charge 30B for local trips, 250B per hour. Motorbike taxis charge the same price. Motorcycles can be rented at travel agencies for about 200B per day. Most agencies can also help you arrange car rental for around 1400B per day.

Trang Beaches & Islands

Think: limestone karsts rising from steamy palm-studded valleys and swirling seas. Trang's beaches are mostly just jumping-off points to the islands, but if you have the time, stop and enjoy the scenery.

The mythical Trang Islands are the last iteration of the Andaman's iconic limestone peaks before they tumble into the sea, and are home to roving sea gypsies.

HAT PAK MENG & HAT CHANG LANG หาดปากเมง/หาดฉางหลาง

Thirty-nine kilometres from Trang in Sikao Amphoe (District), Hat Pak Meng is the main jumping-off point for Ko Ngai. There's a wild-looking stretch of coastline here, and though the beach is scruffy, the backdrop – jutting limestone karsts on all sides that rival the best of Railay and Phi-Phi – is spectacular. The main pier is at the northern end of the beach and there are several seafood restaurants with deck chairs under casuarinas where Rte 4162 meets the coast.

Tour agencies at the jetty organise one-day boat tours to Ko Muk, Ko Cheuk, Ko Ma and Ko Kradan for 900B to 1000B per person (minimum three people), including lunch and beverages. There are also snorkelling day tours to Ko Ngai (750B) and Ko Rok (1200B to 1400B, plus national park fees). Mask and snorkel sets and fins can be rented by the pier for 50B each.

Hat Chang Lang is the next beach south from Hat Pak Meng and it continues the casuarina-backed-beach motif. At the southern end of Hat Chang Lang, where the beachfront road turns inland, is the headquarters of **Hat Chao Mai National Park** (☎0 7521 3260; adult/child under 14yr 200/100B; ⏲6am-6pm).

The 231 sq km park covers the shoreline from Hat Pak Meng to Laem Chao Mai and encompasses the islands of Ko Muk, Ko Kradan and Ko Cheuk plus a host of small islets. In various parts of the park you may see endangered dugong and rare black-necked storks, as well as more common species such as sea otters, macaques, langurs, wild pigs, pangolins, little herons, Pacific reef egrets, white-bellied sea eagles and monitor lizards.

Trang

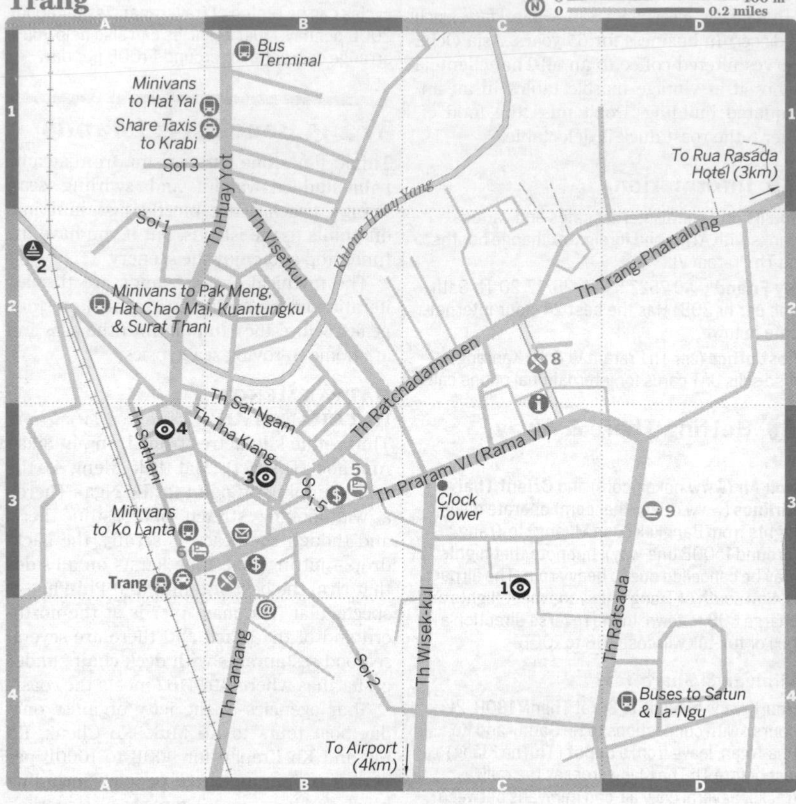

Sleeping

Anantara Sikao HOTEL $$$
(☎0 7520 5888; www.sikao.anantara.com; r 5400-15,400B;) Set on the northern edge of Hat Chang Leng, Anantara's glamorous yet hip vibe has refreshed these old bones (it was once an Amari Resort). Deluxe oceanfront rooms have wood floors, floating desks, flat-screen TVs and amazing views of Pak Meng's signature karsts. There are impressive timber columns and Balinese wood furnishings in the lobby, and the view from its Acqua restaurant is jaw dropping. Take the free shuttle to its guests-only beach club on seductive Ko Kradan.

National Park Headquarters CAMPING GROUND $
(☎0 7521 3260; www.dnp.go.th/index_eng.asp; camping with own tent free, with tent hire 300B, cabins 800-1000B) Simple cabins sleep up to six people and have fans. You can also camp under the casuarinas. You'll find a restaurant and a small shop here, too.

Getting There & Away

There are several daily boats between Pak Meng and Ko Ngai. Boats leave Ko Ngai for Pak Meng (400B) at 9am and return to Ko Ngai at 10am. A long-tail charter is 1200B.

Regular air-con minivans from Th Kha Klang in Trang run to Hat Pak Meng (80B, 45 minutes) and Chao Mai (100B, one hour). Or you can charter a taxi from Trang for around 800B.

The Chao Mai National Park headquarters is about 1km off the main road, down a clearly signposted track.

KO NGAI เกาะไหง (ไห)

The long, blonde, wind-swept beach along the developed eastern coast of Ko Ngai (Ko Hai) extends into blue water with a sandy bottom (perfect for children) that ends at a reef drop-off with excellent snorkelling. Coral and clear waters actually encircle the en-

Trang

Sights

1 Meunram Temple C3
2 Wat Tantayaphirom A2
3 Wet & Dry Market B3
4 Wet & Dry Market A3

Sleeping

5 Koh Teng Hotel B3
6 Sri Trang Hotel A3

Eating

7 Asia Ocha B3
8 Night Market C2

Drinking

9 Coffee Shops D3

tire densely forested island – it's a stunning place. With no indigenous population living here, several spiffy resorts have the whole island to themselves. There are two dive centres (dives from 1500B). Mask and snorkel sets and fins can be rented from resorts for 60B each, sea kayaks for around 150B per hour, or you can take half-day snorkelling tours of nearby islands (850B per person). Internet at the big resorts is slow and costs 100B to 150B per hour.

Even though it's technically a part of Krabi Province, the island's mainland link is with Pak Meng.

Sleeping & Eating

Most places are decidedly midrange and come with restaurants and 24-hour electricity. The boat pier is at Koh Ngai Resort, but if you book ahead resorts on the other beaches will arrange transfers.

Coco Cottages HOTEL **$$**
(☎08 1693 6457, 08 9724 9225; www.coco-cottage.com; bungalows 1650-4700B; ❄📶) As the name suggests, cottages are coconut extravaganzas with thatched roofs, coconut-wood walls and coconut-shell lanterns. Decks and interiors catch plenty of breezes, so air-con isn't necessary. Grab a sea-view fan bungalow if you can. There are bamboo lounges on the beach, massage pavilions, and a terrific restaurant and beachfront bar.

Thanya Beach Resort HOTEL **$$$**
(☎0 7520 6967; www.kohngaithanyaresort.com; bungalows 3500-7600B; ❄@) Ko Ngai's Bali-chic choice has dark but spacious teak bungalows with indoor hot and outdoor country-style bucket showers (don't knock it till you've tried it). Dry in fine linens, then stroll to your seafront terrace and gaze at the palm-dappled lawn, which rolls towards the sea.

Ko Hai Seafood GUEST HOUSE **$$**
(☎08 1367 8497; r 1200B; ❄@⊠) Of the cheaper choices on the beach, these solid bamboo bungalows are easily the most charming. The owners are happy, fun and laid-back, and they have one of the best kitchens on the island. The coconut-milk crab curry with big chunks of de-shelled fresh crab is a dream come true.

Mayalay Resort HOTEL **$$**
(☎08 3530 7523; www.mayalaybeachresort.com; r 2000-3500B; ❄@⊠) A charming resort with huge bungalows, all with double beds plus windowside day beds draped in mosquito nets. The Thai-Western beachside terrace restaurant is a little pricy but the view is sublime and portions are big and tasty.

BUSES TO/FROM TRANG

Buses leave from the Trang **bus terminal** (Th Huay Yot). Air-con buses from Trang to Bangkok cost 600B to 680B (12 hours, morning and afternoon). More comfortable are the VIP 24-seater buses at 5pm and 5.30pm (1050B). From Bangkok, VIP/air-con buses leave between 6.30pm and 7pm.

Other services:

DESTINATION	FARE (B)	DURATION (HR)	FREQUENCY
Hat Yai	110	3	frequent
Krabi	115	2	frequent
Phang-Nga	180	3½	hourly
Phuket	240	5	hourly
Satun	120	3	frequent

Fantasy Resort & Spa HOTEL $$$
(☎0 7520 6960; www.kohhai.com; r 2500-7500B; ❄@📶🏊) A massive Angkor Wat-meets-cheesy-cruise-ship-style place that extends from the beach and up the hillside. The bungalows are comfy but a little gaudy (floral wallpaper matched with red Chinese art). There are also plainer hotel-style rooms up the hill.

Ko Hai Camping CAMPING GROUND $
(☎08 1970 9804; seamoth2004@yahoo.com; tent 600B) Big, clean fan-cooled tent-bungalows on the beach have shared bathrooms and are run by friendly Tu, who also manages the adjacent Sea Moth Dive Center.

Getting There & Away

Ko Ngai Villa runs the daily boats from Ko Ngai to Hat Pak Meng at 9am, returning to Ko Ngai at 10am. Transfers cost 400B (1½ hours). You can also privately charter a long-tail to and from Pak Meng for 1200B, as well as Ko Muk (1200B) and Ko Kradan (1500B).

In the high season, the **Tigerline** (☎08 1092 8800; www.tigerlinetravel.com) high-speed ferry runs between Ban Sala Dan (750B, 30 minutes) on Ko Lanta and Ko Lipe (1400B, four hours), stopping at the pier on Ko Muk. **Satun Pakbara Speedboat Club** (☎0 7475 0389, 08 2433 0114; www.tarutaolipeisland.com) is the more direct and comfortable choice from Ko Lanta (650B, 30 minutes). You can charter a long-tail to Lanta for 2000B.

Ko Muk เกาะมุก

Motoring into Ko Muk is unforgettable whether you land on the sugary white sand bar of **Hat Sivalai** or spectacular **Hat Farang** (aka Hat Sai Yao, aka Charlie's Beach) where jade water kisses a perfect beach. Unfortunately, the lodging options aren't tremendous, and there's a steady stream of Speedo-clad package tourists tramping the beach and even more in the speedboats that buzz to **Tham Morakot** (Emerald Cave) from Ko Lanta. Still, the west-coast sunsets are glorious, it's easy to hop from here to any and every island in the province, and you may be shocked to feel Ko Muk's topography stir something deep and wild in your primordial soul.

Sights & Activities

Tham Morakot (Emerald Cave) is a beautiful limestone tunnel that leads 80m into a *hôrng*. No wonder long-gone pirates buried treasure here. You have to swim or paddle through the tunnel, part of the way in pitch blackness, to a small white-sand beach surrounded by lofty limestone walls; a piercing shaft of light illuminates the beach around midday. The cave features prominently on most tour itineraries, so it can get ridiculously crowded in the high season. Better to arrange a long-tail boat (300B) or rent a kayak (hour/day 150/500B) to zip over to the cave at daybreak or late afternoon when you'll have it to yourself – but note you can't get inside the cave at high tide.

Between Ko Muk and Ko Ngai are the small karst islets of **Ko Cheuk** and **Ko Waen**, both of which have good snorkelling and small sandy beaches.

Princess Divers (☎08 6270 9174) is located at Charlie Beach Resort and the independent **Chill Out Divers** is right behind the resort. Both are recommended and offer one/two dives for 1800/2600B and PADI courses from 10,900B. Chill Out Divers also offers **yoga classes** (250-400B) on the beach.

Koh Muk Nature Resort rents out **mountain bikes** (per day 150B) with maps for self-guided island tours, and you can also spend hours walking through rubber plantations and the island's authentic sea shanty villages (please cover up).

Sleeping & Eating

HAT SIVALAI & HAT LODUNG หาดสิวลัย

The following places are a short walk from either side of the pier. If you're facing the sea, humble, local-flavoured Hat Lodung is to your left after a stilt village and some mangroves; stunning Hat Sivalai wraps around the peninsula to the right.

Sivalai HOTEL $$$
(☎08 9723 3355; www.komooksivalai.com; Hat Sivalai; bungalows incl breakfast 5000-8000B; ❄) Straddling an arrow-shaped peninsula of white sand and surrounded by views of karst islands and the mainland, this location is mind-bogglingly sublime. Elegant thatched-roof cottages are almost encircled with glass doors, so you can let in as much of the view as you want. The vibe is a little cool and the pool is disappointing but the beach offers shallow swimming.

Pawapi Resort GUEST HOUSE $$
(☎08 9669 1980; www.pawapi.com; Hat Sivalai; bungalows incl breakfast 2600B) The upscale bamboo bungalows here are perched on stilts about 1.5m off the ground so that breezes ventilate the room from all sides

and the insanely gorgeous view sits 180 degrees in front of you. It's British-Thai owned and friendly with a restaurant serving good Western and Thai fare and huge breakfasts.

Koh Muk Nature Resort GUEST HOUSE $$
(☎08 1894 6936; www.trangsea.com; Hat Sivalai; bungalows 1500-1800B; ❄) Plain little blue and white concrete bungalows are fronted by two orderly lines of coconut palms just metres away from a gorgeous beach. The resort grows its own organic herbs and veggies, recycles and offers self-guided island bike tours.

Ko Mook Garden Resort GUEST HOUSE $
(☎08 1798 7805; Hat Lodung; bungalows 300B, r 500B) Wooden rooms are large while bamboo bungalows are small and basic. Staying here means you're in with a local family who take guests snorkelling, lend bikes and give out detailed maps of all the island's secret spots.

HAT FARANG หาดฝรั่ง

This is where most of the action is – a blend of travellers and package tourists more liable to relish the calm than to party. More and more places are opening inland from the beach, so shopping around is worthwhile. Most boats will pick up and drop you off here, but if not you'll have to take a 10-minute motorbike taxi to or from the pier (50B).

Charlie Beach Resort HOTEL $$
(☎0 7520 3281/3; www.kohmook.com; bungalows 1200-3100B; ❄@) There's a bunch of different bungalow options, ranging from basic beach shacks to three-star, air-con cottages at this sprawling resort, which dominates the beach and is linked by sandy paths. Skip the restaurant. Staff, although not always helpful, can organise snorkelling tours to Tham Morakot and other islands for around 1000B. Charlie's is open year-round.

Sawasdee Resort GUEST HOUSE $
(☎08 1508 0432; www.kohmook-sawadeeresort.com; bungalows 800B) Unremarkable wooden bungalows with terraces are right on the quiet shady north end of Hat Farang. You're paying for the location – which is sublime.

Rubber Tree Bungalow GUEST HOUSE $$
(☎08 1968 0332; www.mookrubbertree.com; bungalows incl breakfast 800-1990B; ❄@) Inland from the beach, there are cute, peach-tinted air-con cottages; cheaper bamboo bungalows and a large restaurant are high up among the rubber trees.

TOP CHOICE **Ko Yao Restaurant** SEAFOOD $
(meals 100-200B; ⏲breakfast, lunch & dinner) Perched on the cliffs, with wood tables scattered beneath a string of lights, is this family-owned patio restaurant with astounding views. The beer is cold, and the fish is fresh and steamed in a smouldering broth of chilli and lime.

Getting There & Away

Boats to Ko Muk leave from the pier at Kuantungku. There are four daily departures at 8am, 10am, noon and 3pm (100B to 300B, 30 minutes), which make the return trip to the mainland an hour later; the early morning ferry is the cheapest. Minibuses to/from Trang (200B, one hour) meet the boats. A chartered long-tail from Kuantungku to Ko Muk (600B, 30 minutes) and

REMARKABLE RUBBER TREES

If you ever wondered where the bounce in your rubber comes from, wonder no further: unlike money, it grows on trees. All over the Trang region, particularly on the islands floating off its coast, you are likely to come across rubber-tree plantations.

Rubber trees produce the milky liquid known as latex in vessels that grow within the bark of the tree. The trees are 'tapped' by making a thin incision into the bark at an angle parallel with the latex vessels (note that latex isn't the tree's sap). A small cup collects the latex as it drips down the tree. New scores are made every day – you can see these notched trees and collection cups throughout the region.

Latex from multiple trees is collected, poured into flat pans and mixed with formic acid, which serves as a coagulant. After a few hours, the very wet sheets of rubber are wrung out by squishing them through a press. They're then hung out to dry. You'll see these large, yellowish pancakes drying on bamboo poles wherever rubber trees are grown. The gooey ovals are then shipped to processing plants where they are turned into rubber as we know it.

to either Pak Meng or Hat Yao is around 1200B (45 minutes to one hour).

Long-tail charters to Ko Kradan (600B, 30 minutes) and Ko Ngai (1000B, one hour) are easily arranged on the pier or at Rubber Tree Bungalow or Ko Yao Restaurant on Hat Farang.

From November to May, Ko Muk is one of the stops on the speedboats connecting Ko Lanta and Ko Lipe; see p353 for details.

Ko Kradan

เกาะกระดาน

Kradan is dotted with slender, silky white-sand beaches, bathtub-warm shallows and limestone karst views. There are pristine hard and soft corals just off the south coast and a small but lush tangle of remnant jungle inland. Development is happening fast, and while there are now many places to stay on Kradan, all except a select few are overpriced and lack soul.

For internet and boat tickets go to Kradan Beach Resort, the biggest spread of mediocre bungalows on the main beach.

Sleeping & Eating

Seven Seas Resort HOTEL $$$
(☎08 2490 2442; www.sevenseasresorts.com; r 6600-7600B, bungalows 11,750-15,600B; ❄@☎🏊) This stunning small luxury resort has ultra-slick rooms with enormous beds that could sleep four (if you're into that). Beach bums will adore this stretch of sand where cotton hammocks link the curling mangroves. The breezy restaurant, hugging the jet-black infinity pool, serves a mix of Western dishes and excellent southern-style curries. It's a tad pricey, but the amazing staff more than make up for it.

Paradise Lost GUEST HOUSE $$
(☎08 9587 2409; www.koradan.wordpress.com; bungalows 700-1600B, dm 250B) One of the first places built on Kradan and still one of the best, this groovy, inland American-owned bungalow property has easy access to the island's more remote beaches. Small bamboo nests have solid wood floors and shared baths. Larger bungalows are all wood and have private facilities, and dorms are on an open verandah. Its kitchen (dishes 120B to 1800B) is the best on the island.

Kalumé Village GUEST HOUSE $$
(☎08 6905 5034; www.kalumekradan.com; bungalows 900-1500B) Basic bamboo or wooden beach shacks are in a sandy garden steps from blue water. It's Italian run and an honourable effort is made to be environmentally low impact (limited electricity, sustainable materials etc). Our only gripe is the inflated price tag.

Ao Niang Beach Resort GUEST HOUSE $
(☎08 1891 7379; bungalows 800B) Accessed by a jungle track from Paradise Lost or by rounding the corner from the main beach at low tide, this clean, basic place is a wade away from some outrageous snorkelling. The owner goes a little heavy on the Sam Song, but he's a happy guy and was building new, bigger bungalows when we passed. You can also camp here (300B, tent included).

NICE DAY FOR A WET WEDDING

Every Valentine's Day, Ko Kradan is the setting for a rather unusual wedding ceremony. Around 35 brides and grooms don scuba gear and descend to an underwater altar amid the coral reefs, exchanging their vows in front of the Trang District Officer. How the couples manage to say 'I do' underwater has never been fully explained, but the ceremony has made it into the *Guinness World Records* for the world's largest underwater wedding. Before and after the scuba ceremony, the couples are paraded along the coast in a flotilla of motorboats. If you think this might be right for your special day, visit the website www.trangonline.com/underwaterwedding.

Getting There & Away

Daily boats to Kuantungku leave at 9am and noon; tickets include the connecting minibus all the way to Trang (450B). A chartered long-tail from Kuantungku will cost around 800B one-way (45 minutes to one hour); you can also charter boats from Kradan to other islands within the archipelago.

Tigerline (☎08 1092 8800; www.tigerlinetravel.com) connects Kradan with Ko Lanta (750B, 1½ hours) and Hat Yao (750B, one hour). Patpailin Ferry goes to Ko Muk and Ko Ngai (both 500B) then continues to Ko Lanta.

Hat Yao

หาดยาว

A rickety, scruffy fishing hamlet just south of Hat Yong Ling, Hat Yao is sandwiched between the sea and imposing limestone cliffs, and sits at the mouth of a thick mangrove estuary. A rocky headland at the southern end of Hat Yao is pockmarked with caves and there's good snorkelling around the island immediately offshore. The best beach in the area is the tiny **Hat Apo**, hidden away among the cliffs. **Tham Chao Mai** is a vast cave full of crystal cascades and impressive stalactites and stalagmites that can be explored by boat.

Just south of the headland is the Yao pier, the main departure point for Ko Libong and the midpoint in the Tigerline ferry route that connects Lipe to Lanta.

Sleeping & Eating

Haad Yao Nature Resort GUEST HOUSE $
(☎08 1894 6936; www.trangsea.com; r 500-1200B, bungalows 800B; ❄@) Set in the harbour and run by the Lifelong Learning Foundation, an ecological and educational NGO led by enthusiastic naturalists, this place offers a variety of environmentally focused tours in the Hat Yao area. It has large cottages with wide terraces, TV and DVD, simpler motel-style rooms and a few overwater bungalows.

Restaurants THAI, SEAFOOD
Along the beach, north of the limestone headland, is a collection of wooden seafood restaurants selling cheap Thai meals. There is also a handful of tasty harbour restaurants.

Getting There & Around

From here, you can catch one of the regular long-tail boats to Ko Libong (50B, 20 minutes). You can also charter long-tail boats to Ko Libong (800B, 20 minutes) or to Ko Muk (1500B, one hour) each way. Sŏrng·tăa·ou to Trang (70B, one hour) leave when full from the pier and meet arriving boats. **Tigerline** (☎08 1092 8800; www.tigerlinetravel.com) is the area's high-speed ferry service, which docks in Hat Yao for lunch on its way between Lanta (750B, 2½ hours) and Lipe (750B, 2½ hours).

Ko Libong เกาะลิบง

Trang's largest island is just 15 minutes by long-tail from Hat Yao. Less visited than neighbouring isles, it's a peaked, mountainous jungle pearl, known for its captivating flora and fauna more than its thin reddish-brown beaches. The island is home to a small Muslim fishing community and has a few resorts on the west coast.

Sights

Libong Archipelago Wildlife Reserve NATURE RESERVE
(☎0 7525 1932) This reserve on the eastern coast of Ko Libong at **Laem Ju Hoi** is a large area of mangroves protected by the Botanical Department. The grass-filled sea channels here are one of the dugong's last habitats, and around 40 of them graze on the sea grass that flourishes in the bay. The Haad Yao Nature Resort (p341) in Hat Yaho and resorts here on Ko Libong (the reserve is not far from the Libong Beach Resort) offer dugong-spotting tours by sea kayak, led by trained naturalists, for around 1000B. Sea kayaks can also be rented at most resorts for 200B per hour.

Sleeping

Libong Beach Resort HOTEL $
(☎0 7522 5205; www.libongbeachresort.com; bungalows 500-800B; ❄@) This is the only place on the island that's open year-round – rates drop considerably in the low season. There are several options, from bland slap-up shacks behind a murky stream to beachfront and very comfortable varnished wood-and-thatch chalets. It offers a slew of trips, motorbike rental (300B) and internet access (per hour 100B). There's also a dive centre (two dives 3500B) open during the high season.

Le Dugong Resort HOTEL $
(☎08 7972 7228; www.libongresort.com; bungalows 400-900B) The best digs are rustic yet stylish wood-and-bamboo bungalows with terracotta sinks, woven walls and shuttered doors that open the whole room to the sea and setting sun. The lower-end bamboo shacks with shared bathrooms are icky.

Libong Sunset Resort HOTEL $
(☎08 9766 3341; www.libongsunsetresort.com; bungalows 200-800B; ❄) Brand new with a huge deserted restaurant pumping out techno, this resort has very small and basic bamboo bungalows or simple wood or cement bungalows in a sparse garden on the beach.

Getting There & Away

Long-tail boats to Ban Ma Phrao on the eastern coast of Ko Libong leave regularly from Hat Yao (20 minutes) during daylight hours for 50B per person; the long-tail jetty at Hat Yao is just west of the newer Yao pier. On Ko Libong, motorcycle taxis run across to the resorts on the western coast for 100B. A chartered long-tail directly to the resorts will cost 800B each way.

Ko Lao Liang

เกาะเหลาเลียง

Ko Lao Liang is actually two islands right next to each other: Ko Laoliang Nong, the smaller of the two where the only resort is found, and the larger Ko Laoliang Pi, where there's a small fishing settlement. The islands are stunning, vertical karst formations with small white-sand beaches, clear water and plenty of coral close to shore.

The only place to stay is the rock climbing-oriented **Laoliang Island Resort** (☎08 4304 4077; www.laoliangresort.com; per person 1500B). Lodging is in comfy tents equipped with mattresses and fans, right on the beach, and there are plenty of activities on offer, including snorkelling, climbing the islands' karst cliffs and sea kayaking. At night there's a small bar and the restaurant fires up its seafood barbecue regularly – it's like summer camp for grown-ups (although kids are happy here too). Rates include all meals, snorkel gear and sea kayaks.

Tigerline (☎08 1092 8800; www.tigerlinetravel.com) stops just off Ko Lao Liang between Lanta (1400B, 2½ hours) and Lipe (750B, 2½ hours).

Ko Sukorn

เกาะสุกร

Sukorn is a cultural paradise of tawny beaches, light-green sea, black-rock headlands shrouded in jungle, and stilted shack neighbourhoods home to about 2800 Muslim fisher folk – their rice fields, watermelon plots and rubber plantations unfurling on narrow concrete roads. Bike past fields occupied only by water buffalo, through pastel villages where folks are genuinely happy to see you, and sleep soundly through deep, black nights. Sukorn's simple stillness is breathtaking, its authenticity a tonic to the road-worn soul.

With few hills, stunning panoramas, lots of shade and plenty of opportunities to meet locals, renting a bike (150B) is the best way to see the island. Covering up is an absolute must when you leave the beach – be respectful.

Sleeping

TOP CHOICE **Sukorn Beach Bungalows** HOTEL **$$**
(☎0 7520 7707, 08 1647 5550; www.sukorn-island-trang.com; bungalows 1000-2500B; ❄📶) Easily the most professionally run place on this island, the concrete-and-wood bungalows all have comfy verandahs and a long swimming beach out the front, from which you can watch the sun set over outlying islands. The friendly Dutch and Thai owners are chock-full of information, arrange excellent island-hopping tours and offer guided tours of Sukorn (per person 350B). Oh, and the food (mains 180 to 300B) is the best in the Trang Islands.

Sukorn Cabana HOTEL **$$**
(☎08 9724 2326; www.sukorncabana.com; bungalows 800-1300B; ❄@) Sloping landscaped grounds dotted with papaya, frangipani and bougainvillea hold large, clean bungalows with thatched roofs, varnished wood interiors and plush verandahs. The gorgeous beach has stunning views over Ko Petra.

Getting There & Away

The easiest way to get to Sukorn is by private transfers from Trang available with the resorts for 1750B per person. The cheapest way is to take a sŏrng·tăa·ou from Trang to Yan Ta Khao (40 minutes, 60B), then transfer to Ban Ta Seh (45 minutes, 40B), where long-tails (50B) leave from the pier when full.

Otherwise, book a private taxi or sŏrng·tăa·ou from Trang to Ban Ta Seh (800B), where you can charter a long-tail to Ban Saimai (200B), the main village on Ko Sukorn. The resorts are a 20-minute walk or 50B motorcycle-taxi ride from Ban Saimai. You can also charter long-tails directly to the beach resorts (750B).

From Ko Sukorn you can charter long-tails to Ko Lao Liang (1750B), where you can meet the high-speed **Tigerline** (☎08 1092 8800; www.tigerlinetravel.com) ferry that connects Lanta with Lipe and serves all islands in between – including Ko Kradan, Ko Ngai and Ko Muk (1400B).

SATUN PROVINCE

Until recently, Satun was mostly overlooked, but that's all changed thanks to the dynamic white sands of Ko Lipe – a one-time backpacker secret turned mainstream beach getaway. Beyond Ko Lipe the province still hardly rates a blink of the eye as visitors rush north to Ko Lanta or south to Pulau Langkawi, Malaysia. Which means, of course, that they miss the untrammelled beaches and sea caves on Ko Tarutao, the rugged trails and ribbon waterfalls of Ko Adang and the rustic beauty of Ko Bulon Leh.

Largely Muslim in make-up, Satun has seen little of the political turmoil that plagues the neighbouring regions of Yala, Pattani and Narathiwat (see boxed text, p232). Around 60% of people here speak Yawi or Malay as a first language, and the few wát in the region are quite humble and vastly outnumbered by mosques.

Satun สตูล

POP 33,720

Lying in a steamy jungle valley surrounded by limestone cliffs, and framed by a murky river, isolated Satun is a relaxing coastal town where tourism is limited to visa-run traffic, which flows in both directions. Malaysia-based yachties, passing through for cheap repairs in Satun's acclaimed boat yard, are the only travellers who seem to hang around, but if you wander a bit before you leave, you'll see some interesting religious architecture, lots of friendly smiles and plenty of gritty charm.

Sights & Activities

Ku Den Museum MUSEUM

(Satun National Museum; Soi 5, Th Satun Thanee; admission 20B; ⊙8.30am-4.30pm Wed-Sun) Housed in a lovely old Sino-Portuguese mansion, this excellent museum was constructed to house King Rama V during a royal visit but the governor snagged the roost when the king failed to show up. The building has been lovingly restored and the exhibits feature dioramas with soundtracks covering every aspect of southern Muslim life.

Monkey Mountain WALKING

This jungled mound of limestone, teeming with primates, winds around **Spirit Rock**, a kitschy but locally beloved Buddhist shrine; or you could walk over a bridge to stroll through a stilted fishing village just a kilometre from town.

Mangrove Walk WALKING

A self-guided walk along a boardwalk with a river viewpoint behind the football stadium – it's especially popular at sunset.

Tours

On's (p344) offers a one-day **Satun Discoveries trip** (per person 990B). You'll be picked up at 8.30am and shuttled to Tham Phu Pha Pet, where you'll slip into kayaks and paddle through mini-rapids for 7km before relaxing at the Wang Sai Thong waterfall. You can also tack on an overnight stay in its jungle house overlooking the river (1500B). Prices include meals, refreshments and transportation.

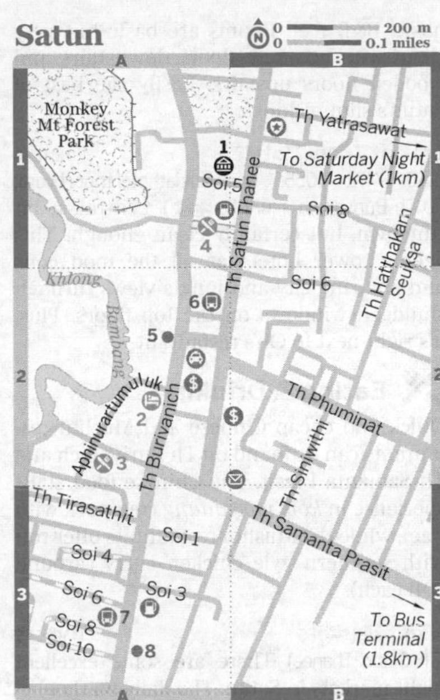

Satun	
Sights	
1 Ku Den Museum	A1
Sleeping	
2 Sinkiat Thani Hotel	A2
Eating	
3 Chinese Food Stalls & Muslim Restaurants	A2
4 Night Market	A1
On's	(see 2)
Information	
5 Immigration Office	A2
Transport	
6 Buses to Trang and Hat Yai	A2
7 Minivans to Hat Yai	A3
8 Sŏrng tăa ou	A3

Sleeping

On's Guesthouse GUEST HOUSE $

(☎0 7473 0469, 08 1097 9783; 1 Soi 1, Th Khuhaprawat; r 200B) This big airy wooden house, about 10 minutes walk from central Satun, has a B&B feel. Rooms are basic but very clean with concrete floors downstairs and wooden floors upstairs. Easily the best of Satun's slim pickings.

Sinkiat Thani Hotel HOTEL $
(☎0 7472 1055; www.sinkiathotel.thport.com; 50 Th Burivanich; r 680B; ❄@) Central, a bit rundown, but certainly clean enough. This ageing tower hotel has all the mod cons and amazing city and jungle views through smudged windows on the top floors. Plus, it's right next to On's restaurant.

Eating & Drinking

Quick and cheap Chinese and Muslim restaurants can be found on Th Burivanich and Th Samanta Prasit. The Chinese food stalls specialise in *kôw mŏo daang* (red pork with rice), while the Muslim restaurants offer roti with southern-style chicken curry (around 50B each).

Night Markets MARKET $
(Th Satun Thanee) There are some excellent night markets in Satun. The daily market begins just north of Satun Tanee Hotel, comes to life around 5pm, and serves great fried fish, squid skewers and spicy, southern-style curries. There's also a much larger Saturday night market on Th Burivanich and a Monday night market 1km from town on Th Yatrasawat.

On's THAI, WESTERN $
(☎0 7473 0469, 08 1097 9783; 48 Th Burivanich; dishes 80-150B; ⊙8am-late; @📶) With its bamboo, sarong-draped tables, leafy front porch and tasty Thai and Western dishes – including chilli con carne and chicken mushroom pie – this is the place to hang out in Satun (which explains the yachtie bar flies). It also has the best travel information in town.

Information

Bangkok Bank (Th Burivanich) Has a foreign-exchange desk and an ATM.

CAT office (Th Satun Thanee) The Communications Authority of Thailand – or Telecom – office; same location as the post office.

Immigration Office (☎0 7471 1080; Th Burivanich; ⊙8.30am-4.30pm Mon-Fri) Handles visa issues and extensions for long termers. It's easier and cheaper for tourists to exit Thailand via the border checkpost at Tammalang pier and immediately re-enter to obtain a new 15-day tourist visa. You will need to catch the boat and enter Malaysia before you come back, however. If you have wheels, hop to Malaysia via Thale Ban National Park.

Post office (cnr Th Satun Thanee & Th Samanta Prasit)

Siam Commercial Bank (Th Satun Thanee) Also has foreign exchange and an ATM.

Getting There & Away

Boat

Boats to Malaysia leave from Tammalang pier, 7km south of Satun along Th Sulakanukoon. Large long-tail boats run daily at 9.30am and 4.30pm to Kuala Perlis in Malaysia (300B one-way, one hour). From Malaysia the fare is M$30.

For Pulau Langkawi in Malaysia, boats leave from Tammalang pier daily at 9.30am, 1.30pm and 4pm (300B, 1½ hours). In the reverse direction, boats leave from Pulau Langkawi at 8.30am, 12.30pm and 3pm and cost M$27. Keep in mind that there is a one-hour time difference between Thailand and Malaysia. You can buy boat tickets for these trips in Satun at the pier.

There's a high-season service to Ko Lipe that departs at 11.30am daily (650B, 1½ hours; December to May). Enquire about tickets at the pier or at On's (p344).

Bus

Buses leave from the **bus terminal** (Th Samanta Prasit), 2km east of the town centre. Air-con services to Bangkok (800B to 1200B, 14 hours) leave at 7am, 7.30am, 3pm and 4pm. Air-con buses to Trang (110B, 1½ hours) leave hourly. There are also a few daily buses to Krabi (220B, four hours) and Phuket (360B, seven hours). Buses to Hat Yai (70B, two hours) and local non-aircon buses to Trang (90B, two hours) will stop and pick up passengers on Th Satun Thanee as they slowly make their way north.

Minivan & Share Taxi

There are regular minivans to the train station in Hat Yai (80B, one hour) from a depot south of Wat Chanathipchaloem on Th Sulakanukoon. Occasional minivans run to Trang, but buses are much more frequent. If you're arriving by boat at Tammalang pier, there are direct air-con minivans to Hat Yai and Hat Yai airport (90B).

Getting Around

Small orange sŏrng·tăa·ou to Tammalang pier (for boats to Malaysia) cost 40B and leave from the 7-Eleven on Th Sulakanukoon 40 minutes before ferry departure. A motorcycle taxi from the same area costs 60B.

Around Satun

PAK BARA ปากบารา

The small fishing community of Pak Bara is the main jumping-off point for the islands in the Mu Ko Phetra and Ko Tarutao Marine National Park. Tourist facilities are slowly improving as Pak Bara becomes increasingly busy with tourists discovering these dazzling isles. The peaceful town has some decent sleeping options and great seafood, but unless you arrive after the boats have gone there's no pressing reason to stick around.

The main road from La-Ngu terminates at the pier where there are several travel agencies, internet cafes, cheap restaurants and shops selling beach gear. There's a brand-new, huge **visitors centre** (☎0 7478 3485) for Ko Tarutao Marine National Park just back from the pier (under construction when we passed), where you can book accommodation and obtain permission for camping. Travel agencies here can arrange tours to the islands in the national park.

Tours

There are several travel agencies near the pier that will vie for your transport custom. **Adang Seatours** (☎0 7478 3338; www.adangseatour.com) is one of the more reliable agencies and also has an ATM. Shop around for kayaking day trips through the impressive caves at **Tham Chet Khok** (per person incl lunch 1800B).

During the high season, the **Satun Pakbara Speedboat Club** (☎0 7478 3643; www.tarutaolipeisland.com) runs speedboat tours to Ko Tarutao, Ko Bulon Leh and Ko Lipe – visit the website for the latest details.

Sleeping & Eating

Best House Resort HOTEL $

(☎0 7478 3058; bungalows 600B; ❄) This place, 100m inland from the pier, has tidy concrete bungalows around a murky pond. Management is super-friendly and helpful with travel tips.

Red Boat THAI, WESTERN $

(☎0 7478 3498; dishes 60-150B; ⏰7am-11pm) Stop here while waiting for your ferry for Western breakfasts, espresso drinks, cocktails or tremendous fried prawns in tamarind sauce.

There are several elementary restaurants and vendors near the Pak Bara pier that serve good Malay Muslim food for 20B to 50B. There's also a series of tasty seafood stalls along the coast south of town that get smoking just before sunset. They're a popular local hang-out on Sundays.

Getting There & Away

BUSES There are hourly buses between 7am and 4pm from Hat Yai to the pier at Pak Bara (90B, 2½ hours). Coming from Satun, you can take an ordinary bus towards Trang and get off at La-Ngu (60B, 30 minutes), continuing by sŏrng·tăa·ou to Pak Bara (20B, 15 minutes).

MINIVANS Air-con minivans leave hourly for Hat Yai (150B, two hours) from travel agencies near Pak Bara pier. There are also minivans to Trang (200B, 1½ hours), which connect to numerous destinations like Krabi (450B, four hours) and Phuket (650B, six hours).

BOATS From 21 October to the end of May there are several speedboats to Ao Pante Malacca on Ko Tarutao and on to Ko Lipe. Boats depart from Pak Bara at 10am, 11am and 12.30pm (return 1200B, 1½ hours); in the reverse direction boats leave fro Ko Lipe at 9.30am, 10am, 12.30pm and 1.30pm. From 16 November these boats also stop at Ko Adang for the same price. For Ko Bulon Leh, boats depart at 12.30pm, arriving in Ko Bulon Leh one hour later (return 800B), before buzzing on to Ko Lipe. If you miss the Bulon boat, you can easily charter a long-tail from local fishermen (1500B to 2000B, 1½ hours). During the wet season, services to Ko Lipe are weather and demand dependent, but usually cut back to three times per week.

KO BULON LEH เกาะบุโหลนเล

This pretty island, 23km west of Pak Bara, is surrounded by the Andaman's signature clear waters and has its share of faultless beaches with swaying casuarinas. Gracious Ko Bulon Leh is in that perfect phase of being developed enough to offer comfortable facilities, yet not so popular that you have to book beach-time days in advance.

The exceptional white-sand **beach** extends along the east coast from Bulone resort, on the northeast cape, to Pansand. At times the beach narrows a bit, especially where it is buffered by gnarled mangroves and strewn with thick sun-bleached logs. But those nooks and crannies make it easy to find a secret shady spot with dreamy views.

Bulon's lush interior is interlaced with a few tracks and trails that are fun to explore – though the dense, jungled rock that makes up the western half remains inaccessible on foot. Bulon's wild beauty is accessible on the southern coast at **Ao Panka Yai**, which is blue and laden with coral gravel. There's good snorkelling around the western headland, and if you follow the trails through remnant jungle and rubber plantations – with eyes wide lest you miss glimpsing one of Bulon's enormous monitor lizards – you'll wind your way to **Ao Muang** (Mango Bay), where you'll find an authentic *chow lair* squid-fishing camp. **Ao Panka Noi**, accessible from the path leading down from Viewpoint Resort, is another fishing village with long-tails docking on a fine gravel beach. Here you'll find beautiful karst views and a clutch of simple but very good restaurants.

Resorts can arrange snorkelling trips (1500B, four hours) to other islands in the Ko Bulon group for a maximum of six people, and fishing trips for 300B per hour. Trips usually take in the glassy emerald waters of **Ko Gai** and **Ko Ma**, whose gnarled rocks have been ravaged by wind and time. But the most stunning sight has to be **White Rock** – bird-blessed spires rising out of the open sea. Beneath the surface is a rock reef crusted with mussels and teeming with colourful fish. Snorkelling is best at low tide. The area's best coral reef is off Laem Son near Bulone Resort, where you can rent masks, snorkels (100B), fins (70B) and kayaks (150B).

Bulone Resort also offers internet (per minute 3B), and battery-charging services for laptops (50B) and digital cameras (10B).

Sleeping & Eating

Most places here shut down in the low season. Those that persevere rent out bungalows at discount rates. For eating, it's worth hiking over to Ao Panka Noi.

Marina Resort HOTEL $$
(☎08 1598 2420, 08 5078 1552; bungalows 500-1000B) Log-built and shaggy with stilted decks, louvred floors and high ceilings, thatched huts never looked or felt so good. There's a tasty kitchen attached to an inviting patio restaurant with cushioned floor seating. The ever-gracious Max will be your wise-guy host. The resort arranges speedboat tickets and snorkelling tours. It's located just inland from Pansand resort.

Bulone Resort HOTEL $$
(☎08 6960 0468; www.bulone-resort.com; bungalows 1250-1650B) Perched on the northeast cape with access to two exquisite stretches of white sand, these cute wooden bungalows have the best beachside location on Bulon. Queen-sized beds come with iron frames and ocean breezes. It has electricity all night long and serves up a tremendous mango smoothie with honey, lime and fresh yoghurt.

Chaolae Homestay GUEST HOUSE $
(bungalows 300B) The fantastic-value classy bungalows have varnished wood interiors, thatched roofs and polished cement bathrooms (with squat toilets). It's blissfully quiet, run by a lovely *chow lair* family and is steps away from decent snorkelling at Ao Panka Yai.

Pansand Resort HOTEL $$
(☎0 7521 1010; www.pansand-resort.com; cottages 1200-1500B; @) Pansand sits on the south end of the island's gorgeous white-sand beach. Brick-and-bamboo bungalows are fan cooled and come with sea views. The actual lodging isn't any better than elsewhere on the island – you're paying for a sublime location and a larger, organised resort setting. Cheaper wooden bungalows are set back in the trees.

Jungle Resort GUEST HOUSE $
(bungalows 150B) You won't find a better deal than this on the Andaman coast: cute, clean, terraced bungalows with attached bathrooms (with squat toilets) sit in a shady inland garden constantly tended by a welcoming *chow lair* family. To get there, ask the boatman to let you off at Ao Panka Yai, walk up through Chaolae Homestay then turn right.

There are a few local restaurants and a small shop in the Muslim village next to Bulon Viewpoint.

Getting There & Away

The boat to Ko Bulon Leh (400B) leaves from Pak Bara at 12.30pm daily if there are enough takers. Ship-to-shore transfers to the beach by long-tail cost 50B – save yourself some sweat and ask to be dropped off on the beach closest to your resort. In the reverse direction, the boat moors in the bay in front of Pansand Resort at around 9am. You can charter a long-tail from Pak Bara for 1500B to 2000B.

From November to May there are two daily speedboats (600B, one hour) from Ko Bulon Leh to Ko Lipe in Ko Tarutao Marine National Park. Boats, which originate in Ko Lanta and make stops in the Trang Islands, depart from in front of the Pansand resort at 1pm and 3pm.

Ko Tarutao Marine National Park

อุทยานแห่งชาติหมู่เกาะตะรุเตา

One of the most exquisite and unspoilt regions in all of Thailand, **Ko Tarutao Marine National Park** (☎0 7478 1285; www.dnp.go.th/

parkreserve; adult/child under 14yr 200/100B) encompasses 51 islands covered with well-preserved virgin rainforest teeming with fauna, and surrounded by healthy coral reefs and radiant beaches.

One of the first marine national parks in Thailand, the main accommodation in the park are small, ecofriendly government-run cabins and longhouses. Pressure from big developers to build resorts on the islands has so far (mostly) been ignored, though concessions were made for the filming of the American reality-TV series *Survivor* in 2001. And there is the minor issue of a private fishing resort on Ko Adang, which is supposed to be off-limits to developers. It was originally slated to open in 2010, but local environmentalists have appealed to the Thai courts to keep it shut.

Rubbish on the islands can be a problem – removal of beach rubbish as well as that generated by visitors only happens sporadically. Do your part and tread lightly out here. Within the park, you can spot dusky langurs, crab-eating macaques, mouse deer, wild pigs, sea otters, fishing cats, tree pythons, water monitors, Brahminy kites, sea eagles, hornbills and kingfishers.

Ko Tarutao is the biggest and most-visited island in the group and is home to the park headquarters and government accommodation. Many travellers choose to stay on Ko Lipe, which has managed to evade the park's protection and is fast becoming a popular and increasingly paved resort island with tourist facilities and bungalows aplenty. Long-tail tours to outlying islands can be arranged through travel agencies in Satun or Pak Bara, through the national park headquarters on Ko Tarutao or through resorts and long-tail boat operators on Ko Lipe. Note that there are no foreign-exchange facilities at Ko Tarutao – you can change cash and travellers cheques at travel agencies in Pak Bara and there's an ATM at La-Ngu.

KO TARUTAO เกาะตะรุเตา

Most of Ko Tarutao's whopping 152 sq km is covered in old-growth jungle, which rises sharply up to the park's 713m peak. Mangrove swamps and typically impressive limestone cliffs circle much of the island, and the western coast is pocked with caves and lined with quiet white-sand beaches. This is one of Thailand's wildest islands. The park entrance fee, payable on arrival, is 200B.

Tarutao's sordid history partly explains its preservation. Between 1938 and 1948, more than 3000 Thai criminals and political prisoners were incarcerated here, including interesting inmates such as So Setabutra, who compiled the first Thai–English dictionary while imprisoned on Tarutao, and Sittiporn Gridagon, son of Rama VII. During WWII, food and medical supplies from the mainland were severely depleted and hundreds of prisoners died from malaria. The prisoners and guards mutinied, taking to piracy in the nearby Strait of Malacca until they were suppressed by British troops in 1944.

There's internet (80B per hour) and wi-fi (50B per hour) at the Ao Pante Malacca Information Centre.

Sights & Activities

The overgrown ruins of the camp for political prisoners can be seen at **Ao Taloh Udang**, in the southeast of the island, reached via a long overgrown track. The prison camp for civilian prisoners was over on the eastern coast at **Ao Taloh Waw**, where the big boats from Satun's Tammalang pier now dock.

Next to the park headquarters at Ao Pante Malacca, a steep trail leads through the jungle to **Toe-Boo Cliff**, a dramatic rocky outcrop with fabulous views towards Ko Adang and the surrounding islands.

Ao Pante Malacca has a lovely alabaster beach shaded by pandanus and casuarinas. If you follow the large stream flowing through here inland, you'll reach **Tham Jara-Khe** (Crocodile Cave), once home to deadly saltwater crocodiles. The cave is navigable for about 1km at low tide and can be visited on long-tail tours from the jetty at Ao Pante Malacca.

Immediately south of Ao Pante Malacca is **Ao Jak**, which has another fine sandy beach; and **Ao Molae**, which also has fine white sand and a ranger station with bungalows and a camp site. A 30-minute boat ride or 8km walk south of Ao Pante is **Ao Son**, an isolated sandy bay where turtles nest between September and April. You can camp here but there are no facilities. Ao Son has decent snorkelling, as does **Ao Makham**, further south. From the small ranger station at Ao Son you can walk inland to **Lu Du Falls** (about 1½ hours) and **Lo Po Falls** (about 2½ hours).

Sleeping & Eating

There's accommodation both at Ao Pante Malacca and Ao Molae, open mid-November to mid-May. Water is rationed, rubbish is (sporadically) transported back to the

Ko Tarutao Marine National Park & Around

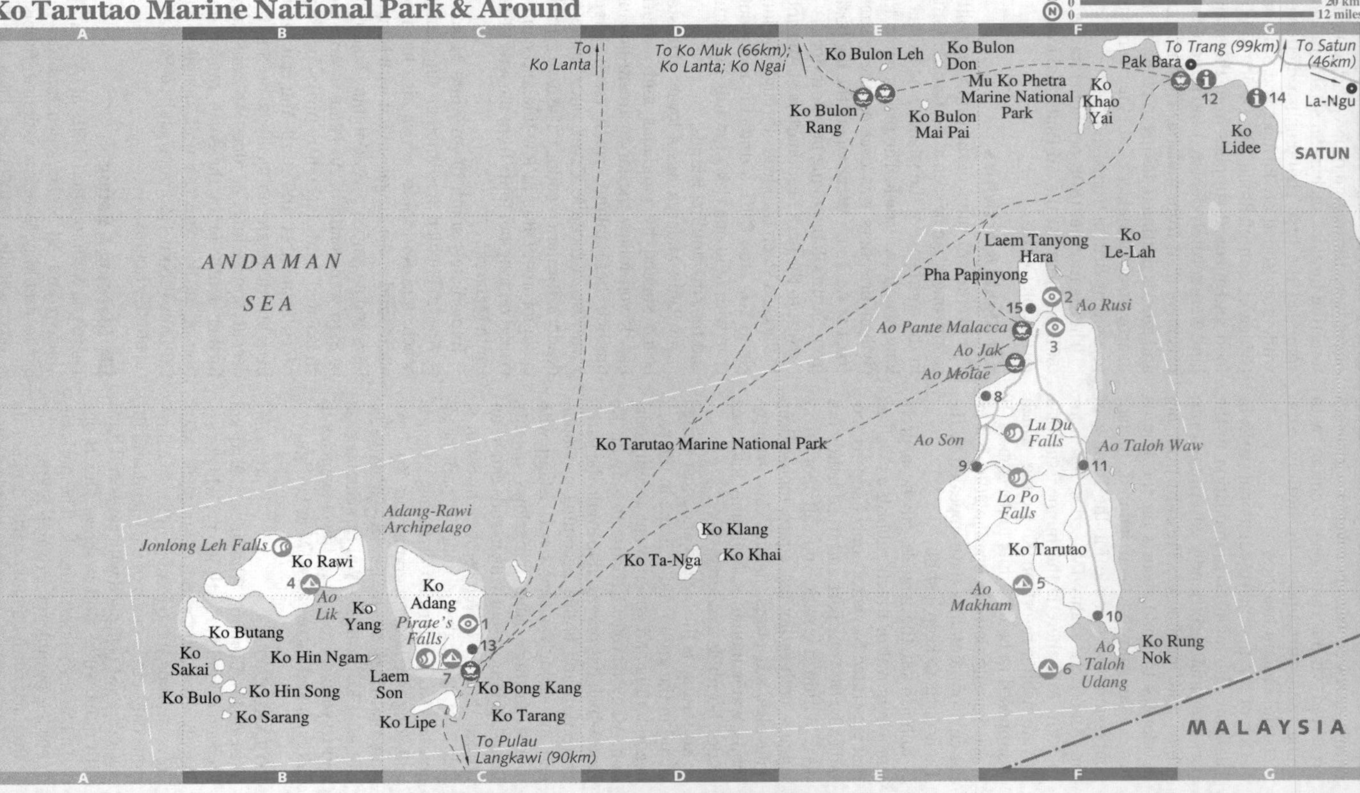

Ko Tarutao Marine National Park & Around

mainland, lighting is provided by power-saving lightbulbs and electricity is available between 6pm and 7am only.

The biggest spread of options is at Ao Pante Malacca, conveniently near all the facilities, where there are **bungalows** (800-1000B), simple **longhouse rooms** (550B) sleeping up to four people with shared bathrooms, and **camp sites** (with tent rental 150B or 375B).

Ao Molae is much more quiet and isolated – and arguably prettier. Recently constructed, rather swanky one- and two-room **duplexes** (r 600-1000B) are right on the beach. Accommodation can be booked at the **park office** (☎0 7478 3485) in Pak Bara. National park entry fees can be paid at Ao Pante Malacca or Ao Taloh Waw.

Camping is also permitted under casuarinas at Ao Molae and Ao Taloh Waw, where there are toilet and shower blocks, and on the wild beaches of Ao Son, Ao Makham and Ao Taloh Udang, where you will need to be self-sufficient. The cost is 30B per person with your own tent, or you can hire tents for 225B. Camping is also permitted on Ko Adang and other islands in the park. Note that local monkeys have a habit of going into tents and destroying or eating everything they find inside – so shut everything tight.

The park authorities run **canteens** (dishes 40-120B; ⏰7am-2pm & 5-9pm) at Ao Pante Malacca and Ao Molae. The food is satisfying and tasty, but you can find beer only at Ao Molae.

Getting There & Around

Boats connecting Pak Bara and Ko Lipe stop at Ko Tarutao along the way; see (p345) for detailed information. The island officially closes from the end of May to 15 September. Regular boats run from 21 October to the end of May; when the boats aren't running, you'll have to charter a long-tail from Pak Bara for 1500B. During the high season, you can also come here on speedboat day tours from Pak Bara for 2000B, including national park fees, lunch, drinks and snorkelling.

With a navigable river and plenty of long paved roads, the island lends itself to self-propulsion: hire a kayak (per hour/day 100B/300B) or mountain bike (50/200B) – or if it's just too darned hot, you can charter a vehicle (per day 600B). Long-tails can be hired for trips to Ao Taloh Udang (2000B), Ao Taloh Waw (1500B), and Tham Jara-Khe or Ao Son for around 800B each.

If you're staying at Ao Molae, take a park car (per person 60B) from the jetty at Ao Pante Malacca.

KO LIPE เกาะหลีเป๊ะ

Ko Lipe is this decade's poster child for untamed development in the Thai Islands. Blessed with two wide white-sand beaches separated by jungled hills, and within spitting distance of protected coral reefs, a few years ago the island was only spoken about in secretive whispers. But then the whispers became small talk, which quickly turned into a roar – you know, the kind generally associated with bulldozers. The biggest losers have

Ko Lipe

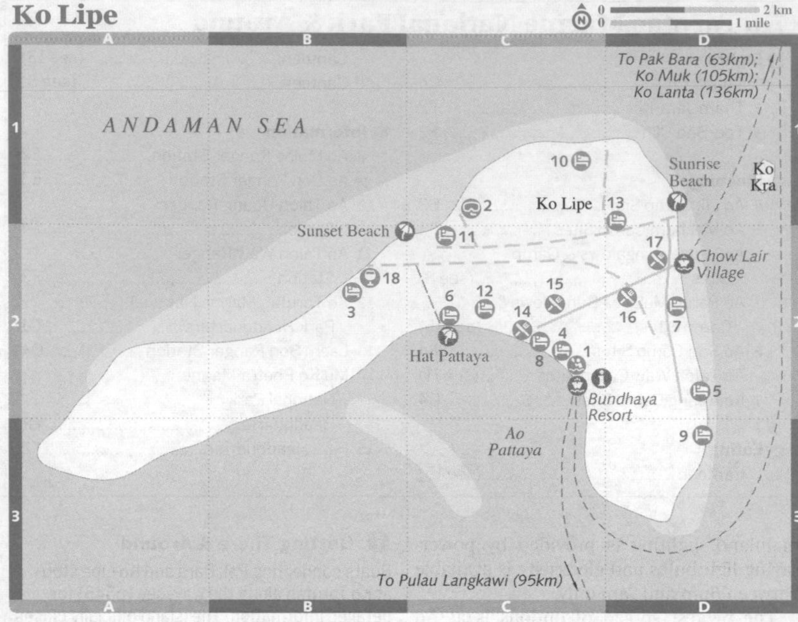

Ko Lipe

Activities, Courses & Tours

- Castaway Divers ....(see 5)
- Forra Dive ....(see 7)
- Forra Dive ....(see 8)
- 1 Islander Sea Sports C2
- 2 Sabaye Divers C1

Sleeping

- 3 Bila Beach B2
- 4 Blue Tribes C2
- 5 Castaway Resort D2
- 6 Daya Resort C2
- 7 Forra Dive D2
- 8 Forra Dive2 ....C2
- 9 Idyllic D3
- 10 Mountain Resort C1
- 11 Porn Resort C2
- 12 Sita Beach Resort C2
- 13 South Sea D1

Eating

- 14 Nong Bank Restaurant C2
- 15 Pee Pee Bakery C2
- 16 Pooh's Bar D2
- 17 Som Tam D2

Drinking

- 18 Mia Luna B2

been the 700-strong community of *chow lair* villagers who sold to a Thai developer.

Yet, given this upheaval, there's still plenty to love about Lipe. The gorgeous white-sand crescent of **Hat Pattaya** on the southern coast has some terrific beach bars, seafood and a party vibe during the high season. Windswept **Sunrise Beach**, another sublime long stretch of sand, juts to the north where you'll have spectacular Adang views. A drawback of both of the busy beaches is the preponderance of long-tails that crowd out swimmers. **Sunset Beach**, with its golden sand, gentle jungled hills and serene bay that spills into the Adang Strait, has an altogether different feel and retains Lipe's wild soul. In between there's an ever-expanding concrete maze of cafes, travel agencies, shops and salons. More resorts are opting to stay open year-round.

There are no banks or ATMs on the island, though several of the bigger resorts can change travellers cheques and cash or give advances on credit cards – all for a hefty fee. Internet is available along the cross-island path for 3B per minute and a few places behind Sunrise beach charge 2B per minute.

Sights & Activities

There's good coral all along the southern coast and around **Ko Kra**, the little island opposite Sunrise Beach. Most resorts rent out mask and snorkel sets and fins for 50B each, and can arrange four-point long-tail snorkel trips to Ko Adang and other coral-fringed islands for around 1500B. The best way to see the archipelago is to hire a local *chow lair* captain. **Islander Sea Sports** (08 7294 9770; per hr/day 100/600B) rents brand-new kayaks on Hat Pattaya.

While it would be a stretch to call the diving here world class, it's certainly very good, with fun drift dives and two rock-star dive sites. **Eight Mile Rock** is a natural amphitheatre of coral-crusted boulders that attracts mantas and whale sharks. **Stonehenge** is popular because of its beautiful soft corals, resident seahorses and rare leopard and whale sharks, and also because it resembles that (possibly) alien-erected monstrosity that inspired Spinal Tap's greatest work. On Sunrise and Pattaya beaches, French-run **Forra Dive** (08 1479 5691, 08 4407 5691; www.forradiving.com), Lipe's least expensive choice, offers PADI Open Water dive courses for 12,800B, and day trips with two dives for 2700B. **Castaway Divers** (08 7478 1516; www.kohlipedivers.com), based on Sunrise Beach, offers PADI and SDI training, and more intimate dive trips (two dives 2800B) off long-tail boats. **Sabaye Divers** (08 9464 5884; www.sabaye-sports.com) is the small Greenfins-certified shop on Sunset Beach owned by a long-time expat.

While it may look inviting, do not try to swim the narrow strait between Lipe and Adang at any time of year. Currents are swift and can be deadly.

Sleeping

Most, but not all, resorts on Ko Lipe close from May to October, when the boats don't run as frequently.

TOP CHOICE Castaway Resort HOTEL $$
(08 3138 7472; www.castaway-resorts.com; Sunrise Beach; bungalows 3500-5000B; @) The roomy wood bungalows with hammock-laden terraces, cushions everywhere, overhead fans and fabulous, modern-meets-naturalistic bathrooms are the most chic on Lipe. The resort is also one of the most environmentally friendly with solar water heaters and lights.

TOP CHOICE Daya Resort HOTEL $
(0 7472 8030; Hat Pattaya; bungalows 500-1000B) One of the few places that's still locally run, the striped bungalows here are your standard slap-up wooden affairs but the beach is fantastic, the flowery back garden charming, and the restaurant has the absolute best and cheapest seafood grill on the island…and that's saying something.

Idyllic HOTEL $$$
(08 1802 5453; www.idyllicresort.com; Sunrise Beach; bungalows 6300-15,000B; @) High design has arrived on Lipe. With slanted roofs, concrete-and-glass walls, flat-screen TVs, a shingled exterior and floating decks out the front, the digs are more like futuristic pods than beach bungalows.

Blue Tribes HOTEL $$
(08 6285 2153; www.bluetribeslipe.com; Hat Pattaya; bungalows 1200-1700B; @) One of Pattaya's more attractive small resorts, its best nests are the two-storey thatched wooden bungalows with a downstairs living room and top-floor bedrooms that have sliding doors opening to sea views.

Bila Beach HOTEL $$
(08 0589 2056; www.bilabeach.com; Sunset Beach; bungalow 1500B) This place has a killer bamboo reggae bar and beachfront restaurant below stylish cliffside bungalows set on and above a tiny, private white-sand cove, which is strewn with boulders and adjacent to Sunset Beach. It's the perfect setting for your hippy honeymoon. It's a short jog over the hill from Pattaya.

Mountain Resort HOTEL $$
(0 7472 8131; www.mountainresortkohlipe.com; Sunrise Beach; bungalows incl breakfast 1300-5000B; @) This big resort has views from its hillside location out over Ko Adang. Winding wooden walkways lead down to the sublime beach on Sunrise Beach's northern sand bar.

Forra Dive HOTEL $$
(08 0545 5012; www.forradiving.com; Sunrise Beach; bungalows 800-1000B) This place captures the look of Lipe's pirate spirit with a range of bamboo bungalows and lofts. The best are large with indoor-outdoor baths and hammock-strung terraces. Divers get

KO LIPE'S METAMORPHOSIS *ADAM SKOLNICK*

Ko Lipe began to change in earnest around five years ago when the sandy cross-island trail was smothered in concrete. However, the seeds of change were planted more than a decade earlier when a Phi-Phi developer named Ko Kyiet approached local *chow lair* (sea gypsy; also spelled *chao leh*) families about their ancestral land. Although deals were struck, they were never completed.

Enter Ko Pi Tong, a Satun native. 'Pi Tong is like Robin Hood', said Kun Pooh of Pooh's Bar and Pooh's Bungalows, a long-time local and one of Lipe's tourism leaders. 'He paid what Kyiet owed the locals plus interest.'

Indeed, Tong went back to the *chow lair* families, most of whom didn't have proper documentation for their land, and offered them lump sums of cash. They accepted, which means that subsequent development was legal and that they participated in their own plight. But it isn't quite that simple.

When Kyiet negotiated the initial deals, he allowed the *chow lair* to keep a slice of their ancestral land. But Tong bought everything. Kun Pan, an elder, who lives in the new cordoned-off *chow lair* village on the hillside above Sunset Beach, offered his account of the situation.

'Before, we had the whole island, we all lived on the beach', said Pan, a silver-haired fishermen with deep lines worn into his leathery brow. 'My brother and I, we not want to sell. The police come and take us to Satun. They said we had no land rights.'

Pooh disputes Pan's claim. He suggests the seaman is confused because 'Tong let [local people] live on the land he bought from them for years'. Tong evicted them relatively recently.

According to Pooh, Tong is now selling the land for many times the purchase price. Clearly, Tong has brought commerce, jobs, infrastructure and wealth into what once was a southern Thai backwater. Furthermore, some *chow lair* families held out, kept their land and launched successful businesses, such as Daya Resort, on their own – a fact that seems to contradict Pan's story. Still, it's hard not to notice that the vast majority of *chow lair* appear left out of the prosperity.

25% off lodging and there's a second location with similar bungalows on Hat Pattaya.

South Sea GUEST HOUSE $
(☎08 0544 0063, 08 1678 9903; Sunset Beach; bungalows 350B) Inland from Sunset Beach, this sunny compound filled with flower and shell mobiles has tiny bamboo huts with small sleeping mats and attached semi-outdoor Thai-style bathrooms.

Porn Resort HOTEL $
(☎08 9464 5765; Sunset Beach; bungalows 500-750B) This collection of weathered bungalows with hard beds is the only resort on imperfect yet golden and swimmable Sunset Beach. It's rustic but the best deal on Lipe for a terrace on a private beachfront.

Sita Beach Resort HOTEL $$$
(☎0 7478 3664; www.sitabeachresort.com; Hat Pattaya; bungalows 6500-9000B; ❄@🛜≋) The most upmarket choice on Hat Pattaya feels a little like a Southern California apartment complex but it's very comfortable with rooms spreading from the beach to high on a hill.

Eating & Drinking

Hat Pattaya's resorts put on nightly fresh seafood barbecues and Daya's is arguably the best. Cheap eats are best found at the roti stands and small Thai cafes along Walking Street, the main paved path.

For drinking, driftwood-clad Rasta bars are found on all beaches. At least some things never change.

Som Tam CAFE $
(Sunrise Beach; dishes 20-50B) There was no name when we passed by, but this tiny cafe on the corner of Walking Street and the Sunrise Beach road serves fantastic *sôm·đam* with lip-smacking fried chicken – a perfect lunch.

Nong Bank Restaurant RESTAURANT $$
(Hat Pattaya; dishes 80-120B; ⏰breakfast, lunch & dinner) This place has a half-dozen tables scattered beneath a tree on the white sand. It serves point-and-grill seafood and a superb yellow curry with crab (120B).

Pooh's Bar RESTAURANT-BAR $
(☎0 7472 8019; www.poohlipe.com) This massive complex was built by a Lipe pioneer and includes bungalows, a dive shop and several restaurants. It's a very popular local expat hang-out, especially in the low season. Each night it projects films onto its big screen.

Pee Pee Bakery BAKERY $
(Hat Pattaya; dishes from 80B; ⏲breakfast, lunch & dinner) The best breakfasts on Lipe include homemade breads and pastries and great people-watching as you dine. A full American set costs 240B.

Mia Luna BAR $
(Hat Pattaya) This is a real pirate bar of hanging painted buoys, driftwood seating and hammocks. It's isolated on its own nugget of white sand near Bila Beach but is only a short walk over the hill from Hat Pattaya. It's also a quiet spot to park a towel in the daytime when partiers are sleeping it off.

ℹ Getting There & Away

From 21 October through to the end of May, several speedboats run from Pak Bara (see p345) to Ko Lipe via Ko Tarutao or Ko Bulon Leh at 9.30am, 11am, 12.30pm and 2pm (550B to 650B, 1½ hours); in the reverse direction boats leave at 9.30am, 10am and 1.30pm. Low-season transport depends on the weather, but there are usually three direct boats per week. A boat charter to Ko Lipe from Pak Bara is a hefty 4000B each way.

Tigerline (☎08 1092 8800; www.tigerlinetravel.com) offers the cheapest high-speed ferry service to Ko Lanta (1500B, 5½ hours), stopping at Ko Muk (1400B, 3½ hours), Ko Kradan (1400B, four hours) and Ko Ngai (1400B, 4½ hours). It departs from Ko Lipe at 9.30am.

The daily and more comfortable **Satun-Pak Bara Speedboat Club** (☎0 7475 0389, 08 2433 0114; www.tarutaolipeisland.com) speedboat departs from Ko Lipe for Ko Lanta (1900B, three hours) at 9am, stopping at Ko Bulon Leh (600B, one hour), Ko Muk (1400B, two hours) and Ko Ngai (1600B, 2½ hours). The same boat makes the return trip from Ko Lanta at 1pm.

Both of these speedboats also offer daily trips to Pulau Langkawi (1200B, one hour) in Malaysia; departure is at 7.30am, 10.30am and 4pm. Be at the immigration office at the Bundhaya Resort early to get stamped out. In reverse, boats leave from Pulau Langkawi for Ko Lipe at 7.30am, 9.30am and 2.30pm Malay time.

No matter which boat you end up deciding to use, you will have to take a long-tail shuttle (per person 50B) to and from the floating pier at the edge of the bay.

KO ADANG & KO RAWI เกาะอาดัง/เกาะราวี

The island immediately north of Ko Lipe, **Ko Adang** has brooding, densely forested hills, white-sand beaches and healthy coral reefs. Lots of snorkelling tours make a stop here, and there are mooring buoys to prevent damage from anchors. Inland are a few short jungle trails and tumbling waterfalls, including the ramble up to **Pirate's Falls**, which is rumoured to have been a freshwater source for pirates (and is more of a river than a waterfall). There are great views from **Chado Cliff**, above the main beach, where green turtles lay their eggs between September and December.

Ko Rawi, a long rocky, jungled ellipse 11km west of Ko Adang, has first-rate beaches and large coral reefs offshore. Camping at Ao Lik is allowed, with permission from the national park authorities. Excellent snorkelling spots include the northern side of **Ko Yang** and tiny **Ko Hin Ngam**, which has underwater fields of giant clams, vibrant anemones and striped pebble beaches. Legend has it that the stones are cursed and anyone who takes one away will experience bad luck until the stone is returned to its source. There is a small restaurant here, but bring your lunch from Lipe, where it's cheaper and (much) tastier. Even a short stop on the island will cost you the park's entrance fee (adult/child 200/100B).

Park accommodation on Ko Adang is located near the ranger station at Laem Son. There are new and attractive **bungalows** (3-9 people 600-1800B), scruffier **longhouses** (3-bed r 300B) with attached bathrooms, and facilities for **camping** (sites per person 30B, with tent hire 250B). A small restaurant provides good Thai meals.

Long-tails from Ko Lipe will take you to Ko Adang and Ko Rawi for 50B per person, although you might have to do a little bargaining.

[illegible]

KO [illegible] & KO [illegible]

[illegible]

Siam [illegible]

[illegible]

GETTING THERE & AWAY

[illegible]

Ferries [illegible]

[illegible]

Understand Thailand's Islands & Beaches

population per sq km

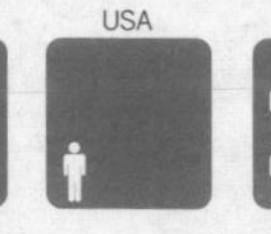

≈ 32 people

Thailand's Islands & Beaches Today

» Population: 66.7 million

» GDP: US$580.3 billion

» GDP per capita: US$8700

» Unemployment: 1.2%

» Education spending: 4.1% of GDP

The Sex Industry

No matter how you cut it, Thailand's most desirable places of leisure – like the islands and beaches – play host to the country's roaring sex industry. It is common to stumble upon prostitutes and touts hawking the skin trade, and while the industry is perhaps far more overt in the Land of Smiles than it is in other nations, one should not misinterpret the fact that Thailand's relationship with prostitution is a long and complicated one.

Today, Thailand has a reputation as being an international sex tourism destination, a designation that began around the time of the Vietnam War. Foreigners are explicitly targeted in the red light districts in Bangkok, Phuket and Pattaya, but there is also a more clandestine domestic sex industry (especially around border towns) and myriad informal channels of sex for hire.

Prostitution is technically illegal, a law declared in the 1960s after much pressure from the UN, but entertainment venues (from go-go bars to massage parlours) are governed by a separate law that allows for nonsexual services. Some analysts have argued that the high demand for sexual services limits the likelihood of the industry being curtailed; limiting abusive practices is the goal of many activists and government agencies.

The International Labor Organisation estimates that a Thai sex worker's salary equals the average wage of a Thai service-industry worker or a mid-level civil servant's job. These economic factors provide a strong incentive for rural, unskilled or uneducated individuals – especially those with financial obligations – to engage in sex work.

Much of Thai society revolves around the importance of family, with many workers, including those in the sex industry, sending home large percentages of their salary. This incoming wealth is often transformed

Dos & Don'ts

» Do take off your shoes when entering a home or temple. Be careful where you put your feet (which are considered filthy in Thailand).

» Don't argue or get visibly angry; you'll cause yourself embarrassment.

» Do stand respectfully for the national anthem.

» Don't criticise the monarchy.

» Do smile: it puts Thais at ease.

» Do dress modestly (cover to the elbows and ankles) for visits to temples or buildings associated with the monarchy.

Top Books

Very Thai (Philip Cornwell-Smith) Colourful photos and essays on Thailand's quirks.

Chronicle of Thailand (William Warren) History of the last 50 years.

belief systems

(% of population)

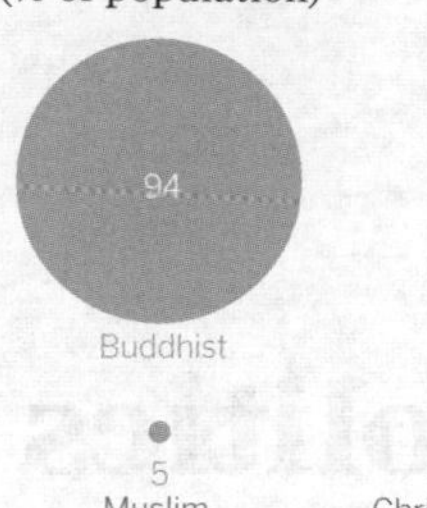

if Thailand were 100 people

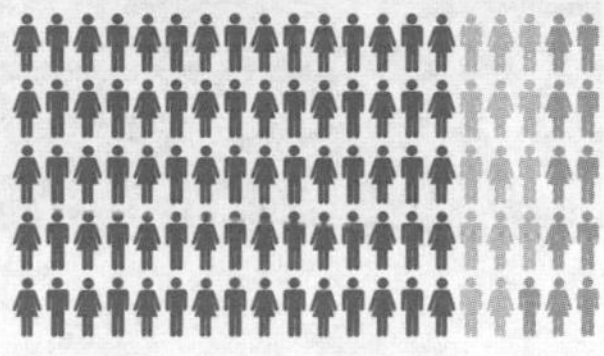

into purchased objects in order to display their child's success in the industry. The unfortunate by-product of such practices is that it further promotes the get-rich-quick sentiment for the next generation of sex workers.

Global Terrorism Analysis (www.jamestown.org/terrorism) publishes online articles about the southern insurgencies.

Southern Separatism

Thailand's south is – mostly – synonymous with golden beaches and sky-scraping palms, but for the regions in the deep south, abutting the Malaysian border, life is far from peaceful. Several of Thailand's southernmost provinces, including Yala, Pattani and Narathiwat, were once part of the sultanate of Pattani, which ruled the region from the 15th century until the turn of the 20th century when Buddhist Siam claimed the land. These areas, however, never truly assimilated to the Thai way of life, and a deep-seeded separatist sentiment has prevailed, even today.

In the 1930s, Thailand closed down the Qu'ranic sharia law courts and the region's Islamic schools, and although Yawi – a local dialect – is spoken throughout the area, it has also been subsequently banned in schools. The squelching of rights, according to the local population, has led to a surge in insurgencies that some pundits call a low-grade civil war.

The 'Patani Mujahedin' network consists of various village-based resistance groups who operate independently to achieve common goals. Believed to consist of roughly 8000 separatists, the groups are known for rarely claiming responsibility for attacks and being reluctant to attack targets outside the deep south. As a result, the conflict has attracted little global interest despite having a profound effect on the region's tourism industry.

Top Films

Uncle Boonmee Who Can Recall His Past Lives (Apichatpong Weerasethakul; 2010) Winner of Cannes 2010 Palm d'Or.

Bangkok Traffic Love Story (Adisorn Tresirikasem; 2009) Romantic comedy with public-transit message.

The Beach (2000) Beautiful Hollywood island utopia, based on the book. Often credited for turning Thailand's beach scene from backpacker to flashpacker.

OK Baytong (2007) Touches on the violence between the Thais and Muslims.

History & Politics

History

Thai history begins as a story of immigrants heading into a frontier land claimed by distant empires for trade, forced labour and patronage. Eventually the nascent country develops its own powerful entities that unite feuding localities and begins to fuse a national identity around language, religion and monarchy. The kings resist colonisation from the expansionist Western powers on its border only to cede their absolute grip on the country when challenged by forces within. Since the transition to a constitutional monarchy in 1932, the military predominantly rules the country with a few democratic hiccups in between. Unravelling Thailand's 20th-century history provides immense insight into the unfolding political drama of today.

Top History Reads

- *Thailand: A Short History* (2003) by David K Wyatt
- *A History of Thailand* (2009) by Chris Baker and Pasuk Phongpaichit
- *Chronicle of Thailand: Headlines Since 1946* (2010) by William Warren

Ancient History

Little evidence remains of the cultures that existed in Thailand before the middle of the 1st millennium AD. *Homo erectus* fossils in Thailand's northern province of Lampang date back at least 500,000 years, and the country's most important archaeological site is Ban Chiang, outside Udon Thani, which provides evidence of one of the world's oldest agrarian societies. It is believed that the Mekong River Valley and Khorat Plateau were inhabited as far back as 10,000 years ago by farmers and bronze-workers. Cave paintings in Pha Taem National Park near Ubon Ratchathani date back some 3000 years.

Early Empires

Starting in the 1st millennium, the 'Tai' people, who are considered the ancestors of the contemporary Thais, began emigrating from southern China into present-day Southeast Asia. These immigrants came in consecutive waves and spoke Tai-Kadai, a family of monosyllabic and tonal

TIMELINE

4000–2500 BC

Prehistoric people develop pottery, rice cultivation and bronze metallurgy in northeastern Thailand.

6th–11th centuries

Dvaravati establish city-states in central Thailand.

9–13th centuries

Angkor extends control across parts of Thailand.

languages said to be the most significant ethno-linguistic group in Southeast Asia. Some settled in the river valleys of modern-day Thailand while others chose parts of modern-day Laos and the Shan state of Myanmar.

They settled in villages as farmers, hunters and traders and organised themselves into administrative units known as *meu·ang,* under the rule of a lord, which became the building block of the Tai state. Over time, the Tai expanded from the northern mountain valleys into the central plains and northeastern plateau, where there existed several important trading centres ruled by various indigenous and 'foreign' empires, including the Mon-Dvaravati, Khmer (Cambodia) and Srivijaya (Malay).

Dvaravati

The Mon dominated parts of Burma, western Thailand and into the central plains. In the 6th to 9th centuries, the Dvaravati culture emerged as a distinct Buddhist culture associated with the Mon people. Little is known about this period but it is believed that Nakhon Pathom might have been the centre and that overland trade routes and trading outposts extended west to Burma, east to Cambodia, north to Chiang Mai and Laos, and towards the northeast, as evidenced by findings of distinctive Dvaravati Buddha images, temples and stone inscriptions in Mon language.

The Dvaravati was one of many Indian-influenced cultures that established themselves in Southeast Asia at the time, but scholars single out the Dvaravati because of its artistic legacy and the trade routes that might have provided an early framework for what would become the core of the modern-day Thai state.

Relief carvings at Angkor Wat depict Tai mercenaries serving in Khmer armies. The Khmer called them 'Syam'. The name was transliterated to 'Siam' by the English trader James Lancaster in 1592.

SYAM

Khmer

While the Dvaravati are a historical mystery, the Khmers were Southeast Asia's equivalent of the Roman Empire. This kingdom became famous for its extravagant sculpture and architecture and had a profound effect on the art and religion of the region. Established in the 9th century, the Khmer kingdom built its capital in Angkor (modern-day Cambodia) and expanded westward across present-day central and northeastern Thailand. Administrative centres anchored by Angkor-style temples were built in Lopburi (then known as Lavo), Sukhothai and Phimai (near Nakhon Ratchasima) and linked by road to the capital.

The Khmer's large-scale construction projects were a symbol of imperial power in its frontier and examples of the day's most advanced technologies. Khmer elements – Hinduism, Brahmanism, Theravada Buddhism and Mahayana Buddhism – mark the cultural products of this period in Thailand.

10th century
Arrival of Tai peoples in Thailand.

1240–1438
Approximate dates of Sukhothai kingdom.

PAUL BEINSSEN/LONELY PLANET IMAGES ©
» Sukhothai Historical Park

Srivijaya

While mainland Thailand was influenced by forces from the north and west, the Malay peninsula was economically and culturally fused to cultures further south. Between the 8th and 13th centuries, the Malay peninsula was under the sway of the confederation of the Srivijaya, which controlled maritime trade between the South China Sea and Indian Ocean. The Srivijaya capital is believed to have been in Palembang on Sumatra.

Of the series of Srivijaya city-states that grew to prominence along the Malay peninsula, Tambralinga established its capital near present-day Nakhon Si Thammarat and adopted Buddhism in the 13th century, while the states further south fell under the influence of Islam, creating a religious boundary that persists to this day. Remains of Srivijaya culture can be seen around Chaiya and Nakhon Si Thammarat. Many art forms of the Srivijaya kingdom, such as *năng đà·lung* (shadow play) and *lá·kon* (classical dance-drama), persist today.

Sacred Landmarks of Note

- » Tham Phraya Nakhon, Khao Sam Roi Yot
- » Sanctuary of Truth, Pattaya
- » Wat Phra Mahathat Woramahawihaan, Nakhon Si Thammarat
- » Khmer temples, Phetchaburi
- » Big Buddha, Phuket

Emerging Tai Kingdoms

In the 13th century, the regional empires started to decline and prosperous Tai city-states emerged with localised power and military might. The competing city-states were ultimately united into various kingdoms that began to establish a Thai identity. Scholars recognise Lanna, Sukhothai and Ayuthaya as the unifying kingdoms of the period.

Lanna

The Lanna kingdom, based in northern Thailand, dates its formation to the upper Mekong River town of Chiang Saen in the middle of the 12th century by King Mengrai, who settled the bickering between neighbouring towns by conquering them. He then migrated south to Chiang Mai (meaning 'new city') in 1292 to establish his capital. The king was a skilled diplomat and forged important alliances with potential rivals, like King Ngam Muang of Phayao and King Ramkhamhaeng of Sukhothai; a bronze statue commemorating this confederation stands in Chiang Mai today. King Mengrai is also credited for successfully repulsing the Mongol invasions in the early 14th century and building diplomatic ties in lieu of future attacks.

The Lanna kingdom is also recognised for its royal patronage of the Sinhalese tradition of Theravada Buddhism, which that is now widely practised in Thailand, and of the distinctive northern Thai culture that persists in the region. The Lanna kingdom never went through an extensive expansion period as it was plagued by dynastic intrigues and wars, especially against Sukhothai and Ayuthaya.

1283
Early Thai script invented by King Ramkhamhaeng of Sukhothai.

1292
Chiang Mai becomes the capital of Lanna.

1351–1767
Reign of Ayuthaya.

1688
King Narai dies and is followed by the Palace Revolution and the expulsion of the French.

Sukhothai

During the 13th century, several principalities in the central plains united and wrested control from the dying Khmer empire, making their new capital at Sukhothai (meaning 'Rising of Happiness'). Thais consider Sukhothai the first true Thai kingdom and the period is recognised as an artistic and cultural awakening.

The most revered of the Sukhothai kings was Ramkhamhaeng, who is credited for developing the modern Thai writing system, which is based on Indian, Mon and Khmer scripts. He also established Theravada Buddhism as the official religion.

In its prime, the Sukhothai kingdom extended as far as Nakhon Si Thammarat in the south, to the upper Mekong River Valley in Laos and to Bago (Pegu) in southern Myanmar. For a short time (1448–86), the Sukhothai capital was moved to Phitsanulok, but by that time another star was rising in Thailand, the kingdom of Ayuthaya.

King Naresuan is portrayed as a national hero and became a cult figure, especially worshipped by the Thai army. His story inspired a high-budget, blockbuster film trilogy, *King Naresuan*, by filmmaker Chatrichalerm Yukol, funded in part by the Thai government.

Ayuthaya

In the mid-14th century, the Ayuthaya kingdom began to dominate the Chao Phraya River basin during the twilight of the Khmer period. It survived for 416 years, defining itself as Siam's most important early kingdom. It had an expansive sphere of influence (including much of the former Khmer empire) and played a fundamental role in organising the modern Thai state and social structure.

With a strategic island location formed by encircling rivers, Ayuthaya grew wealthy through international trade during the 17th century's age of commerce and fortified itself with superior Portuguese-supplied firearms and mercenaries. The river system connected to the Gulf of Thailand and to the hinterlands as well.

This is the period when Western traders 'discovered' Southeast Asia, and Ayuthaya hosted many foreign settlements. Accounts by foreign

FRIENDS OF THE KING

In the 1680s many foreign emissaries were invited to Ayuthaya by King Narai, who was keen to acquire and consume foreign material, culture and ideas. His court placed orders for spyglasses, hourglasses, paper, walnut trees, cheese, wine and marble fountains. He joined the French Jesuits to observe the eclipse at his palace in Lopburi and received a gift of a globe from France's King Louis XIV.

In the 1680s, Narai recruited the services of the Greek adventurer Constantine Phaulkon, who was later accused of conspiring to overthrow the ailing king. Instead, the accusers led a coup and executed Constantine.

1511 Portuguese found a foreign mission in Ayuthaya, followed by other European nations.

1767 Ayuthaya is sacked by the Burmese.

1768 King Taksin establishes a new capital in Thonburi.

1782 Founding of the Chakri dynasty with Bangkok as the new capital.

visitors mention Ayuthaya's cosmopolitan markets and court. In 1690 Londoner Engelbert Campfer proclaimed, 'Among the Asian nations, the kingdom of Siam is the greatest'.

Ayuthaya adopted Khmer court customs, honorific language and ideas of kingship. The monarch styled himself as a Khmer *devaraja* (divine king) rather than Sukhothai's *dhammaraja* (righteous king); Ayuthaya continued to pay tribute to the Chinese emperor, who rewarded this ritualistic submission with generous gifts and commercial privileges.

The glories of Ayuthaya were interrupted by the expansionist Burmese. In 1569 the city had fallen to the great Burmese king, Bayinnaung, but regained independence under the leadership of King Naresuan. Then, in 1765, Burma's ambitious and newly established Kongbaung dynasty pushed eastward to eliminate Ayuthaya as a political and commercial rival. Burmese troops laid siege to the capital for a year before destroying it in 1767. The city was devastated, its buildings and people wiped out. The surrounding areas were deserted. So chilling was this historic sacking and razing of Ayuthaya that the perception of the Burmese as ruthless foes and aggressors still persists in the minds of many Thais to this day.

Landmarks of the Bangkok Era

» Wat Arun

» Wat Phra Kaew and Grand Palace

» Dusit Palace Park

The Bangkok Era

With Ayuthaya in ruins, the line of succession of the kings was broken and chaos ensued. A former general, Taksin, claimed his right to rule, handily defeating potential rivals, and established his new capital in Thonburi, a settlement downriver from Ayuthaya with better access to trade. Consolidating his power, King Taksin, the son of a Chinese father and Thai mother, strongly promoted trade with China.

The king was deposed in 1782 by the military. One of the coup organisers, Chao Phraya Chakri assumed the throne as Phraphutthayotfa Chulalok (r 1782–1809; posthumously known as Rama I) and established the Chakri dynasty, which still rules today. The new monarch moved the capital across the Chao Phraya River to modern-day Bangkok.

The first century of Bangkok rule focused on rebuilding what had been lost when Ayuthaya was sacked. Surviving knowledge and practices were preserved or incorporated into new laws, manuals of government practice, religious and historical texts and literature. At the same time, the new rulers transformed their defence activities into expansion by means of war, extending their influence in every direction. Destroying the capital cities of both Laos and Cambodia, Siam contained Burmese aggression and made a vassal of Chiang Mai. Defeated populations were resettled and played an important role in increasing the rice production of Siam, much of which was exported to China.

Unlike the Ayuthaya rulers, who identified with the Hindu god Vishnu, the Chakri kings positioned themselves as defenders of Buddhism.

1851–68
Reign of King Mongkut (Rama IV) and a period of Western influence.

1855
Bowring Treaty concluded between Siam and Britain stimulating the Thai economy and granting extraterritorial rights to British subjects in Siam.

1868–1910
Reign of King Chulalongkorn (Rama V) and increased European imperialism in neighbouring countries.

1874
Slavery is abolished.

They undertook compilations and Thai translations of essential Buddhist texts and constructed many royal temples.

In the meantime, a new social order and market economy was taking shape in the mid-19th century. Siam turned to the West for modern scientific and technological ideas and reforms in education, infrastructure and legal systems. One of the great modernisers, King Mongkut (Rama IV) never expected to be king. Before his ascension he had spent 27 years in a monastery, founding the Thammayut sect based on the strict disciplines of the Mon monks he had followed. During his monastic career, he became proficient in Pali, Sanskrit, Latin and English and studied Western sciences.

During his reign, Siam concluded treaties with Western powers that integrated the kingdom into the world market system, ceded royal monopolies and granted extraterritorial rights to British subjects.

Mongkut's son, King Chulalongkorn (Rama V) was to take much greater steps in replacing the old political order with the model of the nation-state. He abolished slavery and the corvée system (state labour), which had lingered on ineffectively since the Ayuthaya period. Chulalongkorn's reign oversaw the creation of a salaried bureaucracy, a police force and a standing army. His reforms brought uniformity to the legal code, law courts and revenue offices. Siam's agricultural output was improved by advances in irrigation techniques and increasing peasant populations. Schools were established along European lines. Universal conscription and poll taxes made all men the king's men.

In 'civilising' his country, Chulalongkorn relied greatly on foreign advisers, mostly British. Within the royal court, much of the centuries-old protocol was abandoned and replaced by Western forms. The architecture and visual art of state, like the new throne halls, were designed by Italian artists.

Like his father, Chula was regarded as a skilful diplomat and is credited with successfully playing European powers off one another to avoid colonisation. In exchange for independence, Thailand ceded territory to French Indochina (Laos in 1893, Cambodia in 1907) and British Burma (three Malayan states in 1909). In 1902, the former Pattani kingdom was ceded to the British, who were then in control of Malaysia, but control reverted to Thailand five years later. (The deep south region continues to consider itself an occupied land by the Thai central government.)

Siam was becoming a geographically defined country in a modern sense. By 1902, the country no longer called itself Siam but Prathet Thai (the country of the Thai) or Ratcha-anachak Thai (the kingdom of the Thai). By 1913, all those living within its borders were defined as 'Thai'.

In 1868 King Mongkut (Rama IV) abolished a husband's right to sell his wife or her children without her permission. The older provision, it was said, treated the woman 'as if she were a water buffalo'.

Chulalongkorn (Rama V) enjoys a cult-like devotion due in part to the endearing photographs of him in European dress, ordinary farmer garb or military pomp. He defied tradition by allowing himself to be seen in public by his subjects and to have his image widely disseminated.

Democracy vs Military

In 1932 a group of young military officers and bureaucrats calling themselves Khana Ratsadon (People's Party) mounted a successful, bloodless

1890

Siam's first railway connects Bangkok with Nakhon Ratchasima.

1893

French blockade the Chao Phraya River over disputed Indochina territory, intensify threat of colonisation.

DIANA MAYFIELD/LONELY PLANET IMAGES ©

» Wat Arun (p58) on the Chao Phraya River, Bangkok

coup that marked the end of absolute monarchy and introduced a constitutional monarchy. The leaders of the group were inspired by the democratic ideology they had encountered during their studies in Europe.

In the years after the coup, rival factions (royalists, military, civilians) struggled for the upper hand in the new power regime. Even the People's Party was not unified in its vision of a democratic Thailand, and before general elections were held the military wing of the party seized control of the government. The leader of the civilian wing of the People's Party, Pridi Phanomyong, a French-educated lawyer, was forced into exile in 1933 after introducing a socialist-leaning economic plan that angered the military generals. King Prajathipok (Rama VII) abdicated in 1935 and retired to Britain. Thailand's first general election was held in 1937 for half of the seats in the People's Assembly, the newly instated legislative body. General Phibul Songkhram, one of the leaders of the military faction of the People's Party, became prime minister, a position he held from 1938 to 1944 and again from 1948 to 1957.

PRATHET THAI

Phibul changed the name of the country in 1939 from 'Siam' to 'Prathet Thai' (or 'Thailand' in English); it was considered an overt nationalistic gesture intended to unite all the Tai-speaking people.

Phibul's regime coincided with WWII and was characterised by strong nationalistic tendencies centring on 'nation' and 'Thai-ness'. He collaborated with the Japanese and allowed them to use Thailand as a staging ground for its invasion of other Southeast Asian nations. By siding with the Japanese, the Phibul government was hoping to gain international leverage and reclaim historical territory lost during France's expansion of Indochina. Thailand intended to declare war on the US and Britain during WWII. But Seni Pramoj, the Thai ambassador in Washington and a member of Seri Thai (the Thai Liberation Movement), refused to deliver the formal declaration of war, thus saving Thailand from bearing the consequences of defeated-nation status. Phibul was forced to resign in 1944 and was tried for war crimes.

In an effort to suppress royalist sentiments, Ananda Mahidol, the nephew of the abdicated king, was crowned Rama VIII in 1935, though he was only 10 years old and spent much of his childhood studying abroad. After returning to Thailand, he was shot dead under mysterious circumstances in his bedroom in 1946. In the same year, his brother, His Majesty Bhumibol Adulyadej (pronounced *phuumíphon adunyádèt*) was appointed as the ninth king of the Chakri dynasty, going on to become the longest-reigning king in Thai history, as well as the world's longest-reigning, living monarch.

For a brief period after the war, democracy flourished: full elections for the people's assembly were held, and the 1946 Constitution sought to reduce the role of the military and provide more democratic rights. And it all lasted until the death of King Ananda, the pretext the military used to return to power with Phibul at the helm.

1902
Siam annexes Yala, Pattani and Narathiwat from the former sultanate of Pattani.

1909
Anglo–Siamese Treaty outlines Siam's boundaries.

1913
King Vajiravudh requires all citizens to adopt surnames.

1916
The first Thai university, Chulalongkorn University, is established.

Military Dictatorships

In 1957 Phibul's successor, General Sarit Thanarat, subjected the country to a military dictatorship: abolishing the constitution, dissolving the parliament and banning political parties. In the 1950s, the US directly involved itself in Southeast Asia to contain communist expansion in the region. During the Cold War, the US government gave economic and military support to the Sarit government and continued that relationship with subsequent military dictators, Thanom Kittikachorn and Praphat Charusathien, who ruled from 1964 to 1973. They negotiated a package of economic deals with the USA in exchange for allowing the development of US military bases in Thailand to support the Vietnam War.

By 1973, an opposition group of left-wing activists, mainly intellectuals and students, along with peasants, workers and portions of the middle class, organised political rallies demanding a constitution from the military government. On 14 October that year the military brutally suppressed a large demonstration in Bangkok, killing 77 people and wounding more than 800. The event is commemorated by a monument on Th Ratchadamnoen Klang in Bangkok, near the Democracy Monument. King Bhumibol stepped in and refused to support further bloodshed, forcing Thanom and Praphat to leave Thailand.

In the following years, the left-oriented student movement grew more radical, creating fears among working-class and middle-class Thais of home-grown communism. In 1976 Thanom returned to Thailand (ostensibly to become a monk) and was received warmly by the royal family. In response, protestors organised demonstrations at Thammasat University

Thailand has had 17 constitutions, all rewritten as a result of 18 (this number is debatable) coups. Each reincarnation seeks to allocate power within the branches of government with a bias for the ruling interest (military, royalist or civilian) and against their political foes.

LIBERAL COUNTERWEIGHT

Pridi Phanomyong (1900–83) was a French-educated lawyer and a civilian leader in the 1932 revolution and People's Party. His work on democratic reforms in Thailand was based on constitutional measures and attempts to restrict by law military involvement in Thai politics. He supported nationalisation of land and labour, state-led industrialisation and labour protection. In 1934, he founded Thammasat University. He also served as the figurehead of Seri Thai (the resistance movement against WWII Japanese occupation of Thailand) and was Thailand's prime minister (1946).

Though acknowledged as a senior statesman, Pridi Phanomyong was a controversial figure and a major foe of Phibul and the military regimes. He was accused of being a communist by his critics and forced out of the country under suspicion of regicide. Since the thawing of the Cold War, his legacy has been re-examined and recognised for its democratic efforts and the counterbalancing effects it had on military interests. He was named one of Unesco's great personalities of the 20th-century world in 2000.

1917
Siam sends troops to join the Allies in WWI.

1932
Bloodless coup ends absolute monarchy.

1939
The country's English name is officially changed from Siam to Thailand.

1941
Japanese forces enter Thailand during WWII.

against the perceived perpetrator of the 14 October massacre. Right-wing, anti-communist civilian groups clashed with the students, resulting in bloody violence. In the aftermath, many students and intellectuals were forced underground, and joined armed communist insurgents – known as the People's Liberation Army of Thailand (PLAT) – based in the jungles of northern and southern Thailand.

Prem Tinsulanonda serves as lifelong head of the Privy Council of King Bhumibol and is believed to have been the architect of the 2006 coup.

Military control of the country continued through the 1980s. The government of the 'political soldier', General Prem Tinsulanonda, enjoyed a period of political and economic stability. Prem dismantled the communist insurgency through military action and amnesty programs. But the country's new economic success presented a challenging rival: prominent business leaders who criticised the military's role in government and their now-dated Cold War mentality. Communists, they maintained, should be business partners, not enemies.

It's Just Business

In 1988, Prem was replaced in fair elections by Chatichai Choonhavan, leader of the Chat Thai Party, who created a government dominated by well-connected provincial business people. His government shifted power away from the bureaucrats and set about transforming Thailand into an 'Asian Tiger' economy. But the business of politics was often bought and sold like a commodity and Chatichai was overthrown by the military on grounds of extreme corruption. This coup demarcated an emerging trend in Thai politics: the Bangkok business community and educated classes siding with the military against Chatichai, his provincial business-politicians and their money politics approach to governance.

Without the job of being absolute, King Bhumibol had to find new work so he started the Royal Project Foundation in 1969 to help struggling farmers. The foundation's most lauded effort was eradication of opium cultivation among the northern hill tribes.

In 1992, after reinstating elections, an unelected military leader inserted himself as prime minister. This was met with popular resistance and the ensuing civilian–military clash was dubbed 'Black May'. Led by former Bangkok mayor, Chamlong Srimuang, around 200,000 protestors (called the 'mobile phone mob', representing their rising urban affluence) launched a mass demonstration in Bangkok that resulted in three nights of violence with armed soldiers. On the night of 20 May, King Bhumibol called an end to the violence.

After Black May, a new wave of democracy activists advocated for constitutional reforms. For most of the 1990s, the parliament was dominated by the Democrat Party, which represented the urban middle class and business interests. Its major base of support came from the southern Thai population centres. Formerly port towns, these were now dominated by tourism and exports (rubber, tin and fishing). On the other side of the spectrum were the former pro-military politicians based in the central plains and the people of the agrarian northeast in new provincial

1945
WWII ends; Thailand cedes seized territory from Laos, Cambodia and Malaysia.

1946
King Bhumibol Adulyadej (Rama IX) ascends the throne; Thailand joins the UN.

1957
Sarit Thanarat leads a coup that introduces military rule, which lasts until 1973

1959
The first tourism authority created.

towns who focused on state-budget distribution to their provinces. These political lines exist today.

In 1997, the boom years went bust and the Asian economic crisis unfolded. The country's economy was plagued by foreign-debt burdens, an overextension in the real-estate sector and a devalued currency. Within months of the crisis, the Thai currency plunged from 25B to 56B per US$1. The International Monetary Fund (IMF) stepped in to impose financial and legal reforms and economic liberalisation programs in exchange for more than US$17 billion to stabilise the Thai currency.

In the aftermath of the crisis, the Democrats returned to power uncontested, but were viewed as ineffective as the economy worsened.

Thaksinocracy

In 2000, the economic slump began to ease and business interests eclipsed the military as the dominant political force in Thai politics. The telecommunications billionaire and former police officer, Thaksin Shinawatra, through his Thai Rak Thai (TRT or 'Thai Loving Thai') party, capitalised on the rising nationalism and won a majority in the elections of 2001. Self-styled as a CEO-politician, Thaksin swiftly delivered on his campaign promises for rural development, including agrarian debt relief, village capital funds and cheap health care.

Thanks to the 1997 constitutional reforms designed to strengthen the prime minister's position, his was one of Thai history's most stable elected governments. The surging economy and his bold, if strong-arm, leadership won an outright majority in 2005, effectively introducing one-party rule. His popularity among the working class and rural voters was immense.

In 2006 Thaksin was accused of abusing his powers and of conflicts of interest, most notably in his family's sale of their Shin Corporation to the Singaporean government for 73 billion baht (US$1.88 billion), a tax-free gain thanks to telecommunications legislation that he had helped craft. Demonstrations in Bangkok called for his ousting and on 19 September 2006, the military staged a bloodless coup that forced Thaksin into exile. The TRT Party was dissolved by court order and party executives were barred from politics for five years. As promised, the interim government held general elections in December, returning the country to civilian rule, but the outcome was unsatisfactory to the military and the Bangkok upper and middle classes when Thaksin's political allies won a majority and formed a government led by Samak Sundaravej.

Demonstrations against the Thaksin-aligned government were led by Chamlong Srimuang (Black May activist and former Bangkok governor) and Sondhi Limthongkul (a long-time business and political rival of Thaksin). Their group, the People's Alliance for Democracy (PAD), earned the nickname 'Yellow Shirts' because they wore yellow (the king's

Thaksin was the first prime minister in Thai history to complete a four-year term of office.

THAKSIN

1965
Thailand hosts US military bases during the Vietnam War.

1968
Thailand is a founding member of the Association of Southeast Asian Nations (ASEAN).

1973
Thai students, workers and farmers demonstrate for the reinstallation of a democratic government.

1976
Violent suppression of student movement by the military.

birthday colour) to express their royalist allegiancеs; it was believed that Thaksin was so successfully consolidating power during his tenure that he had designs on the throne or at least interrupting royal succession.

In September 2008, Samak Sundaravej was unseated by the Constitutional Court on a technicality: while in office, he hosted a TV cooking show that the court found to be a conflict of interest. Still not politically satisfied, the Yellow Shirts seized control of Thailand's main airports, Suvarnabhumi and Don Muang, for a week in November 2008 until the military manoeuvred a silent coup and another favourable court ruling that further weakened Thaksin's political proxies. Through last-minute coalition building, Democrat Abhisit Vejjajiva was elected in a parliamentary vote, becoming Thailand's 27th prime minister.

Thaksin supporters organised their own counter-movement as the United Front for Democracy Against Dictatorship, better known as the 'Red Shirts'. Supporters hail mostly from the north and northeast, and include anti-coup, pro-democracy activists as well as die-hard Thaksin fans. There is a degree of class struggle, with some Red Shirts expressing bombastic animosity towards the aristocrats. The Red Shirts' most provocative demonstration came in 2010 after Thailand's Supreme Court ordered the seizure of US$46 billion of Thaksin's assets after finding him guilty of abusing his powers as prime minister. Red Shirts occupied Bangkok's central shopping district for two months and demanded the dissolution of the government and reinstatement of elections. Protest leaders and the government were unable to reach a compromise and in May 2010 the military used forced to evict the protestors, resulting in bloody clashes (91 people were killed) and a smouldering central city (crackdown-related arson caused damage estimated at US$15 billion).

In 2011, general elections were held and Thaksin's politically allied Puea Thai party won a parliamentary majority.

Troubles in the Deep South

Starting in 2001, Muslim separatist insurgents have been waging a low-scale war against the central government in Thailand's southernmost provinces of Pattani, Narathiwat and Yala. These three provinces once comprised the area of the historic kingdom of Patani until it was conquered by the Chakri kings. Under King Chulalongkorn, the traditional ruling elite were replaced with central government officials and bureaucrats from Bangkok. During WWII, a policy of nation-building set out to transform the multi-ethnic society into a unified and homogenous Thai Buddhist nation. This policy was resisted in the deep south and gave birth to a strong separatist movement fighting for the independence of Patani. In the 1980s and '90s, the assimilation policy was abandoned and then-

1979
After three years of military rule, elections and parliament restored.

1980
Prem Tinsulanonda's government works to undermine the communist insugency movement and eventually ends it with a political solution.

1988
Chatichai Choonhavan becomes first elected PM since 1976; trade opens with Indochina.

1991-2
General Suchinda attempts to seize power; King Bhumibol intervenes to halt civil turmoil surrounding 'Black May' protests.

prime minister Prem promised support for Muslim cultural rights and religious freedoms. He also offered amnesty to the armed insurgents and implemented an economic development plan for the historically impoverished region.

The Thaksin regime took another approach to the region, which still ranks among the most economically and educationally depressed in the country. Greater central control was exerted and was viewed as a thinly disguised policy to break up the traditional stronghold of the Democrat Party. The policy succeeded in weakening relations between the local elite, southern voters and the Democrats who had served as their representative in parliament. However, it did not take into consideration the sensitive and tenacious Muslim culture of the deep south. In 2002, the government dissolved the long-standing inspectorate and the army-run joint civilian-police–military border security office – a unit often lauded for maintaining peace and stability and providing a communication link between the Thai government and the southern Muslims. In its place the Thai provincial police assumed control of security, though they lacked perceived moral authority and support of the local population. In 2004, the government responded harshly to demonstrations that resulted in the Krue Se Mosque and Tak Bai incidents, which together cost the lives of at least 180 Muslims, many of them unarmed civilians. In 2005, martial law was declared in the area.

It was widely believed that the 2006 coup, led a by a Thai-Muslim general, could potentially settle the violence in the south but that has not come to pass. Bombings and shootings continue and the region has become a no-go zone.

TROUBLE IN THE TEMPLE FRONTIER

In 2008 Cambodia successfully petitioned Unesco to list the ancient Khmer temple of Phra Wihan ('Preah Vihear' in Cambodian) as an official World Heritage Site. Remote and seemingly insignificant, the temple has long been a contentious issue between Cambodia and Thailand. A 1969 International Court of Justice case awarded Cambodia ownership of the temple, but both countries lay claim to a 4.6 sq-km area surrounding it. Four years since the Unesco decision, troops have been deployed to the border and periodically exchange fire. Running up to the general election of 2011, border tensions increased partly due to competing political interests in both countries. Cambodian leader Hun Sen is viewed as a Thaksin ally and was accused of using the dispute to make the Abhiset government look weak. Meanwhile anti-Thaksin groups in Thailand were accused of exploiting the issue as a nationalistic wedge to discredit pro-Thaksin sentiments. The struggle seems to have fizzled with the Puea Thai electoral win and a 2011 Thai–Cambodian border committee meeting resulted in an official statement of future cooperation.

JACQUES LANGEVIN/SYGMA/CORBIS ©

» Bangkok after the 1992 riots

1997
Asian economic crisis; passage of historic 'people's constitution'.

2001
Thaksin Shinawatra is elected prime minister.

Politics

Government

The Democrat Party (Phak Prachathipat), founded in 1946, is now the longest-surviving political party in Thailand.

Much of the political drama that has unfolded since the 2006 coup involves a long-standing debate about how to structure Thailand's legislative body and, ultimately, who gets greater control. The National Assembly (or parliament of Thailand) currently has 630 members divided into two chambers (House of Representatives and the Senate) with a mix of seats being popularly elected and elected by party vote. The ratio of seats being popularly elected changes with each replacement constitution. The 1997 constitution, dubbed the People's Constitution, called for both chambers to be fully elected by popular vote. This power to the people paved the way for Thaksin and his well-loved Thai Rak Thai party to gain nearly complete control. The military and the elites have since rescinded such a popular structure, often arguing that full democratic representation doesn't work in Thailand.

When Thai voters go to the polls they cast a ballot for the constituency MP (member of parliament) and for their preferred party, the results of which are used to determine individual winners and proportional representation outcomes for the positions assigned by party vote.

The prime minister is the head of the government and is elected via legislative vote by the majority party. Under the most recent constitution, the prime minister must be a sitting MP, though this has not always been the case.

Voting in Thailand is compulsory for all eligible citizens (over the age of 18) but members of the clergy are not allowed to vote. Voter turnout for national elections has steadily increased since the new millen-

SIGNS OF ELECTION

Preceding an election, Thai candidates paper the roadways and electricity poles with political billboards and signs. Traditional posters show the candidate posing seriously in an official uniform but recent trends include ad-like approaches with catchy slogans and evocative imagery.

Always a trendsetter, Chuvit Kamolvisit, former brothel owner turned political whistle-blower, won over voters with his 2011 'Angry Man' campaign ads, featuring him in grimacing and glaring poses expressing frustration and anger with the government. (Incidentally, one of his first acts in office was to expose an illegal Bangkok casino run by high-ranking police.)

Residents complain about the signs' obstruction of traffic but signmakers like the boost in business. All candidate posters are vulnerable to vandalism or theft, but the plastic ones are particularly desired as a makeshift sunshade or roof patch.

2004

Indian Ocean tsunami kills 5000 people and damages tourism and fishing industries; Muslim insurgency reignites in the deep south.

2006

King Bhumibol celebrates 60th year on the throne; Thaksin government overthrown in a coup and prime minister forced into exile.

» King Bhumibol's 60th anniversary celebrations

nium with 78% of registered voters casting ballots in 2007. Charges of vote-buying typically accompany every election. Anecdotally, local party leaders make their rounds through the villages handing out money for the promise of a vote. In some cases, villagers will accept money from competing parties and report that they have no loyalty at the ballot box.

The ballots include a 'no' vote if the voter wishes to choose 'none of the above'. It is also common to 'spoil' the ballot, or disqualify it, by writing on it or defacing it. During the 2005 general election a large number of ineligible ballots contained anti-Thaksin messages.

Media

Southeast Asian governments are not usually fond of uncensored media, but Thailand often bucked this trend during the 1990s, even ensuring press freedoms in its 1997 constitution, albeit with fairly broad loopholes. This ended with the ascension of Thaksin Shinawatra, a telecommunications billionaire, at the beginning of the 21st century. With Thaksin as prime minister and his party holding a controlling majority, the press encountered the kind of censorship and legal intimidation not seen since the 1970s era of military dictatorships. The government filed a litany of defamation lawsuits against individuals, publications and media groups who printed embarrassing revelations about the Thaksin regime.

After the 2006 ousting of Thaksin, the media managed to retain its guarantees of press freedoms in the new constitution, but this was a 'paper promise' that did little to rescue the press from intimidation, lawsuits and physical attacks. Sweeping powers to ensure national security, often invoked against the press, were added to the emergency powers laws that went into effect after the coup.

Press intimidation in Thailand is made easier because of the country's lèse majesté laws – causing offence against the dignity of the monarchy – which carries a jail term of between three and 15 years. Often the media exercises self-censorship with regard to the monarchy, mainly out of respect for the crown, but also out of fear that political enemies will file lèse majesté charges.

Filing of lèse majesté charges has increased since 2006, mainly against political rivals, but also against journalists and even average citizens. Charges have been filed against a Thai Facebook user who posted a negative comment about the king and an overseas Thai who posted translations of a banned book about the king on his blog.

Publications that the government views as presenting an unflattering view of the monarchy are often banned. Several critical issues of *The Economist* have been banned since 2006. Internet censorship is also on the rise and so-called Red Shirt (pro-Thaksin) radio stations based in the northeast have been shut down by the government.

LÈSE MAJESTÉ

Somsak Jiamteerasaku, a university professor long critical of the lèse majesté laws, was arrested after delivering a speech proposing reform measures to the institution of the monarchy. The Thai academic community was surprised that such a politically motivated tool would be applied to previously off-limits intellectuals.

2008
Cambodia successfully petitions Unesco to list Phra Wihan as a World Heritage Site, reigniting border tensions with Thailand.

2008
Yellow Shirt, pro-royalist activists seize Bangkok's international airports, causing weeklong shut-down.

2010
Red Shirt, pro-Thaksin activists occupy central Bangkok for two months; military crackdown results in 91 deaths.

2011
Puea Thai party wins general election; Yingluck Shinawatra becomes Thailand's first female prime minister.

People & Society

Thailand's cohesive national identity provides a unifying patina for ethnic and regional differences that evolved through historical migrations and geographic kinships with ethnically diverse neighbours.

Thailand Demographics

- Population: 66.7 million
- Fertility rate: 1.6
- Percentage of people over 65: 9.2%
- Urbanisation rate: 34%
- Life expectancy: 73 years

Ethnic Makeup

Some 75% of the citizens of Thailand are ethnic Thais, providing a superficial appearance of sameness. But subtle regional differences do exist. In the central plains (Chao Phraya delta), Siamese Thais united the country through historic kingdoms and promulgated its culture and language. Today the central Thai dialect is the national standard and the capital of Bangkok exports unified culture through popular media and standardised education.

The northeast (Isan) has always stood apart from the rest of the country, sharing closer ethnic and cultural ties with Laos and the Thai Lao people. The Isan dialect differs from central Thai, folk beliefs vary and even the local ingredients in *sôm·đam* (spicy papaya salad) mark a cultural shift: *sôm·đam* Lao contains field crabs, while standard *sôm·đam* contains peanuts. In the northeastern provinces that border Cambodia, there is a distinct Khmer influence, as many families migrated across the border during historical tumult. A minority tribe, known as Suay, lives near Surin and Khorat (Nakhon Ratchasima). Suay people are traditional elephant mahouts; with the expansion of the elephant-tourism business many Suay people have relocated across the country for job opportunities.

Thai Pak Tai people define the characteristics of the south. The dialect is a little faster than standard Thai, the curries are a lot spicier, and there is more mixing of Muslim folk beliefs into the regional culture

THE INVISIBLE BURMESE

Due to the ongoing dysfunction of the Myanmar state, there is an increasing exodus of Burmese to Thailand. Approximately 150,000 people have entered the kingdom as political and ethnic refugees but the vast majority are economic migrants (estimated at two to three million, of which less than half are documented). They fill the low-level jobs – fish-processing, construction, and domestic and factory work – that used to employ unskilled northeastern Thai labourers. Many Thais believe that the country needs this imported workforce as the population is ageing faster than it is reproducing.

However, the emerging immigration 'situation' has not been dealt with as swiftly by the government as the private sector. Because many of the Burmese immigrants are residing and working in the country illegally, they are subjected to exploitative relationships with employers that many activists describe as modern-day slavery. The Burmese can't return home due to persecution by the military regime and they can't turn to the Thai authorities in cases of workplace abuse because they would face deportation.

SAVING FACE

Thais believe strongly in the concept of saving face, ie avoiding confrontation and endeavouring not to embarrass themselves or other people (except when it's *sà·nùk* – or 'fun' – to do so). The ideal face-saver doesn't bring up negative topics in conversation, doesn't express firm convictions or opinions, and doesn't claim to have an expertise. Agreement and harmony are considered to be the most important social graces.

While Westerners might find a heated discussion to be good sport, Thais avoid such confrontations and regard any instance where voices are raised as rude and potentially volatile. Losing your temper causes a loss of face for everyone present, and Thais who have been crossed often react in extreme ways.

Minor embarrassments, such as tripping or falling, might elicit giggles from a crowd of Thais. In this case they aren't taking delight in your mishap, but helping you save face by laughing it off.

thanks to the geographic proximity to Malaysia and the historic Muslim population.

If you were to redraw Thailand's borders according to ethnicity and culture, northern Thailand would be united with parts of southern China and northern Myanmar. The traditional homeland of the Tai people was believed to be the Yunnan region of China. There are also many subgroups, including the Shan (an ethnic cousin to the Thais who settled in the highlands of Burma) and the Tai Lü (who settled in Nan and Chiang Rai Province as well as the Vietnam highlands).

People of Chinese ancestry – second- or third-generation Hakka, Teochew, Hainanese or Cantonese – make up 14% of the population. Bangkok and the nearby coastal areas have a large population of immigrants from China who came for economic opportunities in the early to mid-20th century. In northern Thailand there is also a substantial number of Hui-Chinese Muslims who emigrated from Yunnan in the late 19th century.

China and Thailand have long been linked through trade, migration and cultural commonalities. Many families have intermarried with Thais and have interwoven traditional Chinese customs into the predominant Thai culture. Historically, wealthy Chinese introduced their daughters to the royal court as consorts, developing royal connections and adding a Chinese bloodline that extends to the current king. The mercantile centres of most Thai towns are run by Thai-Chinese families and many places in the country celebrate Chinese festivals such as the annual Vegetarian Festival.

The second-largest ethnic minority are the Malays (4.6%), most of whom reside in the provinces of the deep south. The remaining minority groups include smaller percentages of non-Thai-speaking people such as the Vietnamese, Khmer, Mon, Semang (Sakai), Moken (*chow lair,* also spelt *chao leh;* people of the sea, or 'sea gypsies'), Htin, Mabri, Khamu and a variety of hill tribes. A small number of Europeans and other non-Asians reside in Bangkok and the provinces.

Regional Identity

Religion, royalty and tradition are the defining characteristics of Thai society. That Thailand is the only country in Southeast Asia never colonised by a foreign power has led to a profound sense of pride in these elements. However, the country is not homogenous, and in the south a strong cultural identity prevails that is more in tune with the Islamic culture of nearby Malaysia.

THE NICKNAME GAME

At birth Thai babies are given auspicious first names, often bestowed by the family patriarch or matriarch. These poetic names are then relegated to bureaucratic forms and name cards, while the child is introduced to everyone else by a one-syllable nickname. Thai nicknames are usually playful and can be inspired by the child's appearance (Moo, meaning 'pig', if he/she is chubby) or a favourite pastime (Toon, short for 'cartoon' for avid TV-watchers). Girls will typically be named Lek or Noi (both of which mean 'small'). Some parents even go so far as imprinting their interests on their children's names: Golf (as in the sport) and Benz (as in the car).

Before modern political boundaries divided the Malay peninsula into two countries, the city states, sultanates and villages were part of an Indonesian-based Srivijaya empire – with intermingled customs and language – all vying for local control over shipping routes. Many southern Thai towns and geographic names bear the hallmark of the Bahasa language, and some village traditions would be instantly recognised by a Sumatran but not by a northern Thai. Chinese culture is also prominent in southern Thailand, as seen in the numerous temples and clan houses, and it is this intermingling of domestic and 'foreign' culture that defines the south.

Lifestyle

The ordinary life of a southern Thai can be divided into two categories: country and city.

Those in rural areas are typically employed in rubber farming or fishing, though rice and livestock farming are also evident. Rubber farmers live in small, typically inland settlements identified by straight rows of trees and pale sheets of drying latex. Traditional Muslim villages are built directly over the water in a series of connected stilt houses. Because the Andaman Sea had a history of tranquil behaviour, there was no fear of the ocean's wrath, a preconception painfully destroyed by the 2004 tsunami.

Within the cities, life looks a lot like the rest of the country (busy and modern), but the presence of Chinese and Indian merchants marks the uniqueness of southern Thai cities. The commercial centres are also the market towns, where the brightly coloured fishing boats ease into the harbour, unloading the catch and filling the marina with the aroma of fish.

GREETINGS

Instead of a handshake, the traditional Thai greeting is the *wâi* – a prayerlike gesture with the palms placed together.

Family Values

The importance of the family unit in Thai society is immediately apparent to a visitor in the many family-owned and -operated businesses. It is still common to see three generations employed in a family-run guesthouse, or sharing the same house. The elderly are involved in day-to-day life, selling sweets to neighbourhood kids, renting motorcycles to tourists and many other ways. Although tourism has significantly altered the islanders' traditional way of life, the presence of jobs helps to keep many ambitious children from seeking employment on the mainland.

Even the Thai pronouns reflect a strong sense of family. Thais will refer to people in their own generation as an older *(pêe)* or younger *(nórng)* sibling, regardless of bloodline. Sometimes Thais will translate this tribal custom into English, referring to nonfamily members as 'sister' or 'brother', inadvertently amazing foreigners with the vastness of Thai families.

Economy

Due to tourism, fishing, prawn farming and rubber, the south is Thailand's wealthiest region. Most rubber tappers are born into it, inheriting the profession of their fathers and mothers. Prawn and fish farming, on the other hand, are relatively new industries, introduced as an economic development program for rural communities losing ground to commercial fishing operations. The venture proved profitable and Thailand is one of the leading exporters of farm-raised prawn. However, fish farms have been largely unregulated until recently, leading to a host of environmental problems, such as water pollution and the destruction of mangrove forests.

Tourism has undoubtedly had the most tangible impact on the economy of the area, transforming many small villages into bilingual enterprises. Women who would otherwise sell products at market have studied Thai traditional massage, and walk up and down the beach beseeching customers. Other do-it-yourself franchises, so prolific in Thai communities, have been tailored to tourists: shops along beach thoroughfares sell sunscreen and postcards instead of rice whisky and grilled fish, itinerant vendors hawk sarongs and henna tattoos instead of feather dusters and straw brooms, while fishermen sometimes abandon their nets for bigger catches – tourists on snorkelling trips.

Across Thailand, the size of the middle class is growing with successive decades, bridging the gap between rich and poor. Thailand doesn't suffer from poverty of sustenance; even the most destitute Thai citizens can have shelter and food. Rather, the lower rung of Thai society suffers from poverty of material: money isn't available for extensive education, material goods or health care. This is most obvious from an economic perspective: the average Thai income stands at around US$2000 a year, but many in rural provinces earn as little as US$570 a year.

Lifestyle Statistics

» Average age of marriage for a Thai man/woman: 27/24 years

» Minimum daily wage in Bangkok: 206B

» Entry-level government salary: 9000B per month

Religion

Buddhism

Approximately 95% of Thais follow Theravada Buddhism, also known as Hinayana or 'Lesser Vehicle' Buddhism to distinguish it from the Mahayana or 'Great Vehicle' school of Buddhism. The primary difference between the faiths is that Theravada Buddhists believe individuals are

CHOW LAIR

Southern Thailand is home to one of Thailand's smallest ethnic groups, the *chow lair*, literally, 'people of the sea'. Also known as Moken *(mor·gaan)*, or sea gypsies, the *chow lair* are an ethnic group of Malay origin who can be found along coasts as far north as Myanmar and as far south as Borneo. The remaining traditional bands of *chow lair* are hunter-gatherers who are recognised as one of the few groups of humans that live primarily at sea, although in recent years many have turned to shanty-like settlements on various islands. Perhaps as a result of generations of this marine lifestyle, many *chow lair* can hold their breath for long periods of time and also have an uncanny ability to see underwater. Life at sea has also helped them in other ways; during the 2004 tsunami, virtually no *chow lair* were killed, as folk tales handed down from generation to generation alerted them to the dangers of the quickly receding tide, and they were able to escape to higher ground.

The *chow lair* were mostly ignored until recently when their islands became valuable for tourism. Entrepreneurs bought up large tracts of beachfront land and the *chow lair* moved on to smaller, less valuable islands. With these pressures, it was perhaps inevitable that the *chow lair* culture would slowly disappear. Many sea gypsies now make a living ferrying tourists around the islands or harvesting fish for seafood buffets at tourist resorts. One vestige of traditional *chow lair* life you may see is the biannual 'boat floating' ceremony in May and November, in which an elaborate model boat is set adrift, carrying away bad luck.

responsible for their own enlightenment, while Mahayana Buddhists believe society can work together to achieve enlightenment for all.

The ultimate end of all forms of Buddhism is to reach *nibbana* (from Sanskrit, nirvana), which literally means the 'blowing out' or extinction of all desire and thus of all *dukkha* (suffering). Having achieved *nibbana,* an individual is freed from the cycle of rebirths and enters the spiritual plane. In reality, most Thai Buddhists aim for rebirth in a 'better' existence in the next life, rather than striving to attain *nibbana*. To work towards this goal, Buddhists carry out meritorious actions *(tam bun)* such as feeding monks, giving donations to temples and performing regular worship at the local wát (temple). The Buddhist theory of karma is well expressed in the Thai proverb *tam dee, dâi dee; tam chôo·a, dâi chôo·a* (do good and receive good; do evil and receive evil).

There is no specific day of worship in Thai Buddhism; instead the faithful go to temple on certain religious holidays, when it is convenient or to commemorate a special family event. Most temple visits occur on *wan prá* (excellent days), which occur every full and new moon. Other activities include offering food to the temple *sangha* (community of monks, nuns and lay residents), meditating, listening to monks chanting *suttas* (discourses of the Buddha) and attending talks on *dhamma* (right behaviour).

Monks & Nuns

There are about 32,000 monasteries in Thailand and 200,000 monks, many of them ordained for life. Traditionally, every Thai male is expected to spend time as a monk, usually between finishing school and marrying or starting a career. Even His Majesty King Bhumibol served as a novice at Wat Bowonniwet in Banglamphu, Bangkok. Traditionally boys would devote a year or more to monastic life, but these days most people enter the *sangha* for two weeks to three months during *pan·săh* (Buddhist Lent), which coincides with the rainy season.

Women can become *mâa chee* (eight-precept nuns) but this is held in slightly lower regard than the status of male monks, as most Thais believe that a woman can only achieve *nibbana* if she is reincarnated as a man. Both monks and nuns shave their heads and wear robes (orange for men, white for women), give up most of their personal belongings and live on charity. Thais donate generously to the local wát, so monks often live quite comfortable lives.

An increasing number of foreigners are coming to Thailand to be ordained as Buddhist monks or nuns. If you want to find out more, visit the website **Buddha Net** (www.buddhanet.net).

As long as you dress appropriately and observe the correct etiquette (p356) you will be welcome at most monasteries. However, take care not to disturb monks while they are eating or meditating – nothing breaks the concentration quite like tourists snapping photographs!

Islam

Thailand is home to 1.6 million Muslims (just over 4% of Thailand's population), concentrated in the south of the country. Most Thai Muslims are of Malay origin and generally follow a moderate version of the Sunni sect mixed with pre-Islamic animism.

A decade-long revival movement has cultivated stricter Islamic practices and suspicions of outside influences. Under this more strenuous interpretation of Islam, many folk practices have been squeezed out of daily devotions and local people see the mainly Buddhist government and education system as intolerant of their way of life. Schools and infrastructure in the Muslim-majority south are typically underfunded, and frustration with the Bangkok government is sometimes defined as a religious rather than political struggle.

There are mosques throughout southern Thailand but few are architecturally interesting and most are closed to women. If you do visit a mosque, remember to cover your head and remove your shoes.

Other Religions

Half a percent of the population – primarily hill tribes converted by missionaries and Vietnamese immigrants – is Christian, while half a percent is made up of Confucians, Taoists, Mahayana Buddhists and Hindus. Chinese temples and joss houses are a common sight in the south and in Bangkok's Chinatown, and Bangkok is also home to a large, colourful Hindu temple.

Arts

Much of Thailand's creative energy has traditionally gone into the production of religious and ceremonial art. Painting, sculpture, music and theatre still play a huge role in the ceremonial life of Thais and religious art is very much a living art form.

Literature

The most pervasive and influential work of classical Thai literature is the Ramakian, based on the Hindu holy book, the Ramayana, which was brought to Southeast Asia by Indian traders and introduced to Thailand by the Khmer about 900 years ago. Although the main theme remains the same, the Thais embroidered the Ramayana by providing much more biographical detail on arch-villain Ravana (*Thótsàkan* in the Ramakian) and his wife Montho. The monkey-god, Hanuman, is also transformed into something of a playboy.

The epic poem *Phra Aphaimani* was composed by poet Sunthorn Phu (1786–1855) and is set on the island of Ko Samet. *Phra Aphaimani* is Thailand's most famous classical literary work, and tells a typically epic story of an exiled prince.

Modern Thai literature is usually written in Thai, so it isn't very accessible to non-Thais. Modern authors you may find translated include Seni Saowaphong, whose most famous title *Pisat, Evil Spirits* deals with conflicts between the old and new generations. Former prime minister Kukrit Pramoj is another respected author – his collection of short stories, *Lai Chiwit* (Many Lives), and the novel *Si Phandin (*Four Reigns*),* which is set in the era of Rama V, have been translated into English.

Celebrated contemporary writer Pira Sudham was born into a poor family in northeastern Thailand. *Monsoon Country,* one of several titles Sudham wrote in English, brilliantly captures the region's struggles against nature and nurture.

Chart Korbjitti is a two-time winner of the Southeast Asian Writers Award (SEA Write): in 1982 for *The Judgement,* a drama about a young village man wrongly accused of a crime; and in 1994 for a 'mixed-media' novel, *Time.*

SP Somtow has been described as 'Thailand's JD Salinger'. *Jasmine Nights,* Somtow's upbeat coming-of-age novel, fuses traditional ideas with modern Thai pop culture. *Jasmine Nights* won acclaim throughout the world.

Writer Sri Daoruang adapted the Ramayana into modern Bangkok in *Married to the Demon King.* Short stories by modern Thai women writers appear in the collection *A Lioness in Bloom,* translated by Susan Kepner.

The leading postmodern writer is Prabda Yoon, whose short-story collection *Probability* won the 2002 SEA Write award. Although his works have yet to be translated, he wrote the screenplay for *Last Life in the*

Recommended Fiction

- *The Lioness in Bloom: Modern Thai Fiction about Women* (translated by Susan Fulop Kepner)
- *Four Reigns* (Kukrit Pramoj)
- *Bangkok 8* (John Burdett)
- *Fieldwork: A Novel* (Mischa Berlinski)

Universe and other Pen-ek Ratanaruang-directed films, and in 2004 was commissioned by Thailand's Ministry of Culture to write a piece on the 2004 tsunami. The result, *Where We Feel: A Tsunami Memoir by an Outsider,* was distributed free along the Andaman coast.

Another name worth looking out for is Siriworn Kaewkan, whose novels *The Murder Case of Tok Imam Storpa Karde* and *A Scattered World* have recently been translated into English by Frenchman Marcel Barang. In fact Barang, who is also working on an updated translation of *Si Phandin (*Four Reigns*),* is currently the preeminent translator of Thai fiction into English, and several of his translations, including stories by Chart Korbjitti and two-time SEA Write winner Win Lyovarin can be downloaded as e-books at www.thaifiction.com.

Cinema

Thailand has a lively homespun movie industry, producing some very competent films in various genres. The most expensive film ever made in the country, not to mention the highest grossing, was director Prince Chatrichalerm Yukol's epic *Legend of Suriyothai* (2003), which tells the story of a 16th-century warrior princess. But what has propelled Thai viewers to forsake Hollywood imports are generally action flicks such as *Ong Bak: Thai Warrior* and the follow-up *Tom Yum Goong,* directed by Prachya Pinkaew.

Thailand has cropped up in various foreign film festivals over the years, with several critically acclaimed art-house movies. Pen-Ek Ratanaruang's clever and haunting movies, such as *Last Life in the Universe* and *6ixty9ine,* have created a buzz on the film-festival circuit. Apichatpong Weerasethakul leads the avant-garde pack with his Cannes-awarded *Tropical Malady* and *Blissfully Yours.*

LANGUAGE

There is no universally accepted method of transliterating from Thai to English, so some words and place names are spelled a variety of ways.

The Thai government is now actively touting Thailand as a location for foreign film-makers. The most famous film to be made here in recent years was *The Beach* (2000). Based on the Alex Garland novel, it was filmed at Maya Bay on Ko Phi-Phi, Phuket, and several jungle locations near Krabi and Khao Yai National Park. The film caused controversy for allegedly damaging the environment in Maya Bay, which was also a location for the 1995 pirate stinker *Cutthroat Island.* Other famous films made here include the James Bond romp *The Man with the Golden Gun* (1974), which was filmed in Ao Nang Bay, *Good Morning Vietnam* (1987), *The Killing Fields* (1984), *The Deer Hunter* (1978) and *The Hangover II* (2011).

Music

Traditional Thai music may sound a little strange to visitors, as the eight-note Thai octave is broken in different places to the European octave. Thai scales were first transcribed by Thai-German composer Phra Chen Duriyanga (Peter Feit), who also composed Thailand's national anthem in 1932.

The classical Thai orchestra is called the *Ƀèe·pâht* and can include anything from five to 20 musicians. The most popular stringed instrument is the *ja·kêh,* a slender guitar-like instrument played horizontally on the ground, which probably evolved from the Indian *vina.* Woodwind instruments include the *khlùi,* a simple wooden flute, and the *Ƀèe,* a recorder-like instrument with a reed mouthpiece, based on the Indian *shennai.* You'll hear the *Ƀèe* being played if you go to a Thai boxing match. Other popular instruments include the *saw,* a three-stringed fretless instrument, similar to the Japanese *shamisen,* and the *rá·nâht èhk,* a bamboo-keyed xylophone played with wooden hammers.

Perhaps the most familiar Thai instrument is the *kĭm* or hammer dulcimer, responsible for the plinking, plunking music you'll hear in Thai

STOPPING CHILD-SEX TOURISM IN THAILAND

Sadly, Thailand has become a destination for a significant number of foreigners seeking to sexually exploit local children. A range of socioeconomic factors renders many children vulnerable to such abuse, and some depraved individuals seem intent to prey upon this vulnerability.

The sexual abuse and exploitation of children has serious, lifelong and even life-threatening consequences. Child-sex tourism is a crime and a violation of the rights of a child. Strong laws exist in Thailand to prosecute offenders. Many countries also have extraterritorial legislation that allows nationals to be prosecuted in their own country for such crimes.

Responsible travellers can help to stop the scourge of child-sex tourism by reporting suspicious behaviour. Don't ignore it! Your actions may be critical in helping to protect children from future abuse and exploitation.

In Thailand, travellers can report on a dedicated hotline number: ☎1300. If you know the nationality of the individual, you can report to the relevant embassy.

ECPAT (End Child Prostitution & Trafficking; ☎in Bangkok 0 2215 3388; www.ecpat.net) is a global network focusing on these issues with more than 70 affiliate organisations around the world. Its head office is located in Bangkok. ECPAT is actively working to combat child-sex tourism in Thailand and around the world.

Child Wise (www.childwise.net) is the Australian member of ECPAT. Child Wise has been involved in providing training to the tourism industry in Thailand to counter child-sex tourism.

restaurants across the world. The dulcimer resembles a flat harp played with two light bamboo sticks and has an eerie echoing sound. Another unusual Thai instrument is the *kórng wong yài,* a semicircle of tuned gongs arranged in a wooden rack. The double-headed *đà·pohn* drum sets the tempo for the whole ensemble.

The contemporary Thai music scene is strong and diverse. The most popular genre is undoubtedly *lôok tûng* (a style analogous to country and western in the USA), which tends to appeal most to working-class Thais. The 1970s ushered in a new style dubbed *pleng pêu·a chee·wít* (literally 'music for life'), inspired by the politically conscious folk rock of the USA and Europe. The three biggest modern Thai music icons are rock staple Carabao, pop star Thongchai 'Bird' MacIntyre,and *lôok tûng* queen Pumpuang Duangchan, who died tragically in 1995.

Today there are hundreds of youth-oriented Thai bands, from chirpy boy and girl bands to metal rockers, making music that is easy to sing along with and maddeningly hard to get out of your head.

In the 1990s an alternative pop scene – known as *pleng tâi din* (underground music) – grew in Bangkok. Modern Dog, a Britpop-inspired band, is generally credited with bringing independent Thai music into the mainstream, and their success paved the way for more mainstream alternative acts such as Apartmentkunpha, Futon, Chou Chou and Calories Blah Blah. Thai headbangers designed to fill stadiums include perennial favourite Loso, as well as Big Ass, Potato and Bodyslam.

Architecture

Most traditional Thai architecture is religious in nature. Thai temples, like Thai Buddhism, gladly mix and match different foreign influences, from the corn-shaped stupa inherited from the Khmer empire to the bell-shaped stupa of Sri Lanka. Despite the foreign flourishes, the roof lines of all Thai temples mimic the shape of the *naga* (mythical serpent) that protected the Buddha during meditation and is viewed as a symbol of life. Green and gold tiles represent scales while the soaring eaves are the head of the creature.

Traditional teak homes can be seen throughout northern Thailand, but are also present in the capital. The capital's finest teak building is Vimanmek Mansion (p62), said to be the largest golden-teak building in the world. Teak houses are typically raised on stilts to minimise the damage caused by flooding and provide a space for storage and livestock. The whole structure is held together with wooden pegs and topped by sweeping eaves that rise to distinctive gables at either end of the house. Houses are traditionally roofed with glazed tiles or wooden shingles.

In the south, houses have traditionally been simpler, relying heavily on bamboo poles and woven bamboo fibre. You might also see Malay-style houses, which use high masonry foundations rather than wooden stilts.

Architecture over the last 100 years has been influenced by cultures from all over the world. In the south, you can still see plenty of Sino-Portuguese *hôrng tăa·ou* (shophouses) – plastered Chinese-style masonry houses with shops below and living quarters above. Classic examples of this style can be found in Phuket's main city, Phuket Town (p248). Since WWII the main trend in Thai architecture has been one of function over form, inspired by the European Bauhaus movement. As a result, there are lots of plain buildings that look like egg cartons turned on their sides.

Thai architects began experimenting during the building boom of the mid-1980s, resulting in creative designs such as Sumet Jumsai's famous robot-shaped Bank of Asia on Th Sathon Tai in Bangkok, or the Elephant Building off Th Phaholyothin in northern Bangkok.

Recommended Arts Reading

» *The Thai House: History and Evolution* (2002; Ruethai Chaichongrak)

» *The Arts of Thailand* (1998; Steve Van Beek)

» *Flavours: Thai Contemporary Art* (2005; Steven Pettifor)

» *Bangkok Design: Thai Ideas in Textiles & Furniture* (2006; Brian Mertens)

» *Buddhist Temples of Thailand: A Visual Journey Through Thailand's 40 Most Historic Wats* (2010; Joe Cummings)

Painting

Except for the prehistoric and historic cave paintings found in the south of the country, not much ancient formal painting exists in Thailand, partly due to the devastating Burmese invasion of 1767. The vast majority of what exists is religious in nature, and typically takes the form of temple paintings illustrating the various lives of the Buddha.

Since the 1980s boom years, Thai secular sculpture and painting have enjoyed increased international recognition, with a handful of Impressionism-inspired artists among the initial few to have reached this vaunted status. Succeeding this was the 'Fireball' school of artists, such as Manit Sriwanichpoom, who specialise in politically motivated, mixed-media art installations. In recent years Thai artists have again moved away from both traditional influences and political commentary and towards contemporary art, focusing on more personal themes, such as those seen in the gender-exploring works of Pinaree Sanpitak, or Maitree Siriboon's identity-driven work.

Theatre & Dance

Traditional Thai theatre consists of four main dramatic forms: *kŏhn* is a formal masked dance-drama, traditionally reserved for royalty, depicting scenes from the Ramakian; *lá·kon* is dance-drama performed for common people; *lí·gair* is a partly improvised, often bawdy, folk play featuring dancing, comedy, melodrama and music; and *hùn lŏo·ang (lá·kon lék)* is traditional puppet theatre enacting religious legends or folk tales.

Most of these forms can be enjoyed in Bangkok, both at dinner shows for tourists and at formal theatrical performances. There are also some distinctively southern theatrical styles, predating the arrival of Islam on the Malay peninsula. The most famous is *má·noh·rah,* the oldest surviving Thai dance-drama, which tells the story of Prince Suthon, who sets off to rescue the kidnapped Mánohraa, a *gin·ná·ree* (woman-bird) princess. As in *lí·gair,* performers add extemporaneous, comic rhymed commentary. Trang also has a distinctive form of *lí·gair,* with a storyline depicting Indian merchants taking their Thai wives back to India for a visit.

Another ancient theatrical style in the south is shadow-puppet theatre (also found in Indonesia and Malaysia), in which two-dimensional figures carved from buffalo hide are manipulated against an illuminated cloth screen. The capital of shadow puppetry today is Nakhon Si Thammarat, which has regular performances at its festivals. There are two distinctive shadow-play traditions. *Năng đà·lung* uses delicate puppets manipulated by a single puppet master to tell stories from the Ramakian, while *năng yài* (literally, 'big hide') uses much larger puppets with several operators, but is sadly a dying art. Both kinds of puppets are popular souvenirs for tourists.

Food & Drink

There's an entire universe of amazing dishes once you get beyond 'pad thai' and green curry, and for many visitors food is one of the main reasons for choosing Thailand as a destination. Even more remarkable, however, is the love for Thai food among the locals: Thais become just as excited as tourists when faced with a bowl of well-prepared noodles or when seated at a renowned hawker stall. This unabashed enthusiasm for eating, not to mention an abundance of fascinating ingredients and influences, has generated one of the most fun and diverse food scenes anywhere in the world.

Thai Food, by David Thompson, is widely considered the most authoritative English-language book on Thai cooking. Thompson's latest book, *Thai Street Food,* focuses on less formal street cuisine.

The following is a general outline of Thai food; for more specific information about regional Thai eats in Bangkok and southern Thailand, and tips on eating like a local, see p40.

The Four Flavours

Simply put, sweet, sour, salty and spicy are the parameters that define Thai food, and although many associate the cuisine with spiciness, virtually every dish is an exercise in balancing these four tastes. This balance might be obtained by a squeeze of lime juice and a glug of fish sauce, or a tablespoon of fermented soybeans and a strategic splash of vinegar. Bitter also factors in many Thai dishes, and often comes from the addition of a vegetable or herb. Regardless of the source, the goal is the same: a favourable balance of four clear, vibrant flavours.

Staples & Specialities

Rice & Noodles

Rice is so central to Thai food culture that the most common term for 'eat' is *gin kôw* (literally, 'consume rice') and one of the most common greetings is *Gin kôw rĕu yang?* (Have you consumed rice yet?) To eat is to eat rice, and for most of the country, a meal is not acceptable without this staple.

Rice is customarily served alongside main dishes like curries, stir-fries or soups, which are lumped together as *gàp kôw* (with rice). When you

SOMETHING'S FISHY

Westerners might scoff at the all-too-literal name of this condiment, but for much of Thai cooking, fish sauce is more than just another ingredient: it is *the* ingredient.

Essentially the liquid obtained from fermented fish, fish sauce takes various guises depending on the region. In northeastern Thailand, discerning diners prefer a thick, pasty mash of fermented freshwater fish and sometimes rice. Elsewhere, where people have access to the sea, fish sauce takes the form of a thin liquid extracted from salted anchovies. In both cases the result is highly pungent, but generally salty (rather than fishy) in taste, and is used much the same way as the saltshaker in the West.

NOODLE MIXOLOGY

If you see a steel rack containing four lidded glass bowls or jars on your table, it's proof that the restaurant you're in serves *gŏo·ay đĕe·o* (rice noodle soup). Typically these containers offer four choices: *nám sôm prík* (sliced green chillies in vinegar), *nám ƀlah* (fish sauce), *prík ƀòn* (dried red chilli, flaked or ground to a near powder) and *nám·đahn* (plain white sugar).

In typically Thai fashion, these condiments offer three ways to make the soup hotter – hot and sour, hot and salty, and just plain hot – and one to make it sweet.

The typical noodle-eater will add a teaspoonful of each one of these condiments to the noodle soup, except for the sugar, which in sweet-tooth Bangkok usually rates a full tablespoon. Until you're used to these strong seasonings, we recommend adding them a small bit at a time, tasting the soup along the way to make sure you don't go overboard.

order plain rice in a restaurant you use the term *kôw ƀlòw,* 'plain rice' or *kôw sŏoay,* 'beautiful rice'.

You'll find four basic kinds of noodle in Thailand. Hardly surprising, given the Thai fixation on rice, is the overwhelming popularity of *sên gŏo·ay đĕe·o,* noodles made from rice flour mixed with water to form a paste, which is then steamed to form wide, flat sheets. The sheets are folded and sliced into various widths.

Also made from rice, *kà·nŏm jeen* is produced by pushing rice-flour paste through a sieve into boiling water, much the way Italian-style pasta is made. *Kà·nŏm jeen* is a popular morning market meal that is eaten doused with various spicy curries and topped with a self-selection of fresh and pickled vegetables and herbs.

The third kind of noodle, *bà·mèe,* is made from wheat flour and egg. It's yellowish in colour and is sold only in fresh bundles.

Finally there's *wún·sên,* an almost clear noodle made from mung-bean starch and water. Often sold in dried bunches, *wún·sên* (literally 'jelly thread') is prepared by soaking in hot water for a few minutes. The most common use of the noodle is in *yam wún sên,* a hot and tangy salad made with lime juice, fresh sliced *prík kêe nŏo* (tiny chillies), shrimp, ground pork and various seasonings.

Thailand is the world's leading exporter of rice, and in 2010 exported 9.03 million tonnes of the grain.

Curries & Soups

In Thai, *gaang* (it sounds somewhat similar to the English 'gang') is often translated as 'curry', but it actually describes any dish with a lot of liquid and can thus refer to soups (such as *gaang jèut*) as well as the classic chilli paste-based curries for which Thai cuisine is famous. The preparation of the latter begins with a *krê·uang gaang,* created by mashing, pounding and grinding an array of fresh ingredients with a stone mortar and pestle to form an aromatic, extremely pungent-tasting and rather thick paste. Typical ingredients in a *krê·uang gaang* include dried chilli, galangal, lemon grass, kaffir lime zest, shallots, garlic, shrimp paste and salt.

Another food celebrity that falls into the soupy category is *đôm yam,* the famous Thai spicy and sour soup. Fuelling the fire beneath *đôm yam*'s often velvety surface are fresh *prík kêe nŏo* (tiny chillies) or, alternatively, half a teaspoonful of *nám prík pŏw* (a roasted chilli paste). Lemon grass, kaffir lime leaf and lime juice give *đôm yam* its characteristic tang.

Stir-Fries & Deep-Fries

The simplest dishes in the Thai culinary repertoire are the various stir-fries *(pàt),* introduced to Thailand by the Chinese, who are world famous for being able to stir-fry a whole banquet in a single wok.

(CON)FUSION CUISINE

A popular dish at restaurants across Thailand is *kôw pàt à·me·rí·gan,* 'American fried rice'. Taking the form of rice fried with ketchup, raisins and peas, sides of ham and deep-fried hot dogs, and topped with a fried egg, the dish is, well, every bit as revolting as it sounds. But at least there's an interesting history behind it: American fried rice allegedly dates back to the Vietnam War era, when thousands of US troops were based in northeastern Thailand. A local cook decided to take the ubiquitous 'American Breakfast' (also known as ABF: fried eggs with ham and/or hot dogs, and white bread, typically eaten with ketchup) and make it 'Thai' by frying the various elements with rice.

This culinary cross-pollination is only a recent example of the tendency of Thai cooks to pick and choose from the variety of cuisines at their disposal. Other (significantly more palatable) examples include *gaang mát·sà·màn,* 'Muslim curry', a now classic blend of Thai and Middle Eastern cooking styles, and the famous *pàt tai,* essentially a blend of Chinese cooking methods and ingredients (frying, rice noodles) with Thai flavours (fish sauce, chilli, tamarind).

The list of *pàt* dishes seems endless. Many cling to their Chinese roots, such as the ubiquitous *pàt pàk bûng fai daang* (morning glory flash-fried with garlic and chilli), while some are Thai–Chinese hybrids, such as *pàt pèt* (literally 'hot stir-fry'), in which the main ingredients, typically meat or fish, are quickly stir-fried with red curry paste.

Tôrt (deep-frying in oil) is mainly reserved for snacks such as *glôo·ay tôrt* (deep-fried bananas) or *bò·bée·a* (egg rolls). An exception is *blah tôrt* (deep-fried fish), which is a common way to prepare fish.

The authors of Eating Thai Food (www.eatingthaifood.com) have put together an 88-page illustrated PDF guide to identifying and ordering Thai dishes for foreign visitors.

Hot & Tangy Salads

Standing right alongside curries in terms of Thai-ness is the ubiquitous *yam,* a hot and tangy 'salad' typically based around seafood, meat or vegetables.

Lime juice provides the tang, while the abundant use of fresh chilli generates the heat. Most *yam* are served at room temperature or just slightly warmed by any cooked ingredients. The dish functions equally well as part of a meal, or on its own as *gàp glâam,* snack food to accompany a night of boozing.

Nám Prík

Although they're more home than restaurant food, *nám prík,* spicy chilli-based 'dips' are, for the locals at least, among the most emblematic of all Thai dishes. Typically eaten with rice and steamed or fresh vegetables and herbs, they're also among the most regional of Thai dishes, and you could probably pinpoint the province you're in by simply looking at the *nám prík* on offer.

Written, photographed and maintained by the author of this chapter, www.austinbushphotography.com/blog details food and dining in Bangkok and provincial Thailand.

Fruits

Being a tropical country, Thailand excels in the fruit department. *Má·môo·ang* (mangoes) alone come in a dozen varieties that are eaten at different stages of ripeness. Other common fruit include *sàp·bà·rót* (pineapple), *má·lá·gor* (papaya) and *đaang moh* (watermelon), all of which are sold from ubiquitous vendor carts and are accompanied by a dipping mix of salt, sugar and ground chilli.

Sweets

English-language Thai menus often have a section called 'Desserts', but the concept takes two slightly different forms in Thailand. *Kŏrng wăhn,* which translates as 'sweet things', are small, rich sweets that often boast a slightly salty flavour. Prime ingredients for *kŏrng wăhn* include grated coconut, coconut milk, rice flour (from white rice or sticky rice), cooked sticky rice, tapioca, mung-bean starch, boiled taro and various fruits.

Thai sweets similar to the European concept of pastries are called *kà·nŏm*. Probably the most popular type of *kà·nŏm* in Thailand are the bite-sized items wrapped in banana leaves, especially *kôw đôm gà·tí* and *kôw đôm mát*. Both consist of sticky rice grains steamed with *gà·tí* (coconut milk) inside a banana-leaf wrapper to form a solid, almost taffylike, mass.

Although foreigners don't seem to immediately take to most Thai sweets, two dishes few visitors have trouble with are *rođi,* the backpacker staple 'banana pancakes' slathered with sugar and condensed milk, and *ai·đim gà·tí,* Thai-style coconut ice cream. At more traditional shops, the ice cream is garnished with toppings such as kidney beans or sticky rice, and is a brilliant snack on a sweltering Thai afternoon.

Thai Hawker Food by Kenny Yee and Catherine Gordon is an illustrated guide to recognising and ordering street food in Thailand.

Regional Variations

One particularly unique aspect of Thai food is its regional diversity. Despite having evolved in a relatively small area, Thai cuisine is anything but a single entity, and takes a slightly different form every time it crosses a provincial border. For more on the regional specialities of Bangkok and southern Thailand, go to p42 and p43.

Drinks

Coffee, Tea & Fruit Drinks

Thais are big coffee drinkers, and good-quality arabica and robusta are cultivated in the hilly areas of northern and southern Thailand. The traditional filtering system is nothing more than a narrow cloth bag attached to a steel handle. This type of coffee is served in a glass, mixed with sugar and sweetened with condensed milk – if you don't want either, be sure to specify *gah·faa dum* (black coffee) followed with *mâi sài nâm·đahn* (without sugar).

Maintained by a Thai woman living in the US, She Simmers (www.shesimmers.com) is a good source of recipes that cover the basics of Thai cooking.

Black tea, both local and imported, is available at the same places that serve real coffee. *Chah tai,* Thai-style tea, derives its characteristic orange-red colour from ground tamarind seed added after curing.

Fruit drinks appear all over Thailand and are an excellent way to rehydrate after water becomes unpalatable. Most *nám pŏn·lá·mái* (fruit

MUITO OBRIGADO

Try to imagine a Thai curry without the chillies, *pàt tai* without the peanuts, or papaya salad without the papaya. Many of the ingredients used on a daily basis by Thais are recent introductions courtesy of European traders and missionaries. During the early 16th century, when Spanish and Portuguese explorers were first reaching the shores of Southeast Asia, there was also expansion and discovery in the Americas. The Portuguese in particular were quick to seize the exciting new products coming from the New World and market them in the East, and thus most likely introduced such modern-day Asian staples as tomatoes, potatoes, corn, lettuce, cabbage, chillies, papayas, guavas, pineapples, pumpkins, sweet potatoes, peanuts and tobacco.

Chillies in particular seem to have struck a chord with Thais, and are thought to have first arrived in Ayuthaya via the Portuguese around 1550. Before their arrival, the natives got their heat from bitter-hot herbs and roots such as ginger and pepper.

And the Portuguese introduced not only some crucial ingredients to the Thai kitchen, but also some enduring cooking techniques, particularly in the area of sweets. The bright-yellow duck egg and syrup-based treats you see at many Thai markets are direct descendants of Portuguese desserts known as *fios de ovos* ('egg threads') and *ovos moles*. And in the area surrounding Bangkok's Church of Santa Cruz (p63), a former Portuguese enclave, you can still find *kà·nŏm fa·ràng,* a bunlike snack baked over coals.

juices) are served with a touch of sugar and salt and a whole lot of ice. Many foreigners object to the salt, but it serves a metabolic role in helping the body to cope with tropical temperatures.

Beer & Spirits

There are several brands of beer in Thailand, ranging from domestic brands (Singha, Chang, Leo) to foreign-licensed labels (Heineken, Asahi, San Miguel) – all largely indistinguishable in terms of taste and quality. For more on how the Thais drink their beer, see p386.

Domestic rice whisky and rum are favourites of the working class, struggling students and family gatherings, as they're more affordable than beer. Once spending money becomes a priority, Thais often upgrade to imported whiskies. These are usually drunk with lots of ice, soda water and a splash of coke. On a night out, buying a whole bottle is the norm in most of Thailand. If you don't finish it, it will simply be kept at the bar until your next visit.

Where to Eat & Drink

Prepared food is available just about everywhere in Thailand, and it shouldn't come as a surprise that the locals do much of their eating outside the home. In this regard, as a visitor, you'll fit right in.

Open-air markets and food stalls are among the most popular places where Thais eat. In the mornings, stalls selling coffee and Chinese-style doughnuts spring up along busy commuter corridors. At lunchtime, eaters might grab a plastic chair at yet another stall for a simple stir-fry, or pick up a foam box of noodles to scoff down at the office. In most small towns, night markets often set up in the middle of town with a cluster of vendors, metal tables and chairs, and some shopping as an after-dinner mint.

There are, of course, restaurants *(ráhn ah·hăhn)* in Thailand that range from simple food stops to formal affairs. Lunchtime is the right time to point and eat at the *ráhn kôw gaang* (rice-and-curry shop), which sells a selection of pre-made dishes. The more generic *ráhn ah·hăhn đahm sàng* (food-to-order shop) can often be recognised by a display of raw ingredients – Chinese kale, tomatoes, chopped pork, fresh or dried fish, noodles, eggplant, spring onions – for a standard repertoire of Thai and Chinese dishes. As the name implies, the cooks attempt to prepare any dish you can name, a slightly more difficult operation if you can't speak Thai.

WEBSITES

Keep up with the ever-changing food scene in Bangkok by following the dining section of CNNGo's Bangkok pages (www.cnngo.com/bangkok/eat) and BK's restaurant section (http://bk.asia-city.com/restaurants).

A THAI PILSNER PRIMER

We relish the look of horror on the faces of Thailand newbies when the waitress casually plunks several cubes of ice into their pilsners. Before you rule this supposed blasphemy out completely, there are a few reasons why we and the Thais actually prefer our beer on the rocks.

Firstly, despite all the alleged accolades displayed on most bottles, Thai beer does not possess the most sophisticated bouquet in the world and is best drunk as cold as possible. Also, if you haven't already noticed, the weather in Thailand is often extremely hot, another reason it makes sense to maintain your beer at maximum chill. And lastly, domestic brews are generally quite high in alcohol and the ice helps to dilute this, preventing dehydration and one of those infamous Beer Chang hangovers the next day. Taking these theories to the extreme, some places in Thailand serve something called *beea wún*, 'jelly beer', beer that has been semi-frozen until it reaches a deliciously slushy and refreshing consistency.

However, a brief warning: it's a painfully obvious sign you've been in Thailand too long if you put ice in your draught Hoegaarden.

THE RIGHT TOOL FOR THE JOB

If you're not offered chopsticks, don't ask for them. Thai food is eaten with fork and spoon, not chopsticks. When *fa·ràng* (Westerners) ask for chopsticks to eat Thai food, it only puzzles the restaurant proprietors.

Chopsticks are reserved for eating Chinese-style food from bowls, or for eating in all-Chinese restaurants. In either case you will be supplied with chopsticks without having to ask. Unlike their counterparts in many Western countries, restaurateurs in Thailand won't assume you don't know how to use them.

Vegetarians & Vegans

Vegetarianism isn't a widespread trend in Thailand, but many of the tourist-oriented restaurants cater to vegetarians, and there are also a handful of *ráhn ah·hăhn mang·sà·wí·rát* (vegetarian restaurants) in Bangkok and several provincial capitals where the food is served buffet-style and is very inexpensive. Dishes are almost always 100% vegan (ie no meat, poultry, fish or fish sauce, dairy or egg products).

During the Vegetarian Festival, celebrated by Chinese Buddhists in October, many restaurants and street stalls in Bangkok, Phuket and in the Chinese business districts of most Thai towns go meatless for one month.

The phrase 'I'm vegetarian' in Thai is *pŏm gin jair* (for men) or *dì·chăn gin jair* (for women). Loosely translated this means 'I eat only vegetarian food', which includes no eggs and no dairy products – in other words, total vegan.

Thai Food Master (www.thaifoodmaster.com), maintained by a longtime foreign resident of Thailand, contains helpful step-by-step photos that illustrate the making of a variety of Thai dishes.

Habits & Customs

Like most of Thai culture, eating conventions appear relaxed and informal but are orchestrated by many implied rules.

Whether at home or in a restaurant, Thai meals are always served 'family-style' – that is, from common serving platters – and the plates appear in whatever order the kitchen can prepare them. When serving yourself from a common platter, put no more than one spoonful onto your plate at a time. Heaping your plate with all 'your' portions at once will look greedy to Thais unfamiliar with Western conventions. Another important factor in a Thai meal is achieving a balance of flavours and textures. Traditionally, the party orders a curry, a steamed or fried fish, a stir-fried vegetable dish and a soup, taking great care to balance cool and hot, sour and sweet, salty and plain.

Originally Thai food was eaten with the fingers, and it still is in certain regions of the kingdom. In the early 1900s, Thais began setting their tables with fork and spoon to affect a 'royal' setting, and it wasn't long before fork-and-spoon dining became the norm in Bangkok and later spread throughout the kingdom. To use these tools the Thai way, use a serving spoon, or alternatively your own, to take a single mouthful of food from a central dish, and ladle it over a portion of your rice. The fork is then used to push the now food-soaked portion of rice back onto the spoon before entering the mouth.

Bangkok's Top 50 Street Food Stalls, by Chawadee Nualkhair, also functions well as a general introduction and guide to Thai-style informal dining.

Environment

The Land

Thailand's odd shape – bulky and wide up north, with a long pendulous arm draping to the south – has often been compared to the head of an elephant. Roughly the size of France, about 517,000 sq km, Thailand stretches an astounding 1650km along a north–south axis and experiences an extremely diverse climate, including two distinct monsoons from both the southwest and northwest. The north of the country rises into high forested mountains, while the south consists of a long ridge of limestone hills, covered in tropical rainforest.

Bound to the east by the shallow Gulf of Thailand and to the west by the Andaman Sea, an extension of the Indian Ocean, Thailand possesses one of the most alluring coastlines in the world, with exquisitely carved limestone formations above water and tremendously rich coral reefs below. Hundreds of tropical islands of all shapes and sizes adorn the coast, from flat sand bars covered in mangroves to looming karst massifs licked by azure waters and ringed by white sand beaches. Both coasts have extensive coral reefs, particularly around the granitic Surin Islands and Similan Islands in the Andaman Sea. More reefs and Thailand's most dramatic limestone islands sit in Ao Phang-Nga near Phuket. The west coast is of particular interest to divers because the waters are stunningly clear and extremely rich in marine life.

Wildlife

With its diverse climate and topography, it should come as no surprise that Thailand is home to a remarkable diversity of flora and fauna. What is more surprising is that Thailand's environment is still in relatively good shape, particularly considering the relentless development going on all over the country. That said, there are certainly problems; see also p389 on endangered species and p393 on marine environmental issues.

Animals

Animals that live on the coasts and islands of Thailand must adapt to shifting tides and the ever-changing mix of salt and freshwater. Rather than elephants and tigers, keep your eyes open for smaller creatures, such as the odd little mudskipper, a fish that leaves the water and walks around on the mud flats when the tide goes out; or the giant water monitor, a fearsome 350cm-long lizard that climbs and swims effortlessly in its search for small animals.

Without a doubt you will see some of the region's fabulous birdlife – Thailand is home to 10% of the world's bird species – especially sandpipers and plovers on the mud flats, and herons and egrets in the swamps. Look overhead for the sharply attired, chocolate-brown and white Brahminy kite, or scan low-lying branches for one of the region's many colourful kingfishers. You are likely to spot a troop of gregarious and noisy crab-eating macaques, and don't be surprised to see these monkeys swimming from shore. With luck you may glimpse a palm civet, a complexly marbled catlike creature, or a serow, the reclusive 'goat-antelope' that bounds fearlessly among inaccessible limestone crags.

The oceans on either side of the Thai peninsula are home to hundreds of species of coral, and the reefs created by these tiny creatures provide the perfect living conditions for countless species of fish, crustaceans and tiny invertebrates. You can find one of the world's smallest fish (the 10mm-long goby) or the largest (a 10m-long whale shark), plus reef denizens such as clownfish, parrotfish, wrasse, angelfish, triggerfish and lionfish. Deeper waters are home to larger species such as groupers, barracudas, sharks, manta rays, marlin and tunas. You might also encounter turtles, whales and dolphins.

Endangered Species

Thailand is a signatory to the UN Convention on International Trade in Endangered Species of Wild Fauna and Flora (Cites) but the enforcement of these trade bans is notoriously lax – just walk around the animal section of Bangkok's Chatuchak Weekend Market to see how openly the rules are flouted. Due to habitat loss, pollution and poaching, a depressing number of Thailand's mammals, reptiles, fish and birds are endangered, and even populations of formerly common species are diminishing at an alarming rate. Rare mammals, birds, reptiles, insects, shells and tropical aquarium fish are routinely smuggled out to collectors around the world or killed to make souvenirs for tourists.

Many of Thailand's marine animals are under threat, including whale sharks, although they have been seen more frequently in Thai waters recently, and sea turtles, which are being wiped out by hunting for their eggs, meat and shells. Many other species of shark are being hunted to extinction for their fins, which are used to make shark-fin soup.

The rare dugong (also called manatee or sea cow), once thought extinct in Thailand, is now known to survive in a few small pockets, mostly around Trang in southern Thailand, but is increasingly threatened by habitat loss and the lethal propellers of tourist boats.

The Thai government is slowly recognising the importance of conservation, perhaps due to the efforts and leadership of Queen Sirikit, and many of the kingdom's zoos now have active breeding and conservation programs. Wildlife organisations such as the Phuket Gibbon Rehabilitation Centre (p270) are working to educate the public about native wildlife and have initiated a number of wildlife rescue and rehabilitation projects.

Plants

Southern Thailand is chock-full of luxuriant vegetation, thanks to its two monsoon seasons. The majority of forests away from the coast are evergreen rainforests, while trees at the ocean edge and on limestone formations are stunted due to lack of fresh water and exposure to harsh minerals.

The most beautiful shoreline trees are the many species of palm trees occurring in Thailand, including some found nowhere else in the world. All have small tough leaves with characteristic fanlike or featherlike shapes that help dissipate heat and conserve water. Look for the elegant cycad palm on limestone cliffs, where this *ƀlông* (mountain coconut) grows in cracks despite the complete absence of soil. Collected for its beauty, this common ornamental plant is disappearing from its wild habitat.

Thailand is also home to nearly 75 species of salt-tolerant mangroves – small trees highly adapted to living at the edge of salt water.

WHITE ELEPHANT

If anyone in Thailand comes across a white elephant, it must be reported to the Bureau of the Royal Household, and the King will decide whether it meets the criteria to be a royal white elephant.

Standing tiptoe-like on clumps of tall roots, mangroves perform a vital ecological function by trapping sediments and nutrients, and by buffering the coast from the fierce, erosive power of monsoons. This habitat serves as a secure nursery for the eggs and young of countless marine organisms, yet Thailand has destroyed at least 50% of its mangrove swamps to make way for prawn farms and big hotels.

A growing number of overseas tourism companies now insist that Thailand's tourism operators have environmental policies in place before doing business with them.

National Parks

National parks in Thailand are a huge draw for beach visitors. The popular island getaways of Ko Chang and Ko Samet sit just off the mainland along the eastern gulf coast. Ko Tarutao Marine National Park is remote and undeveloped for real back-to-nature vacations. Ao Phang-Nga, north of Phuket, is endlessly photogenic with its limestone cliffs jutting out of the aquamarine water while knotted mangrove roots cling to thick mud flats. Meanwhile the Similan Islands and Surin Islands Marine National Parks, in the waters of the Andaman Sea, have some of the world's best diving.

Approximately 13% of Thailand is covered by 112 national parks and 44 wildlife sanctuaries, which is a very respectable rate by international standards. Of Thailand's protected areas, 18 parks protect islands and mangrove environments. Thailand's parks and sanctuaries contain more than 850 resident and migratory species of birds and dwindling numbers

THAILAND'S NATIONAL PARKS

PARK	FEATURES	ACTIVITIES	PAGE
Mu Ko Chang National Marine Park	archipelago marine park with virgin rainforests, waterfalls, beaches and coral reefs	snorkelling, diving, elephant trekking, hiking	p122
Khao Laem Ya/Mu Ko Samet National Park	marine park with beaches, near-shore coral reefs	snorkelling, diving, boat trips, sailboarding	p111
Kaeng Krachan National Park	mainland park with waterfalls and forests; plentiful birdlife and jungle mammals	bird-watching	p145
Khao Sam Roi Yot National Park	coastal park with caves, mountains, cliffs and beaches; serow, Irrawaddy dolphins and 300 bird species	cave tours, bird-watching, kayaking	p160
Ang Thong Marine National Park	40 scenic tropical islands with coral reefs, lagoons and limestone cliffs	sea kayaking, hiking, snorkelling	p222
Khao Luang National Park	mainland park with forested mountain peaks, streams and waterfalls; jungle mammals, birds and orchids	hiking	p228
Ao Phang-Nga National Marine Park	coastal bay with limestone cliffs, islands and caves; coral reefs and mangroves	sea kayaking, snorkelling, diving	p295
Khao Lak/Lam Ru National Park	coastal park with cliffs and beaches; hornbills, monkeys and bears	hiking, boat trips	p290
Khao Sok National Park	mainland park with thick rainforest, waterfalls and rivers; tigers, monkeys, *rafflesia* and 180 bird species	hiking, elephant trekking, tubing	p288
Laem Son National Park	coastal and marine park with 100km of mangroves; jungle and migratory birds	bird-watching, boat trips	p276

of tigers, clouded leopards, koupreys, elephants, tapirs, gibbons and Asiatic black bears, among other species.

Despite promises, official designation as a national park or sanctuary does not always guarantee protection for habitats and wildlife. Local farmers, well-moneyed developers, and other business interests will often prevail, either legally or illegally, over environmental protection in Thailand's national parks. Islands that are technically exempt from development often don't adhere to the law and there is little government muscle to enforce regulations. Ko Chang, Ko Samet and Ko Phi-Phi are all curious examples of national parks with development problems.

For foreigners, parks charge entry fees of 400B per adult and 200B for children under 14 years. In recent years these rates were doubled, then rescinded on a case-by-case basis, so what you pay may differ from park to park. In some cases the **Royal Forestry Department** (☎0 2561 4292/3; 61 Th Phahonyothin, Chatuchak, Bangkok 10900) rents out accommodation; make reservations in advance as this is a popular option for locals. All parks are best visited in the dry season, particularly marine national parks, which can have reduced visibility in the water during the monsoon.

PARK	FEATURES	ACTIVITIES	PAGE
Similan Islands Marine National Park	marine park with granite islands; coral reefs and seabirds; underwater caves	snorkelling, diving	p293
Sirinat National Park	coastal park with casuarina-backed beaches; turtles and coral reefs	walking, snorkelling, diving	p268
Surin Islands Marine National Park	granite islands; coral reefs, whale sharks and manta rays	snorkelling, diving	p278
Hat Chao Mai National Park	coastal park with sandy beaches, mangroves, lagoons and coral islands; dugong and mangrove birds	sea kayaking, snorkelling, diving	p335
Khao Phanom Bencha National Park	mainland mountain jungle with tumbling waterfalls; monkeys	hiking	p307
Ko Phi-Phi Marine National Park	archipelago marine park with beaches, lagoons and sea-cliffs; coral reefs and whale sharks	sea kayaking, snorkelling, diving	p316
Ko Tarutao Marine National Park	archipelago marine park with remote jungle islands and tropical beaches; monkeys, jungle mammals and birds	snorkelling, hiking, diving	p346
Mu Ko Lanta Marine National Park	archipelago marine park with scenic beaches; coral reefs and reef sharks	sea kayaking, elephant trekking, hiking, snorkelling, diving	p324
Mu Ko Phetra Marine National Park	rarely visited archipelago marine park; dugong, birds and coral reefs	sea kayaking, snorkelling	p344
Tharnbok Korannee National Park	coastal park with mangrove forests and limestone caves; monkeys, orchids and seabirds	sea kayaking	p306

Environmental Issues

Thailand is in a different developmental stage than most Western countries and this affects both the environmental problems and how people react to them. Thailand is wealthier, better developed and more educated than its regional neighbours, so there is an awareness of environmental issues that barely exists in countries such as Cambodia and Myanmar. But that awareness is often limited in scope and, while this is slowly changing, it rarely develops into the sort of high-profile, widespread movements seen in Europe, North America or Australia.

As such most issues have a very low profile, with only the most visible problems, such as pollution, overdevelopment and a lack of adequate planning, making it onto a visitor's radar. Look a little deeper and you'll see the environment has often been the victim in Thailand's rapid modernisation, with short-term considerations usually to the fore. Few Thais see any problem with cutting down mangroves to make prawn farms, or powering their development with energy from dams in Laos and dubious natural gas concerns in Myanmar.

So many well-meaning laws have been put on the books that it might seem Thailand is turning the corner towards greater ecological consciousness. But it has been revealed that corruption and lack of political resolve have severely hampered efforts to enforce these environmental laws. With the deep split within Thai politics showing no signs of being healed and governments having to make all sorts of undesirable concessions just to stay in power, it seems the political will to enforce these laws remains a way off. Ironically, however, this same lack of political stability has also scared off investors.

The Land Environment

The main area in which Asia exceeds the West in terms of environmental damage is deforestation, though current estimates are that Thailand still has about 25% of its forests remaining, which stands up favourably against the UK's dismal 5%. The government's National Forest Policy, introduced in 1985, recommended that 40% of the country should be forested, and a complete logging ban in 1989 was a big step in the right direction. By law Thailand must maintain 25% of its land area as 'conservation forests'. But predictably the logging ban simply shifted the need for natural resources elsewhere. Illegal logging persists in Thailand, though on a relatively small scale. In contrast, in neighbouring Cambodia, Laos and particularly Myanmar, the scale has been huge ever since the 1989 ban. A great number of logs are illegally slipped over the border from these countries.

Despite Thailand being a signatory to Cites, all sorts of land species are still smuggled out of Thailand, either alive or as body parts for traditional Chinese medicines. Tigers may be protected by Thai law, but the kingdom remains the world's largest exporter of tiger parts to China (tiger penis and bone are believed to have medicinal effects and to increase libido). Other animal species are hunted (often illegally) to make souvenirs for tourists, including elephants, jungle spiders, giant insects and butterflies; and along the coast clams, shells and puffer fish.

The government has cracked down on restaurants serving *ah·hăhn Ƀàh* (jungle food), which includes endangered wildlife species such as barking deer, bears, pangolins, gibbons, civets and gaurs. A big problem is that national park officials are underpaid and undertrained, yet are expected to confront armed poachers and mercenary armies funded by rich and powerful godfathers.

The widely touted idea that ecotourism can act as a positive force for change has been extensively put to the test in Thailand. In some instances tourism has definitely had positive effects. The expansion of Thailand's national parks has largely been driven by tourism. In Khao Yai National Park, all hotel and golf-course facilities were removed to reduce damage to the park environment. As a result of government and private-sector pressure on the fishing industry, coral dynamiting has been all but eliminated in the Similan and Surin Islands, to preserve the area for tourists.

However, tourism can be a poisoned chalice. Massive developments around and frequently in national parks have ridden roughshod over the local environment in their rush to provide bungalows, luxury hotels, beach-bars and boat services for tourists. Ko Phi-Phi and Ko Samet are two national parks where business interests have definitely won out over the environment. In both cases, the development began in areas set aside for *chow lair* (also spelt *chao leh;* sea gypsies, the semi-nomadic people who migrate up and down the coast). Ko Lipe in Ko Tarutao Marine National Park and Ko Muk in Hat Chao Mai National Park now seem to be heading the same way.

Rubbish and sewage are growing problems in all populated areas, even more so in heavily visited areas where an influx of tourists overtaxes the local infrastructure. One encouraging development was the passing of the 1992 Environmental Act, which set environmental quality standards, designated conservation and pollution-control areas, and doled out government clean-up funds. Pattaya built its first public wastewater treatment plant in 2000 and conditions have improved ever since.

While Thais generally remain reluctant to engage in broader environmental campaigns, ordinary people are increasingly aware, particularly when they will be affected. Local people have campaigned for years against the building of dams, though usually without success. Damage to a favourite beach during the filming of *The Beach* in Ko Phi-Phi Marine National Park triggered demonstrations around the country and the filming of the US TV show *Survivor* in Ko Tarutao Marine National Park provoked a similar outcry. As a result, strict production and filming bans have been put in place to avoid similar issues in the future. The construction of a petroleum pipeline to Songkhla in 2002 created a remarkable level of grass-roots opposition among ordinary village people.

A group of ecologically engaged Buddhist monks, popularly known as Thai Ecology Monks, have courageously set one of the best examples by using their peaceful activism to empower local communities in their fight against monolithic projects.

The famous white sands of Thailand's beaches are actually tiny bits of coral that have been defecated by coral-eating fish.

The Marine Environment

Thailand's coral reef system, including the Andaman coast from Ranong to northern Phuket and the Surin and Similan Islands, is one of the world's most diverse. Some 600 species of coral reef fish, endangered marine turtles and other rare creatures call this coastline home.

The 2004 tsunami caused high-impact damage to about 13% of the Andaman coral reefs. However, damage from the tsunami was much less than first thought and relatively minor compared to the ongoing environmental degradation that accompanies an industrialised society. It is estimated that about 25% of Thailand's coral reefs have died as a result of industrial pollution and that the annual loss of healthy reefs will continue at a rapid rate. Even around the dive centre of Phuket, dead coral reefs are visible on the northern coast. The biggest threat to corals is sedimentation from coastal development: new condos, hotels, roads and houses. High levels of sediment in the water stunts the growth of coral. Other common problems include pollution from anchored tour boats or other marine activities, rubbish and sewage dumped directly into the sea, and agricultural and industrial run-off. Even people urinating in the water as they swim creates by-products that can kill sensitive coral reefs.

The environmental wake-up call from the tsunami emphasised the importance of mangrove forests, which provide a buffer from storm surges. Previously mangroves were considered wastelands and were indiscriminately cut down. It is estimated that about 80% of the mangrove forests lining the gulf coast and 20% of those on the Andaman coast have been destroyed for conversion into fish and prawn farms, tourist development or to supply the charcoal industry. Prawn farms constitute the biggest threat because Thailand is the world's leading producer of black tiger prawns, and the short-lived, heavily polluting farms are built in pristine mangrove swamps at a terrific environmental and social cost. Prawn farms are big business (annual production in Thailand has soared from 900 tonnes to 277,000 tonnes in the past 10 years), and the large prawn-farming operations are often able to operate in spite of environmental protection laws. Protesting voices rarely get much play in the media.

Contributing to the deterioration of the overall health of the ocean are Thailand and its neighbours' large-scale fishing industries, frequently called the 'strip-miners of the sea'. Fish catches have declined by up to 33% in the Asia-Pacific region in the past 25 years and the upper portion of the Gulf of Thailand has almost been fished to death. Most of the commercial catches are sent to overseas markets and rarely see a Thai dinner table. The seafood sold in Thailand is typically from fish farms, another large coastal industry for the country.

GARBAGE

Students at Dulwich International College in Phuket collected 5000kg of garbage from the beach in a single day; help them out by picking up rubbish whenever you can.

Making a Difference

It may seem that the range of environmental issues in Thailand is too overwhelming, but there is actually much that travellers can do to minimise the impact of their visits, or to even make a positive impact. The way you spend your money has a profound influence on the kingdom's economy and on the profitability of individual businesses. Ask questions up front and take your money elsewhere if you don't like the answers. For instance, a number of large-scale resorts that lack road access transport clients across fragile mud flats on tractors (a wantonly destructive practice), so when booking a room inquire into transport to the hotel. Of the region's countless dive shops, some are diligent about minimising the impact their clients have on the reefs; however, if a dive shop trains and certifies inexperienced divers over living reefs, rather than in a swimming pool, then it is causing irreparable harm to the local ecosystem. As a rule, do not touch or walk on coral, monitor your movements so you avoid accidentally sweeping into coral, and do not harass marine life (any dead puffer fish you see on the beach probably died because a diver poked it until it inflated).

Make a positive impact on Thailand by checking out one of the many environmental and social groups working in the kingdom. If you do some research and make arrangements before arriving, you may connect with an organisation that matches your values, but here are some favourites to start the juices flowing.

The **Wild Animal Rescue Foundation of Thailand** (WAR; ☎0 2712 9715; www.warthai.org; 65/1 3rd fl, Soi 55, Th Sukhumvit, Bangkok 10110) is one of the leading advocates for nature conservation in Thailand and currently runs four wildlife sanctuaries that use volunteers to rehabilitate and return former pets to the wild.

The **Bird Conservation Society of Thailand** (☎0 2691 4816; www.bcst.or.th) provides a plethora of information about the birds of Thailand, offering field trip reports, sightings of rare birds, bird festivals, bird surveys and a birding online forum.

Make a big change by checking out the **Sanithirakoses-Nagapateepa Foundation** (www.sulak-sivaraksa.org), which was started by the 1995 Alternative Nobel Prize winner, Sulak Sivaraksa. This umbrella group is associated with numerous environmental and social justice groups in Thailand including the Foundation for Children, Forum of the Poor, the Thai-Tibet Centre, and Pun Pun, an organic farm and sustainable living centre. These groups offer countless opportunities to help empower local communities, and to get involved in issues important to the people of Thailand. They have also started an alternative college called Spirit in Education Movement (SEM) that offers a spiritually based, ecologically sound alternative to mainstream education.

Other groups promoting environmental issues in Thailand include the following:

Thailand Environment Institute (☎0 2503 3333; www.tei.or.th)
Wildlife Friends Foundation Thailand (☎0 3245 8135; www.wfft.org)
WWF Thailand (☎0 2524 6168; www.wwfthai.org)

Survival Guide

Directory A–Z

Accommodation

Thailand offers a wide variety of accommodation from cheap and basic to pricey and luxurious. Accommodation rates listed in this book are high-season prices. Icons are included to indicate internet access, wi-fi, swimming pools or air-conditioning. If the review doesn't have an air-con icon, assume that there's only a fan.

A three-tiered pricing system has been used in this book to determine budget category (budget, midrange, top end). Room rates under 1000B are budget, under 3000B are midrange and more than 3000B are top end.

In places where spoken English might be limited, it is handy to know the following: *hôrng pát lom* (room with fan) and *hôrng aa* (room with air-con).

Guest Houses

Guest houses are generally the cheapest accommodation in Thailand and can be found all along the backpacker trail. In more remote areas like the eastern seaboard, guest houses (as well as tourists) are not as widespread.

Rates vary according to facilities and location. In provincial towns, the cheapest rooms range from 150B to 200B, and usually have shared bathrooms and rickety fans. Private facilities, air-con and sometimes a TV can be had for 600B to 800B. But prices are much higher in the beach resorts, where a basic fan room starts at 700B to 800B. Many guest houses make their bread and butter from the on-site restaurants that serve classic backpacker fare (banana pancakes and fruit shakes). Although these restaurants are convenient and a good way to meet other travellers, don't judge Thai food based on these dishes.

Most guest houses cultivate a travellers' ambience with friendly, knowledgeable staff and book exchanges. But there are also plenty of guest houses with grumpy, disgruntled clerks who let customers know that they dislike their jobs.

Increasingly, guest houses can handle advance reservations, but due to inconsistent cleanliness and quality it is advisable to always look at a room in person before committing. In tourist centres, there are usually alternatives nearby if your preferred place is full. Guest houses typically only accept cash payments.

Hotels

In provincial capitals and small towns, the only options are often older Thai-Chinese hotels, once the standard in Thailand. Most cater to Thai guests and English is usually limited.

These hotels are multistorey buildings and might offer a range of rooms from midrange options with private bathrooms, air-con and TVs to cheaper ones with shared bath facilities and a fan. In some of the older hotels, the toilets are squats and the 'shower' is a *klong* (large terracotta basin from which you scoop out water for bathing). Although these Thai-Chinese hotels have got tonnes of accidental retro charm, we've found that, unless they've been recently refurbished, they are too old and worn to represent good value compared to guest houses.

In recent years, there has been a push to fill the budget gap for ageing backpackers and young affluent travellers who want the ambience of a guest house with the comforts of a hotel. 'Flashpacker'

BOOK YOUR STAY ONLINE

For more accommodation reviews by Lonely Planet authors, check out http://hotels.lonelyplanet.com. You'll find independent reviews, as well as recommendations on the best places to stay. Best of all, you can book online.

hotels in major tourist towns have dressed up the utilitarian options of the past with stylish decor and more creature comforts.

International chain hotels can be found in Bangkok, Phuket and other high-end beach resorts. Many of these upscale resorts combine traditional Thai architecture and modern minimalism.

Most top-end hotels and some midrange hotels add a 7% government tax (VAT) and an additional 10% service charge. The additional charges are often referred to as 'plus plus'. A buffet breakfast will often be included in the room rate. If the hotel offers Western breakfast, it is usually referred to as 'ABF', meaning 'American breakfast'.

Midrange and chain hotels, especially in major tourist destinations, can be booked in advance and some offer internet discounts through their websites or online agents. They also accept most credit cards, but only a few deluxe places accept American Express.

National Parks Accommodation

Most national parks have bungalows or campsites available for overnight stays. Bungalows typically sleep as many as 10 people and rates range from 800B to 2000B, depending on the park and the size of the bungalow. These are popular with extended Thai families who bring enough provisions to survive the Apocalypse. A few parks also have *reu·an tăa·ou* (longhouses).

Camping is available at many parks for 60B to 90B per night. Some parks rent tents and other sleeping gear, but the condition of the equipment can be poor.

Reservations for all park accommodation must be made in advance through the **central booking system** (☎0 2561 0777; http://web3.dnp.go.th/parkreserve/reservation.asp). Do note that reservations for campsites and bungalows are handled on different pages within the website.

Business Hours

The following are standard hours for different types of businesses in Thailand. Reviews in this book list only variations from these standards. All government offices and banks are closed on public holidays (see p401).

Banks 9.30am to 3.30pm Monday to Friday; ATMs accessible 24 hours.

Bars 6pm to midnight (officially); closing times vary due to local enforcement of curfew laws; bars close during elections and certain religious public holidays.

Clubs (discos) 8pm to 2am; closing times vary due to local enforcement of curfew laws; clubs close during elections and certain religious public holidays.

Government offices 8.30am to 4.30pm Monday to Friday; some close for lunch (noon to 1pm), while others are open Saturday (9am to 3pm).

Live-music venues 6pm to 1am; closing times vary due to local enforcement of curfew laws; venues close during elections and certain religious public holidays.

Restaurants 10am to 10pm; some shops specialise in morning meals and close by 3pm.

Stores Local stores: 10am to 6pm daily; department stores: 10am to 8pm daily. In some small towns, local stores close on Sunday.

Customs Regulations

The **customs department** (www.customsclinic.org) maintains a helpful website with specific information about customs regulations. Thailand allows the following items to enter duty free:

- » reasonable amount of personal effects (clothing and toiletries)
- » professional instruments
- » 200 cigarettes
- » 1L of wine or spirits

Thailand prohibits the import of the following items:

- » firearms and ammunition (unless registered in advance with the police department)
- » illegal drugs
- » pornographic media

COMMISSION HASSLES

In the popular tourist spots you'll be approached, sometimes surrounded, by touts or transport drivers who get a commission from the guest house for bringing in potential guests. While it's annoying for the traveller, this is an acceptable form of advertising among small-scale businesses in Thailand. As long as you know the drill, everything should work out in your favour. Touts get paid for delivering you to a guest house or hotel (whether you check in or not). Some places refuse to pay commissions, so in return the touts will steer customers away from those places (by saying they are closed or burned down). In less scrupulous instances, they'll tell you that the commission-paying hotel is the one you requested. If you meet with resistance, call the guest house for a pick-up, as they are often aware of these aggressive business tactics. See p404 for more information.

Climate

Bangkok

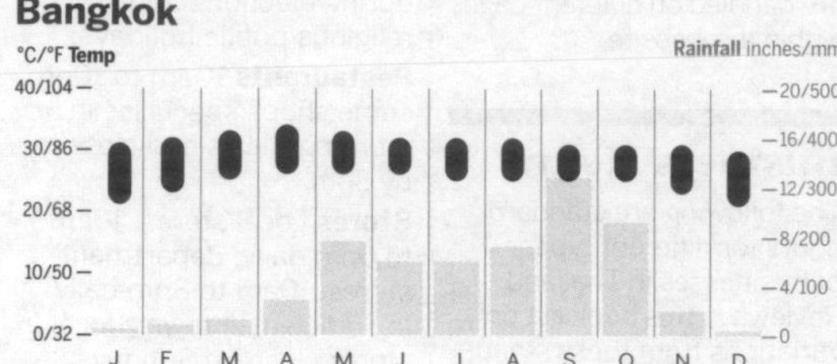

Phuket

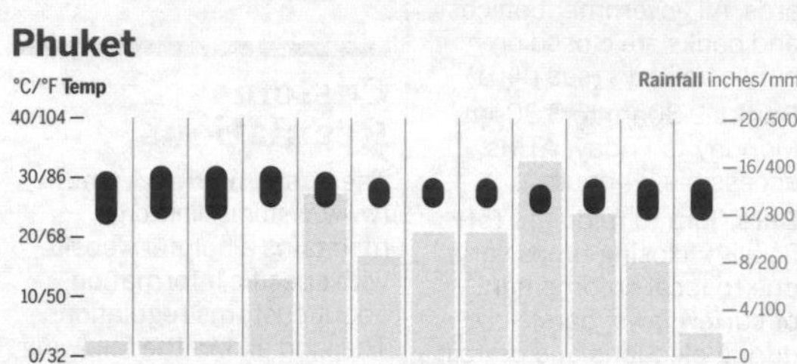

Surat Thani

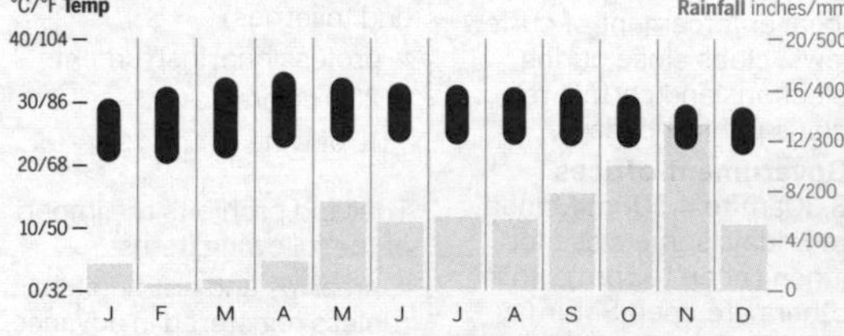

When leaving Thailand, you must obtain an export licence for any antiques, reproductions or newly cast Buddha images (except personal amulets). Submit two front-view photos of the object(s) and a photocopy of your passport, along with the purchase receipt and the object(s) in question, to the **Department of Fine Arts** (☎0 2628 5032). Allow four days for the application and inspection process to be completed.

Electricity

Thailand uses 220V AC electricity; power outlets most commonly feature two-prong round or flat sockets.

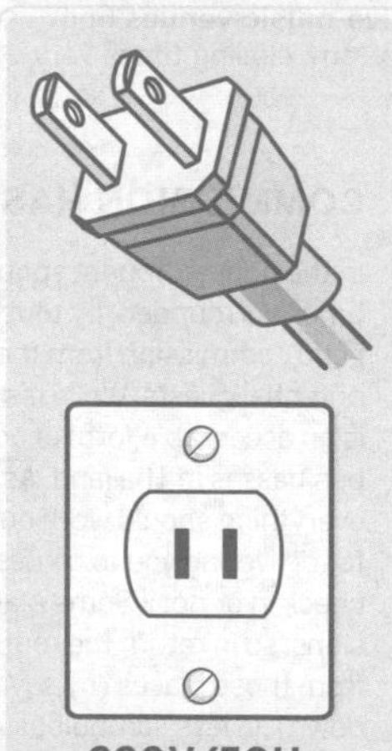

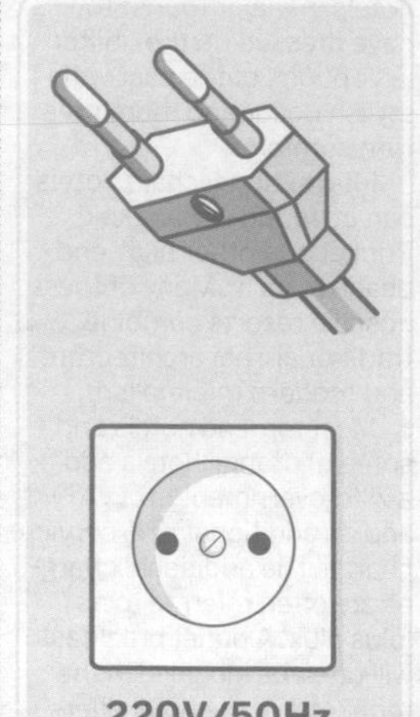

Embassies & Consulates

Foreign embassies are located in Bangkok.

Australia (Map p74; ☎0 2344 6300; www.thailand.embassy.gov.au; 37 Th Sathon Tai)

Cambodia (☎0 2957 5851-2; 518/4 Pracha Uthit/Soi Ramkamhaeng 39)

Canada (☎0 2636 0540; www.thailand.gc.ca; 15th fl, Abdulrahim Bldg, 990 Th Phra Ram IV)

China (☎0 2245 7044; www.chinaembassy.or.th; 57 Th Ratchadaphisek)

Denmark (☎0 2343 1100; www.ambbangkok.um.dk; 10 Soi 1, Th Sathon Tai) Consulates in Phuket and Pattaya.

France Embassy (☎0 2657 5100; www.ambafrance-th.org; 35 Soi 36, Th Charoen Krung); Bangkok Visa & Culture Services (☎0 2627 2150; 29 Th Sathon Tai) Consulates in Phuket and Surat Thani.

Germany (☎0 2287 9000; www.bangkok.diplo.de; 9 Th Sathon Tai)

India Embassy (Map p80; ☎0 2258 0300-6; indianembassy.in.th; 46 Soi Prasanmit/Soi 23, Th Sukhumvit); Indian Visa

PRACTICALITIES

» *Bangkok Post* and the *Nation* are the daily English-language newspapers.

» There are more than 400 AM and FM radio stations; short-wave radios can pick up BBC, VOA, Radio Australia, Deutsche Welle and Radio France International.

» Six VHF TV networks carry Thai programming; TrueVision cable provides international programming.

» The main video format is PAL.

» Thailand follows the international metric system. Gold and silver are weighed in *bàat* (15g).

Application Centre (Map p80; ☎02 6652 9681; www.ivac-th.com; Suite 1503, Glass Haus Bldg, 15th fl, Th Sukhumvit);

Indonesia (Map p70; ☎0 2252 3135; www.kemlu.go.id/bangkok; 600-602 Th Phetchaburi)

Ireland (Map p70; ☎0 2677 7500; www.irelandinthailand.com; 28th fl, Q House, Th Sathon Tai) Consulate only; the nearest Irish embassy is in Kuala Lumpur.

Israel (Map p80; ☎0 2204 9200; bangkok.mfa.gov.il; Ocean Tower 2, 25th fl, 25 Soi 19, Th Sukhumvit)

Japan (☎0 2207 8500; www.th.emb-japan.go.jp; 177 Th Withayu/Wireless Rd)

Laos (☎0 2539 6678; www.bkklaoembassy.com; 502/1-3 Soi Sahakarnpramoon, Pracha Uthit/Soi 39, Th Ramkamhaeng)

Malaysia (☎0 2629 6800; 35 Th Sathon Tai, Bangkok) Consulate in Songkhla.

Myanmar (Burma; Map p70; ☎0 2233 2237; www.mofa.gov.mm; 132 Th Sathon Neua)

Nepal (☎0 2391 7240; www.immi.gov.np; 189 Soi 71, Th Sukhumvit)

Netherlands (Map p70; ☎0 2309 5200; www.netherlandsembassy.in.th; 15 Soi Tonson, Th Ploenchit, Bangkok)

New Zealand (Map p70; ☎0 2254 2530; www.nzembassy.com; 14th fl, M Thai Tower, All Seasons Pl, 87 Th Withayu/Wireless Rd)

Philippines (Map p80; ☎0 2259 0139; www.philembassy-bangkok.net; 760 Th Sukhumvit)

Russia (Map p70; ☎0 2234 9824 www.thailand.mid.ru; 78 Soi Sap, Th Surawong, Bangkok) Consulates in Pattaya and Phuket.

Singapore (☎0 2286 2111; www.mfa.gov.sg/bangkok; 129 Th Sathon Tai, Bangkok)

South Africa (Map p70; ☎0 2659 2900; www.saembbangkok.com; 12A fl, M Thai Tower, All Seasons Place, 87 Th Withayu/Wireless Rd)

Spain (Map p80; ☎0 2661 8284; 23 fl, Lake Ratchada Office Complex, 193 Th Ratchadaphisek)

Switzerland (☎0 2674 6900; www.eda.admin.ch/bangkok; 35 Th Withayu/Wireless Rd)

UK (Map p70; ☎0 2305 8333; ukinthailand.fco.gov.uk; 14 Th Withayu/Wireless Rd) Consulate in Pattaya.

USA (Map p70; ☎0 2205 4049; http://bangkok.usembassy.gov; 95 Th Withayu/Wireless Rd)

Vietnam (Map p70; ☎0 2251 5836-8; www.vietnamembassy-thailand.org; 83/1 Th Withayu/Wireless Rd, Bangkok)

Gay & Lesbian Travellers

Thai culture is relatively tolerant of both male and female homosexuality. There are fairly prominent gay and lesbian scenes in Bangkok, Pattaya and Phuket. With regard to dress or mannerism, lesbians and gays are generally accepted without comment. However, public displays of affection – whether heterosexual or homosexual – are frowned upon. **Utopia** (www.utopia-asia.com) posts lots of Thailand information for gay and lesbian visitors and publishes a guidebook to the kingdom for homosexuals.

Insurance

A travel-insurance policy to cover theft, loss and medical problems is a good idea. Policies offer differing medical-expense options and there is a wide variety of policies available, so check the small print. Be sure that the policy covers ambulances or an emergency flight home.

Some policies specifically exclude 'dangerous activities', which can include scuba diving, motorcycling or even trekking. A locally acquired motorcycle licence is not valid under some policies. Do not dive without diver's insurance.

You may prefer a policy that pays doctors or hospitals directly rather than you having to pay on the spot and claim later. If you have to claim later, make sure you keep all documentation.

Worldwide travel insurance is available at www.lonelyplanet.com/travel_services. You can buy, extend and claim online any time – even if you're already on the road.

Internet Access

You'll find plenty of internet cafes just about everywhere. The going rate is anywhere from 20B to 120B an hour, depending on how much competition there is. Connections tend to be pretty fast and the machines are usually well-maintained. Wireless access (wi-fi) is available in most hotels and guest houses, though staff aren't adept at fixing problems, including when service is down. Wi-fi signal strength deteriorates in the upper floors of a multistorey building, so check to see if your floor has a nearby router.

Legal Matters

In general, Thai police don't hassle foreigners, especially tourists. They generally go out of their way to avoid having to speak English with a foreigner, especially regarding minor traffic issues.

One major exception is drugs, which most Thai police view as either a social scourge against which it's their duty to enforce the letter of the law, or an opportunity to make untaxed income via bribes.

If you are arrested for any offence, the police will allow you the opportunity to make a phone call to your embassy or consulate in Thailand, if you have one, or to a friend or relative, if you don't. There's a whole set of legal codes governing the length of time and manner in which you can be detained before being charged or put on trial, but a lot of discretion is left to the police. In the case of foreigners the police are more likely to bend these codes in your favour. However, as with police worldwide, if you don't show respect, you will make matters worse.

Thai law does not presume an indicted detainee to be either 'guilty' or 'innocent' but rather a 'suspect', whose guilt or innocence will be decided in court. Trials are usually speedy.

The **tourist police** (☎1155) can be very helpful in cases of arrest. Although they typically have no jurisdiction over the kinds of cases handled by regular cops, they may be able to help with translations or with contacting your embassy. You can call the hotline number 24 hours a day to lodge complaints or request assistance with regards to personal safety.

Maps

ThinkNet (www.thinknet.co.th) produces high-quality, bilingual city and country maps, including interactive-map CDs. For GPS users in Thailand, most prefer the Garmin units and associated map products, which are accurate and fully routed.

Money

The basic unit of Thai currency is the baht. There are 100 satang in one baht; coins include 25-satang and 50-satang pieces and baht in 1B, 2B, 5B and 10B coins. Older coins have Thai numerals only, while newer coins have Thai and Arabic numerals. The 2B coin is similar in size to the 1B coin but it is gold in colour. The two satang coins are typically only issued at supermarkets where prices aren't rounded up to the nearest baht.

Paper currency is issued in the following denominations: 20B (green), 50B (blue), 100B (red), 500B (purple) and 1000B (beige).

ATMs & Credit/Debit Cards

Debit and ATM cards issued by a bank in your own country can be used at ATMs in Thailand to withdraw cash (in Thai baht only) directly from your account back home. ATMs are widespread throughout the country and can be relied on for the bulk of your spending cash. You can also buy baht at foreign-exchange booths at some banks.

Thai ATMs now charge a 150B foreign-transaction fee on top of whatever currency conversion and out-of-network fees your home bank charges. That means that ATMs are now a lot more expensive to use than in the past. Before leaving home, shop around for a bank account that has free international ATM usage and reimburses fees incurred at other institutions' ATMs.

Aeon is the only Thai bank that we know of that doesn't charge the 150B usage fee on foreign accounts, but its ATM distribution is somewhat limited – many ATMs are located in Big C stores.

Credit cards, as well as debit cards, can be used for purchases at some shops, hotels and restaurants. The most commonly accepted cards are Visa and MasterCard. American Express is typically only accepted at high-end hotels and restaurants.

To report a lost or stolen credit/debit card, call the following hotlines in Bangkok:

American Express (☎0 2273 5544)

MasterCard (☎001 800 11887 0663)

Visa (☎001 800 441 3485)

Changing Money

Banks or the rarer private moneychangers offer the best foreign-exchange rates. When buying baht, US dollars are the most accepted currency, followed by British pounds and Euros. Most banks charge a commission and duty for each travellers cheque cashed.

Current exchange rates are printed in the *Bangkok Post* and the *Nation* every day, or you can walk into any Thai bank to see a daily rate chart.

See p18 for some information on the cost of travel in Thailand.

Foreign Exchange

As of 2008, visitors must declare arriving or departing with an excess of US$20,000. There are also certain monetary requirements for foreigners entering

Thailand; demonstration of adequate funds varies per visa type but typically does not exceed a traveller's estimated trip budget. It's rare that you'll be asked to produce such financial evidence, but be aware that such laws do exist. The **Ministry of Foreign Affairs** (www.mfa.go.th) can provide more detailed information.

It's legal to open a foreign-currency account at any commercial bank in Thailand. As long as the funds originate from out of the country, there aren't any restrictions on maintenance or withdrawal.

Tipping

Tipping is not generally expected in Thailand. The exception is loose change from a large restaurant bill; if a meal costs 488B and you pay with a 500B note, some Thais will leave the 12B change. It's not so much a tip as a way of saying 'I'm not so money grubbing as to grab every last baht'.

At many hotel restaurants or other upmarket eateries, a 10% service charge will be added to your bill. When this is the case, tipping is not expected. Bangkok has adopted some standards of tipping, especially in restaurants frequented by foreigners.

Photography

Thais are gadget fans and they readily snap pics with cameras or camera phones. Memory cards for most digital cameras are generally widely available in the electronic sections of most shopping malls. In the tourist areas, many internet shops have CD-burning software if you want to offload your pictures. Alternatively, most places have sophisticated enough connections that you can quickly upload digital photos to a remote storage site.

Be considerate when taking photographs of the locals. Learn how to ask politely in Thai and wait for an embarrassed nod.

Post

Thailand has a very efficient postal service and local postage is inexpensive. Typical provincial post offices are open between 8.30am and 4.30pm on weekdays and 9am and noon on Saturdays. Larger main post offices in provincial capitals may also be open for a half-day on Sundays.

Most provincial post offices will sell do-it-yourself packing boxes. Don't send cash or other valuables through the mail.

Thailand's poste restante service is generally very reliable, though these days few tourists use it. When you receive mail, you must show your passport and fill out some paperwork.

Public Holidays

Government offices and banks close on the following days.

1 January New Year's Day

February (date varies) Makha Bucha Day, Buddhist holy day

6 April Chakri Day, commemorating the founder of the Chakri dynasty, Rama I

13–14 April Songkran Festival, traditional Thai New Year and water festival

5 May Coronation Day, commemorating the 1946 coronation of HM the King and HM the Queen

1 May Labour Day

May/June (date varies) Visakha Bucha, Buddhist holy day

July (date varies) Asahna Bucha, Buddhist holy day

12 August Queen's Birthday

23 October Chulalongkorn Day

October/November (date varies) Ork Phansaa, the end of Buddhist Lent

5 December King's Birthday

10 December Constitution Day

31 December New Year's Eve

Safe Travel

Although Thailand is not a dangerous country to visit, it is smart to exercise caution, especially when it comes to dealing with strangers (both Thai and foreigners) and travelling alone. In reality, you are more likely to be ripped off or have a personal possession surreptitiously stolen than you are to be physically harmed.

Assault

Assault of travellers is rare in Thailand, but it does happen. Causing a Thai to 'lose face' (feel public embarrassment or humiliation) can sometimes elicit an inexplicably strong and violent reaction. Often alcohol is the number one contributor to bad choices and worse outcomes.

Women, especially solo travellers, need to be smart and somewhat sober when interacting with the opposite sex, be they Thai or *fa·ràng*. Opportunists pounce when too many whisky buckets are involved. Also be aware that an innocent flirtation might convey firmer intentions to a recipient who does not share your culture's sexual norms

Border Issues & Hot Spots

Thailand enjoys generally amicable relations with its neighbours and most land borders are fully functional passages for goods and people. However, the ongoing violence in the deep south (p232) has made the crossing at Sungai Kolok into Malaysia completely off limits and the entire Muslim-majority provinces (Yala, Pattani and Narathiwat) should be avoided by casual visitors.

Cross-border relations between Thailand and Myanmar have significantly normalised, though borders are subject to closing without warning. Borders are usually closed due to news-making events, like Myanmar's 2010 elections, so keeping abreast of current events prior to arriving at the border will prevent potential problems.

The long-contested area at Khao Phra Wihan (known as 'Preah Vihear' in Cambodia), along the Thai–Cambodian border, is still a source of military clashes and should be avoided until a lasting peace is found.

Check with your government's foreign ministry for current travel warnings.

Drug Possession

It is illegal to buy, sell or possess opium, heroin, amphetamines, hallucinogenic mushrooms and marijuana in Thailand. Belying Thailand's anything-goes atmosphere are strict punishments for possession and trafficking that are not relaxed for foreigners. Possession of drugs can result in at least one year or more of prison time. Drug smuggling – defined as attempting to cross a border with drugs in your possession – carries considerably higher penalties, including execution.

Scams

Thais can be so friendly and laid-back that some visitors are lulled into a false sense of security, making them vulnerable to scams of all kinds. Bangkok is especially good at long-involved frauds that dupe travellers into thinking that they've made a friend and are getting a bargain on highly valuable gem stones (which are actually pretty, sparkling glass).

Follow TAT's number-one suggestion to tourists: 'Disregard all offers of free shopping or sightseeing help from strangers.' These invariably take a commission from your purchases.

Theft & Fraud

Exercise diligence when it comes to your personal belongings. Ensure that your room is securely locked and carry your most important effects (passport, money, credit cards) on your person. Take care when leaving valuables in hotel safes.

Follow the same practice when you're travelling. A locked bag will not prevent theft on a long-haul bus.

When using a credit card, don't let vendors take your credit card out of your sight to run it through the machine. Unscrupulous merchants have been known to rub off three or four or more receipts with one purchase. Sometimes they wait several weeks – even months – between submitting each charge receipt to the bank so that you can't remember whether you've been billed by the same vendor more than once.

To avoid losing all of your travel money in an instant, use a credit card that is not directly linked to your bank account back home so that the operator doesn't have access to immediate funds.

Contact the **tourist police** (☎1155) if you have any problems with consumer fraud.

Touts & Commissions

Touting is a longtime tradition in Asia, and while Thailand doesn't have as many touts as, say, India, it has its share. In Bangkok, túk-túk drivers, hotel employees and bar girls often take new arrivals on city tours; these almost always end up in high-pressure sales situations at silk, jewellery or handicraft shops.

Touts also steer customers to certain guest houses that pay a commission (p399). Travel agencies are notorious for talking newly arrived tourists into staying at badly located, overpriced hotels.

Some travel agencies often masquerade as TAT, the government-funded tourist information office. They might put up agents wearing fake TAT badges or have signs that read TAT in big letters to entice travellers into their offices where they can sell them bus and train tickets for a commission. Be aware that the official TAT offices do not make hotel or transport bookings. If such a place offers to do this for you, then it is a travel agency not a tourist information office.

When making transport arrangements, talk to several travel agencies to look for the best price, as the commission percentage varies greatly between agents. Also resist any high-sales tactics from an agent trying to sign you up for everything: plane tickets, hotel, tours etc. The most honest Thais are typically very low-key and often sub-par salespeople.

Shopping

Many bargains await you in Thailand but don't go shopping in the company of touts, tour guides or friendly strangers, as they will inevitably take a commission on anything you buy, thus driving prices up beyond an acceptable value and creating a nuisance for future visitors.

Antiques

Real Thai antiques are increasingly rare. Today most dealers sell antique reproductions or items from Myanmar. Bangkok is the centre of the antique and reproduction trade.

Real antiques cannot be taken out of Thailand without a permit. No Buddha image, new or old, may be exported without the permission of the Department of Fine Arts. See p397 for information.

Clothing

Clothes tend to be inexpensive in Thailand but ready-made items are not usually cut to fit Westerners' body types. Increasingly, larger-sized clothing is available in metropolitan malls or tourist centres. Markets sell cheap everyday items and are handy for picking up something when everything else is dirty. For chic clothes, Bangkok and Ko Samui lead the country with design-minded fashions. Finding shoes that fit larger feet is also a problem. The custom of returns is not widely accepted in Thailand, so be sure everything fits before you leave the store.

Thailand has a long sartorial tradition, practised mainly by Thai-Indian Sikh families. But this industry is filled with cut-rate operators and commission-paying scams. Be wary of the quickie 24-hour tailor shops; they often use inferior fabric and have poor workmanship. It's best to ask long-time foreign residents for a recommendation and then go for two or three fittings.

Fakes

In Bangkok and other tourist centres there's a thriving black-market street trade in fake designer goods. No one pretends they're the real deal, at least not the vendors. Technically it is illegal for these items to be produced and sold, and Thailand has often been pressured by intellectual-property enforcement agencies to close down the trade. Rarely does a crackdown by the police last and often the vendors develop more surreptitious means of distribution, further highlighting the contraband character of the goods. In Patpong market, for example, vendors might show you a picture of a knock-off watch, you pay for it and they go around the corner to fetch it. They usually come back but you'll wait long enough to wonder.

Furniture

Rattan and hardwood furniture items are often good purchases and can be made to order. Chiang Mai is the country's primary furniture producer with many retail outlets in Bangkok. Due to the ban on teak harvesting and the subsequent exhaustion of recycled teak, 70% of export furniture produced in Thailand is made from parawood, a processed wood from rubber trees that can no longer be used for latex production.

Gems & Jewellery

Thailand is a leading exporter of gems and ornaments, rivalled only by India and Sri Lanka. However, rough-stone sources in Thailand have decreased dramatically, and stones are now imported from Myanmar, Sri Lanka and other countries to be cut, polished and traded.

Although there are a lot of gem and jewellery stores in Thailand, it has become so difficult to dodge the scammers that the country no longer represents a safe and enjoyable place to buy these goods. It is better just to window shop.

Lacquerware

Lacquerware furniture and decorative items were traditionally made from bamboo and teak but these days mango wood might be used as the base. If the item is top quality, only the frame is bamboo and horse or donkey hairs will be wound round it. With lower-quality lacquerware, the whole object is made from bamboo. The lacquer is then coated over the framework and allowed to dry. After several days it is sanded down with ash from rice husks, and another coating of lacquer is applied. A high-quality item may have seven layers of lacquer. The piece is then engraved, painted and polished to remove the paint from everywhere except in the engravings. Multicoloured lacquerware is produced by repeated applications.

From start to finish it can take five or six months to produce a high-quality piece of lacquerware, which may have as many as five colours. Flexibility is one characteristic of good lacquerware: a well-made bowl can have its rim squeezed together until the sides meet without suffering damage. The quality and precision of the engraving is another thing to look for.

Textiles

At Bangkok's Chatuchak Weekend Market (p90) and at many of the popular tourist-friendly markets

MORE ON BARGAINING

If there isn't a sign stating the price for an item, then the price is negotiable. Bargaining for nonfood items is common in street markets and some mum-and-dad shops. Prices in department stores, minimarts, 7-Elevens and so forth are fixed.

Thais respect a good haggler. Always let the vendor make the first offer, then ask 'Can you lower the price?'. This usually results in a discount. Now it's your turn to make a counteroffer; always start low but don't bargain at all unless you're serious about buying.

It helps immeasurably to keep the negotiations relaxed and friendly, and always remember to smile. Don't lose your temper or raise your voice as drama is not a good leverage tool.

throughout the islands and beaches, you can find a slew of traditional textiles from all over the kingdom, including the culturally rich regions of the north.

Fairly nice *bah•đé* (batik) is available in the south in patterns that are more similar to the batik found in Malaysia than in Indonesia.

Telephone

The telephone country code for Thailand is ☎66 and is used when calling the country from abroad. All Thai telephone numbers are preceded by a '0' if you're dialling domestically (the '0' is omitted when calling from overseas). After the initial '0', the next three numbers represent the provincial area code, which is now integral to the telephone number. If the initial '0' is followed by an '8', then you're dialling a mobile phone.

International Calls

If you want to call an international number from a telephone in Thailand, you must first dial an international access code plus the country code followed by the subscriber number.

In Thailand, there are various international access codes charging different rates per minute. The standard direct-dial prefix is ☎001. It is operated by CAT and is considered to have the best sound quality; it connects to the largest number of countries but is also the most expensive. The next best is ☎007, a prefix operated by TOT with reliable quality and slightly cheaper rates. Economy rates are available with ☎008 and ☎009; both of which use Voice over Internet Protocol (VoIP), with varying but adequate sound quality.

The following are some common international country codes: ☎61 Australia, ☎44 UK and ☎1 US.

Many expats use **DeeDial** (www.deedial.com), a direct-dial service that requires a prepaid account managed through the internet. The cheapest service it offers is the 'ring-back' feature, which circumvents local charges on your phone.

There are also a variety of international phonecards available through **CAT** (www.cthai.com) offering promotional rates less than 1B per minute.

Dial ☎100 for operator-assisted international calls or reverse-charges (or collect) calls. Alternatively, contact your long-distance carrier for its overseas operator number, a toll-free call, or try ☎001 9991 2001 from a CAT phone and ☎1 800 000 120 from a TOT phone.

Mobile Phones

The easiest phone option in Thailand is to acquire a mobile phone equipped with a local SIM card.

Thailand is on the GSM network and mobile phone providers include AIS, DTAC and True Move.

You have two phone options. You can buy a mobile phone in Thailand at one of the urban shopping malls or phone stores near the markets in provincial towns. Or you can use an imported phone that isn't SIM-locked (and supports the GSM network). To get started buy a SIM card from one of the carriers (AIS and DTAC are most popular), which includes an assigned telephone number. Once your phone is SIM-enabled you can buy minutes with prepaid phonecards. SIM cards and refill cards (usually sold in 300B to 500B denominations) can be bought from 7-Elevens throughout the country.

There are various promotions but rates typically hover at around 1B to 2B per minute anywhere in Thailand and between 5B and 9B for international calls. SMS is usually 3B per message, making it the cheapest 'talk' option.

If you don't have access to a private phone, you can use a somewhat old-fashioned way to call overseas through a service called Home Country Direct, available at some post offices and CAT centres throughout the country.

Calling overseas through phones in most hotel rooms usually incurs additional surcharges (sometimes as much as 50% over and above the CAT rate); however, sometimes local calls are free or at standard rates. Some guest houses will have a mobile phone or landline that customers can use for a per-minute fee for overseas calls.

There are also a variety of public payphones that use prepaid phonecards for calls (both international and domestic) and, less common, coin-operated pay phones for local calls. Using the public phones can be a bit

3G HERE WE COME, MAYBE?

Thailand's telecommunications companies and state-owned agencies have been wrangling over the 3G (mobile broadband platform) for so many years that the new-generation technology has since been surpassed by 4G. Thailand is the only Asean country not to have the service despite a huge number of smartphone users. In 2010 and 2011, contracts to operate the services were awarded and then suspended by the courts. Approval to import equipment has also been delayed and now it looks like 2012 might be the year of 3G, maybe.

of a pain: they are typically placed beside busy thoroughfares where traffic noise is a problem.

Time

Thailand's time zone is seven hours ahead of GMT/UTC (London). At government offices and local cinemas, times are often expressed according to the 24-hour clock, eg 11pm is written '23.00'.

Toilets

Increasingly, the Asian-style squat toilet is less of the norm in Thailand. There are still specimens in rural places, provincial bus stations, older homes and modest restaurants, but the Western-style toilet is becoming more prevalent and appears wherever foreign tourists can be found.

If you encounter a squat, here's what you should know. You should straddle the two footpads and face the door. To flush use the plastic bowl to scoop water out of the adjacent basin and pour into the toilet bowl. Some places supply a small pack of toilet paper at the entrance (5B); otherwise bring your own stash or wipe the old-fashioned way with water.

Even in places where sit-down toilets are installed, the septic system may not be designed to take toilet paper. In such cases there will be a waste basket where you're supposed to place used toilet paper and feminine hygiene products. Some modern toilets also come with a small spray hose – Thailand's version of the bidet.

Tourist Information

The government-operated tourist information and promotion service, **Tourism Authority of Thailand** (TAT; www.tourismthailand.org), was founded in 1960 and produces excellent pamphlets on sightseeing, accommodation and transport. TAT's head office is in Bangkok and there are 22 regional offices throughout the country. Check the destination chapters for the TAT office in the towns you're planning to visit.

The following are a few of TAT's overseas information offices; check TAT's website for contact information in Hong Kong, Taipei, Seoul, Tokyo, Osaka, Fukuoka, Stockholm and Rome.

Australia (☎02 9247 7549; www.thailand.net.au; Level 2, 75 Pitt St, Sydney, NSW 2000)

France (☎01 53 53 47 00; 90 Ave des Champs Élysées, 75008 Paris)

Germany (☎069 138 1390; www.thailandtourismus.de; Bethmannstrasse 58, D-60311, Frankfurt/Main)

Malaysia (☎603 216 23480; www.thaitourism.com.my; Suite 22.01, Level 22, Menara Lion, 165 Jalan Ampang, Kuala Lumpur, 50450)

Singapore (☎65 6235 7901; c/o Royal Thai Embassy, 370 Orchard Rd, 238870)

UK (☎020 7925 2511; www.tourismthailand.co.uk; 3rd fl, Brook House, 98-99 Jermyn St, London SW1Y 6EE)

USA (☎323 461 9814; 1st fl, 611 North Larchmont Blvd, Los Angeles, CA 90004)

Travellers with Disabilities

Thailand presents one large, ongoing obstacle course for the mobility impaired. With its high curbs, uneven footpaths and nonstop traffic, Bangkok can be particularly difficult. Many streets must be crossed via pedestrian bridges flanked with steep stairways, while buses and boats don't stop long enough even for the fully abled. Rarely are there any ramps or other access points for wheelchairs.

A number of more expensive top-end hotels make consistent design efforts to provide disabled access to their properties. Other deluxe hotels with high employee-to-guest ratios are usually good about accommodating the mobility impaired by providing staff help where building design fails. For the rest, you're pretty much left to your own resources.

Counter to the prevailing trends, **Worldwide Dive & Sail** (www.worldwidediveandsail.com) offers live-aboard diving programs for the deaf and hard of hearing.

Some organisations and publications that offer tips on international travel include the following.

Accessible Journeys (www.disabilitytravel.com)

Mobility International USA (www.miusa.org)

Society for Accessible Travel & Hospitality (www.sath.org)

Visas

The **Ministry of Foreign Affairs** (www.mfa.go.th) oversees immigration and visas issues. Check the website or the nearest Thai embassy or consulate for application procedures and costs.

Tourist Visas & Exemptions

The Thai government allows tourist-visa exemptions for 41 different nationalities, including those from Australia, New Zealand, the USA and most of Europe, to enter the country without a pre-arranged visa.

For those arriving in the kingdom by air, a 30-day visa is issued without a fee. For those arriving via a land border, the arrival visa is 15 days.

Without proof of an onward ticket and sufficient funds for the projected stay any visitor can be denied entry, but in practice this is a formality that is rarely checked.

If you plan to stay in Thailand longer than 30 days (or 15 days for land arrivals), you should apply for the 60-day tourist visa from a Thai consulate or embassy before your trip. Contact the nearest Thai embassy or consulate to obtain application procedures and determine fees for tourist visas.

Non-Immigrant Visas

The Non-Immigrant Visa is good for 90 days and is intended for foreigners entering the country for business, study, retirement and extended family visits. There are multiple-entry visas available in this visa class; you're more likely to be granted multiple entries if you apply at a Thai consulate in Europe, the US or Australia than elsewhere. If you plan to apply for a Thai work permit, you'll need to possess a Non-Immigrant Visa first.

Visa Extensions & Renewals

If you decide you want to stay longer than the allotted time, you can extend your visa by applying at any immigration office in Thailand. The usual fee for a visa extension is 1900B. Those issued with a standard stay of 15 or 30 days can extend their stay for seven to 10 days (depending on the immigration office) if the extension is handled before the visa expires. The 60-day tourist visa can be extended by up to 30 days at the discretion of Thai immigration authorities.

Another visa-renewal option is to cross a land border. A new 15-day visa will be issued upon your return and some short-term visitors make a day trip out of the 'visa run'. See the destination chapters for land border information and border formalities.

If you overstay your visa, the usual penalty is a fine of 500B per day, with a 20,000B limit. Fines can be paid at the airport or in advance at an immigration office. If you've overstayed only one day, you don't have to pay. Children under 14 travelling with a parent do not have to pay the penalty.

Foreign residents in Thailand should arrange visa extensions at the immigration office closest to their in-country address.

Volunteering

There are many wonderful volunteering organisations in Thailand that provide meaningful work and cultural engagement. **Volunteer Work Thailand** (www.volunteerworkthailand.org) maintains a database of opportunities.

Women Travellers

Women face relatively few problems in Thailand. With the great amount of respect afforded to women, an equal measure should be returned.

Thai women, especially the younger generation, are showing more skin than in the recent past. That means almost everyone is now dressing like a bar girl and you can wear spaghetti-strap tops and navel-bearing shirts (if only they were still trendy) without offending Thais' modesty streak. But to be on the safe side, cover up if you're going deep into rural communities.

Attacks and rapes are not common in Thailand, but incidents do occur, especially when an attacker observes a vulnerable target: a drunk or solo woman. If you return home from a bar alone, be sure to have your wits about you. Avoid accepting rides from strangers late at night or travelling around in isolated areas by yourself – common sense stuff that might escape your notice in a new environment filled with hospitable people.

While Bangkok might be a men's paradise to some, foreign women are finding their own Romeos on the Thai beaches. As more couples emerge, more Thai men will make themselves available. Women who aren't interested in such romantic encounters should not presume that Thai men have merely platonic motives. Frivolous flirting could unintentionally cause a Thai man to feel a loss of face if attention is then diverted to another person and, in some cases where alcohol is involved, the spurned man may become unpleasant or even violent.

Transport

GETTING THERE & AWAY

Flights, tours and rail tickets can be booked online at lonelyplanet.com/bookings.

Entering the Country

Entry procedures for Thailand, by air or by land, are straightforward: you'll have to show your passport (see p407 for information about visa requirements) and you'll need to present completed arrival and departure cards. Blank arrival and departure cards are usually distributed on the incoming flight or, if arriving by land, can be picked up at the immigration counter.

You do not have to fill in a customs form on arrival unless you have imported goods to declare. In that case, you can get the proper form from Thai customs officials at your point of entry. See p405 for Thai customs information about minimum funds requirements.

Air

Airports

Bangkok is Thailand's primary international and domestic gateway. There are also smaller airports throughout the country serving domestic and sometimes inter-regional routes.

Suvarnabhumi International Airport (BKK; ☎0 2132 1888) Receives nearly all international flights and most domestic flights. It is located in Samut Prakan – 30km east of Bangkok and 110km from Pattaya. The airport name is pronounced *sù·wan·ná·poom.*

Don Muang Airport (DMK; ☎0 2535 1111) Bangkok's second airport is still used for domestic flights operated by Nok Air and Orient Thai Airlines (formerly One-Two-Go). Be aware of this when booking connecting flights on these airlines.

Phuket International Airport (HKT; ☎0 7632 7230) International Asian destinations include Hong Kong, Singapore and Bali on Air Asia. Direct charter flights from Europe are also available.

Ko Samui Airport (USM; www.samuiairportonline.com) International Asian destinations include Hong Kong, Singapore and Kuala Lumpur.

Airlines

The following airlines fly to and from Bangkok.

Air Asia (☎0 2515 9999; www.airasia.com)

Air Berlin (☎0 2236 9779; www.airberlin.com)

Air Canada (☎0 2670 0400; www.aircanada.com)

Air China (☎0 2634 8991; www.fly-airchina.com)

Air France (☎0 2610 0808; www.airfrance.fr)

CLIMATE CHANGE & TRAVEL

Every form of transport that relies on carbon-based fuel generates CO_2, the main cause of human-induced climate change. Modern travel is dependent on aeroplanes, which might use less fuel per kilometre per person than most cars but travel much greater distances. The altitude at which aircraft emit gases (including CO_2) and particles also contributes to their climate change impact. Many websites offer 'carbon calculators' that allow people to estimate the carbon emissions generated by their journey and, for those who wish to do so, to offset the impact of the greenhouse gases emitted with contributions to portfolios of climate-friendly initiatives throughout the world. Lonely Planet offsets the carbon footprint of all staff and author travel.

Air New Zealand (☎0 2235 8280; www.airnewzealand.com)
Bangkok Airways (☎1771; www.bangkokair.com)
British Airways (☎0 2627 1701; www.britishairways.com)
Cathay Pacific Airways (☎0 2263 0606; www.cathaypacific.com)
China Airlines (☎0 2250 9898; www.china-airlines.com)
Delta Airlines (☎0 2660 6900; www.delta.com)
Emirates (☎0 2664 1040; www.emirates.com)
Eva Air (☎0 2269 6288; www.evaair.com)
Garuda Indonesia (☎0 2679 7371; www.garuda-indonesia.com)
Gulf Air (☎0 2254 7931; www.gulfairco.com)
Japan Airlines (☎0 2649 9520; www.jal.co.jp)
Jetstar Airways (☎0 2267 5125; www.jetstar.com)
KLM-Royal Dutch Airlines (☎0 2610 0800; www.klm.com)
Korean Air (☎0 2620 6900; www.koreanair.com)
Lao Airlines (☎0 2236 9822; www.laoairlines.com)
Lufthansa Airlines (☎0 2264 2400; www.lufthansa.com)
Malaysia Airlines (☎0 2263 0565; www.mas.com.my)
Myanmar Airways International (☎0 2261 5060; www.maiair.com)
Nepal Airlines (☎0 2266 7146; www.nepalairlines.com.np)
Orient Thai Airlines (☎1126; www.flyorientthai.com)
Philippine Airlines (☎0 2263 0565; www.philippineairlines.com)
Qantas Airways (☎0 2236 2800; www.qantas.com.au)
Royal Brunei Airlines (☎0 2637 5151; www.bruneiair.com)
Scandinavian Airlines (☎0 2645 8200; www.flysas.com)
Singapore Airlines (☎0 2353 6000; www.singaporeair.com)
South African Airways (☎0 2635 1410; www.flysaa.com)
Thai Airways International (☎0 2288 7000; www.thaiair.com)
United Airlines (☎0 2353 3939; www.ual.com)
Vietnam Airlines (☎0 2655 4137; www.vietnamair.com.vn)

Tickets

In some cases – when travelling to neighbouring countries or to domestic destinations – it is still convenient to use a travel agent in Thailand. The amount of commission an agent will charge often varies so shop around to gauge the discrepancy in prices. Paying by credit card generally offers protection, because most card issuers provide refunds if you can prove you didn't get what you paid for. Agents who accept only cash should hand over the tickets straightaway and not tell you to 'come back tomorrow'. After you've made a booking or paid your deposit, call the airline and confirm that the booking was made.

Air fares during the high season (December to March) can be expensive.

Land

Thailand shares land borders with Laos, Malaysia, Cambodia and Myanmar. Travel between all of these countries can be done by land via sanctioned border crossings. With improved highways, it is also becoming easier to travel from Thailand to China. See p409 for specific border crossing immigration points and transport summaries.

Bus, Car & Motorcycle

Road connections exist between all of Thailand's neighbours, and these routes can be travelled by bus, shared taxi and private car. In some cases, you'll take a bus to the border point, pass through immigration and then pick up another bus or shared taxi on the other side. In other cases, especially when crossing the Malaysian border, the bus will stop for immigration formalities and then continue to its destination across the border.

Train

Thailand's and Malaysia's state railways meet at Butterworth (93km south of the Thai–Malaysian border), which is a transfer point to Penang (by boat) or to Kuala Lumpur and Singapore (by Malaysian train).

There are several border crossings for which you can take a train to the border and then switch to automobile transport on the other side. The Thai–Cambodian border crossing of Aranya Prathet to Poipet and the Thai–Laos crossing of Nong Khai to Vientiane are two examples.

Another rail line travels to the Malaysian east-coast border town of Sungai Kolok,

TRAVELLING BY BOAT TO/FROM THAILAND

You can cross into and out of Thailand via public boat from the Andaman coast to the Malaysian island of Langkawi.

All foreign-registered private vessels, skippers and crew must check in with the relevant Thai authorities as soon as possible after entering Thai waters. Although major ports throughout Thailand offer port check-ins, most leisure-boating visitors check in at Phuket, Krabi, Ko Samui, Pranburi or Pattaya. Before departing from Thailand by boat, you must also check out with immigration, customs and the harbourmaster.

but because of ongoing violence in Thailand's deep south we don't recommend this route for travellers.

Border Crossings

Cambodia

Cambodian tourist visas are available at the border for US$20, though some borders charge 1200B. Bring a passport photo and try to avoid the runner boys who want to issue a health certificate or other 'medical' paperwork for additional fees.

Hat Lek to Krong Koh Kong (p123) The coastal crossing for travellers heading to/from Ko Chang/Sihanoukville.

Pong Nam Ron to Pailin (p118) A backdoor route from Ko Chang (via Chanthaburi) to Battambang and Angkor Wat.

The most direct land route between Bangkok and Angkor Wat is Aranya Prathet to Poipet. Several more remote crossings include O Smach to Chong Chom (periodically closed due to fighting at Khao Phra Wihan) and Chong Sa to Ngam Choam, but they aren't as convenient as you'll have to hire private transport (instead of a share taxi) on the Cambodian side of the border.

China

With an increase in infrastructure the interior of southern China is now linked with Laos and northern Thailand, making it possible to travel somewhat directly between the two countries. You'll need to arrange your Chinese visa prior to departure, ideally in Bangkok or Chiang Mai.

The two main crossings are Chiang Khong to Mengla and Chiang Saen to Jinghong. It was once also possible to travel overland from the Thai town of Mae Sai through Myanmar and across the border near Mong La to the Chinese town of Daluo, but this border has been closed since 2005.

Laos

It is fairly hassle-free to cross into Laos from northern and northeastern Thailand. Lao visas (US$30 to US$42) can be obtained on arrival and applications require a passport photo.

The main transport gateway to Laos is the first Thai–Lao Friendship Bridge at Nong Khai to Vientiane. Other crossings include Chiang Khong to Huay Xai, Mukdahan to Savannakhet, Hakhon Phanom to Tha Khaek and Chong Mek to Vangtao.

Remote crossings include Bueng Kan to Paksan, Tha Li to Kaen Thao and Ban Huay Kon to Muang Ngeun.

Malaysia

Malaysia, especially the west coast, is easy to reach via bus, train and even boat.

Hat Yai to Butterworth (p231) The western spur of the train line originating in Bangkok terminates at Butterworth, the mainland transfer point to Penang. Less popular these days due to unrest in the deep south.

Ko Lipe to Pulau Langkawi (p353) Boats provide a convenient high-season link between these two Andaman islands.

Satun to Pulau Langkawi/Kuala Perlis (p344) Boats shuttle from this mainland port to the island of Langkawi and the mainland town of Kuala Perlis.

Other crossings include Hat Yai to Padang Besar and Sungai Kolok to Kota Bharu (p236), but we don't recommend taking these routes due to the violence in the deep south.

Myanmar

Most of the land crossings into Myanmar have restrictions that don't allow full access to the country. Border points are also subject to unannounced closures, which can last anywhere from a day to years.

Ranong to Kawthoung (p272) This is a popular visa-renewal point in the southern part of Thailand.

The Mae Sai to Tachileik crossing is the only crossing through which foreigners can travel beyond the border town, although travel is limited and subject to extensive regulations. Many travellers use this borders to renew their Thai visas as it is convenient to Chiang Mai and Chiang Rai. Other crossings include Mae Sot to Myawadi and Three Pagodas Pass, both of which were closed at the time of research.

GETTING AROUND

Air

Hopping around the country by air continues to be affordable. Most routes originate from Bangkok, but Ko Samui and Phuket all have a few routes to other Thai towns. See p410 for routes and estimated costs; for airline contact information, see the respective city sections.

Thai Airways International operates many domestic air routes from Bangkok to provincial capitals. Bangkok Air is another established domestic carrier. Orient Thai Airlines and Nok Air are the domestic budget carriers.

Boat

The true Thai river transport is the *reu·a hăhng yow* (long-tail boat), so-called because the propeller is mounted at the end of a long drive shaft extending from the engine. Long-tail boats are a staple of transport on rivers and canals in Bangkok and neighbouring provinces.

Air Fares & Train Routes Map

Between the mainland and islands in the Gulf of Thailand or the Andaman Sea, the standard craft is a wooden boat, 8m to 10m long, with an inboard engine, a wheelhouse and a simple roof to shelter passengers and cargo. Faster, more expensive hovercraft or jetfoils are available in tourist areas.

Bus & Minivan

The bus network in Thailand is prolific and reliable, and is a great way to see the countryside and sit among the locals. The Thai government subsidises the Transport Company *(bò·rí·sàt kŏn sòng),* usually abbreviated to Baw Khaw Saw (BKS). Every city and town in Thailand linked by bus has a BKS station, even if it's just a patch of dirt by the side of the road.

By far the most reliable bus companies in Thailand are the ones that operate out of the government-run BKS stations. In some cases the companies are entirely state-owned; in others they are private concessions.

We do not recommend using bus companies that operate directly out of tourist centres, such as Bangkok's Th Khao San, because of repeated instances of theft and commission-seeking stops. Be sure to read the Dangers & Annoyances sections in the relevant destination chapters to be aware of bus scams and problems.

Increasingly, though, minivans are the middle-class option. Minivans are run by private companies and because their vehicles are smaller they can depart from the market (instead of the out-of-town bus stations) and will deliver guests directly to their hotel. Just sit in the back so you don't see the driver's daredevil techniques!

Bus Classes

The cheapest and slowest are the *rót tam·má·dah* (ordinary fan buses) that stop in every little town and for every waving hand along the highway. Only a few of these ordinary buses, in rural locations or for local destinations, still exist since most have been replaced by air-con buses.

The bulk of the bus service consists of faster, more comfortable air-con buses, called *rót aa* (air bus). Longer routes offer at least two classes of air-con buses: 2nd class and 1st class. The latter have toilets. 'VIP' and 'Super VIP' buses have fewer seats so that each seat reclines further; sometimes these are called *rót norn* (sleeper bus).

It is handy to bring along a jacket, especially for long-distance trips, as the air-con can turn the cabin into a deep freeze.

The service on these buses is usually quite good and on certain routes sometimes includes a beverage service and video, courtesy of an 'air hostess', a young woman dressed in a polyester uniform.

On overnight journeys the buses usually stop somewhere en route for 'midnight *kôw đôm*', when passengers are awakened to get off the bus for a free meal of rice soup.

Reservations

You can book air-con BKS buses at any BKS terminal. Ordinary (fan) buses cannot be booked in advance. Privately run buses can be booked through most hotels or any travel agency, but it's best to book directly through a bus office to be sure that you get what you pay for.

Car & Motorcycle

Driving Licence

Short-term visitors who wish to drive vehicles (including motorcycles) in Thailand need an International Driving Permit.

Fuel

Modern petrol (gasoline) stations are in plentiful supply all over Thailand wherever there are paved roads. In more-remote, off-road areas *ben·sin/nám·man rót yon* (petrol containing benzene) is usually available at small roadside or village stands. All fuel in Thailand is unleaded, and diesel is used by trucks and some passenger cars. In 2007, Thailand introduced several alternative fuels, including gasohol (a blend of petrol and ethanol that comes in different octane levels, either 91% or 95%) and compressed natural gas, used by taxis with bifuel capabilities. For news and updates about fuel options, and other car talk, see the website of **BKK Auto** (www.bkkautos.com).

BICYCLE TRAVEL IN THAILAND

For travelling just about anywhere outside Bangkok, bicycles are an ideal form of local transport – cheap, nonpolluting and slow-moving enough to allow travellers to see everything. Bicycles can be hired in many locations, especially guest houses, for as little as 50B per day, though they aren't always high quality. A security deposit isn't usually required.

Bicycle touring is also a popular way to see the country; most roads are sealed and have roomy shoulders. Because duties are high on imported bikes, in most cases you'll do better to bring your own bike to Thailand rather than purchasing one there. No special permits are needed for bringing a bicycle into the country, although it may be registered by customs – which means if you don't leave the country with your bicycle, you'll have to pay a customs duty. It's advisable to bring a well-stocked repair kit.

Hire

Cars, jeeps and vans can be rented in most major cities and airports from local companies as well as international chains. Local companies tend to have cheaper rates than the international chains, but their fleets of cars tend to be older and not as well maintained. Check the tyre treads and general upkeep of the vehicle before committing.

Motorcycles can be rented in major towns and many smaller tourist centres from guest houses and small mum-and-dad businesses. Renting a motorcycle in Thailand is relatively easy and a great way to independently tour the countryside. For daily rentals, most businesses will ask that you leave your passport as a deposit. Before renting a motorcycle, check the vehicle's condition and ask for a helmet (which is required by law).

Many tourists are injured riding motorcycles in Thailand because they don't know how to handle the vehicle and are unfamiliar with the road rules and conditions. Drive slowly, especially when roads are slick, to avoid damage to yourself and to the vehicle, and be sure to have adequate health insurance. If you've never driven a motorcycle before, stick to the smaller 100cc step-through bikes with automatic clutches. Remember to distribute weight as evenly as possible across the frame of the bike to improve handling.

Insurance

Thailand requires a minimum of liability insurance for all registered vehicles on the road. The better hire companies include comprehensive coverage for their vehicles. Always verify that a vehicle is insured for liability before signing a rental contract; you should also ask to see the dated insurance documents. If you have an accident while driving an uninsured vehicle, you're in for some major hassles.

Road Rules & Hazards

Thais drive on the left-hand side of the road (most of the time!). Other than that, just about anything goes, in spite of road signs and speed limits.

The main rule to be aware of is that right of way goes to the bigger vehicle; this is not what it says in the Thai traffic law, but it's the reality. Maximum speed limits are 50km/h on urban roads and 80km/h to 100km/h on most highways – but on any given stretch of highway you'll see various vehicles travelling as slowly as 30km/h and as fast as 150km/h. Speed traps are common along Hwy 4.

Indicators are often used to warn passing drivers about oncoming traffic. A flashing left indicator means it's OK to pass, while a right indicator means that someone's approaching from the other direction. Horns are used to tell other vehicles that the driver plans to pass. When drivers flash their lights, they're telling you not to pass.

In Bangkok traffic is chaotic, roads are poorly signposted, and motorcycles and random contra flows mean you can suddenly find yourself facing a wall of cars coming the other way.

Outside the capital, the principal hazard when driving in Thailand, besides the general disregard for traffic laws, is having to contend with so many different types of vehicles on the same road – trucks, bicycles, túk-túk ('pronounced *đúk đúk*) and motorcycles. This danger is often compounded by the lack of working lights. In village areas the vehicular traffic is lighter but you have to contend with stray chickens, dogs and water buffaloes.

Hitching

Hitching is never entirely safe in any country and we don't recommend it. Travellers who decide to hitch should understand that they are taking a small but potentially serious risk. Hitching is rarely seen these days in Thailand, so most passing motorists might not realise the intentions of the foreigner standing on the side of the road with a thumb out. Thais don't 'thumb it'; instead when they want a ride they wave their hand with the palm facing the ground. This is the same gesture used to flag a taxi or bus, which is why some drivers might stop and point to a bus stop if one is nearby.

In some of the national parks without public transport, Thais are often willing to pick up a passenger standing by the side of the road.

Local Transport

City Bus & Sŏrng•tăa•ou

Bangkok has the largest city-bus system in the country. The etiquette for riding public buses is to wait at a bus stop and hail the vehicle by waving your hand palm-side downward. You typically pay the fare once you've taken a seat or, in some cases, when you disembark.

Elsewhere, public transport is provided by *sŏrng·tăa·ou* (a small pick-up truck outfitted with two facing rows of benches for passengers). They sometimes operate on fixed routes, just like buses, but they may also run a share-taxi service where they pick up passengers going in the same general direction. In tourist centres, *sŏrng·tăa·ou* can be chartered just like a regular taxi, but you'll need to negotiate the fare beforehand. You can usually hail a *sŏrng·tăa·ou* anywhere along its route and pay the fare when you disembark.

Depending on the region, *sŏrng·tăa·ou* might also run a fixed route from the centre of town to outlying areas or even points within the provinces. Sometimes these vehicles are larger six-wheeled vehicles (sometimes called *rót hòk lór*).

Mass Transit

Bangkok is the only city in Thailand to have an above-ground and an underground light-rail public transport

SĂHM·LÓR & TÚK-TÚK

Săhm·lór are three-wheeled pedicabs that are typically found in small towns where traffic is light and old-fashioned ways persist.

The modern era's version of the human-powered săhm·lór is the motorised túk-túk. They're small utility vehicles, powered by screaming engines (usually LPG-powered) and a lot of flash and sparkle.

With either form of transport the fare must be established by bargaining before departure. In tourist centres, túk-túk drivers often grossly overcharge foreigners so have a sense of how much the fare should be before soliciting a ride. Hotel staff are helpful in providing reasonable fare suggestions.

Readers interested in pedicab lore and design may want to have a look at Lonely Planet's hardcover pictorial book *Chasing Rickshaws*, by Lonely Planet founder Tony Wheeler.

system. Known as the Skytrain and the Metro respectively, both systems have helped to alleviate the capital's notorious traffic jams.

Motorcycle Taxi

Many cities in Thailand have *mor·đeu·sai ráp jâhng* (100cc to 125cc motorcycles) that can be hired, with a driver, for short distances. If you're empty-handed or travelling with a small bag, they can't be beaten for transport in a pinch.

In most cities, you'll find motorcycle taxis clustered near street intersections, rather than cruising the streets looking for fares. Usually they wear numbered jerseys. Fares tend to run from 10B to 50B depending on distance and you'll need to establish the price beforehand. The exception is in Bangkok where the soi motorcycle taxis are a standard 10B.

Taxi

Bangkok has the most formal system of metered taxis. In other cities, a taxi can be a private vehicle with negotiable rates. You can also travel between cities by taxi but you'll need to negotiate a price as few taxi drivers will run a meter for intercity travel.

Train

Thailand's train system connects the four corners of the country and is most convenient as an alternative to buses for the long journey north to Chiang Mai or south to Surat Thani.

The 4500km rail network is operated by the **State Railway of Thailand** (SRT; ☎1690; www.railway.co.th) and covers four main lines: the northern, southern, north-eastern and eastern lines. All long-distance trains originate from Bangkok's Hualamphong station.

Classes

The SRT operates passenger trains in three classes – 1st, 2nd and 3rd – but each class varies considerably depending on whether you're on an ordinary, rapid or express train.

1st class In 1st class, passengers have private cabins, which are available only on rapid, express and special-express trains.

2nd class The seating arrangements in a 2nd-class, non-sleeper carriage are similar to those on a bus, with pairs of padded seats, usually recliners, all facing towards the front of the train. On 2nd-class sleeper cars, pairs of seats face one another and convert into two fold-down berths. The lower berth has more headroom than the upper berth and this is reflected in a higher fare. Children are always assigned a lower berth. There are air-con and fan 2nd class carriages, and 2nd-class carriages are only found on rapid and express trains.

3rd class A typical 3rd-class carriage consists of two rows of bench seats divided into facing pairs. Each bench seat is designed to seat two or three passengers, but on a crowded rural line nobody seems to care. Express trains do not carry 3rd-class carriages at all. Commuter trains in the Bangkok area are all 3rd class.

Costs

Fares are determined by a base price with surcharges added for distance, class and train type (special-express, express, rapid, ordinary). Extra charges are added if the carriage has air-con and for sleeping berths (either upper or lower).

Reservations

Advance bookings can be made from one to 60 days before your intended date of departure. You can make bookings in person from any train station. Train tickets can also be purchased at travel agencies, which usually add a service charge to the ticket price. If you are planning long-distance train travel from outside the country, you should email the **State Railway of Thailand** (passenger-ser@railway.co.th) at least two weeks before your journey. You will receive an email confirming the booking. Pick up and pay for tickets an hour before leaving at the scheduled departure train station.

It is advisable to make advanced bookings for long-distance sleeper trains from Bangkok to Surat Thani, especially around Songkran in April and the peak tourist-season months of December and January.

For short-distance trips you should purchase your ticket at least a day in advance for seats (rather than sleepers).

Partial refunds on tickets are available depending on the number of days prior to your departure you arrange for a cancellation. These arrangements can be handled at the train station booking office.

Station Services

You'll find that all train stations in Thailand have baggage-storage services (or cloak rooms). Most stations have a ticket window that will open between 15 and 30 minutes before train arrivals. There are also newsagents and small snack vendors, but no full-service restaurants.

Most train stations have printed timetables in English, although this isn't always the case for smaller stations. Bangkok's Hualamphong station is a good spot to load up on timetables.

Health

Health risks and the quality of medical facilities vary depending on where and how you travel in Thailand. The majority of major cities and popular tourist areas are well developed with adequate and even excellent medical care. Travel to remote rural areas can expose you to some health risks and less adequate medical care.

Travellers tend to worry about contracting exotic infectious diseases when visiting the tropics, but such infections are far less common than problems with pre-existing medical conditions such as heart disease, and accidental injury (especially as a result of traffic accidents).

Becoming ill in some way is common, however. Respiratory infections, diarrhoea and dengue fever are particular hazards in Thailand. Fortunately most common illnesses can be prevented or are easily treated.

The following advice is a general guide and does not replace the advice of a doctor trained in travel medicine.

BEFORE YOU GO

Pack medications in clearly labelled original containers and obtain a signed and dated letter from your physician describing your medical conditions, medications and syringes or needles. If you have a heart condition, bring a copy of your electrocardiography (ECG) taken just prior to travelling.

If you take any regular medication bring double your needs in case of loss or theft. In Thailand you can buy many medications over the counter without a doctor's prescription, but it can be difficult to find the exact medication you are taking.

Insurance

Even if you're fit and healthy, don't travel without health insurance – accidents *do* happen. You may require extra cover for adventure activities such as rock climbing or diving, as well as scooter/motorcycle riding. If your health insurance doesn't cover you for medical expenses abroad, ensure you get specific travel insurance. Most hospitals require an upfront guarantee of payment (from yourself or your insurer) prior to admission. Inquire before your trip about payment of medical charges and retain all documentation (medical reports, invoices etc) for claim purposes.

Vaccinations

Specialised travel-medicine clinics are your best source of information on which vaccinations you should consider taking. Ideally you should visit a doctor six to eight weeks before departure, but it is never too late. Ask your doctor for an International Certificate of Vaccination (otherwise known as the yellow booklet), which will list all the vaccinations you've received. The **Centers for Disease Control** (CDC; www.cdc.gov) has a traveller's health section that contains recommendations for vaccinations. The only vaccine required by international regulations is yellow fever. Proof of vaccination will only be required if you have visited a country in the yellow-fever zone within the six days prior to entering Thailand. If you are travelling to Thailand *from* Africa or South America you should check to see if you require proof of vaccination.

Medical Checklist

Recommended items for a personal medical kit include:

» antifungal cream, eg Clotrimazole

» antibacterial cream, eg Muciprocin

» antibiotic for skin infections, eg Amoxicillin/Clavulanate or Cephalexin

» antibiotics for diarrhoea include Norfloxacin, Ciprofloxacin or Azithromycin for bacterial diarrhoea; for giardiasis or amoebic dysentery take Tinidazole

» antihistamine – there are many options, eg Cetrizine for daytime and Promethazine for night

» antiseptic, eg Betadine
» antispasmodic for stomach cramps, eg Buscopan
» contraceptives
» decongestant
» DEET-based insect repellent
» oral rehydration solution for diarrhoea (eg Gastrolyte), diarrhoea 'stopper' (eg Loperamide) and antinausea medication (eg Prochlorperazine)
» first-aid items such as scissors, Elastoplasts, bandages, gauze, thermometer (but not one with mercury), sterile needles and syringes (with a doctor's letter), safety pins and tweezers
» hand gel (alcohol based) or alcohol-based hand wipes
» ibuprofen or another anti-inflammatory
» indigestion medication, eg Quick Eze or Mylanta
» laxative, eg Coloxyl
» migraine medicine – for migraine suffers
» paracetamol
» Permethrin to impregnate clothing and mosquito nets if at high risk
» steroid cream for allergic or itchy rashes, eg 1% to 2% hydrocortisone
» sunscreen, hat and sunglasses
» throat lozenges
» thrush (vaginal yeast infection) treatment, eg Clotrimazole pessaries or Diflucan tablet
» Ural or equivalent if you are prone to urine infections

IN TRANSIT

Deep Vein Thrombosis

Deep vein thrombosis (DVT) occurs when blood clots form in the legs during long trips such as flights, chiefly because of prolonged immobility. The longer the journey, the greater the risk. Though most blood clots are reabsorbed uneventfully, some may break off and travel through the blood vessels to the lungs, where they can cause life-threatening complications.

The chief symptom of DVT is swelling or pain of the foot, ankle or calf, usually, but not always, on one side. When a blood clot travels to the lungs, it may cause chest pain and difficulty in breathing. Travellers with any of these symptoms should immediately seek medical attention.

To prevent the development of DVT on long flights you should walk about the cabin, perform isometric compressions of the leg muscles (ie contract the leg muscles while sitting) and drink plenty of fluids (nonalcoholic). Those at higher risk should speak with a doctor about extra preventive measures.

Jet Lag & Motion Sickness

Jet lag is common when crossing more than five time zones; it results in insomnia, fatigue, malaise or nausea. To avoid jet lag try drinking plenty of fluids (nonalcoholic) and eating light meals. Upon arrival, seek exposure to natural sunlight and readjust your schedule. Some people find melatonin helpful but it is not available in all countries.

Sedating antihistamines such as dimenhydrinate (Dramamine) and Prochlorperazine (Phenergan) are usually the first choice for treating motion sickness. Their main side effect is drowsiness. A herbal alternative is ginger. Scopolamine patches are considered the most effective prevention.

IN THAILAND

Availability & Cost of Health Care

Bangkok is considered the nearest centre of medical excellence for many countries in Southeast Asia. Private hospitals are more expensive than other medical facilities but offer a superior standard of care and English-speaking staff. Such facilities are listed under Information in the city and some other sections of this book. The cost of health

FURTHER READING

» **International Travel & Health** (www.who.int/ith) Health guide published by the World Health Organization (WHO).

» **Centers for Disease Control & Prevention** (www.cdc.gov) Country-specific advice.

» Your home country's Department of Foreign Affairs or the equivalent; register your trip, a helpful precaution in the event of a natural disaster.

» *Healthy Travel – Asia & India* (by Lonely Planet) Includes pretrip planning, emergency first aid, and immunisation and disease information.

» *Traveller's Health: How to Stay Healthy Abroad* (by Dr Richard Dawood) Considered the 'health bible' for international holidays.

» *Travelling Well* (by Dr Deborah Mills) Health guidebook and website (www.travellingwell.com.au).

» *Healthy Living in Thailand* (published by the Thai Red Cross) Recommended for long-term travellers.

care is relatively cheap in Thailand compared to most Western countries.

Self-treatment may be appropriate if your problem is minor (eg traveller's diarrhoea), you are carrying the appropriate medication and you are unable to attend a recommended clinic or hospital.

Buying medication over the counter is not recommended, because fake medications and poorly stored or out-of-date drugs are common.

Infectious Diseases

Cutaneous Larva Migrans

This disease, caused by dog or cat hookworm, is particularly common on the beaches of Thailand. The rash starts as a small lump, and then slowly spreads like a winding line. It is intensely itchy, especially at night. It is easily treated with medications and should not be cut out or frozen.

Dengue Fever

This mosquito-borne disease is increasingly problematic throughout Southeast Asia, especially in the cities. As there is no vaccine it can only be prevented by avoiding mosquito bites. The mosquito that carries dengue is a daytime biter, so use insect-avoidance measures at all times. Symptoms include high fever, severe headache (especially behind the eyes), nausea and body aches (dengue was previously known as 'breakbone fever'). Some people develop a rash (which can be very itchy) and experience diarrhoea. The southern islands of Thailand are particularly high-risk areas. There is no specific treatment, just rest and paracetamol – do not take aspirin or ibuprofen as they increase the risk of haemorrhaging. See a doctor to be diagnosed and monitored.

Dengue can progress to the more severe and life-threatening dengue haemorrhagic fever; however, this is very uncommon in tourists. The risk of this increases substantially if you have previously been infected with dengue and are then infected with a different serotype.

Hepatitis A

The risk in Bangkok is decreasing but there is still significant risk in most of the country. This food- and water-borne virus infects the liver, causing jaundice (yellow skin and eyes), nausea and lethargy. There is no specific treatment for hepatitis A. In rare instances, it can be fatal for those over the age of 40. All travellers to Thailand should be vaccinated against hepatitis A.

Hepatitis B

The only sexually transmitted disease (STD) that can be prevented by vaccination, hepatitis B is spread by body fluids, including sexual contact. In some parts of Thailand up to 20% of the population are carriers of hepatitis B, and usually are unaware of this. The long-term consequences can include liver cancer, cirrhosis and death.

HIV

HIV is now one of the most common causes of death in people under the age of 50 in Thailand. Always practice safe sex, and avoid getting tattoos or using unclean syringes.

Influenza

Present year-round in the tropics, influenza (flu) symptoms include high fever, muscle aches, runny nose, cough and sore throat. Flu is the most common vaccine-preventable disease contracted by travellers and everyone should consider vaccination. There is no specific treatment, just rest and paracetamol. Complications such as bronchitis or middle-ear infection may require antibiotic treatment.

Leptospirosis

Leptospirosis is contracted from exposure to infected surface water – most commonly after river rafting or canyoning. Early symptoms are very similar to the flu and include headache and fever. It can vary from a very mild ailment to a fatal disease. Diagnosis is made through blood tests and it is easily treated with Doxycycline.

Malaria

There is an enormous amount of misinformation concerning malaria. Malaria is caused by a parasite transmitted by the bite of an infected mosquito. The most important symptom of malaria is fever, but general symptoms such as headache, diarrhoea, cough or chills may also occur – the same symptoms as many other infections. A diagnosis can only be made by taking a blood sample.

Most parts of Thailand visited by tourists, particularly city and resort areas, have minimal to no risk of malaria, and the risk of side effects from taking antimalarial tablets is likely to outweigh the risk of getting the disease itself. If you are travelling to high-risk rural areas (unlikely for most visitors), seek medical advice on the right medication and dosage for you.

Travellers are advised to prevent mosquito bites by taking these steps:

» Use a DEET-containing insect repellent on exposed skin; natural repellents such as citronella can be effective, but must be repeatedly applied.

» Sleep under a mosquito net, ideally impregnated with Permethrin.

» Choose accommodation with screens and fans.

» Impregnate clothing with Permethrin in high-risk areas.

» Wear long sleeves and trousers in light colours.

» Use mosquito coils.

» Spray your room with insect repellent before going out for your evening meal.

Measles

This highly contagious viral infection is spread through coughing and sneezing. Most people born before 1966 are immune as they had the disease in childhood. Measles starts with a high fever and rash and can be complicated by pneumonia and brain disease. There is no specific treatment. Ensure you are fully vaccinated.

Rabies

This uniformly fatal disease is spread by the bite or lick of an infected animal – most commonly a dog or monkey You should seek medical advice immediately after any animal bite and commence post-exposure treatment. Having a pre-travel vaccination means the post-bite treatment is greatly simplified.

If an animal bites you, gently wash the wound with soap and water, and apply iodine-based antiseptic. If you are not pre-vaccinated you will need to receive rabies immunoglobulin as soon as possible, followed by five shots of vaccine over 28 days. If pre-vaccinated you need just two shots of vaccine given three days apart.

STDs

The sexually transmitted diseases most common in Thailand include herpes, warts, syphilis, gonorrhoea and chlamydia. People carrying these diseases often have no signs of infection. Condoms will prevent gonorrhoea and chlamydia but not warts or herpes. If after a sexual encounter you develop any rash, lumps, discharge or pain when passing urine seek immediate medical attention. If you have been sexually active during your travels, have an STD check on your return home.

Typhoid

This serious bacterial infection is spread through food and water. It gives a high and slowly progressive fever, severe headache, and may be accompanied by a dry cough and stomach pain. It is diagnosed by blood tests and treated with antibiotics. Vaccination is recommended for all travellers spending more than a week in Thailand, or travelling outside the major cities. Be aware that vaccination is not 100% effective so you must still be careful with what you eat and drink.

Traveller's Diarrhoea

Traveller's diarrhoea is by far the most common problem affecting travellers – up to 50% of people will suffer from some form of it within two weeks of starting their trip. In over 80% of cases, traveller's diarrhoea is caused by a bacteria (there are numerous potential

RARE BUT BE AWARE

Avian Influenza Most of those infected have had close contact with sick or dead birds.

Filariasis A mosquito-borne disease that is common in the local population; practise mosquito-avoidance measures.

Hepatitis E Transmitted through contaminated food and water and has similar symptoms to hepatitis A; can be a severe problem in pregnant women. Follow safe eating and drinking guidelines.

Japanese B Encephalitis Viral disease transmitted by mosquitoes, typically occurring in rural areas; vaccination is recommended for travellers spending more than one month outside cities or for long-term expats.

Meliodosis Contracted by skin contact with soil. Affects up to 30% of the local population in northeastern Thailand. The symptoms are very similar to those experienced by tuberculosis (TB) sufferers. There is no vaccine but it can be treated with medications.

Strongyloides A parasite transmitted by skin contact with soil; common in local population. It is characterised by an unusual skin rash – a linear rash on the trunk that comes and goes. An overwhelming infection can follow. It can be treated with medications.

Tuberculosis Medical and aid workers and long-term travellers who have significant contact with the local population should take precautions. Vaccination is recommended for children spending more than three months in Thailand. The main symptoms are fever, cough, weight loss, night sweats and tiredness. Treatment is available with long-term multi-drug regimens.

Typhus Murine typhus is spread by the bite of a flea; scrub typhus is spread via a mite. Symptoms include fever, muscle pains and a rash. Following general insect-avoidance measures and doxycycline will also prevent them.

culprits), and responds promptly to treatment with antibiotics.

Here we define traveller's diarrhoea as the passage of more than three watery bowel movements within 24 hours, plus at least one other symptom such as vomiting, fever, cramps, nausea or feeling generally unwell.

Treatment consists of staying well hydrated; rehydration solutions such as Gastrolyte are the best for this. Antibiotics such as Norfloxacin, Ciprofloxacin or Azithromycin will kill the bacteria quickly.

Loperamide is just a 'stopper' and doesn't get to the cause of the problem. It can be helpful, for example if you have to go on a long bus ride. Don't take Loperamide if you have a fever or blood in your stools. Seek medical attention quickly if you do not respond to an appropriate antibiotic.

Giardia lamblia is a parasite that is relatively common in travellers. Symptoms include nausea, bloating, excess gas, fatigue and intermittent diarrhoea. 'Eggy' burps are often attributed solely to giardiasis. The treatment of choice is Tinidazole, with Metronidazole being a second-line option.

Amoebic dysentery is very rare in travellers but may be misdiagnosed by poor-quality labs. Symptoms are similar to bacterial diarrhoea. You should always seek reliable medical care if you have blood in your diarrhoea. Treatment involves two drugs; Tinidazole or Metronidazole to kill the parasite in your gut and then a second drug to kill the cysts. If left untreated complications, such as liver abscesses can occur.

Environmental Hazards

Food

Eating in restaurants is the biggest risk factor for contracting traveller's diarrhoea. Ways to avoid it include eating only freshly cooked food, and avoiding food that has been sitting around in buffets. Peel all fruit and cook vegetables. Eat in busy restaurants with a high turnover of customers.

Heat

Many parts of Thailand are hot and humid throughout the year. For most people it takes at least two weeks to adapt to the hot climate. Prevent swelling of the feet and ankles as well as muscle cramps caused by excessive sweating by avoiding dehydration and excessive activity in the hot hours of the day.

Heat stroke is a serious medical emergency and requires immediate medical treatment. Symptoms come on suddenly and include weakness, nausea, a hot dry body with a body temperature of over 41°C, dizziness, confusion, loss of coordination, fits and eventually collapse and loss of consciousness.

Insect Bites & Stings

Bedbugs live in the cracks of furniture and walls and then migrate to the bed at night to feed on you. You can treat the itch with an antihistamine. Lice inhabit various parts of your body but most commonly your head and pubic area. Transmission is via close contact with an infected person. They can be difficult to treat and you may need numerous applications of an anti-lice shampoo such as Permethrin. Pubic lice are usually contracted from sexual contact.

Ticks are contracted when walking in rural areas. They are commonly found behind the ears, on the belly and in armpits. If you have had a tick bite and experience symptoms such as a rash at the site of the bite or elsewhere, fever or muscle aches you should see a doctor. Doxycycline prevents tick-borne diseases.

Leeches are found in humid rainforest areas. They do not transmit any disease but their bites are often intensely itchy for weeks afterwards and can easily become infected. Apply an iodine-based antiseptic to any leech bite to help prevent infection.

Bee and wasp stings mainly cause problems for people who are allergic to them. Anyone with a serious allergy should carry an injection of adrenaline (eg an Epipen) for emergencies. For others, pain is the main problem – apply ice to the sting and take painkillers.

Parasites

Numerous parasites are common in local populations in Thailand, but most of these are rare in travellers. The two rules to follow to avoid parasitic infections are to wear shoes and to avoid eating raw food, especially fish, pork and vegetables. A number of parasites are transmitted via the skin by walking barefoot, including strongyloides, hookworm and cutaneous *larva migrans*.

Skin Problems

Prickly heat is a common skin rash in the tropics, caused by sweat being trapped under the skin. Treat by taking cool showers and using powders.

Two fungal rashes commonly affect travellers. The first occurs in the groin, armpits and between the toes. It starts as a red patch that slowly spreads and is usually itchy. Treatment involves keeping the skin dry, avoiding chafing and using an antifungal cream such as Clotrimazole or Lamisil. The fungus *Tinea versicolor* causes small and light-coloured patches, most commonly on the back, chest and shoulders. Consult a doctor.

Cuts and scratches become easily infected in humid climates. Immediately wash all wounds in clean water and apply antiseptic.

If you develop signs of infection, see a doctor. Coral cuts can easily become infected.

Snakes

Though snake bites are rare for travellers, there are over 85 species of venomous snakes in Thailand. Always wear boots and long pants if walking in an area that may have snakes. First aid in the event of a snake bite involves 'pressure immobilisation' using an elastic bandage firmly wrapped around the affected limb, starting at the hand or foot (depending on the limb bitten) and working up towards the chest. The bandage should not be so tight that the circulation is cut off, and the fingers or toes should be kept free so the circulation can be checked. Immobilise the limb with a splint and carry the victim to medical attention. It is very important that the victim stays immobile. Do not use tourniquets or try to suck the venom out.

The Thai Red Cross produces antivenom for many of the poisonous snakes in Thailand.

Sunburn

Even on a cloudy day sunburn can occur rapidly. Use a strong sunscreen (at least factor 30), making sure to reapply after a swim, and always wear a wide-brimmed hat and sunglasses outdoors. Avoid lying in the sun when the sun is at its highest in the sky (10am to 2pm). If you become sunburnt stay out of the sun until you have recovered, apply cool compresses and take painkillers for the discomfort. One per cent hydrocortisone cream applied twice daily is also helpful.

JELLYFISH STINGS

Box jellyfish stings range from minor to deadly. A good rule of thumb, however, is to presume a box jellyfish is dangerous until proven otherwise. There are two main types of box jellyfish – multi-tentacled and single-tentacled.

Multi-tentacled box jellyfish are present in Thai waters – these are potentially the most dangerous and a severe envenomation can kill an adult within two minutes. They are generally found on sandy beaches near river mouths and mangroves during the warmer months.

There are many types of single-tentacled box jellyfish, some of which can cause severe symptoms known as the Irukandji syndrome. The initial sting can seem minor; however severe symptoms such as back pain, nausea, vomiting, sweating, difficulty breathing and a feeling of impending doom can develop between five and 40 minutes later. There has been the occasional death reported from this syndrome as a result of high blood pressure causing strokes or heart attacks.

There are many other jellyfish in Thailand that cause irritating stings but no serious effects. The only way to prevent these stings is to wear protective clothing, which provides a barrier between human skin and the jellyfish.

First Aid for Severe Stings

For severe life-threatening envenomations the first priority is keeping the person alive. Stay with the person, send someone to call for medical help, and start immediate CPR if they are unconscious. If the victim is conscious douse the stung area liberally with vinegar – simple household vinegar is fine – for 30 seconds. For single-tentacled jellyfish stings pour vinegar onto the stung area as above; early application can make a huge difference. It is best to seek medical care quickly in case any other symptoms develop over the next 40 minutes.

Australia and Thailand are now working in close collaboration to identify the species of jellyfish in Thai waters, as well as their ecology – hopefully enabling better prediction and detection of the jellyfish.

Thanks to Dr Peter Fenner for the information in this boxed text.

Travelling with Children

Thailand is relatively safe for children from a health point of view. It is wise to consult a doctor who specialises in travel medicine prior to travel to ensure your child is appropriately prepared. A medical kit designed specifically for children includes paracetamol or Tylenol syrup for fevers, an antihistamine, itch cream, first-aid supplies, nappy-rash treatment, sunscreen and insect repellent. It is a good idea to carry a general antibiotic (best used under medical supervision) – Azithromycin is an ideal paediatric formula used to treat bacterial diarrhoea, as well as ear, chest and throat infections.

Good resources are the Lonely Planet publication *Travel with Children;* for those spending longer away Jane Wilson-Howarth's book *Your Child's Health Abroad* is excellent.

Women's Health

Pregnant women should receive specialised advice before travelling. The ideal time to travel is in the second trimester (16 and 28 weeks), when pregnancy-related risks are at their lowest. Avoid rural travel in areas with poor transportation and medical facilities. Most of all, ensure travel insurance covers all pregnancy-related possibilities, including premature labour.

Malaria is a high-risk disease in pregnancy. Advice from the World Health Organization (WHO) recommends that pregnant women do *not* travel to those areas with Chloroquine-resistant malaria. None of the more effective antimalarial drugs is completely safe in pregnancy.

Traveller's diarrhoea can quickly lead to dehydration and result in inadequate blood flow to the placenta. Many of the drugs used to treat various diarrhoea bugs are not recommended in pregnancy. Azithromycin is considered safe.

In Thailand's urban areas, supplies of sanitary products are readily available. Your personal birth-control option may not be available so bring adequate supplies. Heat, humidity and antibiotics can all contribute to thrush. Treatment of thrush is with antifungal creams and pessaries such as Clotrimazole. A practical alternative is one tablet of fluconazole (Diflucan). Urinary-tract infections can be precipitated by dehydration or long bus journeys without toilet stops; bring suitable antibiotics for treatment.

Language

WANT MORE?

For in-depth language information and handy phrases, check out Lonely Planet's *Thai Phrasebook*. You'll find it at **shop .lonelyplanet.com**, or you can buy Lonely Planet's iPhone phrasebooks at the Apple App Store.

Thailand's official language is effectively the dialect spoken and written in central Thailand, which has successfully become the lingua franca of all Thai and non-Thai ethnic groups in the kingdom.

In Thai the meaning of a single syllable may be altered by means of different tones. In standard Thai there are five: low tone, mid tone, falling tone, high tone and rising tone. The range of all five tones is relative to each speaker's vocal range, so there is no fixed 'pitch' intrinsic to the language.

- » **low tone** – 'Flat' like the mid tone, but pronounced at the relative bottom of one's vocal range. It is low, level and has no inflection, eg bàht (baht – the Thai currency).
- » **mid tone** – Pronounced 'flat', at the relative middle of the speaker's vocal range, eg dee (good). No tone mark is used.
- » **falling tone** – Starting high and falling sharply, this tone is similar to the change in pitch in English when you are emphasising a word, or calling someone's name from afar, eg mâi (no/not).
- » **high tone** – Usually the most difficult for non-Thai speakers. It's pronounced near the relative top of the vocal range, as level as possible, eg máh (horse).
- » **rising tone** – Starting low and gradually rising, sounds like the inflection used by English speakers to imply a question – 'Yes?', eg săhm (three).

The Thai government has instituted the Royal Thai General Transcription System (RTGS) as a standard method of writing Thai using the Roman alphabet. It's used in official documents, road signs and on maps. However, local variations crop up on signs, menus etc. Generally, names in this book follow the most common practice.

In our coloured pronunciation guides, the hyphens indicate syllable breaks within words, and some syllables are further divided with a dot to help you pronounce compound vowels, eg mêu·a-rai (when).

The vowel a is pronounced as in 'about', aa as the 'a' in 'bad', ah as the 'a' in 'father', ai as in 'aisle', air as in 'flair' (without the 'r'), eu as the 'er' in 'her' (without the 'r'), ew as in 'new' (with rounded lips), oh as the 'o' in 'toe', or as in 'torn' (without the 'r') and ow as in 'now'.

Most consonants correspond to their English counterparts. The exceptions are Ƀ (a hard 'p' sound, almost like a 'b', eg in 'hip-bag'); đ (a hard 't' sound, like a sharp 'd', eg in 'mid-tone'); ng (as in 'singing'; in Thai it can occur at the start of a word) and r (as in 'run' but flapped; in everyday speech it's often pronounced like 'l').

BASICS

The social structure of Thai society demands different registers of speech depending on who you're talking to. To make things simple we've chosen the correct form of speech appropriate to the context of each phrase.

When being polite, the speaker ends his or her sentence with kráp (for men) or kâ (for women). It is the gender of the speaker that is being expressed here; it is also the common way to answer 'yes' to a question or show agreement.

The masculine and feminine forms of phrases in this chapter are indicated where relevant with 'm/f'.

Hello. สวัสดี sà-wàt-dee
Goodbye. ลาก่อน lah gòrn
Yes. ใช่ châi
No. ไม่ mâi
Please. ขอ kŏr
Thank you. ขอบคุณ kòrp kun
You're welcome. ยินดี yin dee
Excuse me. ขออภัย kŏr à-pai
Sorry. ขอโทษ kŏr tôht

How are you?
สบายดีไหม sà-bai dee măi
Fine. And you?
สบายดีครับ/ค่า แล้วคุณล่ะ sà-bai dee kráp/kâ láa·ou kun lâ (m/f)
What's your name?
คุณชื่ออะไร kun chêu à-rai
My name is ...
ผม/ดิฉันชื่อ... pŏm/dì-chăn chêu ... (m/f)
Do you speak English?
คุณพูดภาษาอังกฤษได้ไหม kun pôot pah-săh ang-grìt dâi măi
I don't understand.
ผม/ดิฉันไม่เข้าใจ pŏm/dì-chăn mâi kôw jai (m/f)

ACCOMMODATION

Where's a ...? ... อยู่ที่ไหน ... yòo têe năi
campsite ค่ายพักแรม kâi pák raam
guesthouse บ้านพัก bâhn pák
hotel โรงแรม rohng raam
youth hostel บ้านเยาวชน bâhn yow-wá-chon

Do you have a ... room? มีห้อง ... ไหม mee hôrng ... măi
single เดี่ยว dèe·o
double เตียงคู่ đee·ang kôo
twin สองเตียง sŏrng đee·ang

air-con แอร์ aa
bathroom ห้องน้ำ hôrng nám
laundry ห้องซักผ้า hôrng sák pâh
mosquito net มุ้ง múng
window หน้าต่าง nâh đàhng

Question Words

What? อะไร à-rai
When? เมื่อไร mêu·a-rai
Where? ที่ไหน têe năi
Who? ใคร krai

DIRECTIONS

Where's ...?
... อยู่ที่ไหน ... yòo têe năi
What's the address?
ที่อยู่คืออะไร têe yòo keu à-rai
Could you please write it down?
เขียนลงให้ได้ไหม kĕe·an long hâi dâi măi
Can you show me (on the map)?
ให้ดู (ในแผนที่) ได้ไหม hâi doo (nai păan têe) dâi măi
Turn left/right.
เลี้ยวซ้าย/ขวา lée·o sái/kwăh

It's ... อยู่ ... yòo ...
behind ที่หลัง têe lăng
in front of ตรงหน้า đrong nâh
near ใกล้ๆ glâi glâi
next to ข้างๆ kâhng kâhng
straight ahead ตรงไป đrong ɓai

EATING & DRINKING

I'd like (the menu), please.
ขอ (รายการอาหาร) หน่อย kŏr (rai gahn ah-hăhn) nòy
What would you recommend?
คุณแนะนำอะไรบ้าง kun náa-nam à-rai bâhng
That was delicious!
อร่อยมาก à-ròy mâhk
Cheers!
ไชโย chai-yoh
Please bring the bill.
ขอบิลหน่อย kŏr bin nòy

I don't eat ... ผม/ดิฉันไม่กิน ... pŏm/dì-chăn mâi gin ... (m/f)
eggs ไข่ kài
fish ปลา ɓlah
red meat เนื้อแดง néu·a daang
nuts ถั่ว tòo·a

Key Words

bar	บาร์	bah
bottle	ขวด	kòo·at
bowl	ชาม	chahm
breakfast	อาหารเช้า	ah-hăhn chów
cafe	ร้านกาแฟ	ráhn gah-faa
chopsticks	ไม้ตะเกียบ	mái đà-gèe·ap
cold	เย็น	yen
cup	ถ้วย	tôo·ay
dessert	ของหวาน	kŏrng wăhn
dinner	อาหารเย็น	ah-hăhn yen
drink list	รายการเครื่องดื่ม	rai gahn krêu·ang dèum
fork	ส้อม	sôrm
glass	แก้ว	gâa·ou
hot	ร้อน	rórn
knife	มีด	mêet
lunch	อาหารกลางวัน	ah-hăhn glahng wan
market	ตลาด	đà-làht
menu	รายการอาหาร	rai gahn ah-hăhn
plate	จาน	jahn
restaurant	ร้านอาหาร	ráhn ah-hăhn
spicy	เผ็ด	pèt
spoon	ช้อน	chórn
vegetarian (person)	คนกินเจ	kon gin jair

Signs

ทางเข้า	**Entrance**
ทางออก	**Exit**
เปิด	**Open**
ปิด	**Closed**
ที่ติดต่อสอบถาม	**Information**
ห้าม	**Prohibited**
ห้องสุขา	**Toilets**
ชาย	**Men**
หญิง	**Women**

with	มี	mee
without	ไม่มี	mâi mee

Meat & Fish

beef	เนื้อ	néu·a
chicken	ไก่	gài
crab	ปู	ƀoo
duck	เป็ด	ƀèt
fish	ปลา	ƀlah
meat	เนื้อ	néu·a
pork	หมู	mŏo
seafood	อาหารทะเล	ah-hăhn tá-lair
squid	ปลาหมึก	ƀlah mèuk

Fruit & Vegetables

banana	กล้วย	glôo·ay
beans	ถั่ว	tòo·a
coconut	มะพร้าว	má-prów
eggplant	มะเขือ	má-kĕu·a
fruit	ผลไม้	pŏn-lá-mái
guava	ฝรั่ง	fa-ràng
lime	มะนาว	má-now
mango	มะม่วง	má-môo·ang
mangosteen	มังคุด	mang-kút
mushrooms	เห็ด	hèt
nuts	ถั่ว	tòo·a
papaya	มะละกอ	má-lá-gor
potatoes	มันฝรั่ง	man fa-ràng
rambutan	เงาะ	ngó
tamarind	มะขาม	má-kăhm
tomatoes	มะเขือเทศ	má-kĕu·a têt
vegetables	ผัก	pàk
watermelon	แตงโม	đaang moh

Other

chilli	พริก	prík
egg	ไข่	kài
fish sauce	น้ำปลา	nám ƀlah
ice	น้ำแข็ง	nám kăang

noodles	เส้น	sên
oil	น้ำมัน	nám man
pepper	พริกไทย	prík tai
rice	ข้าว	kôw
salad	ผักสด	pàk sòt
salt	เกลือ	gleu·a
soup	น้ำซุป	nám súp
soy sauce	น้ำซีอิ๊ว	nám see-éw
sugar	น้ำตาล	nám đahn
tofu	เต้าหู้	đôw hôo

Drinks

beer	เบียร์	bee·a
coffee	กาแฟ	gah-faa
milk	นมจืด	nom jèut
orange juice	น้ำส้ม	nám sôm
soy milk	น้ำเต้าหู้	nám đôw hôo
sugar-cane juice	น้ำอ้อย	nám ôy
tea	ชา	chah
water	น้ำดื่ม	nám dèum

EMERGENCIES

Help!	ช่วยด้วย	chôo·ay dôo·ay
Go away!	ไปให้พ้น	ɓai hâi pón

Call a doctor!
เรียกหมอหน่อย rêe·ak mŏr nòy

Call the police!
เรียกตำรวจหน่อย rêe·ak đam·ròo·at nòy

I'm ill.
ผม/ดิฉันป่วย pŏm/dì-chăn ɓòo·ay (m/f)

I'm lost.
ผม/ดิฉันหลงทาง pŏm/dì-chăn lŏng tahng (m/f)

Where are the toilets?
ห้องน้ำอยู่ที่ไหน hôrng nám yòo têe năi

SHOPPING & SERVICES

I'd like to buy ...
อยากจะซื้อ ... yàhk jà séu ...

I'm just looking.
ดูเฉย ๆ doo chĕu·i chĕu·i

Can I look at it?
ขอดูได้ไหม kŏr doo dâi măi

How much is it?
เท่าไร tôw-rai

That's too expensive.
แพงไป paang ɓai

Can you lower the price?
ลดราคาได้ไหม lót rah-kah dâi măi

There's a mistake in the bill.
บิลใบนี้ผิดนะครับ/ค่ะ bin bai née pìt ná kráp/kâ (m/f)

TIME & DATES

What time is it?	กี่โมงแล้ว	gèe mohng láa·ou
morning	เช้า	chów
afternoon	บ่าย	bài
evening	เย็น	yen
yesterday	เมื่อวาน	mêu·a wahn
today	วันนี้	wan née
tomorrow	พรุ่งนี้	prûng née
Monday	วันจันทร์	wan jan
Tuesday	วันอังคาร	wan ang-kahn
Wednesday	วันพุธ	wan pút
Thursday	วันพฤหัสฯ	wan pá-réu-hàt
Friday	วันศุกร	wan sùk
Saturday	วันเสาร์	wan sŏw
Sunday	วันอาทิตย์	wan ah-tít

TRANSPORT

Public Transport

bicycle rickshaw	สามล้อ	săhm lór
boat	เรือ	reu·a
bus	รถเมล์	rót mair
car	รถเก๋ง	rót gĕng
motorcycle taxi	มอร์เตอร์ไซค์รับจ้าง	mor-đeu-sai ráp jâhng
plane	เครื่องบิน	krêu·ang bin
train	รถไฟ	rót fai
túk-túk	ตุ๊ก ๆ	đúk đúk

Numbers

1	หนึ่ง	nèung
2	สอง	sŏrng
3	สาม	săhm
4	สี่	sèe
5	ห้า	hâh
6	หก	hòk
7	เจ็ด	jèt
8	แปด	bàat
9	เก้า	gôw
10	สิบ	sìp
11	สิบเอ็ด	sìp-èt
20	ยี่สิบ	yêe-sìp
21	ยี่สิบเอ็ด	yêe-sìp-èt
30	สามสิบ	săhm-sìp
40	สี่สิบ	sèe-sìp
50	ห้าสิบ	hâh-sìp
60	หกสิบ	hòk-sìp
70	เจ็ดสิบ	jèt-sìp
80	แปดสิบ	bàat sìp
90	เก้าสิบ	gôw-sìp
100	หนึ่งร้อย	nèung róy
1000	หนึ่งพัน	nèung pan
10,000	หนึ่งหมื่น	nèung mèun
100,000	หนึ่งแสน	nèung săan
1,000,000	หนึ่งล้าน	nèung láhn

When's the ... bus?	รถเมล์คัน ... มาเมื่อไร	rót mair kan ... mah mêu·a rai
first	แรก	râak
last	สุดท้าย	sùt tái
next	ต่อไป	đòr bai

A ... ticket, please.	ขอตั๋ว ...	kŏr đŏo·a ...
one-way	เที่ยวเดียว	têe·o dee·o
return	ไปกลับ	bai glàp

I'd like a/an ... seat.	ต้องการ ที่นั่ง ...	đôrng gahn têe nâng ...
aisle	ติดทางเดิน	đìt tahng deun
window	ติดหน้าต่าง	đìt nâh đàhng

platform	ชานชาลา	chan-chah-lah
ticket window	ช่องขายตั๋ว	chôrng kăi đŏo·a
timetable	ตารางเวลา	đah-rahng wair-lah

What time does it get to (Chiang Mai)?
ถึง (เชียงใหม่) กี่โมง — tĕung (chee·ang mài) gèe mohng

Does it stop at (Saraburi)?
รถจอดที่ (สระบุรี) ไหม — rót jòrt têe (sà-rà-bù-ree) măi

Please tell me when we get to (Chiang Mai).
เมื่อถึง (เชียงใหม่) กรุณาบอกด้วย — mêu·a tĕung (chee·ang mài) gà-rú-nah bòrk dôo·ay

I'd like to get off at (Saraburi).
ขอลงที่(สระบุรี) — kŏr long têe (sà-rà-bù-ree)

Driving & Cycling

I'd like to hire a/an ...	อยากจะ เช่า ...	yàhk jà chôw ...
4WD	รถโฟร์วีล	rót foh weel
car	รถเก๋ง	rót gĕng
motorbike	รถ มอร์เตอร์ไซค์	rót mor-đeu-sai

I'd like ...	ต้องการ ...	đôrng gahn ...
my bicycle repaired	ซ่อมรถ จักรยาน	sôrm rót jàk-gà-yahn
to hire a bicycle	เช่ารถ จักรยาน	chôw rót jàk-gà-yahn

Is this the road to (Ban Bung Wai)?
ทางนี้ไป (บ้านบุ่งหวาย) ไหม — tahng née bai (bâhn bùng wăi) măi

Where's a petrol station?
ปั๊มน้ำมันอยู่ที่ไหน — bâm nám man yòo têe năi

How long can I park here?
จอดที่นี้ได้นานเท่าไร — jòrt têe née dâi nahn tôw-rai

I need a mechanic.
ต้องการช่างรถ — đôrng gahn châhng rót

I have a flat tyre.
ยางแบน — yahng baan

I've run out of petrol.
หมดน้ำมัน — mòt nám man

GLOSSARY

ah·hăhn – food
ah·hăhn Ƀàh – 'jungle food'; usually refers to dishes made with wild game
ah·hăhn Ƀàk đâi/ ah·hăhn pàk tâi – southern Thai food
ao/ow – bay or gulf

bâhn/ban – house or village
bàht – traditional measure for gold and silver, equivalent to 15g
bòht – central sanctuary or chapel in a Thai temple
BTS – Bangkok Mass Transit System (Skytrain)

CAT – Communications Authority of Thailand
chedi – stupa; monument erected to house a Buddha relic
chow lair/chao leh/ chow nám – sea gypsies

đa·làht/tàlàat – market
dhamma – right behaviour and truth according to Buddhist doctrine
đròrk – see *tràwk*
đrùđ jeen/Trùt Jiin – Chinese New Year

fa·ràng – foreigner of European descent; guava

ga·teu·i/kàthoey – 'ladyboy'; transvestites and transsexuals
gò – see *ko*

hàht/hat – beach
hôrng/hâwng/hong – room or chamber; island caves semisubmerged in the sea

ìsan/ìsăhn – general term for northeastern Thailand

jataka – stories of the Buddha's previous lives
jeen/jiin – Chinese

kàthoey – see *ga·teu·i*
khao/kŏw – hill or mountain
klong/khlong/khlawng – canal
ko/koh/gò – island
Kun/Khun – honorific used before first name

laem/lăam – geographical cape
lá·kon – classical Thai dance-drama
lí·gair Ƀàh/lí·keh pàa/ lí·gair bòk – Thai folk dance-drama
longyi – Burmese sarong

masjid/mátsàyít – mosque
meu·ang/muang – city
moo·ay tai/muay·thai – Thai boxing
MRT – Metropolitan Rapid Transit (Metro); the underground railway in Bangkok

nám – water or juice
nám đòk/náam tòk – waterfall
năng đà·lung – Thai shadow theatre; movies
nibbana – nirvana; the 'blowing out' or extinction of all desire and thus of all suffering
nóy/noi – small

ow – see *ao*

pàk tâi/Ƀàk đâi – southern Thailand
Pali – language derived from Sanskrit, in which the Buddhist scriptures are written
pìi-phâat – see *Ƀèe·pâht*
prá/phrà – monk or Buddha image
prang/Ƀrang – Khmer-style tower on temples

Ƀàk đâi – see *pàk tâi*
Ƀèe·pâht/pìi-phâat – classical Thai orchestra
Ƀrang – see *prang*

ráhn goh·Ƀêe/ráhn ko-píi – coffee shops (southern Thailand)
râi – an area of land measurement equal to 1600 sq m
Ramakian – Thai version of India's epic literary piece, the Ramayana
reu·a hăhng yow/reua hăang yao – long-tail taxi boat
reu·an tăa·ou – a longhouse
reu·sĕe/reusĭi – Hindu rishi or sage
rót aa – blue-and-white air-conditioned buses
rót tam·má·dah – ordinary bus (no air-con) or ordinary train (not rapid or express)

săh·lah/sala/saalaa – open-sided, covered meeting hall or resting place
săhm·lór/săamláw – three-wheeled pedicab
săhn jôw/săan jâo – Chinese shrine or joss house
sangha – brotherhood of Buddhist monks; temple inhabitants (monks, nuns and lay residents)
sà·nùk – fun
soi – lane or small street
Songkhran – Thai New Year, held in mid-April
sŏrng·tăa·ou/ săwngthăew – small pickup truck with two

benches in the back, used as bus/taxi

SRT – State Railway of Thailand

stupa/chedi – domed edifice housing Buddhist relics

suttas – discourses of the Buddha

tàlàat – see *đa·làht*

TAT – Tourism Authority of Thailand

tha/tâh/thâa – pier, landing

Thai Ɓàk đâi – also *Thai pàk tâi;* southern Thais

thâm/tâm – cave

thànŏn – street, road, avenue (we use the abbreviation 'Th' in this book)

tràwk/trok/đròrk – alley, smaller than a soi

Trùt Jiin – see *đrùđ jeen*

túk-túk – motorised *săhm·lór*

vipassana – Buddhist insight meditation

wâi – palms-together Thai greeting

wan prá – Buddhist holy days which coincide with the main phases of the moon (full, new and half) each month

wang – palace

wát – temple, monastery

wí·hăhn/wihan/viharn – counterpart to *bòht* in Thai temples, containing Buddha images but not circumscribed by sema stones

yài – big

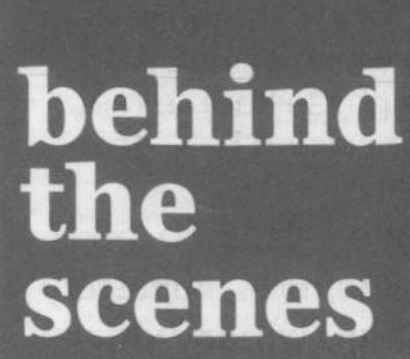

SEND US YOUR FEEDBACK

We love to hear from travellers – your comments keep us on our toes and help make our books better. Our well-travelled team reads every word on what you loved or loathed about this book. Although we cannot reply individually to postal submissions, we always guarantee that your feedback goes straight to the appropriate authors, in time for the next edition. Each person who sends us information is thanked in the next edition – the most useful submissions are rewarded with a selection of digital PDF chapters.

Visit **lonelyplanet.com/contact** to submit your updates and suggestions or to ask for help. Our award-winning website also features inspirational travel stories, news and discussions.

Note: We may edit, reproduce and incorporate your comments in Lonely Planet products such as guidebooks, websites and digital products, so let us know if you don't want your comments reproduced or your name acknowledged. For a copy of our privacy policy visit lonelyplanet.com/privacy.

OUR READERS

Many thanks to the travellers who used the last edition and wrote to us with helpful hints, useful advice and interesting anecdotes:

Ralph Bain, Reinier Bakels, Gavin Bartle, Saskia Beijering, Rachel Cooper, Yvonne Degen, Sara Forssell, Brandon Hausmann, Anique Landre, Anne Myles, William Seager

AUTHOR THANKS

Brandon Presser

As always, a big thank you to the Bambridges for the best home away from home on this (lonely) planet. In the islands, a very special thanks goes out to Matt Bolton and Crystal. A big thank you also goes out to China Williams for successfully (re)launching our Thailand content, to Celeste and Austin for their diligence, to Ilaria for always striving to keep things fresh for our readers, and to Joanne and Sasha Fachay for always putting a smile on my face even when the deadlines loomed large.

Celeste Brash

Huge thanks to my husband Josh and my kids who I missed so much on this extra-long trip. In Phuket thanks to Celine Masson, Lauren Ladky, Jade in Surin and Aleksander Bochenek; fellow Lonely Planet authors Adam Skolnick, Lisa Dunford and Greg Bloom for expert support; to Bodhi Garrett, master of the best places, and to Starlight on Phayam and Dick on Sukorn. And Brandon and Ilaria for keeping this crazy book together.

Austin Bush

Thanks to talented Lonely Planeters Ilaria Walker, David Connolly and Bruce Evans; fellow writers Celeste Brash and Brandon Presser; and the kind folks on the ground in Bangkok including Joe Cummings, Greg Glachant, Craig Harrington, Richard Hermes, Natchaphat Itthi-chaiwarakom, Maher Satter, David Thompson, Pailin Wedel and Patrick Winn.

ACKNOWLEDGMENTS

Climate map data adapted from Peel MC, Finlayson BL & McMahon TA (2007) 'Updated World Map of the Köppen-Geiger Climate Classification', *Hydrology and Earth System Sciences*, 11, 163344.

Cover photograph: Ang Thong Marine National Park, Thailand, Mikel Bilbao/Getty Images ©

Many of the images in this guide are available for licensing from Lonely Planet Images: www.lonelyplanetimages.com.

THIS BOOK

This 8th edition of *Thailand's Islands & Beaches* was coordinated by Brandon Presser, who wrote the Plan Your Trip (with the exception of Eat & Drink Like a Local) and Understand chapters (with the exception of Food & Drink) as well as the Survival guide. Brandon also researched and wrote the Ko Samui & the Lower Gulf chapter. Brandon was assisted by an extraordinary pair of Thailand aficionados: Celeste Brash (Phuket & the Northern Andaman Coast, Ko Phi-Phi & the Southern Andaman Coast) and Austin Bush (Bangkok, Eat & Drink Like a Local, Food & Drink). The Health chapter is based on that supplied by Trish Batchelor and the Environment chapter is based on that supplied by David Lukas. Maher Sattar came through with the goods at the last moment and wrote the Cambodia's South Coast content for the Ko Chang & Eastern Seaboard chapter.

This guidebook was commissioned in Lonely Planet's Melbourne office, and produced by the following:

Commissioning Editor Ilaria Walker

Coordinating Editor Elin Berglund

Coordinating Cartographers Xavier Di Toro, Valentina Kremenchutskaya, Alex Leung

Coordinating Layout Designer Carol Jackson

Managing Editors Bruce Evans, Anna Metcalfe, Martine Power, Dianne Schallmeiner

Managing Cartographers Adrian Persoglia, Amanda Sierp

Managing Layout Designers Chris Girdler, Jane Hart

Assisting Editors Gordon Farrer, Cathryn Game, Kate Mathews, Amanda Williamson, Simon Williamson

Assisting Layout Designer Paul Iacono

Cover Research Naomi Parker

Internal Image Research Aude Vauconsant

Language Content Annelies Mertens

Thanks to Yvonne Bischofberger, Ryan Evans, Yvonne Kirk, Karyn Noble, Trent Paton, Gerard Walker, Wendy Wright

NOTES

000 Map pages
000 Photo pages

000 Map pages
000 Photo pages

J

K

000 Map pages
000 Photo pages

000 Map pages
000 Photo pages

000 Map pages
000 Photo pages

how to use this book

These symbols will help you find the listings you want:

- Sights
- Beaches
- Activities
- Courses
- Tours
- Festivals & Events
- Sleeping
- Eating
- Drinking
- Entertainment
- Shopping
- Information/ Transport

These symbols give you the vital information for each listing:

- Telephone Numbers
- Opening Hours
- Parking
- Nonsmoking
- Air-Conditioning
- Internet Access
- Wi-Fi Access
- Swimming Pool
- Vegetarian Selection
- English-Language Menu
- Family-Friendly
- Pet-Friendly
- Bus
- Ferry
- Metro
- Subway
- Skytrain
- Train

Reviews are organised by author preference.

Look out for these icons:

- TOP CHOICE — Our author's recommendation
- FREE — No payment required
- A green or sustainable option

Our authors have nominated these places as demonstrating a strong commitment to sustainability – for example by supporting local communities and producers, operating in an environmentally friendly way, or supporting conservation projects.

Map Legend

Sights

- Beach
- Buddhist
- Castle
- Christian
- Hindu
- Islamic
- Jewish
- Monument
- Museum/Gallery
- Ruin
- Winery/Vineyard
- Zoo
- Other Sight

Activities, Courses & Tours

- Diving/Snorkelling
- Canoeing/Kayaking
- Skiing
- Surfing
- Swimming/Pool
- Walking
- Windsurfing
- Other Activity/ Course/Tour

Sleeping

- Sleeping
- Camping

Eating

- Eating

Drinking

- Drinking
- Cafe

Entertainment

- Entertainment

Shopping

- Shopping

Information

- Bank
- Embassy/ Consulate
- Hospital/Medical
- Internet
- Police
- Post Office
- Telephone
- Toilet
- Tourist Information
- Other Information

Transport

- Airport
- Border Crossing
- Bus
- Cable Car/ Funicular
- Cycling
- Ferry
- Metro
- Monorail
- Parking
- Petrol Station
- Taxi
- Train/Railway
- Tram
- Other Transport

Routes

- Tollway
- Freeway
- Primary
- Secondary
- Tertiary
- Lane
- Unsealed Road
- Plaza/Mall
- Steps
- Tunnel
- Pedestrian Overpass
- Walking Tour
- Walking Tour Detour
- Path

Geographic

- Hut/Shelter
- Lighthouse
- Lookout
- Mountain/Volcano
- Oasis
- Park
- Pass
- Picnic Area
- Waterfall

Population

- Capital (National)
- Capital (State/Province)
- City/Large Town
- Town/Village

Boundaries

- International
- State/Province
- Disputed
- Regional/Suburb
- Marine Park
- Cliff
- Wall

Hydrography

- River, Creek
- Intermittent River
- Swamp/Mangrove
- Reef
- Canal
- Water
- Dry/Salt/ Intermittent Lake
- Glacier

Areas

- Beach/Desert
- Cemetery (Christian)
- Cemetery (Other)
- Park/Forest
- Sportsground
- Sight (Building)
- Top Sight (Building)

OUR STORY

A beat-up old car, a few dollars in the pocket and a sense of adventure. In 1972 that's all Tony and Maureen Wheeler needed for the trip of a lifetime – across Europe and Asia overland to Australia. It took several months, and at the end – broke but inspired – they sat at their kitchen table writing and stapling together their first travel guide, *Across Asia on the Cheap*. Within a week they'd sold 1500 copies. Lonely Planet was born.

Today, Lonely Planet has offices in Melbourne, London and Oakland, with more than 600 staff and writers. We share Tony's belief that 'a great guidebook should do three things: inform, educate and amuse'.

OUR WRITERS

Brandon Presser

Coordinating Author, Ko Samui & the Lower Gulf Growing up in a land where bear hugs are taken literally, this wanderlust-y Canadian always craved swaying palms and golden sand. A trek across Southeast Asia as a teenager was the clincher — he was hooked, returning year after year to scuba dive, suntan and savour spoonfuls of spicy *sôm·đam* (papaya salad). After leaving his job at the Louvre, Brandon joined the glamorous ranks of eternal nomadism and became a full-time freelance travel writer. He's since co-authored over 35 guidebooks for Lonely Planet, from Iceland to Thailand and many 'lands' in between. Visit www.brandonpresser.com for more on Brandon.

Celeste Brash

Phuket & the Northern Andaman Coast, Ko Phi-Phi & the Southern Andaman Coast Celeste first arrived in Thailand as a student of Thai language, history and culture at Chiang Mai University. She's come back many times since and has done the gamut from wild nights on Ko Phang-Ngan to weeks of silence at Wat Suanmok. Her writing has appeared in numerous publications from Travelers' Tales books to the *LA Times* and *Islands* magazine. She's contributed to around 30 Lonely Planet guides but her heart is irrevocably stuck on Southeast Asia. When not in exotic places, she and her family live in Portland, Oregon. Find her on the web at www.celestebrash.com.

Austin Bush

Bangkok Austin Bush came to Thailand in 1998 on a language scholarship at Chiang Mai University. The lure of city life and a need for employment and spicy food eventually led Austin to Bangkok. City life, employment and spicy food have managed to keep him there since. He's a native of Oregon and a writer and photographer who often focuses on food; samples of Austin's work can be seen at www.austinbushphotography.com

Published by Lonely Planet Publications Pty Ltd
ABN 36 005 607 983
8th edition – Jul 2012
ISBN 978 1 74179 964 4

10 9 8 7 6 5 4 3 2 1
Printed in China